Jews of Poland

MACHT ARBEIT FREI?

German Economic Policy and Forced Labor of Jews in the General Government, 1939–1943

WITOLD W. MĘDYKOWSKI

Boston
2018

Jews of Poland
Series Editor ANTONY POLONSKY (Brandeis University)

Library of Congress Cataloging-in-Publication Data: the bibliographic record for this title is available from the Library of Congress at https://lccn.loc.gov/2018036422

© Academic Studies Press, 2018
ISBN 978-1-61811-956-8
ISBN 978-1-61811-597-3 (electronic)

Book design by Kryon Publishing Services (P) Ltd.
www.kryonpublishing.com

Academic Studies Press
28 Montfern Avenue
Brighton, MA 02135, USA
P: (617)782-6290
F: (857)241-3149
press@academicstudiespress.com
www.academicstudiespress.com

This publication is supported by

An electronic version of this book is freely available, thanks to the support of libraries working with Knowledge Unlatched. KU is a collaborative initiative designed to make high quality books Open Access for the public good. The Open Access ISBN for this book is 978-1-61811-907-0. More information about the initiative and links to the Open Access version can be found at www.knowledgeunlatched.org.

To Luba, with special thanks and gratitude

Table of Contents

Acknowledgements	v
Introduction	vii

Part One

Chapter 1: The War against Poland and the Beginning of German Economic Policy in the Occupied Territory	1
Chapter 2: Forced Labor from the Period of Military Government until the Beginning of Ghettoization	18
Chapter 3: Forced Labor in the Ghettos and Labor Detachments	74
Chapter 4: Forced Labor in the Labor Camps	134

Part Two

Chapter 5: The War in the East: Galicia during the First Weeks of the War	181
Chapter 6: Jewish Labor in Galicia	193
Chapter 7: Jewish Labor in the Shadow of the *Aktion Reinhardt*	221
Chapter 8: War Industry Requirements in the Face of Annihilation of the Workforce	246
Chapter 9: Harvest Festival (*Erntefest*)—Extermination of the Remaining Jews in the District of Lublin	273
Conclusion	292
List of Abbreviations	320
Archival Sources	323
Maps	326
Tables	333
Photographs	364
Bibliography	381
Index	407

Acknowledgements

This research, as with any academic inquiry, would not be possible without the support of many people and institutions that over the past years have assisted me in its completion.

Firstly, I would like to express my deepest gratitude to Professor Daniel Blatman, the supervisor of this research project at the Hebrew University of Jerusalem. Prof. Blatman has been my academic teacher for many years, starting from my studies at Tel Aviv University and during my subsequent studies at the Institute of Contemporary Jewry at the Hebrew University of Jerusalem. Many of his courses have given me not only knowledge regarding the Holocaust, but also an understanding of the processes and mechanisms which functioned during the Holocaust period, as well as before and afterwards.

I would like to thank Professors Dalia Ofer, Moshe Zimmermann from the Hebrew University, as well as Professor Dan Michman from Bar Ilan University and Yad Vashem, who assisted me during this research. I would also express my deep gratitude to the late Professor David Bankier, who was a brilliant teacher and researcher, but who is unfortunately no longer with us.

During my studies at the Institute of the Contemporary History at the Hebrew University of Jerusalem, I had the privilege of being a student of such researchers as late Professors Israel Gutman, Ezra Mendelsohn and many other outstanding scholars, who provided me with knowledge and inspiration which led me to follow their footsteps and study the Holocaust. I am very grateful to Professor Eli Lederhendler, Mrs. Tzipi Bibelnik, from the Institute of Contemporary Jewry, and Ms. Alma Lessing from the Authority of Research and Development at the Hebrew University. I would like to thank my colleagues at Yad Vashem, whose assistance was very helpful.

The German Foundation "Remembrance, Responsibility and Future" (*Die Stiftung "Erinnerung, Verantwortung und Zukunft,"* or EVZ) supported this research in Germany in the framework of International Research Project on

Forced Labor during the National Socialist regime. Thanks to this support, I was able to visit archives in Germany and Poland as well as to attend conferences in Schwanenwerder and Berlin. In particular, I would like to thank Dr. Martin Salm, Mr. Günter Saathoff, Mr. Martin Bock as well as Ms. Ekaterina Engel, Ms. Judith Blum, Ms. Anna Henk, and Ms. Veronika Sellner. I wish to express my gratitude to other institutions which supported my research during its early stages: the Institute of Contemporary Jewry, The Leonid Nevzlin Research Center for Russian and Eastern European Jewry, The Dinur Center for Research in Jewish History at the Hebrew University of Jerusalem, and the Avraham Margaliot Foundation at Yad Vashem.

During my research, I used material from the Military Archives in Freiburg, The Federal Archives in Germany, the State Archives in Lublin, the Institute of National Remembrance (IPN), the Yad Vashem Archives and many collections from various archives around the world copied by and stored at the Yad Vashem Archives. I had the opportunity to consult the research literature in the following libraries: the Bloomfield Library at Mt Scopus, the Jewish National Library, the Yad Vashem Library, The National Library in Warsaw and others.

I would like to thank my colleagues, Prof. Stephan Lehnstaedt and Dr. Klaus-Peter Friedrich, who helped me in obtaining several important sources, Mr. Jarosław Suproniuk who graphically prepared the maps, and Yochanan Amichai, a specialist in German sources.

I am very grateful to Yad Vashem Photo Archives in Jerusalem and the National Digital Archives (NAC) in Warsaw.

Finally, yet importantly, my family members were witnesses of the long hours spent on writing—the hours I was not able to give to them. I would like to thank them for their patience and support.

Introduction

This book examines various questions concerning the forced labor of Jews in the General Government. Since labor in general provides means of subsistence, it is important to the economy and existence of any society. However, in this case we are dealing not only with labor but "forced labor" in the times of war and the Holocaust. This was one of the greatest catastrophes of the Jewish people and with no doubt one of the blackest times of the history of the humanity. Therefore, the concepts of subsistence and labor in this period take new and important meaning, especially if terms like "labor," "productivity," and "utility" are the ones which could have played a role in saving the lives of able-bodied Jews from imminent destruction. The key term here is "forced labor" (*Zwangsarbeit*) because, apart from some variants, it was the word employed for the labor of Jews during most of the period of the General Government's existence and, in general, this term was one of the most widely used during World War II. But the question is not only semantics; rather, our goal is to examine the the real meaning hidden behind this term. This idea was first conceived in the official documents of the General Government in the autumn of 1939 but, quite quickly, other words were adopted to supplement or clarify the meaning. Perhaps, a term that better reflects the meaning of such labor is the word "slave labor" (*Sklavenarbeit*), although the Nazi official establishment tried to avoid its use.

The period of utilization of forced labor in the General Government can be divided into two key phases that will be examined:

- a period when Jews worked as a means to obtain a bare subsistence
- a period when Jews worked as a means to save themselves from immediate destruction

The first period begins with the outbreak of the war and ends with the beginning of the *Aktion Reinhardt*. It important to stress that during this period most of the Jews in occupied Poland and, in particular, in the territory of the General Government were still alive. Moreover, during that period more and more Jews were deported from the territory of Warthegau and other formerly Polish territories annexed to the Reich as well as from the Reich itself (from Vienna, Stettin, and other places). Therefore, the problem of finding work that could provide means of subsistence concerned millions of Jews. Contemporary research still does not dedicate enough space and attention to this question.

Additionally, our research aims to understand the role that forced labor played in the economic policies of the German authorities in the General Government. War economy has its rules, its limitations, and its regulations, making it different from a free market capitalist economy. To complicate matters, in the ghettos of the General Government there existed a particular economic system, which could be described as "forced economy." It was very different from the general economic system outside the ghettos, which also had its limitations and regulations. However, this "forced" economic system was also limited by general legal restrictions, such as rationing of means of energy, restrictions concerning the functioning of the market, and so on. The people inside the ghettos were struggling with additional legal restrictions, which limited their movement, transfer of money, and so forth. This system forced the Jews to work under the conditions of hunger and lack of raw materials. In some cases, the workers were not able even to feed themselves and their families. They were underpaid and exploited. This economic system requires further research, however.[1]

The second period, starting with the *Aktion Reinardt*, begins a completely new phase in the life of the Jews in the General Government as well in other areas of Nazi-occupied Central and Eastern Europe. This period is marked by the partial liquidation of the ghettos, accompanied by brutal *Aktionen*, and by the beginning of mass deportation to the death camps, so that most of the Jews at this time faced danger of imminent annihilation. The only ones who could hope for a prolongation of their existence were able-bodied men and women who could work for the Germans. The Jews faced a choice: to work or to perish. Not all Jews were able to work; thus, this question was irrelevant to most of them. However, in many cases, even those

---

1 Witold Mędykowski, "Der jüdische Kampf um Lebensunterhalt in den Ghettos des Generalgouvernements," in *Lebenswelt Ghetto: Alltag und Soziales Umfeld während der nazionalsozialistischen Verfolgung*, ed. Imke Hanse Katrin Steffen, and Joachim Tauber (Wiesbaden: Harrassowitz Vlg., 2013), 230.

not particularly abled, old, or underaged made all the possible effort in order to work. We will, however, examine closely whether the work really meant survival or not. This question is quite important, since not all working Jews survived. Was the Nazi policy in this regard consistent during the examined period, and who were the people or organizations making those decisions? The aim of this research is also to identify these actors, the conflicting objectives of their activities, the competition among them, and even their opposing interests. The use of a monolithic understanding of the SS turns out to be incorrect in the case of the General Government. Moreover, even from a broader perspective, the SS, as well as its different agencies, seems to be less monolithic.

Forced labor in general and forced labor of Jews in particular were also important in the context of migrations inside the Third Reich as well as in territories occupied by Nazi Germany in Europe. Frequently mentioned are foreign laborers, including concentration camp prisoners and forced laborers, among them the Jews. For example, in 1944, 7.1 million foreign workers were employed in Nazi Germany.[2] According to Wolfgang Benz, "A total of about 15 million Soviet citizens had been recruited into the one or other forms to perform work for the German side."[3] We do not have the exact numbers for all the occupied territories but, surely, we may speak about tens of millions of forced laborers performing daily work for the Nazi regime. In this case, the General Government may serve as a case study. It is a very complex case, but especially important because the General Government suffered Nazi occupation during an especially long period, which allowed the Nazis to develop special policies concerning the territory's multiethnic population, which included ethnic Germans. The Nazi authorities introduced new migration policies, settlement of ethnic Germans, a Jewish policy that involved construction of more death camps than anywhere in Europe and annihilation measures such as *Aktion Reinhardt*. Their legislation also aimed at developing the region's armament industry. Close examination of the developments in the General Government may answer many questions concerning the Nazi policy in general and SS policy in particular. Although the General Government was conceived as an independent administrative unit, it was, however, a playground of multiple actors within the German administration

---

2 Wolfgang Benz, "Zwangsarbeit im nationalsozialistischen Staat: Dimensionen—Strukturen—Perspektiven," in *Dachauer Hefte* 16 (2000): 4.
3 Ibid., 6.

on different levels, in the Reich proper, the SS, the Wehrmacht, among the German entrepreneurs, as well as, to lesser extent, the Polish entrepreneurs and the Jewish institutions and individuals.

From autumn 1942 forward, forced labor was increasingly used in the German armament industry. Because of the importance of this industry for the Third Reich's war effort, working there took on a new meaning. These protected workplaces could save lives. However, the controversy between the Wehrmacht and the SS in this matter was not a new problem. It existed in the Reich since the beginning of the war and reemerged periodically. It seems that this controversy remained unsolved until the very end of the Third Reich.

During the last twenty-five years, the question of forced labor during the Nazi period has become a subject not only of intensive research but also a battlefield of various theories and theses. Many researchers have advanced arguments for this or that position, trying to explain the meaning of forced labor policies that led to the annihilation of millions of people, among them most of the European Jewish population. Thus, labor, forced labor, and the war economy are directly linked to the key questions surrounding the very nature of the Nazi State. We hope that this research may contribute to this larger historical debate.

BEGINNING OF THE WAR

The use of forced labor in the 1930s serves as a basis for the analysis of the development of forced labor in Polish territory during the period of hostilities and military administration. The creation of the General Government in October 1939 initiated a period of exploitation of forced labor of the Jews. Hans Frank,[4] and subsequently the higher SS and police leader in the General Government, Friedrich-Wilhelm Krüger,[5] created a legal basis for exploitation of the Jews.

---

4 Hans Frank (1900–1946), founder of the Academy of German Law, Member of the Reichstag and Minister without portfolio. In September 1939 he was nominated by General Gerd von Runstedt as the chief of the civil administration (*Chef der Zivilverwaltung*) by the Army Group South. Since October 26, 1939, Frank served as the general governor for the occupied Polish territories (*Generalgouverneur für die besetzten polnischen Gebiete*). Arrested by American troops on May 3, 1945, he was tried before the International Military Tribunal in Nuremberg. He was sentenced to death on October 1, 1946, and executed on October 16, 1946.

5 Friedrich-Wilhelm Krüger (1894–1945) became on October 4, 1939 HSSPF "Ost," then HSSPF in the General Government. Since May 1942 he was also Secretary of State

During that period, the civil administration started working together with the SS, the organization formally responsible for Jewish affairs. This was the period of relative stability, when the Jewish population ruled by the General Government was untouched, apart from the victims of the war who fell in 1939. For this population, the main problem was the need to adapt to the new reality and reorganize its economic activity.

The beginning of the war against the Soviet Union was an important and decisive event during the period of German occupation. Previously, the Nazis had held military control during a relatively stable period when, despite economic difficulties, the majority of the Jewish community was preserved. Operation Barbarossa marked the launch of the massacres of Jews on an immense scale, with the first mass executions of Jews by the *Einsatzgruppen*.[6] Later, the onset of *Aktion Reinhardt* started mass extermination in the death camps.

Although the mass murder by the *Einsatzgruppen* took place within other eastern territories, only in the newly created Galicia District—the fifth district of the General Government—did they precede the beginning of *Aktion Reinhardt* by several months. In the course of *Aktion Reinhardt*, mass deportations to death camps followed. These deportations were often accompanied by violent actions; mass executions were also undertaken in many small towns.

---

for Security Affairs in the General Government (*Staatssekretär für das Sicherheitswesen im Generalgouvernement*). From November 1943 to April 1944, he headed the 7th *SS-Freiwilligen-Gebirgs-Division* "Prinz Eugen" in occupied Jugoslavia, then the 6th *Gebirgs-Division* "Nord" and the 5th *SS-Freiwilligen-Gebirgskorps*. Since February, he was Himmler's Plenipotentiary of Southeastern Front, then in April and May, he became the commander of police unit *Kampfgruppe der Ordnungspolizei bei der Heeresgruppe Süd*, and since May 1—the commander of *Heeresgruppe Ostmark*. He committed suicide in an American prison in Gundertshausen on May 10, 1945.

6 Helmut Krausnick, *Hitlers Einsatzgruppen: Die Truppe des Weltanschauungskriege 1938–1942* (Frankfurt a. M.: Fischer Taschenbuch-Verlag, 1985); Dieter Pohl and Andrej Angrick, *Einsatzgruppen C and D in the Invasion of the Soviet Union* (London: Holocaust Educational Trust, 2000); Patrick Dempsey, *Einsatzgruppen and the Destruction of European Jewry* (Eastbourne: P.A. Draigh Publishing, 2003); Yitzhak Arad, Shmuel Krakowski, and Shmuel Spector, eds., *The Einsatzgruppen Reports: Selections from the Dispatches of the Nazi Death Squads' Campaign against the Jews, July 1941–January 1943* (New York: Holocaust Library, 1989); P. Klein, ed., *Die Einsatzgruppen in der besetzten Sowjetunion 1941/1942: Die Tätigkeits- und Lageberichte des Chefs der Sicherheitspolizei und des SD* (Berlin: Edition Hentrich, 1997); Richard Rhodes, *Extermination: La machine nazie: Einsatzgruppen, a l'Est, 1941–1943* (Paris: Autrement, 2004); French L. MacLean, *The Field Men: The Officers Who Led the Einsatzkommandos—the Nazi Mobile Killing Units* (Atglen, PA: Schiffer Military History, 1999).

The transition from a period of relative stability to a period of mass destruction put into question the meaning of work in general, including labor and forced labor. During this period, labor had received an additional dimension. It ceased to be merely a means to acquire the basic means for subsistence. Now it became a way to survive. Those who worked had their existence justified; those did not work became useless and, as such, were led to their deaths.

After the first period of deportation to extermination camps, smaller ghettos (*Restghetto*) were created in many places. These were forced labor camps of sorts. In addition, new labor camps were established. In the second period of deportation, from the spring of 1943 onward, it was not the ability to work that determined survival. In addition, it was necessary to actively convince the Germans that work done by the Jews was necessary in order to increase manufacturing production and to release Germans capable of fighting from production plants. This convincing took place in various ways: through personal initiative of establishment and efforts of production, working in order to fulfill German needs, offering bribes to authorities, and so forth.

Other groups besides the Jews were interested in prolonging the business activity of Jewish enterprises, labor camps, and small ghettos. German actors also had a keen interest in maintaining the existence of Jewish firms and Jewish labor. This research also aims to identify these actors, as well as conflicting objectives of their activities, competition, and opposing interests. I argue that only one organization, the SS, was interested in the total destruction of the Jews. All other German organizations were opposed to this decision or were neutral. However, there remains an important question to ask: how did it happen that the organization carrying out such an absurd program—not only from a moral and human point of view, but also from an economic, strategic, and logistic viewpoint—almost fully realize that annihilation plan?

Those who were saved from the destruction were forced to work in the framework of labor camps and concentration camps in appalling living and work conditions, which ultimately caused their death. The prisoners in the camps were also worked to death. Such conditions created by the administration of labor and concentration camps were intentional, part of the policy called "extermination through labor" (*Vernichtung durch Arbeit*).

DEFINITIONS

The starting point of a discussion on forced labor is to give a definition. One of the basic definitions describing forced labor is given in Article 2 of the Convention of the 16 International Labor Organization, signed in Geneva in 1930, and reads as follows:

1. For the purposes of this Convention the term *forced or compulsory labor* shall mean all work or service which is exacted from any person under the menace of any penalty and for which the said person has not offered himself voluntarily.[7]

The English term "forced labor" has its equivalent in German—*Zwangsarbeit*. However, in terms of Nazi legislation, *Arbeitspflicht* were also used. The last term may be translated into English as "duty of labor" or "obligation of labor." In the correspondence of German offices in the General Government, we find yet another term: *Judenarbeitspflicht*, synonymous to *Zwangsarbeit*.[8] A rarer term in the context of forced labor for Jews is *Pflichtarbeit*, translated as "labor under obligation."[9] There is yet another term, which was seldom used in the Nazi time: *Sklavenarbeit*, translated to English as "slave labor."[10]

In order to discuss the question of slave labor, we should provide a definition of slavery. According to the Slavery Convention in 1926, slavery is the following: "The status or condition of a person over whom any or all of the powers attaching to the right of ownership are exercised."[11] It is important to mention that Germany was one of signatories of this convention. The definition of a slave according to the New Lexicon Webster's Dictionary of the English Language is as follows: "a person who is the property of, and completely subject to another person, a person victimized by another...."[12] This definition will also be useful as we examine the questions of forced labor, duty of labor, and slave labor of Jews during the Holocaust.

---

7 Convention concerning Forced or Compulsory Labor signed in Geneva during the Fourteenth Session of the General Conference of the International Labor Organisation on June 10, 1930.
8 Documents of Governor of Lublin District (GDL). YVA-JM.12307, 59.
9 YVA-JM.12331, Der Kreishauptmann des Kreises Jasło, Jasło, den 2 Juni 1940, Lagebericht über die Zeit von Mitte Mai 1940 bis Ende Mai 1940, scan 75.
10 Albert Speer, *Der Sklavenstaat: Meine Auseinandersetzungen mit der SS* (Stuttgart: DVA, 1981).
11 *Encyclopaedia Britannica* (Chicago: Encyclopaedia Britannica Lts, 1953), vol. 20, 786.
12 *The New Lexicon Webster's Dictionary of the English Language* (New York: Lexicon Publications Inc., 1989), 933.

The use of prisoners of war was in flagrant disregard of the rules of international law, particularly Article 6 of the Regulations annexed to The Hague Convention Number 4 of 1907, which states that the tasks of prisoners of war shall have no connection with the operations of war.[13]

The Geneva Convention of 1929 was adopted in times of peace, and while it provides for situations of war, this document does not discuss forced labor of ethnic groups at risk of total extermination. Hence, further discussion will be needed to define more clearly what forced labor was understood to be during the Holocaust. Can paid work be considered forced labor? Or working in ghettos in exchange for food? According to Jens-Christian Wagner, "the undifferentiated use of the term 'forced labor' leads to an equation of the living and working conditions of such widely differing groups as, for example, Dutch civilian workers, Soviet prisoners of war and Jewish concentration camps inmates. What is more, the definition of 'force' is also subjective and, finally the degree of force used in any given case could also vary. For example, many prisoners of war were assigned the status of civilian worker at some point during the war, but were still forced to work in Germany."[14] Wagner tries to draw a general definition of forced labor: "...the term 'forced labor' will be used to denote all cases in which the laborer was forced to work against his/her will with coercive measures of non-material nature."[15] Other researchers confirm the use of the term "forced labor" in differing contexts and different meanings, which requires further research.[16]

However, the above definition does not, and cannot, exhaustively explain the issue of forced labor, as it does not take into account other factors beyond the physical compelling to perform work and the lack of payment. Consideration should also be given to the matter of terminology as well as the issue of the circumstances in which the work was done. With the onset of *Aktion Reinhardt*, when most Jews were deported to death camps, new types of forced labor camps came into being. They were more similar to concentration camps and appeared where forced labor turned into slave labor.

---

13 International Military Tribunal, *Nazi Conspiracy and Aggression, Opinion and Judgment* (Washington, DC: US Government Printing Office, 1947), vol. 1, 911. Hereafter as IMT, Red Series.

14 Jens-Christian Wagner, "Forced Labor in the National Sozialist Era—an Overview," in *Forced Labor: The Germans, the Forced Laborers and the War*, ed. Volkhard Knigge et al. (Weimar: Gedenkstätten Buchenwald und Mittelbau-Dora, 2010), 180.

15 Ibid.

16 Stephan Lehenstaedt, "Die deutsche Arbeitsverwaltung im Generalgouvernement und die Juden," *Vierteljahrshefte für Zeitgeschichte* 3 (2012): 416.

In the discussion of forced labor, many terms are used that require clarification and verification. Such terms as described above are "forced labor," "slave labor," "labor camp," "economics of the ghetto," and others. Such terminology will appear throughout this work, but the meaning of certain terms changes in practice, which can lead to confusion or misunderstanding of the contents of the documents. It is necessary to check the significance of individual terms and determine whether it remains the same or changes over time.

The following analysis of the idea of "forced labor" is based on tracing its development. We have to check whether it underwent evolution and, if yes, then in which direction: whether this evolution was due to the development of this concept or to practical considerations that affected this idea. We do not approach the forced labor of Jews as a subset of forced labor in general, meaning that Jews should work just as other population groups should work. The very fact that the one regulation was established for Jews and another for the Poles testifies that there was no equality and that for the Jews there was a different kind of work and a different ideological basis for its establishment. However, legislation gives only a partial answer to the question of why there were differences in the types of forced labor. It is also about the fact that besides coercion to work, the implementation of this notion was changing. The very idea of what "forced labor" should be was also evolving. According to Wagner:

> ... in the twelve years of Nazi rule, the economic, political and social framework conditions of forced labor gradually changed: it was constantly adapted to the changing requirements of the Nazi power machinery, and took on increasing economic importance over the course of the war.[17]

The framework of forced labor of Jews in October 1939 in the General Government was very different from the scheme of forced labor in October 1943. This also concerned the forced labor of Poles and other nationalities. It is therefore important to examine the mutual correlation of ideas and praxis. Reference groups that can be used are concentration camp prisoners, POWs (including Soviet POWs), Polish workers and Polish forced laborers, *Ostarbeiter*, youth brigade of *Baudienst*, workers of the *Organisation Todt* (OT), and DAF workers.

For analytic purposes, we may make a comparison with other areas of Central and Eastern Europe under German occupation: part of Warthegau, *Reichskommissariat Ukraine*, and *Reichskommissariat Ostland*. A partial analogy can be made between the working conditions of forced laborers and the

---

17 Wagner, "Forced Labor," 181.

working conditions in the camps in the Reich. Assessment of other areas, which spent less time under the German occupation or where the branches of the Nazi state apparatus were not so well developed, does not seem appropriate.

In the discussion of forced labor, it is also important to raise issues of economic models applied in occupied territories. In these areas, a war economy was introduced, which was an extension of the model that prevailed in Germany before the war. It was a planned economy where, despite the existence of private property, the state regulated the production profile, allotted raw materials, and often was the recipient of the finished products. The state also controlled the level of profit. In order to function well in such a system, companies struggled for large military orders, receiving allocations of raw materials and forced laborers. Forced labor meant cheap labor, which was important for the computation of profits. If all other factors were regulated by the state, reducing labor costs could significantly affect the amount of profit, and a sudden increase in labor cost could incur great losses. Additionally, in large ghettos, a certain isolated economic system existed. It had its circumstances and its characteristics, even though it was associated with the external environment. It was a forced system created by existing legislation that isolated and persecuted the Jews. The ghetto was not based on an autarchic system, because there was no sufficient economic basis and no natural resources; therefore, it was dependent on an exchange with the external environment.

This research demonstrates the *modus operandi* of the Nazi system of power, which suffered from massive bureaucracy, conflicts of interest between different institutions, and a total destruction of human and moral values—all of which led to extensive degeneration.

This research intends to show the fate of Jews in the Nazi system as compared to other population groups, especially the Poles. The Jews showed great activity and initiative, at least during the first stretch of the war. Later on, the Jews became more passive because they had no possibility of influencing decisive factors. Their actions lacked any characteristic of collective activity, but rather presented individual or small group initiatives. Uprisings and revolts of the Jews in the General Government did not contribute to the improvement of their situation; on the contrary, they accelerated the extermination. However, the Jews saw undisputed successes in their struggles and, despite their final subjugation, achieved a great moral victory.

Adopting a macro perspective on the problems of forced labor and economic policy in the General Government, this research gives few examples of individual actions and approaches. Yet, despite this limitation, the human element is revealed. The victims of the forced labor system had to function under great pressure; in many cases they depended only on luck. Nonetheless, they also had some possibilities to manipulate their situation, despite the apparently restricted possibility of any action or initiative.

Although it is not a treatise on morality, undoubtedly this work will illustrate an inhumane and cruel battle against a people who, due to their origin, religion, or ethnicity, had been deprived of the right to live. Even so, they tried to survive and believed it was possible. Their struggle against evil and a belief in human values helped some of the persecuted to survive. This work can serve as a case study of the exploitation of social, ethnic, and religious groups defenseless against modern state mechanisms. Our research shows to what extent such exploitation can, in the absence of a democratic apparatus, affect a balance of power in a country.

THE TYPES OF FORCED LABOR: CATEGORIZATION

Our in-depth discussion is accompanied by an appendix that contains statistical tables supplying quantitative backup data for our assertions. Two maps are also provided to help the reader visualize the scope and boundaries of the General Government. We can define different forms of forced labor by classifying cases by the place of execution, ethnic composition of forced laborers, type of work, organizing agent, economic sector, the form of the regime, the form of coercion and so forth. Later in the discussion, many of these terms and forms will be used on a regular basis.

Forced labor, in terms of organizational forms, can be divided into the following types: work in places of residence, ghettos, labor camps and other types of camps, outposts or labor detachments (in German, *Dienststellen*, or, in Polish, *placówki*).

Evolution of forced labor due to the progressive restrictions of freedom can be divided into the following categories: obligation to work (*Arbeitspflicht*), forced labor (*Zwangsarbeit*), and slave labor (*Sklavenarbeit*).

> Categorization of the camps can be made according to the following criteria:
> - Period of their existence: temporary (provisory), permanent, working commandos.
> - Ethnic composition: Jewish (*Julag* or *Judenlager*), non-Jewish, mixed.
> - Parent/organizing agent: SS, Army (*Wehrmacht, Heeres, Luftwaffe*), civil administration, private firms.

- Typical names, which include: *Arbeitslager* (labor camp), *Zwangsarbeitslager* (ZAL, forced labor camp), *Julag* (Jewish camp), *Straflager* (penal camps), and *Kriegsgefangenenlager* (POW camp).
- Forms of work, depending on the industry: infrastructure (roads, railways, bridges, water management), industry (military, civil, heavy industry, light industry), mining, agriculture (field work, support for existing property).

In classifying by paid wages, cases of forced labor can be divided into work for no compensation, work in exchange for full pay, and work in exchange for accommodations.

Another ground for division is the nature of employment: hired workers (*pracownicy wolnonajemni*), workers performing forced labor (substitutions for those originally called up to perform forced labor), penal workers (prisoners, convicts, prisoners of concentration camps), and prisoners of war (POWs).

FORCED LABOR IN OCCUPIED POLAND

Jews were first forced to work at the beginning of the occupation, so that a concept of forced labor was required early in the course of war. When during war it is necessary to perform some urgent work, civilians are often conscripted for this purpose. We have to mention the German anti-Semitic propaganda campaigns in September 1939, and the direct contact between German soldiers with Orthodox and traditional Jews, with whom they were not intimate in Germany. This contact plus the propaganda made possible the German soldiers' practical application of the German experience directly on the object of the propaganda. In wartime, there were additional elements in play as well—force and vulnerability.

When the creation of the General Government was proclaimed on October 26, 1939, two important pieces of legislation were published that announced the introduction of forced labor for Jews (*Zwangsarbeit*) and the obligation to work for the Poles (*Arbeitspflicht*). This last term poses some difficulties, because in Germany there was also an obligation to work for the Germans. Nevertheless, it is difficult to compare the situation of Germans in Germany and that of people in annexed or occupied territories, such as the situation of Poles in the General Government. Particularly difficult was the situation of Poles in the areas annexed to the Reich, where they were deported en masse and persecuted. In the General Government, in the initial period of occupation, the Poles were the majority population; therefore, their persecution was more political than economic. However, after a while, when there was an increased demand for labor in Germany, the initial obligation to work often evolved into forced labor. Polish workers, especially in Germany, were subject to many restrictions. In particular, this concerned the rural population which, in the early years of the occupation, was not obliged to work (although later the situation was exacerbated). A special form of forced labor was labor battalions, bearing the name of the Polish Service of Construction in the General Government (*Polnischer Baudienst im Generalgouvernement*), which mobilized young men of military age.[18] Similar organizations were created for the Mountaineers (*Goralische Heimatsdienst*), whom the German authorities wanted to isolate from the rest of the Poles; furthermore, they were considered a separate ethnic group. The Ukrainians in the General Government worked in the Ukrainian Homeland Service (*Ukrainischer Heimatdienst* or *Ukrains'ka Sluzhba Bat'kivschyni*). These organizations were modeled after the German labor battalions of the Reich Labor Service (*Reichsarbeitsdienst*, RAD).

A separate form of forced labor was the work of prisoners of concentration camps (*KZ Häftlinge*) and detainees in prisons, who during the war were also transferred to concentration camps or penal labor camps administered by the SS and police leaders in the districts. Throughout the war, convicts were sent to concentration camps for the time required to serve their sentence. These prisoners could be released after completing their punishments. Later, releases from the concentration camps were annulled and prisoners' sentences were not limited in time, becoming life imprisonment. Penal labor camps organized by the SS commanders and police leaders in the districts of the General Government were intended for both Poles and Jews.

REVIEW OF RESEARCH LITERATURE

The first post-war text concerning forced labor during World War II and the Holocaust appeared by 1946.[19] The author of this text not only gave a general description of different of Nazi camps, but also attempted to make a classification of labor camps. The article also contains one of the first lists of labor camps in post-war Poland. It is quite characteristic that most post-war publications in Poland did not use wartime administrative division, but rather the new regional

---

18 Mścisław Wróblewski, *Służba Budowlana (Baudienst) w Generalnym Gubernatorstwie 1940–1945* (Warsaw: PWN, 1984).
19 Zofia Czyńska and Bogumił Kupść, "Obozy zagłady, obozy koncentracyjne i obozy pracy na ziemiech polskich w latach 1939–1945," *BGKBZNwP* I (1946): 11–62.

division in districts (*województwa*). It was without doubt influenced by a regional network of the branches of the main Commission for Investigation of Nazi Crimes in Poland (*Główna Komisja Badania Zbrodni Hitlerowskich w Polsce*, GKBZHP). The bulletin of the Main Commission (*Biuletyn GKBZHP*) published some other articles concerning forced labor and labor camps.[20] In the post-war period, there were books published concerning economic aspects of the German occupation in Poland. Among the researchers writing on those subjects were authors linked to the Western Institute in Poznań and Main Commission: Wacław Jastrzębowski,[21] Tadeusz Kłosiński,[22] and Czesław Łuczak.[23] During the following years more books appeared about the Holocaust period, but already written in the spirit of Stalinism.[24] Their authors emphasized the importance of the communist organizations and interpreted history according to Marxist ideology. In the beginning of the 1950s, Tatiana Berenstein begun to publish numerous articles, many of which explored economic exploitation of Jews and forced labor.[25] At the end of the 1950s, she began to write about labor camps for Jews in the district of Lublin[26] and continued during the 1960s with an article about Jewish forced labor in Warsaw,[27] followed by work on extermination and forced labor of Jews in the district of Galicia.[28] In the 1960s and 1970s, the Jewish Institute in Warsaw (ŻIH), which continued the work of the Central Jewish Historical Commission from 1944–1947, became practically the only institution researching the

---

20 Zdzisław Łukaszewicz, "Obóz pracy w Treblince," *BGKBZNwP* III (1947): 107–22.
21 Wacław Jastrzębowski, *Gospodarka niemiecka w Polsce 1939–1944* (Warsaw: Czytelnik, 1946).
22 Tadeusz Kłosinski, *Polityka przemysłowa okupanta w Generalnym Gubernatorstwie* (Poznań: Instytut Zachodni, 1947).
23 Czesław Łuczak, *Przyczynki do gospodarki niemieckiej w latach 1939–1945* (Poznań: Instytut Zachodni, 1949).
24 Artur Eisenbach, *Hitlerowska polityka eksterminacji Żydów jako jeden z przejawów imperializmu niemieckiego* (Warsaw: ŻIH, 1953).
25 Tatiana Brustin-Berenstein, "Hitlerowskie dyskryminacje gospodarcze wobec Żydów w Warszawie przed utworzeniem getta," *BŻIH* 2/4 (1952): 156–90; Tatiana Brustin-Berenstein, "O hitlerowskich metodach eksploatacji gospodarczej getta warszawskiego," *BŻIH* 4/8 (1953): 3–52; Tatiana Brustin-Berenstein, "O niektórych zagadnieniach gospodarczych w tzw. Generalnej Guberni w świetle 'Dziennika Franka,'" *BŻIH* 9–10 (1954): 236–87.
26 Tatiana Brustin-Berenstein, "Obozy pracy przymusowej dla Żydów w dystrykcie lubelskim," *BŻIH* 24 (1957): 3–20.
27 Tatiana Brustin-Berenstein, "Praca przymusowa Żydów w Warszawie w czasie okupacji hitlerowskiej," *BŻIH* 45–46 (1963): 42–93.
28 Tatiana Brustin-Berenstein, "Eksterminacja ludności żydowskiej w dystrykcie Galicja (1941–1943)," *BŻIH* 61 (1967): 3–58; Tatiana Brustin-Berenstein, "Praca przymusowa ludności żydowskiej w tzw. Dystrykcie Galicja (1941–1944)," *BŻIH* 69 (1969): 3–45.

Holocaust and Judaism in Poland. Apart from the books published by the Institute, the *Biuletyn ŻIH* (BŻIH) became the main scientific journal where this research was published. Besides Berenstein, BŻIH published articles written by Brenner,[29] Datner,[30] and Rutkowski.[31] In mid-1965, the journal *Zeszyty Majdanka* was launched by the State Museum in Majdanek, which quickly became one of the most important scientific journals concerning the period of World War II and the Holocaust. This journal featured articles about economic exploitation,[32] forced labor,[33] POWs,[34] and the German administration in occupied Poland.[35] In the 1960s and beyond, BGKBZHP (*Biuletyn Głównej Komisji Badania Zbrodni Hitlerowskich w Polsce*, or, in English, Bulletin of the Main Commission for Investigation of Nazi Crimes in Poland) continued to publish articles on economic aspects of the German occupation and forced labor, but mainly concerning Poles or the general population.[36]

In the 1960s and 1970s, important books were published about economic aspects of the German occupation. One of the leading scholars of that period was Czesław Madajczyk, who published, among others, monumental works such as *Polityka III Rzeszy w okupowanej Polsce*[37] and *Faszyzm i okupacje*.[38]

---

29 L. Brener, "O pracy przymusowej ludności żydowskiej w Częstochowie w okresie okupacji hitlerowskiej," *BŻIH* 22 (1952): 45–60.
30 Szymon Datner, "Sonderkommando 1005 i jego działalność ze szczególnym uwzględnieniem okręgu białostockiego," *BŻIH* 100 (1976): 63–78.
31 A. Rutkowski, "Hitlerowskie obozy pracy dla Żydów w dystrykcie radomskim," *BŻIH* 17–18 (1956): 106–26.
32 Bronisław Wróblewski, "Obóz w Budzyniu," *Zeszyty Majdanka* 5 (1971): 179–189.
33 Czesław Madajczyk, "Lubelszczyzna w polityce okupanta," *Zeszyty Majdanka* 2 (1967): 5–18; Czesław Rajca, "Lubelska filia Niemieckich Zakładów Zbrojeniowych," *Zeszyty Majdanka* 4 (1969): 237–300; Józef Kasperek, "Początki organizacji i działalności urzędów pracy na Lubelszczyźnie (październik 1939—styczeń 1940)," *Zeszyty Majdanka* 6 (1972): 130–150; Józef Kasperek, "Zarys organizacyjny Arbeitsamtów w dystrykcie lubelskim w latach 1939–1944," *Zeszyty Majdanka* 7 (1973): 94–117; Józef Kasperek, "Metody werbunku do przymusowych robót w III Rzeszy na terenie dystryktu lubelskiego w latach 1939–1944," *Zeszyty Majdanka* 8 (1975): 52–99; Mścisław Wróblewski, *Służba Budowlana*.
34 Szymon Datner, "Obozy jenieckie na Lubelszczyźnie w latach okupacji niemieckiej," *Zeszyty Majdanka* 3 (1969): 235–37.
35 Czesław Szczepańczyk, "Centralny Urząd Rolniczy—Landwirtschaftliche Zentralstelle," *Zeszyty Majdanka* 7 (1973): 121–58.
36 Szymon Datner, "Wywóz ludności polskiej na roboty niewolnicze do Niemiec," *BGKBZHP* XVI (1967): 17–64; Szymon Datner, "Zbrodnie Wehrmachtu na jeńcach wojennych w zakresie pracy," *BGKBZHP* XVII (1967): 7–100.
37 Czesław Madajczyk, *Polityka III Rzeszy w okupowanej Polsce* (Warsaw: PWN, 1970).
38 Czesław Madajczyk, *Faszyzm i okupacje 1938–1945: Wykonywanie okupacji przez państwa Osi w Europie*, vol. 1, *Ukształtowanie się zarządów okupacyjnych* (Poznań: Wydawnictwo Poznańskie, 1983), and vol. 2, *Mechanizmy realizowania okupacji* (Poznań: Wydawnictwo Poznańskie, 1984).

Madajczyk also wrote some important studies about Generalplan Ost[39] and the General Government.[40] Czesław Łuczak also researched economic aspects of the occupation.[41] During the 1970s, more books were published about the monetary and fiscal policy of the German authorities in Poland by Franciszek Skalniak[42] and Karol Ostrowski.[43] In 1976, Alfred Konieczny published an important collection of documents on forced labor of Poles.[44] It is important to stress that during the communist period in Poland, there was a tendency to speak about Poles or Polish citizens (including Polish Jews) and not Jews. Toward the end of 1970s and the beginning of the 1980s, important books were published about forced labor and the German arms industry in the district of Kielce by Kaczanowski,[45] Meducki,[46] and Pietrzykowski[47]. Herbert Szurgacz published in 1979 his study about forced labor of Poles under the Nazi occupants in 1941.[48] One of the most important publications of this period in Poland was an encyclopedia or lexicon of Nazi camps in the Polish territories from 1939 to 1945, published in 1979.[49] This book gave very short descriptions of many camps, including labor camps for Poles and for Jews, which until then were literally unknown. During the 1980s, relatively few publications appeared concerning the question of forced labor and various

---

39 Czesław Madajczyk, *Generalplan Ost* (Poznań: Instytut Zachodni, 1962).
40 Czesław Madajczyk, *Generalna Gubernia w planach hitlerowskich: Studia* (Warsaw: Państwowe Wydawnictwo Naukowe, 1961).
41 Czesław Łuczak, *Polityka ludnościowa i ekonomiczna hitlerowskich Niemiec w okupowanej Polsce* (Poznań: Wydawnictwo Poznańskie, 1979).
42 Franciszek Skalniak, *Polityka pieniężna i budżetowa tzw. Generalnego Gubernatorstwa narzedziem finansowania potrzeb III Rzeszy* (Warsaw: Ministerstwo Sprawiedliwości. Główna Komisja Badania Zbrodni Hitlerowskich w Polsce, 1976); Franciszek Skalniak, *Stopa życiowa społeczeństwa polskiego w okresie okupacji na terenie Generalnego Gubernatorstwa* (Warsaw: Ministerstwo Sprawiedliwości. Główna Komisja Badania Zbrodni Hitlerowskich w Polsce, 1979).
43 Karol Ostrowski, *Hitlerowska polityka podatkowa w Generalnym Gubernatorstwie* (Krakow: PWN, 1977).
44 Alfred Konieczny, ed., *Praca przymusowa Polakow pod panowaniem hitlerowskim, 1939–1945, Wybór źródeł i opracowanie* (Poznań: Instytut Zachodni, 1976).
45 Longin Kaczanowski, *Hitlerowskie fabryki śmierci na Kielecczyźnie* (Warszawa: Książka i Wiedza, 1984).
46 Stanisław Meducki, *Przemysł i klasa robotnicza w dystrykcie radomskim w okresie okupacji hitlerowskiej* (Krakow: PWN, 1981).
47 Jan Pietrzykowski, *Łowy na ludzi: Arbeitsamt w Częstochowie* (Katowice: Wydawnictwo Śląsk, 1968).
48 Herbert Szurgacz, *Przymusowe zatrudnianie Polaków przez hitlerowskiego okupanta w latach 1939–1945: Studium prawno-polityczne* (Wroclaw: Ossolineum, 1971).
49 Czesław Pilichowski, ed., *Obozy hitlerowskie na ziemiach polskich 1939–1945: Informator encyklopedyczny* (Warszawa: PWN, 1979).

aspects of the Nazi economy during the war. Likely, this was due to the period of great changes that took place in Poland in the beginning of the 1980s and the development of new trade and the political movement of Solidarity. Moreover, on December 13, 1981 a state of emergency was announced, which included the return of censorship and great limitations of movement and possibilities of travel abroad, as well as lack of open use of the archives. It should be stressed that until the end of the 1980s, most researchers engaged in research of the period of Nazism were in some way linked to the establishment—only because of this did they have open access to the archives. Many of those researchers were employees of the Main Commission for Investigation of Nazi Crimes in Poland (GKBZHP) and martyrological museums at Auschwitz, Majdanek, and Stutthof. Jewish researchers and researchers of Polish origin dealing with Jewish subjects were active mainly in the Jewish Historical Institute in Warsaw. Among the few publications of the 1980s, we may quote those of Krzysztof Dunin-Wasowicz,[50] himself a survivor of Nazi camps, Ryszard Gicewicz,[51] or Władysław Misiuna.[52]

The 1990s saw the new research of Józef Marszałek, a scholar employed at the State Museum in Majdanek.[53] His important work on forced labor camps in the General Government was published in 1998,[54] after his early and unexpected death in 1995. A summary of his research was published in English in 2001.[55] Also in the 1990s, yet another researcher from Lublin, named Tadeusz Radzik, published his papers and a book about the Lublin ghetto.[56]

---

50 Krzysztof Dunin-Wasowicz, "Forced Labor and Sabotage in the Nazi Concentration Camps," *The Nazi Concentration Camps* (1984): 133–42.
51 Ryszard Gicewicz, "Obóz pracy w Poniatowej (1941–1943)," *Zeszyty Majdanka* 10 (1980): 88–104.
52 Władysław Misiuna, "Wspomnienia o dziewczętach z obozu pracy dla Żydów w Radomiu," *BŻIH* 1/149 (1989): 91–99.
53 Józef Marszałek, "Rozpoznanie obozów śmierci w Bełżcu, Sobiborze i Treblince przez wywiad Armii Krajowej i Delegatury Rządu Rzeczypospolitej Polskiej na Kraj," *BGKBZHP XXXV* (1993): 36–52; Józef Marszałek, "The camp of Zarzecze near Nisko in the system of Jewish labor camps," in *Akce Nisko* (1995): 139–147; Józef Marszałek, "System obozów śmierci w Generalnym Gubernatorstwie i jego funkcje (1942–1943)," *Zeszyty Majdanka* 17 (1996): 17–35.
54 Józef Marszałek, *Obozy pracy w Generalnym Gubernatorstwie w latach 1939–1945* (Lublin: Państwowe Muzeum na Majdanku, 1998).
55 Józef Marszałek, "Labor camps in the General Government, 1939–1945," *Pro Memoria* 11 (2001): 37–42.
56 Tadeusz Radzik, "Praca przymusowa ludności żydowskiej na przykładzie obozu pracy w Bełżcu w 1940 r.," in *Żydzi i judaizm we współczesnych badaniach polskich: Materiały z konferencji, Kraków, 21–23 XI 1995*, ed. Krzysztof Pilarczyk (Krakow: Księgarnia Akademicka Wydawnictwo Naukowe, 1997), 307–19; Józef Marszałek, *Lubelska dzielnica zamknięta* (Lublin: Wydawnictwo UMCS, 1999).

Since the beginning of the new century, many researchers of the younger generation begun to publish their books and articles. In 2001, Barbara Engelking and Jacek Leociak published their monumental work on the Warsaw Ghetto.[57] In 2003, Barbara Engelking and her colleagues established a new Center for Holocaust Research at the Institute of Philosophy and Sociology of the Polish Academy of Sciences. Since then, the members of the Center, as well as many other researchers, have published many books and articles on the Holocaust in Poland. For example, Marta Janczewska published her study about forced labor camps in the district of Warsaw.[58] Edward Kopówka,[59] Sebastian Piątkowski,[60] and Krzysztof Gibaszewski[61] also published books and articles about different labor camps in the General Government. Beata Macior-Majka published a book on *Generalplan Ost* and its economic and political aspects.[62] Witold Mędykowski published a study concerning forced labor of POWs during World War II.[63] Although Anna Ziółkowska's research concerned not the General Government but Warthegau, she also explored the transfer of workers from Warthegau to the General Government, and thus her work is worth mentioning.[64]

In 2009, two researchers from the State Museum in Majdanek, Wojciech Lenarczyk and Dariusz Libionka, published one of the first books containing studies and documents on the Operation *Erntefest*, during which about 42,000 were executed on November 3 and 4, 1943 in Majdanek, Poniatowa, and Trawniki. This volume also contains some articles about labor camps

---

57 Barbara Engelking and Jacek Leociak, *Getto warszawskie: Przewodnik po nieistniejącym mieście* (Warsaw: Wydawnictwo IFiS PAN, 2001).
58 Marta Janczewska, "Obozy pracy przymusowej dla Żydów na terenie dystryktu warszawskiego," Prowincja noc (2007): 271–320.
59 Edward Kopówka, "Obozy pracy przymusowej w Szczeglacinie i Bartkowie Nowym k. Siedlec," *Kwartalnik Historii Żydów* 204 (2002): 515–19.
60 Sebastian Piątkowski, "Obóz pracy w Bliżynie (1942–1944)," *Zeszyty Majdanka* 21 (2001): 97–112; Sebastian Piątkowski, "Żydowscy robotnicy przymusowi w radomskiej fabryce obuwia 'Bata' (1941–1943)," Kwartalnik Historii Żydów 227 (2008): 322–33.
61 Krzysztof Gibaszewski, HASAG: Historia obozu pracy w Skarżysku Kamiennej (Skarżysko Kamienna: Muzeum im. Orła Białego, 2011).
62 Beata Macior-Majka, *Generalny Plan Wschodni: Aspekt ideologiczny, polityczny i ekonomiczny* (Krakow: Avalon, 2007).
63 Witold Mędykowski, "Pomiędzy euforią a klęską: Polityka zatrudnienia jeńców wojennych w przemyśle zbrojeniowym III Rzeszy," *Łambinowicki Rocznik Muzealny* 31 (2008): 7–28.
64 Anna Ziółkowska, "Obozy pracy przymusowej dla Żydów w Poznańskiem w czasie okupacji Hitlerowskiej," *Żydzi i judaizm we współczesnych badaniach polskich* II (2000): 313–23; Anna Ziółkowska, *Obozy pracy przymusowej dla Żydów w Wielkopolsce* (Poznań: Wydawnictwo Poznańskie, 2005).

liquidated during this action, such as Majdanek, Lipowa 7 in Lublin,[65] Poniatowa,[66] Trawniki, Dorohucza,[67] and Budzyń.[68]

On the other hand, the literature outside Poland concerning economic aspects and forced labor had a different trajectory. Already, during the war, books appeared dealing with economic exploitation and forced labor.[69] During the first years after the war, coming to terms with Nazism was determined by a number of significant events—namely, the International Military Tribunal in Nuremberg in 1945–1946, during which many leaders of Nazi Germany were put on trial. Among them were people responsible for the economy and forced labor, such as Hermann Göring, Albert Speer, Alfred Rosenberg, Fritz Sauckel, and Hans Frank. After the main trial, smaller trials took place during the years 1945–1949, some of them concerned with different aspects of economic life and exploitation of forced labor. Worth mentioning is the trial of Oswald Pohl and WVHA, and the trials of Friedrich Flick, Alfred Krupp, and IG-Farben. The trial of Oswald Pohl and WVHA in particular touched many economic aspects of exploitation of forced and slave labor of prisoners in concentration camps. As a consequence of the Nuremberg trials, thousands of documents were published that would serve as a basis for future research.[70]

During the postwar period, many important books appeared about World War II, Nazism, and the resistance. A study of fundamental importance was published in 1961 by Raul Hilberg.[71] This monumental work was based on thousands of documents captured by the Americans and stored in Alexandria. Yet another important event took place the same year: the Eichmann Trial in Jerusalem, during which many Jewish witnesses appeared. The Nuremberg and Jerusalem trials changed perspectives on Nazism and marked a new period

---

65 Wojciech Lenarczyk, "Obóz pracy przymusowej dla Żydów przy ul. Lipowej w Lublinie (1939–1943)," *Erntefest 3-4 listopada 1943—zapomniany epizod Zagłady*, ed. Wojciech Lenarczyk and Dariusz Libionka (Lublin: Państowe Muzeum na Majdanku, 2009), 37–71.
66 Ryszard Gicewicz, "Obóz pracy w Poniatowej (1941–1943)," in Lenarczyk and Libionka, *Erntefest*, 211–28.
67 Witold Mędykowski, "Obóz pracy dla Żydów w Trawnikach," in Lenarczyk and Libionka, *Erntefest*, 183–210.
68 Wojciech Lenarczyk, "Obóz pracy przymusowej w Budzyniu (1942–1944)," in Lenarczyk and Libionka, *Erntefest*, 261–86.
69 John Price, *Organised Labor in the War* (New York: A. Lane, 1940).
70 *Trial of the Major War Criminals before the International Military Tribunal, 14 October 1945–1 November 1946* (Nuremberg: International Military Tribunal, 1947).
71 Raul Hilberg, *The Destruction of the European Jews* (Chicago: Harper & Row, 1961).

in Holocaust research. In the 1960s and 1970s, many new documents and studies were published. Among them are the diaries of Adam Czerniakow,[72] documents from the Lublin ghetto,[73] and the monumental work of Yeshayhu Trunk, entitled *Judenrat*.[74]

Among the researchers who began to study economic aspects of the Nazi period was Georg Enno. He published in 1963 a study of economic enterprises of the SS.[75] He was followed by a researcher from East Germany, Eva Seeber, who in 1964 published a book about the labor of Polish citizens, especially from the General Government, employed in the German war economy.[76] A year later, Hans Buchheim and Martin Broszat published the book *Anatomie des SS-Staates*, where one chapter was dedicated to Nazi concentration camps, including forced labor of the prisoners.[77] In 1968, Edward Homze published a book about foreign labor in Nazi Germany.[78] The same year, Dieter Pezina published his book about policy of autarchy in Nazi Germany, which was intended to protect Germany from international blockade.[79]

During the 1980s and 1990s, Götz Aly and Susanne Heim published a number of studies concerning the reasons for extermination of Jews. Those discussions were a kind of continuation of *Historikerstreit*, which took place in Germany in the 1980s.[80] In 1983, Götz Aly published a study entitled *Sozialpolitik und Judenvernichtung: Gibt es eine Ökonomie der Enlösung?*[81]

---

72 Adam Czerniakow, *Warsaw Ghetto Diary* (Jerusalem: Yad Vashem, 1968).
73 Nachman Blumental, ed., *Documents from the Lublin Ghetto: Judenrat without Direction* (Jerusalem: Yad Vashem, 1967).
74 Isaiah Trunk, *Judenrat: The Jewish Councils in Eastern Europe under Nazi Occupation* (New York: Macmillan, 1972).
75 Enno Georg, *Die Wirtschaftlichen Unternehmungen der SS* (Stuttgart: Deutsche Verlags-Anstalt, 1963).
76 Eva Seeber, *Zwangsarbeiter in der faschistischen Kriegswirtschaft: die deportation und Ausbeutung polnischer Burger unter besonderer Berücksichtigung der Lage der Arbeiter aus dem sogenannten Generalgouvernement (1939–1945)* (Berlin: VEB Deutscher Verlag der Wissenschaften, 1964).
77 Martin Broszat, "Nationalsozialistische Konzetrationslager 1933–1945," in *Anatomie des SS-Staates*, ed. Martin Broszat (Freiburg: Walter-Verlag, 1965).
78 Edward L. Homze, *Foreign Labor in Nazi Germany* (Princeton, NJ: Princeton University Press, 1967).
79 Dieter Petzina, *Autarkiepolitik im Dritten Reich: Der nationallsozialistische Vierjahresplan* (Stuttgart: Deutsche Verlags-Anstalt, 1968).
80 Martin Broszat and Saul Friedlaender, "A Controversy about the Historicization of National Sozialism," *Yad Vashem Studes* 19 (1988): 1–47.
81 Götz Aly et al., *Sozialpolitik und Judenvernichtung: Gibt es eine Ökonomie der Enlösung?* (Berlin: Rotbuch Verlag, 1983).

During the following years, Götz Aly and Susanne Heim published a number of other studies in German and English dealing with the questions of social policy, economy, forced labor, rationalization, planning, and the extermination of Jews.[82] Christian Gerlach also studied the link between the problem of nourishment and extermination.[83] In the mid-1980s, one of the leading researchers of forced labor in Nazi Germany, Ulrich Herbert, began to publish his works.[84] During the 1990s, a number of new researchers published their works concerning German administration, forced labor, and the murder of Jews.[85]

In 1993, a young German researcher named Dieter Pohl began to publish his works. Pohl begun his career with a study of the Lublin District.[86]

---

82 Götz Aly and Susanne Heim, "The Economics of the Final Solution: A Case Study from the General Government," *Simon Wiesenthal Center Annual* 5 (1988): 3–48; Götz Aly and Susanne Heim, eds., *Bevölkerungsstruktur und Massenmord: Neue Dokumente zur deutschen Politik der Jahre 1938–1945* (Berlin: Rotbuch Verlag, 1991); Götz Aly, *Endlösung: Völkerverschiebung und der Mord an den europäischen Juden* (Frankfurt a. M.: Fischer, 1995) (English edition: *"Final Solution": Nazi Population Policy and the Murder of European Jews* [London: Arnold, 1999]); Aly Götz and Susanne Heim, *Vordenker der Vernichtung: Auschwitz und die deutschen Pläne für eine neue europäische Ordnung* (Frankfurt a. M.: Fischer, 1995) (English edition: *Architects of Annihilation: Auschwitz and the Logic of Destruction* [London: Weidenfeld and Nicolson, 2002]).

83 Gerlach, Christian, *Krieg, Ernährung, Völkermord: Forschungen zur deutschen Vernichtungspolitik im Zweiten Weltkrieg*, Hamburger Edition, Hamburg, 1998.

84 Urlich Herbert, *Fremdarbeiter: Politik und Praxis des Ausländer Eisatzez in der Krieg des Dritten Reiches* (Berlin: J. H. W. Dietz, 1986); Urlich Herbert, *Arbeit, Volkstum, Weltanschauung: Über Fremde und Deutsche im 20. Jahrhundert* (Frankfurt a. M.: Fischer, 1995); Urlich Herbert, *Hitler Foreign Workers: The Forced Foreign Labor in Germany under the Third Reich* (Cambrigde: Cambridge University Press, 1997); Urlich Herbert, *Nationalsozialistische Vernichtungspolitik 1939–1945: Neue Forschungen und Kontroversen* (Frankfurt a. M.: Fischer, 1998); Urlich Herbert, "Zwangsarbeiter im 'Dritten Reich' und das Problem der Entschädigung: Ein Überblick," in *Die politische Ökonomie des Holocaust* (2001): 203–38.

85 Konrad Kwiet, "Forced Labor of German Jews in Nazi Germany," *Leo Baeck Institute Year Book* 36 (1991): 389–410; Richard Breitman, *The Architect of Genocide: Himmler and the Final Solution* (London: Bodley Head, 1991).

86 Dieter Pohl, *Von der 'Judenpolitik' zum Judenmord: Der Distrikt Lublin des Generalgouvernements 1939–1944* (Frankfurt a. M.: Lang, 1993); Dieter Pohl, "Rola dystryktu lubelskiego w 'ostatecznym rozwiązaniu kwestii żydowskiej,'" *Zeszyty Majdanka* 18 (1997): 7–24; Dieter Pohl, *Nationalsozialistische Judenverfolgung in Ostgalizien 1941–1944: Organisation und Durchfürung eines staatlichen Massenverbrechens*, Studien zur Zeitgeschichte (München: R. Oldenbourg Verlag, 1997); Dieter Pohl, "Die Ermordung der Juden im Generalgouvernement," *Nationalsozialistische Vernichtungspolitik* (1998): 98–121; Dieter Pohl, "Die Grossen Zwangsarbeitslager der SS- und Polizeiführer für Juden im Generalgouvernement 1942–1945," in *Die nationalsozialistischen Konzentrationslager: Entwicklung und Struktur*, ed. Christopher Dieckmann (Göttingen: Wallstein Vlg, 1998), 415–438; Dieter Pohl, "Ukrainische Hilfskräfte beim Mord an den Juden," in *Täter der Shoah:*

In the mid-1980s, yet another leading scholar of the Holocaust, Christopher Browning, began to publish.[87] However, his important studies concerning the path to the final solution and question of labor were published later—in the 1990s and during the first decade of the twenty-first century.[88] His monumental study, titled *The Origins of the Final Solution: The Evolution of Nazi Jewish Policy, September 1939–March 1942*, was published in 2004.[89] During the 1990s, other scholars took interest in forced labor and labor camps. Among them was an Israeli scholar, herself a survivor of the HASAG labor camp in Skarżysko Kamienna and in Leipzig, Felicja Karay. Her study, *Death Comes in Yellow: Skarżysko-Kamienna Slave Labor Camp*,[90] deals not only with the labor camp in Skarżysko-Kamienna, but also with the functioning of the HASAG Company and a complex of many different labor camps in the district of Radom. In her other studies she researched additional labor camps in the General Government and other territories.[91] Since the early 1990s, Wolf Gruner has written a series of publications concerning forced labor in Nazi

---

Fanatische Nationalsozialisten oder ganz normale Deutsche?, ed. Gerhard Paul (Göttingen: Wallstein Vlg, 2002); Dieter Pohl, "Die '*Aktion Reinhard*' im Licht der Historiographie," in: *Aktion Reinhardt* (2004): 15–47; Dieter Pohl, "Die Stellung des Distrikts Lublin in der 'Endlösung der Judenfrage,'" in: *Aktion Reinhardt* (2004): 87–107.

87 Christopher Browning, *Fateful Months: Essays on the Emergence of the Final Solution* (New York: Holmes and Meier Publishers, 1985).

88 Christopher Browning, "Nazi Germany's Initial Attempt to Exploit Jewish Labor in the General Government: The Early Jewish Work Camps 1940–41," *Die Normalität des Verbrechens* (1994): 171–85; Christopher Browning, *The Path to Genocide: Essays on Launching the Final Solution* (Cambridge: Cambridge University Press, 1998); Christopher Browning, "Jewish Workers in Poland: Self-Maintenance, Exploitation, Destruction," in *Nazi Policy, Jewish Workers, German Killers*, ed. Christopher Browning (Cambridge: Cambridge University Press, 2000), 58–88; Christopher Browning, "Jewish Workers and Survivor Memories: The Case of the Starachowice Labor Camp," in Browning, *Nazi Policy*, 89–115; Christopher Browning, "'Alleviation' and 'Compliance': The Survival Strategies of the Jewish Leadership in the Wierzbnik Ghetto and Starachowice Factory Slave Labor Camps," *Gray Zones* (2005): 26–36.

89 Christopher Browning, with contributions by Jurgen Matthaus, *The Origins of the Final Solution: The Evolution of Nazi Jewish Policy, September 1939–March 1942* (Lincoln: University of Nebraska Press, 2004).

90 Felicja Karay, *Death Comes in Yellow: Skarżysko-Kamienna Slave Labor Camp* (Amsterdam: Harwood Academic Publishers, 1996).

91 Felicja Karay, "Spór między władzami niemieckimi o żydowskie obozy pracy w Generalnej Guberni," *Zeszyty Majdanka* 18 (1997), 27–44; Felicja Karay, "The Conflict among German Authorities over Jewish Slave Labor Camps in the General Government," *Yalkut Moreshet* (1999): 1–28; Felicja Karay, "Women in the Forced-Labor Camps," in *Women in the Holocaust*, ed. Dalia Ofer, Lenore J. Weitzman (New Haven: Yale University Press, 1998), 285–309; Felicja Karay, "Żydowskie obozy pracy w czasie 'akcji Reinhardt,'" in *Akcja Reinhardt. Zagłada Żydów w Generalnym Gubernatorstwie*, ed. Dariusz Libionka (Warsaw: IPN,

Germany and the occupied territories.[92] More focused studies on Galicia were published by Thomas Sandkühler.[93] At the end of the 1990s, Bogdan Musial published important studies concerning the German administration of the General Government as well as the decision-making process leading to the Aktion Reinhardt.[94] In 1998, Hedwig Singer published her essential book about Organisation Todt.[95] The same year also saw the publication of an important lexicon of Nazi concentration camps, labor camps, and labor *kommandos*.[96]

Since the beginning of the twenty-first century, there has been an intensive development of research concerning forced labor, mainly in Germany and neighboring countries. Jan Erik Schulte published his important studies, continuing his thesis of extermination through labor.[97] During the

---

2004), 248–60; Felicja Karay, "Heaven or Hell? The Two Faces of the HASAG-Kielce Camp," *Yad Vashem Studies* 32 (2004): 269–321.

92 Wolf Gruner, "Der Beginn der Zwangsarbeit für arbeitslose Juden in Deutschland 1938–39," *Zeitschrift für Geschichtswissenschaft* 37/2 (1989): 135–151; Wolf Gruner, "Terra Incognita?: The Camps for Jewish Labor Conscription (1938–1943) and the German Population," *Yad Vashem Studies* 24 (1994): 3–42; Wolf Gruner, *Der geschlossene Arbeitseinsatz deutscher Juden: Zur Zwangsarbeit als Element der Verfolgung 1938–1943* (Berlin: Metropol Vlg., 1997); Wolf Gruner, *Die Organisation von Zwangsarbeit für Juden in Deutschland und im Generalgouvernement 1939–1943, eine vergleichende Bestandsaufnahme* (Berlin: Stiftung Topographie des Terrors, 1995); Wolf Gruner, *Jewish Forced Labor under the Nazis: Economic Needs and Racial Aims, 1938–1944* (Cambridge: Cambridge University Press, 2006).

93 Thomas Sandkühler, *"Endlösung" in Galizien: Der Judenmord in Ostpolen und die Rettungsinitiativen von Bertold Beitz, 1941–1944* (Bonn: Dietz, 1996); Thomas Sandkühler, "Zwangsarbeit und Judenmord im Distrikt Galizien des Generalgouvernements: Die Rettungsinitiativen von Berthold Beitz," in *Konzentrationslager und deutsche Wirtschaft 1939–1945*, ed. Hermann Kaienburg (Opladen: Leske and Budrich, 1996), 239–62; Thomas Sandkühler, "Das Zwangsarbeitslager Lemberg-Janowska 1941–1944," in *Die nationalsozialistischen Konzentrationslager* II (1998): 606–35; Thomas Sandkühler, "Rozpoczęcie 'ostatecznego rozwiązania kwestii żydowskiej' w Generalnym Gubernatorstwie na przykładzie dystryktu galicyjskiego w latach 1941–1942," *Zeszyty Majdanka* 19 (1998): 7–33.

94 Bogdan Musiał, *Deutsche Zivilverwaltung und Judenverfolgung im Generalgouvernement: Eine Fallstudie zum Distrikt Lublin, 1939–1944* (Wiesbaden: Harrassowitz Verlag, 1999); Bogdan Musiał, "The Origins of 'Operation Reinhardt': The Decision-Making Process for the Mass Murder of the Jews on the Generalgouvernement," *Yad Vashem Studies* (2000).

95 Hedwig Singer, *Organisation Todt* (Osnabrück: Biblio), 1998.

96 Martin Weinmann, Ane Kaiser, and Ursula Krause-Schmidt, eds., *Die Nationalsozialistische Lagersystem (CCP)* (Frankfurt a. M.: Zweitausendeins, 1998).

97 Jan Erik Schulte, "Zwangsarbeit für die SS—Juden in der Ostindustrie GmbH," in *Ausbeutung, Vernichtung, Öffentlichkeit*, ed. Norbert Frei (Munich: Saur, 2000); Jan Erik Schulte, *Zwangsarbeit und Vernichtung: Das Wirtschaftsimperium der SS: Oswald Pohl und das SS-Wirtschafts-Verwaltungshauptamt 1933–1945* (Padeborn: Ferdinand Schöningh, 2001).

same period, other authors published studies supporting the same idea.[98] In the first decade of the twenty-first century, many studies appeared concerning the Nazi economy, and in particular, the economic enterprises of the SS (such as the volumes written by Allen and Fear).[99] Among the other authors writing about the Nazi economy were Wolfgang Benz,[100] Herman Kaienburg,[101] Ingo Loose,[102] and others.[103] In those years, several biographies of Odilo Globocnik were also published, which naturally deal the with economic enterprises that he headed.[104] Studies by Finder, Bender, Browning, and Wenzel were dedicated to labor camps in the General Government.[105] In 2005, Wolfgang Benz and Barabra Distel published a multivolume book about Nazi concentration camps, which also explored labor camps.[106] In 2008, an important collection of documents from the

---

98 Joel Kotek, Pierre Rigoulot, eds., *Das Jahrhundert der Lager: Gefangenschaft, Zwangsarbeit, Vernichtung* (Berlin: Propyläen, 2001); Jörg Echtenkamp, *Die deutsche Kriegsgesellschaft: 1939 bis 1945: Politisierung, Vernichtung, Überleben*, vol. 1 (Stuttgart: DVA, 2004); Andrej Angrick, "Annihilation and Labor: Jews and Thoroughfare IV in Central Ukraine," in *The Shoah in Ukraine: History, Testimony, Memorialization*, ed. Ray Brandon, Wendy Lower (Bloomington: Indiana University Press, 2008), 190–223.

99 Michael Thad Allen, *The Business of Genocide: The SS, Slave Labor and the Concentration Camps* (Chapel Hill: University of North Carolina Press, 2002); Jeffrey Fear, "The Business of Genocide: The SS, Slave Labor and the Concentration Camps," *Business History Review*, June 30, 2004.

100 Benz, "Zwangsarbeit im nationalsozialistischen Staat," 3–17.

101 Hermann Kaienburg, "Zwangsarbeit von Juden in Arbeits- und Konzentrationslagern," in *"Arisierung" im Nationalsozialismus*, ed. Irmtrud Wojak and Peter Hayes (Frankfurt a. M.: Campus Verlag, 2000), 219–40; Hermann Kaienburg, *Die Wirtschaft der SS* (Berlin: Metropol, 2003).

102 Ingo Loose, "Credit Banks and the Holocaust in the 'Generalgouvernement,' 1939–1945," *Yad Vashem Studies* 34 (2006): 177–218.

103 Joachim Neander, "The SS and the Economics of Genocide," *Yad Vashem Studies* 32 (2004): 449–67; Hans-Christian Petersen, *Bevölkerungsökonomie—Ostforschung—Politik: eine biographische Studie zu Peter-Heinz Seraphim (1902–1979)* (Osnabrück: Fibre, 2007).

104 Joseph Poprzeczny, *Globocnik—Hitler's Man in the East* (London: McFarland & Company, 2004); Berndt Rieger, *Creator of Nazi Death Camps: The Life of Odilo Globocnik* (London: Valentine-Mitschell, 2007).

105 Gabriel N. Finder, "Jewish Prisoner Labor in Warsaw after the Ghetto Uprising, 1943–1944," *Polin* 17 (2004): 325–51; Mario Wenzel, "Ausbeutung und Vernichtung: Zwangsarbeitslager für Juden im Distrikt Krakau 1942–1944," *Dachauer Hefte* 23 (2007): 189–207; Christopher Browning, *Remembering Survival: Inside a Nazi Slave Labor Camp* (New York: W. W. Norton, 2010); Sara Bender, "Jewish Slaves in Forced Labor Camps in Kielce, September 1942–August 1944," *Polin* 23 (2011): 437–63.

106 Wolfgang Benz, Barbara Distel, eds., *Der Ort des Terrors: Geschichte der nationalsozialistischen Konzentrationslager*, vol. 1–9 (Munich: Beck, 2005).

Nazi period began to be compiled in a volume, edited by Susanne Heim, Ulrich Herbert, Hans-Dieter Kreikamp, Horst Müller, Dieter Pohl, and Hartmut Weber.[107] During that period, few research works concerning particular districts of the General Government were written or published. Among those that appeared, especially significant are the dissertation of David Silberklang about the Lublin District,[108] the work of Jacek Andrzej Młynarczyk about the district of Radom,[109] and Sara Bender's study about Kielce and its surroundings, published in Hebrew.[110]

After 2010, the research of forced labor intensified due, among other causes, to research launched by the Foundation "Remembrance, Responsibility and Future" (*Stiftung Erinnerung, Verantwortung und Zukunft*, EVZ). A catalogue of the exhibition "Forced Labor" appeared in 2010, containing some important overviews written by leading researchers.[111] In 2013, two books were published by the participants of this program.[112] In the same year, a volume edited by Dieter Pohl and Tanja Sebta was published[113] containing some essential studies by the participants of the historical program of the EVZ.[114] In 2013,

---

107 Susanne Heim, Ulrich Herbert, Hans-Dieter Kreikam pet al., eds., *Die Verfolgung und Ermordung der europäischen Juden durch das nationalsozialistische Deutschland 1933–1945*, vol. 1–7 (Munich: R. Oldenbourg Verlag, 2008–2012).

108 David Silberklang, *The Holocaust in the Lublin District*, PhD thesis (Jerusalem, 2003, subsequently published as *Gates of Tears: The Holocaust in the Lublin disctrict* (Jerusalem: Yad Vashem, 2013).

109 Jacek Andrzej Młynarczyk, *Judenmord in Zentralpolen: Der Distrikt Radom im Generalgouvernement 1939–1945* (Warsaw: Deutsche Historische Institut, and Darmstadt: Forschungstelle Ludwigsburg der Universität Stuttgart, 2007).

110 Sara Bender, *Be-Eretz Oyev: The Jews of Kielce and the Vicinity during World War II—1939–1945* (Jerusalem: Yad Vashem, 2012). An English version is due to appear in 2018 (Boston: Academic Studies Press).

111 Wagner, "Forced Labor"; Andreas Heusler, "*Forced Labor* in the Nazi War Economy: The Genesis of a Research Genre," in Knigge et al., *Forced Labor*, 194–201; Dieter Pohl, "Forced Labor in Occupied Eastern Europe—A Research Overview," in Knigge et al., *Forced Labor*, 202–7; Manfred Grieger, "Extermination and Work under the Nazi System of Forced Labor," in Knigge et al., *Forced Labor*, 208–19.

112 Dierl Florian, Janjetović Zoran, and Linne Karsten, *Pflicht, Zwang und Gewalt: Arbeitsverwaltungen und Arbeitskräftspolitik im deutsch besetzten Polen und Serbien 1939–1944* (Essen: Klartext, 2013). Dieter Steinert, *Deportation und Zwangsarbeit: Polnische und sowjetische Kinder im nazionalsozialistischen Deutschland und im besetzten Osteuropa 1939–1945* (Essen: Klartext, 2013).

113 Dieter Pohl and Tanja Sebta, ed., *Zwangsarbeit in Hitlers Europa: Besatzung-Arbeit-Folgen* (Berlin: Metropol, 2013).

114 Dieter Pohl and Tanja Sebta, "Nationalsozialistische Zwangsarbeit außerhalb des Deutsches Reiches und ihre Folgen," in Pohl and Sebta, *Zwangsarbeit in Hitlers Europa*, 13–22; Ulrich Herbert, "Zwangsarbeit im 20. Jahrhundert," in Pohl and Sebta, *Zwangsarbeit in Hitlers*

a young German researcher working on various aspects of forced labor, an author of many articles about forced labor, Stephan Lehnstaedt,[115] edited *Arbeit in den nationalsozialistischen Ghettos* with Jürgen Hensel, which contains various studies concerning the General Government and the question of forced labor in general.[116] At the end of 2013, yet another volume appeared, edited by Imke Hansen, Katrin Steffen, and Joachim Tauber, with articles concerning forced labor and economic life in the ghettos of Eastern Europe.[117] Some recent studies explore compensations for forced labor in camps and ghettos.[118]

Europa, 23–36; Karsten Linne, "Struktur und Praxis der deutschen Arbeitsverwaltung im besetzten Polen und Serbien," in Pohl and Sebta, *Zwangsarbeit in Hitlers Europa*, 39–61; Mario Wenzel, "Die Arbeitslager für Juden im Distrikt Krakau des Generalgouvernements 1940–1941," in Pohl and Sebta, *Zwangsarbeit in Hitlers Europa*. 173–194.

115 Stephan Lehnstaedt, "Die deutsche Arbeitsverwaltung im Generalgouvernement und die Juden," in *Vierteljahrshefte für Zeitgeschichte* 60 (2012): 409–40; Stephan Lehnstaedt, "Jewish Labor in the Smaller Ghettos in the Warthegau Region," in *Yad Vashem Studies* 38/2 (2010): 47–84; Stephan Lehnstaedt, "Coercion and Incentive: Jewish Ghetto Labor in East Upper Silesia," in *Holocaust and Genocide Studies* 24 (2010): 400–430.

116 Stephan Lehnstaedt, "Zwischen Profitgier, Überleben und Rente: Überlegungen zu einer Geschichte der *Arbeit in nationalsozialistischen Ghettos*," in Arbeit in den nationalsozialistischen Ghettos, ed. Jürgen Hensel and Stephan Lehnstaedt (Osnabrück: Fibre, 2013), 11–29; Witold Mędykowski, "Wie überdauerte ein Ghetto? Mikroökonomische Aspekte," in Hensel and Lehnstaedt, *Arbeit*, 53–69; Ingo Loose, "Die Bedeutung der Ghettoarbeit für die nationalsozialistische Kriegswirtschaft," in Hensel and Lehnstaedt, *Arbeit*, 71–90; Giles Bennett, "Die Arbeitsbedingungen der Warschauer Juden 1941–1942: Max Bischof und die Transferstelle Warschau," in Hensel and Lehnstaedt, *Arbeit*, 91–110; Stephan Lehnstaedt, "Generalgouvernment: Ideologie und Ökonomie der Judenpolitik," in Hensel and Lehnstaedt, *Arbeit*, 159–80; Mario Wenzel, Die Umwandlung von Ghettos in Zwangsarbeitslager für Juden: Das Beispiel des Distrikts Krakau im Generalgouvernement 1942–1944," in Hensel and Lehnstaedt, *Arbeit*, 361–73.

117 Stephan Lehnstaedt, "Jüdische Arbeit in Generalgouvernement, Warthegau und Ostoberschlesien," *Lebenswelt Ghetto: Alltag und Soziales Umfeld während der nationalsozialistischen Verfolgung*, ed. Imke Hansen, Katrin Steffen, and Joachim Tauber (Wiesbaden: Harrassowitz Vlg., 2013), 210–25; Mędykowski, "Der jüdische Kampf um Lebensunterhalt," 226–41; Wolfgang Benz, "Ghetto: Topographie—Strukturen—Funktion," in Hansen et al., *Lebenswelt Ghetto*, 24–36; Martin Dean, "Regional Pattern of Ghettoisation in the Annexed and Occupied Territories of the Third Reich," in Hansen et al., *Lebenswelt Ghetto*, 37–51.

118 Constantin Goschler, "The Struggle for Recognition and Compensation of Forced Laborers," in *Forced Labor: The Germans, the Forced Laborers and the War*, ed. Volkhard Knigge et al. (Weimar: Stiftung Gedenkstätten Buchenwald u. Mittelbau-Dora, 2010), 230–41; Stephan Lehnstaedt, *Geschichte und Gesetzesauslegung: Zu Kontinuität und Wandel des bundesdeutschen Wiedergutmachungsdiskurses am Beispiel der Ghettorenten* (Osnabrück: Fibre, 2011); Stephan Lehnstaedt, "Ghetto Labor Pensions: Holocaust Survivors and Their Struggle for Compensation in the 21st Century," *Kwartalnik Historii Żydów* 283 (2011): 191–210.

Part One

CHAPTER 1

The War against Poland and the Beginning of German Economic Policy in the Occupied Territory

THE OBJECTIVES OF THE WAR

One Germany's objectives during the Second World War was economic expansion in the new territories, which was generally referred to as *Lebensraum*. However, this concept represented much more than merely territory. It was, first of all, "living space for the German economy," bringing with it, apart from territory, a labor force, raw materials, and agricultural production. On May 10, 1939, the chief commander of the armed forces sent a letter to various OKW departments that was signed by Hitler. Attached to the letter were the "Instructions for the conduct of war and the economic security of their own."[1] Thus, parallel to the preparations for the military, were preparations for sustainability in economic terms. A conference in the Reich's Chancellery was held on May 23, 1939 to summarize preparations in economic terms. The report from this meeting was called the "Schmundt protocol."[2] During his speech, Hitler recalled again the validity of *Lebensraum* and said that the war was not really because of Gdańsk and the Corridor, but its objective was extension of living space in the east.[3] Also in other occasion, during a meeting with Mussolini in

---

1 IMT, *Red Series* (C-120), vol. 1, 692.
2 IMT, *Red Series* (L-79), vol. 1, 693.
3 IMT, *Red Series* (C-120), vol. 1, 693.

August 1939, Hitler said: "For economic reasons also, Germany needed the foodstuffs and timber from these eastern regions."[4]

In addition to the planned use of resources from the conquered territories, the exploitation of vast numbers of foreign workers was planned even before Germany went to war and was an integral part of the plan for waging an aggressive war. On May 23, 1939, a meeting was held in Hitler's study at the Reich's Chancellery. Hermann Göring, Erich Raeder, and Wilhelm Keitel were present. According to the minutes of this meeting, Hitler stated: "... the possession of extensive areas in the east will be advantageous. We shall be able to rely upon record harvests, even less in time of war than in peace. The population of non-Germans will perform no military service and will be available as a source of labor."[5]

Hitler did not think too highly of the Polish army; however, he feared that the delivery of arms from Western countries might weaken German supremacy. He was also speaking about the ethnic composition of Poland, which according to him, was composed of 14.5 million people belonging to various minorities like Germans, Byelorussians, Lithuanians, Jews, and Ukrainians. Not all Poles were, according to him, "fanatics." He believed that such a large proportion of non-Poles significantly reduced the fighting strength of Poland. Therefore Poland could be "struck to the ground" in a very short time.[6] In conclusion, the fundamental objectives of the war against Poland were winning of war and the occupation of the Polish "living space." Detailed instructions on how to conduct the war and the management of the new living space had been issued in August, September, and October 1939.

Hitler's speech at a meeting of senior commanders of the Wehrmacht, which took place in Hitler's residence in Obersalzberg on August 22, 1939,[7] produced one of the most important documents relating to the conduct of the war in Poland. At this time, all preparations for war had been completed. Before making a final decision concerning the attack on Poland, Hitler rejected proposals of peaceful solution, blaming Poland for rejecting German demands. Speaking to senior commanders, Hitler said: "Destruction of Poland is in the foreground. The aim is elimination of living forces, not the arrival at a certain line. Even if war should break out in the west, the destruction of Poland shall be

---

4 IMT, *Red Series* (TC-77), vol. 1, 697.
5 IMT, *Red Series* (L-79), vol. 1, 875–76.
6 IMT, *Red Series* (TC-77), vol. 1, 696.
7 The Obersalzburg Speech. On August 22, 1939, Hitler addressed his commanders-in-chief at Obersalzburg, in IMT, *Red Series* (1014-PS), vol. 1, 702.

the primary objective."[8] Hitler pointed out that the decision to attack Poland had been taken already in the spring.[9] Hitler explicitly said that the causes for the attack would be presented, regardless whether it was true or not. "When starting and leading a war, not justice but victory counts."[10] Hitler also spoke about economic aspects of the war. "We need not be afraid of a blockade. The east will supply us with grain, cattle, coal, lead and zinc. It is a big arm, which demands great efforts."[11] Given this, it was in a signed agreement with the Soviet Union that he said "They [Edouard Daladier and Neville Chamberlain] will not go beyond a blockade. Against that we have our autarchy and the Russian raw materials."[12]

One of the most important passages is located at the point where Hitler stopped the discussions about the war was to address the behavior of German soldiers on the battlefield and his plans for population of conquered Poland. Hitler said: "Our strength lies in our quickness and brutality [. . .]. I have given the command and I shall shoot everyone who utters one word of criticism [. . .] and so for the present, only in the east have I put my death-head formations in place with the command relentlessly and without compassion to send into death many women and children of Polish origin and language. Only thus can we gain the living space (*Lebensraum*) that we need."[13] Then Hitler continued: "For you, gentlemen, fame and honor are beginning as they have not for centuries. Be hard; be without mercy; act more quickly and brutally than the others. The citizens of western Europe must tremble with horror. That is the most human way of conducting a war. For it scares the others off."[14]

Those words uttered to senior commanders leave no doubt as to the intentions of Hitler concerning the behavior of his troops and the conduct of war. It was to be brutal, involving the physical destruction of the enemy, which involved not only combatants, but civilians as well. Commanding violent behavior suggests that it will not be punished—quite the contrary. Therefore, the instructions for the conduct of war were released and passed on to the

---

8 Ibid.; IMT, *Red Series* (798–PS).
9 Ibid.
10 Ibid.
11 Ibid.
12 Ibid.
13 IMT, *Red Series* (1014-PS), vol. 1, 702; IMT, *Red Series* (798-PS); E. L. Woodward and Rohan Riftlep, eds., *From Documents on British Foreign Policy 1919–1939*, 3rd series (London: HMSO, 1954), vol. 7, 258–60.
14 IMT, *Red Series* (1014-PS), vol. 1, 702; Woodward and Riftlep, *From Documents*, vol. 7, 258–60.

soldiers. Of course, Hitler fulfilled his promises regarding both the reward of the soldiers and their impunity. At the beginning of October 1939, amnesty was announced for crimes committed by German soldiers during the campaign in Poland.[15]

When the war broke out, Hitler spoke in the Reichstag, where he explained the reasons for this war, charging Poland with complete responsibility. His statement, quoted below, is a denial of what he said at a secret meeting with senior commanders in Obersalzberg. On September 1, 1939 he said:

> ... I will not wage war against women and children. I have ordered my air force to restrict itself to attacks on military objectives. If, however, the enemy thinks he can draw from that *carte blanche* on his side to fight by the other methods he will receive an answer that will deprive him of hearing and sight.[16]

Hitler continued:

> ... and from now on, bombs will be met with bombs. Whoever fights with poison gas will be fought with poison gas. Whoever departs from the rules of humane warfare can only expect that we shall do the same. I will continue this struggle, no matter against whom, until the safety of the Reich and its rights are secured.[17]

On the same day, September 1, 1939, Hitler made a speech to the German armed forces, in which he also presented reasons for starting the war. He said:

> I can see no other way but from now onwards to meet force with force. The German Armed Forces, with firm determination, will take up the struggle for the honor and the fundamental rights of the German people. I expect every soldier to be conscious of the high tradition of the eternal German soldierly qualities and to do his duty to the end. 'emember always and in any circumstances that you are the representatives of the National Socialist Greater Germany. Long live our people and the Reich.[18]

---

15 "Decree of Amnesty of the Führer and Chancellor of the Reich, of October 4, 1939," in Szymon Datner, *Crimes Committed by the Wehrmacht during the September Campaign and the Period of Military Government* (Poznań: Instytut Zachodni, 1962), 44.
16 *Speech by Hitler in Reichstag*, September 1, 1939.
17 Ibid.
18 IMT, *Red Series* (TC-54), vol. 1, 721.

In the speeches of August 22 and September 1, 1939, Hitler did not mention the Jews, but his attitude on this issue was obvious to all. On January 30, 1939, in his speech, Hitler told the Reichstag:

> The Jewish race was created by God only for the purpose of being in a certain percentage of a parasite living body on the productive and the work of other nations. The Jewish race will have to adapt itself to sound constructive activity as other nations do, or sooner or later it will succumb to a crisis of an inconceivable magnitude. [...] Today I will once more be a prophet: If the international Jewish financiers in and outside Europe should succeed in plunging the nations once more into a world war, then the result will not be the Bolshevization of the earth, and thus the victory of Jewry, but the annihilation of the Jewish race in Europe![19]

BEGINNING OF THE WAR

The war began on September 1, 1939, at 4:45 a.m., with a cannonade from the cruiser Schleswig-Holstein on Westerplatte.[20] The German aviation began bombing cities and military facilities. The German army crossed the Polish border, attacking from three directions simultaneously: from the north: from west Pomerania and east Prussia, from the west, and in the south from the territory of Slovakia.[21] Before the attack, the Germans prepared a series of actions of sabotage and instigated hostile ethnic groups, for example Ukrainians.[22] On the same day, Hitler spoke to the Reichstag assembly, explaining objectives of the war. He presented them as follows:

> I am determined: first, resolve the question of Danzig, second the question of the corridor, and thirdly, to ensure that in relation to Germany there will

---

19 Yitzhak Arad, Yisrael Gutman et al., eds., *Documents on the Holocaust: Selected Sources on the Destruction of the Jews of Germany and Austria, Poland and the Soviet Union* (Jerusalem: Yad Vashem, 1987), 134–35.
20 Andrzej Albert (Wojciech Roszkowski), *Najnowsza historia Polski 1914–1993*, vol. 1 (London: Plus Publications Ltd., 1994); Gerhard L. Weinberg, *A Worlsd at Arms: A Global History of World War II* (Cambridge: Cambridge University Press, 2005); Madajczyk, *Polityka III Rzeszy w okupowanej Polsce.*
21 BA-MA, RW5-150, 172/673–172/677.
22 BA-MA, RW5-699, 2–3.

be a reversal of Polish position, which will provide peaceful coexistence and security!²³

In the meantime, the situation deteriorated, and the Polish armies were in constant retreat. Warsaw became increasingly threatened by attack from the north, which forced the evacuation of the Polish government, state institutions, and the Bank of Poland's gold reserves from Warsaw. On September 6, Chief Commander Marshal Edward Śmigły-Rydz and his staff left the capital and moved to Brest. On the same day Colonel Roman Umiastowski, in a dramatic appeal, asked the young men to leave the capital for the east, where he called for the organization of a new line of defense.²⁴ Political leaders of party representatives also came to the east. Umiastowski's appeal had far-reaching effect: in addition to thousands of men who went east, whole families went in the same direction, in an atmosphere of fear and panic. The situation on the roads became even more difficult and refugees became an easy prey for the German airmen, who attacked civilian refugee columns. At that time, from September 7 to 9, the Soviet authorities announced mobilization in the European part of USSR.

On September 17, 1939, at 2.00 in the night, the Commissariat of Foreign Affairs called for the Polish Ambassador to give him a notice informing that in the morning the Red Army had begun crossing the Polish border in its entire length in order to "take care of people in western Ukraine and western Belarus." In this situation, Marshal Edward Śmigły-Rydz commanded the Polish troops not to fight the Red Army troops. On the night of September 17 to 18, the Polish commander-in-chief crossed over the Romanian border. The Red Army disarmed Polish troops and captured the soldiers and officers. Only in some places did struggle break out between the Polish and Soviet troops. Some units, mainly from the region of Polesie, returned in the direction of the west intending to support the defense of Warsaw and in order not fall into the hands of the Red Army and be disarmed in the process. However, those units failed to get to Warsaw. In the meantime, as a result of heavy bombing that caused many

---

23 Doc. 2322-PS, Hitler's address to the Reichstag on the outbreak of war, September 1, 1939; USA-39; Adolf Hitler, *The Essential Hitler: Speeches and Commentary*, ed. Max Domarus and Patrick Romane (Wauconda, IL: Bolchazy-Carducci, 2007).

24 L. Dobroszycki, M.M. Drozdowski, M. Getter, A. Słomczyński, eds., *Cywilna obrona Warszawy we wrześniu 1939, Dokumenty, materiały prasowe i relacje* (Warszawa: PWN, 1964); Marian Porwit, *Obrona Warszawy, Wrzesień 1939: Wspomnienia i fakty* (Warsaw: Czytelnik, 1959); Mieczysław Ciepielewicz and Eugeniusz Kozłowski, eds., *Obrona Warszawy 1939 we wspomnieniach* (Warsaw: MON, 1984); Mieczysław Ciepielewicz i Eugeniusz Kozłowski, eds., *Wrzesień 1939 w relacjach i wspomnieniach* (Warsaw: MON, 1989).

casualties and large damage, and the lack of food, water, and electricity, on September 26, 1939 it was decided to surrender Warsaw. The act of capitulation was signed on September 28, 1939. Soon, German troops entered the city. In the last days of September sporadic fighting was still going on. On October 5, 1939, Special Operational Group (SGO) "Polesie" under the command of General Franciszek Kleeberg capitulated, which marked the end of the war in Poland.

OPERATION *TANNENBERG*

In 1939 German directions in order to carry out the extermination of the Polish leadership echelon (*Liquidierung der polnischen Führungsschicht*) and intelligentsia got the codename *Unternehmen Tannenberg*. In May 1939, in the Main Office of the SD (*Sicherheitsdienst*), the head of the German Police, Reichsführer SS Heinrich Himmler, established a special cell called *Zentralstelle II/P (Polen)*, whose task was to draw up proscription lists of Poles (*Sonderfahndungsbuch Polen*)[25] who were considered particularly dangerous to the Third Reich. They were political activists; representatives of the clergy; leaders of political parties; people of science and culture; activists and fighters for the Polish state in disputed territories, from World War I, where plebiscites and armed uprisings (Śląsk/Schlesien, Poznań/Posen, Pomorze/Pommern) took place. On those lists were the names of 61,000 Poles.[26] In July 1939, an agreement was reached between *Oberkommando des Heeres* (OKH) and the head of *Sicherheitspolizei* and SD Reinhard Heydrich. Under the agreement, each of the five armies prepared to attack Poland was to obtain *Einsatzgruppe*, consisting of a Gestapo, Kripo (*Kriminalpolizei*), and SD men. After the outbreak of war in the first half of September, a further three sub-groups of about 2,700 people operating similarly were added.

At a conference held on September 21, 1939, referring to the ongoing operation *Tannenberg*, convened by the *Einsatzgruppen*, Heydrich said:

> Solving of the Polish question—as has been repeatedly indicated—is to be varied: one way in relation to the leadership (Polish intelligentsia), another in relation to the workers and the lower layers of the Polish population. There are still no more than 3% of political leaders in the occupied territories.

---

25 *Sonderfahndungsbuch Polen* (Berlin: Reichskriminalpolizeiamt Berlin C2, Wederscher Mark 5/6, 1939).

26 Ryszard Majewski, *Waffen SS: Mity i rzeczywistość* (Wroclaw: Zakład Narodowy im. Ossolińskich, 1977), 53.

> And these 3% must be neutralized and sent to concentration camps. The *Einsatzgruppen* should draw up a list, on which they should place outstanding leaders and also lists containing the average layer of the Polish society: teachers, clergy, nobility, legionnaires, returning officers, and so forth. They must be arrested and deported to the remaining district (*Restraum*).[27]

Heydrich clearly expressed his murderous intentions. Interesting is the fact that in spite of obtaining the proxies for the elimination of elements deemed undesirable, he continued his provocative actions in order to cause difficulties and even paralyzing court actions. At the conference on September 21, 1939, he ordered:

> Executions should be used only in case of necessary self-defense or in cases of attempts of escape. All other matters should be transferred to the martial courts. You should load military courts with so many applications, that they could not manage to deal with this C [Chef, i.e., Reinhard Heydrich] wants him to submit all the judgments of the military courts, ending with no conviction to death penalty.[28]

The *Einsatzgruppen* operating in Poland, in addition to the tasks relating to the liquidation of Polish activists, intellectuals and leaders also had duties concerning the Jews.[29] One of their obligations was causing forced migration of Jews to the Soviet zone in the first weeks of war, when the demarcation line between the German and Soviet occupation zone was not yet determined. Forcing resettlement on Jews took place by issuing specific instructions to leave the immediate locality. Particularly cruel to the Jews was the *Einsatzgruppe* under the command of Udo von Woyrsch, who committed numerous crimes, including in the vicinity of Przemyśl.[30] "Already in 1939, soon after the entry into Przemyśl, Germans gave an example of their methods of bandits slaughtering five hundred Jews, mostly from the intelligentsia."[31]

---

27 Document from the Conference in Security Police Office of September 21, 1939, BŻIH 49 (1964): 68–73.
28 Ibid.
29 Jochen Böhler, "Nazi Anti-Jewish Policy during the Polish Campaign: The Case of the Einsatzgruppe von Woyrsch," *German Studies Review* 24 (2001): 35–54; Alexander B. Rossino, *Hitler Strikes Poland: Blitzkrieg, Ideology and Atrocity* (Lawrence: University Press of Kansas, 2003), 88–120.
30 Böhler, "Nazi Anti-Jewish Policy."
31 YVA, M.49.E/1938, 1, testimony of Marian Bień.

IDEOLOGICAL ATTITUDE OF GERMAN SOLDIERS TOWARDS THE JEWS

The beginning of the war ushered in a sharp change in the life of the Jewish population in Poland. Persecution of Jews in Germany and the territories occupied by Germany after 1938 now threatened Polish Jews, who were much more numerous than the Jewish communities of Germany, Austria, and the Protectorate. Polish Jews were also different from their brethren in the above-mentioned countries, where not all Jews were traditional and not all of them differentiated themselves from the rest of the country's population, even though the Jews who lived traditionally made up a fairly large faction of the Jewish community. For Polish Jews, the Germans invented a special term: *Ostjuden*—Eastern Jews, which indicated geographic area inhabited by those Jews, but also evoked a specific cultural meaning. It conjured up a different type of Jew: traditional in terms of clothing, appearance, including beards and side locks, but also traditional in terms of language and behavioral education. For a casual viewer, in many cases, the difference was enormous. While German Jews were not often distinguished by their appearance, in Poland the situation was completely different. Elements such as the appearance and behavior of traditional Jews were used in German propaganda for years. Especially since Hitler seized power, the anti-Semitic propaganda increased. Books, newspapers, and posters with cartoons where stylized images of Jews were portrayed were printed in millions of copies. Some features and characteristics of the Jewish body were much exaggerated: the propaganda materials showed great curved noses, odd-looking faces, beards and side locks. Often, such propaganda items were presented next to idealized drawings of the Aryan type: tall, athletic, with simple features and light hair, and neatly dressed. It was not only drawings and photos in newspapers and books that launched this type of the German man. There were also other means of propaganda everywhere—in film, painting, and sculpture. The work of Arno Breker is one of the best examples.[32]

The propaganda and the political climate of Germany from the years 1933–1939 affected the consciousness of the young generation of Germans. After the elimination of pre-Hitler youth organizations and the establishment of Hitler Youth and related organizations such as BDM and *Jungvolk*, the majority of adolescents came under Hitler's influence for a longer or shorter

---

[32] Jürgen Trimborn, *Arno Breker—Der Künstler und die Macht: die Biographie* (Berlin: Aufbau, 2011); B. John Zavrel, *Arno Breker—His Art and Life* (New York: Amherst, 1985); Peter Adam, *The Art of the Third Reich* (London: Harry N. Abrams Inc, 1992).

period of time. Germans born in 1919, for example, who reached the age of 20 in 1939, spent a greater part of their youth in the above-mentioned organizations. These organizations not only dealt with sporting activities, developed interests, organized trips outside the city and summer camps, but also educated the German youth in the spirit of Nazism. In 1930s, the German youths spent the greater part of their time in school and in the Hitler Youth organizations in order to reduce the impact of the family. This educational activity was intentionally propagated by the Nazi leadership. The official propaganda and youth organizations exerted very strong influence on young people. Their activities had a great effect on the generation, which grew up in 1930s and became soldiers during the war of 1939, and supposedly caused generational differences in the prevailing mood of the Wehrmacht.[33]

A generation of young Germans educated in an atmosphere of anti-Semitic propaganda and convinced of its superiority was mobilized and sent to war against Poland. In the period preceding the war, German propaganda against Poland was very intense[34] and focused not only on the Free City of Gdańsk and the "Corridor." It also alleged the persecution of Germans in Poland. Poland had been presented as a country that persistently acted unreasonably. Moreover, Poland had never enjoyed a positive evaluation from the Germans. Above all, Germany, irrespective of the reigning system and the ruling government, never reconciled with the loss of the lands, which belonged to Germany prior to the World War I, in favor of Poland. Therefore, slogans such as *Lebensraum*, used by Hitler, gained social acceptance quite easily. The Polish economy was regarded as primitive; the common term "Polish economy" (*polnische Wirtschaft*) meant mismanagement, mess, and laziness.[35] In German eyes, Poland was a hostile country that wanted to prevent the development of Germany. These two important elements of consciousness—anti-Semitism and the hatred of Poland—accompanied the German forces that invaded Poland in September 1939.

The Jews were depicted in German propaganda as parasites who profited from the hard work of others. They did not do the work themselves but

---

33 Jochen Böhler, *Zbrodnie Wehrmachtu w Polsce: Wrzesień 1939: Wojna totalna* (Kraków: Znak, 2009), 37–41.
34 Ibid., 41–45.
35 Eugeniusz Cezary Król, *Polska i Polacy w propagandzie narodowego socjalizmu w Niemczech 1919–1945* (Warsaw: ISP PAN-Collegium Civitas-Rytm, 2010); Götz Aly and Susanne Heim, "The Holocaust and Population Policy: Remarks on the Decision on the Final Solution," *Yad Vashem Studies* 24 (1994): 48–55.

gathered the fruits of hard labor done by other people. Their exploitation of others did not apply solely to economic benefits, but also to political and social ones. The actions of Jews in culture and the arts were considered as causing constant disgrace. Therefore, according to the propaganda, it was necessary to root out the Jews and get rid of them in order to protect the German people, the German culture, the economy, education, the administration, and so forth. In turn, the Poles were depicted as rough and thriftless people who should also learn from the German work ethic.

The beginning of the war also established the confrontation between propaganda and reality. It was an eye-to-eye meeting with the population in Poland and encounter with the Jews, who represented about 10% of the population. However, in cities and towns their percentage was significantly higher and amounted to several dozen percent. Therefore, the German newcomers were under the impression that there was a massive concentration of Jews in Poland. Many German soldiers met traditional Jews, whom so far they had only seen in the form of propaganda, for the first time in their lives.

Another important element accompanying the invasion of Poland (and later, the other countries of Central and Eastern Europe), was the contrast between what Germany wanted to achieve—to get rid of the Jews, to remove them from German society—and between what they actually found. As German control was established on new territories, the number of Jews under German rule did not reduce: on the contrary, the invaders only found more Jews.

After a period of fighting, German troops came in contact with many civilians. This encounter displayed an entire range of attitudes. The expression of these opinions was discovered in letters written to the soldiers' families in Germany. Large collections of correspondence have survived in archives.[36] A great number of German soldiers adopted the objectives of the war and considered it just and fair, designed to protect ethnic Germans. In relation to the local population—Poles and Jews—they felt contempt and hatred. Together with all the nation, they felt good and worthy to rule others, sure that their mission was to spread "civilization" in the east.[37]

---

36 O. Buchbender and R. Sterz, eds., *Das andere Gesicht des Krieges: Deutsch Feldpostbriefe 1939–1945* (Munich: C. H. Beck, 1982); Alexander Rossino, "Destructive Impulses: German Soldiers and the Conquest of Poland," *Holocaust and Genocide Studies* 11, no. 3 (Winter 1997): 351–65.

37 Rossino, "Destructive Impulses," 353.

VIOLENCE AGAINST THE JEWS

In order to collect weapons and ammunition in the occupied areas of the Poland, on September 12, 1939, the chief commander of the German armed forces, Walther von Brauchitsch, issued regulations to the civilians, calling for an immediate delivery of all weapons and ammunition to the nearest military and police posts. According to the regulation, storage of weapons and ammunition would be punished by death. Similarly, any acts of violence towards German soldiers were to be punished by death. Judgment, and its execution by the court, would take place immediately.[38]

Thereafter, an addendum was issued to the regulation of the Decree of September 12, 1939.[39] Regulations to ban the possession of weapons had become the basis for the search for hidden arms and ammunition by German soldiers. The sweep for the arms was conducted in public buildings as well as in private homes. In practice, it gave the Germans unlimited permission to enter homes and private residence and to take stock. During the search for weapons, robbery of private property was commonplace. German soldiers "preferred" Jewish homes where everything of value was robbed.

> [. . .] looting took place in the city of [Warsaw] after the victory. The opportunity to take—and take more—is carried out gradually in the city in search of weapons inspections. These revisions, in some cases are carried out quite decently; in others, they are used for mass looting. This is the rule in Jewish neighborhoods—but not only there.[40]

Provocations and pretexts were employed in relation to the possession of weapons or taking part in armed resistance. Reinhard Heydrich wrote in a well-known *Schnellbrief* of September 21, 1939, inter alia: "As a justification for the concentration of Jews in cities should be administered, according to authoritative information, they took part in the partisan attacks and robbery."[41]

---

38 The regulation on the possession of weapons on the September 12, 1939, issued by the supreme commander of Armed Forces von Brauchitsch.
39 Ordinance to supplement the Ordinance on the possession of weapons on September 21, 1939 (*Verordnungsblatt für die besetzten Gebiete in Polen*, 9); Second Order of the supreme commander of the Armed Forces to supplement the Ordinance on the possession of weapons on October 6, 1939 (*Verordnungsblatt für die besetzten Gebiete in Polen*, 32).
40 Ludwik Landau, *Kronika lat wojny i okupacji*, vol. 1, *Wrzesień 1939–listopad 1940* (Warsaw: PWN, 1962), 25.
41 "Instructions by Heydrich on Policy and Operations Concerning Jews in the Occupied Territories, September 21, 1939," in Arad and Gutman, *Documents on the Holocaust*, 173–78;

The method of searching for weapons is reflected in many testimonies of Jewish witnesses, who described the brutality with which the searches were carried out. German soldiers did not even care to justify their behavior in order to search for weapons. In practice, the searches were merely a common form of looting.

One of the methods aimed at protecting the German forces against the attacks by "partisans"[42] or hidden soldiers was taking hostages who were chosen from well-known personalities in occupied cities or representatives of municipalities. Among the hostages were also prominent Jews. The German troops announced that in case of attacks they would shoot the hostages. The arrest of hostages, in practice, served not only security exigencies, but often was used as an instrument of pressure on the local society, especially in order to force the local society or community to pay contributions or provide other material benefits. One of witnesses said: "On September 5, 1939 the German army entered Strzemieszyce. They began the persecution of Jews; they took hostages, tortured and beat them in order to get as much gold as possible."[43]

Imposition of contributions on the civilian population of the occupied land was a legitimate act of the occupation forces in accordance with international law.[44] Contributions, however, were designed to meet the needs of occupying troops. According to the international norms, requests for contributions should be issued in writing by a general commander of the troops. They should be distributed proportionally, according to the most recent taxation. In World War II, contributions were often imposed on the Jewish community which did not take into account a balanced contribution of the population of a specific area of the occupied country. Such a way of collecting contributions can be considered collective responsibility. International law prohibited the use of collective responsibility in the form of fines.[45] Levying contributions was

---

T. Berenstein, A. Eisenbach, A. Rutkowski, ed., *Eksterminacja Żydów na ziemiach polskich w okresie okupacji hitlerowskiej: Zbiór dokumentów* (Warsaw: Żydowski Instytut Wydawniczy, 1957), 27.

42 Böhler, *Zbrodnie Wehrmachtu*, 135–78.

43 YVA, M.49.E/1553, 2, testimony of Jerychem Frajman.

44 Marian Flemming, "Traktowanie ludności cywilnej i jeńców podczas działań wojennych w świetle norm prawa międzynarodowego," *BGKBZHP XXII* (1987): 67; Convention (IV) Respecting the Laws and Customs of War on Land, Signed at Hague, 18 October 1907., Art. 51, in *The Laws of Armed Conflicts: A Collection of Conventions, Resolutions and Other Documents*, ed. Dietrich Schindler and Jiří Toman (Geneva: Henri Dunant Institute, 1988), 90.

45 Flemming, "Traktowanie ludności cywilnej"; Convention (IV) Respecting the Laws and Customs of War on Land, Signed at Hague, 18 October 1907, Art. 50, in Schindler and Toman, *The Laws of Armed Conflicts*, 89–90.

a prevalent phenomenon in September 1939, as illustrated by testimonies of many witnesses from different regions of the country. Usually, the specified amount of time given to the population to collect and deliver the contribution did not exceed more than a few days. Contributions were imposed on the population of Lublin, Strzemieszyce,[46] Jaworzno, Kraśnik, and Izbica, as well as many other cities. In Jaworzno, in accordance with the accepted principles of imposing contributions, the following order was given by the military commander of the city:

> During this time, the military commander of the city announced imposing contribution on the Jews; at the same time they detained eight people as hostages, who were important among the Jewish community, including me among them. After the payment of the contribution we were released.[47]

The following are excerpts from testimonies pertaining to a number of cities: "Germans laid upon the Jews a contribution of 500,000 zł. The *Judenrat* had to collect this sum and at an indicated date the contribution had been paid."[48] The same was true in Kraśnik:

> In September 1939, Germans entered Kraśnik. Then in our city there were about 8,000 Jews. Mostly craftsmen, merchants and workers, there were also many belonging to intelligentsia. Germans asked for contribution for the next few days. Then we had to give them silver and brass.[49]

In some towns, the contribution was only a first step towards the systematic looting of Jewish property. This is illustrated by an example from Izbica:

> The Germans who came first to Izbica were motorcycle patrols; one of their first steps was a pogrom. On the first day of the occupation several Jews were killed. Two days later they imposed contribution on us. Jews had to pay it and a few days later the Germans issued a decree that Jews

---

46 YVA, M.49.E/1553, 2, testimony of Jerychem Frajman.
47 YVA, M.49.E/3424, 1, testimony of Paulina Klein.
48 YVA, M.49.E/1295, 2, testimony of Franciszek Mandelbaum, Lublin
49 YVA, M.49.E/1516, 1, testimony of Abraham Olender.

had to deliver all the gold they had. After that they ordered the Jews to deliver their goods and valuable papers. After finishing that action they gave three more days for delivering all these items and announced that if they find gold, any goods or valuable papers by somebody, he will be killed on the spot. After a few days they began to conduct mass searches in Jewish homes. If they found even the smallest piece of a material, they shot and no excuse helped.[50]

International law forbade looting of private property belonging to the civilian population and it could not be confiscated. Nevertheless, the law allowed confiscation of goods for the occupying army. However, such confiscation should be tailored to the resources of the country.[51] Still, in the case of requisition, the army that was carrying it out was obliged to give receipts or payment for the confiscated property. In many cases during World War II, requisitions took the form of looting, which made it difficult to distinguish between lawful and unlawful seizure of property. There also was a progressive deterioration of the German soldiers' moral standards in relation to the Jewish civilians. This is illustrated by the case of Łańcut: "On September 9, 1939, the Germans entered to Łańcut. Initially, it was the Wehrmacht. Soldiers went to the Jewish shops and took things paying the minimum price."[52] In the above-quoted testimony, the German soldiers initially paid for the goods, although they preferred low prices. Therefore, this case can be treated as a sale; however, the merchants were forced to sell goods for prices much lower than the actual value of the goods. Nevertheless, merciless looting soon began. "A few days later, civilian authorities and the Gestapo came [to Łańcut]. Afterwards began the inspection of Jewish homes, taking valuables, furniture, clothing, bedding, etc."[53] In this case we have to admit that the sales were carried out by soldiers, while the looting was performed by the policemen, but, when taken together with other evidence, it also confirms the progressive deterioration of moral standards.

---

50 YVA, M.49.E/1518, 1, testimony of Hejnoch Nobel.
51 Flemming, "Traktowanie ludności cywilnej"; Convention (IV) Respecting the Laws and Customs of War on Land, Signed at Hague, 18 October 1907., Art. 46, in Schindler and Toman, *The Laws of Armed Conflicts*, 89.
52 YVA, M.49.E/1501, 1, testimony of Diana Grinabaum.
53 Ibid.

Ludwik Landau also wrote about the looting in his journal:

> Searches for weapons and radios were (and still are) in the Jewish neighborhoods and in the form, associated, more or less, with open robbery: the things taken are, as a rule, furs and often other valuable items. Even in non-Jewish districts, people often talk about questions posed [by the German soldiers]: *Sind Sie Jude* or *Sind Sie Pole?* Depending on the response, the variety of things seized changes. I do not think that the soldiers doing that were fanatic supporters of Hitler or sophisticated robbers: they simply belonged to a common—maybe the most widespread in most of societies—type of man, not particularly firm in his beliefs, weak, giving rise to prevailing currents, and acted under these conditions [of the war and occupation]. They were demoralized and unable to resist the temptation of an easy win of such desirable valuables in their daily struggle for existence.[54]

Ludwig observed that:

> [b]oth this looting and harassment of the people were certainly not ordered by their commanders; however, without a doubt, this situation in so many instances occurred with the approval of their officers, and in any case, they were not prosecuted with any particular severity. In individual cases, it happened to obtain effective intervention of an officer—apparently a general policy trend of the occupiers—was rather looking at these abuses through spread fingers—unless it had already exceeded the extent possible.[55]

Apart from the above-described individual killings of Jews, in some towns, mass killings also took place shortly after the entry of the German troops.[56] A well-known case of violence against the Jews during the September campaign was the case of Końskie.[57] Another one, the massacre in Częstochowa, on

---

54 Landau, *Kronika lat wojny i okupacji*, 27–28.
55 Ibid., 26.
56 Jochen Böhler, *Auftrakt zum Vernichtungskrieg: Die Wehrmacht in Polen 1939* (Frankfurt a. M.: Fischer Taschenbuch Verlag, 2006), 194–97.
57 Jochen Böhler, ed., *Grösste Härte...: Verbrechen der Wehrmacht in Polen, September-Oktober 1939* (Osnabrück: Deutsches Historisches Institut, 2005), 121–23.

September 4, 1939 was so fierce that it was later known as "Bloody Monday."[58] One of the victims described it in the following manner:

> The Germans [...] gathered the entire male population of the city in the Old Market and from there they were scurried into a so-called cathedral. When we were entering the church, they began to shoot us with machine guns and rifles. Some hundreds of us were killed then on the spot. There were about 400 injured. I got a bullet in the right side; the wound was luckily not serious, since the bullet passed through my body.[59]

---

58   Liber Brenner, *Widerstand un Umekum in Tschenstochover Geto* (Warsaw: Yidisher Historisher Institut in Pojlin, 1950), 6.
59   YVA, M.49.E/1567, 1, testimony of Henoch Diamant.

CHAPTER 2

Forced Labor from the Period of Military Government Until the Beginning of Ghettoization

On September 1, 1939 the chief of the Armed Forces (OKH) Walther von Brauchitsch issued a special order.[1] He declared that the German army would have absolute power over all occupied areas. Von Brauchitsch added, "The Wehrmacht will not consider the [civil] population as his enemy. All practices will be respected." Von Brauchitsch's order also touched upon economic matters: "The country's economy and public administration will continue to further its operation or will be rebuilt."[2] Until then, it was announced that all provisions relating to the occupied areas would be published in *Bekanntmachung über das Verordnungsblatt für die besetzten Gebiete in Polen*.[3]

Further detailed orders followed the order of September 1, 1939 that declared the punishment of activities hostile to the German army. On September 5, 1939, Walther von Brauchitsch released the next order creating special courts (*Sondergerichte*) to examine crimes committed in the occupied areas of Poland.[4] On the same day, September 5, 1939, German criminal

---

1 Walter von Brauchitsch, "Aufruf des Oberbefehlshabers des Heeres Vom 1. September 1939," in *Zbiór rozporządzeń władz niemieckich*, ed. Witold Święcicki and Feliks Zadrowski (Warsaw: n.p., 1940), 11–12.
2 Ibid.
3 "Bekanntmachung über das Verordnungsblatt für die besetzten Gebiete in Polen. Vom 1. September 1939," in Święcicki and Zadrowski, *Zbiór rozporządzeń władz niemieckich*, 12.
4 "Verordnung des Oberbefehlshabers des Heeres über Sondergerichte im besetzten polnischen Gebiet. Vom 5. September 1939," in Karol Marian Pospieszalski, *Ziemie wcielone* (Poznań: Instytut Zachodni, 1952), 40–43; YVA-O.21/1, 4.

law was introduced in the occupied territories[5] as well as a decree regarding punishment for juveniles.[6]

Entering Poland, the German army took power from the hands of local representatives. Temporarily they acted as the units' patrol officers who later passed control to senior officers. Subsequently, the head of the civil administration (*der Chef der Zivilverwaltung*, CdZ) of the High Command of the Army (*Armeeoberkommando*) nominated heads of local civil administration.[7] At that time they were called *Landräte* (district/county administrators). The *Einsatzgruppen* were subsequently transformed into police functionaries in local police stations.[8] Upon entering a new village, one of the first procedures was to impose measures to ensure the security of the German forces. For this purpose, posters announcing takeover by the German army were created immediately after the end of fighting, or when the troops entered a village, thereby both informing the public and preserving the peace. Despite this, an atmosphere of fear reigned. One of Jewish women recalled those moments:

> After entering the city [Rzeszów] posters in Polish and German were put in public places, to appeal to the public that they behave peacefully and not be afraid, since they [Germans] came to make order (it seems that in those appeals there was nothing about the Jews). I do not remember the exact content of the poster, or the first or later, because in the city was in such a climate of fear and uncertainty that we lived constantly in panic. I was scared and worried about the children. Still, there were incidents of killings and beatings by the Germans. I stopped to go out in the street, I did not even do necessary matters and purchases but all was arranged by my Jewish hostesses, where I was living.[9]

Any action against the German army was punished severely, usually by death. Immediately after the entry, the authorities collected weapons and ammunition. In order to ensure the peace, hostages were taken, threatening

---

5   "Verordnung über Einführung deutschen Strafrechts. Vom 5. September 1939," in Pospieszalski, *Ziemie wcielone*, 44
6   "Verordnung über die Aburteilung von Taten Jugendlicher. Vom 10. September 1939," in Pospieszalski, *Ziemie wcielone*, 45.
7   AIPN, NTN, 196/270, 10–22.
8   *Einsatzgruppen* were transformed subsequently into police functionaries in local police stations.
9   YVA, M.49.E/1549, 1–2, testimony of Stefania Rosenberg.

throughout that in the event of any hostile action, hostages would be executed. Hostages in several villages were both Poles and Jews. In addition, the invaders often demanded a payment of contributions. It seems that the nuisance contributions were especially acute for the Jews. It was precisely because of this that they were particularly preferred.

On September 25, 1939, Hitler's decree regarding the appointment of the military administration in occupied Poland (*Erlass des Führers über die Organisation der Militärverwaltung des besetzten ehemals polnischen Gebiete*) was announced.[10] It is important to note that it occurred before the end of hostilities and the capitulation of Warsaw. According to this decree, full authority was transferred to the supreme commander of land forces, who in turn set up a military administration headed by the commander-in-chief "East," General Gerd von Rundstedt. The military headquarters was in Spała. In the area of Poland occupied by the Germans, four military districts were established: West Prussia, Poznań, Łódź, and Kraków. Their commanders were respectively: Artillery General Heitz, Colonel General von Vollard-Bockelberg, General Gerd von Rundstedt, and Colonel General Wilhelm von List. Their appointment combined the supreme command of land forces with the command of the military administration "East." Hitler also nominated the heads of the civil administration (*Verwaltungschef*) for each of the military districts. They were respectively Gauleiter Albert Forster in West Prussia, the Senate President of the Free City of Gdańsk Arthur Greiser in the Poznań District, and Reich Minister Arthur Seyss-Inquart in Kraków. The head of the civil administration (*Oberverwaltungschef*) under the supreme commander "East" and the head of civil administration in the district of Łódź was Reich Minister Dr. Hans Frank.

As the supreme head of the civil administration, Hans Frank[11] publicly expressed his ideas concerning the economic and political future of Poland, according to which he wished to proceed. During an interview given on October 3, 1939, he said:

> Poland can only be administered by utilizing the country through means of ruthless exploitation, deportation of all supplies, raw materials, machines, factory installations, etc., which are important for the German

---

10 "Erlass des Führers über die Organisation der Militärverwaltung in den besetzten ehemals polnischen Gebiete, z 25 września 1939 r."; Mieczysław Brones, "Niektóre problemy grabieży ekonomicznej w Polsce dokonywanej przez Wehrmacht w okresie 1.9–25.10.1939 r.," *BGKBZHP XVIII* (1968): 46–79.

11 Schenk, Dieter, *Hans Frank: Hitlers Kronjurist und Generalgouverneur* (Frankfurt a. M.: S. Fischer, 2006).

war economy, availability of all workers for work within Germany, reduction of the entire Polish economy to the absolute minimum necessary for bare existence of the population, closing of all educational institutions, especially technical schools and colleges in order to prevent the growth of the new Polish intelligentsia. Poland shall be treated as a colony; the Poles shall be the slaves of the Greater German World Empire.[12]

Continuing the interview, Frank added: "It was most important now to make available as soon as possible raw materials, machines and workers to the German industry, which was short in all of these." Most important, however, in Frank's opinion, was the fact that by destroying the Polish industry, its subsequent reconstruction after the war would become more difficult, if not impossible, so that "Poland would be reduced to its proper position as an agrarian country which would have to depend upon Germany for importation of industrial products."[13] At that time there had been no final decision yet regarding the organization of the territory of Poland in terms of administration. In September, the ideas of the creation of a reduced Polish state which would be dependent on the Third Reich circulated among the German leaders, but later those ideas were abandoned. Frank in his speech had in mind such a reduced country (*Reststaat*).

At the first conference with Department Heads of the General Government on December 2, 1939, Frank stated: "Decisive in the administrative activities of the General Government is the will of the Führer that this area shall be the first colonial territory of the German nation."[14] At the same meeting Frank explained:

> Principally it can be said, regarding the administration of the General Government: This territory in its entirety is booty of the German Reich, and it thus cannot be permitted that this territory shall be exploited in its individual parts, but that the territory in its entirety shall be economically used and its entire economic worth redound to the benefit of the German people.[15]

On October 3, 1939, the chief commander of the land forces issued an instruction regarding the armament policy of the Wehrmacht on Polish land as

---

12 Interview with Hans Frank, in IMT, *Red Series* (EC-344-16 and 17), vol. 2, 632.
13 IMT, *Red Series* (EC-344-16 and 17), vol. 2, 642.
14 IMT, *Red Series* (2233-K-PS), vol. 2, 632–33.
15 IMT, *Red Series* (2233-K-PS), vol. 2, 642.

well as regarding the designation of the commander-in-chief "East" and the establishment of the Inspectorate of War Economy. It was stated inter alia that: "In the field of industrial policy, the main goal is the extreme exploitation of industry producing raw materials (such as iron, non-ferrous metal, oil, coal), the security of existing industrial facilities and verifying which should start the production for the benefit of the economy of the Third Reich; in principle, only those goods should be produced, which are indispensable for the German war economy. By contrast, production of unnecessary goods should be eliminated, because it uses raw materials in the process of production, so needed in the Reich."[16]

On October 5, 1939, together with the new structure of the military administration of OKW and in agreement with the OKH, the Inspectorate of War Economy was established, with the task of organizing the economy of war in areas of occupied Poland. The head of the inspectorate (*Inspekteur der Wehrwirtschafts-Inspektion Ober-Ost*) was Colonel Nagel. Branches of the War Economy Inspection (*Wehrwirtschaftsstelle*) were subordinated to the Inspectorate. In the future General Government, there was an office in Kraków, whose head was Lt. Col. Elsässer. Branches (*Außenstelle*) in Warsaw, Kielce, Lublin, and Rzeszów were subsequently established. On October 5, 1939, OKH issued an order concerning the coordination of work on establishing the type and quantity of raw materials, semi-finished, and finished products in occupied Poland. Therefore, General Bührmann was nominated for this purpose as a plenipotentiary for the detection of raw materials (*Beauftragter für die Rohstofferfassung*). He was subordinate to the supreme commander "East" and was included in the Inspectorate of War Economy.

From the very beginning of the war, the representatives of the German armament industry and the *CdZ*, who were advancing towards the front line, were conducting reconnaissance and organizing protection of all industrial establishments that were useful to the German economy. Interesting, in this context, is the disparity between the ideas of Hitler and, as a consequence, of Frank on that subject, contrasting with the vision of people closely related to the armament industry and war production of the Reich. The reconnaissance of Polish industry took place throughout the 1930s, but was particularly intense in 1939. For example, in July of that year, a special report entitled: "The most important chemical plants in Poland," whose author was Illgner from the IG-Farben, was prepared.[17]

---

16 Brones, "Niektóre problemy," 54.
17 Ibid., 54.

Particularly active was Staff of War Economy inside OKW (*Wehrwirtschaftsstab—Oberkommando der Wehrmacht*) which was led by General Georg Thomas. In 1939, the Wehrmacht issued a publication under the title "War Economy of The Polish Republic"[18] that included maps on the scale of 1:300,000, containing important information concerning economic facilities, transportation lines, electricity plants, and so forth. The same year, detailed statistical data on the population of Poland was published.[19]

Even after the beginning of hostilities and gradual occupation of more and more areas, people specifically designated for this task were preparing in-depth reports on the Polish economy. This investigation could include, for instance, a report for Fitzner and Hütter,[20] or information about the plant in Skarżysko-Kamienna.[21] Reports on population policy were also prepared.[22] These reports were used as the basis for decisions regarding economic policies in areas of occupied Poland. The reconnaissance and identification by the Wehrmacht and factors associated with CdZ, were also involved in protection before devastation and nomination of people responsible—even on a temporary basis—in order to maintain the facilities in readiness so they could continue their operation and production.

Reich Minister Dr. Hans Frank was appointed governor general of the Polish Occupied Territories by Hitler's decree dated October 12, 1939. The deputy of the governor general was Reich minister, Dr. Arthur Seyss-Inquart. The scope of their executive power was defined by Hitler as follows:

> The territories occupied by German troops shall be subject to the authority of the Governor General of the occupied Polish territories, except insofar as they are incorporated within the German Reich. [. . .] The Governor

---

18 Ibid., 47.
19 *Statistisches Gemeindeverzeichnis des bisherigen polnischen Staates: mit Berücksichtigung der am 28. September 1939 festgelegten Grenze der deutschen und sowjetrussischen Reichsinteressen* (Berlin: Selbstverlag der Publikationstelle, 1939).
20 Mieczysław Wrzosek, "Raporty Hütera i Fitznera o sytuacji w Zagłębiu Śląsko-Dąbrowskim w okresie 3 września–20 października 1939 r.," *BGKBZHP* XIX (1968): 165–245; Janusz Gumkowski, and Kazimierz Leszczyński, "Generalne Gubernatorstwo w oczach Niemca (Sprawozdanie dra Blaschka z podróży służbowej do Generalnego Gubernstorstwa w dn. 21–26 sierpnia 1942 r.)," *BGKBZHP* XV (1965), 126–63;
21 Werkbericht, Skar.-Kam., 19.9.1939, MA, Wi ID 1/165a, 215–17, in Karay, *Death Comes in Yellow*, 9.
22 "Die Frage der Behandlung der Bevölkerung der ehemaligen polnischen Gebiete nach rassenpolitischen Gesichtspunkten in Program narodowościowy Rassenpolitischen-Amt'u z 1939 roku na ziemiach polskich," *BGKBZHP* IV (1948): 133–71; NO-3732,

General shall be directly responsible to me. All branches of the administration shall be directed by the Governor General.[23]

Hitler added:

There is no authority here in the General Government which is higher as to rank, influence, and authority than that of the Governor General. Even the Wehrmacht has no governmental or official functions of any kind in this connection; it has only security functions and general military duties—it has no political power whatsoever. The same applies here to the Police and SS. There is here no state within a state, but we are the representatives of the Führer and of the Reich. In final conclusion, this applies also to the Party which has here no far-reaching influence except for the fact that very old members of the National Socialist Party and loyal veterans of the Führer take care of general matters.[24]

The decree suggests that Hans Frank had absolute power in the General Government, subordinate only to Hitler. Subsequently, in practice, it turned out that despite the aspirations of Hans Frank, his power was not absolute and various other factors, particularly the SS and SD, constantly undermined his authority. Despite his high position in the party, Hans Frank proved to be an insufficiently strong personality and his decisions and policy were influenced strongly by decision-making factors in the Reich. At least in the initial period of taking of power, Frank's speeches were characterized by repeating ideas presented earlier by Hitler, Hermann Göring, and others. This also applies to his declarations concerning economic policy.

On October 19, 1939, Göring gave instructions on the economic policy in the occupied areas.[25] He said among other things:

The General Government must export all the raw materials, scrap metal, machinery, and so forth. In one word everything that can benefit the war economy of Germany. Companies that are not absolutely necessary should be transferred to Germany, unless they require too much time or use of them in their location by carrying out German military orders would be more purposeful.[26]

---

23 IMT, *Red Series* (2537-PS), vol. 2, 629.
24 IMT, *Red Series* (2233-PS), vol. 2, 630.
25 *Trial of the Major War Criminals before the International Military Tribunal*, Doc. 410–EC, 482.
26 Brones, "Niektóre problemy," 54.

On October 20, 1939 a meeting between Adolf Hitler and Wilhelm Keitel took place, in which General Walter Warlimont was also present. During that meeting, the shape of future relations between the Reich and the occupied areas of Poland was discussed. Hitler repeated that in the Polish territories there could not be two administrations. The General Government's administration should not be dependent on Berlin; rather, it should take responsibility for the management of land. Hitler believed that one of the tasks of this administration would be conducting a racial struggle free from any legal constraints, and the methods used in the General Government would be completely different than in other areas of Germany.

Speaking about the future of Poland's economy, Hitler said:

> It is not the task of the administration to make Poland into a model province or a model state of the German order or to put her financially or economically on a sound basis. The Polish intelligentsia must be prevented from forming a ruling class. The standard of living in the country is to remain low; we only want to draw labor forces from there. Poles are also to be used for the administration of the country. [...] The Governor General is to give the Polish nation only bare living conditions and is to maintain the basis for military security. [...] The Polish economy [*polnische Wirtschaft*] must be allowed to develop.[27]

In addition, General Government was to receive deported Jews and Poles from the Reich. Therefore, the collaboration of General Government with the new provinces of the Reich (annexed territories) was required, in accordance with Heinrich Himmler's new responsibilities as a plenipotentiary for the strengthening of Germany.[28]

DECISIONS CONCERNING JEWS AND THE ECONOMY

The first decisions of economic nature concerning the Jews were taken almost immediately after entry into the occupied towns. However, they were not coordinated by the military authorities. These decisions were a result of German economic policy towards the Jews in Germany, which was a model of their position regarding the occupied Polish territories. The German troops entered

---

27 IMT, *Red Series* (864-PS), vol. 2, 631–32.
28 "Erlass des Führers und Reichskanzlers zur Festigung deutschen Volkstums. Vom 7. Oktober 1939," in Pospieszalski, *Ziemie*, 176–78; BGKBZHP XII (1960): 34–35

Kraków on September 6, 1939. On the same day, regulations concerning the Jews were issued, regarding movable and immovable property.[29] Two days later, another decree by the head of the civil administration about the marking of all enterprises belonging to the Jews was issued.[30] The decree sought to protect Jewish property in order to ease the subsequent acquisition of that property by the German authorities. Marking Jewish shops was serving the same goal. Interim measures aimed at eliminating Jews from economic life and taking over their property by trustees had been issued in other cities. In Częstochowa such an order was issued by the mayor of the city on September 15, 1939.[31] A similar order was issued in Jędrzejów[32] and other places.

Reinhard Heydrich issued instructions concerning the Jewish problem in the occupied territories in the *Schnellbrief* of September 21, 1939 to the heads of all the *Einsatzgruppen*, the Security Police, and SD.[33] In this way, Reinhard Heydrich was taking responsibility for dealing with all Jewish matters in the newly occupied areas. The essential task of the *Einsatzgruppen*, the Security Police, was not dealing with Jewish issues, but providing security in the rear areas of the front line.[34] They were responsible for the arrest and liquidation of known leaders and local political activists who were, according to the criteria

---

29 "Verordnung des Chefs der Zivilverwaltung, die eine Verlagerung und übertragung des jüdischen beweglichen und unbeweglichen Vermögens in den besetzten Gebiet verbietet. 6. September 1939, Krakau," *Faschismus—Ghetto—Massenmord: Dokumentation über Ausrottung und Widerstand der Juden in Polen während des Zweiten Weltkrieges*, Tatiana Berenstein, Artur Eisenbach, et al. (Berlin: Rütten & Loenig, 1960), 165.

30 "Rozporządzenie szefa Zarządu Cywilnego w sprawie znakowania wszystkich przedsiębiorstw należących do Żydów, 8 września, 1939, Kraków," in Eisenbach and Rutkowski, *Eksterminacja Żydów*, 69.

31 "Befehl Nr 7 des Chefs der Zivilverwaltung beim Wehrkreisbefehlshaber in Tschenstochau an die Landräte und Bürgermeister über die Ausschaltung der Juden aus dem Wirtschaftsleben, 15. September 1939, Tschenstochau," in Berenstein, Eisenbach, et al., *Faschismus—Ghetto—Massenmord*, 166.

32 "Auszug aus dem wöchentlichen Lagebericht des Landrats Glehn in Jędrzejów an den Chefs der Zivilverwaltung, Außenstelle Radom, über die Einsetzung von Treuhändern für jüdische Betriebe, 21. Oktober 1939, Jędrzejów," in Berenstein, Eisenbach, et al., *Faschismus—Ghetto—Massenmord*, 167.

33 "Instructions by Heydrich on Policy and Operations Concerning Jews in the Occupied Territories, September 21, 1939," in Arad and Gutman, *Documents on the Holocaust*, 173–78; Eisenbach and Rutkowski, *Eksterminacja Żydów*, 21–29.

34 Rossino, *Hitler Strikes Poland*; Alexander B. Rossino, "Nazi Anti-Jewish Policy during the Polish Campaign: The Case of the Einsatzgruppe Woyrsch," in *German Studies Review* 24 (2001): 35–54; Krausnick, *Hitlers Einsatzgruppen*.

of the occupying forces, characterized by anti-German attitudes and could become organizers of an armed resistance.[35]

As a result of the conference of September 21, 1939, and discussions which took place there, it was revealed that Reinhard Heydrich planned to organize the life of the Jews in occupied Poland at a very rapid pace, overestimating the capabilities of the *Einsatzgruppen*. It is important to add that, despite the fact that the war was not yet over, a significant part of the territory of Poland was occupied by the Germans. Further, the eastern provinces of Poland were occupied by Soviet troops and the result of that war was not yet known. It was a risky decision, based on the position of the western powers, who were not really interested in opening an additional front in the west. For Heydrich, it was evident at that time, what the fate of the territories belonging to Germany until the beginning of the Second World War would be. They were to be annexed to Germany. Therefore, in the first part of the *Schnellbrief* he clearly distinguished those areas from other territories (areas not implicitly occupied by the USSR). Heydrich was well informed on the location of the demarcation line between the Germany and the Soviet Union.

Heydrich's *Schnellbrief* indicates, on the one hand, a certain euphoria and haste. Issued decisions were not based on sufficient knowledge regarding the size and quantity of Jewish communities in the area. Decisions concerning the concentration of Jews in designated areas were not fully rational. Resettlement of hundreds of thousands of Jews in a very short time seemed to be an impossible task. It would require preparation accommodation in new places of residence. Subsequent deportations from Warthegau in the General Government after November 1939, when thousand of Poles and Jews were deported, created very serious problems and protests from the part of receiving authorities. If, however, the concentration was not feasible, remained the question remained as to why these tasks had been given to the *Einsatzgruppen* involving several hundred men. If the resettlement was aimed to facilitate the administration and control of Jewish matters, it was certain that so massive a resettlement could only cause chaos and inconvenience rather than validation of the situation.

If, on the other hand, it was a matter of eliminating the Jews, no concrete methods and means were presented. The only way of reducing the number of the Jews would be to cause the forced migration from the area of southern Poland to the area of Eastern Galicia, which was under the Soviet administration.

---

35 Kazimierz Leszczyński, "Działalność Einsatzgruppen Policji Bezpieczeństwa na ziemiach polskich w 1939 w świetle dokumentów," *BGKBZHP* XXII (1971): 7–281.

The primary task concerning Jewish matters given to the *Einsatzgruppen* was consolidating Jewish communities with fewer than 500 inhabitants, into larger towns where the absorption would take place.[36] Such a task was impossible under the circumstances of war and the initial organizational period of the German administration in the occupied territories. In the introduction to his *Schnellbrief*, Heydrich spoke about the ultimate objective, which appeared to be quite distant. According the content of the *Schnellbrief*, it was suggested that this goal was very close. An immediate deportation of thousands of Jews could paralyze transport, the economy, cause devastation of property, and disrupt the equilibrium in which they lived. Despite difficulties in the functioning of the supply system, the population, as a rule, had some supplies at home. Sudden deportation would constitute an enormous burden on the administration, on the system of assistance and on providing supplies, as usually happens in such situations. Heydrich could not have meant liquidation of the Jews at that time. It may be assumed that Heydrich believed it would be possible to shift a significant number of Jews across the border into the Soviet zone. Such tasks had been set before the *Einsatzgruppen* acting in southern Poland. This was taken into account, since Heydrich recommended only an approximate census of the Jewish population east of Kraków. Such a census, which contained detailed information about age and occupations of Jews, was necessary in order to facilitate the exploitation of the Jewish labor force. Concentration of Jews in the larger towns would facilitate the administration of that labor force.

The task set before the *Einsatzgruppen* had been carried out by creating Jewish Councils of Elders, which were to be an essential tool "of exact and timely implementation of any order issued" by the German authorities.[37] The Councils of Elders were to be composed of up to twenty four people, depending on the size of the municipality. The councils had been given the responsibility for conducting a census of the population according to the age, sex, and professional groups. An important part of the *Schnellbrief* concerned securing German economic interests. This certainly reflected the instructions given by the plenipotentiary of Göring's Four-Year Plan. Also, Heydrich treated this matter extremely carefully. As apparent from the wording of his *Schnellbrief*, he was ready for far-reaching concessions regarding that issue.

Among other things, in order to meet the needs of the army, he was ready to leave the "Jewish merchants who, in the absence of other options, must remain

---

36 Eisenbach and Rutkowski, *Eksterminacja Żydów*, 26.
37 Ibid., 26–27.

due to the necessity of providing supplies for the army."[38] Also, as a result of "defending the interests of the German economy in the occupied areas, it is necessary, of course, to allow for the time being, Jewish industries and factories of essential importance for life, for the purposes of the war effort and the Four-Year Plan."[39] However, this was a temporary solution until Aryanization[40] and the evacuation of the Jews. Similarly, it was necessary to ensure securing the harvest in the fields and making certain that all necessary field works and sowing of winter corn crops would be done. Worthy of note is that in the minutes of the meeting of September 21, 1939 the following was written: "This is necessary that Jews will disappear from the village as a small settler. This action must be carried out within the next 3–4 weeks."[41]

Particularly interesting is the fourth part of the *Schnellbrief*, in which Heydrich required to carry out the census of Jews in different areas according to previously chosen age groups and professional categories, to indicate places and determine the time for the transfer of Jews. He also he ordered the *Einsatzgruppen* to perform a reconnaissance of industrial plants owned by Jews. It was necessary to "give a list of all Jewish branches and industrial plants with essential for life and for the purposes of war and the Four-Year Plan"[42] in the given area. Heydrich called for reports on the types of plants, including the possibility of transforming them into factories of basic importance for the war objectives or the Four-Year Plan. He indicated as well in which order they should be aryanized, without causing any damage and whether those performing Aryanization could be Germans or Poles. He also demanded reporting the number of Jewish employees in the plant, whether they were in positions of management and whether the plant could lead normal production after the evacuation of Jews.

Heydrich's instructions, particularly concerning the drawing up of lists of establishments owned and managed by Jews and submitting recommendations on their further use in the war economy was a kind of curiosity. First of all,

---

38 Ibid., 27.
39 Ibid.
40 It is important to mention that the Schnellbrief of Heydrich was not the first document regerding the Aryanization. In the order of September 15, 1939 signed by General Rüdiger, was said: "The Jews shall only be involved in economic life in order to absolutely exclude them from the future and transfer their enterprizes to the Aryans." See "Armeeoberkommando. Der Chef der Zivilverwaltung, Tagesbefehl Nr 7, Tschenstochau, den 15. September 1939," AIPN, NTN, 196/270, 13.
41 Eisenbach and Rutkowski, *Eksterminacja Żydów*, 27.
42 Ibid., 27.

the *Einsatzgruppen* were neither competent in economic matters nor in recommending transformation in the production and management profile. It appears to be a sort of usurpation regarding competencies in economic matters. In addition, in actuality, other organizational units that had the task of gathering information and registration of industrial plants and stock of raw materials for the further use in the war effort were active.

Heydrich did not write in the *Schnellbrief* that the *Einsatzgruppen* were acquiring these plants for the SS, as was the case of the Wehrmacht that tried to take over plants and transfer them to their respective companies and to begin war production. Also, private companies expecting gigantic profits hurried up to be ahead of others in the takeover of plants. In the final analysis, the SS was not the first and not the only organization interested in economic exploitation of the new occupied areas of Poland. However, only at the end of 1939 did the SS begin to deal with organized labor camps in Lublin. Moreover, the SS was relatively late in taking over and creating new companies in comparison to other institutions.

FORCED LABOR OF JEWS DURING THE MILITARY ADMINISTRATION

The issues concerning forced labor were regulated by the International Convention on Forced Labor of 1930, prepared by the International Labor Organization. Article 2 of the Convention defined the term forced labor, as "work or service required of any person under the threat of any penalty to which the person does not offered himself voluntarily."[43] However, Section 2 of Article 2 referred to the exceptions stating that "any work, required in times of emergencies, that is to say, during war or the threat of disasters or misfortunes [...] which might endanger the existence or the well-being of all or part of the population"[44] was acceptable. Fragments of the Conventions relating to war were not well defined and allowed a broad margin of interpretation. Article 9 of the Convention provided a number of such cases. During the war, the competent authority may order execution of forced labor in addition to the above-mentioned threats. This was likewise the case in situations where such work was in the interest of the local people, where such work was a necessity, and when it was hard to get volunteer laborers in order to perform a particular job. According to Article 11, people under age 18 and above 45 should not be called to perform forced labor.

---

43 *Forced Labor Convention*, 1930.
44 Ibid.

Forced Labor in the Ghettos and Labor Detachments • CHAPTER 2 | 31

In practice, during the military administration, chaos reigned in the field of forced labor. Immediately after the entry of the German troops into newly occupied areas, rampant aggression was applied against the Jews and forced labor was one of aspects of that aggression.[45] One can observe a lack of any rules as far as labor was concerned. Jews were caught on the streets and led to work. Many testimonies described cases in which the basic purpose of forced labor was humiliating, as the object of harassment and abuse of Jews—such as, cleaning toilets with one's bare hands, cleaning the streets, and so on. The work was, as a rule, accompanied by beatings. On occasion religious Jews were humiliated by having their beards forcefully being shaved off, their side locks violently cut, or by removing any other symbols associated with the Jewish religion and tradition. Additional steps were aimed at humiliating Jews, for instance, forcing them to do useless work, where the only goal was harassment and abuse.

Particularly severe were the first days of the occupation. For the Jewish population living in areas of western Poland, it had already occurred at the beginning of September 1939. One of the witnesses described the entering of Germans into Olkusz on September 4, 1939 in the following manner:

> [. . .] there began a flood of tribulation and persecution of Jews. Immediately the Jewish population had to appear for public works, where supervisors beat and tortured them in a murderous way. Day by day from early morning till late evening, Jews often did useless work, beaten by Nazi criminals for which this sight served as entertainment.[46]

Thr first moments of the occupation in Siemianowice were described in a similar way:

> Germans search for everybody and force them to do public works. Jewish women must with brooms and rags march in the streets of the city and clean public toilets. Whoever does not have rags must do the work with bare hands.[47]

The same was true in Lublin, where immediately after the entry of the Germans, Jews were forced to do particularly humiliating work connected with cleaning manure and public toilets: "Soon after entering, the Germans started

---

45   YVA, M.49.E/1295, 2, testimony of Franciszek Mandelbaum z Lublina; YVA, M.49.E/1442, 1, testimony of Rywka Grynwald; YVA, M.49.E/4600, 1, testimony of Józefa Korniło, Tarnów;
46   YVA, M.49.E/1551, 1, testimony of Efraim Parasol.
47   YVA, M.49.E/1545, 1–2, testimony of Dawid Pinkus.

to mistreat us. We had to work; sometimes they made us clean toilets with bare hands."[48] The prevalence of degrading works is confirmed in other testimonies: "In 1939, when Germans entered Rejowiec [...] the first day they ordered us to gather. They ordered us to remove mud with hands, clean toilets etc. They tortured and beat us and several elderly men were killed. We had to report to work every day."[49] The same was true in Warsaw:

> The enemy picks Jews particularly for the most distasteful work—cleaning toilets, scrubbing floors, and other jobs of this sort. And there was an occurrence that I heard of from a youth—"It happened to me, myself!" he said. They caught him for work and ordered him to clean out filthy places and gave him no tools. When he asked for tools, they advised him to do it with his hands and to use his coat in place of a vessel. When he objected to this, they beat him.[50]

The primary method of recruitment for forced labor was the arrest of Jews in the street[51] or going from house to house to draw men.[52] In many cases, young women, girls,[53] and boys were taken to work.[54] Jews, who understood the danger that threatened them in forced labor, stopped going on the streets to avoid the chase after forced laborers; they fled or remained hidden at home. During forced labor, Jews were not only beaten, but there were even cases of murder.[55] In his diary Ludwik Landau noted:

> The same way as in relation to the general population, a mix of problems resulting from abuse and as the consequence of conscious policy, when it concerns the attitude of the occupiers to the Jewish population. [...] Especially Jews were called to perform various kinds of forced labor: recruitment is carried out by asking the question *Sind Sie Jude?* in cases of doubt. It was without being asked that question, when the origin of the person raised

---

48 YVA, M.49.E/1444, 1, testimony of Rywka Rosenblum.
49 YVA, M.49.E/1445, 1, testimony of Józef Feifermacher.
50 Chaim Kaplan, *Scroll of Agony: The Warsaw Diary of Chaim Kaplan* (Bloomington: Indiana University Press, Bloomington and Indianapolis, 1999), 48.
51 YVA, M.49.E/1476, 1, testimony of Chaim Hirszman.
52 YVA, M.49.E/1443, 1, testimony of Maria Rosenzweig.
53 YVA, M.49.E/1565, 1, testimony of Goldhust Blanka.
54 YVA, M.49.E/1445, 1, testimony of Józef Feifermacher.
55 YVA, M.49.E/1476, 1, testimony of Chaim Hirszman.

no doubts. I saw in those days at the military hospital a few men brought to unload coal to the basement: they were all Jews in long *chałats*.[56]

German soldiers exploited the situation of occupation and inspired terror by using the Jews to perform various services. One such activity was washing cars.[57] Among the jobs that were included in the category of permitted works by the International Labor Convention, was the work done during the war for the benefit of the general public. In many places, such work meant filling up the anti-aircraft ditches and removing barricades, which were made during the war in many towns.

Ludwik Landau wrote in his diary about the situation in Warsaw:

> The population is forced to procure various personal services, of course without any remuneration. At the time when German troops entered Warsaw, the entire city was covered with a network of barricades. Germans demanded removing these barricades. Since the Executive Municipal Board did not answer fast enough or not quite vigorously enough to the request, the Germans accelerated the progress of these works, detaining men passing in the streets. At times, they even searched for men at home. In many cases they 'caught' only Jews to do the work by asking passersby to show their identity documents; even old people were not exempt. Somebody told me, about a case of dragging an old man, a former senator [of the Polish Republic], on the street and forcing him to dig. Obviously, however, it is not confined only to the Jews. In the same way, men were taken in the streets, as well as from their homes, to perform forced labor.[58]

The Jews were preferred by the Germans, which proved that they treated them in a unique way, different from the rest of the Polish public. Chaim A. Kaplan wrote on October 10, 1939 the following: "Only Jews are taken for forced labor. Young, energetic, muscular Poles stand and mock from afar the Jews who kneel under the burden of their toil."[59]

The identification of Jews could involve certain difficulties, particularly when related to non-orthodox Jews, who in many cases were not different in

---

56 Landau, *Kronika lat wojny i okupacji*, vol. 1, 27.
57 YVA, M.49.E/1512, 1–2, testimony of Chaim Nadel.
58 Landau, *Kronika lat wojny i okupacji*, vol. 1, 26–27.
59 Kaplan, *Scroll of Agony*, 48.

appearance from the rest of society. Therefore, harassment in the initial period of the military occupation referred specifically to Orthodox Jews,[60] who were dressed in traditional attire, with beards and side locks.[61] "Eyewitnesses tell that even military officers and high officials are not ashamed to chase after an old Jew with scissors in their hands, to cut off his beard."[62] It was easy to distinguish them from others. Sometimes detained were poor, Orthodox Jews, who were in lines for the free food, as Chaim A. Kaplan wrote in his diary: "A broken Jew, standing in a food line for long hours, was picked up for a twenty-four-hour work detail, hungry and thirsty as he was."[63] It was only later that the authorities obliged the Jews to wear the Star of David, which, inter alia, facilitated the rapid identification of all Jews. Nevertheless, persecution was not limited only to the people, but also to the symbols and everything bringing to mind the Jewish religion. Germans would enter synagogues and houses of prayer in order to remove Jews praying there and take them into forced labor.[64] The aim was not only to humiliate them by showing lack of respect for their religion, but also to humiliate them physically, abusing them by pulling them away from prayer to work. Often those taken were old men, who were physically unable to work. Some Jews, already at the beginning of the occupation, forfeited their health because of forced labor.[65]

Germans were also well informed about the Jewish holidays, and they particularly tormented the Jews on those days. During the holiday of Rosh Hashana, on September 14, 1939, the Jews in Częstochowa were drawn from the synagogue and forced to work.[66] In Warsaw during a morning prayer of "... Shemini Atzeret, a hundred and fifty men were pulled out of the Mława Street synagogue, herded into a truck, and taken to enforced labor."[67] In Kraków, "on the Day of Atonement, they [Germans] raided the Jewish quarter. Cars stood next to the bridge at the end of Starowiślna Street, on which Jews who were caught were loaded, while all that action was accompanied by beating and derision. They took them to work. They returned in the evening badly beaten."[68]

---

60 Ibid., 45.
61 Ibid.
62 Ibid., 54.
63 Ibid., 45.
64 YVA, M.49.E/1549, 1–2, testimony of Stefania Rosenberg.
65 YVA, M.49.E/1565, 1, testimony of Goldhust Blanka.
66 Liber Brenner, *Widerstand un Umekum in Tschenstochover Geto* (Warsaw: Yidisher Historisher Institut in Pojlin, 1950), 8.
67 Kaplan, *Scroll of Agony*, 45.
68 YVA, M.49.E/1474, 1, testimony of Ester Fefer.

The humiliation and ill-treatment of Jews was accompanied by taking photographs, which took place in many cities in Poland. In various archives, many such photographs showing humiliated and harassed Jews taken by German soldiers are stored. The witness from Tarnów recalled: "Jews with beards were photographed on the streets while their beards were being torn off."[69]

Forced labor took the form of humiliation and persecution. Still, the occupational authorities faced the necessity to bring certain order on the streets and had to use local manpower to remove barricades and debris of destroyed houses. In some cities, like Warsaw, where fighting was intense, most of the streets were blocked with barricades made of brick, stones, tram wagons, destroyed cars, and other objects. In many places anti-aerial trenches had to be covered. Due to heavy bombing and sieges, in many cities squares, courtyards, and public gardens were turned to graves for people who died during the fighting. Those graves owould be removed. In many Polish towns, carcasses of horses, widely used for transportation and by the Polish army, also had to be removed from the streets. Due to destruction of local administration, organizational chaos and lack of available manpower, German military authorities used their powers in order to mobilize local citizens by force. In places where Jews did not live, the local Polish population was mobilized to perform urgent works, but in places of mixed population, the Jews were frequently preferred, which gave an occasion to humiliate them. Mobilization of local inhabitants during the military period to perform the most urgent works could serve as a solution during the initial period of the occupation, and in no way could substitute for organized labor.

JEWISH ORGANIZED LABOR

Prolonged roundups of Jews on the streets of cities, in homes, and synagogues for forced labor had become a highly widespread phenomenon and impossible to bear. Chaotic roundups of Jews forced to work fully confused their economic and social lives. Because of the roundups, some Jews stopped going out in the streets. Apolinary Hartglas recalled this period in the following words:

> One of the most troubling economic measures was this: the picking up of people in the streets, or in their homes, for forced labor. This situation robbed the Jews of all opportunity of carrying on any kind of activity—no business, no office run by Jews can operate, because neither the owner nor

---

69   YVA, M.49.E/4600, 1, testimony of Józef Korniło, Tarnów.

the employees can be sure that they will get to their place of work. Even the employees of the Jewish Council are picked up while they are on their way to work.[70]

In many cities the *Judenräte* simultaneously came to the conclusion that it was necessary to take the initiative into their own hands and came up with a proposal to establish special labor detachments or work battalions, in order to ensure the continued supply of a work force for the German institutions. Such a solution would ensure the cessation of random roundups of Jews. Quite often these people were unable to do hard work that could cause exhaustion, disability, and even death. The orders of Reinhard Heydrich given to the *Einsatzgruppen*, concerning the census of the Jewish population, were supposed to determine not only their number, but also the quantity of Jews able to work, dividing the Jews into categories according to age and profession. In most cases, these orders were not completed. In Lublin, however, the registration of those able to work had been carried out on October 25, 1939—one day before the proclamation of the General Government.[71]

The work battalions appeared from mid-October 1939. The *Judenrat* in Warsaw was established in the middle of October. Already on October 19, 1939, the *Judenrat* promised the security police recruitment of a required number of Jewish workers together with the necessary tools. The next step of regulating forced labor was the establishment of labor battalions. Labor battalions were responsible for the recruitment and assignment of Jewish workers according to the requests sent by the SS and police.

> Czerniaków offered to supply a certain number of workers if only they [the German authorities] would stop seizing whoever comes to their hands in the streets for forced labor. [...] Finally they agreed that the *Judenrat* will supply five hundred laborers a day, and that captures on the street will stop. Tomorrow will be the first day of this new arrangement. The *Judenrat* will pay each worker four złoty a day out of its treasury.[72]

The first group of 360 workers was ready on October 21, 1939.[73]

---

70   Arad and Gutman, *Documents on the Holocaust*, 189; Apolinary Hartglas, *Na pograniczu dwóch światów* (Warsaw: Rytm, 1996), 279–30.
71   APL, RŻL-8, 39.
72   Kaplan, *Scroll of Agony*, 55.
73   Tatiana Berenstein, "Praca przymusowa Żydów w Warszawie," 44.

Already in mid-October, the Jewish Council in Lublin send a request to the German *Arbeitsamt* proposing regulation on the assignment of Jewish workers for various German institutions. The *Judenrat* promised to deliver 100 workers in exchange for cessation of arrests of Jews in the streets.[74] In fact, the Lublin *Judenrat* created a Labor Department on October 20, 1939.[75] The office was supposed to recruit the required number of Jewish workers and pay them wages from funds of the community, according to the established tariffs. Until end of March daily payment was as follows: single man: 2.5 zł; married man: 3 zł; married man supporting more than four family members: 3.5 zł; single woman: 2.5 zł; married woman: 3.5 zł.[76] At that time, for many refugees and deportees from other areas, that kind of employment gave a chance of gaining at least a minimal means for supporting themselves and their families.

DEVELOPMENT OF GERMAN LEGISLATION ON FORCED LABOR IN THE INITIAL PERIOD OF GENERAL GOVERNOR'S RULE

With the proclamation on October 26, 1939, the governor general of the General Government (*Generalgouvernement*), Dr. Hans Frank issued a series of acts. Two of them related to labor issues. The new authorities introduced obligatory labor (*Arbeitspflicht*) for the Polish population[77] and compulsory labor (*Arbeitszwang*) for the Jewish population.[78] Regulation on the introduction of compulsory labor for the Jewish population was issued on the same day when the establishment of the General Government for the occupied Polish territories was proclaimed. It is not clear why this regulation was adopted as one of the first regulations of the new governor general. It can be, however, assumed that the matter of Jewish forced labor, and labor in general, was one of the most important issues for the newly created administrative unit. Regulation on the introduction of compulsory labor for the Polish population of the General Government was no less important for the new authority. Considering the economic policy, the introduction of forced labor and

---

74 APL, RŻL-8, 47. Report on the activity of the [Jewish] Council [in Lublin] for the period September 1, 1939 until August 31, 1940.
75 Ibid., 39.
76 Ibid., 49.
77 "Verordnung über die Einführung des Arbeitspflicht für die polnische Bevölkerung des Generalgouvernements. Vom 26. Oktober 1939," *VBlGG*, 5; Karol Marian Pospieszalski, *Hitlerowskie "prawo" okupacyjne* (Poznań: Instytut Zachodni, 1952), vol. 2, 306–7.
78 "Verordnung über die Einführung des Arbeitszwangs für die jüdische Bevölkerung des Generalgouvernements. Vom 26. Oktober 1939," *VBlGG*, 6; Pospieszalski, *Hitlerowskie "prawo" okupacyjne*, vol. 2, 560.

compulsory labor was one of the steps in the direction of further measures for the economic exploitation of the conquered population. A confirming fact is high unemployment that was recorded at that time. It was a result of military operations and related damage, administrative changes and creating of new customs borders, lack of raw materials and fuels, chaos in the market. All those factors caused economic crisis and in consequence, economic stagnation and high unemployment.[79] Therefore, it was difficult in this period to introduce forced labor or, rather, require full employment. Since this was impossible, the authorities could on this basis remove surplus of labor force to Germany. Already at the end of 1940, many factories returned to work. According to the *Kreishauptmann* of Jędrzejów:

> The factories are still working to capacity and operate extremely profitable. It would be desirable if a decision was made soon about the future of the formerly Jewish factories that have been set into operation and good shape again by the *Kreishauptmann* [of Jędrzejów] and his staff, since there are rumors in circulation about nonsensical profits of the trustees that were not reciprocated.[80]

In Starachowice, the situation of employment of Jews was also improving considerably:

> As far as I could assess, 530 workers have been newly employed in October by the local Erzbergbau-GmbH (Ore Mining-East Ltd.). One has to take into account a further requirement of skilled labor in the local mines and smelting works in the near future. The activity of the local branch [in Starachowice] of the *Arbeitsamt* Radom can be called brisk. During the period under review, ca. 1,000 placements were carried out. The Jews were put on work detail in road construction, in work for the Water Management office, in agriculture and forestry, in mining and other places (army, administration and so forth).[81]

---

79 BA-MA, RW23-8, Rüstungswirtschaftlicher Lagebericht für 7.–28. October 1939, 134.
80 YVA, JM-814, Der Kreishauptmann des Kreises Jędrzejów, Lagebericht für August 1940, September 5, 1940, scan 320.
81 YVA, JM-814, Der Kreishauptmann des Kreises Starachowice, Lagebericht für Oktober 1940, scan 769.

By issuing separate orders for the Poles and the Jews, the authorities made formal distinctions between Polish and Jewish populations in ethno-racial terms. Other ethnic groups, such as the Ukrainians, were not included in those acts. The reason was not only the relatively low numbers of other groups, but also the idea that these groups could be used as a political tool in the event of a possible expansion to the east. The German population, after the occupation of the country, became a privileged group. Separate laws for the German population were issued.[82]

It is important to emphasize that with the introduction of the above-mentioned regulations for Poles and Jews, there was no clear definition of the term "Jew." This definition was introduced for the first time on July 24, 1940.[83] Probably, the German authorities at that time did not feel a need for such a definition, and it seemed obvious to them who was a Jew and who was not, or they relied on data registered in Polish documents. Representatives of the German administration were familiar with the legislation existing in Germany at that time, so the definitions of ethnicity were self-evident to them and probably were used in a somewhat subconscious manner. For example, the regulation on the marking of Jewish men and women in the General Government of November 23, 1939[84] does not contain such a definition. Instead, the regulation of head of the Warsaw District of November 25, 1939[85] stipulates that "under this ordinance shall be considered as a Jew, person which: 1. which belonged or belongs to the Jewish community; 2. whose father or mother belong or belonged to the Jewish community." Similar definition was published by the chef of the district of Kraków, Wächter, on November 18, 1939, where he stated that "according to this regulation the Jews is: 1) that who is or was of Mosaic faith; 2) that person, whose father or mother are or were of Mosaic faith."[86] Those are simplified definitions, incompatible with the Nuremberg laws as well as with later regulations of the governor general. A definition of a "Pole" or a "Ukrainian" did not appear in the official documents

---

82 *Das Arbeitsrecht des Generalgouvernements: Die Regelungen der Arbeitsbedingungen, insbesondere der Lohngestaltung im Generalgouvernement, Zusammengestellt und erlaeutert von Regierungsrat dr. iur. Heinz Melies* (Krakow: Burgverlag, 1943).

83 "Verordnung über die Bestimmung des Begriffs 'Jude' im Generalgouvernement. Vom 24. Juli 1940," in Pospieszalski, *Hitlerowskie "prawo" okupacyjne*, vol. 2, 558–59; "Official definition of the term 'Jew' in the General Government, July 24, 1940," in Arad and Gutman, *Documents on the Holocaust*, 214–15; VBlGG, 1940, 231–32.

84 Święcicki and Zadrowski, *Zbiór rozporządzeń*, 226–27.

85 Ibid., 227–28.

86 YVA-JM.12306, Rozporządzenie—Znamionowanie Żydów w okręgu Krakowa, scan 485.

as well. Therefore, the Poles were defined on the basis of the elimination of the possibility of belonging to the German or Jewish ethnic groups. Between German and Polish ethnic groups, there was certain mobility in connection with the introduction of the status of *Volksdeutsche*.[87] Over time, the criteria for membership of this group were alleviated, thus increasing the possibility of changing of the status of many people, who did not have any legal base to define their belonging. Similar was the admission of the Ukrainian ethnic group to the General Government. Belonging to this group gave numerous membership privileges; so the number of Ukrainians in the General Government in the initial period of occupation grew to large sizes.[88]

Issuing of legal acts for various groups of Polish citizens was held without a definition of the governor general "citizenship," which had further consequences. The German authorities allowed the deportation of Polish or Jewish population from other areas and treated them the same way as inhabitants of the General Government. In this case, it would be more appropriate to use the term "inhabitant" and not "citizen."

The regulation concerning the introduction of identity documents in the General Government uses the term "total Polish population in the General Government" (*Gesamte polnische Bevölkerung des Generalgouvernements*).[89] However, § 1, Section 2 contains a provision: "The identity card (*Kennkarte*)... provides information on name, birth and ancestry, marital status, occupation, religion and nationality of its owner. It is equipped with a fingerprint."[90] This way, when Jewish religion was registered in the identity card, the Jews were distinguished. However, it was an indication based on religious affiliation rather than nationality. In such cases a person of Jewish origin, belonging to the Christian religion, could avoid categorization as Jewish. This, of course, depended on the origin of the records and names of parents. Strongly Jewish

---

87 "Verordnung über die Einführung einer Kennkarte für deutsche Volkszugehörige im Generalgouvernement. Vom 26. Januar 1940," in Pospieszalski, *Hitlerowskie "prawo" okupacyjne*, vol. 2, 174–75.

88 Fritz Arlt, *Die ukrainische Volksgruppe im Generalgouvernement, Regierung des Generalgouvernements* (Krakau: n.p., 1940); Fritz Arlt, *Polen-, Ukrainer-, Judenpolitik im Generalgouvernement für die besetzten polnischen Gebiete 1939/40 und im Oberschlesien 1941/43 und im Freitheitskampf der unterdrückten Ostvölker: Errinerungen eines Insiders* (Lindhorst: Täge, 1995).

89 "Verordnung über die Einführung on Kennkarten im Generalgouvernement. Vom 26. Oktober 1939," in Pospieszalski, *Hitlerowskie "prawo" okupacyjne*, vol. 2, 375.

90 Ibid., vol. 2, 375. See § 1 (2). "Die Kennkarte gibt insbesondere Auskunft über Namen, Geburt und Abstammung, Familienstand, Beruf, Religion und Staatszugehörigkeit des Kennkarteninhabers. Sie ist mit einem Fingerabdruck zu versehen."

names and family names could indicate Jewish origin and thus arouse suspicion of the officials or the police.

The German authority was an occupation authority, formed as a result of winning the war.[91] Through the nomination of Dr. Hans Frank on the post of governor general, Hitler entrusted him with all the executive power.[92] In terms of structures of power, the governor general was directly subject only to Hitler.[93] On the basis of Hitler's decree of October 12, 1939, the governor general had also full legislative power.[94] Regulation of the obligation to work for the Poles (*Arbeitspflicht*) is important for further discussion, as a benchmark, and permits us to compare the status of workers in these two groups of occupied populations in conquered Poland: Poles and Jews. The text of the regulation of October 26, 1939 determined that all the inhabitants of the General Government of Polish nationality from 18 to 60 years of age are subject to public work. In the same document it was stated that the Jews were subjected to a special regulation. Persons who could demonstrate having constant and "useful" employment from the social point of view were not invoked to perform the obligation to work. In paragraph 3 of the regulation it is said that "the public obligation of work will be performed in particular on the on farms, construction and maintenance of public buildings, construction of roads, waterways and railways, regulation of rivers and work intended to meliorate agricultural conditions."[95] The regulation further provides that any person subjected to the obligation of work will receive salary, "according to the just rates." According to this regulation, further provisions were the responsibility of the head of the Labor Department in the Office of the Governor General (*Abteilung des Arbeit im Amt des Generalgouverneurs für die bestzte polnische Gebiete*). At the head of this office stood *Reichshauptamtsleiter* Dr. Max Frauendorfer.[96]

---

91 "Erste Verordnung über den Aufbau der Verwaltung der besetzten polnischen Gebiete. Vom 26. Oktober 1939, § 1," in Pospieszalski, *Hitlerowskie "prawo" okupacyjne*, 54.
92 "Erlass des Führers und Reichskanzlers über die Verwaltung der besetzten polnischen Gebiete. Vom 12. Oktober 1939, § 3," in Pospieszalski, *Hitlerowskie "prawo" okupacyjne*, 52.
93 Ibid.
94 "Erste Verordnung über den Aufbau der Verwaltung der besetzten polnischen Gebiete. Vom 26. Oktober 1939, § 7," in Pospieszalski, Karol Marian, *Hitlerowskie "prawo" okupacyjne*, vol. 2, 57.
95 "Verordnung über die Einführung des Arbeitspflicht für die polnische Bevölkerung des Generalgouvernements. Vom 26. Oktober 1939," in Pospieszalski, Karol Marian, *Hitlerowskie "prawo" okupacyjne*, vol. 2, 307; Święcicki and Zadrowski, *Zbiór rozporządzeń*, 194.
96 JD Max Frauendorfer (1909–1989) since October 1, 1939 until November 18, 1939 was Trustee for Labor Affairs (*Reichstreuhander der Arbeit*), then President of the Main Department of Labor (*Leiter des Hauptamtes Arbeit im Generalgouvernement*). Due to the

Regulation concerning compulsory labor for Poles has suggested that employees not having a job and representing unused labor force could be utilized to carry out public works, mainly in the reconstruction and expansion of infrastructure, agriculture, and the regulation of rivers. This indicated the plans of the German government for the occupied Polish areas. As a result of the war there was extensive damage to bridges, roads, and railways, which had to be rebuilt as soon as possible, both for strategic and economic reasons. However, the problem of regulation of rivers was different from the repair and expansion of infrastructure. It indicated significant understanding of the new administration in matters of Polish agriculture and pointed to the existence of plans for the transformation of Polish agriculture into more intense and extension existing farmland areas. It should be noted that such discussion took place in October 1939, which was meaning that the work could begin no sooner than six months later.[97]

Regulation regarding the introduction of compulsory labor for the Jewish population of the General Government of October 26, 1939, announced the introduction of compulsion to work (*Arbeitszwang*) for the Jewish population with an immediate effect on the date of publication of the regulation. Further the document stated in paragraph 1 that: "for this purpose the Jews are organized in detachments of forced labor."[98] Higher SS and Police Commander (HSSPF) in the General Government Friedrich-Wilhelm Krüger was responsible for further implementing of the rules. In contrast to instructions of obligation to work for the Polish population, the regulation concerning the Jews did not mention anything more specific about locations of forced labor. It seems that the regulation on Jewish forced labor was, on the one hand, issued too early and on the other hand, too late. At the time of issuing of the regulation, October 26, 1939, the authorities apparently wanted to emphasize the division of the occupied society on the Poles and the Jews. Their rights and obligations were different. Even in case of terminology concerning the matters of labor, different terms were used and they were not synonyms. At the moment of the establishment of the General Government, a number of different rules for Poles

---

    conflict with Higher SS and Police Leader in the General Government Friedrich-Wilhelm Krüger, he was released of his duty and transferred to Waffen-SS. After a short leave, he was employed by Fritz Sauckel as his Plenipotentiary in Holland.

97 "Verordnung über die Einführung des Arbeitspflicht für die polnische Bevölkerung des Generalgouvernements. Vom 26. Oktober 1939, § 3," in Pospieszalski, *Hitlerowskie "prawo" okupacyjne*, vol. 2, 307.

98 "Verordnung über die Einführung des Arbeitszwangs für die jüdische Bevölkerung des Generalgouvernements. Vom 26. Oktober 1939, § 1," in Pospieszalski, *Hitlerowskie "prawo" okupacyjne*, vol. 2, 560.

and Jews were issued, but the regulations concerning forced labor appeared to be the most significant. Hans Frank did not specify the scope of labor more closely, as was the case of the Polish population, the way of its implementing, and its goals, whether economic or other. Furthermore, it was not stated, as it was in the case of Poles, whether all Jews were forced to perform forced labor, which age group was to perform forced labor and whether Jews employed in other companies also had to perform forced labor, or whether this legislation only concenrned the unemployed. Soon after the establishment of the General Government, new regulations appeared relating to employment law and protection of employment, containing no distinction between Poles and Jews, which would mean that all employment contracts valid on August 31, 1939 remained in force, also in the case of the Jews.[99]

It should be emphasized that at the time of issuing the regulation on forced labor for Jews, such labor was performed by thousands of Jews in the General Government every day. During this period, however, kidnapping Jews from the street to forced labor continued. Sometimes they were taken away from their current places of employment to do other work. The most active factor in this procedure was the SS and police, though the Wehrmacht was also involved in the kidnapping of Jews from the streets, places of employment or homes. As the rule, the works where the Jews were forcibly brought were mostly dirty works, very difficult, and degrading.

An important point of regulation of October 26, 1939 concerning the introduction of forced labor for Jews was revealed in § 2. This paragraph stated that "the necessary measures for implementation of this regulation will be adopted by the higher SS and police leader."[100] This meant that forced labor of Jews were to be regulated not by civilian labor offices but by the SS. It was also a confirmation that Jewish affairs in general were in the hands of the SS. This decision was in the spirit of earlier documents, especially telegraphic message sent by Heydrich, to all operational groups (*Einsatzgruppen*) of the Sipo in Poland, from September 21, 1939, where he transferred in the hands

---

99 "Erste Durchführungsverordnung zur Verordnung vom 25. Oktober 1939 über die Eiführung der Arbeitspflicht für die polnische Bevölkerung des Generalgouvernements. Vom 31. Oktober 1939," in Pospieszalski, *Hitlerowskie "prawo" okupacyjne*, vol. 2, 308.

100 "Verordnung über die Einführung des Arbeitszwangs für die jüdische Bevölkerung des Generalgouvernements. Vom 26. Oktober 1939," in Pospieszalski, *Hitlerowskie "prawo" okupacyjne*, vol. 2, 560.

of the *Einsatzgruppen*[101] all the matters concerning organization of Jewish councils and other matters related to Jews. Operational groups of the Security Police became later a part of the Reich Security Main Office (*RSHA*) that was established on September 22, 1939. In Germany, for example, Jewish affairs were in the hands of the Gestapo: *Referat* B4 of the division IV. In the General Government the same system of dealing with Jewish matters was introduced as in Germany.

The consequences of all Jewish matters, including labor issues, being handled by the SS and the police were far-reaching. First of all, these were not the actions of the civilians, but of the police, which have obviously influenced the treatment of the Jewish workers. During the mobilization of workers, organization of labor, and its supervision, brutal police methods were often used. In addition, the SS and the police could not deal with the issues of forced labor of Jews in a professional manner. Brutality and the use of force did not ensure the rational use of labor resources. The consequence of this state of affairs was the lack of coordination between civilians, and SS and police agents, leading to numerous conflicts and irrational and uneconomical actions. The use of police methods was aimed at unlimited exploitation of the Jews in the initial period of Nazi occupation, but it led to further consequences and created undue burdens, and even a financial overload of the Jewish communities in the General Government.

LABOR OFFICES (*ARBEITSÄMTER*)

Responsible for organization of labor were the labor offices (*Arbeitsämter*), which were created in general in October 1939. However, already on September 14, 1939 the *Chef der Zivilverwaltung* established labor offices in Tarnowiec, Lubliniec, Częstochowa, Wieluń, Piotrków, Radomsko, Kielce, Radom, and Końskie.[102] In the General Government, 23 labor offices were created and in addition 70 branches of labor offices (*Nebenstellen*) were set up.[103] From the part of the government for organization of labor in the General Government, the Labor Department of the Office of the Governor General (*Die Abteilung des Arbeit im*

---

101 "Schnellbrief," 21 September 1939, in Pospieszalski, *Hitlerowskie "prawo" okupacyjne*, vol. 2, 532–36.

102 Armeeoberkommando. Der Chef der Zivilverwaltung, Tagesbefehl Nr 6, Tshcenstochau, den 14. September 1939. AIPN, NTN, 196/270, 11.

103 Max Freiherr Du Prel, *Das Deutsche Generalgouvernement Polen: Ein Überblick über Gebiet Gestaltung und Geschichte* (Krakow: Buchverlag Ost GmbH, 1940), 288.

Amt für die Generalgouverneurs besetzten polnischen Gebiete) was responsible. Later, the name "Labor Department" (*Abteilung Arbeit*) was replaced by "the Main Department of Labor" (*Hauptamt Arbeit*). At the head of the department stood *Reichshauptamtsleiter* Dr. Max Frauendorfer. Basically, department activities were divided into four groups.[104] The first dealt with the issues relating to trusteeship of industrial plants (*Treuhänder*); the second dealt with the management and administration of labor matters (*Arbeitseinsatz*), and to this group were subjected labor offices; the third group dealt with issues of social protection (*Sozialversicherung*), with particular emphasis on the needs of the population associated with damage caused by the war; and the fourth group dealt with issues relating to housing and population settlements issues (*Wohnung- und Siedlungswesen*).[105] To the head of the Labor Department were subjected appropriate positions at the level of heads of district offices. At the head of the Labor Department in the districts stood chefs of departments (*Leiter der Arbeit Abteilungen bei den Chefs der Distrikt*). Labor offices were engaged in tasks related to inspection of labor, keeping of statistics of unemployed and employment, as well as mandatory employment of unemployed to obligatory labor (*Arbeit Pflicht*) in the case of non-Jewish population. Labor offices also mobilized Polish workers for work in German agriculture and industry in the Third Reich.

Labor offices registered all able-bodied Poles, shaped working conditions, and were engaged in the provision of forced laborers to the Reich. During the initial period of the occupation until the summer of 1940 and from mid-1942, the Jewish population was not subject to the labor offices, because the SS and the police dealt with their issues. In the autumn of 1939 shipment of Polish workers to the Reich began. According to the reports Polish population tried to evade the mobilization to work in the Reich. The *Kreishauptmann* of Jasło reported in July 1940: "By night police action only a very small part of the required workers can be detected incidentally. The eligible people are not to be found at home even during the night, but they spend the night in the woods or at friends and relatives in other villages. The fear to go to the Reich, has its basis in the most absurd rumors that Polish farm workers are to be used in part on the theater of war or in danger zones, on the other—apart from Poles' reluctance before work—in reports that come to the relatives from the Reich from the farm workers sent there."[106]

---

104 Max Freiherr Du Prel, ed. *Das Generalgouvernement* (Würzburg: K. Triltsch, 1942), 135–40.
105 Ibid., 286.
106 YVA-O.53/101, Der Kreishauptmann des Kreises Jasło, Jasło, den 2. Juni 1940, Lagebericht über die Zeit von Mitte Mai 1940 bis Ende Mai 1940, scans 74–76.

Systematic registration and shipment of Polish workers took place since 1940. In fact, the shipment of Polish workers to Germany could create an impression of much harder persecution of Poles then the Jews. The *Kreishauptmann* of Jasło wrote: "The Jews pride themselves that they can do their work here, they do not need to go to in the Reich, where they would live in chaos of the war. Even though the enforcement exerted by the police had little effect on the deployment of farm workers because of the aforementioned circumstances, I would consider it inappropriate to abandon doing so. This would undoubtedly be interpreted by the Poles as backing off or conceding of the German administration."[107] On the other hand, the *Kreishauptmann* of Końskie reported:

> The Polish population welcomed the removal of 16 to 25-year-old Jews for forced labor with particular satisfaction. Until now, the Jews triumphed over the Poles, because the Poles were sent to Germany as seasonal workers, while they could stay here. In addition, they troubled the Poles with rumors about the cession of their homeland to the Russians. With the crackdown on the Jewish forced laborers the rumors were quashed abruptly.[108]

The German authorities tried initially to persuade the Poles about the benefits and job prospects in the Reich, however soon it became clear that voluntary mobilization of Poles failed and the Germans begun to use force in order to mobilize required quantity of Polish laborers. Already in 1940 Polish resistance against their labor mobilization grew. The *Kreishauptmann* of Puławy wrote in his report: "The employment of labor of the Polish population lately meets a growing resistance. One has the impression as if certain powers worked methodically against the willingness to work, and made counter-propaganda. For example, in one community of 200 requested workers 8 men reported for work, in another community, of 300 requested workers 27. Concerning the coercive measures, some expressed they would rather be imprisoned than work for a few pennies. In an agricultural business, the workers demanded a pay-rise from the manager, threatening to go on strike. That didn't happen because I arrested the ringleaders and interpreters."[109]

Labor offices below the district level did not coincide with the administrative division of districts into *Kreishauptmannschaften* and *Stadthauptmannschaften*,

---

107 Ibid.
108 YVA-O.53/101, Der Kreishauptmann von Końskie, Lagebericht, September 9, 1940, scan 2.
109 YVA, JM-814, Der Kreishauptmann des Kreises Puławy, Lagebericht für Oktober 1940, Puławy, den 6. November 1940, scan 826.

but were created in larger towns. For example, in the district of Warsaw, labor offices were established in Warsaw, Siedlce, Sochaczew, Mińsk Mazowiecki and Skierniewice. Each of these offices had branches (*Nebenstellen*). The biggest number of branches was in Warsaw (nineteen in total).[110] Labor offices could assign people to work or impose an obligation on each municipality to indicate a certain number of workers. Control of labor was performed using the labor cards (*Arbeitskarte*), introduced at the end of 1940, in which the employer typed employment data. The employees received certificates of occupation (*Beschäftigunsnachweis*) from the employment office that had a work card.

One of the most important tasks of labor offices was to mobilize workforce (*Arbeitseinsatz*). Authorities could exercise control over the administration of the workforce through the introduction of registration of workers. In addition, the labor offices exercised control over the flow of labor force from one to the other jobs. This was done under the regulation on restriction of changes of workplaces of February 22, 1940.[111] The labor offices could express their disagreement to change jobs thus controlling both size and quality of employment in specific industries or crafts. Labor offices also identified reserves of the workers, which could be sent to work in the Reich. Writing about tasks of labor offices in 1940, Max Frauendorfer mentioned the need to send to the Reich 100,000 Polish workers for work in German industry and agriculture.[112]

Simultaneous resumption of economic activity in the General Government resulted in increasing need to regulate the flow of workers to particular sectors of the economy and individual companies.

LEGAL STATUS OF JEWS AND POLES CONCERNING FORCED LABOR

The term "forced labor" (*Zwangsarbeit*), which is crucial in the present work, requires further explanation. In the official German documents and regulations the term appears for the first time in the Regulation of Dr. Hans Frank, on October 26, 1939. This term was used widely for several years and did not change within that time until the end of the war, but its content underwent

---

110 Skorwider, Danuta, "Organizacja władz niemieckich na terenie dystryktu warszawskiego w latach 1939–1945," in *Raporty Ludwiga Fischera gubernatora dystryktu warszawskiego 1939–1944*, ed. Krzysztof Dunin-Wąsowicz (Warsaw: Książka i Wiedza, 1987), 62.
111 Verordnung über die Beschränkung des Arbeitsplatzwechsels, 22. Februar 1940.
112 Dr. Frauendorfer, "Organisation des Arbeitseinsatzes," in Du Prel, *Das Deutsche Generalgouvernement Polen*, 291.

continuous change. The first meaning, used by Frank, seems to mean that Jews not only should work, but must work, while in the case of Poles, it seems a kind of recommendation, or determination of direction. Under this Regulation, the Poles were supposed to have a permanent place of employment. There was, however, a substantial part of rural population in Poland, which was not officially employed in any other place than in their farms. The Germans had thus less control of this part of the General Government population. Nevertheless, according to German economic analysis, the Polish countryside was overpopulated and subsequently became a reservoir for mobilisation of Polish workers to be sent to the Reich. In the case of Jews, without any doubt, they had to work. In the official documents there is no explanation of reasons to issue forced labor provision, or as to why there was such a differentiation between Jews and Poles. Frank does not mention the elements of German propaganda, which defined the Jews as parasites, using the work of others, or as exploiters. The text of the Regulation of October 26, 1939 is laconic, and one can get the impression that the authors of this regulation do not really know what content they could insert into its framework. In the case of the Poles, a few days after issuing the regulation on the obligation to work, further implementing rules appeared, whereas in the case of the Jews, another month and a half passed before such regulations were published.

First supplementary directive to the Regulation of October 26, 1939, regarding the introduction of compulsory labor for the Polish population in the General Government, was issued on October 31, 1939,[113] that is, five days after the proclamation of the General Government and the introduction of the obligation of labor. The regulation was signed by Dr. Krohn, head of the Labor Department. Under this regulation, the labor office was to forward the laborers required to appropriate jobs institutions and employment may be terminated only with the permission of the labor office. For non-compliance with the obligation of work, punishments of prison terms and fines were to be implemented. Wages for the work were to be determined by the chief of the district (*Distriktchef*) or the head of the labor office.

On the same day, another regulation was issued, signed by Governor General Hans Frank: regulation to normalize the conditions of labor and to protect in the General Government.[114] Under this Regulation, any legislation relating to working conditions and workers' protection remained in force as

---

113 Święcicki and Zadrowski, *Zbiór rozporządzeń*, 195–97.
114 Ibid., 189–91.

long as they did not change the regulation of October 31, 1939. In addition, all collective agreements between employees and employers were left unchanged. However, heads of districts acquired a right to influence the contracts, regulating wages by means of tariffs. In case of regulations which went beyond the boundaries of districts, decisions on tariffs were taken by the head of the Department of Labor. Similarly, additional rules and regulations were to be issued by the head of Department of Labor. The regulation issued by Hans Frank abolished the existing regulation issued by the Head of Administration by the supreme commander "East" on the normalization of conditions of labor and the protection of work on the occupied Polish areas of September 17, 1939.[115] Already on November 1, 1939 the first guideline implementing the Regulation of October 31, 1939 appeared.[116] The guideline was issued by Dr. Krohn, director of the Labor Department in the General Government, in order to regulate tariffs of salaries issues in the General Government. According to this guideline, district chefs had to submit all tariffs of salaries applicable in their districts to Krohn. These tariffs were to be published in the Official Regulations of the General Governor and the Department of Labor in the Office of the Governor General had to keep a register of tariffs (*Tarifregister*). In addition, all collective agreements in force on August 31, 1939 were to be added to the register of tariffs. On the other hand, on November 16, 1939, a second guideline appeared.[117] It standardized regulations on working conditions of workers and employees in the public service.

Regulation on broadening the obligation to work for the Polish population in the General Government, dated December 14, 1939,[118] expanded the duty to work for the Polish population to young people from 14 to 16 years old. So far, the obligation to work was applicable to adolescents as young as 16 years old. This provision also ensured that the working conditions were adapted to the physical abilities of young people. On December 16, 1939 the Regulation on granting allowances for the unemployed appeared.[119] Compensations could be paid to people able to work who were not employed and not responsible for that situation. However, the payment of unemployment benefits could be contingent on completion of the work requirements (public works). Jews were excluded from the benefit of unemployment

---

115 *Verordnungsblatt fur die besetzten Gebiete in Polen*, 56.
116 Święcicki and Zadrowski, *Zbiór rozporządzeń*, 191–93.
117 Ibid., 193–94.
118 Ibid., 197–98.
119 Ibid., 198–99.

assistance. Paragraph 2.1 says that "in cases of poverty they [Jews] are to be send to the Jewish welfare organizations."[120]

THE DECISIONS OF THE HSSPF FRIEDRICH-WILHELM KRÜGER IN DECEMBER 1939

Even before the issuance of two implementation decrees on December 11 and 12, 1939, HSSPF Friedrich-Wilhelm Krüger said on December 8: "The problem of forced labor of Jews cannot be solved in a satisfactory manner from day to day. The starting point in this regard is the establishment of records of the Jews—men aged from 14 to 50 years. It would also determine the current occupation by the Jews, precisely because in these areas Jews provided all kinds of crafts and would be a pity if these forces were not utilized in useful manner. In order to do this careful planning was required. As for now, we should create Jewish labor detachments and hire workers, where there is this urgent need. The task of district heads (*Distiktchef* or *Distriktgouverneur*) would be to formulate such needs."[121] The above quotation shows clearly that at the beginning of December, the German authorities had no concept of using forced labor of Jews and the previous acts were deprived of any realistic possibility of their implementation. The only real proposal was to create labor detachments in order to exploit them for the most urgent tasks.

The first provision for implementing of Regulation of October 26, 1939 with the introduction of compulsory labor for the Jewish population of the General Government on December 11, 1939 was issued by the HSSPF Friedrich-Wilhelm Krüger.[122] In its content, in principle, it does not concern the problems of work but rather addresses questions related to issues of movement restrictions of the Jewish population in the General Government. According to this provision with effect from January 1, 1940, all Jews residing in the General Government were prohibited from changing their place of residence without permission. All the Jews who came to the General Government

---

120 Ibid.
121 "Wypowiedź HSSPF Krügera na posiedzeniu kierowników wydziału rządu General Government w sprawie pracy przymusowej Żydów," in Eisenbach and Rutkowski, *Eksterminacja Żydów*, 203–4.
122 "Erste Durchführungsvorschrift zur Verordnung vom 26. Oktober 1939 über die Einführung des Arbeitszwanges für die jüdische Bevölkerung des Generalgouvernements. Vom 11. Dezember 1939," *VBlGG*, 1939, 231; Pospieszalski, *Hitlerowskie "prawo" okupacyjne*, vol. 2, 560–62.

within 24 hours after arrival had to register at the mayor's office or inform the Jewish council about that fact. Moreover, the provision introduced a curfew from 9:00 p.m to 5:00 a.m. During those hours, one could move on the streets only after obtaining written permission. Exclusively, section 4 of the provision concerned forced labor, and that was because all the Jews violating the rules of this provisions were to be "immediately sent to severe long-term labor service" (*langdauerende Arbeitszwangsdienst*).[123] However, apart from forced labor Jews could also be punished under other laws. The first executive order treated forced labor as an element of punishment.

The second supplementary direction to the Regulation of October 26, 1939, regarding the introduction of compulsory labor for the Jewish population of the General Government, was issued on December 12, 1939,[124] and concerned the preparation of an inventory. According to the first paragraph of this provision, all Jewish residents of the General Government from age 14 to 60 were obliged to perform forced labor. It should be noted that in a regulation issued two days later the duty of work for Poles also extended the group of subjected to labor from the age of 14,[125] in contrast to previous orders requiring the work form the age of 16. Friedrich-Wilhelm Krüger announced that forced laborers would be assigned to work according to their professions and skills. In order to conduct the registration of Jews for forced labor, all male Jews aged 12 to 60 years had to present themselves to the registration. They were to be called by the mayors or the *Kreis*-and *Stadthauptleute* to appear before the relevant territorial *Judenrat* in order to register in a special card index (*Erfassungkartei*).[126] Mayors were responsible for the proper conduct of the registration process. According to this ordinance, not labor offices but the *Judenräte* had to carry out the registration process of the Jewish workers under the supervision of the mayors, that is, in practice, the municipalities. However, the process of mobilization of the workers registered to work was to take place on special call of the German authorities. Paragraph 4 of the provision of December

---

123 Święcicki and Zadrowski, *Zbiór rozporządzeń*, 231.
124 "Zweite Durchführungsvorschrift zur Verordnung vom 26. Oktober 1939 über die Einführung des Arbeitszwanges für die jüdische Bevölkerung des Generalgouvernements. (Erfassungvorschrift) Vom 12. Dezember 1939," *VBlGG*, 1939, 246; Pospieszalski, *Hitlerowskie "prawo" okupacyjne*, vol. 2, 562–64.
125 Święcicki and Zadrowski, *Zbiór rozporządzeń*, 197–98.
126 Bericht für den Monat März 1940. Abt. Innere Verwaltung, Judenreferat VIII. A letter about transfering by Kreishauptleute of card index of Jews performing forced labor, which will be transfered to Kraków, YVA- O.53/101, 2.

12, 1939 did not specify what kind of authority Germans had to summon the Jewish workers to perform labor.[127]

Paragraph 5 of the provision specifies how to prepare the Jewish workers to perform forced labor. The workers called upon had to be present themselves in a specific collection point on time. They also had to bring with them food for two days and two clean sheets. Holders of workshops had to come to the assembly point with tools. Morevoer, they had to pre-notify the *Judenrat*. At the same time, the regulations forbade Jews to sell, rent, or transfer their own tools, workshops, or machinery without prior written permission of *Kreis-* or *Stadhauptmann*. For failure to appear on gathering points, submitting false or incomplete data, or situation of inability to work, the transgressions were punishable by imprisonment for 10 years. A similar punishment was to be applied towards the members of the *Judenrat* and other people who obstructed the process of registration and attendance for forced labor or were hiding the requested person. Again, responsible for the execution of these orders were the mayors (*Bürgermeister*) via the *Judenräte*.

The provisions of December 12, 1939 theoretically only could regulate the registration and administration of the Jews requested to perform forced labor. In practice, those regulations were unclear and vaguely worded. City offices and the *Judenrat* were esponsible for the execution of the foregoing provisions. It was unclear, however, who and when had to perform forced labor, where it would take place and how it would be organized. As suggested in paragraph 5 of the provisions of December 12, 1939, it can be assumed that the workers coming with the supply for two days could be sent to labor camps or long-distance facilities. It was significant, however, that the HSSPF in the General Government, being a part of police apparatus, transferred the implementation of these laws and control of its implementation to the civil authorities apart from the labor office. For the administration of forced labor of Polish Jews the municipalities and the *Judenräte* were responsible, in practice.

At the time the HSSPF issued the implementing rules, the actual situation in the General Government was completely different of that depicted in the document. Individual *Judenräte* carried out the register of those who were able to work. These registrations were performed in Warsaw, Lublin and other cities. Similarly, there were the labor departments of the *Judenräte* that dealt

---

127 "Zweite Durchführungsvorschrift zur Verordnung vom 26. Oktober 1939 über die Einführung des Arbeitszwanges für die jüdische Bevölkerung des Generalgouvernements. (Erfassungvorschrift) Vom 12. Dezember 1939, § 2," in Pospieszalski, *Hitlerowskie "prawo" okupacyjne*, vol. 2, 563.

with the matters of labor on an ongoing basis of forced labor. In some cities, labor battalions (*bataliony pracy*) had been already created, which were used to perform forced labor. They were organized primarily in order to avoid the so-called "wild" arrests of Jews on the streets in order to perform the most varied of works. These "wild" arrests had a very negative impact on the opinion of the Jewish public.

After the two provisions of December 11 and 12, which were very general in their nature and still devoid of detailed guidance on the organization of labor, new detailed regulations were not issued until January 20, 1940. On that day were issued the orders for the *Judenräte* on registration and mobilization of forced labor (*Dienstbefehl an die Judenräte für die Erfassung und Gestellung der Juden zur Zwangsarbeit*).[128] The fact that nearly 40 days passed between those regulations indicated the lack of haste and lack of organization and coordination on issues of forced labor of Jews. Systematic forced labor of Jews was also impracticable due to continuous economic stagnation and the severe winter. Practical exploitation of Jewish workforce could take place only during late spring 1940. It was dependent, obviously, on the type of work performed. Working in the industry was much less dependent on climatic conditions than the work on infrastructure and agriculture, but Polish industry was still in a state of stagnation due to the disruption of the supplies of raw materials and energy as well as the disruption of production processes due to war damages, change of management, and disruption of connections between producers and the market.

The order of January 20, 1940 concerned the method of registration and mobilization of Jews to forced labor.[129] This order was sent directly to the *Judenräte*, whose chairman and members had been held responsible for the execution of the order. Those, who did not obey the order, were threatened with imprisonment for 10 years. This last detail requires attention, as it demonstrates the time perspective of the occupational authorities, who evidently supposed that the occupied Polish territory would still be an integral part of the areas under German control after decades. Supervision of implementing of orders was in the hands of mayors and *Kreis-* and *Stadhauptleute*. Basically, the order concerned two principal issues: registration and appointment for forced labor. Case registration was to be done by making records. Each candidate to forced labor should have appropriate card. Cards were produced in 6 colours.

---

128 "Dienstbefehl an die Judenräte für die Erfassung und Gestellung der Juden zur Zwangsarbeit. Vom 20. Januar 1940," in Pospieszalski, *Hitlerowskie "prawo" okupacyjne*, vol. 2, 565–68.
129 Ibid.

Each colour corresponded to a professional group. Cards were made for all men from 12 to 60 years. In the case of health problems preventing work, it was necessary to carry out a medical examination by a doctor employed by a *Judenrat*, and appropriate medical certificate was be attached to the card. Cards were filled on the basis of information supplied by the subjects of registration of Jews, verified by members of the *Judenrat*. These files had to be the primary instrument for the administration of forced labor of Jews.

The Jewish workers were summoned for forced labor with mediation of the *Judenräte*, who were also responsible for timely appearance of workers on gathering points. Workers presenting themselves to forced labor had to be clean and deloused. They had also been provided with two sheets, extra clothing, coat, two pairs of shoes (if possible, long boots), three shirts, three pants, three pairs of stockings, a pair of gloves, two towels, a comb and brush, a set of cutlery, and food for two days. All these items had to be packed in a laundry bag or suitcase. In the case of poor Jews, *Judenräte* had to take care of their supplies.[130]

The workers had to bring with them light tools, while heavier tools and machines had to be prepared for transportation and the appropriate authorities had to be informed. All belonging to the groups of those called for forced labor factories, plants, and other possessions, such as the right to lease, were to be reported to *Kreis*-or *Stadhaupleute* through the mayor, having confirmed the truth of these declarations. The letters from the mayors had to indicate to whom, during the absence of their owners, was entrusted the property or how it should be protected by the authorities.[131]

The order for *Judenräte* concerning calling for registration and for forced labor enables us to follow intentions of the German authorities concerning forced labor of Jews in the General Government. First of all, they did not inform which amount of time or workdays was necessary to perform such work and who was supposed to perform this work. The recommendations presented above create the impression that the forced labor was to be performed during a few days. However, it seems that its duration, according to the intention of HSSPF, was to last longer, perhaps weeks or months. Labor camps, however, were not mentioned in this document. Perhaps the author of the document was referring to long-distance workplaces, not necessarily the labor camps. Work would be done away from home because, as indicated by the directives; the workers had to appear with two sets of bed linen or several sets of underwear. Directives to

---

130 Pospieszalski, *Hitlerowskie "prawo" okupacyjne*, 567.
131 Ibid., 567–68.

provide the tools and machines, such as sewing machines or lathes, clearly testified to the intentions to create special plants for the Jews. This was confirmed by the guidelines of administration concerning protection of the factories or other Jewish businesses and real estate, which could be of importance only during periods of prolonged absence of the owners.[132] However, any practical steps were not undertaken in order to create such plants for Jews at the turn 1940. The above-mentioned regulations were issued in order to register and bring to a state of readiness the Jewish labor force rather than to ensure its practical use.

THE PROCESSES OF ECONOMIC EXPLOITATION OF JEWS IN THE GENERAL GOVERNMENT

The Nazi policy towards Jews in the General Government was patchy and uncoordinated. On the one hand, from the very beginning of the civil administration in the General Government, two parallel processes—discrimination and exploitation—took place. These processes in many cases were contradictory, since discriminatory provisions hindered both the production capacity of the Jews and the rational use of their workforce. Therefore, economic exploitation was not the primary purpose of this policy, since it had not been carried out in a way that ensures maximum efficiency. Nazi policy towards the Jews could be described as more discriminatory and punitive than operational. These orders were designed not only to discriminate against Jews, but also to gradually limit the economic opportunities of Jews in the General Government.

The regulation of November 28, 1939 concerning the establishment of the *Judenräte* defined their function clearly:

> It is the duty of the Judenrat through its chairman or his deputy to receive the orders of the German Administration. It is responsible for the conscientious carrying out of orders to their full extent. The directives it issues to carry out these German decrees must be obeyed by all Jews and Jewesses.[133]

The Regulation of November 28, 1939 did mention the *Judenräte*, regardless of whether they had such name or not. The *Judenräte* continued administration of Jewish communities of pre-war period and fulfilled many social and

---
132 Ibid., 567.
133 "Verordnung über die Einsetzung von Judenräten. Vom 28. November 1939," in Pospieszalski, *Hitlerowskie "prawo" okupacyjne*, vol. 2, 551.

organizational tasks. During the military occupation and the early days of the General Government, many Jewish councils often gained new members, and their composition usually changed. However, in many cases, a majority of the prominent pre-war Jewish activists found themselves in new councils of the Jewish communities. During the military administration and the initial period of General Government, Jewish councils were modified and took over most administrative functions, which previously resided at the discretion of the municipalities.

GERMAN ECONOMIC POLICY IN THE GENERAL GOVERNMENT

At the end of October 1939, a few weeks after the end of the war in Poland, the economy in areas that were in the General Government's borders remained paralysed, due to lack of raw materials, fuels, disruption of production processes, and market failure. Because of this situation, there was high unemployment,[134] especially among Jews. Any provisions on the obligation to labor and forced labor were unnecessary or unviable. First, the introduction of compulsory labor and forced labor in the current situation of unemployment and economic stagnation was impracticable. The population was interested in returning to work which simply was not available. Moreover, Jews arrested in order to perform forced labor, and the responsible authorities, at least for the time being, did not intend to obey the rules. The absurdity of this situation is also made evident by the fact that the HSSPF, the most active agent in the persecution of Jews, responsible for detention of Jews for the purpose of forced labor, also issued regulations to ensure the proper performance of forced labor. The SS continued the wild roundups of Jews and in this respect belonged to the category of most insubordinate elements. HSSPF was not a professional responsible for economic matters as well as the entire apparatus of the RSHA. The SS had large competence in Jewish affairs. Their experience and power over the fate and lives of Jews allowed the SS to collect a large resource of gratuitous workforce and, therefore, to create economic organizations. These organizations could function and generate huge profits, not thanks to excellent economic administration, but rather due to unlimited exploitation of prisoners and Jews.

---

134 BA-MA, RW23-7, Rüstungswirtschaftlicher Lagebericht für 28. October–10. November 1939, 7.

Forced Labor in the Ghettos and Labor Detachments • CHAPTER 2

Since the beginning of the war and the occupation, development of Jewish exploitation continued. However, at the end of 1939 these processes had not yet fully develped. If there had been a real need to issue the implementing rules, it would have taken place much faster. Nevertheless, in the months of October and November 1939, German administration at different levels was still under construction and was not able to manage excess manpower. HSSPF actually issued rules implementing the Regulation on the introduction of compulsory labor only on December 11 and 12, 1939. However, these rules were very general and did not explain how the whole mechanism could function.

Economic planning in the General Government took place in two ways. On one hand, there still remained the earlier concept of the General Government as a colony of Germany, which should provide labor forces, raw materials, and agricultural products. Hans Frank was under considerable pressure from the part of economic factors in Germany, to which, apparently, he could not resist. He expressed his hesitation inter alia in a letter to Göring dated January 25, 1940:

> In view of the present requirements of the Reich for the defense industry, it is at present fundamentally impossible to carry on a long term economic policy in the General Government. Rather, it is necessary so to steer the economy of the General Government that it will, in the shortest possible time, accomplish results representing the maximum that can be gotten out of the economic strength of the General Government for the immediate strengthening of our capacity for defense. In particular the following performances are expected of the total economy of the General Government—supply and transportation of at least 1 million male and female agricultural and industrial workers to the Reich—among them at least 750,000 agricultural workers of which at least 50% must be women-in order to guarantee agricultural production in the Reich and as a replacement for industrial workers lacking in the Reich.[135]

On the other hand, the Armament Inspectorate of the Wehrmacht since the beginning of the occupation identified Polish industrial plants belonging to the war industry sector as well as many plants producing equipment necessary for the army—for example plants producing optic lenses and optic

---

135 Letter of Hans Frank to Göring of January 25, 1940 (1375-PS), IMT, *Red Series*, vol. 3, 925–29.

equipment.[136] The aim of this action was using Polish war industry plants for the benefit of the German war production.[137]

In order to facilitate the economic exploitation of the General Government, the German authorities confiscated both raw materials and Polish and Jewish enterprises. The first regulation on this confiscation of raw materials and products, defining the framework for plunder, was issued by General von Brauchitsch in October 1939. The Governor General Regulation of November 15, 1939 ordered the confiscation of assets of the Polish state.[138] According to the regulation of January 24, 1940, it was possible to confiscate personal property for public purposes.[139] This regulation also provided confiscation of ownerless assets, that is, belonging to people who did not reside in the General Government. The right to confiscate the assets belonged to the district governor or an institution authorized by him. Jewish assets were enfranchised entirely. For the seizure of assets there was appointed a trustee (*Treuhänder*). The Regulation of January 24, 1940 provided great flexibility in the appropriation of private assets by the German administration, the SS, and the police. Confiscation of enemy property, that is, the property that belonged to countries with which the German Reich was at war, or to nationals of those countries, was governed by the regulation of August 31, 1940.[140] War industry plants were, however, confiscated on the basis of Hitler's decree and transferred to the Wehrmacht.[141]

The management of Polish state property belonged to the Department of Trust of the Main Economic Department (*Hauptabteilung Wirtschaft*) of the General Government and to trust departments in the districts. However, the property of the Polish Railways (PKP) was taken over by the Eastern Railway (*Ostbahn*). The Trust Department ordered confiscation of private companies and municipal real estate. As a result of the transfer of the above powers in the area of agricultural land and property by the Trust Department, these matters were administered by the Main Department of Food and Agriculture (*Hauptabteilung*

---

136 BA-MA, RW23-7, Liste der bis heute besuchten 19 Rüstungs- 3 Versorgungsbetriebe, 15. November 1939, 34–35.
137 BA-MA, RW23-7, Rüstungswirtschaftlicher Lagebericht für 29. October–18. November 1939, 4–6; BA-MA, RW23-7, Rüstungswirtschaftlicher Lagebericht für 29. October–18. November 1939, 4–6.
138 VBlGG, 1939, 37; *Doc. Occ.*, vol. 6, 128–129.
139 VBlGG, 1940, vol. 1, 23–28, 62; *Doc. Occ.*, vol. 6, 253.
140 VBlGG, 1940, vol. 1, 265–72.
141 BA-MA, RW23-7, Rüstungswirtschaftlicher Lagebericht für 15. Juli–13. August 1940, 106.

Ernährung und Landwirtschaft). For this purpose, a special Board of Real Estates (*Liegenschaftsverwaltung*) had been established.[142] Forests were under the management of the Department of Forestry (*Abteilung Forsten*).

Companies which were not liquidated had difficulties in economic activity. The governor's general orders of April 23, 1940 hampered the acquisition, establishment, and development of Polish enterprises.[143] According to this regulation, it was necessary to obtain authorization of the German administration not only to acquire industrial or agricultural enterprises, but also for the purpose of acquisition of shares, the extension of the existing workplace, establish subsidiaries, and launch existing but inactive companies. This was associated with the rationalization of the German economy and shortages of raw materials and especially fuel. The top-down regulation eliminated enterprises which were small, unprofitable, and consuming large quantities of raw materials and fuel, or were producing the goods for the market, or were inconsistent with the standards, priorities, and plans of the Reich.[144]

In order to recreate the economics of the General Government, reconstruction and infrastructure development was necessary. This task was undertaken by the Department of Civil Engineering (*Bauwesen*) in the Office of the Governor General, led by Bauder. The department was divided into groups of road and bridge construction (*Gruppe Straßen-und Brückenbau*), group for construction of waterways (*Gruppe Wasserstraßen*) and group for high constructions (*Gruppe Hochbau*). The group for construction of roads and bridges was represented in the following cities: Kraków, Kielce, Lublin, Mińsk, Radom, Rzeszów, Warsaw, and Zamość. The enitre existing road network was divided into three categories: highways, district roads, and county roads (*Durchgangsstraßen, Distriktstraßen und Kreisstraßen*). Until the beginning of winter 1939 and 1940, the group was able to fix just about 800 km roads of the first category. Plans for 1940 provided reconstruction of 1000 km of former national roads in order to pass them to the first category, with a width of 6 and 7.5 m, and remodelling or construction of 250 bridges.[145]

---

142 Lageberichte, governor of the Kraków District, February 17, 1941. In the district, there were 184 *Liegenschaften* having 68202 ha of land, of which 122 were administered by the German administration and 62 (8946 ha) were leased. YVA-O.53/101, 3

143 *VBlGG*, 1940, vol. 1, 171–74; *Doc. Occ.*, vol. 6, 253.

144 BA-MA, RW23-2, Die wesentliche Probleme, ihre Entwicklung und ihre Lösung im 4. Vierteljahr 1942, 6–7, 42; BA-MA, RW23-5, Geschichte der Rü In im GG (1. Juni 1940–31. Dezember 1941), 67.

145 Du Prel, *Das Deutsche Generalgouvernement Polen*, 296.

The river road construction was expected to begin in 1940; particularly extensive works were to be done in order to use Wisła River as a waterway. According to a protocol:

> The General Governor speaks about the great task of regulating the Wisła. It would concern a length of 900 km which has not been worked on, partly at all, partly since more than 50 years. The regulation of the Wisła would give a long-term opportunity to employ a large number of workers in a useful manner.[146]

The German authorities estimated that about 1800 km of rivers could be used as waterways in Poland, while only about 800 km were used in reality until then. In order to adapt rivers for water transport their level had to be regulated, that is, proper embankments had to be built and the river current deepened, and in some places dams and culverts had to be built. At the end of the year a considerable part of those plans had been completed. For example, the *Kreishauptmann* of Puławy wrote in his report in December 1940: "Apart from the tasks in the sapper units, which is important for the armed forces, substantial roadwork was done on the communal, *Kreis-*, district, and through roads, the through road Puławy-Lublin was broadened, and the bridges were enhanced by new constructions. Apart from that, considerable work was done on the *Kreis-* and communal roads."[147] In addition, the administration planned to build water berms along the rivers in order to offset the risk of flood in spring time. Likewise, it was necessary to build adequate safeguards in order to discharge the ice damming, which resulted in floods or destroyed bridges. German plans were more far-reaching, because they projected construction of the Wisła-Bug canal near Dęblin, which would allow connection of river navigation network between Poland and Russia, that is, the creation of channel Dnieper-Wisła.[148]

The Regional Planning Department (*Abteilung Raumordnung*) of the General Government coordinated economic planning, and was headed by Dr. Schepers. From the standpoint of the department, the area of the General

---

146 YVA-JM.21 (3508214_08004009), *Hans Frank's Diary*, vol. 15, R. 5, Beschprechung von Fragen der Einsiedlung von Polen und Juden in das Generalgouvernement, den 15. Januar 1941, scan 15.
147 YVA, JM-814, Der Kreishauptmann des Kreises Puławy, Lagebericht für November 1940, Puławy, den 7. Dezember 1940, scan 1028.
148 Du Prel, *Das Deutsche Generalgouvernement Polen*, 296.

Government was evaluated as an important area of interest for the German Reich (*wichtiges deutsches Interessengebiet*). The purpose of this department was to get acquainted with Polish spatial development plans, gathering statistics, and creating a new regional plan for the General Government to craft an organic connection with the Reich. For this purpose, in addition to the Regional Planning Department at the Office of the Governor General, three branches were initially created in the districts of Lublin, Radom, and Warsaw. A Statistical Office was added to the Planning Department in Kraków, which fulfilled the tasks of the Central Statistical Office (*Statistische Zentralstelle für das Generalgouvernement*). Similarly, there was also a Cartographic Office (*Zentralkartenstelle für das Generalgouvernement*).[149] The Regional Planning Department, according to *Oberregierungsrat* Dr. Schepers, did pioneering work in order to create a new order for the needs of the Third Reich.[150] In practice, the department integrated development plans in various economic and political areas, such as planning for population settlements (*Siedlungsplanung*), planning for exploitation of the resources in terms of industrial, forestry, agriculture, and transport, taking into account the needs of the Wehrmacht.

The situation in the field of agriculture was evaluated very poorly. First, the Polish countryside was overpopulated, Polish agriculture (at least according to German specialists) was inefficient, and productivity per worker in agriculture was very low. The peasants produced primarily for their own needs and only a small part of the output reached the market. A better organization of agriculture was hindered by highly fragmented fields; and therefore, it was necessary to regroup land. In addition, many areas required improvement of water infrastructre in order to enlarge quantity of arable land. Melioration of water conditions required, on one side, the regulation of many rivers, such as construction of embankments preventing floods and canals and thus removing large quantities of water in the springtime, enabling increased cultivation. According to the head of the Food and Agriculture Department of the General Government, Körner, over the next four years (1940–1944) circa 700 thousand hectares of land had to be meliorated.[151] This problem was dealt with by the Office of Water (*Wasserwirtschaftsamt*). Moreover, it was necessary to intensify agriculture with increased fertilization, switch to the market production, providing adequate breeding and seed materials, increased use of machinery in

---

149   Ibid., 277–78.
150   Ibid.
151   Ibid., 273.

agriculture through mechanization, provision of modern machinery, and electrification of agriculture. To ensure greater supply of electricity, the construction of new hydroelectric power plants in Rożnów was necessary. The German authorities argued that it was necessary to regulate the market for agricultural products. According to Körner, the pre-war situation was inadmissible, when the market for agricultural products and the seeds was dominated by Jews, and a new pricing policy for agricultural products was to be developed.[152]

Despite the negative attitude towards Jews, saturated with propaganda and anti-Semitism, evaluation of Jewish labor force was not uniform. At the basis of the decision on forced labor of Jews was their evaluation as exploiters who avoid heavy physical labor. Therefore, regulations concerning employment of Jews mentioned educational purpose of forced labor. However, these opinions were based mainly on the propaganda. Upon arrival at the General Government, the opinions of many high-ranking German officers underwent a modification. One of them was HSSPF Friedrich-Wilhelm Krüger, who spoke at a meeting of heads of department of the General Government about forced labor of Jews.[153] He said: "precisely in these areas [in the General Government] Jews provided all kinds of crafts and would be a pity if these forces were not utilized in a useful manner."[154]

INITIATIVES OF GLOBOCNIK

Despite the transfer of control over the Jewish affairs to the hands of the SS, it would seem that a leading factor in the field of exploitation of Jewish labor would still be the civil administration. Many civil administration departments were dealing with the economy, such as the Department of Economics, Department of Construction, Department of Food and Agriculture, Department of Regional Planning, and others, created for both planning and ongoing management of the economy of the General Government. In one of his statements, HSSPF Friedrich-Wilhelm Krüger said, ". . . we should create Jewish detachments and hire where there is this urgent need. The task of the head of the district would by ascertainment of any needs."[155] In turn, the instruction of January 20, 1940

---

152 Ibid., 272–74.
153 Statement of HSSPF Krüger at a meeting of heads of government departments of the General Government on the forced labor of Jews, in Eisenbach and Rutkowski, *Eksterminacja Żydów*, 203–4.
154 Ibid.
155 Ibid.

stated that the orders for Jewish forced laborers would be made exclusively through the appropriate *Kreis-* and *Stadhauptleute*. This expression indicates that, despite the formal control over Jewish affairs by the SS, civilian factors played a decisive role in case of economic issues. However, things went a bit differently because of some SS activity, especially on the part of the SSPF in the district of Lublin, Odilo Globocnik.[156] The matters concerning the use of forced labor of Jews would become, over the next two years, the cause of numerous disputes, primarily between the SS and civil administration, even though there were other actors involved such as Wehrmacht and private entrepreneurs. Nevertheless, the divisions between different interest groups were much more complicated and many complex lines of divisions could be drawn.

Already by the end of 1939, the SSPF Odilo Globocnik took the initiative to utilize forced labor of Jews. Thanks to his promptness, he overtook other actors, such as the civil administration and even the HSSPF in the General Government Friedrich-Wilhelm Krüger. It should be noted that, despite his relatively low position in the Nazi hierarchy, Globocnik found himself in a key position thanks to the special ties of friendship with RFSS Himmler and the tasks the latter granted to him. Globocnik was entrusted directly by Himmler with one of the most important tasks: the implementation of the *Aktion Reinhardt*, thus avoiding the Nazi hierarchy.[157] Globocnik was formally subordinate to HSSPF Friedrich-Wilhelm Krüger, and he, in turn, to Governor General Hans Frank. However, thanks to close ties with Himmler, Globocnik was able to contact the RFSS directly and with his support, in many cases, was allowed to operate independently. Thanks to his special position, he had not reckoned with the head of the Lublin district. In some areas, Globocnik established administrative structures subordinate to himself, similar or even identical to the official authorities, which became a source of numerous conflicts and overlapping jurisdiction.

The factor that served as a catalyzer in the process of exploitation of Jewish workforce was the "exemption" from the POW camps of Jewish prisoners,

---

156   Odilo Globocnik (1904–1945) since May 28, 1938 gauleiter of Vienna, removed from the post on January 30, 1939 because of transactions done in foreign currency. On November 9, 1939 he was nominated on the post of SSPF in Lublin District. He was responsible for organizing and execution of *Aktion Reinhardt*. Released from the post of SSPF in Lublin District in September 1943, transferred to Triest and nominated for the post of HSSPF for the operations on Adriatic seaside. Arrested on May 31, 1945 and committed suicide on the same day.

157   Poprzeczny, *Globocnik—Hitler's Man in the East*; Rieger, *Creator of Nazi Death Camps*; Zygmunt Mańkowski, "Odilo Globocnik und die Endlösung der Judenfrage," *Studia Historiae Oeconomicae* 21 (1994): 147–55.

ex-soldiers of the Polish army. This process began in autumn 1939, the Jewish POWs were forced to sign their agreement to take advantage of the exemption, and then they could return to their hometowns. Releasing of Jews was only apparently beneficial, because it really meant the termination of their prisoner of war status, protected by international conventions. Liberated Jews were seen as civilians, subject to any discriminatory provisions relating to the Jews.[158] The Jewish officers who had not been released, at least in part, survived to the end of the war in POW camps for officers (*Offizierslager* or, abbreviated, *Oflag*).[159]

Prisoners of war who came from the areas under Soviet occupation were not released. Many among these prisoners were transferred to Lublin between December 1939 and February 1940. Prisoners who arrived to Lublin were placed in a camp on 7 Lipowa Street. In the area converted into a camp, there were previously stables for horses in several barracks. After the September 1939 campaign, these barracks were converted into workshops, where Jews from Lublin worked in the framework of forced labor. In the area of Lublin, there were essentially two permanent places where forced labor was performed: in the barracks at 7 Lipowa Street and in the areas of aircraft factory Plage-Laśkiewicz. From the autumn of 1939 forward, the barracks at the 7 Lipowa Street served as a gathering place for Jewish forced laborers in Lublin. Some of the workers were employed in workshops located in the barracks, and some in other places of employment in Lublin. The arrival of Jewish prisoners of war caused the transformation of the infrastructure at 7 Lipowa Street into a labor camp. This was one of the first labor camps in the General Government. However, even after the creation of 7 Lipowa Street labor camp, it was also a workplace of the Jewish workers coming there every day from the ghetto. Essentially, the labor camp at 7 Lipowa Street served as an exemplary camp for exploitation of Jewish forced labor in the Lublin district. This camp contributed substantially to the exploitation of Jewish manpower through the preparation of cadres, which were used later as a staff in other labor camps in the Lublin district, mainly in the complex of labor camps around Bełżec, and after the beginning of the Operation Barbarossa in Lwów in the labor camp at Janowska Street.[160] In February 1940, the camp commandant at 7 Lipowa Street was *SS-Sturmbannführer* Hermann Dolp, who later became commandant

---

158 Shmuel Krakowski, "The Fate of Jewish Prisoners of War in the September 1939 Campaign," *Yad Vashem Studies XII* (1977): 297–333.
159 YVA-O.3/3632. Testimony of Artur Loewenstein.
160 Sandkühler, *"Endlösung" in Galizien*; Sandkühler, "Das Zwangsarbeitslager Lemberg-Janowska 1941–1944"; Michał Borwicz, *Uniwersytet zbirów* (Krakow: CKŻP, 1946).

of the camp complex near Bełżec. He was replaced by Franz Bartetzko, who later became deputy commander of the Trawniki labor camp. After February 1940, the connandant was *SS-Untersturmführer* Horst Riedel. His deputy was Wolfgang Mohwinkel.

When HSSPF Friedrich-Wilhelm Krüger issued his hesitant and inexact instructions on the use of Jewish labor force in December 1939 and January 1940, a workshop in Lublin already functioned, and a labor camp on 7 Lipowa Street was being established. However, the process of exploitation of Jewish forced labor was more complex because of vague division of competences. The case of Lublin is very important for further understanding the development of the situation in all the General Government. In the hierarchy of the civil administration, the authority for Jewish affairs was the sub-division of Population and Social Affairs (*Bevölkerung und Fürsorge*, BuF), part of the Department of Internal Affairs. In this particular department, there was a position of clerk for Jewish affairs (*Judenreferent*). At the level of the General Government, the post of the first referent for Jewish affairs was occupied by Dr. Heinrich Gottong. However, positions of clerks for Jewish affairs was also created at the level of district civil administration. In addition, employment offices also had certain powers in cases of forced labor of Jews. In the case of Lublin District, a competitive *Jüdische Referat* had been established in the office of SS and police leader. In this way, two offices for Jewish affairs functioned parallelly: one in the office of the chief of the district (subsequently district governor), headed by Richard Türk, and the other in the office of SSPF, headed by Dr. Karl Hofbauer.

With the support of the SSPF Odilo Globocnik, Karl Hofbauer consolidated the majority of Jewish affairs under his own authority, including issues related to forced labor. Despite the regulation issued by Hans Frank on October 26, 1939 that transferred to Hofbauer the competences of issuing of implementing regulations by HSSPF, which could be understood as the transfer of all matters relating to the forced labor of Jews, the issue of competence remains unclear. The HSSPF Friedrich-Wilhelm Krüger said in one of his speeches that the task of district chief would be identifying need for the employment of Jewish forced laborers.[161] In turn, in the instruction of January 20, 1940 he stated that summons of Jewish forced laborers will be made exclusively through the appropriate *Kreis-* and *Stadhauptleute*.

---

161 Statement of HSSPF Krüger at a meeting of heads of government departments of the General Government on the forced labor of Jews, in Eisenbach and Rutkowski, *Eksterminacja Żydów*, 203–4.

However, in the Lublin district, it was the desk for Jewish affairs in the office of the SSPF that took over the matters of Jewish manpower available at the district. This had far-reaching consequences: the availability of the Jewish workforce in Lublin allowed Globocnik to undertake a long project of the construction of border fortifications. The German authorities decided to dig an anti-tank trench in order to create a line of defense in the strip of land between the rivers Bug and San. This line of defense was to secure the eastern border areas of the German occupation against possible attack by the Soviet Union during the campaign in western and northern Europe. Nevertheless, even after victory over France, Belgium, and the Netherlands, the construction of these fortifications had not stopped. They were part of the German long-term strategic plans. Globocnik, who undertook the work on the fortifications, exploited not only Jewish workers from the Lublin district, but also from other districts of the General Government, which gave him a special position of leadership in the use of Jewish labor. His initiatives were later used in the economic activities of such SS companies as DAW[162] and OSTI.

During a meeting on April 22, 1940, according to the minutes of the conference:

> *Brigadeführer* Globocnik discussed at the outset of the conference Jewish desk [in his office], its aims and objectives. In short words, he presented the situation that existed before the creation of the desk, mobilization of Jews for forced labor took place in a manner that absolutely could not be maintained—several workers had been simply seized off the street; there was no guarantee that one could obtain required number of regular workers. One took the Jews from another job; matter of food and maintenance of family members was unclear and so on. Bad results obtained using these methods and the conviction that without systematic planning one cannot ever do more work prompted the commander of the SS and the police to create a separate *Referat* that would address all issues relating to the Jews, and especially would have to develop a plan for Jewish forced labor utilization. Implementation of plans concerning the utilization of forced labor had been submitted to *Selbstschutz*. These innovations have already led to a whole range of achievements, which primarily include snow

---

162 Various companies established by Globocnik were linked with each other. For example, DAW used to provide building material and different dervices to the *Fleischerei des SS und Polizeiführers* in Lublin. On October 18, 1941 they set a bill for performed works for 122.25 zł. YVA-JM.12333, 495.

removal and daily job placement led by *Selbstschutz* in Lublin in the city and beyond its borders.163

One can agree with the statement that before the establishment of the Jewish desk [in the office of the SSPF] there was no proper coordination on forced labor and that there was no guarantee that adequate number of workers would be provided. The Jews' avoidance of forced labor was motivated, among other factors, by ill-treatment of the Jewish workers in the workshops at Lipowa 7 at the hands of their supervisors who were subordinate to Globocnik. Similarly, arresting casual laborers from the street was usually done by the SS or *Selbstschutz* under the authority of the same Globocnik. Functioning of the Jewish desk in the SSPF office did not improve the situation of the Jewish workers, whose fate was very difficult and subsequently even tragic. Without any doubts, the Jewish desk enabled systematic planning of investments on much larger scale.

The protocol further noted:

> While the job is not in area of residence, one intends to put the workers in the camps, especially when it comes to larger works. Cost of accommodation and meals will cover religious community; this way we can also have to our disposition Jewish property, to which otherwise we wouldn't be able to reach. Supply of food and clothing will be provided by Jewish women and Jews already unable to work hard. Strict separation of sex Groups will be carried on. Since the work force is completely or almost free, this will allow us magnification already not too big budgets of individual departments.164

The purpose of Globocnik's activity became thus clear: he planned unlimited exploitation of Jewish manpower while incurring the least cost. The Jewish communities had to cover all costs of maintenance and provisioning facilities workers. Forced labor in Globocnik's meaning was to become an instrument of power and drain all the means at the hands of Jews. At the same time, however, the needs of the Jewish community had not been considered. It was one-sided thinking that sooner or later had to lead to pauperization of Jewish communities and their bankruptcy.

---

163 The minutes of the meeting at SS and Police Leader in the Lublin District O. Globocnik with managers in the Office of District Governor on forced labor of the Jewish population, Lublin, April, 22, in Eisenbach and Rutkowski, *Eksterminacja Żydów*, 207–8.

164 Ibid.

Indeed, the exploitation of Jewish workers who were treated as free labor and dumping the responsibility for all logistic matters onto the Jewish communities resulted in drainage of manpower and material means. The consequence of this was economic weakness of the Jewish communities and their total pauperization.[165] The communities bearing the costs of maintenance and provisioning of the Jewish workers at the same time were losing possibility of receiving from those workers any taxes and any benefits. Morevoer, the issue of aid to families of Jewish forced laborers did not find any appropriate solution. The costs were born by the social assistance budget of the Jewish communities. This meant that the budgetary situation of Jewish communities in the General Government became catastrophic. While the SS and other German institutions used free Jewish labor, Jewish communities with overburdened budgets turned for help to the General Government. Budget deficits of the Jewish communities would be covered by the budget of the General Government, which was in contradiction with the principle of self-financing. To prevent this situation, the civil administration had to create new regulations.

THE AGREEMENT OF JULY 4, 1940

Existing conflict concerning the exploitation of Jewish forced labor and the question of competences had led to a meeting between Hans Frank and HSSPF Friedrich-Wilhelm Krüger in order to establish clear rules for the use of Jewish labor. On July 4, 1940, Hans Frank met with Friedrich-Wilhelm Krüger in order to reach an agreement concerning the division of competences between the SS and civil administration. The decision had been made in consultation with various departments. On July 5, 1940, the Office of the Governor General published a circular letter,[166] sent to all the heads of labor departments at the district chefs, as well as to all heads of labor offices in the General Government. According to this agreement, the Jewish card index or *Judenkartei* was to be transferred to labor offices, which, in turn, would have to be responsible for the management of this card index and for assembling data concerning the required quantity of Jewish workers. The main objective was to improve the exploitation of labor force in the General Government.

---

165 Circular Lester of the Jewish Self-Assistance (ŻSS), nr. 19 concerning provision of food and money by the local German administration. YVA-JM.1501, scan 630.
166 Pospieszalski, *Hitlerowskie "prawo" okupacyjne*, 568–72.

Forced Labor in the Ghettos and Labor Detachments • CHAPTER 2 | 69

The German institutions were obliged to pay the Jewish workers' wages according to the official tariff, which was 20% less than the rate for Polish workers. However, Jews employed in labor camps of the SS, according to the new regulations, would not receive any wages.[167] The *Judenräte* would maintain families of workers closed in labor camps. The document underlined that responsibility over measures concerning registration of Jewish forced laborers, rules of movement and registration of population remained in the area of competencies of higher SS and police leader.

As a result of the agreement, the civilian authorities established a *Judeneinsatzstelle* (Jewish Forced Labor Office) within the district labor offices (*Arbeitsämter*) in July 1940. This office partly took over the functions of the labor offices of the *Judenräte*. Jewish officials from *Judenräte* were employed at the *Judeneinsatzstellen* in order to facilitate their work. According to the report of the *Kreishauptmann* of Puławy,

> ... for a special census of the Jews, deployment offices (*Einsatzstellen*) under Jewish administration were established, so that indeed every usable Jew can be deployed to a service benefiting the general public. Here, too, every measure ensues by coercion, if necessary. For this purpose, a *Judenlager*, established in Puławy, was reorganized as a forced labor camp (*Zwangsarbeitslager*).[168]

The implementation of the agreement met many difficulties, and further memos and letters were required forcing various German institutions to act according to the instructions. As stated by Dr. Max Frauendorfer during the conference of the Labor Department on August 6, 1940,

> There are arguments from various directions, that the remuneration for Jews was too high. Dr. Frauendorfer [head of the Department of Labor] emphasizes that on principle the remuneration of 80% [of the tariff for Polish workers] should be retained, otherwise the preservation of the Jewish employees is not guaranteed. If feasible, a piecework system should be implemented, and in cases of time pay accelerating incentives.[169]

---

167 Ibid., 571.
168 YVA, JM-814, Der Kreishauptmann des Kreises Puławy, Lagebericht für November 1940, Puławy, den 7. Dezember 1940, scan 1028.
169 YVA-JM.2700, Protokoll über die Judeneinsatzbesprechung vom 6. August 1940 [...] bei der Abteilung Arbeit im Amt des Generalgouverneurs, scan 3.

On August 20, 1940 Frauendorfer sent a letter to the commander of the Wehrmacht in the General Government, to the higher SS and police leader, and the commander of the Security Police about non-implementation of the instruction.[170] Likewise, chief of the Warsaw District, Dr. Ludwig Fischer[171] sent circular letter about new system of employment of Jews on August 20, 1940.[172] But the reason this agreement was ignored by certain institutions was obvious. Since July 1940, all German institutions that needed Jewish forced labor had to pay for it when previously they had the workers gratis. Previously, the *Judenräte* paid the workers' wages, transportation, tools, maintaining of their families, which caused financial bankruptcy[173] of many *Judenräte* and literally paralyzed their functioning.[174] The statistics show that after July 1940, requests for Jewish forced laborers dropped significantly. In Lublin, for example, the average daily number of forced laborers reached its highest point in July 1940 with 967. In August 1940, the average daily number was only 232.[175]

The agreement of July 4, 1940 exempted the SS and police from payment of wages for Jews in their camps, so Globocnik could freely use thousands of laborers and perform grandiose projects for no cost from his side. Great projects of 1940 are linked to "Otto Program"—the plan for constructing strategic roads and other elements of infrastructure.[176] All sectors of the economy of the General Government were to participate in implementation of the plan. The realization of the plan had to be concluded in spring 1941, prior to the attack

---

170 Berenstein, "Praca przymusowa Żydów w Warszawie," 52.
171 Ludwig Fischer (1905–1947) since October 26, 1939 chef of the Warsaw District; since April 25, 1941 governor of the Warsaw District. Fled from Warsaw on January 17, 1945, arrested on May 10, 1945, extradited to Poland on March 1946, sentenced to death on March 3, 1947, and executed on March 8, 1947 in Warsaw.
172 Berenstein, "Praca przymusowa Żydów w Warszawie," 52.
173 Critical conditions of the Jewish communities were caused by various reasons; among them, big influx of refugees from Warthegau, general pauperization because of the German policy and the result of the war: economic difficulties, drive of labor force to labor camps, as well as other reasons. In fact, many Jewish communities were dependent on the help of Jewish Self-Assistance, joint (until the end of 1941) and even subventions from German local administration on the county level. YVA-JM.1588, scans 79, 81, 83, and ff. In the questions of material support, the Jewish Self-Assistance turned also to *Reichsvereinigung der Juden* in Deutschland. YVA-JM.1588, scan 84; Letter of February 10, 1942, Lublin. YVA-JM.1574, scans 10 and ff.
174 Report of Höller, chef of the Cracow District, in Eisenbach and Rutkowski, *Eksterminacja Żydów*, 212.
175 Tadeusz Radzik, *Lubelska dzielnica zamknięta* (Lublin: Wydawnictwo UMCS, 1999), 101.
176 Hans Frank, *Okupacja i ruch oporu w dzienniku Hansa Franka 1939–1945*, vol. 1 (Warsaw: Książka i Wiedza, 1970), 243.

on the Soviet Union; however, the works were still not completed in February 1941. According to the report of *Kreishauptmann* of Mińsk Mazowiecki: "The outside work also suffered heavily in February [1941] due to bad weather. The preparatory work for the 'Otto Program' nevertheless continued on increased scale."[177] Improvement of the infrastructure in the framework of the "Otto Program," especially of railways and roads, facilitated transportation of coal, coke, and raw materials. It also ameliorated economic conditions of the General Government, facilitating development of industry, including war industry.[178] The "Otto Program" required great quantity of labor force, in particular the Jewish labor force which already at the end of 1940 was in deficit. According to the chef of the Lublin District:

> The implementation of the "Otto Program" is confronted with difficulties concerning the procurement of laborers. The 600 Jews provided by the *Judenlager* Bełżec were mostly unfit for work. The subsequently requested 1,000 laborers have not yet arrived, so that all construction sites are currently working with too few personnel. To be added are the familiar transport problem of the *Ostbahn*. On October 8, the Wieprz Bridge in Łysobyki was opened to traffic.[179]

The construction of roads, bridges, and railways also required large groups of physical workers, not necessary qualified ones, which would be able to perform hard work under control of a limited number of engineers and supervisors. Those workers were supposed to be kept in number of camps and moved from place to place according to progress of the work. The model of Globocnik's camps was quite appropriate for these purposes and had to be enlarged.

Alongside Globocnik's camps, another important institution exploiting Jewish forced labor was the Water Inspection Office (*Wasserwirtschaftsamt*).[180] In nearly every county of Lublin district, this office created their own camps (more than 27 camps in total), with at least 5,000 Jewish workers.[181] The Water

---

177 YVA-JM.814, Mińsk Mazowiecki, 5. März 1941, Monatsbericht, scan 1330.
178 BA-MA, RW23-7, Rü In im GG, Lagebericht für Oktober 1940, 151.
179 YVA, JM-814, Der Chef des Distrikts Lublin im Generalgouvernement, Lagebericht für Oktober 1940, Lublin, den 6. November 1940, scan 782.
180 In a report, *Wasserwirtschaftstelle* Lublin requested 22,000 workers. YVA-O.53/sc. 58.
181 Berenstein, "Obozy pracy przymusowej"; Marszałek, *Obozy pracy w Generalnym Gubernatorstwie*; "10,000 Żydów buduje nasypy i rowy: Melioracje w Dystrykcie Lubelskim—ponad 30 obozów pracy," *Gazeta Żydowska*, August 9, 1940, 10.

Inspection Office in Radom[182] established at least 14 camps. Other labor camps in the Radom district included work in quarries, road construction, in forests, removing of ruins, construction of ramparts along Wisła River, digging of peat, production of bricks, and agriculture.[183] This kind of campt existed before the new type of camp attached to factories became prevalent in 1942. Most of the camps established in 1940 and 1941 were set up to perform specific work and existed for a limited period of time. Camps along the roads or rivers moved according to the progress of work. In many places camps for seasonal work in agriculture were set up.[184]

In places of residence, in big cities, forced labor evolved into new organizational types due to the closure of ghettos. Initially, the number of workers taken out of the ghettos was reduced because of organizational problems. Jewish workers left ghettos in ordered, organized groups and worked in different places called outposts, work places, or labor detachments. They were guarded and counted before leaving and after returning to the ghettos. In 1941, with the closure of big ghettos, more and more firms began to develop their activity inside the ghettos, reducing all kind of costs in this way.

During the period of two years, we observe significant changes in German concepts and practical forms of forced labor of Jews in the General Government, according to changing needs and conditions. From the initial period of military occupation forward, there was no clear policy regarding forced labor, and chaos prevailed. The attitude towards the Jews was based on ideological view of the Jews. Every German institution, and even individuals, could arrest, intimidate, and coerce Jews to do any work. Hans Frank, on the first day of his rule, issued a decree regarding forced labor. However, the German administration was not ready and able to implement this decree, partly because of uncompleted organization of administration[185] and lack of intentions to rebuild the economic life in occupied Poland. Thus, till the springtime of 1940 they needed mainly workers in services.

---

182 "Żydzi osuszają bagna: Jak się pracuje w Jedlance pod Radomiem," *Gazeta Żydowska*, August 17, 1940, 4.
183 Rutkowski, "Hitlerowskie obozy pracy dla Żydów."
184 Note from the visit to the estates in Nieprześno, Janiszowcie, as well as to Bochnia and Wiśnicz Nowy concerning the labor in agriculture on July 21, 22, 23, 1941. YVA-JM.1588, scan 38. A note on the activity of " 'Toporol', Kraków, November 21, 1941. YVA-JM.1588, scans 39–41.
185 The chef of the Kraków District Wächter nominated only on December 13, 1939 Landkomissare in Myślenice and Gorlice, as well as Stadtkommissare in Rzeszów and Bochnia. YVA-JM.12277, 5.

Only in the late spring and summer of 1940 were the Germans able to launch great projects in the field of infrastructure, fortifications, and agriculture. However, their intentions to do it in an orderly manner, despite systematic registration, failed, mainly because of internal frictions between civil administration and the SS. Even the agreement of July 4, 1940, and in consequence transfer of administration of forced labor to the *Arbeitsämter*, did not reach its goal. The SS, and most of all Globocnik, managed to exempt the SS-administered camps from payment of Jewish laborers and from providing minimal living conditions for them. This led to the exploitation of Jews for no compensation and harsh conditions for Jewish workers, leading to mistreatment and death, even some workers could return to their places of residence.[186] The dichotomy of the SS's attitude compared to other factors became clearly visible already in thet early stage of occupation.[187] The model of temporary, dispersed camps disappeared after summer 1941 and was substituted by permanent camps in the vicinity of factories. After the beginning of deportations, reduced ghettos became, in practice, a kind of labor camps. Yet, in places of residence, as a consequence of July 1940 agreement and the closure of large ghettos, forced labor remained in the form of labor commandos, while most production was transferred inside the ghettos.

---

186 Report of Zörner, chef of the Lublin District, November 6, 1940, in Eisenbach and Rutkowski, *Eksterminacja Żydów*, 221.
187 Karay, "The Conflict among German Authorities."

CHAPTER 3

Forced Labor in the Ghettos and Labor Detachments

Labor in both the ghettos and labor detachments is discussed here together because forced labor occurred in all places of residence, even though individual or group employment was performed inside and outside the ghetto. The main difference lies in the fact that outside the ghetto, usually organized working groups were sent to carry out work under guard. These groups departed in the morning and returned in the evening after working. However, the institution of forced labor in the ghettos and labor detachments is just one aspect of a broader issue that included all types of work and business within the Jewish economy during the German occupation. In the present chapter, the issues of forced labor and self-employment (*praca wolnonajemna*) will be discussed. However, we have to take into account the fact that the Jewish economy during the Nazi occupation was not free, due to the existing legislation, which not only limited businesses greatly, but also resulted in a restriction of personal liberty and freedom of movement that actually forced the Jews into a specific state of affairs. Jews as a persecuted ethnic group, even in the case of free rent (*wolny najem*), were not only in a forced situation, but had been seen as inferior in relation to other population groups. Therefore, in addition to what is formally called forced labor, other work, even the free hiring, was de facto forced labor due to the prevailing conditions. In addition, Jewish working groups were usually subordinate to a non-Jewish superior, and that caused more negative consequences for the Jews.

Prior to the determination of competence in the employment of the Jewish labor force, certain patterns of informal exploitation of the Jewish labor began to emerge. As mentioned above, the Jews were arrested in order to perform the clean-up jobs, transportation, and other work on the use and repair of equipment of these works, as well as different jobs for German military units and institutions. This work required skilled human resources capable of executing such works as well as a constant flow of those workers in sufficient quantities. Stopping passersby on the street would supply a sufficient number of workers, but it provided neither healthy workers, nor those having the appropriate qualifications. In spite of these drawbacks, during the first months of occupation, random people were typically stopped on the streets in order to be exploited for work. Because most often it concerned military units, the SS and police, and not the civil business organizations, this practice had a tendency towards ruthlessness and did not promise economic benefits to the arrested.

ESTABLISHMENT AND ACTIVITY OF THE *JUDENRÄTE*

One of the first Jewish institutions created by the German authorities was the Jewish council (*Judenrat;* pl. *Judenräte*). Superficially, it might appear that the Jewish Council was a continuation of the pre-war Jewish community organization of Poland. The similarity stems from the fact that both the new and pre-war Jewish community organizations dealt with the internal affairs of Jewish residents. Moreover, some leaders of Jewish communities also served as important functionaries in the Jewish council during the interwar period as well as in the Jewish administration during the occupation. On the other hand, the *Judenrat* was, primarily, a German institution, created by the occupation authorities to carry out their commands and to exercise the administrative functions of the Jewish communities and ghettos. In some localities, such as in Warsaw, the German authorities (Gestapo) disbanded the Jewish council on October 4, 1939 and appointed in its place a Council of Elders.[1] Among the principal documents serving as a basis for the creation of Jewish councils was Heydrich's telegraphic message of September 21, 1939, which contained specific instructions:

> Councils of Jewish Elders.
> 1) In each Jewish community a Council of Jewish Elders is to be set up which, as far as possible, is to be composed of the remaining authoritative personalities and rabbis. The Council is to be composed of up to 24 male Jews (depending on the size of the Jewish community). The Council is to be made fully responsible, in the literal sense of the word,

---

1 Arad and Gutman, *Documents on the Holocaust*, 188; B. Mintz and L. Klausner, eds., *Sefer ha-Zeva'ot* [Book of Abominations] (Jerusalem: R. Mass, 1945), vol. 1, 1–2.

for the exact and prompt implementation of directives already issued or to be issued in the future.

2) In case of sabotage of such instructions, the Councils are to be warned that the most severe measures will be taken.[2]

An additional task of the Jewish councils, according to the instructions of Heydrich, was to conduct a census of all Jews by gender and age groups: up to 16, from 16 to 20, and over 20. Jewish councils were also to be responsible for the assemblage of Jews in the cities. According to the statement: "They are to be made personally responsible for the evacuation of the Jews from the countryside."[3] And further: "The Councils of Elders in the concentration centers are to be made responsible for the appropriate housing of the Jews arriving from the countryside."[4] Despite the very limited task of the Jewish councils, their most significant feature was that they were created by the German authorities in order to perform administrative functions. It is important to underline personal responsibility for carrying out the instructions of the German authorities. However, despite the fact that the Jewish councils were set up by the Germans, the continuity of personnel and lack of other Jewish institutions meant that the Jewish councils, since their inception, were forced to take upon themselves considerable administrative and organizational functions, even if in formal terms they were not compelled to do so.

The regulation issued on November 1939 by Governor General Dr. Hans Frank concerning the establishment of Jewish councils, in fact, changed nothing in comparison with Heydrich's telegraphic message of September 21, 1939. Hans Frank ordered that in communities (*Gemeinde* in German, or *gminy* in Polish) of up to 10,000 people a council of 12 members was to be set up; in communities over that number the council would have 24 members. Members of the community had to choose the councils, and the Jewish council in turn was to choose from among its members a chairman and his deputy. Council elections were to be held no later than December 31, 1939, and elected council

---

2 Instructions by Heydrich on policy and operations concerning Jews in the occupied territories, September 21, 1939. See Arad and Gutman, *Documents on the Holocaust*, 174; Eisenbach and Rutkowski, *Eksterminacja Żydów*, 21–29.

3 Instructions by Heydrich on policy and operations concerning Jews in the occupied territories, September 21, 1939. See Arad and Gutman, *Documents on the Holocaust*, 174; Eisenbach and Rutkowski, *Eksterminacja Żydów*, 21–29.

4 Instructions by Heydrich on policy and operations concerning Jews in the occupied territories, September 21, 1939. See Arad and Gutman, *Documents on the Holocaust*, 175; Eisenbach and Rutkowski, *Eksterminacja Żydów*, 21–29.

members were to be submitted for approval to the local German authorities (*Kreishauptmann* or *Stadthauptmann*).⁵ Paragraph 5 of this regulation defines the tasks of the board as follows:

> The Jewish council is obliged to accept orders from the German authorities by means of its chairman or his deputy. It accounts for the correct and conscientious carrying out of these orders. Jewish men and Jewish women have to obey instructions given by it and to comply with German regulations.⁶

In addition to this regulation, two other executive orders were issued on April 25 and June 7, 1940.⁷ In light of these provisions, all commands had to be directed to the Jewish councils through county governors (*Stadthauptmann* or *Kreishauptmann*). The orders, however, did not specify anything about forced labor.

Nevertheless, the Jewish councils, despite the responsibilities set before them by the occupation authorities, had reached a crossroads of different tasks and expectations on the part of the Jewish institutions and the Jewish community. The newspaper *Gazeta Żydowska* worded this clearly:

> The Council is responsible for dealing with the obligations that the authorities have imposed on the Jewish public, and at the same time it conveys to the authorities the requirements of this same population. In this way, the Council has become the sole representative and mediator between the Jewish population and the authorities. For this purpose, it has been conferred with certain rights, and authority in some matters. The Council has become the central place where all the various Jewish affairs are organized. This gives it certain rights but also imposes duties. The maintenance of balance between these rights and duties is a difficult task, but an important one, and the satisfactory relationship between the Council and the public depends on its achievement.⁸

The balance between the commands of the German authorities, which were coercive in relation to the Jewish people, and between the expectations

---

5   *VBlGG*, 1939, no. 9, 72; Eisenbach and Rutkowski, *Eksterminacja Żydów*, 74.
6   Eisenbach and Rutkowski, *Eksterminacja Żydów*, 74.
7   *VBlGG*, 1940, vol. 2, 249, 387.
8   *Gazeta Żydowska*, December 23, 1940, 206.

of the Jewish community that Jewish councils would take care of all the communities' problems, was difficult and sometimes impossible. In addition, problems associated with the provision of financial resources, for current activity of the councils and its administration and for social welfare and health care while under general impoverishment and increased morbidity, were acute. In fact, from the onset, Jewish councils had no choice but to deal with different issues and tried to reconcile different and conflicting interests.

From the beginning until the end of their activity, the Jewish councils struggled with financial problems. This was related to the overall economic situation of the Jewish community. During the war, Jewish communities had many different expenses, and at the beginning of the occupation, many Jewish communities were haunted by Wehrmacht officers or officers of the SD, who compelled them to pay heavy levies (*kontrybucje*) and taxes. Jewish communities were forced to pay large sums of money and even jewellery. Usually, hostages were taken from among the representatives of the community, under threat of being shot in the event of non-payment of an expected sum. Chaim A. Kaplan summarized this situation in the following words: "The *Judenrat* [in Warsaw], which was orphaned when its money was stolen and its appointed president (commissar) [Maurycy Mayzel] fled, attempted to organize the matter of seizing people for labor."[9]

The practice of imposing high contribution fees on the Jewish community meant that in the early period of its activity, Jewish councils were deprived of cash and were still forced to spend large sums of money for welfare assistance of refugees, and to people affected by the war. Already during the war, many Jewish families lost their homes in the bombing, and many others lost their breadwinners who had been mobilized, died, or injured. In the autumn of 1939, the Jewish councils had to build financially functioning mechanisms. The basis of their income originated from a variety of taxes that had always been difficult to collect. Thus, revenues of the Jewish councils were small, while expenses grew at a quick pace. Economic stagnation and legislation by the German authorities, which sought to eliminate Jews from the economy, caused rapid impoverishment, although the Jewish population still had cash holdings in the initial period of the occupation. Moreover, the economic system of the occupational forces was calculated on the exploitation of the Jews, which further reduced the communities' income. For example, Aryanization of businesses, shops, and houses resulted in loss of revenue and receipts of rent, while on the other hand, free forced labor deprived Jews of wages.

---

9 Entry of October 20, 1939, in Kaplan, *Scroll of Agony*, 55.

The occupation authorities, busy with the persecution of Jews, did not need to pay attention to the normal functioning of the economy and the role Jews played in it. In face of the difficulties the implementation of the Jewish councils caused, the situation did not change until the summer of 1940. Despite Hans Frank's and Friedrich-Wilhelm Krüger's agreement on payment for Jewish forced labor, Jews employed in the SS-managed labor camps did not receive payment for their work from the German authorities. Thanks to that, Globocnik was able to continue to manage tens of thousands of Jewish forced laborers, placing the burden of the cost of living and wages of these workers on the Jewish councils in general, and on the Jewish Council in Lublin in particular.[10]

The Jewish Council in Warsaw, as many others, was in a difficult financial situation. On March 25, 1940, Adam Czerniaków wrote in his diary, "Our cashbox is empty. I owe the Labor Battalion 90,000 zł, hospital officials 25,000, and registration officials 50,000 zł."[11] A few months later, Adam Czerniaków's diary entry stated:

> We worked out a plan of payments of arrears for the Labor Battalion. The amount overdue on July 1, 1940 is 482,011 zł, including 282,563 to the workers. The loan received from our emigration account is 300,000 zł. If again the matter of the ghetto does not turn around, we may somehow find the way out from this trap. Unfortunately, I'm afraid that we cannot safely operate.[12]

The Jewish councils attempted to solve their financial problems in different ways such as imposing taxes on the Jewish population and issuing food vouchers, in addition to requests made to the Jewish councils for medical examinations to determine workers' ability to perform forced labor, and so on. A relatively large source of their revenue was from charges for replacements during forced labor roundup. In Warsaw, it depended on the status of a person's property: the person who was better off had to pay higher fees. In 1941 in Lublin, 4,260 people were paying for their replacements. However, with the time and pauperization of the population less and less people were able to pay for their replacement and in

---

10 APL, RŻL-47, 23–25. Report from the activity of the Central Camps Council in Bełżec for the period June 13 until December 5, 1940.
11 Entry of March 25, 1940 in Marian Fuks, ed., *Adama Czerniakowa dziennik* (Warsaw: PWN: 1983), 96.
12 Entry of June 30, 1940 in Fuks, *Adama Czerniakowa dziennik*, 126.

Lublin in 1942 only 2,587 people were still able to pay for the replacement.[13] However, all these measures were insufficient, and the Jewish councils still remained in a deficit. Therefore, they asked the commercial banks for loans[14] secured with real estate. When these loans were not enough, the Jewish councils tried to get grants from the General Government. There was the fear that the General Government administration would be forced to subsidize the Jewish councils, and that would compel German institutions to pay a fee for using Jewish forced labor through the mediation of labor offices.

In the area of economic activity, the performance of Jewish councils was diversified and depended on the quality of people in key positions. Jewish councils did not have a uniform pattern of fiscal operation, and various councils had different structures. Most of them were engaged in economic activity via departments of economy, forced labor, and finance. Departments of economy in different councils had either active or passive styles of operation. Passive *Judenräte* usually dealt with the issue of licenses for economic activity or business litigation and regulation. Active *Judenräte* in times of crisis, unemployment, and widespread impoverishment tried to pursue a dynamic policy of employment through the organization of workshops and assistance in creating associations of craftsmen. Those associations allowed their members to avoid the limitations of keeping accounts and making financial transactions, obtain permits to travel outside the place of residence, procure orders for their production, raw materials, and energy.

LABOR BATTALIONS

With incessant arrests of Jewish passersby on the streets, the Jewish councils in many towns, parallel in time and independently of one another, concluded that the question of labor supply to various German institutions was inevitable. In such a situation, to avoid the arrests of random passersby, the best solution was to organize several workers each day and deliver them according to a specific demand by the German institutions.[15] Chaim A. Kaplan wrote in his diary:

> The *Judenrat* [. . .] attempted to organize the matter of seizing people for labor. Czerniaków offered to supply a certain number of workers if only they

---

13 Report of the activity of the Commission and Department of Labor for February 1942, APL, RŻL, syg 6, 90.
14 Letter to the Bank Związku Spółek Zarobkowych A.G. in Kraków, October 11, 1940. YVA-JM.1588, scan 128.
15 Entry of October 20, 1939, Kaplan, *Scroll of Agony*, 55.

would stop seizing for forced labor whoever comes to hand in the streets. They scarcely listened to this proposal, merely explained in passing that it was not detailed enough. Finally they agreed that the *Judenrat* will supply five hundred laborers a day, and that the street captures will stop. Tomorrow will be the first day for this new arrangement. [. . .] Let us see if they find people willing to work, if the *Judenrat* can meet its obligation, and if the conqueror will be satisfied with the new arrangement. If, heaven forbid, the contract with the enemy doesn't succeed, the evil will be worse than it has been up to now. We have all become orphans. Out of the depths I called thee.[16]

In many places such as Warsaw and Lublin, special labor detachments were created. These groups had different names—in Warsaw, for instance, they were called the labor battalions. An important note is the fact that the organization of Jewish labor detachments arose even before the proclamation of the General Government. Therefore, the decision of Hans Frank and the announcement of the regulation regarding Jewish forced labor did not in effect change the situation. Forced labor of Jews took place before the proclamation of the General Government as well as after it. Frank's regulation was purely formal and mostly propagandistic. However, in the case of the *Judenräte*, they initiated organizing groups of Jewish workers to reduce the number of random arrests on the streets of elderly people, of unable to work, and the ill. Yet, among the arrested also were people employed on a permanent basis who held the relevant documents. In those cases, the documents were either not accepted or ignored. In some instances, among the arrested Jews forced to work were also the employees of the Warsaw *Judenrat*.

Labor battalions performed huge quantities of labor. For example, the Labor Battalion in Warsaw performed only in the first half year of 1940 as much as 1,200,000 workdays, with approximately 8,000 workers employed every day.[17]

Organization of permanent working groups funded by *Judenräte* was an important proposal because it was a quick response to rapidly changing economic conditions. Notwithstanding the existing and growing restrictions on Jewish economic activity, the Jews were taking initiatives. The quotation from the report of *Kreishauptmann* of Jędrzejów may shed some light to the attitude of some German officials towards Jewish economic initiatives:

> I have received requests from several companies to license Jewish traders, respectively to support those licensed by higher authorities

---

16 Ibid.
17 "Warszawska Gmina Żydowska przy pracy," *Gazeta Żydowska*, August 9, 1940.

in their business. Until now I refused to comply with these requests. In my County the Jews have been collected in special quarters where they lead their own life, among others to render them harmless in all aspects. In the beginning of my activities I tried to employ Jews in individual cases in the economy. I experienced the greatest failures. The Jews took the opportunity to instigate their Polish staff and for profiteering wherever they could. They tried with all their means to establish a network extending beyond the local labor office that they did not use for its proper tasks but for obscure profiteering. This profiteering has stopped almost totally now that I let the Jews lead their own lives in special quarters. Now again, the Jews shall have the opportunity to travel about in the district, for example, to buy skins, to buy scrap material and so forth, even to use the railway, and on top of that my support is requested. The result of this will undoubtedly be, as proven by experience, that the Jews will bring the black market and profiteering to bloom again, even the network that has fortunately been torn will be woven again immediately and the activities of the *Kreishauptmann* [of Jędrzejów] will secretly be thwarted.

The Poles will again be grateful objects of exploitation and secret coworkers of the Jews, as it used to be before. This risk is much greater than the financial advantages the companies can expect when they make use of the cunning, deviousness, and unscrupulousness of the Jews. Everywhere I employed Aryans, especially evacuated Poles, instead of the Jews, I could push the Jews out. I can lend my hand to support Jewish traders and buyers only if the companies can prove to me that Aryans cannot do the same jobs. And even if their financial success will not be as big as with the Jews, the damage prevented by not licensing the Jews is much bigger than the financial loss through Aryan rather than Jewish work.

I cannot help but notice that it was more financial reasons that lead to the re-employment of the Jews than responsible investigation if the Jews can be substituted by Aryans, even risking a certain financial loss.[18]

The Jews in conditions of constant economic discrimination could only respond to new and constantly changing regulations, in order to find their proper niche. Because it was not possible to change or cancel German practices and orders, including random arrests, they had to adapt to those practices so as to reduce their perniciousness. Forced labor in places of residence, when

---

18 YVA, JM-814, Der Kreishauptmann des Kreises Jędrzejów, Lagebericht für August 1940, September 5, 1940, scans 327–28.

speaking of organized working groups, was not to be paid for by the German authorities and institutions. To reward the labor of the workers, the *Judenräte* paid their wages from their own resources. Chaim A. Kaplan wrote in his diary: "The Judenrat will pay each worker four złoty a day out of its treasury."[19] In other areas, the heads of local administration decided what kind of Jewish work should be paid or not. The *Kreishauptmann* of Jasło wrote in his report of May 1940:

> The Jewish obligation to work will be done here on a rotational basis for every Jew who is able to work (regardless of whether he is employed), business owner, or an employee will be obliged to perform compulsory labor. The *Judenräte* will set up Jewish Labor Offices, which are under the supervision of the Labor Office in Jasło and works according to my instructions. Requirements of Jewish workers have to be directed to the Labor Office in Jasło; compulsory labor in the public interest is not paid. Jews working, on the other hand, at an authorized service station or a company receiving benefits of such work as car washing, gardening, legged of spaces, that that are not dedicated to the public transport must be paid. The institution performing the work is required to pay for it.[20]

Non-payment for forced labor was overt exploitation of the Jews, because not only were the Jews subject to economic discrimination, which was intended to eliminate them from the country's economy, but also since the authorities benefitted from Jewish labor without paying for it. It was a seemingly absurd situation. However, its significance was as follows: the Jews were banned from the country's economy not in an absolute way but by means of their declassification, which in the end led to their impoverishment due to the maximum use of their material resources in addition to their physical labor.

Labor battalions, or labor detachments established in different localities of the General Government, seemed to be at first fragile and instable institutions that depended upon the temporary satisfaction of German demands for labor. However, they appeared to be an important institution and, therefore, continued their work after the proclamation of both the General Government and the top-down organization of forced labor by the German authorities in the General Government.[21]

---

19   Entry of October 20, 1939, in Kaplan, *Scroll of Agony*, 55.
20   YVA-O.53/101, Der Kreishauptmann des Kreises Jasło, Jasło, den 2 Juni 1940, Lagebericht über die Zeit von Mitte Mai 1940 bis Ende Mai 1940, scans 74–76.
21   AIPN, NTN, 196/270, 10–22.

REGISTRATION OF JEWS FOR FORCED LABOR

Judenrat labor departments were required under the regulations of December 11 and 12, 1939, and supplementary regulations from January 1940, to conduct a registration of all Jews and to determine their ability to work. This process, especially in large cities with their large Jewish communities had encountered persistent difficulties. These resulted from evading registration and attempting to obtain exemption from forced labor due to illness. It was fully justified because the German authorities' attitude towards Jews and the persecution of Jews in the streets and public places was widely known. Many Jews were direct participants in forced labor or had at least witnessed it. Forced labor was often meaningless and demeaning. Therefore, the registration process, in large communities, was long and lasted for weeks. Repeatedly avoiding the registration process resulted in incomplete or inaccurate data.

The mere fact that one had to register resulted in great anxiety among Jews:

> There is deep concern over the forced labor camps. The Jewish community will perform from the third [of February 1940] the registration of all [the Jews] from the age of 12; the information will be transferred to the Municipal Board. Six groups will operate—five in Poland and one in East Prussia. The five groups are employed near Wisła.[22]

In Warsaw, the first registration took place between February 5 to 14, 1940, when 121,265 people reported.[23] A few days later, the next registration took place.

> February 19 [1940]. News of the re-registration to forced labor. In each place there will sit a Jewish doctor responsible for the diagnosis of disease. The Jewish community is responsible for the statements of registrants. All artisans and industrialists should submit their tools. They [the Germans] will print those statements in German at the expense of the Jewish community.[24]

---

22 Entries of January 28–30, 1940 in Emanuel Ringelblum, *Kronika getta warszawskiego: wrzesień 1939–styczeń 1943*, ed. Artur Eisenbach (Warszawa: Czytelnik, 1988), 85–86.
23 Ibid.
24 Entries of February 21, 22, and 23, 1940, in Ringelblum, *Kronika getta warszawskiego: wrzesień 1939–styczeń 1943*, 96.

This second registration listed Jews between the ages of 16 and 25, while others were to be registered at a later date. "Please report tools. Supervisors of the Council of Elders (*Ältestenrat*) of the Jews are responsible for the [veracity of the] information."[25]

After registering, based on a special card-index, the Jews received a summons to appear for forced labor. The spring directory of those capable of working also served as a reference for summoning Jews to forced labor camps. Data regarding the scale of dodging forced labor is provided in Ludwik Landau's chronicle:

> The second recruit concerns people who avoided the warrants distributed by the Labor Battalion. Of 90,000 people about 6,000 paid money for the replacements, about 25,000 did not come to work, and two thirds did not respond to the summons at all. From among the "stubborn" a sample of several hundred people were chosen to act on behalf of the others. The Jewish community selected only bachelors, removing family men from the list. Those who were chosen were supposed go to the camp designated after medical examination.[26]

Ludwig Fischer also wrote in his report about the registration of forced labor:

> The Jewish census that was ordered by Higher SS and Police Commander in Kraków and was planned as a prelude to the great action of forced labor is now almost complete. There are 250,000 Jewish men total who are subject to the work [to be forced laborers], and the entire directory was divided according to particular professions.[27]

Special labor departments of *Judenräte* were created in order to deal with taking orders and delivering appropriate numbers of workers for forced labor. In large cities, such as Warsaw, the labor battalions were subjected to the Labor Department, which were directly responsible for the organization and supervision of the working groups that were to be sent to the appropriate outposts. The problem of showing up, supervision, and attempts of exemption from

---

25 Ibid.
26 Entry of August 13, 1940, in Landau, *Kronika lat wojny i okupacji*, vol. 1, 637.
27 Dunin-Wąsowicz, *Raporty Ludwiga Fischera*, 196.

forced labor at any cost led to constant conflicts and great corruption. In addition, forced laborers initially did not receive remuneration for their work. This placed the members of the *Judenrat* in an uncomfortable position: on the one hand, they were required to fulfil the commands of the German authorities, and on the other hand, the Jewish community sensed their pressure and suspected them of corruption. The chairman of the *Judenrat* in Warsaw, Adam Czerniaków, who had repeatedly reorganized labor battalions, wrote about it.[28] One of ways to avoid forced labor in Warsaw was by counterfeiting stamps. The counterfeiters were subjected to corporal punishment. The forgers were sent for prolonged forced labor.[29] News of counterfeiting stamps that would exempt people from forced labor even reached the Gestapo, which conducted its own investigation into this issue.[30] On June 10, 1940, Adam Czerniaków wrote in his diary,

> The Gestapo on Labor Battalion. They are apparently investigating counterfeit stamps of the [Labor] Battalion. Those arrested explained that, after all, they only cheated the [Jewish] community. Thrown out of the hospital, administration officials denounced the office of allegedly hiding information regarding those forced to work.[31]

The above quotation illustrates how much emotion and tension had been created around the subject of forced labor. Gestapo investigation, mutual denunciations, forgery, and corruption were all on the agenda. In an almost overt manner, large sums of money were required for exemption from the forced labor. Adam Czerniaków noted inter alia: "In the filth Battalion—extortion of money from people (Lekachmacher paid 100 zł for May; they required 400 zł from him)."[32]

The extent of evasion from forced labor and problems in recruiting workers, to the outposts as well as to work in labor camps, prompted further street arrests. For example, in Lublin in February 1942, of about 430 workers a day obliged to perform forced labor, only 35 came. In other words, of 12,044 workdays, only 968 workdays were actually done. Given the fact that 790 people were paid for

---

28 Entries of April 20–May 1, 1940, in Ringelblum, *Kronika getta warszawskiego*, 129; Entry of April 15, 1940 in Fuks, *Adama Czerniakowa dziennik*, 105; Entry of May 5, 1940, in Fuks, *Adama Czerniakowa dziennik*, 109.
29 Entry of May 6, 1940, in Fuks, *Adama Czerniakowa dziennik*, 110.
30 Entry of June 1, 1940, in Fuks, *Adama Czerniakowa dziennik*, 118.
31 Entry of June 10, 1940, in Fuks, *Adama Czerniakowa dziennik*, 119–20.
32 Entry of May 19, 1940, in Fuks, *Adama Czerniakowa dziennik*, 113.

their work [790 × 4 weeks = 3,160] and absence in amount of 822 workdays was justified, it gives only 40 percent workdays of 12,044 expected.[33] Emanuel Ringelblum wrote about the situation in the following words:

> Recently Jewish catchers (section leaders) from the Jewish community are going around. They face a gate, suddenly run into [the house], the Jews are hiding in the doorways, and there they are dealt with by the policemen. A week ago, on April 20 [1940], there was a terrible raid to capture workers. They were pulling people from the trams and out of the flats.[34]

Sometimes those arrests were selective in nature; and only a particular group of people was stopped. "From Gertner's restaurant they pulled all the Jews to work. On the streets, no one moved. They surrounded Kercelak [market place], and all were taken to work; likewise, in the trams."[35] Sometimes they selected only women: "Today, September 19 [1940] they seized the women, but only the very elegant, those wearing lipstick, to perform hard labor—apparently, to dig potatoes."[36] The German authorities loved to "celebrate" all kinds of Jewish religious holidays by the persecuting Jews.[37] Particularly on those special days, they tried to humiliate the Jews. In Lublin, for example, in order to prevent wild arrests on the streets on Rosh Hashanah and Yom Kippur, the Forced Labor Department of the *Judenrat* mobilized a special reserve group of workers, paid by the *Judenrat*, to be ready to answer any request for forced laborers in those days.[38]

In the towns where large and medium construction sites were located close to Jewish communities or ghettos, Jewish workers left for work in the morning and returned home in the evenings. In a report we can learn about such project near Włodawa. According to the Water Management inspector:

> In Włodawa itself it is not a camp, but a construction site of the Water Management, where about 400 Jewish workers are employed. The working

---

33 Report of the activity of the Commission and Department of Labor for February 1942, APL, RŻL, syg 6, 88.
34 Entries of April 20–May 1, 1940, in Ringelblum, *Kronika getta warszawskiego*, 132.
35 Entries of May 2, 4, 6, 7, and 8, 1940 in Ringelblum, *Kronika getta warszawskiego*, 135.
36 Entries of September 17, 18, and 19, 1940, in Ringelblum, *Kronika getta warszawskiego*, 152.
37 APL, RŻL-41, 41, Letter written by the head of Department of Forced Labor of December 23, 1941.
38 Ibid.

hours are 48 hours per week. Sometimes Sundays are also workdays. All Jewish workers on this construction site made a good impression physically, but clothing and footwear were very poor. For the Jewish workers, there have already been procured rubber boots by the Water Management. Moreover, on this construction site, there were 6 *Reichsdeutsche* foremen who oversee the Jews during the work. For the Jewish workers, good tools were also provided.[39]

In addition to labor battalions organized in some cities, Jews were often employed to perform cleaning work. In autumn, it was elimination of debris from the streets. From the first snowfall, it began to be customary to hire Jews to shovel the snow on roads and sidewalks in the cities.[40] In the early 1940s, winters in the Polish territories were very severe, characterized by frosts and heavy snow. After a major snowfall, most of the roads became impassable and required treatment. In rural areas, snow removal was the responsibility of local authorities, while in urban areas, Jews were commonly employed. The Jews were used to remove snow not only during the winter of 1939 and 1940, but also in following years.[41] One of the Jewish chroniclers wrote about this in the following way:

> When snow begins to fall, we have additional trouble. According to the agreement between the *Judenrat* and the government, the Jews are liable for the forced labor of snow removal throughout the whole city. Every morning several hundred Jews, at the "order of the *Judenrat*," go out to forced labor. You can recognize them not only by the "Jewish insignia" on their sleeves, but also by "their gestures" and by the sorrow implanted on their faces. They receive no pay for this, not even food. The Gentiles, too, are required to work, but they are paid.[42]

The German administration and various German institutions and service companies that were subject to the municipally created cleaning enterprise (*Zakład Oczyszczania Miasta*, ZOM) marked the beginning of organized labor

---

39 YVA-JM.2700, Vermerk, Lublin, November 19, 1940, Report from the inspection of Water Inspection forced labor camps in Siedlicze, Sawin, and Włodawa, scan 33.
40 Entry of March 6, 1940, in Ringelblum, *Kronika getta warszawskiego*, 99.
41 "Obowiązek uprzątania śniegu w Krakowie," *Gazeta Żydowska*, January 7, 1940, 3; "Obrazek krakowski: śnieg... śnieg," *Gazeta Żydowska*, January 17, 1940, 3.
42 Entry of March 4, 1940, in Kaplan, *Scroll of Agony*, 129.

detachments in the places where Jews lived. This was associated with the stabilization of the situation. It must not be forgotten that in the General Government several divisions of the Wehrmacht, military police, and civil police were stationed. Polish airports were transformed into the German military airfields. Most of these institutions needed workers to do a variety of jobs and they often benefitted from Jewish labor. This was due to their position and discriminatory attitude towards Jews as well as the ease with which it was possible to arrest Jews without the risk of being punished. At least in the initial period of the occupation, the German authorities tried not to provoke the Polish population unnecessarily. It was only after 1942 that intensified mass arrests of Poles for forced labor took place. In the years 1939 to 1942, the easiest way to get workers free of charge was to apprehend Jews. By using that method to mobilize workers, not only the Jews complained, but so did the representatives of the German administration. In the report of Ludwig Fischer, the governor of the Warsaw District, the following text can be found:

> We must again conclude that the troops, making independent roundups in the Jewish quarter, greatly interfere with normal employment. Managers of workplaces every day complain that their Jewish workers are delayed for hours or do not show up for work at all because they were arrested or stayed in their flats due to the ongoing roundup. In order to satisfy the requirements of military facilities in an orderly fashion at all times, it is expected to introduce an obligation to work for all Jews between the ages of 14 to 60. According to this, anyone who does not have permanent employment will be required to serve 2–5 days a month, for which he will receive remuneration.[43]

The problem of roundups was difficult to solve. Despite attempts to regulate forced labor, many German institutions felt completely unpunishable and therefore continued to hold on to Jews for work.

WORKSHOPS

For many of the *Judenräte*, the best solution was to create workshops in which Jews were employed in order to satisfy the demand for services from German institutions. In some places those workshops were called "urban workshops" (Germ. *Städtische Werkstätte*; Pol. *warsztaty miejskie*). Establishment of workshops

---

43 Dunin-Wąsowicz, *Raporty Ludwiga Fischera*, 405.

prevented wild roundups, helped to stabilize the employment of Jews, and even gave prospects for further development. Workshops dealt not only with repairs but also with production of new items that could be sold on the open market.

It is difficult to determine the origins of the proposal to create workshops and whether it had come from the Jews themselves, or whether the idea developed earlier within the circles of the German authorities. The chapter on forced labor camps describes the creation of workshops in former military barracks of the Lipowa Street No. 7 in Lublin. Already from the autumn of 1939, on the order of SSPF Globocnik, workshops of this kind—in which Jewish workers from Lublin were employed—had been functioning. Such workers arrived to work every day and left in the evening. Numerous workshops were set up by the Germans in the autumn of 1939 and in the beginning of 1940. However, it seems that most often workshops were created at the initiative of the Jews themselves, although establishing them required approval from the authorities.

Workshops were created in the cities like Lublin,[44] Warsaw,[45] Bochnia,[46] Zamość,[47] Kielce,[48] Częstochowa,[49] Tarnów,[50] Wieliczka,[51] and others. They were also a response to attempts to exclude Jews from the Polish economy, thereby leaving them destitute. Aryanization of Jewish businesses, shops and stores, and registration of machines and tools was a very dangerous process; therefore, creation of workshops, with the assistance of the *Judenräte*, allowed the salvaging of some of the tools and machines that were still owned by Jews. Jews could also make use of existing buildings to create workshops and thus continue to keep them under their management. For example, "In Międzyrzec [...] workshops were built in the streets, from which, as is feared, the Jews will be removed in connection with the intention of creating a ghetto."[52] Top-down organization of workshops by the *Judenräte* allowed circumventing all the bureaucratic and legal constraints, such as, the financial appropriation

---

44 APL, RŻL-8, 40–41. Report from the activity of the [Jewish] Council [in Lublin] for the period from September 1, 1939 to August 31, 1940. The workshops in Lublin were created already in December 1939 and employed 300 workers.
45 "Z Warszawy: Wytwórczość żydowska," *Gazeta Żydowska*, September 3, 1941, 3.
46 "Z miast i miasteczek: Bochnia," *Gazeta Żydowska*, July 7, 1941, 2.
47 YVA-O.33/322, testimony of Mieczysław Garfinkiel, 12; YVA-O.3/2940, testimony of Lea Białowicz, 1–11.
48 "Placówka dla rzemieślników-fachowców w Kielcach: Nowe warsztaty kamsznicze," *Gazeta Żydowska*, December 10, 1940, 4
49 "Zbiorowe warsztaty w Częstochowie," *Gazeta Żydowska*, August 21, 1942, 2.
50 "Wiadomości z Tarnowa," *Gazeta Żydowska*, May 20, 1941, 4.
51 Henryk Schönker, *Dotknięcie Anioła* (Warsaw: Ośrodek Karta, 2005, 113).
52 Entry of April 13, 1940, in Ringelblum, *Kronika getta warszawskiego*, 125.

of bank accounts that would have been insurmountable for individual entrepreneurs. Ludwig Fischer wrote, furthermore, in his report about the improvement of employment among the Jews:

> Compared with the last month (February 1941), the employment of Jews has improved. Many thousands of unemployed Jewish artisans received jobs again thanks to the establishment of large workshops. At the moment, in the Jewish quarter, there still are about 62,000 unemployed Jews willing to work, including 28,000 artisans. There is an effort to incorporate into the production process those able-bodied Jews. [. . .] In this connection, the Jewish quarter, in which all Jews must present themselves for the examination conducted by Jewish doctors will be carefully inspected. Jews who are classified as "unfit" [to work] will be re-examined by German physicians.[53]

Workshops developed relatively quickly; however, in the larger towns many Jewish workers were unable to secure employment. In big cities, the numbers of workers employed ranged from several hundred to several thousand. "The craft workshops in the Jewish quarter of Warsaw employed in June [1941] an average of 2,325 artisans daily."[54] Shortly afterwards, we find information about an increase in the number of workers in workshops:

> When it comes to economic issues, it should be noted that the number of workers employed in the workshops has grown to approximately 3,000 people. However, in general, there are still doubts about whether the economic potential of the Jewish quarter in the near future will develop, so that in a stricter separation from the outside world—it could use the surplus production in order to cover the necessities of peoples' lives.[55]

Development of workshops was initially slow, but in the summer of 1940, it became increasingly dynamic. Since the spring of 1941, in connection with the preparation for Operation Barbarossa when the need to increase supplies for the army had grown, the demand for supplies and labor was very high.[56]

---

53 Dunin-Wąsowicz, *Raporty Ludwiga Fischera*, 294.
54 Ibid., 343.
55 Ibid., 375–76.
56 In his report, the governor of the district Lublin wrote about poor condition of people deported from Warthegau. The new migrants to Lublin were 5,000 Poles and 2,000 Jews, many of whom were unable to work. Moreover, 1540 Jews from Kraków also came to the district. At the same time, firms constructing roads needed 20,000 workers: *Bauleitung der Flugwaffe*

In addition to workshops, artisan craft unions were created, which were gradually able to unite small businesses into big economic conglomerates. In Warsaw, such organizations included, for instance, the Association of Jewish Artisans (*Związek Rzemieślników Żydowskich*)[57] and Jewish Industrial Supply Company Ltd. (*Spółka Dostawcza Przemysłu Żydowskiego z o.o.*, or, in German, *Lieferungsgesellschaft des jüdischen Gewerbes GmbH*). The Association of Jewish Artisans was active also in Kraków[58] and other places. Until end of July 1940 it registered 2381 masters (*majstrowie*), 4360 assistants (*pomocnicy*), 588 apprentices (*czeladnicy*), and 287 pupils (*praktykanci*). All registered artisans received personal documents and were enlisted in one of seven basic categories: wood workers, building, textile, food processing, metal workers, leather processing, and general artisans.[59] The arrangement of economic relations with the Jewish district in Warsaw was followed by establishment of the Society of German Companies Warsaw, Ltd. (*Deutsche Firmen Gesellschaft Warschau GmbH*), which was supposed to unite many German industrial companies. That society was the first to take care of all contracts in order to ensure employment of the Jews.[60]

Some Jewish communities attempted to develop the possibility of work in agriculture, despite limited possibilities. The *Judenrat* in Warsaw was in the best situation, as it managed to renew activity of the agricultural farm in Grochów, which before the war belonged to *He-Chalutz*. It was a relatively large farm, possessing about 38 hectares of land and buildings. After the beginning of the war, the farm was devastated and all the animals from there were slaughtered or stolen. However, after investing a lot of work, the farm was restored and employed 60 young people in the ages from 16 to 23. All its products were destined for the market.[61] There were also similar agricultural Jewish farms outside the General Government, for example, in Będzin.[62] In Tarnów, a group

---

requested 8,000 to 10,000 workers, and *Wasserwirtschaft* requested 22,000 workers. See Lagebericht of the Governor of the Lublin District, March 6, 1941. YVA-O.53/101, scans 47–50.

57 "Zespolenie rzemieślników żydowskich," *Gazeta Żydowska*, December 10, 1940, 6.
58 "Rejestracja rzemieślników żydowskich w Krakowie," *Gazeta Żydowska*, July 30, 1940, 3.
59 Ibid.
60 Dunin-Wąsowicz, *Raporty Ludwiga Fischera*, 290.
61 "Ferma rolnicza w Grochowie," *Gazeta Żydowska*, August 6, 1940, 2; "Ferma rolnicza w Grochowie," *Gazeta Żydowska*, September 13, 1940, 6.
62 "Ferma rolna pod Będzinem: Dzień pracy na fermie," *Gazeta Żydowska*, October 23, 1940, 2

of young people volunteered to the work in agriculture and was sent by the labor office to the estate Łęg and Partyń, near Żabno.[63]

CHANGES IN THE MECHANISM FOR PROCUREMENT OF FORCED LABOR AND SALARY

In early spring of 1940, some measures were taken in order to reduce the unpredictability of certain German institutions, especially the police and the army, who carried out arrests for forced labor on the streets, in homes, and at places of Jewish worship; there was an attempt to regulate that problem on the local level by requiring the German authorities to direct requests for workers to the local administration. "In Kraków a copy of the regulation that the Jews can be taken to work only through the Jewish community had been received; this means that other forms of forced labor are prohibited."[64] Similar information is included in a report by Ludwig Fischer (May 9, 1940), who wrote: "The matter of giving orders to *Judenräte* by the German offices was regulated. From then on, the Jewish forced laborers should be obtained only by means of the mayors or heads of cities."[65] Despite the regulation, some chiefs of local administration still supported arrests of Jews for forced labor. The *Kreishauptmann* of Puławy wrote in his report:

> On behalf of a strong performance of the employment of labor and the fastest possible accomplishment of the building projects, coercive measures were imposed and implemented, because despite the decree of the *Arbeitsamt* only ca. 40 % of the men called upon reported. The 40 men who were unwilling to work were brought to the forced labor camp Kazimierz. The length of stay of these indolent men in the forced labor camp is limited to 3–4 weeks. After that ensues service obligation to a new workplace to vacate the camp for other indolent elements. This measure proved to be successful throughout.[66]

It seems that other chiefs of local administration also used punitive measures freely. The *Kreishauptmann* of Jasło reported about initial failure of

---

63 "Grupa młodzieży w Tarnowie zgłasza się do robót rolnych," *Gazeta Żydowska*, September 6, 1940, 5.
64 Entries of March 9, 12, 15, and 16, 1940, in Ringelblum, *Kronika getta warszawskiego*, 104.
65 Raport of May 9, 1940, Dunin-Wąsowicz, *Raporty Ludwiga Fischera*, 196.
66 YVA, JM-814, Der Kreishauptmann des Kreises Puławy, Lagebericht für November 1940, Puławy, den 7. Dezember 1940, scan 1028.

mobilization of Jewish workers, and about punitive measures directed towards the whole Jewish Community in Jasło:

> After I had to make in recent weeks the observation that the local Jews had been challenging in their appearance and in particular the *Judenrat* destined to deal with compulsory labor of Jewish workers did not complete allocated quotas, I have arrested 150 Jews in a prompt police action on May 25, 1940. These Jews were housed 2 days without food in a larger room; on the third day they had to work for 12 hours. On the same day the following notice was published in Jasło:
>
> "The Jewish community in Jasło has failed to comply with my orders and shirked all of the work.
>
> In addition to earlier adopted measures, I order therefore that as of today, Saturday, May 25, 1940 no Jew, not a Jewess, and not a Jewish child may go out on the streets in Jasło. Also looking out from the windows is strictly prohibited.
>
> Against the Jews who do not adhere to this arrangement, the strongest measures will be adopted.
>
> Jasło, May 25, 1940, the County Chief in Jasło
>
> Signed: Dr. Losacker"
>
> Compliance with the house arrest was monitored strictly. The Jewish community has strictly adhered to the arrangement that triggered joyful echo in the Polish population. The Jews endeavor since that time to adhere strictly to the instructions.[67]

Allocation of forced labor through local governors was meant to regulate the manner of mobilization and the introduction of control over the distribution of labor. Naturally, governors passed their orders on to the *Judenräte*, which were required to obey them. Already at that time, it was clear that forced labor, in the form as introduced in the autumn of 1939, did not work and that the situation had to be changed. Economists who dealt with forced labor, however, clashed with the conservative attitudes of party ideologues that had a poor grasp of the economy. It is shown by the following information taken from the reports of Hans Frank:

> Head of the Department of Labor [Dr. Frauendorfer] made the request to allow the Jews to seek employment on their own. This request must

---

67 YVA-O.53/101, Der Kreishauptmann des Kreises Jasło, Jasło, den 2. Juni 1940, Lagebericht über die Zeit von Mitte Mai 1940 bis Ende Mai 1940, scans 74–76.

be firmly rejected, because it is contrary to the decree of the Governor General, which allows the employment of Jews only in the context of forced labor.[68]

However, in the summer of 1940, there was no other choice than to develop the employment of Jews and fix remuneration for their work. If the system of non-paid forced labor were continued, it would be necessary to ensure a budget that could cover the expenses associated with maintaining Jewish communities. This would not be accepted by anyone of importance in the General Government administration. As discussed earlier, the agreement of July 4, 1940 between Hans Frank, representing the civilian administration, and Friedrich-Wilhelm Krüger, representing the police and SS, undoubtedly Dr. Frauendorfer's suggestion, among others, had merit. Thanks to that agreement, German institutions were forced to pay wages to the Jews for forced labor and at the same time, employment opportunities of the Jews in the system of free hiring (*praca wolnonajemna*) were developed. Information about the change towards the use of forced labor of Jews was reflected in the release of information. Ludwik Landau, a renowned economist and observer of the reality of war, wrote, with surprise, in his diary about these modifications. He noted:

> In Lublin a new meeting of administrative leadership of the district was held. Upon examination of cases mentioned in *Warschauer Zeitung* . . . regarding the matter of the employment of Jews, besides forced labor for "running away from work and criminal Jewish elements," oddly enough, normal placement by labor offices for the jobs paid according to tariff rates and resulting in the compulsory insurance was discussed; even while speaking about forced labor, bonuses are mentioned for better performance: is there a desire to leave good farewell memories?[69]

THE COLLECTORS OF RECYCLED RAW MATERIALS

There was a special group of Jews, who were distinguished from all other groups—Jewish collectors of recycled materials. Emanuel Ringelblum wrote

---

68 Minutes of the meeting dedicated to the entirety of police matters related to the security situation in the General Government, Krakow, May 30, 1940, in Frank, *Okupacja i ruch oporu*, vol. 1, 208.
69 Entry of July 20, 1940, in Landau, *Kronika lat wojny i okupacji*, vol. 1, 595.

about them: "A larger number of Jews—say, a thousand—has received the green armband, which authorizes the collection of [scrap] metal. They shall be exempt from compulsory labor. They do not wear Jewish armbands."[70] This policy was completely opposite to the previous elimination of the Jews from the trade. In November 1940, the chef of the Lublin District wrote in his report: "The Jewish iron trade is off. All Jewish stores were taken over by the Aryans."[71] At the same time, the authorities employed thousands of Jews to collect scrap iron and metal. The quantities of scrap and metal were quite considerable. For example, the Kreishauptmann of Puławy reported in September 1940: "In the course of scrap and metal collection, 500,000 kg scrap and 20,000 kg of metal in total were shipped out of the County area. 300,000 kg of scrap and 1,000 kg of metal are currently awaiting shipment."[72]

Those Jews had an advantage because they could move freely throughout the General Government. In another place, Ringelblum wrote, "In Międzyrzec, workers employed to produce the bristles [przy szczecinie], are considered economically useful Jews. They can drive around the country."[73] The fact that they have authorization to move out of places designated for Jews seemed to be highly exceptional at the beginning of the occupation because of the importance of their work, but those Jews were able to move freely around the country also in 1942, when liquidation of the ghettos and deportations to death camps began. Their freedom of movement continued even in the first half of 1943, when most of the concentrated small ghettos were completely liquidated.[74]

The German economy, especially after the campaign in Western Europe, and to a greater extent after the start of the war with the USSR, was cut off from supplies of many key raw materials due to the blockade. Raw materials such as non-ferrous metals were very important for war production, so the Germans were looking for the possibility of obtaining non-ferrous metals from scrap taken from various old and useless items. However, the raw material collectors were searching not only for metal. They collected scrap iron, paper, rags, and many other raw materials. Collecting groups, consisting of a few people, in

---

70 Entry of April 13, 1940, in Ringelblum, *Kronika getta warszawskiego*, 124.
71 YVA-JM.814, Der Chef des Distriks Lublin im Generalgouvernement, Lagebericht für Oktober 1940, Lublin, den 6. November, 1940, scan 783.
72 Der Kreishauptmann des Kreises Puławy, Lagebericht für August 1940, den 7. September 1940, scan 184.
73 Ringelblum, *Kronika getta warszawskiego*, 125.
74 YVA, JM-1478. This document contains lists of names of some thousands Jewish 'rags-collectors' in different counties of the Lublin District.

general had horse-drawn carriages available, which roamed the area and actively searched for raw materials, or re-purchased them at low prices, delivering them later to special warehouses. Such depots were, for example, in Okęcie and in Warsaw, where workers from the Labor Battalion sorted scrap and loaded it on wagons.[75]

The Germans even created a special facility called the raw material office (*Rohstoffstelle*), whose task was to coordinate the collection of raw materials. The development of these facilities was very dynamic throughout the General Government; they coordinated the work of several thousand such collectors of raw materials. In one of the entries in his diary, Adam Czerniaków wrote:

> This morning, the community lieutenant from the *Rohstoffstelle* [raw material office] came by and paid workers 4,000 zł for 3 days of work. He also handed out 1,500 green armbands to functionaries working for them and to workers with the appropriate *Ausweis*.[76]

In 1942–1943, the raw materials were so sought after that the act of collection had become a lucrative activity. Special companies were founded for that purpose; one of the most famous among them was Victor Kremin's company. It operated mainly in the Lublin District and Galicia. The scale of the collection is reflected in some sources. According to a report in 1941, 47,369 tons of scrap iron were collected in the General Government.[77] According to information published in *Gazeta Żydowska*, an official Jewish newspaper published in Galicia, 3,000,000 kg of wastepaper were collected in 1942. About 3,500 people were employed there to collect wastepaper, rags, and other raw materials.[78] The following excerpt from Ludwig Fischer's report explains why the collection of rags was so important. Felt was produced by using special equipment for shredding rags and the new material was then used in cloth manufacture. Ludwig Fischer wrote about the difficulties of the textile industry:

> The situation of the textile industry has deteriorated further. Some plants—among them one of the largest in the district, an artificial silk factory in Chodaków—had to stop production due to lack of fuel. Furthermore, owing to the suspension of Jewish rag collectors, the influx of

---

75 Entry of April 26, 27, 1940, in Ringelblum, *Kronika getta warszawskiego*, 128.
76 Entry of April 6, 1940, in Fuks, *Adama Czerniakowa dziennik*, 103.
77 BA-MA, RW23-5, Geschichte der Rü In im GG (1. Juni 1940–31. Dezember 1941), 127.
78 "3 miliony makulatury z Okręgu Galicji," *Gazeta Żydowska*, August 30, 1942, 1.

rags, which in recent months was in average of 70,000 kg, fell to 14,000 kg. Everything is ready to replace the Jewish traders by Poles.[79]

WORKING CONDITIONS IN THE OUTPOSTS

Working conditions in the outposts depended largely upon the institution organizing the work and its relation to the Jews. On the other hand, conditions were generally poor. The workers were subjected to harassment by the police and SS troops that engaged them to work. They were often beaten. Somewhat better conditions prevailed in outposts that were managed by civil institutions. The Jewish workers were employed in these outposts usually from dawn to dusk. They should have received meals; however, it did not always happen, or time for dinner was insufficient. In some other outposts, workers did not receive meals at all, and the Jewish workers had to work throughout the day while hungry, or bring food with them. In one of the entries to his diary, Adam Czerniaków wrote:

> Workers who did not report for labor in the outposts are caught on the streets. They tried to escape because they weren't given food but 2.80 zł instead [as a substitute of food]. I applied to Kamlah [a German official] to feed [them]. For now, no avail. The Jewish masses facing the immensity of Jewish misery are quiet and composed. [...] It is said that there is no inflation, but it is expensive. No one considers the fact that a worker cannot live on 2.80 zł.[80]

The workers employed in the outposts performed all sorts of work depending upon the needs. For example: "To work outside the Jewish quarter [in Warsaw], the Jews are directed in columns, which everyday number about 2,000 people, to perform a variety of ancillary works for different agencies."[81] Such works could involve clearing rubble of buildings destroyed during a bombing, repairing buildings,[82] unloading and demolition work,[83] sorting metal scrap,[84] and so forth. Jews were also employed in the ZOM (Department

---

79 Dunin-Wąsowicz, *Raporty Ludwiga Fischera*, 239.
80 Entry of July 8, 1941, in Fuks, *Adama Czerniakowa dziennik*, 199.
81 Dunin-Wąsowicz, *Raporty Ludwiga Fischera*, 278.
82 Entries of May 2–9, 1940, in Ringelblum, *Kronika getta warszawskiego*, 138.
83 Dunin-Wąsowicz, *Raporty Ludwiga Fischera*, 457.
84 Entries of April 26 and 27, 1940, in Ringelblum, *Kronika getta warszawskiego*, 128.

of Municipal Cleaning Services), which at certain times needed up to 1,000 workers per day.[85]

The positive side of the work on the outposts, from the Jewish point of view, was the possibility of trading with other workmen or people outside the ghetto. This was especially important after the closure of the ghetto, when opportunities to import food into the ghetto were limited. Delivery of food to the ghetto was a key issue—decisive when considering survival in the ghetto.

At this point, an explanation is required as to why the Germans limited official food supplies and combated smuggling and illegal trade in food. This was related to the war economy and the role of the General Government in the economy of the Third Reich. Since the General Government had to exercise a subordinate role and to serve as a reservoir of raw materials, food, and labor for the Third Reich, it was necessary to obtain a surplus of food by reducing the consumption of the non-German population living under the General Government. Therefore, the official ration of food was possible only through the use of special vouchers (*karty żywnościowe*). The war economy of the Third Reich functioned in a system of allocating resources, where all agricultural production was to be under control and its transfer could take place only through authorized channels from producer to consumer. Therefore, black market trade interfered with the functioning of the official distribution of food and meant that large quantities of food circulated outside the official circuit, controlled by the German administration. This, in turn, lowered the amount of reserves that the economy of the General Government could donate to the Third Reich. The Jews were especially blamed for the existence of black market trade, although Jewish involvement in it was very limited in comparison to the Polish population that participated in the black market. The Polish urban population living in big cities particularly suffered from serious deficiencies of food. The Jews, in turn, in order to survive, had to use black market trade to make up for the food shortages.

During the growing isolation of the ghettos, the products brought into the ghetto by the workers employed in the outposts outside the ghetto served as a major source of food supply. Ringelblum wrote in his chronicle: "People working outside the ghetto are standing at every step [on the streets]. They bring full bags of bread and other products."[86] In another place, he wrote: "Some Jews penetrated the Aryan side thanks to the Polish outposts in the ghetto. Then, the

---

85 Entry of April 8, 1940, in Fuks, *Adama Czerniakowa dziennik*, 103.
86 Entries of November 29–December 2, 1940, in Ringelblum, *Kronika getta warszawskiego*, 209.

German factories in the ghetto employed Jews and Poles who worked alongside one another (Kurt Rohrich, KG Schultz, Brauer, and others); it was thought that Polish workers would take the place of Jewish workers later on. Jews provided with Aryan papers joined the group of Polish workers."[87] The incidence of employees smuggling from food establishments was also known to the German authorities. This information was featured in reports by Ludwig Fischer:

> The Polish peasants and traders continued to sell large quantities of bread and other foods to Jews working outside the ghetto. Those Jews were bringing enormous quantities of food with them into the Jewish quarter and selling it there at astronomical prices.[88]

However, the German authorities tried their best to hamper business, and, therefore, undertook additional measures to restrict trade, increase control, and reduce workers' contacts with the local population centres. In one of the subsequent reports, Fischer stated:

> Jewish columns that have been most actively engaged in black market trade, can now cross the border of the Jewish residential district only through two special gateways where they are subjected to strict control. Outside the Jewish quarter, an operating column can move only under the supervision the Wehrmacht and SS. Probably even now, goods are smuggled by secret ways into the Jewish quarter, but black market trade, compared to the previous period, is insignificant. We can therefore conclude that by creating the Jewish residential district significant progress was achieved in combating trafficking.[89]

TRANSFER TO GHETTOS

One of the most important processes, hardly noticed by the researchers, was the transfer to the Jewish quarters. As a result, one of the most dramatic practices of looting of Jewish property took place. Already before the establishment of the ghettos, most Jews lost their businesses. In most cases, it was purely ideological and not an economically motivated decision. For example,

---

87 Emanuel Ringelblum, *Stosunki polsko-żydowskie w czasie drugiej wojny światowej: Uwagi i spostrzeżenia*, ed. Artur Eisenbach (Warsaw: Czytelnik, 1988), 78–79.
88 Dunin-Wąsowicz, *Raporty Ludwiga Fischera*, 240.
89 Ibid., 254.

the *Stadtkommissar* of Ostrowiec wrote in his report: "Jewish businesses that were possible to transfer to trustees (*brauchbar*) have received a trustee or shall still get a one. The purpose is to bind the Jewish capital and expand a decent business."[90] The German authorities were very interested in taking over the Jewish apartments, especially in the city and town centers. According to the report by *Kreishauptmann* of Opatów:

> For the near future, 1,000 people are announced for resettlement in the *Kreis*. They will be accommodated in several villages. To remedy the housing shortage in the main town and to secure the housing needs of employees of the Reich and the administration, conveniently located, spacious but partly destroyed houses with 1 or 2 rooms will be quickly repaired. The *Kreissparkasse* (County Savings Bank) will cover the costs. In contrast to that, the construction of new homes starts only reluctantly. In communities affected by war damage the reconstruction of damaged houses achieved a nice progress. In the district's main town Opatów, the *Kreishauptmann* initiated a systematic de-judification [*Entjudung*] and arranged in preparation that the Jews have to leave the spacious market square apartments. In this context, the ghetto will be established as convenient as possible. It is questionable if the simultaneously prescribed decrease of the number of Jews of about 2,500 can be effected by December 1 [1940] because a migration to other districts is not feasible.[91]

The *Stadthauptmann* of Częstochowa also reported extensively on the problems of housing and eviction of Jews from their apartments:

> It may be connected to the fact that there are more German troops deployed in the General Government and hence in the town of Tschenstochau (Częstochowa), that the present quarters are insufficient and I had to arrange for new quarters in a greater extent. This initiative occurred not without frictions. Jewish houses that are suited for military quarters are not existent anymore, so that I had to revert to Poles as well. I did this in the following manner: I moved scattered Jews from their houses, confiscated their furniture and allocated the houses with the furniture to those

---

90 YVA-JM.814, Stadtkommissar der Stadt Ostrowiec an den Herrn Kreishauptmann in Opatów, Lagebericht für August 1940, Ostrowiec, den 5. September 1940, scan 309.
91 YVA, JM-814, Der Kreishauptmann des Kreises Opatów, District Radom, Lagebericht für August 1940, Opatów, den 7. September 1940, scans 306–7.

> Polish families that were evacuated from a cohesive block of houses. Since the accommodation of the troops that are now coming to Tschenstochau is for long-term, my position is that the troops must have decent winter quarters. I also intend to arrange for decent permanent living quarters for those German civilian officers and personnel that partly still live in very poor housing.⁹²

During the formation of ghettos and the move into them, many families who found themselves outside the designated boundaries of the Jewish neighbourhoods, lost their entire life's possessions, including property that had accumulated over generations. During the transfer into the ghetto in Kraków, furniture was primarily sold since when it was being thrown out of their apartments, owners could not take furniture with them, especially given the very short time left at their disposal and the scarcity of new apartments. Many, mostly from the intelligentsia and without the possibility of work, were forced to sell their belongings to obtain necessary monetary resources for basic living.⁹³ Transfer to the ghetto was connected with losing a large part, if not a complete loss, of property that caused a sudden and almost total impoverishment of displaced Jews. .⁹⁴ The consequences of this act were in many cases immediate, but sometimes they became apparent later. The rapid transfer of refugees made them destitute. This was true, for example, in the case of the evacuation of Jews from the western counties of the Warsaw District to the Warsaw Ghetto.⁹⁵ In other cities rapid impoverishment ensued as well.

> The Jewish population of Kraków rapidly was becoming more and more impoverished. This process was particularly intensified among the pensioners, the disabled, as well as among unemployed civil servants, and especially among the growing numbers of displaced.⁹⁶

---

92 YVA, JM-814, Tschenstochau, Bericht für den Monat August 1940, September 14, 1940, scans 338–39.
93 Aleksander Biberstein, *Zagłada Żydów w Krakowie* (Krakow: Wydawnictwo Literackie, 1985), 31.
94 Barbara Engelking and Jacek Leociak, *Getto warszawskie: Przewodnik po nieistniejącym mieście* (Warsaw: Wydawnictwo IFiS PAN, 2001), 453.
95 *To Live with Honor and Die with Honor: Selected Documents from the Warsaw Ghetto Underground Archives "O.S." (Oneg Shabbath)*, ed. Joseph Kermish (Jerusalem: Yad Vashem, 1986), 537.
96 Biberstein, *Zagłada Żydów w Krakowie*, 32.

The process of impoverishment of a well-established Jewish merchant, who was taken to a forced labor camp, became sick, and had his life in danger, all due to a series of anti-Jewish measures, is illustrated by the following fragment of a report:

> At the request of Israel Grünwald addressed by Dr. Bieberstein, I visited him in the epidemic hospital and stated: Grünwald, Israel, born January 29, 189[?], Son of Isaac and Sarah b. Neugröschl, permanent residence in Gorlice, a month ago had been assigned to the camp in Płaszów, the father of two children—according to his claims, he is a merchant and ran a haberdashery shop until May [1942], which store was sequestrated by the authorities, together with the entire inventory and revenues from this shop are made on a blocked account, so that his wife and children are in complete poverty and are not able to come to his aid material. He is entirely without funds, without any footwear (no. 43), starving, because the hospital board is insufficient. Dr. Bieberstein gained for him free lunches in *Beit Lechem*, but he didn't receive them because no one brought them to him. He asked to intervene in that matter, to obtain for him the bread and shoes.
>
> On my request, director Mrs. Feuerstein sent ward of the Institute for Orphans, with whom I went to *Beit Lechem* and there I have learned that they promised to give meals only two days a week, Mondays and Thursdays. I pledged to send lunches for the petitioner. At my request, they gave him a free dinner today.[97]

Transfer to the ghetto had many consequences. Firstly, it resulted in the deterioration of the displaced Jews' situation and brought about the creation of the poorest sectors of society. Since then, people became dependent on their work, selling the rest of their belongings, until finally they were dependent on the support of Jewish welfare institutions, if available. As a rule, during the planning process for the ghettos, the worst neighbourhoods were chosen. They were mostly in areas with poor infrastructure and buildings in the worst condition. Further degeneration took place owing to the concentration of large numbers of Jews into a small congested area. According to a report sent to the government of the General Government: "Most of the Jews are settled on the outskirts. The rental prices got into complete disarray. The Jews pay

---

97 YVA-JM.1581, ŻSS, Notatka, Kraków, August 16, 1942, scan 230.

extraordinary high rental prices."[98] This process of crowding the Jewish population was also a process of depriving them of property and freeing up Jewish homes for other purposes. The unoccupied apartments and houses were earmarked for offices and housing for German officials, German settlers, Poles expelled from other districts, and refugees. Empty homes sometimes became the target of looting. Many Jewish residences were passed on to the Board of Trustees (*Zarząd Powierniczy*).

For example, in Zamość, Jews were transferred to the so-called Nowa Osada, which was described by one witness in the following words:

> The Nowa Osada was [. . .] composed mostly of small, wooden houses. At the time of transfer, of course, better houses were occupied by the Polish population. For us, there were the worst slums and huts left by the poor Jews, many thousands of whom left Zamość in 1939, along with the Soviet troops. [. . .]; the need to locate people could not be avoided—wherever—in factory premises, shops and halls. There were no waterworks or sewers; people used public wells. Then, as part of the Polish population moved from Nowa Osada to Zamość, flats vacated by Jews (*mieszkania pożydowskie*), were used and some relief was felt. The housing situation deteriorated significantly again, however, after the arrival of the first transports of Jews from abroad.[99]

Losses of property during the transfer of Jews to ghettos were huge. In terms of material value, this stage was undoubtedly one of the most painful for the Jews and caused the sudden impoverishment of the population. For example, during the evacuation of Jews from the western counties of the Warsaw District, the whole towns became *judenrein*. This meant not only that property belonging to the Jewish communities was in the hands of non-Jews, but also that private property was taken away from individual Jews. This hapened in concerned shops and workshops that had not yet been aryanized, as well as private homes with all their possessions. During the transfer to ghettos, there was virtually no way for the Jews to convert their possessions into capital. The situation forced upon the Jews caused the sudden decline in the market value both of real estate as well as movable property, and so even in cases of the sale of property, the Jews were not able to get a fair price for the offered items or for their real estate.

---

98 YVA, JM-814, Abt. Innere Verwaltung, Auszug aus den Lageberichten der Kreis- und Stadthauptleute für August 1940, Krakau, den 30. September 1940, scan 349.
99 YVA-O.33/322, testimony of Mieczysław Garfinkiel, 11–12.

Transfer to the ghettos was made in a hurry, usually within a few days.[100] In such a short time, there were transport difficulties caused not only by the great demand for moving belongings, but also increased haulage prices. In the new places of residence, there was such crowding that Jews could take only the most basic everyday items with them when they were transferred. Previously introduced rules on bank account ownership and market diffuclties during the occupation led to substantial losses of cash resources. Therefore, during the transfer to ghettos, the Jews were able to bring a maximum of 5–10% value of their pre-war resources of cash and valuables. In most cases, less than 5% seems more correct. When the Jews moved into the ghetto, what could serve as a basis for their maintenance were the remnants of their resources and their labor.

Jews whose apartments were already in the ghettos were in a much better situation; at least temporarily, they managed to keep their property. It allowed them a more prosperous life because they could sell off their property for a longer period, and thus remain at a better standard of living. They did not undergo sudden impoverishment and had a longer time to adapt to the new conditions. Thanks to this, they were in better shape both physically and mentally during the critical period of deportation to the camps and escape from the ghetto to the Aryan side.

An extremely important factor in the early days of the ghettos was their isolation from the external environment. This was particularly evident in the Warsaw Ghetto. As a rule, smaller ghettos were less isolated from their surroundings. Some provincial ghettos remained "open" up to the end of their existence. In the case of the ghetto in Zamość, in spite of its isolation, going out of the ghetto was not a problem. In the words of a witness:

> At first [in May 1941], there were no restrictions regarding the movement of Jews in Zamość, but soon such a ban was issued. This prohibition wore a rather symbolic character, since many Jews worked in Zamość or in various outposts outside the city and all those, in accordance with an agreement concluded by us with the German authorities, had the right to leave Nowa Osada and enjoy free movement in Zamość on the basis of a pass issued by the Jewish council.[101]

---

100 For example, in Kielce Mayor's Regulation was published on March 31, 1941, while the completion date of transfer to the ghetto was set on April 5, 1941. See Regulation of Mayor of Kielce Drechsel on the creation of the ghetto, Kielce, March 31, 1941, in Eisenbach and Rutkowski, *Ekstermnacja Żydów*, 117.

101 YVA-O.33/322, testimony of Mieczysław Garfinkiel, 13.

And the witness continued:

> The fact that the Jewish quarter until the last minute was not closed can be explained only by efforts of the Jewish council, supported by regular donations and payments, which permitted a large number of Jewish laborers, who had to constantly leave the [Jewish] quarter, to work outside the quarter.[102]

These two factors—transfer to ghettos and isolation—had a major impact on the economic conditions of the Jews. They not only robbed the Jews of most movable and immovable property, but they also isolated them from the external environment in economic terms, thereby creating a kind of economic enclave in the economic system of the General Government. This produced a new type of economic system in isolated ghettos. Creating economic enclaves resulted in the reduced quality of life of the Jews in their surroundings and allowed the increased exploitation of both human and material resources. The flow of raw materials and goods across those borders gave additional benefits to intermediaries and created a hedge against prices,[103] resulting in inflated payments for raw materials and products, including food from and outside the ghetto, while at the same time, making all products and raw materials from the ghetto became cheaper.[104]

The labor force in the ghettos was less expensive because of high unemployment. The products of the ghetto, in order to remain competitive, also had to be cheaper than in the outside market, even after deducting the cost of delivery through the walls of the ghetto. The same principle also applied to the trade and services in the ghetto. Goods sold in the ghetto, as well as services, needed to be very cheap to allow a profit chain for intermediaries—yet still remain cheaper than the product on the outside.

ACQUIRING THE MEANS OF SUBSISTENCE IN THE EARLY DAYS OF THE GHETTO

Earning a living in the ghetto can be divided into several key areas. In the early days of the ghetto, the livelihood of many Jews was from trade and services. The reason for this was, among other things, the fact that development of

---

102 Ibid., 18.
103 Engelking, Barbara and Jacek Leociak, *Getto warszawskie*, 472.
104 Ibid., 375.

production on a large scale in the new economic environment required time and not merely because of the lack of appropriate conditions and equipment. It was also an arduous procedure because it required complex processes associated with creating an entire network of links between markets and producers, solving a number of problems associated with the acquisition of raw materials, procuring adequate equipment, labor, the creation of distribution networks, and so forth. No less important was obtaining the relevant licenses and the establishment of appropriate contacts to enable the flow of cash or barter exchange.

All these circumstances meant that trade had become the easiest and fastest way to earn a living. Together with the relatively poor isolation of ghettos from the general public or the existence of places for the exchange of goods with the outside populace, the ghetto became a supplier of a multitude of local and external market goods.[105] It is worthwhile to pay attention to the fact that under the conditions of the occupation, the production of some consumer goods actually ceased entirely or was very limited.[106] This situation created a huge market for used items. One could virtually sell and buy everything. Much of this involved footwear and clothing, including underwear. Residents of the ghettos sold almost everything in bulk; however, it was at the expense of reducing their own resources, for example, leaving only one set of clothes for themselves, while selling all the rest. Many goods from the ghetto reached the external market. Trade in used goods took place during the entire period of the ghetto existence. The increased supply of certain goods was also associated, in a tragic way, with the fate of Jews in the ghettos. For instance, during the period of increased mortality, the remaining items of the dead appeared on the market. Arrival of Jews from abroad to transit ghettos in the Lublin District was reflected in the increased supply of rare and luxury goods. Finally, during the partial liquidation of the ghettos, once again, a variety of goods appeared on the market.

With the phenomenon of trafficking in closed ghettos—that is, those ghettos where the population was locked inside and not able to freely leave it—additional trade related economic activities developed, namely, smuggling of goods, also known as *szmugiel* in Polish (from Germ. *Schmuggel*). Henryk Bryskier describes this new type of economic activity in the following words:

> There is a new industry—smuggling. Individuals deprived of sources of income on the Polish side, decided to go by trams through the ghetto

---

105 Engelking, Leociak, *Getto warszawskie*, 454, 378.
106 Dunin-Wąsowicz, *Raporty Ludwiga Fischera*, 527, 596.

and, with risk, dropped off food packages at agreed points where their Jewish partners in smuggling expected them. This resulted in fairly substantial profits, given the huge price differences. In addition to these rather numerous small smugglers, entire organizations with vast sums and balances were created.[107]

Labor was also an important means of obtaining funds to survive. Jews living in ghettos worked inside or outside the ghetto. Groups of Jews were employed in various German institutions, so-called *placówki* (outposts, labor detachments),[108] or labor camps. Inside the ghetto, Jews were given jobs by *Judenräte*, by the Jewish police, and by other institutions. Jews also worked in the private sector, mainly in the crafts. In addition, Jews were obligated to perform forced labor, mainly in labor camps and German institutions. Despite the fact that Jews worked in labor camps as well as outside the ghetto, the effect of this, in many cases, was negative for their families who remained in the ghetto and for the ghetto economy in general. This was mainly because working in labor camps and some external labor detachments did not bring any payment or at best resulted in a very low salary.[109] Taking labor forces from the ghettos was a drain of productive elements from the ghetto society, which caused the deterioration of the overall balance of productivity in the ghettos.

During the transfer of Jews to ghettos and their isolation, a sudden shift in job opportunities took place. Throughout this period, extremely high unemployment emerged in the ghettos, along with a surplus of specialists in certain fields.[110] However, over time, the Jews adjusted to life in the ghettos. One of the witnesses of those events describes his feelings in this manner:

> We all thought that we were surrounded by a Chinese wall; that we were lost; that we would die of hunger. Indeed, many people perished and [...] even more died at this time. This is due to the prevailing conditions: an epidemic of typhus, hunger, and overpopulation. However, to date, most of the Jews adapted to these conditions.[111]

---

107 Henryk Bryskier, *Żydzi pod swastyką, czyli getto w Warszawie w XX wieku* (Warsaw: Aspra, 2006), 49.
108 Engelking and Leociak, *Getto warszawskie*, 154, 396–97.
109 Ibid., 154.
110 Ibid., 381, 463.
111 Kermish, *To Live with Honor*, 535–36.

ADAPTING TO ECONOMIC CONDITIONS IN THE GHETTOS

The process of rapid adaptation of Jews to the conditions in the ghetto took place thanks to the extraordinary ingenuity and initiative of the Jews. In this process, not only institutions of the *Judenräte* were involved, but also, and perhaps above all, were involved Jewish entrepreneurs. Adjusting to new conditions included an intensive search for raw materials, machines, and tools, analysis of market needs, or initiating new demand by offering various goods and services.

In most of the ghettos, there was not a sufficiently large internal market that could provide a self-sufficient economy. In the case of the Warsaw Ghetto, when it was closed up, there were approximately 350,000 Jews inside and there was a relatively large internal market. Moreover, such a large community required a complex and extensive administration. It should be noted that during the Nazi occupation, the *Judenrat* was much more complicated than the institutions of Jewish communities before the war, because the *Judenrat* had to concentrate in its hands all the administrative functions of the pre-war Jewish communities, and, in addition, to act as municipal offices and police, as well as perform other administrative functions that, before the war, were filled by government offices. Therefore, the *Judenrat* was also one of the biggest employers of Jews. For example, in December 1940, in the Częstochowa Ghetto, numbering at its peak about 42,000 people, 676 of them were employed by the *Judenrat*. In this period, the number of employees represented an escalating trend.[112] However, the ghettos had to not only maintain themselves, but also provide manpower and to make available funds in order to pay for various fees, taxes, contributions,[113] and bribes.[114] For their survival, the ghettos had to abandon an autarchic economic system and to begin export goods, services, and labor in order to obtain food, raw materials, energy, and so forth. Therefore, even in the Warsaw Ghetto, the autarchic economy could no longer exist. In small ghettos isolation from the external area was practically impossible.

---

112 YVA-O.6/348, Tab. no. 1.
113 YVA-O.33/322, testimony of Mieczysław Garfinkiel, 15.
114 According to the witness, "the biggest financial problem of the [Jewish] Council was the need to invent how to cover the increasing costs associated with bribery, gifts, and other expenses for the various dignitaries and higher and lesser Gestapo officers, the German police, gendarmes, and officials. As it turned out, it was the only way, the only platform of understanding, on which could be arranged relations, the only way to acquire relative peace." See YVA-O.33/322, testimony of Mieczysław Garfinkiel, 16.

The transition from trade to production took place in all the ghettos. This process was the easiest in small provincial ghettos, where the majority of Jewish artisans, even in the interwar period and in the first months of the occupation, were working as craftsmen for the non-Jewish population. Jews engaged in trade were in a much more difficult situation because in the Aryanization process they had lost many stores and stock of goods and cash. Some Jews dealing in trade switched to illicit trade, mainly on a relatively small scale. Others began to sell different goods on the streets or started to work as peddlers. Developing trade in the ghetto environment depended on the possibility of finding new customers as well as establishing contacts with regular commercial clients or individual customers. Since there was a very limited supply of consumer goods, given the constant food rationing and control of other products that were difficult to obtain, the black market grew rapidly.[115]

Most of the Jews previously dealing in trade had to switch to services, crafts, or production for the non-Jewish market. This production consisted of different fields, depending on local needs. In small provincial ghettos most traditional areas of service and craftsmanship, such as shoemaking, tailoring services, saddler, blacksmithing, and repair of tools were needed. In the cities, the list of areas in which there was a need had greatly expanded and included more technologically related fields. The urban market was more receptive because of the higher concentration of population and a greater range of requirements. In addition, urban Jews could sell not only to the local residents, but also to the rural population from the surrounding area, German officials, and German companies.

DEVELOPMENT OF WORKSHOPS

In large ghettos, the development of productive activity was associated with the demand for laborers and with orders from German officers and German institutions for services provided by artisans. This development was uneven. In different places, workshops were created for residents of the ghettos to provide work. Under the existing provisions of the General Government, any new businesses had to be approved by the authorities and be registered in the commercial register. In order to obtain the permit, the person assuming charge of the company would have to demonstrate his Aryan origin, thereby making it impossible for Jews to set up new businesses or to transform existing ones, since all

---

115 BA-MA, RW23-8, Tabelle über den Verhältnissen von amtlichen Preisen uns Scheichhandelspreisen nach dem Stande vom Marz 1941, 96.

companies had to be registered.[116] In addition, provisions concerning the operation of bank accounts also prevented Jews from making financial transactions that were necessary for doing business. Due to that situation, at the beginning of the occupation, the establishment of workshops and production enterprises were arranged by the economic departments of the *Judenräte*. Such workshops were created independently in different localities. Adam Czerniaków wrote in his diary about attempts to open a locksmith shop, a tailor shop, and a corsetry workshop in Warsaw in mid-December 1939.[117] In early January 1940, the first decisions on the production profile of workshops in Warsaw were taken.[118] In Warsaw, besides the *Judenrat*, the workshops were established by the ORT, where in the middle of 1940, 120 workers were employed. The organization intended to open professional courses and attempted to receive the authorization during the school year of 1939 and 1940. However, such authorization, came only in August 1940. ORT planned therefore to open professional courses for artisans and courses preparing for work in agriculture in Warsaw and other towns of the General Government.[119] Organization of professional courses for Jews continued to develop also in 1941. There were some courses preparing to work in agriculture,[120] but most of the courses concerned manufacturing and industrial production.[121]

Economic initiatives came from a variety of factors which influenced the operation of such workshops. In some cities, the establishment of a workshop was initiated by the representatives of the *Judenrat* and entrepreneurs. Although initiatives to set up a framework to permit use of existing economic potential in the ghettos took different organizational form, their main goal was quite similar. We can show it using some examples of small ghettos like Bochnia or Zamość and a bigger ghetto of Częstochowa. For example, in Zamość, a workshop was initiated by the *Judenrat* in order to cope with the continuing orders for the execution of various works for German functionaries and institutions.[122] However, an additional goal of the organizers of the workshop in Zamość was to keep buildings belonging to the Jewish community in Jewish hands and to

---

116 *Wiadomości Gospodarcze*, January 31, 1940, in Eisenbach and Rutkowski, *Eksterminacja Żydów*, 159.
117 Entry of December 15, 1939 in Fuks, *Adama Czerniakowa dziennik*, 71.
118 According to the entry of January 8, 1940, they intended to produce metal beds. In Fuks, *Adama Czerniakowa dziennik*, 76.
119 "Z działalności T-wa 'ORT,'" *Gazeta Żydowska*, October 24, 1940, 3.
120 YVA-JM.1501, scans 620–21.
121 *Jüdische Handwerker-Ausbildungskurse für Erwachsene und Jugendliche*. YVA-JM.1501, scans 610–19.
122 Adam Kopciowski, *Zagłada Żydów w Zamościu* (Lublin: Wyd. UMCS, 2005).

protect them from damage. The chairman of the *Judenrat* in Zamość, Mieczysław Garfinkiel,[123] put it this way:

> Wondering before the exodus [to the area designated for the ghetto] over the fate of synagogues and other Jewish public edifices, located in Zamość, which would inevitably be doomed to annihilation and destruction after our departure, I had an idea. I made an agreement with Zygmunt Zipser,[124] a local industrialist (as I later realized, contrary to appearances, he helped during the occupation of Poles and Jews); and in all the synagogues and other buildings in the public domain of the Jews, he founded, with the help of the *Judenrat*, carpentry and furniture workshops. Thanks to that, these buildings were saved from burning and destruction, which was the fate [of Jewish public buildings] in almost all Polish cities, and among others in Warsaw and Lublin.[125]

The *Judenrat* in Bochnia set up urban workshops (Germ. *Städtische Werkstätten*; Pol. *warsztaty miejskie*) in order to provide new jobs for the Jews and to encourage production.[126] Development of workshops in the ghettos was a type of compensation for the earlier prohibitions on Jewish businesses outside the ghettos and forced Aryanization. These were precisely workshops, in which establishments and functioning experts in different fields of economy took part and that led to the launch of production under the aegis of the *Judenrat*. All formalities relating to the creation of those enterprises and financial transactions with companies outside of the ghetto were organized with the assistance or mediation of the *Judenrat*. Without this, no financial transactions would have been possible due to restrictions on Jewish bank accounts.

Particularly important was the creation of workshops after the transfer and closure of the ghettos. In the case of the Kraków ghetto, Jews were transferred to the Podgórze District, which was a small area surrounded by walls and deprived

---

123 Despite the fact that *Judenräte* and Jewish Self-Assistance (ŻSS) were two separate organizations and the ŻSS had to be financially and organizationally independent, the head of Zamość *Judenrat* was also the head of ŻSS, registered as Mendel Garfinkiel. The official name of the ŻSS in Zamość was Jewish Self-Assitance, Jewish Assistance Committee Zamość (in Polish, *Żydowska Samopomoc Społeczna, Żydowski Komitet Opiekuńczy Powiatowy w Zamościu*, or, in German, *Jüdische Soziale Selbsthilfe, Jüdisches Hilfskomitee Kreis Zamość*). A letter from ŻSS Kraków to Mendel Garfinkiel, October 29, 1940. YVA-JM.1551, scan 479.
124 The context shows that this was a person of German descent.
125 YVA-O.33/322, testimony of Mieczysław Garfinkiel, 12.
126 "Z miast i miasteczek: Bochnia," *Gazeta Żydowska*, July 7, 1941, 2.

of not only facilities, but also having only a small internal market and a negligible reserve of goods and raw materials. After the expulsions in June 1941, Jewish shops, workshops and enterprises beyond the walls were closed down. Therefore:

> On the initiative of the Association of Jewish Artisans in Kraków, communities (*Gemeinschaften*) of tailors, furriers, cobblers, and other skilled workers, were established, which since then began to operate in workshops, located in a former chocolate factory "Optima" on Węgierska Street, which [also] had great facilities at Krakusa Street and premises on Targowa Street. These communities had their representation at Słowacki Avenue 26, called *Zentrale für Handwerks-Lieferungen*, which took orders from the Germans and Poles. Until then, most Jews left the ghetto every day in order to work in German factories that were housed in barracks close to those factories. Individual passes were no longer issued. Contact with the city and thus the ability to purchase food, became extremely difficult.[127]

The creation of workshops by communities of craftsmen was contingent on their members contributing their machines and work to those communities. On the other hand, the Housing Committee of the Jewish Community allocated appropriate accommodations to the Association of Craftsmen—as mentioned, the building of a former chocolate factory "Optima" at Krakusa Street and two other facilities. Because it was believed that working in the craftsmen's association could prevent the deportation from Kraków, many, not only craftsmen, but also many white-collar workers, tried to get a job there. According to statistics of employment, in the ghetto the number of office workers decreased in favor of craftsmen.[128]

DEVELOPMENT OF PRODUCTIVE ACTIVITIES

In large ghettos, the development of productive activity was associated with the demand for laborers and orders from German functionaries and German institutions for services to be provided by artisans.[129] This development was irregular. The workshops were created in order to provide employment for residents of the

---

127 Katarzyna Zimmerer, *Zamordowany świat: Losy Żydów w Krakowie, 1939–1945* (Krakow, Wydawnictwo Literackie, 2004), 126.
128 Biberstein, *Zagłada Żydów w Krakowie*, 61–62.
129 Betr Notiz, Produktivisierung der Juden in den Grossstadten des Generalgouvernements. YVA-JM.1588, scan 42.

ghettos depending on their various abilities, so that the type of workshops set up was different from place to place. Economic initiatives came from a variety of sources, which influenced the operation of such workshops. In some cities, the establishment of a workshop was initiated by representatives of the *Judenrat* and entrepreneurs. For example, in Zamość, the workshops were introduced by the *Judenrat* to cope with the continuing orders for the implementation of various works for officers and German institutions.[130] The *Judenrat* in Bochnia established workshops[131] to provide new jobs for the Jews and develop production.

Expansion of workshops in the ghettos was a kind of compensation for the earlier prohibitions on Jewish businesses out of their ghettos and forced Aryanization. It was precisely the establishment of workshops, supervised with expert help, that led to the launch of production under the aegis of the *Judenrat*. All formalities relating to the creation of enterprises and financial transactions with companies outside of the ghetto were organized with the assistance or mediation of the *Judenrat*. Without this, any financial transactions would not be possible, or at least, would be very difficult due to restrictions on the conduct of Jewish bank accounts.

PRIVATE INITIATIVE

Engineer Bryskier stated that the "[...] private initiative, therefore, gave more scope for expansion of profit, than the relatively narrow section of official actions."[132] By his account, all the activities of an official character were always late. However, one cannot entirely agree with this view, since at least at early stage of development, workshops or crafts associations sponsored by official factors were very important simply because they allowed the establishment of official Jewish business in the ghettos, at a time when it was otherwise impossible to register enterprises. Only in the wake of this came the development of economic activity in the ghettos and the creation of companies of various kinds, including private Jewish companies.

An example of private initiative was described by Emanuel Ringelblum:

> One of the most characteristic phenomena in the ghetto is establishment in Warsaw of about 50 looms. [The founders] are usually from Łódź.

---

130 Kopciowski, *Zagłada Żydów w Zamościu.*
131 Sandkühler, *"Endlösung" in Galizien: Der Judenmord in Ostpolen und die Rettungsinitiativen von Bertold Beitz, 1941–1944* (Bonn: Dietz, 1996), 214.
132 Jerzy Winkler, "Getto walczy z niewolą gospodarczą," *BŻIH* 35 (1960): 67–68.

They produce their products, understandably illegally: various *cajgi* [textiles], quilts, et cetera. It is a testimony of remarkable adaptation to the conditions. Obtaining the yarn is not an easy thing.[133]

Testimony of the development of entrepreneurship can be seen by the amount of fees paid for permits in order to conduct business in Częstochowa. For example, in 1940 the following quantities of industrial-tax cards were purchased: 1,101 in the field of trade, 866 in crafts, and 265 in industry.[134]

Outside the ghetto, Jewish businesses that had undergone a process of Aryanization also operated. In some cases, it was a pure formality and non-Jews, having no knowledge or experience in leading companies, were engaged in contacts with other institutions and agencies. Their task was limited primarily to signing documents while company executives and the entire production were still in Jewish hands. In such cases, the Jews could be officially hired as employees of the company. These companies generally were located outside the ghettos, but provided employment for the inhabitants of the ghettos.

A key factor in enabling the competitiveness of production in the ghettos was using all available resources. Almost every superfluous thing in the ghetto could be used to produce something else. The Jews gathered rags, remnants of wool, glass, scrap metal, ferrous metals, paper, and other waste. Thanks to the ingenuity of Jewish businesses, many of these recycled materials could be used for further production. For example, grass was used to manufacture mattresses; old watches, after dismantling, served as a source for spare parts to repair other watches;[135] leather and fur remnants were used to fabricate gloves. Many products in the ghetto were created thanks to the ingenuity of specialists from various fields of technology: engineers, chemists, or craftsmen. For instance, Alexander Donat, a trained chemist, was producing briquettes from coal dust and sulfur candles, whichhad been used in the ghetto for disinfection.[136]

> There was not a single profession, in which a Jewish craftsman could not profit from existing opportunities. In the second half of 1941, the demand for different goods increased, especially for iron beds, so metal workers had lot of work. The main supplier was the "Balbinder" company (Twarda Street 8). Running out of new raw materials, the workers used all kinds of

---

133 Ringelblum, *Kronika getta warszawskiego*, 339.
134 YVA-O.6/348, drawing no. 29.
135 Winkler, "Getto walczy z niewolą gospodarczą," 64.
136 Aleksander Donat, *The Holocaust Kingdom: A Memoir* (New York: Talman Co, 1978), 37.

old iron pipes. Therefore, at that time an upsurge in prices in the market for pipes, particularly gas pipes, was reported.[137]

In the ghettos the production of prohibited goods should be distinguished from illegal manufacturing. Illegal production, also referred to as the "gray economic zone,"[138] was the production of items in factories or workshops that were not registered in the *Judenrat* as establishments engaged in business activities. Owners of such facilities or those working from home did not pay taxes and were not registered as employed. The end of the underground economy in the Warsaw Ghetto was marked by the great deportation action in 1942. After this period, there were only shops realizing military orders.[139]

Yet another advantage of the ghetto was the fact that Jewish enclaves and zones could be proclaimed "threatened with typhoid fever," which resulted in reducing the direct control of the German authorities.[140] Therefore, production of illicit goods[141] developed in the ghettos that were tightly controlled by the occupation authorities associated with the production of allocated or prohibited products. Among the manufacturing and services produced were: meat processing,[142] leather tanning, milling of grain,[143] bread bakeries, production of soap,[144] tire retreading, and the like. In such cases, the non-Jewish partners from outside the ghettos, who gained huge profits from the illegal production, were very interested in providing raw materials and distributing the finished products.

In general, it is difficult to estimate the volume of production and exports from the ghettos, because of the lack of statistical data and large-scale illegal production and marketing. Production was home-based, on a high volume, consumed low energy, and used cheap raw materials. For example, the manual production of sweaters, gloves, and socks was very popular. One witness described the production of gowns from sheets, which occupied his entire

---

137 Winkler, "Getto walczy z niewolą gospodarczą," 84.
138 Engelking and Leociak, *Getto warszawskie*, 395.
139 Ibid., 396.
140 YVA-O.33/322, testimony of Mieczysław Garfinkiel, 19.
141 Engelking and Leociak, *Getto warszawskie*, 383.
142 "Jewish butchers in the ritual slaughter house located in a building opposite the tannery of the Altman Family ran great risk of slaughter calves purchased in the country. At slaughter of bigger cattle they benefit from barns of their neighbors—Poles." Ryszard Adamczyk, *Izbicy dni powszednie—wojna i okupacja: Pamiętnik pisany po latach* (Lublin: Norbertinum, 2007), 73.
143 Ita Diamant, *Moja cząstka życia* (Warszawa: Twój Styl, 2001), 82.
144 The decree of the head of the Warsaw District on of the seizure of fatty materials and soap, dated November 18, 1939, in Święcicki and Zadrowski, *Zbiór rozporządzeń władz niemieckich*, 181–83.

family consisting of several people.[145] Old linen was bought, dyed, cut, and sewn at home. The facilitator who bought the old sheets also sold the finished products. Such home-production remained outside official statistics and can hardly be estimated.

The profitability of Jewish businesses and the cottage industry in the ghettos was quite low. Production required long work hours under difficult societal conditions in order to earn only a meager living. In some cases, despite the hard work, the money earned was not enough to survive.[146] Inadequate nutrition and impoverishment caused marginalization of those who were not able to make a living. Thus, even working Jews could fall into poverty. This situation prevailed in the Warsaw Ghetto from when it was enclosed until early 1942, when welfare institutions were unable to help the growing number of Jews who could not support themselves and were dying from starvation. The lack of food caused Jews from the Warsaw Ghetto to escape. The German authorities had troubles to cope with this phenomenon. During internal discussions the problem of escapees was much exaggerated. During the discussion at the office of chief of the Lublin District a report by the Warsaw authorities, was mentioned, according to which, every day about 5,000 Jews escape from the Warsaw Ghetto, of whom probably a part return, but the rest hangs out in the adjoining districts. Initially the director of the labor office requested that apprehended Jews should be put for a while in quarantine in Lublin prison. There was also a request to supply Jews apprehended by police or gendarmerie officers to the district towns or their prisons, due to lack of police forces.[147] Already at that period the German authorities tended to take the strictest measures:

> It was determined that following on from a request of the Governor, he put forward in the last main session, after which any Jew who is not in possession of valid identity documents will be shot immediately, the Governor obtains the required consent of the Governor General. Afterwards, this decree is to be brought to the *Judenrat* in Warsaw to its knowledge.[148]

One way to circumvent the restrictions on the Jews was by subcontracting. Formally, the "Aryan" firms signed contracts, procured raw materials, dealt

---

145 Engelking and Leociak, *Getto warszawskie*, 378.
146 Ibid., 463.
147 YVA-JM.12331, Notiz für Brigadeführer über die Besprechung beim Amtschef am 8. August 1941, 10 Uhr ist festzuhalten, scam 221.
148 Ibid.

with distribution of final products, and handled financing and other similar activities, while companies in the Jewish ghettos were involved in the production process. This activity was associated with a common interest. Some non-Jewish companies, in order to be able to compete in the outside market, had to cut prices as well as other elements influencing the cost of production. One important aspect of production expenditure was the cost of labor. Therefore, the use of cheap labor in the ghettos gave, on the one hand, the possibility for non-Jewish firms to compete in the market, and on the other hand, it gave more employment opportunities to those in the ghettos. "During the war, the Jewish craftsman, due to the nature of things, had to be cheaper, because, when the economic cycle was switched off, he was looking for a possibility of earning [a living] at any cost. This fact was exploited by newly created Christian contractors (*nakładca chrześcijański*) who entrusted their delivery to a Jewish craftsman."[149]

Isolation of craftsmen producing different goods in the ghetto for direct recipients contributed to the division of roles for producers and intermediaries. This division was inevitable because small producers were not yet able to deal in parallel with issues of production, finding ways of transfer to the Aryan side, and distribution. Manufacturers in the ghetto also remained dependent on raw materials and opportunities that could expand their market, which, in their case, was crucial. Because the internal market of the ghetto was very limited, the distribution of products in the outside market, or finding contractors who depended upon their production, was vital. It is worth paying attention to the fact that the majority of production in the ghetto was intended for the external market. Often, in such a situation, a whole chain of relationships was created. On the one hand, the non-Jewish manufacturers struggling with the competition were looking for opportunities to cut costs. Such prospects were available in any ghetto, especially in large ghettos with a sizeable potential labor force. The labor force in the ghettos, particularly in isolated ones, was much cheaper than the non-Jewish labor force outside the ghettos.

In the ghetto, there was no free market of labor and payment. Due to their isolation, the Jewish workers were not able to move freely, and mechanism of regulation of supply and demand of labor did not exist. As a consequence of the restrictions against the Jews, there was a surplus of labor in the ghettos in relation to available employment. In such circumstances, many Jews were ready to perform any work, even in return for a wage below the average level and,

---

149 Winkler, "Getto walczy z niewolą gospodarczą," 70.

in some cases, in exchange for food.[150] The manufacturer outside the ghetto, who could directly or through intermediaries mobilize Jews from the ghetto to work in the sub-contracting system, used, on the one hand, cheap labor in the ghetto, and on the other hand, distributed finished products outside the ghetto. This gave him an advantage over other producers.[151] He could charge lower prices for finished products. In so doing, such a manufacturer became more competitive, while his profit margin could be greater than that of other producers using a non-Jewish labor force, which was inherently more expensive. The difference in rates between non-Jewish and Jewish artisans ranged from 25% to 30%. Therefore, using a Jewish labor force was for the external producers very attractive. In the case of bulk supplies such a difference in the cost of labor could produce very large profits.[152] Nonetheless, the desire to exploit cheap labor in the ghettos also had its positive results, since an increase in demand for some products that could be produced in the ghetto caused an increase in demand for labor in the ghetto, which gave employment to growing numbers of Jews. Growth in demand for labor, especially for specialized labor, could cause an increase in wages of Jewish workers.

Despite the prevailing bad opinion, and contrary to appearances, the role of intermediaries was very important in the organization of the production and marketing chain, linking the ghetto with the external world. The most common accusation against the intermediaries was exploitation of Jewish workers. Undoubtedly, this was, to a large extent, justified, because in many cases, intermediaries were the factor that controlled the situation at the ghetto and its link with the external world. In cases when a non-Jewish contractor had no direct contact with large numbers of laborers working for him (and often there was no contact at all), the intermediaries were the masters of the situation, because they were able to choose the workers and to dictate their own terms. Of course, on a global scale, the market within the ghetto set the prices, but in individual cases, agents were able to exert pressure on specific workers. Similarly, in the case of entrepreneurs from the outer world, intermediaries with a network of agents and knowledge of relations inside the ghetto, could put pressure on enterprisers. Nevertheless, it had to be reasonable, because businessmen could turn to other intermediaries.

The role of intermediary in the production process under contract was to create links between the entrepreneur providing the raw materials and

---

150 Engelking and Leociak, *Getto warszawskie*, 393.
151 Winkler, "Getto walczy z niewolą gospodarczą," 67.
152 Ibid., 70.

the producers. A clever agent could make a series of relationships with workers, provide continued supplies of raw materials, and control the manufacturing process. This had a significant impact on the quantity of production. The action mechanism of home-production work can be defined in a simplified manner as follows:

> [. . . the] Jewish producer, in spite of some form of independence, was primarily a home-producer. His autonomy is expressed as follows: 1) the artisan receives money from his contractor, which was paid in advance for the execution of the contract rather than raw and auxiliary materials, that being a fundamental feature of cottage industries; 2) in cases where even the carpenter receives raw materials, they were treated as cash, which is then deducted from total order value.[153]

ILLEGAL PRODUCTION AND TRADE

In practice, it turned out that the ratio between official and unofficial export was just like relationship of official provision of food and the actual supply. In effect, the ghetto still maintained business relationship with the Aryan side. The economic ties created long before the war had not ceased, even after the walls dividing the ghetto from the Aryan world grew higher and higher. In addition to the official production for the German army, and in general for the German market, the ghetto used for production its existing supply of raw materials, as well as raw materials smuggled into the ghetto from the Polish market. These materials were obtained from the stores of companies in Tomaszów Mazowiecki, Częstochowa, Łódź, and other cities. Needless to say, they were received in an illegal way from allocations of raw materials for these companies. Jewish industrialists and craftsmen showed incredible ingenuity in finding alternative products instead of the absent materials. For the Aryan market everything was produced as it had been before the war. Weaving factories produced excellent fabrics from wool stolen from the factories of Częstochowa, from the "Wola" factory in Warsaw and other cities. *Tallitot* were dyed and made into scarves, sweaters, and other articles of clothing. Production of scarves for women, sweaters, jackets for peasants, and other items developed. The locals made them from old clothes (*ciuchów*) that were bought in great quantities in a huge square on Gęsia Street (also called Gęsiówka), where a massive sale took place, gradually making the Jewish

---

153 Ibid., 72.

population needy. Day after day, special agents of various companies bought up in Gęsiówka thousands of pounds of old sheets and old clothes.[154]

Gęsiówka became the center of trade of old clothes from Warsaw and other cities. On the Polish market traders rushed a large shipment of old things (*Werterfassung*), amounting to 20,000 kg, from Lublin, acquired with the liquidation of the ghettos in the Lublin region. All these old clothes underwent dyeing in a special installation on Niska Street or in private homes,[155] and then a variety of patterns were printed on them. The manufacturing industry, organized by former entrepreneurs from Łódź, flourished. Woolen stockings and gloves of cotton blended with wool were produced there. Cotton haberdashery, wool, and leather industries prospered. Pressed cardboard suitcases were prepared from remnants of old books and all kinds of other materials. A large-scale brush industry also developed. Brushes were made—apart from bristles—from old beaters, with goose feathers and similar rubbish, which was carefully collected in the ghetto. This industry employed several thousand workers. Mattresses for troops and for the Aryan side were made of various *Ersatz* resources. Illegal tanneries processed smuggled leather to the ghetto. Children, 6–10 years old, produced toys in bulk in private homes, attics, basements, and other such locations. From aircraft debris "imported" into the ghetto, the aluminum industry (production of bowls, spoons, and other private consumption goods) developed. In addition, stoves, hinges, and other steel articles were made in the ghetto for the Aryans. Shoes with wooden soles and upper parts of pressed cardboard were mass-produced. Beautiful pipes and cigar boxes were made from processed wood.[156] There was a booming chemical industry, pharmaceutical industry, processing of fats business, oil manufacturer, soap factory, and other enterprizes, as well as developed wood industry (i.e., sawmills and production of furniture), a rubber industry, and the like.

> Even after the action in July (1942), when the whole business collapsed due to the deportation of three hundred fifty thousand Jews from Warsaw, the ghetto still was able to produce for the Polish market, but to a lesser extent. This production took place under the guise of the newly established "shops," employing the remainder of the Warsaw Jews. From soldiers' trousers the "shops" produced thousands of pairs of trousers for the rural population,

---

154 Ringelblum, *Stosunki polsko-żydowskie*, 57–58.
155 Ibid.
156 Ibid.

naturally, after dyeing the material. Besides, windbreakers were made from trousers. And so was the manufacture in almost all "shops." Both the import of raw materials and export of the finished goods were performed by means of smuggling, in which the help of *Transferstelle*, created officially for the exchange of goods with the Aryan side, was instrumental. These rather small factories worked from cellars, in disguised rooms, in specially built shelters, and other locations. By day, it was not possible in any way to know that at night there is an active factory! The owners of these companies had to pay various "leeches," preying on the economic organism of the Jewish population. One branch of the Gestapo in the Jewish Quarter—the Authority for Combating Usury and Huckstering [*Urząd Walki z Lichwą i Paskarstwem*]— the so-called "Thirteen" [*Trzynastka*], *Preisüberwachungsstelle* [The Office for Price Surveillance], and police agents who were active in Polish police stations in the ghetto belonged to these "leeches."[157]

THE TRANSFORMATIONS IN THE ACQUISITION OF MATERIAL RESOURCES

Within a few years of the ghettos' existence, many significant changes occurred in the ways to acquire the means of survival. Despite the initial high turnover of trade in this area, there was a depletion of stock for sale, and, therefore, a gradual decrease of trade in favor of labor. There was also a gradual increase in both the number of employees and their percentage in the Jewish population between the spring of 1942 and the final liquidation of the ghettos in the summer of 1943. That was followed by mass deportations to death camps when ghettos were transformed into so-called "small ghettos." These were, for all intents and purposes, turned into forced labor camps. During that period the employed ghetto population proportionally increased. For example:

> At the end of the existence of the Jewish Community in Zamość, over 70% of Jews, both men and women were employed in various locations. We gave false certificates to children younger than 14 stating that they were older in order to place them at some outpost through *Arbeitsamt*, and in this way, for the time being, to save them from destruction.[158]

---

157   Ibid.
158   YVA-O.33/322, testimony of Mieczysław Garfinkiel, 31.

In this last period of the ghettos—in the spring of 1942, and until the summer of 1943, a drastic reduction in the number of elderly people, children, and women running households ensued. In some small ghettos, the percentage of employees reached almost 100% due to the elimination of children, the elderly, and the sick. This period was also marked by an increasing loss of ability to make independent business decisions by Jewish entrepreneurs and Jewish institutions, in favor of external actors. In the Warsaw Ghetto, such actors were German companies working for the army, the best-known among which were the companies of Walter Caspar Többens and Fritz Schultz. They had state-of-the-art modern assemblies and focused on a variety of professionals engaged in various activities. With time, these professionals were concentrated in specific areas, and the production units were transformed into factories, or, more appropriately, workshops. In some shops, the work was divided into various specialized activities; in others, mostly fur and tailors' workshops, the greatest part of the activities were performed by the artisans producing finished products.[159] In shops, most decisions were taken by the German businessmen and Jews that constituted the main labor force.

As stated above, with the depletion of items for sale, the share of labor in the ratio of acquiring material resources in order to enable the maintenance of the ghetto increased. In the final stages of the ghetto, labor was the main source of income and the "small ghettos" had become a reservoir of cheap labor. Along with this process of changes in the proportion of income, the autonomy of action of entrepreneurs and artisans from the ghettos gradually declined. In the early days of the ghettos, the *Judenrat*'s great initiative in adapting the production profile for opportunities of entrepreneurs and artisans was evident in the ghettos. In the later period, in the shadow of deportation to death camps, possessing documents that confirmed official employment, preferably in production for the army, had become increasingly important. Organization of work passed into the hands of German officials, who directed the Jews to various institutions. The development of the shops was also a reflection of this process. German companies took the workers together with their equipment, such as sewing machines. Many times in the last period of the ghettos, employees not only brought the equipment with them, but also paid fees just to be accepted to work and to receive certificates of employment, which were to protect them from deportation to death camps.

---

159 Helge Grabitz, *Letzte Spuren: Ghetto Warschau, SS-Arbeitslager Trawniki, Aktion Erntefest: Fotos und Dokumente über Opfer des Endlösungwahns im Spiegel der historischen Ereignisse* (Berlin: Hentrich, 1988), 23–27.

As in many areas of production, manufactured items required intensive manual labor. The share of labor costs in calculating the unit cost of product was high and ranged, for example, in carpentry from 30% to 50% of production costs.[160] The value of production carried out by Jews in ghettos in many cases amounted to quite a bit. Because of the various tracks of goods: the official, illegal, internal market, and production for the army without formal factors (as in the case of the Warsaw Ghetto *Transferstelle*), it is difficult to make detailed calculations, and it certainly would require extensive research. In one case, a person working in the Statistics Department of the Warsaw Jewish Council gave the monthly data showing the volume of production.

> The value of such supplies in the craft of carpentry was at certain times 4–5 million zł per month; in the brush industry—about 3 million zł. So with only those two branches of export, although important, there was a yield of 7 million zł per month. Add to this export for military purposes of tinsmithing, upholstery, metal industry, and so forth, plus a huge array of illegal exports to the private Aryan market. No exaggeration, if we estimate the total exports of 10 million zł a month.[161]

As Winkler suggests, "assuming that in total labor is 30–40%; it appears that it has provided the ghetto with 3–4 million zł [salary] per month, and so several times more than the 'shops' and similar enterprises."[162]

Undoubtedly, the value of labor and production carried out by the Jews was significant in the economy of the General Government. It should be born in mind that the statistics from the period of occupation does not show a true picture of Jewish participation in the economy and not only because of the lack of data. Even if we take into account the existing partial data, the value of Jewish participation will also be underestimated because several factors will reduce the value of work and production. Importantly, the official rate paid for the work of the Jews constituted 80% of the rate paid to the Poles.[163] It should also be taken into account

---

160 Winkler, "Getto walczy z niewolą gospodarczą," 73.
161 The German authorities have assessed the turnover of the Warsaw Ghetto at 8–9 million zł per month, Document no. 108, June 18, 1942, Kraków, Minutes of the meeting of the state police on security situation in the General Government and the relationship between the administration and the police in connection with the establishment of the State Secretariat for Security Affairs, in Frank, *Okupacja i ruch oporu*, 479.
162 Winkler, "Getto walczy z niewolą gospodarczą," 67.
163 APL, RŻL-6, Stundenlöhne der Arbeiter und Arbeiterinnen—Lohnordnung, 1941, 80.

that forced labor was not paid for or payment was from the Jews' own resources through the *Judenrat*. In addition, different rates were used for work on the "free" market in the ghettos. Considering the existing situation of constraints in the ghettos, the "market" value of Jewish labor was much lower than in the real free economy. The difference between the fair value of labor in the ghettos and the value of work outside the ghettos created a profit for intermediaries and organizations that relied on Jewish labor. It should be taken into account that the wages of the General Government, both official and of the free market, did not reflect the true value of wages, since the Polish population was economically exploited as well. Function of the labor market in relation to the goods market may serve as a comparative example. In the General Government, there was a well-developed alleged "black market" of food, and not only of food. The market price was disproportionate in relation to salaries of German arms factories that paid workers the official rates. This resulted in a frequent reduction of work, as these factories responded to the price of additional food or provided free lunches in order to encourage workers to work.[164] Despite the significant exploitation of Jews, over time the adaptation to the conditions of the ghetto transpired. One witness said that after adjusting to living in the ghetto, mastering the methods of production, and the creation of a distribution network, despite poverty, one could survive for a long time, measured in months and years.[165] Unfortunately, this period was very short, since the extermination of the Jews was soon to begin.

In discussing the economic issues of the ghettos, it would be worthwhile to consider a few remarks of Jerzy Winkler,[166] who was a graduate of economics from the University of Vienna and who until the great deportation had been an employe of the Statistics Department of the *Judenrat* in Warsaw. He wrote:

> [. . .] under the concept of the "ghetto," we understand here not territorially closed Jewish quarter, and not a period that closely coincides with the consequences of November 16, 1940 [closure of the Warsaw Ghetto], but rather the entire period of war when Jews were excluded from free economic activity. It must be assumed that the endurance before the creation and closure of the ghetto became a natural source of this economic movement, which in this framework subsequently developed.[167]

---

164 Meducki, *Przemysł i klasa robotnicza*, 156–59.
165 Engelking and Leociak, *Getto warszawskie*, 378.
166 Winkler, "Getto walczy z niewolą gospodarczą," 55–86.
167 Ibid., 56.

Despite the walls surrounding the ghetto, the Jews were seeking to acquire material resources, both through trade and work together with the normal desire to break the isolation. This was expressed in the statements of those involved in economic activity:

> Locked in the ghetto, a Jewish merchant and artisan had to do something to stay alive. A Polish entrepreneur, even though everything was open to him, had to use Jewish labor to profit. Admittedly, the Jew was exploited in every field but his flexibility overcomes the obstacles and walls. He worked at a loss, but stuck to the surface of life, proving by his existence that Jewish positions cannot be completely eliminated from the rump of Polish economic life.[168]

In another passage, the author stated: "... inherent economic forces in the ghetto blow up the narrow walls."[169]

The economy of the ghetto was unstable due to isolation, because of its limited domestic market, limited supplies of raw materials, and lack of energy. These conditions forced the Jews in the ghettos to adjust the production profile to the existing conditions, using accessible materials or manufacturing goods that required cheap and available materials. The production profile was characterized by low energy consumption and high share of labor, using simple tools and machines. However, the great amount of work required long hours under poor conditions.[170] On the other hand, in order to ensure competitiveness in the market, products had to be cheap. Erroneous management of the ghetto forced Jews to innovate, simplify production methods, and seek new industries. Isolated economy required a special mode of operation, in which a large part of the Jewish population was involved. That system was the main battleground between Nazi policies of exploitation, extermination of the Jews, and the struggle for survival through work. However, the objectives of the economic system, formed mainly by external conditions, were not economical. The main economic goal was to survive, and all funds were dedicated to this purpose. Production and profits were just a by-product of the economic system.

---

168 Ibid., 86.
169 Ibid., 56.
170 Engelking and Leociak, *Getto warszawskie*, 379.

PRODUCTION IN THE WARSAW GHETTO

Establishment of the ghettos always had its supporters and opponents, even among the German administration. Waldemar Schön, the head of the Department of Resettlement in the Warsaw District, in his lecture on January 20, 1941, proclaimed:

> It was clear that this idea [of establishment of the ghetto] must at first appear to be incapable of execution, owing to the specific and extremely complicated conditions in the city of Warsaw. Objections were raised on various sides and in particular by the City Administration. It was argued that the forming of a ghetto would cause serious disruption to industry and the economy. As about 80 percent of all the skilled labor was Jewish, it was indispensable and could not be shut away. Finally, it was argued that the feeding of the Jews would not be possible if they were concentrated in a closed area.[171]

Despite all such arguments, the Warsaw Ghetto had been established. Nevertheless, we have to admit that, in fact, the establishment of the ghetto caused disruption of the economy, serious shortage of a skilled labor force, and great difficulties in providing food. At the peak of the famine, about 5,550 Jews died there in one month (July 1941).[172] This happened not because the Jews were not capable of earning a living, but because they were forcibly cut off from the general labor force and the food market, and they received starvation food rations. Continuing his speech, Waldemar Schön said:

> The Department for Interior Administration in the office of the Governor General on August 20, 1940, confirmed that it was necessary to establish Jewish areas of residence, but these would not be hermetically closed ghettos, but Jewish districts, which would permit just enough economic contact with the Aryan surroundings to keep the Jewish quarter viable.[173]

---

171 From a lecture by Waldemar Schön, head of the Department of Resettlement in the Warsaw District on the steps leading to the establishment of the Warsaw Ghetto, January 20, 1941, in Arad and Gutman, *Documents on the Holocaust*, 224.
172 Dunin-Wąsowicz, Raporty Ludwiga Fischera, 376.
173 From a lecture by Waldemar Schön, Head of the Department of Resettlement in the Warsaw District on the steps leading to the establishment of the Warsaw Ghetto, January 20, 1941, in Arad and Gutman, Documents on the Holocaust, 222.

This quotation explains in rather general terms the intention of the ghettoization policy, but it does not explain the actual application of this policy. In fact, in May 1942, 3,636 people died in the Warsaw Ghetto.[174] The correlation between effective labor and the provision of food was well understood by Heinz Auerswald, the commissar of the Warsaw Ghetto; however, there was a lack of coordination between the official food ration policy and the General Government authorities. This policy was expressed, although ironically, by the governor general, Hans Frank:

> The Jews for us also represent extraordinarily malignant gluttons. We have now approximately 2,500,000 of them in the General Government—perhaps, with the Jewish crossbreeds, and everything that goes with them, 3,500,000 Jews.[175]

The basic difference between the ghettos and the world outside their walls was that the Polish population was always able to buy additional food, which was not possible in the ghetto, thus causing famine. Official food rations and the policy of exaggerated isolation were deadly for ghetto inhabitants. On September 26, 1941 Heinz Auerswald said:

> ... the quantity of legally supplied foodstuffs is far from enough to counter the acute starvation in the Jewish quarter effectively. The quantity of foodstuffs smuggled into the Jewish quarter is not small, but owing to the high cost, it is available only to the wealthier section of the Jews. If there is to be any successful large-scale exploitation of Jewish labor, it will be necessary to increase their food supply considerably.[176]

Continuing, Auerswald said:

> The increase in the food supply described above was insufficient to stop the rise in the number of deaths resulting from the generally wretched condition of the Jews since the beginning of the war. [...] It is seen that in August [1941], for the first time mortality remains unchanged at the level

---

174 Dunin-Wąsowicz, *Raporty Ludwiga Fischera*, 530.
175 IMT, *Red Series* (2233-D-PS), vol. 1, 1007. On the same subject see Christopher Browning, "From Ethnic Cleansing to Genocide," in Browning, *Nazi Policy*, 22–25.
176 From a report by Auerswald, commissar of the Warsaw Ghetto, September 26, 1941, in Arad and Gutman, *Documents on the Holocaust*, 246.

of the previous month. Improved nutrition appears now to be having its effect. This is confirmed by preliminary figures for September, which indicate that [the final figures] for this month will scarcely exceed the figures for each of the past two months.[177]

The situation concerning food provision and increased production improved in the second half of 1941, and continued in this way until the beginning of the great deportation in July 1942.

Regarding the Warsaw Ghetto, as well as other ghettos, an important external factor causing the improvement was the discovery of their production capacity by the Wehrmacht. With stabilization of the economy and the winning campaigns on the Western Front, many German units were placed in the General Government. The military formations were obliged to cover their needs for different items within the General Government. Quartermasters, therefore, started to look for suppliers that could provide various items needed for the army. Military units permanently residing in the area contributed to establishing business contacts and stabilizing contracts affecting the increased yield.[178] Production for the army was privileged, which meant the army not only made supplies available, but also provided a market for manufactured goods. The stable situation on the front line also called for better equipment of the soldiers' barracks, causing a demand for furniture and other everyday objects, for example, brushes.

Many units were moved to the General Government when, in the summer of 1940 after the campaign in Western Europe, the front was stabilized. From that summer until the beginning of Operation Barbarossa, increasing numbers of soldiers regularly entered the General Government. A particularly strong arrival came in the spring of 1941. At that time, a period of great economic growth in the area was noted. This had an impact on increased military orders for many products and services. During that period, the demand for labor for the construction of various facilities such as barracks, airports, roads, bridges, and others was also amplified. Housing in general and public buildings, in particular, had to be adapted for the army. This work also required the labor of many artisans. The Jews were employed in many craftsmanship assignments, but they particularly preferred requests for finished products, since work—often in the form of forced labor—was low-paid, or, as was in the case of labor camps in the Lublin region, was not paid in any way.[179] Forced labor caused

---

177 Ibid.
178 Winkler, "Getto walczy z niewolą gospodarczą," 69.
179 BA-MA, RH53-23-27, Lublin, September 23, 1940, 148–49; APL, RŻL-8, 54.

financial detriment to the Jewish communities because, in many cases, the Jewish communities had to pay for work done in labor camps and to the institutions that exploited those Jewish workers.

In a time of increased military contracts—in 1940 and 1941—well-developed German companies did not yet exist in the General Government, so most orders were given to Polish companies. These, in turn, were interested not only in increased profits, but also in cooperation of the Jewish craftsmen. In this way, simple entrepreneurs became more competitive in the market, allowing them to capture the bulk of the contracts. In some cases, Polish firms were not able to realize bigger contracts without adding to the number of workers.[180] The military issued increasing demands for furniture for their barracks. In many cases, soldiers were placed in public buildings such as schools or offices, which were not suited for the army. Then, these buildings had to be provided with beds or bunks, cabinets, tables, and the like. The amounts of furniture needed for the army were enormous, given the fact that a large number of army divisions and air force units involved in Operation Barbarossa were stationed in the General Government territory. Furniture was delivered within a short time. Its production was quick and, in general, of poor quality, but the requirements were also not particularly high, because they concerned products intended for short-term use. Therefore, suppliers met the demands of providing huge amounts of furniture by looking for producers that might fill such orders. In this way, some Polish companies created partnerships with Jewish craftsmen, thereby becoming subcontractors.[181]

According to Jerzy Winkler, "The period of peak supply in the field of carpentry falls in the first half of 1941. Turnover in this period reached 4–5 million per month (including the value already in the raw materials at market prices)."[182] After the beginning of the war with the Soviet Union, there was a sudden drop in demand, because most military units moved to the east, leaving their accommodations in the General Government. Therefore, many firms changed their production profile. Orders for barracks supplies stopped, but more and more office furniture and equipment for hospitals, such as tables, stools, desks, and wardrobes were ordered. Besides, fine sets of furniture were produced for the German officials in the General Government.[183]

---

180 Winkler, "Getto walczy z niewolą gospodarczą," 69–70.
181 Ibid., 71.
182 Ibid., 72.
183 Ibid.

The brush industry was almost entirely dominated, if not monopolized, by Jewish producers. It developed first of all in Warsaw in the first half of 1940. Since then, the industry expanded in a very dynamic manner. Most of the brush industry production in Warsaw was intended for the German army, although some of the production reached the general market. In 1941, about 2,000 Jewish families in Warsaw earned a living from the brush industry.[184] Mass production of brushes meant that manufacturers in the Warsaw Ghetto held a monopoly in this field through market operation mechanisms. In this case, they practically took over of the entire production of brushes in the manner described below. Huge orders for the German army from the spring of 1940 were responsible for the strong growth of the brush industry. Thus, there had been interest in businesses outside of the ghetto for this kind of production. To reduce production costs and become competitive in the market, Polish or German entrepreneurs entered into an agreement with companies in the Jewish ghetto that carried out the production. In this case, the Aryan company acted as a contractor, engaged in providing the ghetto with raw materials and receiving finished goods. Taking advantage of cheap labor for mass production, companies cooperating with producers in the ghetto had gained an advantage in the market, because, by reducing production costs, they could offer lower unit prices than other producers. The decline in market prices caused many companies that manufactured the same brush to go under and they discontinued production. Thus, only Jewish companies and Aryan companies closely cooperating with them remained in the market.

Military orders had become a stimulus for mass production, with contracts amounting to hundreds of thousands of brushes per month. This allowed obtaining the necessary raw material allocations and ensured a steady market. The quality of the products was low, but the unit price of the product was also low, and it did not prevent the placing of new orders for brushes. It is possible that some of the military orders were the result of corruption, as suggested by some witnesses active in the economic field during the occupation.[185] Sales of mass-produced supplies to the army enabled production development on such a magnitude that it was possible to redirect a significant part of that production to the general market and control it in its totality. In this way,

---

184 Ibid., 77.
185 Ibid.

producers held a Jewish monopoly in both the supplies to the troops as well as in the private market.[186] As Winkler explains:

> It is difficult to estimate the brush production quantitatively. One time, a larger supply of brushes ranged from five hundred thousand different pieces. There were periods (September and October 1941) when the ghetto was producing about 25,000 brushes daily. Prices of individual brushes are different, which makes it difficult to determine the value of total exports. However, one can assume that in periods of high volume supply of brushes, the ghetto produced for about 3 million złoty per month.[187]

The main difference between the woodworking industry and the brush industry was the issue of providing the raw material. In carpentry, military orders were dependant on the official provision of raw material supplies; however, the brush industry received less aid. While it was possible to provide wood for brushes, which even in mass production was not required in large quantities, a much bigger problem was caused by other raw materials, which were scarce. Without doubt, the matter of providing raw materials for brushes was a factor in the prevailing tide of competition among the Jewish producers. Seeing the provision of raw materials as a great opportunity, the Jews started the whole process of collecting and processing raw materials to manufacture brushes. Most of these raw materials came from recycled materials or had substitutes. To quote Winkler:

> In this area, Jewish brush manufacturer[s], as above noted, revealed a high degree of inventiveness, starting with the uses of each *Ersatz*, thus: goose feathers, some species of straw, some species of veneer, reed (reworked old beaters, bamboo sticks, and baskets), and so called *pierzawę* (part of feathers).[188]

Undoubtedly, the value of labor and production carried out by the Jews was significant in the German economy. It should be born in mind that the statistics from the occupation period does not show a true picture of Jewish

---

186 Ibid.
187 Ibid., 82.
188 Ibid., 80–81.

participation in the economy, and not only because of the lack of data. The wages, both official and "free market," did not reflect the real value of wages for work performed.

Despite significant exploitation of the Jews, adaptation to the conditions of the ghetto evolved in which the source of livelihood was work. In one of the notes from the Ringelblum Archive, we find the following words:

> It is quite clear that the basis of existence of the [Jewish] quarter is not imaginary wealth, nor the existing stock and the hidden goods, nor finally the notorious "Jewish dollars," but above all, productive labor.[189]

The Jews adapted to the conditions of ghetto life, mastered the methods of production, and established a distribution network. Thanks to that, and despite their poverty, they could endure long periods of time. On the other hand, it was not economic policy, but the ideological stance of the highest authorities of the Third Reich that prompted the decision to liquidate the ghettos and perpetrate the mass extermination of Jews in Poland. Just a few survived in hiding, while the others endured in concentration camps and forced labor camps in conditions over which they did not have the slightest influence.

---

189 AŻIH, AR 1/250 (103), 4.

CHAPTER 4

Forced Labor in the Labor Camps

From September 1939 to the beginning of winter, only the most important work of repairing roads and bridges was performed. Part of the work was done by German technical services—*Technische Nothilfe* (TN). During the war, these services were used, for example, to build makeshift bridges, or repair communications. Some activities of TN were not strictly and exclusively related to the military.[1] After the military campaign of September 1939, TN was still engaged in repairing electrical wiring, gas, and other such works. However, the main task of TN was to ensure technical assistance during the war and immediately after the war. After the war, following the organization of the civil administration, TN was replaced by other services. Some of the urgent works in the field of infrastructure were also performed by Reich Labor Service (*Reichsarbeitsdienst*, RAD). However, extensive work in the field of economy and infrastructure could not be carried out by TN or RAD, because people mobilized to perform these services were diverted from their regular jobs in the Reich, to which they returned after the period of mobilization. Similarly, RAD was not designed to perform a wide range of works in the occupied territories. Later in the war, a lot of engineering work was performed by officers and prisoners within the *Organization Todt*.

At the end of the military administration and with the proclamation of the General Government on October 26, 1939, intensive planning of economic development began. A group of young German economic experts and planners came together in the departments of planning and management. They intended to develop General Government economy, despite initial intentions of unlimited

---

1 Tagesbefehl nr. 6, Armeekommando, Der Chef der Zivilverwaltung, Tschenstochau, September 14, 1939, AIPN, NTN, 196/270, 12.

exploitation of raw materials and labor. Creation of this loosely associated group was associated with a way to recruit professionals for various positions in the newly established administrative structure. Frequently they had previous personal contacts.[2] These mostly young people saw potential for advancement in taking responsible positions and implementing their knowledge and their ideas.

Therefore, in autumn of 1939, extensive work was undertaken in the field of regional planning and economic exploitation. This work covered a few basic areas: reconstruction and development of infrastructure, work on projects involving the military field—such as the construction of airfields, training areas, fortifications,[3] and projects relating to agriculture, particularly relevant among which were projects in water management and reconstruction and development of the industry. After the General Government was established, its administration was not completely established in the initial period. The two months remaining until the end of the year were too short of a time to implement any new projects. In addition, weather conditions did not allow any work beyond necessary repairs and maintenance of acceptable state of communication. Extensive works in many industries: communications, agriculture, water management, and so forth, were planned for the year 1940. These works required a high expenditure of labor. In addition, they were to take place in remote areas, far from urban centers. Therefore, it was decided to create work camps to provide on-site permanent contingent workforces. Because it was necessary to prepare appropriate economic plans, in practice it was impossible to undertake any work on a large scale in 1939.

However, in the autumn of 1939, no formal regulations on working in the camps were issued. In the first implemented regulation of December 11, 1939, it was only mentioned in paragraph 6 that the Jews who transgress the provisions mentioned in the regulation "will be sent immediately to the strict long-standing labor service."[4] However, the implemented regulation did not specify whether the work would take place in the labor camps. On the basis of the second

---

2 Aly and Heim, "The Economics of the Final Solution"; Aly and Heim, "The Holocaust and Population Policy."
3 "January 30, 1940, Berlin. From the speech of the head of the Reich Security Main Office, Heydrich and senior SS and police commander in the General Government Krüger, presented at a Berlin conference, concerning the forced resettlement of Polish and Jewish population of Warthegau to General Government," in Eisenbach and Rutkowski, *Eksterminacja Żydów*, 44.
4 "December 11, 1939, Kraków, The first executive order of the higher SS and police leader in the General Government, Krüger on compulsory labor for the Jewish population," in Eisenbach and Rutkowski, *Eksterminacja Żydów*, 205–6.

regulation issued by the HSSPF in the General Government Friedrich-Wilhelm Krüger on December 12, it can be assumed that he meant the work in the camps.[5] First of all, in paragraph 1 of the regulation of December 12, Krüger set the length of labor for two years. However, in case of failure to achieve the educational aim (*erzieherischer Zweck*), this period could be extended.[6]

In the same piece of legislation in paragraph 2, Krüger pointed to the possibility of creating labor camps:

> [the Jews] subject to forced labor are employed, in order to use their labor, according to their profession, if this is possible, and are put to work in the camps. Those able to work do not find an employment corresponding fully to their abilities.[7]

Speaking of forced labor and its educational purposes was confusingly similar to the "educational" goals of the concentration camps in Nazi Germany before the war.[8] Besides, it would be difficult to imagine how the educational aim could be realized outside the labor camps in the General Government, indicating the inconsistency of this argumentation. The regulation of December 12 in section 5 sets out the items that the workers should carry with them, including lunch for two days and two clean sheets, which implies at least a two-day period of forced or compulsory labor.[9] In turn, the regulation of January 20, 1940 in the section concerning mobilization to work also lists items that people called for forced labor should bring with them. These include: two sheets, extra clothing, a coat, two pairs of shoes, three shirts, three pants, three pairs of stockings [socks], pair of gloves, two towels, a comb and a brush, cutlery, and food for two days.[10]

---

5 "Zweite Durchführungsvorschrift zur Verordnung vom 26. Oktober 1939 über die Einführung des Arbeitszwanges für jüdische Bevölkerung des Generalgouvernements. Vom 12. Dezember 1939, in Pospieszalski," *Hitlerowskie "prawo" okupacyjne*, 562.
6 Ibid.
7 Święcicki and Zadrowski, *Zbiór rozporządzeń władz niemieckich*, 232; Pospieszalski, *Hitlerowskie "prawo" okupacyjne*, vol. 2, 562–63.
8 Martin Broszat, "The Concentration Camps 1933–45," in *Anatomy of the SS State*, ed. Helmut Krausnick et al. (London: Collins, 1968), 402–7.
9 "Zweite Durchführungsvorschrift zur Verordnung vom 26. Oktober 1939 über die Einführung des Arbeitszwanges für die jüdische Bevölkerung des Generalgouvernements. (Erfassungvorschrift) Vom 12. Dezember 1939," *VBlGG*, 1939, 246; Pospieszalski, *Hitlerowskie "prawo" okupacyjne*, vol. 2, 562–64.
10 "Dienstbefehl an die Judenräte für die Erfassung und Gestellung der Juden zur Zwangsarbeit. Vom 20. Januar 1940," in Pospieszalski, *Hitlerowskie "prawo" okupacyjne*, vol. 2, 567.

This list is also compiled of objects needed at least for two or three days, but these objects could also serve for a much longer stay.

In the winter of 1939 to 1940 no labor camps existed in the General Government except for POW camps, which had place for more people, and could provide the newcomers with food and work. As a result of the September 1939 campaign, about 450,000 Polish POWs, including about 60,000 Jews, were captured by the Germans, which caused considerable problems for the German administration.[11] Therefore, the use of Jewish forced labor could take place close to home, or in labor camps created on *ad hoc* basis.

FIRST LABOR CAMPS

The labor camp at 7 Lipowa Street in Lublin was created in December 1939 by the SSPF in the Lublin District, *SS-Gruppenführer* Odilo Globocnik.[12] This camp was set up in already existing barracks and sports grounds of the Academic Sports Association (*Akademicki Związek Sportowy*, AZS). In hindsight, we can say that it was a typical labor camp, but with an unusual mixed character. In the existing barracks, craft workshops originally were created: carpentry, locksmith, shoe repair, tailoring, and watchmaking. There were also working groups responsible for the work on the expansion of the camp. The Jews of Lublin served as a workforce at the camp.

The structure at 7 Lipowa Street would have consisted of typical craft workshops. It is not for the fact that already in February 1940 the German authorities had begun to send transports of POW, essentially making it a camp. The newcomers were Jews who were billeted on the spot. Lublin received Jewish POWs who came from Polish eastern territories occupied by the Soviet Union.[13] Up to December 1940, the 7 Lipowa Street camp served as a transit camp for POWs, and the prisoners spent a relatively short time in the camp. After a few days or weeks, they were dismissed or sent away. Releasing Jewish

---

11 S. Kisielewicz, "Żydzi polscy w obozach jenieckich Rzeszy Niemieckiej w czasie II wojny światowej," *BŻIH* 3 (1999): 3; Krakowski, "The Fate of Jewish Prisoners of War," 299.
12 Marta Grudzińska and Violetta Rezler-Wasielewska, "Lublin, Lipowa 7: Obóz dla Żydów— polskich jeńców wojennych (1939–1943)," *Kwartalnik Historii Żydów* 4/228 (2008): 490–514.
13 Initially, the prisoners were promised to be repatriated, but the agreement in this case was not working. While other Jewish prisoners, coming from areas under the control of the Germans, were released. It should be noted that such a release from bondage automatically made them lose their status as prisoners of war. Notable exemptions are Jewish officers who survived the camps by the end of the war.

POWs from the camp was conditional upon a declaration from residents of Lublin, who had to confirm that they were willing to take the prisoners for a living.[14] An additional element that transforms the complex at 7 Lipowa Street into a camp was that the Jewish workers were prevented from returning to their homes for the night. These steps were taken due to the difficulty in ensuring the presence of a Jewish labor force, as many Jews tried to evade forced labor.

In the early days of the General Government's existence, there were no clear ideas of how Jewish labor could be used in the camps. Therefore, the camp at 7 Lipowa Street also had no clearly defined functions. Newly created workshops were primarily aimed at providing skilled workforce to support the police, military, and civilian German institutions. Similar workshops were set up in many other cities in the General Government.[15] The workshops were located in existing barracks or other industrial or storage buildings, and the workers came to the workplace. Only after the Jewish POWs were transported to 7 Lipowa Street, it did become a closed camp. However, in many respects the camp at 7 Lipowa Street served as a model for many other camps that were created in 1941. This regarded also the camp staff, which gained experience used subsequently in other camps, especially in the complex of labor camps in Bełżec and later in the camp at Janowska Street in Lwów. Until mid-1940, guarding functions at the camp were performed by *Selbstschutz* (self-defense units), under the command of Walter Gunst, Ludolf von Alvensleben, Franz Bartetzko, Horst Riedel, and Wolfgang Mohwinkl.[16] In addition to the obligation to provide labor, the *Judenrat* in Lublin was also responsible for other matters relating to the maintenance of the camp. Organization of workshops in the labor camp at 7 Lipowa Street undoubtedly influenced the decision of Globocnik to continue creating similar facilities of this type.[17] He was not the only one who worked towards the creation of labor camps, but certainly he became a pioneer in the field, not only because of the number of camps he set up in his district, but also due to the high number of workers in these camps.

---

14 Prisoners released from the camp were required to surrender their uniform, and thus lose their POW status.
15 Similar workshops can be found in Warsaw, Kraków, Bochnia, Zamość, and other cities.
16 Lenarczyk, "Obóz pracy przymusowej."
17 Grudzińska and Rezler-Wasielewska, "Lublin, Lipowa 7"; Silberklang, *The Holocaust in the Lublin District*; Jacob Frank, *Himmler's Jewish Tailor: The Story of Holocaust Survivor Jacob Frank* (Syracuse: Syracuse University Press, 2000); Browning, "Nazi Germany's Initial Attempt"; Poprzeczny, *Globocnik—Hitler's Man in the East*; Rieger, *Creator of Nazi Death Camps*; Tuvia Friedman, *Himmlers Teufels-General SS- und Polizeiführer Globocnik in Lublin: Dokumenten-Sammlung* (Haifa: Center of Documentation for Israel, 1977).

CATEGORIZATION OF LABOR CAMPS

Labor camps can be divided in terms of the organizing factor of the camps, the nature of the work, the camp regime, and the ethnic composition of the workers and prisoners.[18] This last factor requires further explanation, as it causes much confusion. Jewish labor camps often had the following names: labor camp (*Arbeitslager*), forced labor camp (*Zwangsarbeitslager*), Jewish camp or camp for Jews (*Judenlager*), labor camp for Jews (*Judenarbeitslager*), collective camp (*Sammellager*), camp for certain tasks (*Einsatzlager*), and administrative labor camp (*Verwaltungarbeitslager*).[19] In terms of ethnic composition, we can categorize the labor camps established in the General Government as Polish, Jewish, and mixed. Among the latter were representatives of other nationalities, including Gypsies and Ukrainians. During the early days of the occupation, the majority of inmates in labor camps were Jews, both in numerical terms as well as in terms of number of camps designed exclusively for them. According to Józef Marszałek, among the 850 labor camps existing in the General Government during the occupation, 400 contained only Jews, and in 200, Jews were one of the many ethnic groups.[20]

In terms of the regime, we can distinguish regular camps, labor camps (*Arbeitslager*), and penal camps (*Straflager*). Regular camps were created in order to perform specific work regarding economy and infrastructure of the General Government, such as work on roads and bridges, railways, work on the regulation of rivers and land drainage, and agricultural work. Labor camps had in most cases strict regime, although the difference between regular camps

---

18 Czyńska and Kupść, "Obozy zagłady, obozy koncentracyjne i obozy pracy na ziemiech polskich w latach 1939–1945"; Pilichowski, *Obozy hitlerowskie*; Weinmann, Kaiser, and Krause-Schmidt, eds., *Die Nationalsozialistische Lagersystem*; Pohl, "Die Grossen Zwangsarbeitslager der SS- und Polizeiführer für Juden im Generalgouvernement 1942–1945"; A. Ungerer, *Verzeichnis von Ghettos, Zwangsarbeitslagern und Konzentrationslagern: Vorgelegt nach Beschluss den Vertreter den obersten Wiedergutmachungsbehörden und der Entschädigungsgerichte den Länder Baden-Württemberg, Bayern und Hessen* (Munich: n.p., 1955); Allen, *The Business of Genocide*; Gruner, "Terra Incognita?"; Allen, *Jewish Forced Labor*; Łukaszewicz, "Obóz pracy w Treblince."

19 Marszałek, *Obozy pracy w Generalnym Gubernatorstwie*, Pilichowski, ed., *Obozy hitlerowskie*; Edward Dziadosz and Józef Marszałek, "Więzienia i obozy w dystrykcie lubelskim w latach 1939–1944," *Zeszyty Majdanka* 3 (1969): 54–125; Zygmunt Mańkowski, "Obozy zagłady na terenie dystryktu lubelskiego, ich system i funkcje," *Zeszyty Majdanka* 17 (1996): 39–49; Czyńska and Kupść, "Obozy zagłady, obozy koncentracyjne i obozy pracy na ziemiech polskich w latach 1939–1945."

20 Marszałek, *Obozy pracy w Generalnym Gubernatorstwie*, 12.

and labor camps remained quite fluid. A large group of labor camps was created for Poles who were obliged to work under the regulation of duty of labor of October 26, 1939 (even without this regulation, unemployed Poles were sent to the camps). Camps in this case should be treated as temporary residences of employees performing certain works. The second group of forced labor camps was created especially for Jews. These camps were known under various names, among others: labor camp for Jews (*Arbeitslager für Juden*), Jewish camp (*Judenlager*), or *Julag* for short. According to Józef Marszałek, during all the time of existence of the General Government, it had 491 such camps, which accounted for 58% of all labor camps. The largest development of such camps was noted in 1942, when in all districts together, there were 322 labor camps for Jews.[21] Some of them existed only for several weeks or months, others lasted some years. Their number and development were closely linked to the Nazi policy towards the Jews: with the extermination of Jews, the number of camps decreased.

Penal labor camps (*Strafarbeitslager*) were mixed in terms of ethnicity. In general, these camps contained people who were sent there for a limited period of time, accused of evasion of the obligation to work, not paying the contingents of agricultural products,[22] illicit trafficking, and other criminal offenses.[23] Jews who had committed various offenses were also sent to such camps. These camps had strict criminal regime and offered extremely heavy works. The prisoners were sent to work in quarries, drainage, and road-building.

STATUS OF WORKERS

The status of the Jewish workers in the camps requires further explanations. The Jews, according to existing regulations, were required to perform forced labor. At the same time, the official regulations limited stay of Jews outside the areas designated for them—that is, in Jewish residential districts. Staying in other places was only possible for Jews who had special permits. However, despite these limitations, they could move freely in designated areas. The labor

---

21 Ibid., 14.
22 YVA-JM.814, The Kreishauptmann of the County of Puławy wrote in his report that everybody who did not deliver 100% of contingents would be sent to a penal camp. Lagebericht, Kreishauptmann des Kreises Puławy, Lagebericht für Oktober 1940, Puławy, scan 821.
23 "December 9, 1940, Lublin, part of the report of the Lublin District Governor to Division of Interior Affairs of the Office of the Governor General about draconian repression of the peasants for non-delivery of quotas," in Frank, *Okupacja i ruch oporu*, vol. 1, 312–13.

departments of the Jewish councils appointed them to work in labor camps. Some workers reported on a voluntary basis. Others were arrested and transported to labor camps against their will. Formally speaking, they were not prisoners, unlike the prisoners in the penal camps. Workers in the ordinary labor camps could be treated as hired workers (*wolnonajemni*), and indeed, in many places (particularly in agricultural labor camps), they were treated in this way and their freedom of movement was not limited. They could leave the camp. In some camps the workers remained unguarded, but they could not permanently leave the camps without permission, because it had severe consequences.[24]

In most SS camps the situation was fundamentally different. There, the workers were treated as prisoners, although they did not have this formal status.[25] Certainly, it was a result of the attitude of the SS to the Jews. Many SS men were trained in German camps before the war. They were a highly indoctrinated group, so that their attitude towards the Jews was particularly negative and they were inclined to use repressive methods. Jews in the SS labor camps could not leave the camps. Workers went to work in groups under heavy guard. All attempts to escape were thwarted. The workers were shot when trying to escape. In cases of capture during a raid on refugees, they were publicly punished, in some cases by death. Prisoners were beaten and humiliated during the work. Jewish workers in labor camps designed to perform drainage work were treated like prisoners: they were held in custody and were subjected to severe discipline of the camp.[26]

The main problem here is still the matter of terminology. Labor coercion in camps was due to the racist Nazi system, which treated the Jews as inferior race. As such, Jews had to be subjected to exacerbated treatment, discrimination, and criminalization, and eventually completely destroyed. Such treatment of the Jews resulted from the alleged harm they caused that could not be corrected by educational methods. Jews were sent to labor camps mainly as a result of racist policies and not after commission of certain crimes. They were preferred as a labor force in early labor camps due to their availability. Because

---

24 A note of ŻSS about a case of arresting 70-years-old father in Działoszyce, because his son fled from a labor camp in Kostrze near Kraków. YVA-JM.1581, scan 119.
25 Situation of prisoners changed with the development of labor camps. For example, the camp at the 7 Lipowa Street in Lublin, although organized by the SSPF Globocnik, went through various stages. In the early months of its existence the Jewish laborers and POWs in this camp had freedom of movement. With time only, this freedom was limited.
26 Łukaszewicz, "Obóz pracy w Treblince."

of the racial policy, they were eliminated from the Polish economy, then in the situation of unemployment, lack of sources of income, and overcrowding of the Jewish quarters, they could be forcibly mobilized and sent to the labor camps to do the worst and hardest works. Most of the labor camps were not punitive camps,[27] but despite that, their administration applied severe punitive measures and harsh discipline.

Usually, the term "prisoner" refers to a person in custody or camp who has committed a crime or suspected of a crime. Political prisoners are and were considered a separate category of prisoners who were detained as a result of differing political views and not as a result of some offense. The Jews were locked in prison camps and treated like prisoners in consequence of discriminatory provisions under the racist ideology. In contrast to other inmates, the difference in their status was mainly due to the fact that the Jews were treated as prisoners, although from the formal point of view they were not prisoners. They did not have any designated period of residence in the camp, because there were not sent there on the basis of a sentence. They could also be released from the camp. Indeed, after the completion of their tasks, in general seasonal work, most of the prisoners were released to their original settlements. Some Jewish workers were released from the camps for health reasons.

THE COMPLEX OF LABOR CAMPS IN BEŁŻEC

The complex of labor camps in Bełżec and the surrounding area had a significant impact on the development of labor camps in the General Government, so their discussion is important for understanding the processes associated with the use of forced labor of Jews.[28] Labor camps in Bełżec and the surrounding area have been created for fortification works, so-called *Grenzgraben*, between the rivers Bug and San, on a territory of several dozen kilometers. These lines of defense were planned specifically by Wehrmacht.[29] Most of the demarcation line between the areas occupied by Germany and the Soviet Union ran along the natural boundaries: the rivers Narew, Bug, and San, while the

---

27 One of the best known punitive camps was the labor camp in Treblinka, established by the governor of the Warsaw District, Ludwig Fischer on November 15, 1941. This order was retroactive and was actually valid since September 1, 1941. YVA-JM.12307, 136.
28 Silberklang, *The Holocaust in the Lublin District*, 102–27; Radzik, "Praca przymusowa"; Radzik, *Lubelska dzielnica zamknięta*.
29 BA-MA, RH53-23-56, Oberbefehlshaber Ost, Sicherung des Gebietes Oberost, Lodsch, den 6. Dezember 1939, 104–15.

southern part of the line took place in mountainous terrain. The remaining part of the line that separated these two areas was not supported by any natural borders. Therefore, it was decided to fortify this sector of the demarcation line by digging anti-tank trenches in conjunction with other means of defense. It is difficult to accurately reconstruct the decision-making process on this matter, but already in January 1940, Himmler suggested[30] that the army high command (OKH) use about 2.5 million Jews to build fortifications along the Soviet border.[31] This decision was supported by Heydrich at a conference in Berlin on the resettlement of population from Warthegau. He expressed the need to organize a network of labor camps for hundreds of thousands of Jews, for the construction of these fortifications.[32] At the turn of 1939 and 1940, when the plans for the invasion in Western Europe were already accepted, it has become extremely important to secure the eastern border against a possible surprise attack by the Soviet Union.[33] Despite previously signed agreements of August 23, 1939 and a basic understanding on the division of spheres of influence in Eastern Europe, the attack on Western Europe would have been a violation of the balance of power against the USSR. Therefore, the reactions of this country could not be entirely predictable.

The section of the borderline between the Bug and the San was the most important, as it could be the perfect place for an invasion by land. The German strategy of *Blitzkrieg* prescribed massive attacks mainly with armored forces, with the support of troops and mechanized infantry.[34] To perform such attacks, it was necessary to transfer the majority of forces on the Western Front, thereby exposing the eastern border. Similar measures were used in 1939, when the western border of Germany remained almost devoid of troops. Preparation of

---

30 From a discussion on the compulsory evacuation of the Jewish Population of the Wartheland to the Government-General, January 30, 1940. NO-5322; Arad and Gutman, *Documents on the Holocaust*, 183–85.
31 Madajczyk, "Lubelszczyzna w polityce okupanta," 6.
32 "In connection with that matter, *SS-Gruppenführer* Heydrich mentions that the construction of the shaft and other projects in the east will enable concentration of hundreds of thousands of Jews in forced labor camps," January 30, 1940, Berlin, From the speech of the head of the Reich Security Main Office, Heydrich and Higher SS and Police Commander in the General Government Krüger, presented at a conference in Berlin, dedicated to the forced resettlement of Polish and Jewish population of Warthegau to the General Government, in Eisenbach and Rutkowski, Eksterminacja Żydów, 45.
33 BA-MA, RH53-23-56, Oberbefehlshaber Ost, Sicherung des Gebietes Oberost, Lodsch, den 6.12.39, 104–15.
34 Len Deighton, *Blitzkrieg: From the Rise of Hitler to the Fall of Dunkirk* (New York: Knopf, 1980), 213–20; 241–313.

the fortification line against any attack could give a chance to defend the eastern border (even with a small force) and allow the Germans to gain time to bring extra troops.

An additional argument on the use of the Jews to build fortifications was the fact that the Jews deported from Warthegau had no chance of any employment in the General Government. In a situation of economic stagnation and high unemployment,[35] there were greater opportunities to find employment for Jewish labor in public works. Such tendency had already been seen in 1938 in Germany, when as a result of mass arrests of Jews following *Kristallnacht*, the sudden inflow of large amounts of manpower to the concentration camps was an important factor in the development of prisoners' labor and development of companies that employed it. Similarly, in this case, the inflow of large amounts of labor and the need to carry out large-scale works in the area were important factors in the decision to set up labor camps.

It was possible to start work before the spring of 1940. For this purpose, SSPF Odilo Globocnik established a special unit for the construction of fortifications (*SS-Grenzsicherungs-Baukommando*), based in Bełżec. Originally, construction of fortifications on the stretch of 140 km between the rivers Bug and San were planned. An essential element of these fortifications was to be an anti-tank ditch of 7.5 m wide and 2.5 m deep. Discussions about the validity of border fortifications were also conducted at the meetings of the leadership of the General Government.[36] In one of his speeches, HSSPF Friedrich-Wilhelm Krüger described the intentions of the construction of fortifications

---

35   In fact, deported Jews caused lot of problems to the authorities of the General Government because of lack of accommodation for thousands of arriving *ausgesiedelte Juden*. During January, the number of people searching employment in the district of Kraków increased from 19,616 to 23,586. 6127 places were offered, and assistance in searching for employment was given to 14,304; among them 2,411 were Jews. See in Der Chef des Distrikts Krakau. Lagebericht für Januar 1941, 17. Februar 1941, YVA-O.53/101, scan 26.

36   August 9, 1940, Kraków, Minutes of meeting held on August 6, 1940, in the Department of Labor of the General Government, devoted to forced labor of the Jewish population: "The meeting was held under the chairmanship of Frauendorfer, assisted by representatives of the General Directorate of Eastern Railway, the higher SS and police leader in the General Government, the commander of the Security Police, Security Service of the General Government, and certain departments of General Government—[Department of] Food Supplies and Agriculture, Economy, Construction, Forestry, and Labor Departments in the offices of heads of Kraków, Warsaw, Lublin, and Radom Districts, and Labor Office (department of Employment Jews) in Kraków and other departments." In April 1940 the German authorities ordered the resettlement of Jews from Krakow to various places in the districts of Krakow and Lublin. The Lublin Jews were to be employed in the fortification works. See Eisenbach and Rutkowski, *Eksterminacja Żydów*, 217–18.

in following words: "In consultation with the Supreme Commander of the East are organized now works for the Jews near the so-called green border between the Bug and San, yet as an experiment; the future will prove what results it will produce."[37]

The first group of 1,140 prisoners at Bełżec was composed of Gypsies deported from Germany, *Protektorat*,[38] and Gypsies who were arrested in the General Government, brought to Bełżec in late May 1940.[39] The first group of 100 Jews arrived to Bełżec on May 29, 1940;[40] and before August 14, 1940, the camp already contained 350 Jews from Lublin and Piaski. However, the great influx of Jewish workers to a labor camp in Bełżec was only in mid-August 1940.[41]

The organizational model of the camp at Bełżec[42] reflects Globocnik's ideas. Despite the criticism of irrational use of Jewish labor as it was expressed at the meeting in April 1940,[43] Globocnik himself contributed to a no less irrational attitude towards that labor force, directed against Jewish institutions in general. It is worthwhile to consider a possible cause of such attitude. From the

---

37 June 7, 1940, Kraków, Minutes of the meeting on economic issues—situation of hunger in the Polish population, the task of the German police, policy towards the Jewish population in the General Government, in Frank, *Okupacja i ruch oporu*, vol. 1, 223.

38 At the January meeting, which was attended by Seyss-Inquart and Krüger, one of the items discussed was relocating 30,000 Gypsies from Germany and eastern marches to the General Government. January 30, 1940, Berlin. From the speeches of the head of the Reich Security Main Office, Heydrich, and the higher SS and police commander in the General Government, Krüger, presented at a conference in Berlin and dedicated to the forced resettlement of Polish and Jewish population of Warthegau to General Government, in Eisenbach and Rutkowski, *Eksterminacja Żydów*, 45.

39 Radzik, "Praca przymusowa," 308; Janusz Peter, "W Bełżcu podczas okupacji," in *Tomaszowskie za okupacji*, ed. Janusz Peter (Tomaszów: Nakł. Tomaszowskiego Towarzystwa Regionalnego, 1991), 180.

40 APL, RŻL-8, 52, Report from the activity of the [Jewish] Council [in Lublin] for the period September 1, 1939 until August 31, 1940.

41 Beginning of September 1940, Warsaw, Report of the Warsaw District governor, Ludwig Fischer for August 1940, about situation of the Jews sent to labor camps in the Lublin region, in Eisenbach and Rutkowski, *Eksterminacja Żydów*, 218–19; September 7, 1940, Lublin, Report of the Department of the Interior Office of the Lublin District Governor for August, 1940 about the use of Jewish labor and difficulties of planned employment of the Jewish professional labor forces because of arbitrary moves of the commander of SS and police, Globocnik, in Eisenbach and Rutkowski, *Eksterminacja Żydów*, 219–20.

42 Radzik, "Praca przymusowa," 310.

43 Krzysztof Pilarczyk, ed., *Żydzi i judaizm we współczesnych badaniach polskich: Materiały z konferencji, Kraków, 21–23 XI 1995* (Krakow: Księgarnia Akademicka Wydawnictwo Naukowe, 1997), 308; Peter, "W Bełżcu podczas okupacji," 180.

very beginning of his activity in Lublin, Globocnik tried to exploit the Jews. He did not take into account the many other economic factors. First of all, the continuous exploitation of the Jews and shifting all the costs of forced labor on them had its limits. Going beyond such limits not only accelerated impoverishment of the Jewish society, but also caused the collapse of Jewish institutions. Another important element of the unlimited exploitation of the Jews by Globocnik was paralysis of many important economic assets and facilities in the General Government.[44] Perhaps, Globocnik deliberately tried to push forward his interests, hoping that other people will deal with the problems he created. However, shifting costs and responsibility on the Jews had their source also in official documents. It was Friedrich-Wilhelm Krüger, who in his regulations of December 1939 and January 1940 required the *Judenräte* to supply the poor Jewish workers.[45]

Organizing his camps, Globocnik intended not only to exploit Jewish workers for free, but also to pass on to the *Judenräte* any responsibility for their administration and financing. In this way, he exploited Jewish community both through people able to work and financially, by shifting costs on them. The drainage of able-bodied Jews to the labor force caused a serious economic weakening of the Jewish community in Jewish residential areas and ghettos, creating imbalance between working and not working people.[46] In this way, Globocnik received not only free labor, but also escaped administrative costs. In addition, he objected to the agreement of July 4, 1940 between Friedrich-Wilhelm Krüger and Hans Frank, who required from German institutions hiring Jews to pay for their work. Globocnik was exempted from paying the wages to Jews who worked in his labor camps.

The organization of the camps complex in Bełżec was conducted in accordance with Globocnik's idea of unlimited use of the Jews. Although the SS was responsible for the organizational framework and for the engineering service of the camp, matters related to workers were entirely left to the Jews. The Jews had to supply labor to the camps. However, this did not end their role. The Jews were responsible for the organization, activities, and funding of the camp.

---

44 September 7, 1940, Lublin, Report of the Department of the Interior Office of the Lublin District Governor for August, 1940 about the use of Jewish labor and difficulties of planned employment of the Jewish professional labor forces because of arbitrary moves of the commander of SS and police, Globocnik, in *Eksterminacja Żydów*, 219–20.
45 Ibid.
46 N. Rosen, "The Problem of Work in the Jewish quarter—July 1942," *To Live with Honor and Die with Honor: Selected Documents from the Warsaw Ghetto Underground Archives "O.S." (Oneg Shabbath)*, ed. Joseph Kermish (Jerusalem: Yad Vashem, 1986), 259.

Forced Labor in the Labor Camps • CHAPTER 4 | 147

The condition of the camps and their bad organization was noticed by the civil administration and reported to the General Government in Kraków. For example, the *Kreishauptmann* of Zamość wrote in his monthly report in September 1940:

> It is known that in order to create the border fortifications, large Jewish forced labor camps, which were set up [in the area of Bełżec], have grown greatly in the last period. The sanitary and general conditions are, of course, quite primitive. Recently complaints have been lodged by the Wehrmacht, which I have forwarded to the solely responsible SS-Office in Lublin. In the management of Jewish camp, only the Department of Food and Agriculture is a participant when it has to make the necessary allocations for the catering.[47]

In those conditions, the physical state of the workers was quickly deteriorating and after a few months the released workers were totally unable to work. For example:

> The Jews who were sent from the Jewish camp Bełżec to the water management authority, unfortunately, had to be dismissed again, as they had been extremely exploited by the agency then responsible for the measure (SS) and are now totally unable to work. The further use of these Jews is impossible, even in future.[48]

COMMITTEE OF THE CAMP AT BEŁŻEC

The first group of Jews sent to the camp at Bełżec was from Lublin, and Bełżec itself was within the province of Lublin. Therefore, the Jewish Council in Lublin took action to care for the workers from their area.[49] So, the decision was made on June 1, 1940 to establish the Department of External Labor Camps. However, the German camp headquarters in Bełżec also set up a so-called Committee (*Gremium*),[50] which was a representation of the Jewish community. Task of the committee was "to organize the camp services and to

---

47 Der Kreishauptmann des Kreises Zamość, Lagebericht, Zamość, den 10. September 1940, scan 172.
48 YVA-JM.2700, Vermerk, 20. November 1940, Betr: Arbeiteinsatz von Juden, scans 40–41.
49 Radzik, "Praca przymusowa," 311.
50 APL, RŻL-8, 52, Report on the activity of the [Jewish] Council [in Lublin] from September 1, 1939 to August 31, 1940.

gain material means of subsistence in order to maintain the camp."[51] Members of the Committee were composed of members of the Jewish Council in Lublin, headed by its President Engineer Henryk Bekker. The Committee was to prepare the rooms for the workers, providing food, transport, medical care, and provision of correspondence and parcels.

According to Globocnik's idea, the Jewish community should bear all costs associated with camp maintainance. The money was to be transferred by the Jewish Council of the Lublin district. Therefore, the committee requested that 57 Jewish councils transfer money for this purpose. However, only 9 of them sent money. By September 1, 1940, 37,178 zł were spent on the camps, of which only 10,525 zł were sent by the Jewish councils of the district.[52] The rest was covered by the Jewish Council in Lublin. The money came from tax collections and the Jews of Lublin. Lack of cooperation from the Jewish councils in the district of Lublin has caused many conflicts between them and the Jewish Council in Lublin. First of all, the cost of living in most parts of the camp fell on the Jewish community in Lublin. This uneven burden-sharing, given the bad economic situation of the Jewish population, worsened their condition.

This situation was well-known to the German authorities. During the meeting devoted to the security situation in the General Government, the following minutes were recorded:

> If we will continue to use the robbery tactics against Jewish communities, then one fine day, millions of Jews will become a burden to the General Government. Finally, we cannot let them to die of hunger. The means available to Jewry are quite limited; as in the General Government there are no more rich Jews, mostly Jewish proletariat has remained on the spot. The speaker therefore considers that a fundamental decision on the supervision of the Jewish Councils of Elders and religious communities would be highly desirable. Security Police is by no means interested in additional hassle, but practice has shown that the current procedure in this section was not appropriate.[53]

---

51 Radzik, "Praca przymusowa," Radzik, Tadeusz, "Praca przymusowa ludności żydowskiej na przykładzie obozu pracy w Bełżcu w 1940 r.," in *Żydzi i judaizm we współczesnych badaniach polskich: Materiały z konferencji, Kraków, 21–23 XI 1995*, ed. Krzysztof Pilarczyk, Księgarnia Akademicka Wydawnictwo Naukowe, Kraków, 1997, 311.
52 Pilarczyk, *Żydzi i judaizm*, 307–19.
53 May 30, 1940, Kraków, Minutes of the police conference dedicated to issues of the security situation in the General Government. In Frank, *Okupacja i ruch oporu*, 211.

To ensure the influx of the workforce, Dr. Frauendorfer organized a meeting of the Labor Department in Kraków on August 6, 1940. It was not possible to send thousands of Jewish workers to perform fortification works in the camps in the area of Bełżec without any coordination and cooperation with labor offices. During the conference, there was a discussion concerning demands for Jewish workers in the General Government.

At the meeting, problems with the recruitment of labor force were discussed. The original design of employing 2.5 million Jews was totally unrealistic. Such evaluation of the available labor force was unfounded and not supported by any calculations. Even providing much more modest number of Jewish workers exceeded the capabilities of the Lublin district, which is why it was necessary to call a conference of the Labor Department—to provide Jewish workers from other districts.

At the beginning of the discussion about Bełżec camps, strategic reasons for building the belt of fortifications were mentioned. However, the strip of fortification had not been completed before the end of the campaign in Western Europe. Winning the campaign and changing the strategic balance in favor of Germany did not cause the abandonment of the construction of the strip of fortifications. In response to the campaign in Western Europe, the USSR began to implement the provisions of the Ribbentrop-Molotov pact, annexing Bessarabia and Northern Bukovina, and proceeding to the direct occupation of the Baltic States. Despite these steps, there was not any hostile action or deterioration of relations between Germany and the USSR. Germany had no reason to suspect the USSR of offensive action. However, the construction of fortifications belt was the result not only of immediate threat, but rather of long-term strategic plans that played an important role in land-defense system. Therefore, despite the winning campaign and stable relations with the Soviet Union, the German authorities continued to work on the belt of fortifications in the Bełżec area.

The head of the Labor Department under the chief of the District Lublin stated that

> ... the demand for labor at construction projects related to water management could be covered by the district [...] but it is impossible to get accurate data on the number of Jews who can be mobilized to work on the basis of the filing of the Jewish cards. Recently there have been noticed considerable uncertainties in cooperation with SS.[54]

---

54 YVA-JM.2700, Protokoll über die Judeneinsatzbesprechung vom 6. August 1940 [...] bei der Abteilung Arbeit im Amt des Generalgouverneurs, scan 6.

According to Dr. Hofbauer's assessment, 10,000 Jewish workers had to be mobilized immediately in Lublin.[55] As stated by the head of the Labor Department under the chief of the District Warsaw, in August 1940 about 6,000 to 8,000 Jews were employed. After meeting the demand of the district, a significant number of Jews can be sent to the fortification works in the district of Lublin.[56] The representative of the district of Kraków stated:

> Kraków District cannot send workers because of the high demand in the district. There is a great need to provide workers for the roads and the construction of a hydroelectric dam in Rożnów, which is also covered by the district. Therefore, it is not possible to send Jewish workers to Lublin.[57]

In the case of Lublin, the most important was the demand for 2,700 Jewish laborers to be employed at the water management, and then at the construction of fortifications.[58] It was agreed that districts of Warsaw and Radom would immediately set transports to district of Lublin, and district of Kraków primarily would cover the demand of hydroelectric dam in Rożnów, and later, if possible, would send workers to Lublin for the construction of border fortifications.[59]

In order to increase the number of workers, on August 14 to 16, 1940 mass roundups were held in various towns[60] of Lublin District,[61] as well as in other districts. Here are just two examples of correspondence on this matter and lack of communication between the SS, labor offices, and civil administration:

> On the night between November 14 and 15, 1940, a police raid (*Razzia*) took place, where 250–300 Jews were arrested. The Labor Office in Lublin is registering Jews, but the SS is disturbing, since it conducts police raids

---

55 Ibid.
56 Ibid., scan 5.
57 Ibid.
58 Ibid., scan 4.
59 Ibid.
60 Lageberichte, Kreshauptmann des Kreises Chełm, September 9, 1940. Information about 374 Jews arrested during Special Action (*Sonderaktion*) of August 14, 1940, who were later brought by train to Bełżec. YVA-O53/101, 3.
61 Letter of August 20, 1949 to Frauendorfer about the arrests of Jews. YVA-JM.12307, scans 40–41. The Governor of the District Lublin Zörner ordered the Arbeitsamt in Lublin to cooperate with the police. This letter describes sending 5500 Jews to build border fortifications. No Jews were sent to the road-building firms (*Strassenbau*) or water administration (*Wasserwirtschaft*).

without informing other institutions. [...] most of the Jews have regular identity cards issued by the Labor Office in Lublin, but the SS does not take this fact into consideration.[62]

In another document, the chef of the Labor Office in Łuków

... reported by telephone that today a police raid occurred in the county of Radzyń. The SS has detained 60 Jews, who were shipped off to Lublin. The documents were not taken into consideration by the SS, despite valid stamps. Part of those Jews was employed by the German authorities. Further police raids in Radzyń County are expected. The *Kreishauptmann* of Radzyń informed Governor Zörner about this matter.[63]

As a result of these raids, more than 10,000 Jews arrived to Bełżec.[64] The haste and vehemence of the action meant that people unable to work also wound up in Bełżec. As was also agreed during the conference in Kraków: "As the camps in Lublin [District] are infested with lice, shipments will not be passed delousing. Jews will be examined by Jewish doctors, and those unable [to work] will be further examined by SS physicians or contracted physicians."[65] They were devoid of any personal items, essential in the camp.[66] Since this action was organized by the police, in most cases labor offices did not participate in it. In some cases, they did not really know about the action. In fact, there is a correspondence to Globocnik from labor offices complaining that this wild action did not permit the checking of the Jewish card index (*Judenkartei*) taken over by the labor offices after the agreement between Friedrich-Wilhelm Krüger and Hans Frank concerning administration of Jewish forced labor by the labor offices. This meant that many arrested workers were already employed or unfit for this kind of work.[67] The number of Jewish workers in Bełżec had increased to about 11,000[68]. The camps in

---

62   YVA-JM.2700, 15.11.1940, Vermerk, scan 27.
63   Ibid., scan 28.
64   APL, RŻL-8, 52, Report on the activity of the [Jewish] Council [in Lublin] from September 1, 1939 to August 31, 1940.
65   YVA-JM.2700, Protokoll über die Judeneinsatzbesprechung vom. 6 August 1940 [...] bei der Abteilung Arbeit im Amt des Generalgouverneurs, scan 4.
66   Radzik, "Praca przymusowa," 309.
67   YVA-JM.12307, scans 45, 50.
68   Vermerk, August 20, 1940. Probably due to quantity of Jews arrested in different districts and sent to the district of Lublin and lack of appropriate facilities, Globocnik decided to send

Bełżec now hosted many thousands of Jews from other districts. For example, 2975 workers in the camps were from Lublin,[69] and about 5,200 workers came from Warsaw District. The others came mainly from the district of Radom.[70] Jewish workers from the other districts were shipped to the district of Lublin, despite high demand in other regions. The *Kreishauptmann* of Skierniewice wrote in his report:

> In the County Skierniewice high demand for workers to perform melioration works continued in August, and could hardly be covered. [. . .] 200 Jews were sent to the assembly place in Warsaw for the work enterprises in Lublin.[71]

THE COMPLEX CAMPS IN BEŁŻEC

The arrival of many thousands of workers led to the rapid growth of camps not only in Bełżec but also in the surrounding area.[72] Most of the shipments arrived within three days. As a result of this action, the following camps were established: Bełżec-Dwór (Bełżec-Manor), Bełżec-Młyn (Bełżec-Mill), Bełżec-Parowozownia (Bełżec-Roundhouse), and the camps in Cieszanów, Lipsk, Płazów, and Dzików. Accommodation in Bełżec and other places was not suitable for such a large number of workers. After few days, most of workers were placed in the camps. 2,800 workers remained in Bełżec,[73] 2,086 people arrived in Lipsk; 1,250 people went to Płazów; 3,000 people to Cieszanów, and 1,000 people to Dzików.[74]

---

a part of Jewish workers to perform works for *Wasserwirtschaftamt*. He ordered to send 65% of workers to Bełżec complex and 35% to be deployed by the labor offices in the district of Lublin. YVA-JM.12307, scan 43.
69   APL, RŻL-6, 72, Annex nr 5, Forced labor of Lublin's Jews in 1940 in the city of Lublin and outside.
70   On August 19, 1940, 1192 Jews from Ostrowiec, Radom, and Warsaw arrived in Lublin. See YVA-JM.12307, 49. On August 20, 1940, 500 Jews from Radom arrived in Lublin. See YVA-JM.12307, scans 40–41. Kiełboń, Janina, "Deportacje Żydów do dystryktu lubelskiego," *Zeszyty Majdanka* 14 (1992): 69–70; Radzik, "Praca przymusowa," 310.
71   YVA-JM.814, Kreishauptmannschaft des Kreises Skierniewice, Lagebericht, September 9, 1940, scan 283.
72   Radzik, "Praca przymusowa," 310.
73   APL, RŻL-47, 25. Report on the activity of the Central Camps Council in Bełżec from June 13 to December 5, 1940.
74   Ibid.

The sudden arrival of thousands of workers to Bełżec as a result of raids from August 14 to 16, 1940 caused a crisis in the camp. The arrival of so many people was not in any way prepared for, and not agreed with the committee. Accommodation was not ready; there was lack of food and money. This resulted in the collapse of the functioning of the committee. The committee, consisting of several representatives on the spot while other members were away from Bełżec, could not meet the new requirements of the organization; therefore, on August 21, the Central Camp Council in Bełżec was established.[75]

Organizational changes concerning new methods of the operation of camps concerned Bełżec and Lublin. As in Bełżec the committee ceased to exist and the Central Camp Council appeared in its place, so also in Lublin a Committee for Aid to Workers in the Camps was established. The Committee had asked for assistance from other Jewish councils.[76] In Warsaw and Lublin conferences of Jewish communities were held, but without significant results. According to the calculations, 60% of all money spent on the maintenance of the camps in Bełżec (amounting to about 100,000 zł) was covered by the *Judenrat* in Lublin, while only about 15% of workers in the camps came from Lublin.[77]

In addition to Camp at 7 Lipowa Street in Lublin and the camps in Bełżec, many other labor camps arose after the spring of 1940. These camps had different structures, which will be discussed below. As a basis for the establishment of labor camps, the regulation issued by Hans Frank on October 26, 1939 was always mentioned. This document introduced forced labor for Jews between the ages of 18 to 60 years. On December 12, 1939 the age threshold had been lowered to 14 years of age. In the same piece of legislation, in paragraph 2, Friedrich-Wilhelm Krüger pointed to the possibility of creating labor camps.[78] However, no legal document dealing exclusively with the establishment and organization of labor camps had been issued.

Some labor camps for Jews were created by SSPF. Under Frank's regulation of October 26, 1939, all responsibility for Jewish forced labor was transferred to HSSPF, which allowed the SS and police in various districts to create labor

---

75　Pilarczyk, *Żydzi i judaizm*, 311.
76　"O obozach pracy w Lublinie," *Gazeta Żydowska*, September 3, 1940, 2; "Zorganizowanie pomocy dla obozów pracy: Co zdziałała Rada Żydowska w Warszawie," *Gazeta Żydowska*, October 11, 1940, 2; "Akcja pomocy dla przebywających w obozach pracy," *Gazeta Żydowska*, October 14, 1940, 2; "Z obozów pracy: Akcja zbiórkowa na rzecz obozów pracy w Warszawie," *Gazeta Żydowska*, December 3, 1940, 2
77　Radzik, "Praca przymusowa," 312.
78　Pospieszalski, *Hitlerowskie "prawo" okupacyjne*, vol. 2, 562–63.

camps. Camps in Bełżec and its surroundings in the district of Lublin were set up on this basis. Forced labor camps subjected to SS and police leaders were created in other districts as well.[79]

THE CAMPS ESTABLISHED BY THE CIVIL ADMINISTRATION

The administration in most of the labor camps was in the hands of the relevant German institutions. The complex in Bełżec was an exception in this respect, because it was a big camp complex performing important strategic tasks and run by the SS, where most of the administrative work was performed by Jews.[80] Typically, the division of the camp administration was as follows: in the camps under the management of SS and police commander in the district, the authority which exercised command in the camp was made up of SS members. Guard functions were in the hands of SS auxiliary services made mostly of Ukrainians and other nationalities (after June 1941). Guard service at the beginning of the camps in Lublin District was also *Selbstschutz* units composed of *Volksdeutsche* (ethnic Germans).[81] According to the report by an *Abwehr* officer:

> Custody is completely inadequate, in the camp as well as at work. In the camps of Lipsko, Płazów, and Cieszanów the *Volksdeutsche* are currently active, but they do not have sufficient numbers to prohibit deliberate border crossings, especially at work. So I observed in Lipsko, shortly before 6 p.m., two gangs of 40 men each mustering up on a road 10 m from the border, without any guard near. The groups were mustered and tallied by Jewish wardens. In Bełżec there are only two guards with rifles and in the tower two guards with a machine gun at hand to watch the allegedly 6 km road to work and 3.000–4.000 men. But in this woodland one can only see a part of the road from the tower. So here, too, border crossings are easily possible. In Lipsko, once again, four people have crossed the border on September 22 [1940]. If, despite this insufficient watch, the number of transgressions is relatively small, it is due to the fact that most people have relatives on this side, and they don't want to lose connection with their relatives, or they fear retaliatory measures against their relatives. On the other hand, it is the supervision of the Jewish watch, who are afraid of reprisals if they lose men from their group. Often the incertitude about

---

79 Łukaszewicz, "Obóz pracy w Treblince."
80 Marszałek, *Obozy pracy w Generalnym Gubernatorstwie*.
81 Lenarczyk, "Obóz pracy przymusowej," 39.

the Russians' attitude towards escapees might curtail the inclination to escape. Customs officials are of the opinion that Jews are generally shot by the Russians. In one instance, a customs official observed three escaped Jews waving their hands from the other side, and shortly after shots were heard, so it was assumed that these Jews were shot by the Russian border patrol. The German command dealt with the administration of the camps, but the office support functions were performed by the prisoners. All work in camps linked to the maintenance was performed by prisoners.[82]

The tasks for which the camps were created were in the hands of professional staff: mainly engineers and technicians. In labor camps, where Jewish workers performed only auxiliary works, the essential work was performed by firms responsible for carrying out the tasks. Those firms provided professional management: managers, engineers, and supervisory workers, as well as average technical supervision—technicians and craftsmen. Usually, some part of the work was performed by wage-earning Polish workers. However, in those cases where most of the work was done by Jewish workers, only technical supervision was performed by German or Polish engineers and foremen employed by the company. The German administration, as a part of the organization structure of the General Government, supervised the work of several camps or in a particular area.

RECRUITMENT TO LABOR CAMPS

Recruitment to labor camps took place in the Jewish quarters and was organized by the Labor Departments of the *Judenräte*. Based on previously prepared files, men, mostly aged 18–25, were chosen to work in the camps. Soon, however, the maximum age was raised to 35 years.[83] According to the regulations issued by the HSSPF Friedrich-Wilhelm Krüger of December 11 and 12, 1939, the Jews had to perform forced labor. The initial practice was to serve one day a week for free in the framework of forced labor. However, working in the camps was different. Due to the remoteness of the place, this work had to be carried out continuously. Distance from home and family caused additional difficulties. Therefore, the call to work in labor camps posed a serious dilemma

---

82 BA-MA, RH53-23-27, Tgb. Nr. 1433/40 gIIIC, Judenlager an der Grenze, Lublin, 24.9.40, 145–47.
83 Kermish, *To Live with Honor*, 250.

before the Jews.[84] Naturally, failing to appear for work in the camps led to specific consequences. It should be emphasized that during the summer of 1940, when the first groups of workers were recruited, the work in the camps was an unknown phenomenon, and many of those called to the work agreed to go, for the prospect of having jobs and income. For many displaced people from the territories annexed to the Reich and deported to the General Government, who did not have any background information, the opportunity to work in the camps, where they would get food and payment, seemed tempting.[85]

The workers chosen for labor camps received personal summons and had be present at rallying points with specific items of equipment. Some of the summoned tried to obtain an exemption, which was associated with obtaining appropriate medical certificate or paying the appropriate sum of money. From the first days of forced labor, the practice of substitutions was developed in the area. However, finding substitutes for work in the camps was much more difficult. This resulted, on the one hand, in increased corruption, because people having material means attempted to pay money in order to avoid shipment to the camp; and on the other hand, it caused increased exploitation of weaker and poorer Jews, who belonged to the lowest social strata of society. From among those called to work in the camps, many people did not present themselves due to medical exemptions, because they paid, or simply because they did not bother to find excuses. Lack of adequate numbers of workers meant that those absent or exempted had to be replaced with other recruits. The possibility of shipment to the camps caused the Jews to find other permanent places of employment, which was also noticed in the province. The *Stadkomissar* of Ostrowiec wrote: "There are already several hundred skillful Jews who were sent by the labor office to Lublin. This is a success that there are many Jews now, who are more willing to come to work in order not be sent [to the labor camps in Lublin]. They also make more effort to get permanent work."[86]

In the first phase of recruitment to the camps in the summer of 1940, particularly in the Warsaw Ghetto, there was a very high unemployment, not only because of the lack of jobs. The influx of refugees and deportees from other locations, in the early days of the areas incorporated into the Reich, only increased the number of residents, even worsening the employment situation. Many refugees did not have the means to feed themselves, so for some of them

---

84 Rosen, "The problem of work," 258.
85 Ringelblum, *Kronika getta warszawskiego*, 200.
86 YVA-JM.814, Stadtkommissar der Stadt Ostrowiec an den Herrn Kreishauptmann in Opatów, Lagebericht für August 1940, Ostrowiec, den 5 September 1940, scan 309.

work in the camps seemed to be the only chance. Therefore, in the initial stage of the recruitment many of the unemployed people who did not have means of support reported to work in the camps.[87] Intelligentsia was particularly vulnerable because their previous jobs were now useless; moreover, they often lacked the knowledge and experience in carrying out other work and therefore they simply became unskilled workers. The difficult situation concerning employment was also known to the German civil administration. In the report delivered to the Secretary of the State Dr. Josef Bühler we find the following information: "7,604 Jews were sent to labor and 9,000 were still available at the end of this month; at the end of October, around 2,000 workplaces were still open for Jews."[88] However, with the spread of news about difficult conditions in labor camps, disease, and violence, even the unemployed displaced people began to avoid reporting to work, which resulted in arrests of men and their forceful transfer to work in the camps.[89]

A common way of recruiting labor was arrests[90] of random passersby on the streets of the Jewish quarters. Arrests were also made during the night.[91] Usually, transported men were taken to rallying points where they waited until a sufficient number of people could be collected for further transportation to the camp. At the collection points they had to pass a medical inspection, after which those unable to perform hard physical work were released. According to the report by the *Kreishauptmann* of Opatów:

> Various actions to secure the provision of Jewish labor by the *Arbeitsamt* did not always achieve the desired success because the listed people were almost without exception untraceable. A totally unsuspected action with the support of the Wehrmacht came off best.[92]

---

87 Rosen, "The problem of work," 258; Henryk Bryskier, *Żydzi pod swastyką czyli getto w Warszawie w XX wieku* (Warsaw: Oficyna Wydawnicza ASPRA-JR, 2006), 63–64.
88 YVA-JM.814, Blatt zum Schreiben an Staatssekretär Dr. Bühler vom 18 November 1940, Judeneinsatz, scan 483.
89 Bryskier, *Żydzi pod swastyką*, 63–64.
90 Vermerk, October 10, 1940, concerning arrest of Jews in Lublin for performing the works on Krakowskie Przedmieście. YVA-JM.12307, 51. A letter of December 10, 1941 mentions a *Razzia*, during which 500 Jews were arrested. The medical services and labor office had infirmation about the action, however, the latter did not have any decisive power. YVA-JM.12307, 59.
91 "Six weeks in a forced labor camp," AR I/399, in Kermish, *To Live with Honor*, 270; H. Huberband, "Dynasy—Summer of 1940," in Kermish, *To Live with Honor*, 262.
92 YVA, JM-814, Der Kreishauptmann des Kreises Opatów, District Radom, Lagebericht für August 1940, Opatów, den 7 September 1940, scans 306–7.

According to the data contained in Rosen's report from the Warsaw Ghetto, about 60% of all summoned were found unable to work in the camps. The reason for this was their bad health condition or emaciation resulting from malnutrition.[93] But medical control was not always carried out. During the great wave of arrests of August 14–16, 1940, thousands of Jews were arrested and transported to labor camps without any medical control. Only in the camps it became clear that many of them were unable to work. The arrested were led under guard from assembly points to the train station, where the transports departed. In the case of local camps, some dozens of kilometers away, the prisoners could also be transported on trucks.[94] Upon arrival at the camp, frequent beatings and abuse of newcomers took place in the first moments.

In some cases, Jews unable to work were intentionally sent to the camps. For example, on October 22, 1940, Stalag II B Hammerstein, near Königsberg, sent 1,550 Jewish prisoners of war to the train station Ryki, from where they should march to Biała Podlaska.[95] In fact, only about 800 POWs arrived for the Water Management Inspection and the Constructions Management of the Luftwaffe (*Bauleitung der Luftwaffe*) in Biała Podlaska;[96] and among those 800 Jews from Königsberg, 250 were crippled and sick. They had to be released and transferred to the Assistance Committee at the *Judenrat* in Biała Podlaska.[97] From further correspondence on this matter we learn that

> ... among other [Jewish] POWs from Hammerstein, 200 Jews had prostheses and were unable to work. They should be released and the costs [of their transport] will be covered by the Water Management and Luftwaffe. The problem is that they come from the lands of the Russians—they are destitute and without clothes. Due to bad weather and lack of clothes, a great part of the Jews does not work, and there is decline in performance. Please contact the BuF to get assistance.[98]

---

93 Rosen, "The problem of work in the Jewish quarter—July 1942," in Kermish, *To Live with Honor*, 258.
94 Kermish, *To Live with Honor*, 262–63, 270–71.
95 YVA-JM.2700, Chef des Districts Lublin, 24 Oktober, 1940. Arbeitseinsatz Kriegsgefangenen Juden, scan 20.
96 YVA-JM.2700, Arbeitseinsatz der jüd. Bevölkerung, Biała Podlaska, October 28, 1940, scan 21.
97 YVA-JM.2700, A letter from the Department Labor, Referat II to the Department of Internal Administration, Subdivision BuF, November 5, 1940, Arbeitseinsatz Kriegsgefangenen Juden, scan 22.
98 YVA-JM.2700, 13.11.1940, Amt des Generalgouverneurs, Abteilung Arbeit, Einsatz der Juden, an den Herrn Leiter der Abteilung Arbeit beim Chefs des Distrkits Lublin, scan 26.

As in many other cases, the Jewish POWs were treated by the Wehrmacht as a burden, and therefore every possible way of getting rid of them seemed acceptable, even by sending the infirm to labor camps.

In some places agreements between the police at the labor offices and the civil administration were made to end police raids. For example, in Lublin, the chief of the Lublin District wrote a letter on November 11, 1940:

> All police stations shall, when they need Jewish workers, contact the Department of Labor on the allocation of the required number of workers. The Department of Labor, in turn, ensures further processing of this request by way of negotiation with the labor offices. If the department of Labor or competent Labor Office will not provide the necessary number of workers within the required time, the police can independently detect the Jews by the way of a police raid. In what number and in which locations Jews shall be tracked forcibly by the police, will be established together with the Department of Labor or relevant Labor Office.
>
> In particularly urgent cases, the police can independently decide to conduct police raids on Jews. In this case, however, it is necessary to provide timely and immediate information to the Labor Office or Labor Department. These forces may only be used temporarily, and must be replaced by the Jews properly mobilized by the Labor Offices. The Labor Offices are obliged to inform in advance the competent *Kreis-* or *Stadthauptmann* about the proposed measures.[99]
>
> ... During the police raids on Jews, the police will detain no Jews that have the newly introduced work permit (brown card with the Star of David).[100]

LIVING CONDITIONS IN CAMPS

The living conditions in labor camps varied greatly depending on the type of camp. The hardest were in the camps of Bełżec and the surrounding area, which were under the direct management of the SS and were designed to construct very heavy earthworks. They were very large camps numbering several thousand workers who came there in very short period of time. The

---

99 YVA-JM.2700, Der Chef des Distrikts Lublin, Lublin, am 28.11.1940. Wegen Zusammenarbeit der Polizei mit der Abteilung Arbeit beim Distriktschef und den Arbeitsämtern über Fragen des Judeneinsatz, scan 56.
100 Ibid.

camp infrastructure was not originally prepared to receive such large numbers of people, so the new arrivals were placed in primitive conditions in a room suddenly adapted to the needs of workers. The situation in other camps was difficult as well because most of the temporary labor camps were created at random in the field, in public buildings, or service buildings not designed to accommodate people. This was basically the rule, and only in some cases did workers build special barracks. Most barracks were constructed in areas remote from villages.

The fundamental problem of labor camps in the first years of the occupation was their temporary character, which meant that they did not have a well-organized infrastructure. Most of the work performed during this period took place in the field. After the execution of the works, the inmates were transferred to another place to continue their work. In such cases, either the whole camp was moved, or the route march to the place of work was lengthened. In better situations were probably small labor camps designated to carry out field work in agriculture. Usually, they were located in agricultural estates, in barns or other areas,[101] but the ruling regime there was not as severe as in the larger SS camps or in the camps for amelioration works, construction, road construction, and others. In the camps designed to perform agricultural work, there was a better board and the supervisor did not bully the workers to such an extent. In such camps, supervisors were usually regular workers of the property and not members of *Selbstschutz* or Ukrainian formations, and they treated the Jewish workers more mildly. Some labor camps in agriculture were not guarded at all. For example, Jews in Lublin were mobilized for summer work in agriculture from mid-June to mid-August. In more than 30 estates, 770 men and 59 women worked for 0.50 zł per day plus accommodation. There was no lack of volunteers for such works.[102] However, even if some camps were unguarded, this did not mean that there was a possibility to run away, because in such cases both the fleers and their families in places of residence were threatened by serious consequences.

Particularly severe living conditions prevailed in the camps of Bełżec complex and the camps performing drainage work. They were the result of extreme exploitation of Jewish labor force by authorities who did not have the skills to

---

101 Extract from a letter of a nurse from the camp in Oszczów of September 26, 1940, Eisenbach and Rutkowski, *Eksterminacja Żydów*, 223.
102 APL, RŻL-47, 54–55. Report on the activity of the Central Camps Council in Bełżec from June 13 to December 5, 1940.

deal with the economy and proper organization of labor. SSPF Odilo Globocnik was responsible for Bełżec camps complex. For the rest the responsible authority was the Water Management Inspection; however, the ill-treatment of the workers was the result of 'exploitory attitude'[103] of both the SS and economic authorities involved. During the meeting on April 22, 1940, Globocnik said: "Unless labor place is not in the area of residence, we intend to put the workers in the camps, especially when it comes to larger works. The cost of living and food will be covered by the [Jewish] religious community, in this way we can also have the Jewish property, which otherwise we could not grab. The food and clothing will be supplied by Jewish women and Jews already unable to work. Strict separation of sexes will be conducted."[104] Globocnik also stated: "As the work force is completely or almost free, we will be able to increase the relatively small budgets of individual departments."[105]

The exploitation of the Jews was made difficult by the chaos that prevailed in the area of their employment, as noted by Bruno Streckenbach at the meeting on May 30, 1940:

> The authority of the *Sicherheitspolizei* (Security Police) over the Jews, however, has been gradually somewhat restricted, since all political organizations and formations used a Council of Elders and religious communities in a completely chaotic manner. Without setting any plan, it had been ordered to send work force; moreover, it was arbitrarily demanded that the Council of Elders provides a variety of objects—sometimes even amounts of money. In that case, a clear decision must be taken. First we must solve the problem which authorities are to exercise oversight over the Jewish Councils of Elders—*Stadthauptmann*, district head, mayor, or the Security Police. The speaker has a specific reason to believe the latter case is the most appropriate.[106]

---

103 The organizations exploiting forced labor of Jews were interested in performing certain labor at minimal cost and exploiting Jewish workers to the maximum, disregarding their health, living conditions, and safety.
104 Lublin, April 22, 1940, Statement of HSSPF Krüger at Meeting of Heads of Government Departments of the General Government, dedicated to the Forced Labor of Jews, in Eisenbach and Rutkowski, *Eksterminacja Żydów*, 209.
105 Eisenbach and Rutkowski, *Eksterminacja Żydów*, 209–10.
106 Speech of Streckenbach (May 30, 1940, Kraków). Minutes of the police conference dedicated entirety of matters related to the security situation in the General Government, in Frank, *Okupacja i ruch oporu*, vol. 1, 210.

Further, Streckenbach said:

> The Security Police, seeking to regulate such matters [the use of Jewish labor], by no means intended to secure all the benefits that we can pull of the Jews, nor the seizure of the fattest bites. It strictly observes the framework set out in the order on requisition. It receives funding from the Reich and does not feel the need to accumulate wealth, the more so since we do not find any administrative or technical considerations that support this. Therefore, the speaker proposes to solve the problem by transferring the Jewish Council of Elders and all the Jews put together under the supervision of the Security Police and address to it any request from the Jews.[107]

Discussions on the question of to whom Jews were to be subjected lasted for a long time and caused many disputes between the various authorities. Even the agreement of July 4, 1940, between Frank and Krüger did not end the dispute, which lasted until the end of the war, even when the number of Jews was very limited.[108] Unfortunately, this agreement of July 4, 1940 left Globocnik free to manage the Bełżec camps and exploit the Jews residing there. The situation in other camps was also very difficult. The authorities' willingness to work as scheduled in order to execute planned works at the lowest cost meant that individual institutions and offices responsible for these camps were not interested in their conditions. Isolation of camps, lack of proper control,[109] abuse from the guards, and the prevailing corruption meant that in most of camps, the conditions were quite tragic.

Conditions deteriorated with the passage of time spent by the Jewish workers in the camps. Since they received no new clothes or shoes, but stayed in what they had brought with them or on themselves, after a short time, their situation was desperate. Here is a brief description of the situation in Bełżec:

> Poverty in the camp is terrible. I cannot describe it. Naked, barefoot, and hungry, and in addition, sick—they are not people, they are walking shreds. One has to see. This is not a camp that was few weeks after its

---

107 Ibid.
108 Karay, "The Conflict among German Authorities."
109 Even if there were external controls, they did not improve the situation of workers for a long time. See "Six Weeks in a Forced Labor Camp," 275.

creation. Everyone washes their hands; no one can help them—because there is no money.¹¹⁰

The vast majority of camps in the Lublin area performed drainage works: regulation of rivers and streams. During this work, most inmates dug canals and drainage ditches, strengthened levees, and equipped them with wicker edges. The work lasted many hours a day—practically from dawn to dusk. Much of the work was carried out in water, but

> ... inmates employed in this work did not receive any special clothing or shoes for work in water; the type of work forced them to stand 8–10 hours a day in the water. They could not dry their clothes and had to remain in wet clothes due to lack of clothes and spare linen. When working in the water without shoes and bottom clothing, especially exasperating were the leeches, which terribly bit their feet.¹¹¹

Some camps managed by the Water Management office were visited by inspectors, who delivered special reports on this matter. As one report goes:

> In Siedlicze Camp, there are about 200 Jewish workers, including about 60 Jews from Warsaw, and 50 Jews from *Arbeitsamtsbezirk* Siedlce. All Jewish workers in that camp made a relatively good impression, they were well-dressed and had reasonably good shoes. The camp itself is guarded by an *SS-Scharführer* and Ukrainian auxiliary police. The good nutrition is provided with the help of the Jewish Council of Siedlicze. Meat rations are not administered, because this cannot be obtained. The accommodation rooms were clean and tidy. Furnaces were also available in accommodation. In about 3 weeks the works of water management in Siedlicze will be completed and the foreign Jews will be dismissed. The *Judenrat* of Siedlicze has informed me that in the spring 1941, it can provide about 200 Jewish volunteers for the Water Management in Lublin.

---

110 Extract from Report on the Camp at Bełżec (late November), end of 1940, Warszawa, Excerpts from a paper prepared by the desk handling camps by the Labor Battalion in Warsaw, on the inhuman conditions in labor camps for Jews in the Lublin, in Eisenbach and Rutkowski, *Eksterminacja Żydów*, 224.

111 End of 1940, Warszawa. Excerpts from a paper prepared by the desk handling camps by the Labor Battalion in Warsaw, on the inhuman conditions in labor camps for Jews in the Lublin, in Eisenbach and Rutkowski, *Eksterminacja Żydów*, 222.

> The camp no. 2 in Sawin housed about 250 Jews. These Jews (mostly from Warsaw) were released on November 17, 1940, after completion of the work. The camp is located in a former Polish school and is solidly built. The rooms are very large and in good condition. Furnaces are also available. This camp will be set up by the Water Management Lublin as winter camp, with about 100 Jews employed, which shall bring the tools of the Water Management in order. Mr. Holzheimer made every effort to ensure that only Jews from Lublin, mainly carpenters and joiners, will be employed there. The wages are paid according to the tariff rates and the Jews also get food. I have promised Mr. Holzheimer to settle down this matter with the Labor Office in Lublin.[112]

However, *Oberregierungsrat*, the author of a memorandum to the Labor Department in Kraków, had a slightly less optimistic impression in comparison to the above report. He wrote:

> I have further checked the abilities of the Jewish workers in the camps of the Water Management Office and found that these workers are very poorly provided with clothing and shoes. The Department of Water Management Inspection adopts all effort to provide these Jewish workers with shoes and clothing. To date, they did not succeed. Rubber boots have been bought only for the Jewish workers who perform their work in the ditches. The health status of Jews employed by the Water Management is consistently regarded as good. The Jewish workers are paid according to tariff and will also get more food. Jewish doctors are present in almost all camps. [...] To prevent a serious accident with the Jewish workers in the future, it would be appropriate if aid in form of clothing and shoes were allocated for the Jewish workers. From here, unfortunately, no remedy can be found in this matter.[113]

The work that Jewish workers performed was very difficult; besides, there were many other inconveniences, such as the distance to be overcome between the camps and places of work:

> All kinds of work required a great effort on the part of workers [whose] work day lasted 8–10 hours. Conditions of work were very inconvenient: the need

---

112 YVA-JM.2700, Vermerk, Lublin, November 19, 1940, Report of Water Inspection on forced labor camps in Siedlicze, Sawin, and Włodawa, scans 33–34.
113 YVA-JM.2700, Vermerk, 20.11.1940, Betr: Arbeiteinsatz von Juden, scans 40–41.

to stay in the water or on wet meadows, the long route march to the workplace, where the distance from the camp was from 4–6 km up to 12 km (Dzików).[114]

Another passage describes the work conditions during the drainage:

> The work was to smooth down with spades the surface of a canal; [and that's] hard work since we were unused to it. But we were quite nicely stimulated by our overseers. The stomachs behaved wildly with only 180 grams of bread in them. As if this were not enough, it started raining badly, and quite soon water mingled with our sweat in the sogged clothes. They stopped us only toward 3 p.m., and our hungry, wet, perspiring and shivering party started dragging feet back to camp, carrying on the way the first few gravely ill.[115]

Working in the camps was a typical example of overuse of labor, having nothing to do with rational planning, based on economic calculation. Predatory exploitation was based on lack of interest in the physical condition of workers, their nutrition, providing the appropriate clothing, footwear, and tools. Most of the work was performed using the most primitive tools. Here is an excerpt of speech on this subject:

> In other camps road works were performed: bringing and unloading material (stone, cement, and gravel), breaking stones, [and] paving. And here the work was carried out using very primitive tools or directly with bare hands while appropriate tools, assigned in sufficient numbers, could have greatly improved this work. One of the easiest works in the camps was earthworks (excavation and construction of embankments).[116]

Food in the labor camps was often bad and did not provide enough energy for workers doing heavy physical work. From a letter of a nurse staying in the camp in Oszczów we can learn how meals looked for the hard-working workers:

> They get up at 4, at 6 they go to work—they work up to 4 p.m. The diet consists of black coffee without sugar and, apparently, 1/2 kg of bread (in

---

114 Eisenbach and Rutkowski, *Eksterminacja Żydów*, 222–23.
115 "Six Weeks in a Forced Labor Camp," 271.
116 End of 1940, Warsaw, Fragments of the work carried out by the desk handling camps in the Labor Battalion in Warsaw, on the inhuman conditions in labor camps for Jews in the Lublin region, in Eisenbach and Rutkowski, *Eksterminacja Żydów*, 222.

fact it is less), and when they get back from work, 1/2 liter of soup, which in addition to porridge, potatoes, and peas has to include 50 g of meat per capita (this is calculated with the bones). And this is all the food they have during the two meals I mentioned. No fat—only as much is attached to meat, and this is certainly very little.[117]

Alexander Biberstein describes the ration of the Jewish workers in labor camps where Jews from Kraków lived: "The daily diet consisted of 100–150 grams of bread, black colored water called coffee, given twice a day, and a soup of turnip or rotten beets, with individual potatoes, most often previously frozen in the winter.[118]

As follows from the above descriptions, food in the camps was very bad. It was mainly bread, vegetables, and potatoes served in insufficient quantities. All this was greatly diluted with water—whether in the form of soup or coffee. Meat and fat, if at all, were given in negligible amounts. In terms of calories, the food was far from enough for people doing heavy physical work in harsh weather conditions. According to a report of the Jewish Self-Assistance,

> Without the aid in the form of feeding, the results of staying in the camp must become devastating for those workers. 200 grams of bread and a fairly thin soup is much below the minimum in order to manage to do so heavy and unhealthy work. Those who may receive home help are a very small percentage. Only 8 people reported for paid lunches issued by the caretaker.[119]

The result of malnutrition was a continuous deterioration of the physical conditions of the workers. Hard work, harassment, and bad food very quickly weakened the workers so that after a few weeks the results of their situation became visible. Add to this poor housing, as the workers lived in cramped conditions, poor sanitation, lack of spare clothing, and dirt everywhere. Lice and bedbugs multiplied in the camps, which did not only weaken the workers, but also helped spread diseases, especially typhus.[120] As a result, the workers very quickly succumbed to exhaustion, different diseases, and injuries and

---

117 Extract from a letter of a nurse from the camp in Oszczów, September 26, 1940, in Eisenbach and Rutkowski, *Eksterminacja Żydów*, 223.
118 Biberstein, *Zagłada Żydów w Krakowie*, 28.
119 YVA-JM.1581, ŻSS, Notatka z odwiedzin obozu pracy w Koszczu dnia 17 i 18 kwietnia br., Kraków, April 19, 1942, scans 120–21.
120 YVA-JM.12331, Notiz für Brigadeführer über die Besprechung beim Amtschef am 8. August 1941, 10 Uhr ist festzuhalten, scan 221.

accidents at work. In some camps, there were whole weeks when most of the workers were unable to work.

One of the witnesses describing the stay in the labor camp mentioned the overwhelming feeling of hunger, which always accompanied them:

> The hunger has suppressed every other thought and banned all sensation, one does not think of anything else, not even of one's helpless, closest, and most loved people. All that fills one's thoughts is a dream: "To eat!" [. . .] our desires went no further than to black bread and potatoes, in all our wolfish craving. Hunger! It tortured us day and night, never letting up, not even in our fleeting nap—for a deep sleep was unknown to us now, amidst the cold and the lice. [. . .] And again the hunger! At rising and going to sleep, at work and after work, before eating and after. A steady companion is nagging—a killer![121]

The problem of insufficient food and its poor quality was not only a result of corruption and lack of control. Additional factors were mentioned by Emanuel Ringelblum in his diary:

> The scandal of forced labor camps became clearer and clearer. It turns out that the German company that undertook the execution of those works receives 2 zł for each worker and spends only 1.08 zł per day on the food. Doing so, it makes savings at the employees' expense.[122]

In the later period of existence of labor camps, mainly in 1942, and especially in the District of Kraków, the main force aiding the workers in labor camp became the Jewish Self-Assistance. According to a report:

> We stand up to this position that one cannot leave these campers, and it is our duty to help them according to our resources and opportunities. Besides, the Jewish Self-Assistance does not neglect any means to influence the Jewish Councils and Delegations from which the campers are recruited to come with precious help, such as food and clothing for their workers.[123]

---

121 "Six Weeks in a Forced Labor Camp," 273.
122 Entries of September 6, 7, 8, and 9, 1940, in Ringelblum, *Kronika getta warszawskiego*, 148.
123 YVA-JM.1581, ŻSS, Notatka z przewodniczącym Gminy żydowskiej p. Dr. Rozenzweigiem. Kraków, May 10, 1942, scans 732–33.

Paralell to the Jewish Community in Lublin, which became a kind of umbrella organization and supreme Jewish council in the district of Lublin, the Jewish Community in Kraków felt the same towards the Jewish camps in that district. Although the local *Judenräte* were invited, asked, and encouraged to assist the workers in the camps coming from their communities, those *Judenräte* were not always willing or able to bring relief to their countrymen. The Jewish Self-Assistance reported on this matter:

> We have extensively discussed this case, pointing to the fact that the workers located in the vicinity of Kraków in quantity 1,500 people suffer of malnutrition, hunger, and bad accommodation. Until now the communities, where these workers come from, did not give them considerable assistance, except Działoszyce, which sent one parcel. We emphasized that the most important order of the day would be to run the kitchen in Wola Duchacka to allow serving the campers extra soup at lunch time, when the workers are outside the camp. The Committee of Women in Wola Duchacka wants to take on that matter, but this committee should be assisted and, above all, we should mobilize funds for this purpose. Rosenzweig pointed out that the municipality as well as the Jewish community in our area, which gives money in a substantial way to maintain necessary institutions, are not able to nourish better workers coming from Miechów and Kraków Counties.[124]

According to a report of the Jewish Self-Assistance, the Jewish Community of Kraków took the responsibility of aiding Jewish workers in labor camps:

> After a long discussion, Dr. Rosenzweig showed that it is difficult to commit to the full board of campers and in the end agreed with our position that population of Kraków should help those campers and for this reason he is ready to allocate a subsidy of 1,000 zł granted outside the monthly amount to the popular kitchen in the Wola Duchacka for boarding campers. He also mentioned that to relieve the misery of campers we divided or assured more than 100 pairs of clogs, 50 sets of underwear, and several pairs of pants.[125]

---

124 Ibid.
125 Ibid.

Housing conditions of the Jewish workers were also a reflection of their exploitation. Alexander Biberstein describes the living conditions of the Jews from Kraków in labor camps:

> [The people] deported to forced labor camps were placed in barracks not adapted to live in: not heated, with no latrines and other sanitary facilities, no doctors and medicines, hellish nutrition; they were beaten, dirty, often sleeping on the bare ground, and had different diseases.[126]

Workers from Kraków District were assisted by the representatives of the Jewish Social Self-Assistance (ŻSS). In a report there was description of very hard conditions in labor camps in Winnica, Kostrze, and Płaszów. Young men particularly needed new clothes, underwear, and shoes.[127] Similar descriptions of the harsh conditions we can find in the case of the Jewish worker sent from Warsaw to work in the camp:

> We sleep in a big brick horse-barn, on straw unclear blankets. Some have brought little pillows from home, but the majority put their pants or shirts under their heads. By now lean and sunburnt bodies are getting up from all the pallets. They put on torn and mostly dirty underwear and even shabbier clothes.[128]

Similar information can be found in official Jewish reports prepared by the medical committee:

> [The conditions] are in generally fatal, the worst in Narol. The room is completely unfit to accommodate so many people, dark and dirty, although very big. Up to 30% of workers do not have shoes, pants, and shirts. They sleep all on the floor, without straw.[129]

The above descriptions show that in most labor camps housing conditions were very poor. Sometimes workers were placed in public buildings such as

---

126 Biberstein, *Zagłada Żydów w Krakowie*, 28.
127 YVA-JM.1581, PDF frame 105.
128 "Our Day in the Camp," in Kermish, *To Live with Honor*, 267.
129 From the annex nr. 5, Report of medical visit in the camps of Bełżec group (mid-September 1940), in Eisenbach and Rutkowski, *Eksterminacja Żydów*, 223–24.

synagogues,[130] but usually in warehouses, stables, and barns, where they slept on straw in cramped conditions. Everywhere was the impression of temporariness. The camps were not solidly planned and prepared; in most cases they had primary planning of the work schedule as well as technical and engineering plans. The matters regarding workers were the least important. Workers were placed in temporary spaces, not prepared for such a large number of people, which resulted in narrowness. There was no adequate sanitation. Workers often did not have the opportunity to wash and change clothes, which meant that they continued to remain in the same clothes, both during work and after work, or even while sleeping. Not having spare clothes, they could not wash or disinfect what they had.[131]

Especially in the camps, where difficult, debilitating work and malnutrition prevailed, many workers succumbed to disease, or had traumas and injuries; and that resulted in their inability to work. In the camps of Bełżec complex, doctors who could provide care and examine patients were available, but they had limited options: there was no money for medicine.[132] In smaller camps there was no health care; assistance could be provided by doctors from the neighboring village, on the condition that the inmates obtained authorization to go to the doctor. Because many sick Jewish workers met with harassment and were accused of simulation by their supervisors and guards, they often preferred to hide illness or injury and continue work, and reported inability to work only in obvious cases. Heavy physical work, often without adequate clothing and tools, and weakening due to malnutrition caused frequent diseases and traumas. Drainage, in particular, was the cause of many illnesses. The Jews working there worked for many hours in cold water reaching about their knees, not having proper footwear.

Staying in cramped random buildings favored the spread of disease. This is part of the description of one camp of the Bełżec complex:

> . . . everywhere damaged roofs, windows without glass, and terrible narrowness. For example, in a room with dimensions of 5×6 m, 75 people sleep on the floor, one on the other. Under these conditions, there is obvi-

---

130 "Impressions from a Labor Camp," in Kermish, *To Live with Honor*, 269.
131 Ibid.
132 Kraków ŻSS was distributing considerable quantities of medicine in the district, which was then distributed in the ghettos and labor camps; however, it was insufficient. As an example, see confirmation of receiving shipment of medicine by the ŻSS in Lublin in December 1941. YVA-JM.1574, scan 75.

ously no question of undressing. In addition, there is too little soap, and even water is acquired with difficulty. Patients lie and sleep together with the healthy wardens. At night, they cannot go out of the barracks, so that all the natural needs must be dealt with on the spot. No wonder that under these conditions a lot of cases of disease appear. It is very difficult to get time off work even for 1 day. So the sick must also go to work.[133]

Similar conditions prevailed in Oszczów,[134] also in the Lublin region. Here is a detailed description of this camp:

> The center of the camps was the village Oszczów, where we currently reside under the command of the district physician in consultation with the municipality of Hrubieszów. Workers live in barns—50–100 in each—and they work 10 hours a day. We have not enough shirts, pants, shoes, and soap. Workers should be mainly fed bread, fat, and *kasza* (porridge). These products can be obtained in Hrubieszów or in nearby villages. As for the drugs, one has to specify each item carefully. The Warsaw boys live in terrible poverty. Many of them walk barefoot, despite cold weather, because we do not have shoes. We perform 40 wound dressings of arms and legs daily for wounds from accidental injuries by spade, pickaxe, and other tools, and soreness because of dirt. The dressings [bandage] run out rapidly in spite of the extreme savings.
>
> Given the great difficulty in combating lice (no underwear and soap, and crowded rooms), it is imperative to build a disinfectant furnace at expense of 3,000 zł. Among the patients, there are numerous cases of dysentery and now there is a fear that typhus will spread. The boys sleep in sheds, the barns are completely open and cold, the boys cannot breathe, and there are lice, lice, and lice again. They are so dirty and ragged, that the greatest pauper in Warsaw looks *Vornehm* [elegant, noble] in comparison with them. Few people have two spare sets of underwear, and a lot of people have never changed their shirt and pants. Chaff, which was once straw, is also horribly polluted. The people wear rags so terrible that they no longer resemble clothes.[135]

---

133 From the annex nr. 5, Report of medical visit in the camps of Bełżec group (mid-September 1940), in Eisenbacj and Rutkowski, *Eksterminacja Żydów*, 224.
134 YVA, O.3/3180, testimony of Jakow Jachimowicz, 5–6.
135 Extract from a letter of a nurse from the camp in Oszczów, September 26, 1940, in Eisenbach and Rutkowski, *Eksterminacja Żydów*, 223.

The description of the situation in the labor camps given above demonstrates the fatal organization on the part of the German authorities. They were not in the least interested in improving or stabilizing these conditions. Rather, all indicates that they did not show even minimal interest in working and living conditions of the laborers, despite numerous attempts at intervention[136] on the part of Jews.[137] The most important were economic plans implemented with minimal funding from the budget. This was consistent with the idea of Globocnik, who wanted to shift all costs onto the Jews. Other institutions have followed in his footsteps. The repressive attitude towards the Jewish workers was reflected in the lack of control over the conditions in which they were living. In most cases, the technical staff was not interested in the conditions of Jewish life. The fate of the Jews was in the hands of various camp commanders, who became masters of life and death. The workers depended on them to determine whether the sick inmates will be exempt from work. They influenced the attitude of the guards to the prisoners, sanitary and living conditions, and access to medical care. In the summer of 1940, the workers unable to work in the camps were not yet selected for physical elimination, but already present were the first signs of murderous tendencies on the part of the commanders and the guards. This became most evident when the workers escaped. The punishment was severe, because in the eyes of the staff the workers were already prisoners of labor camps. Here is a description of some attempted escapes:

---

136 One of the organizations that had the fullest information on Jewish labor camps was ŻSS. On January 9, 1942, Lublin ŻSS received a letter asking for detailed information concerning labor camps in the district—such as the number of workers, relation of work and renumeration, accommodation, nutrition, treatment, and sanitary conditions. The central office in Kraków asked for exact and detailed information, based on written documents, letters, and protocols. They also wanted to know the names of all commanders, guards, and the institutions taking care of the inmates (*obozowicze*) and their families. Moreover, they asked to send requests and complains. YVA-JM1574, scan 50.

137 For example, in the camp organized by the company *Siemens Bau-Union* in Płaszów and at the airport in Kraków, there were 70 workers from Książ Wielki (50 young men and 20 young women), who were living and working in severe conditions. On May 7, 1942, Kraków ŻSS came to talk with the director of the company. The director answered that there is a Jewish physician, Dr. Kohn, who, according to the agreement with the Social Security, is treating the workers. If the representatives of the ŻSS had further requests, they were invited to use the post or call the manager of the construction site, engineer Müller. In order to improve the conditions, ŻSS tried to establish a kitchen for the workers. They also tried to arrange a meeting with Dr. Kohn. Besides, they tried to order wooden shoes with the help of the companies employing the workers because those companies were able to overcome the system of reglamentation.

The less food, the more beatings, the more split heads, the more bloodied and ill people, the more murderous the blows, [and] the wilder the Polish guards.[138] This caused a wave of desertions; people were fleeing from camp. One morning, the commandant gave a speech, saying we should not desert, things will turn better, but if the desertions continue, there will be fatal results. This was illustrated by such example that inspired fear about deserting. [He suddenly] appeared pulling a wheelbarrow with the bodies of the two brothers.[139]

Commanders of the camps felt comfortable when they could punish escape. The workers, on their part, felt helpless. Although there was contact between many labor camps and the Jewish communities from which the workers came, it was very limited. The Jews were too weak to let their interventions have effect. Sometimes the visits of commissions or arrival of doctors gave hope, but those hopes proved to be unreliable. Below is an example of such situation:

> The arrival of the doctors in our camp raised hope that the savage guards, free of any restraint until now, will have to cease their brutal beating. This was a mistake. After their arrival as before, and even in their presence, there was no end to flogging and beating, with sticks and with clubs, on our backs and heads. Bodies of bloodied inmates used to fall to the ground and be carried away by nurses. The doctors were helpless in the face of those spectacles, quite unexpected and surprising, but there was never time enough for any treatment: the guards kept supplying them with business. [. . .] They [doctors] intervened with the commandant of the camp and quietly tried to convince him of the beatings that increased the number of sick and dead—all to no avail.[140]

The German authorities knew quite well the conditions that were in the camps, but were unwilling to improve those conditions. Their fear mainly regarded the possibility of outbreak of epidemics. According to a German report:

> In Płazów, for example, the *Judenlager* is situated in the center of the village on the main road. The enclosure is on both sides of the village

---

138 According to an announcement of the Warsaw District governor (February 17, 1941), the camps guards (*Lagerschutz*) coud be recruited from Poles, Ukrainians, and Belorussians. See Ekspertyza Historycznej Komisji Żydowskiej, AIPN, NTN, 196/59, 190.
139 "Six Weeks in a Forced Labor Camp," in Kermish, *To Live with Honor*, 272.
140 Kermish, *To Live with Honor*, 272–73.

brook, so the Jews wash their lice infested clothes in the brook and thus put the local residents at risk. If it is not feasible, because of lack of supervision, to enforce the use of the camps latrines, then any control during work on the *Himmlergraben* is impossible. There exists an order that every Jew has to carry a spade when going to defecate. But very often this doesn't happen. Thus, walking in this area is risky for the residents and the customs officials. If despite this the cases of contagious diseases are relatively few, according to information by the Jewish physicians, this may be caused partly by the season, and partly by the tenacity of the inmates. However, the last 10 days there have been several cases of dysentery. The sick people from the camps were taken care of in the Polish military hospital in Tomaszów. Since that hospital can accommodate only 94 patients, the staff surgeon of the regiment based in Tomaszów was ordered by his commander to find other accommodation for the sick Jews. A building complex between Tomaszów and Narol has already been inspected. The sick Jews shall be placed there, and Jewish physicians shall take care of them. The customs officials of the offices close to the Jewish work places and camps have been vaccinated yesterday by staff surgeon Schiller. He and the town commander (*Ortskommandant*) of Tomaszów see a growing danger of epidemics when the weather gets worse. This would not happen if the Jews were discharged on the November 1, 1940, as the *Lagerkommandant* in Płazów and other man of the watch assume.[141]

As already mentioned in this work, repressive attitude towards the Jewish workers from the part of the German authorities meant that they had practically no possibility to appeal their commanders' decisions. Since the camps were located in the provinces, far from major urban agglomerations, the commanders of the camps felt that they could go unpunished. Attempts to intervene, as described above, ended in nothing, because the camp commanders and guards were more interested in economic results than in reworking their repressive attitudes towards Jews. Both commanders and camp staff were corrupt. They benefited from their privileged position and stole food rations from the camp kitchens, leaving only bread and potatoes for the workers, and often in already truncated quantities.

Testimony confirming the difficult food situation in the camps is also provided by statements from residents of these villages where Jewish labor camps were located. Jewish workers were asking people for a piece of

---

141 BA-MA, RH53-23-27, Tgb. Nr. 1433/40 gIIIC, Judenlager an der Grenze, Lublin, September 24, 1940, 145–47.

bread.[142] Another witness confirms that Jewish workers were starving and did not despise any food. In the words of the witness:

> . . . prisoners very often asked me to give them something to eat: even when I carried food for pigs, they did not let me go, and took with their hands from the bucket and ate. Usually I had to throw potatoes through the wire, and the prisoners ate them.[143]

The Jewish inhabitants of the villages next to the labor camps tried to help them.[144]

In the report of ŻSS of June 20, 1941, we find at least a partial explanation as to why the work in the camps, especially drainage work, was so devastating and why the Jews were so often employed for these works:

> Water and drainage works exhaust the human body so far, that the period of employment of Polish workers, even before the war, when food was quite normal, could not exceed three weeks, after which there would have been interruption or replacement of workers. It is thus clear that the work of the Jews, already malnourished and exhausted by the war, which lasted already 20 months, could not be efficient in conditions of poor nourishment, often taking a form of real hunger, and lead to disastrous consequences to health and even life of campers.[145]

This is confirmed by another passage from that report, about Przyrów:[146]

> In Przyrów (Radomsko County) the working conditions are terrible. The workers stand all day up to their knees in swampy ground or even in water. Often, they are beaten and do not receive any food. Before the war it was very difficult to keep the Polish workers there, even though they were paid 8 zł a day.[147]

---

142 YVA-TR.17/316, 5–6, Ko80/66/15; YVA-TR.17/222.
143 YVA-TR.17/316, 8–9, Ko80/66/15.
144 "Impressions from a Labor Camp," AR1/414, in Kermish, *To Live with Honor*, 269.
145 June 30, 1941, Kraków, Report of the Bureau of Jewish Social Self-Assistance in the General Government to the authorities of the General Government on the situation of Jews in labor camps, in Eisenbach and Rutkowski, *Eksterminacja Żydów*, 228–30.
146 YVA, O.3/3180, testimony of Jakow Jachimowicz, 5. This testimony confirms very hard condition in Przyrów.
147 Eisenbach and Rutkowski, *Eksterminacja Żydów*, 230.

Not only the drainage work was devastating. In other camps where hard work was performed the workers were starving. For example, in a camp in Stąporków (Końskie County), Jews employed in heavy and exhaustive works did not receive any food during working hours, and were paid only 3 zł a day.[148]

The bad situation in terms of food caused numerous interventions from members of the *Judenräte*. Not all of them could greatly alter the situation; however, *Judenräte* in smaller towns were able to have a significant impact on improving conditions at the local level, even if they did not have access to higher German authorities. In the case of the Warsaw *Judenrat*, its activities were at least partially effective. Adam Czerniaków says in his diary that after representatives of the *Judenrat* and the commander of *Lagerschutz* visited the camps in order to check the conditions there, they confirmed that:

> Eating is below any criticism. The workers were to receive 180 g of bread, 1–1.3 kg of potatoes, sugar, marmalade, meat, coffee, and so forth. They receive no potatoes, and [only] 120–150 g of bread. No fats. The firm Juske, [Three] Crosses Square 23, reduces *lon* [wages] for food, taking double prices in relation to the quota price of the product. [. . .] The workers usually provide good material [i.e., they are in good condition]. Everything depends on the nourishment.[149]

In another entry, Czerniaków wrote: "The conditions [in the camps] are terrible. No one can endure a month. Companies steal food [from the workers]. Beating will not stop. Performance [effectiveness] of hard work is, in fact, small."[150] Czerniaków went to Auerswald. He was even received by Governor Fischer. According to him, Fischer "says his goal is not starving Jews. Ration may be increased; work or *obstalunki* [tasks] for the workers will come."[151]

Jewish Welfare Committees actively helped the Jewish workers and sought to improve working conditions and increase their rations. This assistance was funded by the Jewish councils because the workers were paid very low wages that were not sufficient for food.[152] Workers also received food

---

148 Ibid., 228–30.
149 Entry of May 10, 1941, in Fuks, *Adama Czerniakowa dziennik*, 179.
150 Ibid., 184.
151 Ibid., 184.
152 June 30, 1941, Kraków, Report of the Bureau of Jewish Social Self-Assistance in the General Government to the authorities of the General Government on the situation of Jews in labor camps, in Eisenbach and Ritkowski, *Eksterminacja Żydów*, 228–30.

parcels and clothing. With help from the outside, the conditions were significantly improved.¹⁵³

> The Committee of aid to workers in this camp [in Zagacie (Końskie County)] assigned to them—as long as there are enough means—additional 50 g of bread a day and 10 zł a week. Housing conditions are good: workers are placed in barracks and equipped with sufficient number of bunks. They wash or bathe twice a day. The cleanliness is exemplary. Generally, they are treated tolerably.¹⁵⁴

Similar interventions led to improvements in other camps. For example:

> In the labor camp in Dąbrowice (near Skierniewice), camp guards were removed and replaced by Jewish police. As a result, productivity [of work] has increased by 50%. German company therefore increased rations.¹⁵⁵

RELEASE FROM THE CAMPS

Sick and physically tired prisoners could be released from the labor camps and sent back to their places of residence.¹⁵⁶ The release depended largely on the treatment of workers by camp authorities. Where the camp regime was more severe, the release of unable workers was more difficult. In extreme cases there was no release at all. Then the Jewish workers, even after the onset of the disease were forced to work hard, causing starvation and death.¹⁵⁷ The authorities of some camps, with designated sections of the work, tried to perform their tasks at all cost, regardless of the health status of the workers. Another limiting factor

---

153 Bryskier, Żydzi pod swastyką, 63–64.
154 Ibid.
155 Entry of May 20, 1941, in Ringelblum, Kronika getta warszawskiego, 289.
156 Bryskier, Żydzi pod swastyką, 63–64; APL, RŻL-48, 12, Judenrat in Lublin, Abteilung für Zwangsarbeit, Hilfskomitie für die Arbeitenden in den Arbeitslagern, Delegatur in Belzec, September 11, 1940; APL, RŻL-48, 137–45, Register of cases of death in labor camps (in the Lublin District, September–beginning of December 1940). 169 cases were entered in the Register. Moreover, the same file includes a sheet dated November 3, 1940, listing 23 Jews, who died in hospitals after transportation from labor camps. There were also reports about 300 Jews who died of exaustion in the Warsaw Ghetto after returning from labor camps. See Ekspertyza Historycznej Komisji Żydowskiej, AIPN, NTN, 196/59, 185.
157 Bryskier, Żydzi pod swastyką, 63–64.

was the bad availability of additional workers to replace the released inmates,[158] and, therefore, the camp commanders sought to exploit their Jewish workers to extremes. In some cases, the release from the camps happened thanks to the activity of the Jewish community. For example, the visit of a representative of the *Judenrat* in Częstochowa, Bernard Kurland, to the camp in Oszczów and other camps, his negotiations with commanders of the camps, use of bribes, and procurement of medical certificates resulted in release of many workers. They returned in several trains to Częstochowa at the end of 1940 and the beginning of 1941.[159]

In some camps, due to a high degree of disease and mortality, the number of workers was strongly reduced, which led to liquidation of the camps. In the words of one witness:

> ... after the departure of the first party of the sick, there remained for work only some 50 men, not counting the functionaries, the technicians, overseers, and administrators. No new people came to work, so everybody understood that the camp was to be liquidated, and this is what happened.[160]

CLOSURE OF LABOR CAMPS

Most of the labor camps for Jews established in 1940 were seasonal camps, which were designed to perform a variety of seasonal work in the open air. Weather and climate determined the ability to perform such work. In Bełżec camps, digging anti-tank ditches was possible until late autumn, but only before the severe rain showers. The advent of cold weather meant that digging works became impossible. Melioration works—digging channels and embankments to prevent floods or changing the flow of rivers by digging fragments of new riverbeds—were also regulated by weather conditions. These works began in late spring when the water level dropped enough in wetlands. The work was completely impossible, however, with the advent of the rains and cold, when water level simultaneously increased. When cold and rainy autumn came, the continued maintenance of the camps became useless and the Jewish workers

---

158 Entries of September 6, 7, 8, and 9, 1940, in Ringelblum, *Kronika getta warszawskiego*, 146–47.
159 YVA, O.3/3180, testimony of Jakow Jachimowicz, 5–6.
160 "Six Weeks in a Forced Labor Camp," in Kermish, *To Live with Honor*, 275.

were gradually dismissed to their places of residence. According to the report from Water Management:

> On 176 construction sites, there are 8,395 workers employed, namely: 5,950 Poles, 1,824 *Baudienst*, and 621 Jews. The number of workers diminished by ca. 1,000 men, because since December 1 this year [1940], most of the construction sites are discontinued. 14 activities on ca. 423 hectares were terminated. On 25 construction sites, contractors are appointed. Here, ca. 100 km of embankments enlargement works are carried out, 267 km river regulation, and torrent control on 18 mountain torrents.[161]

Labor camps created in 1940 were temporary. They were mostly established in existing buildings where workers were placed. The tasks, for which the camps were created, were seasonal field works. Such works could not be performed during the winter, and the existence of the camps during this period became redundant. According to the decision of the German authorities, all labor camps in Warsaw District were closed on June 18, 1941.[162] All the Jews employed there were released and returned to their places of residence.

One of the consequences of the existence of labor camps for Jews was widely prevalent fear and terror, which led to rumors about what happened in the camps and what conditions were there. Ringelblum wrote in his diary the following:

> [...] The Jewish population is impressed with the terrible news from labor camps— from which a lot of people who escaped or were released due to illness come to Warsaw, among other places. The main cause of death accidents (91 deaths until May 6 [1941]) is the terrible treatment of campers by the majority of Ukrainians camp guard, as well as bad, just starving food supply. [...] The worst was in Kampinos Forests [*Puszcza Kampinoska*], which recorded 37 victims, amounting to 10% [of the campers]. The camp guards simply stole the campers' food (18 g of bread, watery soup, and a glass of black coffee). Those who returned from the camps died on the premises of the Jewish community [in Warsaw]. Some of them were shot while fleeing from the camp. The camp regime is terrible. The returning

---

161 YVA, JM-814, Blatt zum Schreiben an Staatssekretär Dr. Bühler vom 18 Dezember 1940, scan 887.
162 "Rozwiązanie obozów pracy," *Gazeta Żydowska*, June 24, 1941, 2.

men are completely exhausted. Some are still under influence of severe psychotic camp experience and tremble at the sight of every man in uniform. [...] You can imagine the mood of those who need to go to the camps. People from transport, which went yesterday (May 5 [1941]), raised a veritable revolt, refusing to go [to camp]. We now understand how to trust their promises that the camp will be better than last year.[163]

The fact that many Jews were unable to do hard physical work was well known to the highest German authorities in the General Government. The chef of the Lublin District wrote in his report in November 1940:

From the *Judenlager* Bełżec, 4,331 Jewish forced laborers were released and employed in road construction and buildings of the "Otto Program." Their condition was such that they could not be considered as totally fit for work. The OKW Berlin allocated 800 former Jewish-Polish prisoners of war to work on the airfield Biała [Podlaska]. 250 (of them) could not be utilized because of invalidity.[164]

From a report to the State Secretary Dr. Josef Bühler, dated December 1940:

The physical condition hampers their [Jews] employment; in many cases their use for the earthwork they are slated for is impossible. Their outfit with work wear is inadequate; many companies refuse the employment of Jews because of their earlier experience. During November, 8,286 Jews were placed to work.[165]

---

163 Entry of May 6–11, 1941, in Ringelblum, *Kronika getta warszawskiego*, 279–80.
164 YVA, JM-814, Der Chef des Distrikts Lublin im Generalgouvernement, Lagebericht für Oktober 1940, Lublin, den 6 November 1940, scan 782.
165 YVA, JM-814, Blatt zum Schreiben an Staatssekretär Dr. Bühler vom 18. Dezember 1940, scan 900.

Part Two

CHAPTER 5

The War in the East: Galicia during the First Weeks of the War

THE POLITICAL AND IDEOLOGICAL PLANS FOR THE EASTERN AREAS AND ITS IMPLEMENTATION AT THE BEGINNING OF OPERATION BARBAROSSA

Prior to the formulation of any practical plans of armed conflict with the Soviet Union, there already existed a basic ideological conflict between Nazi Germany and the USSR. Germany during the Weimar Republic and the USSR enjoyed a relatively good relationship, despite the restrictions imposed on Germany that prevented the development of the armed forces and production of certain weapons. In the 1920s, the Soviet paradigms were precisely implemented by German military experts to test new weapons. Despite the maintenance of diplomatic relations after Hitler's rise to power in Germany, communist ideology, also called Bolshevism, became the object of many attacks by Hitler. In one of his speeches in 1935, he said:

> Bolshevism destroys not only private property but also private initiative and the readiness to shoulder responsibility. It has not been able to save millions of human beings from starvation in Russia, the greatest Agrarian State in the world. National Socialists and Bolshevists both are convinced they are a world apart from each other and their differences can never be bridged. Apart from that, there were thousands of our people slain and maimed in the fight against Bolshevism. If Russia likes Bolshevism, it is

not our affair, but if Bolshevism casts its nets over to Germany, then we will fight it tooth and nail.¹

Only after winning the campaign in Western Europe could Hitler consider turning against the USSR. As early as August 1940, in the highest circles of power, information concerning commencement of preparations for war with the USSR began to circulate.

> On August 14, the Chief of *Wi Rü* [*Wirtschaft Rüstung*—Armament Production Management], during a conference with *Reichsmarschall* Göring, was informed that the Führer desired punctual delivery to the Russians only until spring 1941. Later on we would have no further interest in completely satisfying the Russian demands. This allusion moved the Chief of *Wi Rü* to give priority to matters concerning the Russian War Economy.²

It is worth mentioning that economic exchange with the Soviet Union was very important, since the naval blockade of Germany caused difficulties in obtaining important raw materials for the war economy. This message showcases the double-faced German policy towards the USSR. On the one hand, Germany was preparing for war against the Soviet Union; on the other hand, its war production was based on raw materials obtained from the USSR. We may also see, from the following quotation, the importance of commerce with the USSR:

> To date the Russian deliveries have been a very substantial support of the German war economy. Since the new economic agreements have become valid, Russia has delivered raw materials for more than 300 million Reichsmark; this includes grain for approx. 100 million Reichsmark. So far Russia has received an equivalent amounting to only approx. 150 million Reichsmark. [...] Our only economic connection with Iran, Afghanistan, Manchukuo, China, Japan, and beyond that to South America, is the way through Russia, which is being exploited to an increasing degree for German raw material imports.³

---

1 Hitler's Speech, May 21, 1935.
2 IMT, *Red Series* (2353-PS), vol. 1, 796.
3 Memorandum concerning economic contact with USSR, Berlin, September 28, 1940, signed by Schnurre (3579-PS), in IMT, *Red Series*, vol. 1, 278.

The war with the USSR did not only have its ideological and strategic goals, but also economic ones. This mainly concerned the war economy. Until the outbreak of the war, the Germans received supplies of raw materials from the Soviet Union. However, with the outbreak of hostilities these supplies ceased to arrive. Therefore, the extension of hostilities was dangerous to Germany, as it could quickly lead to the exhaustion of stocks of raw materials and the collapse of German war production. For that reason, one of the most important tasks in the occupied territories was to recognize the economic objectives of strategic importance and, as soon as possible, to start the required work. For this purpose, already in November 1940, the chief of the *Wi Rü* along with secretaries of State Körner, Neumann, Backe, and General von Hanneken were informed by the *Reichmarschal* of the action planned in the east.

> By reason of these directives the preliminary preparations for the action in the east were commenced by the office of *Wi Rü* at the end of 1940:
> 1. Obtaining a detailed survey of the Russian Armament industry, its location, its capacity and its associate industries.
> 2. Investigation of the capacity of various big armament centers and their dependency one on the other.
> 3. Determine the power and transport system for the industry of the Soviet Union.
> 4. Investigation of sources of raw materials and petroleum (crude oil).
> 5. Preparation of a survey of industries other than armament industries in the Soviet Union.[4]

These points were concentrated in one big compilation called "War Economy of the Soviet Union" and illustrated with detailed maps and other materials. Furthermore, a card index was to be made containing all the important factories in Soviet Russia and a German-Russian lexicon for economics for the use of the German War Economy Organization.[5]

By the end of February 1941, preliminary planning had proceeded to a point where a broader plan of organization, recognition, and protection of war production objectives in the occupied territories had to be prepared. General Thomas held a conference with his subordinates on February 28, 1941 to

---

4 IMT, *Red Series*, vol. 1, 809.
5 Ibid.

prepare such a plan. A memorandum of this conference, classified "top secret" and dated March 1, 1941, reads as follows:

1. The whole organization is to be subordinate to the Reich Marshal. Purpose: Support and extension of the measures of the Four-Year Plan.
2. The organization must include everything concerning war economy, excepting only food, which is already under special responsibility of State Secretary Backe.
3. It should be clearly stated that the organization is to be independent of the military or civil administration. Close cooperation is welcome, but instructions should be directed from the central office in Berlin.
4. The scope of activities is to be divided in two steps:
   a. Accompanying the advancing troops directly behind the front lines, in order to avoid the destruction of supplies and to secure the removal of important goods.
   b. Administration of the occupied industrial districts and exploitation of economically complimentary districts.
5. In view of the extended field of activity, the term "war economy inspection" is preferable instead of armament inspection.
6. In view of the great field of activity, the organization must be generously equipped and personnel must be correspondingly numerous. The main mission of the organization will consist of seizing raw materials and taking over all important concerns. For the latter mission, reliable people from German concerns will be suitably interposed from the beginning, since successful operation from the beginning can only be performed by the aid of their experiences. (For example, lignite, ore, chemical supplies, and petroleum).[6]

PREPARATIONS FOR WAR WITH THE USSR

Preparations for Operation Barbarossa took a long time: in essence, they began at the end of the campaign in Western Europe and Norway. At that time, decisions concerning the treatment of prisoners of war and Jews became more radical. Already on February 26, 1941, Hermann Göring said in an interview with General Georg Thomas that one must quickly dispose of Bolshevik leaders. On March 13, 1941, it was decided to entrust this specific task resulting

---

6 IMT, *Red Series*, vol. 1 (1317-PS), 810–11.

from the struggle between two opposing political systems to Heinrich Himmler, enabling the use of the *Einsatzgruppen*. Heinrich Himmler was, according to this directive, to act in a manner independent of the Wehrmacht, although the functional area of activities of his operational groups (*Einsatzgruppen*) coincided with the frontline zone, where the administrative authority belonged to the army. The army high command was to help operational groups in their tasks. The commanders dealing with the agreement concerning the division of competences were the main army Quartermaster General Eduard Wagner and *SS-Gruppenführer* Reinhard Heydrich. The Commissars' Order of June 6, 1941 gave a basis not only to eliminate political commissars, but primarily to disregard existing rules of warfare and the "purity of arms." The first part of the instruction stated that in the struggle against Bolshevism it was ". . . not expected that the enemy act in accordance with the rules of warfare and international law."[7]

In addition to the existing directives concerning division of powers between the Wehrmacht and special operational groups (*Einsatzgruppen*), on July 2, 1941, Reinhard Heydrich issued an instruction for the elimination of selected groups on Soviet territories occupied by German troops.[8] In this instruction, inter alia, it was written:

> 4) Executions. All the following are to be executed: Officials of the Comintern [...], top and medium-level officials [...], People's Commissars; Jews in Party and State employment, and other radical elements (saboteurs, propagandists, snipers, assassins, inciters, etc.).[9]

INVASION

On June 22, 1941, Nazi Germany, supported by Romanian, Hungarian, and Slovak troops in the south, launched Operation Barbarossa and began military operations against the USSR. Soviet troops were surprised by the fierce attack. Unprepared for war, they were not able to resist their enemy and began to retreat in disarray. During the first few weeks, the German troops advanced

---

7 Extract from the Commissar's Order for the Operation Barbarossa, June 6, 1941, NOKW-484; Arad and Gutman, *Documents on the Holocaust*, 376.
8 Extracts from guidelines by Heydrich for higher SS and police leaders in the Occupied Territories of the Soviet Union, July 2, 1941, Arad and Gutman, *Documents on the Holocaust*, 378; see the same document in YVA, O.54/53-1.
9 Ibid.

deep into the territory under Soviet control and took over most of the Polish territories that had been occupied by Soviet troops after September 17, 1939. Among those territories was also the future Galicia District that encompassed part of the former province of Lwów, Stanisławów, and Tarnopol.

The Red Army, unable to face the German troops, began a disorderly retreat. Only in a number of fortified positions did longer resistance take place. However, the *Luftwaffe* managed in its operational sphere to reach and destroy the majority of Soviet aircraft still on the ground, which gave the Germans almost complete domination in the air. The German Air Force destroyed not only military facilities, but also other objects of strategic importance, such as road and rail bridges, communication centers, and other important installations. A powerful armored thrust forward meant that in many cases, small Soviet units did not manage to escape and remained at the front line. Individual soldiers or smaller units were captured by the German rearguard units. Thousands of Soviet soldiers fell into German custody. By the autumn of 1941, that number had turned into millions.

At that time, the Soviet penitentiaries were filled with prisoners from recent waves of arrests in June 1941. The Soviet authorities in larger cities, who could not or did not want to evacuate prisoners and, on the other hand, did not want to free them, had decided to liquidate the inmates. In this way, thousands of prisoners were murdered in the prisons in Lwów, Stanisławów, Tarnopol, and many other places. Shortly before the arrival of the German troops in Galicia, several thousand prisoners were murdered, and their bodies were left in closed prisons and areas of mass executions.

Simultaneously, in many towns where there were no Soviet troops, or where they managed to withdraw and the German troops had not yet entered, a vacuum of power was created which started to fill up at the local level by self-proclaimed Ukrainian authorities.[10] These were more or less armed militias made up of local people. The local Ukrainian population, who hated the Soviet authorities and had, perhaps, hopes of establishing an independent state supported by Germany, was favorable to them. Then again, during the chaos after the withdrawal of Soviet troops and authorities, hatred towards the Jews erupted again. Unarmed Jews, who identified with Soviet powers, suddenly became the embodiment of the hatred towards the Soviets. The vacuum of

---

10 Ukrainian Nationalist Movement (OUN), as well as its paramilitary organization, was in close contact with the German authorities during the period of 1939–1941, and relayed them a lot of information on the situation in the part of Ukraine occupied by the Soviets after September 17, 1939. See Bericht über die Lage in der Westukraine unter der jetzigen Sowjetherrschaft, Krakau, 13 November, 1939. YVA-JM.12306, scans 687–741.

power in many rural areas and a renewed outbreak of hatred, in general, sparked anti-Semitic pogroms.[11] In some localities, rural councils convened to make conscious decisions about the murder of Jews. Not all such decisions were implemented, but the mere fact that they were made testified to the attitude towards the Jews even before the entrance of the Germans. With the German troops, Ukrainian battalions also entered.[12] Their significance was largely symbolic; however, it indicated political options of these organizations and testified to attempts of establishing a temporary Ukrainian government by the assailant.

THE ACTIVITIES OF THE *EINSATZGRUPPEN*

The *Einsatzgruppen* began to operate in the areas occupied by the Soviet Union from 1939, as well as in the Soviet Union itself.[13] In Eastern Galicia *Einsatzgruppe* C acted under the command of *SS-Brigadeführer und Generalmajor der Polizei* Dr. Otto Rasch, who was replaced at the end of 1941 by *SS-Brigadeführer und Generalmajor der Polizei* Dr. Max Thomas, the commander of *Einsatzgruppe* C until 1943. In accordance with the guidelines of RSHA chief Reinhard Heydrich, *Einsatzgruppen* were responsible for murder of communists and Jews.

Einsatzgruppen, together with local militias and with the cooperation of local people, systematically murdered Jews in many towns of Galicia. Information on this subject may be found in the reports sent by the Wehrmacht. One of these reports describes how the actions of liquidation of the Jews by the *Einsatzgruppen* were conducted in cooperation with the local police:

> Immediately following the military operations, the Jewish population remained undisturbed at first. It was only weeks, in some cases months,

---

11 Witold Mędykowski, *W cieniu gigantów: Pogromy 1941 r. w byłej sowieckiej strefie okupacyjnej. Kontekst historyczny, społeczny i kulturowy* (Warsaw: ISP PAN, 2012).
12 The Ukrainian Legion was composed of two batallions—"Roland" and "Nachtigall," and was commanded by Theodor Oberländer and, from the Ukrainian side, by Roman Shukhevich.
13 Helmut Krausnick, *Die Truppe des Weltanschauungskrieges: Die Einsatzgruppen der Sicherheitspolizei und des SD 1938–1943* (Stuttgart: Deutsche Verlags-Anstalt, 1981); P. Klein, ed., *Die Einsatzgruppen in der besetzten Sowjetunion 1941/1942. Die Tätigkeits- und Lageberichte des Chefs der Sicherheitspolizei und des SD* (Berlin: Edition Hentrich, 1997); Arad, Krakowski, and Spector, *The Einsatzgruppen Reports*; Trials of War Criminals before the Nuerenberg Military Tribunals, vol. 4, The Einsatzgruppen Case, [Green Series], Nuernberg, 1946–1949; H. H.Wilhelm, *Die Einsatzgruppe A der Sicherheheitspolizei und des SD 1941/42* (Frankfurt a. M.: Fischer Verlag, 1996); MacLean, *The Field Men*; Dempsey, *Einsatzgruppen and the Destruction*.

later that systematic shooting of the Jews was carried out by units of the Order Police specially set up for this purpose. This *Aktion* moved in the main from east to west. It was carried out entirely in public, with the assistance of Ukrainian militia; in many cases, regrettably, also with the voluntary participation of members of the Wehrmacht. These *Aktionen* included aged men, women, and children of all ages, and the manner in which they were carried out was appalling. The gigantic number of executions involved in this *Aktion* is far greater than any similar measure undertaken in the Soviet Union up to now. Altogether about 150,000 to 200,000 Jews may have been executed in the section of the Ukraine belonging to the RK [*Reichskommissariat*]; up to now no consideration was given to the interests of the economy.[14]

Despite many statements in various documents quoted above, from the very beginning it was completely clear that economic interests were in the background, while ideology dominated. As in the beginning of the war, not only political commissars, but civilian population, who were only presumed to be communists, were usually shot en masse because nobody tried to prove anything. Soviet POWs were mostly treated in an inhumane manner. Their increased mortality could already be observed after several months, especially during the winter of 1941–1942. The POWs, many of whom were reservists, could have proved to be an excellent source of labor that was totally lost. The same was true in regard to Jews—in addition, they were particularly skilled workers. This problem was noted even in the *Einsatzgruppen* reports. Here is an example from such report:

> After the carrying out of the first large-scale executions in Lithuania and Latvia the total elimination of the Jews already proved to be impossible there, at least at the present time. As a large part of the skilled trades is in Jewish hands in Lithuania and Latvia, and some (grazers, plumbers, stove builders, shoe makers) are almost entirely Jewish, a large proportion of the Jewish craftsmen are indispensable at present for the repair of essential installations, for the reconstruction of destroyed cities, and for work of military importance. Although the employers aim at replacing Jewish

---

14 From a Wehrmacht Report on the Extermination of the Jews in Ukraine, Inspector of Armament in the Ukraine (December 2, 1941) to the Office of Wi Rü [Industrial Armament Department] OKW [High Command of the Wehrmacht] General of the Infantry Thomas (PS-3257), in Arad and Gutman, *Documents on the Holocaust*, 418.

labor with Lithuanian or Latvian workers, it is not yet possible to replace all the Jews presently employed, particularly in the larger cities. In cooperation with the labor exchange offices, however, Jews who are no longer fit for work are picked up and will be executed shortly in small *Aktionen*.[15]

The Inspector of Armaments in Ukraine reported the fact that mass executions of Jews brought immediate and irreparable harm to the war economy. He also was aware that ideology superceded all other interests. Nevertheless, he tried to propose a solution for the partial elimination of the Jewish labor force. Worth emphasizing is the fact that he did not present any type of moral arguments, but only "practical" considerations:

> To sum up, it could be said that the solution of the Jewish Question as carried out in the Ukraine, evidently motivated by ideological principles, has the following consequences:
> a. Elimination of some, in part superfluous, eaters in the cities.
> b. Elimination of a part of the population that undoubtedly hated us.
> c. Elimination of urgently needed craftsmen, who were in many cases indispensable for the requirements of the Wehrmacht.
> d. Consequences, in connection with foreign propaganda, which are obvious.
> e. Adverse effects on troops, which in any case have indirect contact with executions.
> f. Brutalizing effects on the units (Order Police), which carry out the executions.[16]

THE IMPORTANCE OF OPERATION BARBAROSSA FOR THE GENERAL GOVERNMENT

Issuing instructions to proceed with the Otto Program was the first step in implementing the strategy of preparation for the invasion of the Soviet Union. However, the idea of using the territory of General Government as a base to

---

15 Extracts from a report by Einsatzgruppe A in the Baltic Countries, October 15, 1941 (L-180), in Arad and Gutman, *Documents on the Holocaust*, 392.
16 From a Wehrmacht Report on the Extermination of the Jews in Ukraine, Inspector of Armament in the Ukraine (December 2, 1941) to the Office of Wi Rü [Industrial Armament Department] OKW [High Command of the Wehrmacht] General of the Infantry Thomas, in Arad and Gutman, *Documents on the Holocaust*, 418–19; PS-3257.

attack the east significantly preceded the release of specific directives. Already in the autumn of 1939, Hitler defined his plan to use Polish territories that were not incorporated into the Reich, as a series of strategic objectives. According to this plan, a high level of infrastructure, especially roads, railways, and the like, in the General Government had to be maintained. Already then, work on the modernization of national and regional roads was started. The Otto Program, though, covered many areas of the economy, not just transportation. The General Government was to hold one of the largest concentrations of German troops before the attack on the USSR. Therefore, in the first half of 1941, especially in the spring, an extensive work effort was performed in order to prepare military bases. For this purpose, accommodations for millions of soldiers, repair garages, equipment, fuel supplies, airports, and other army facilities had to be prepared. Concentrated military units required ongoing upkeep and maintenance. The General Government was also obliged to provide food for millions of soldiers. It was necessary to set up military hospitals as well as other arrangements.

On the one hand, all these works constituted an economic burden, because they required intense labor, while raw materials and food had to be delivered exclusively by the General Government. On the other hand, large orders for the military resulted in development of the economic situation in the General Government. For example, the need to prepare accommodation for the soldiers caused an increase in orders for wooden furniture. As the Polish companies that received contracts were also interested in greater profits, they looked for cheap labor, which often could be found in the ghettos. For example, in the spring of 1941, a huge increase in the production of wooden furniture in the Warsaw Ghetto could be noticed.

The outbreak of the German-Soviet war was also of great importance for the General Government, because this area became close to front zone with a high concentration of troops. Thus, the General Government changed from a peaceful area to the rear of the front line, forced to provide many products and supplies for the army. In the wake of the Operation Barbarossa, Governor General Dr. Hans Frank explained:

> With the proceeding victory of our marvelous armed forces in the East, in a time of great courage and most excellent probation of German soldiership, we, who have the honor to be so distinguished by the Führer to act as a bridge between the opening gigantic space in the East and the closed realm of our people, see the noble duty to think solely of this task. No one will take this land of the Poles away from us again. We will facilitate

here for all Germans a reconstruction on the foundations we built, which shall be a glorious work. I am looking forward to calling the German settlers back to Galicia and to begin the task of regulating the Wisła in a completely different perspective; I am looking forward to the plan and the realization of the plan of a navigable connection between Wisła, San and Dniestr, through which we will develop gigantic transport routes everywhere. The General Government will be a balanced entity in East and West, North and South.[17]

However, from a political point of view, the shift of the front to the east and reaching new areas also meant new opportunities to solve demographic problems. This concerned first of all the Jews, since the acquisition of new territories could mean finding new evacuation places. Until then, the General Government was playing that role in the region, hosting deported Jews in both the Reich and the Protectorate.[18] Many gauleiters could boast that their administration areas became *judenrein*. For example, Gauleiter of Warthegau Arthur Greiser attempted to cleanse his *Gau* by deporting Jews and Poles to the General Government.

Hans Frank wrote, inter alia, in his diary:

> During the conversation, which I had with the Führer at the Reich Chancellery three days before the entering [the territory of Soviet Russia], the Führer told me, among other things, that Jews were the first to leave the General Government. In the next days I will issue an order on the initiation of preparations for the evacuation of the Warsaw Ghetto. We have to make every effort to remove, as soon as possible, the Jews of the General Government. In the spirit of Hitler's own words, in the future the General Government will not be a place of their final concentration, but only a transit camp.[19]

Hans Frank, who previously occupied a rather secondary position of the governor general, attempted to acquire more meaning and importance.

---

17 YVA-JM.21 (3508214_08004009), *Hans Frank's Diary*, vol. 15, R. 5, Wirtschaftstagung, den 22. Juli 1941, scans 134–35.
18 YVA-JM-1476 (AIPN, GDL-5) lists of names transported from Wien and Stettin to the district Lublin.
19 Frank *Okupacja i ruch oporu*, vol. 1, 374; YVA-JM.21 (3508214_08004009), *Hans Frank's Diary*, vol. 15, R. 5, Wirtschaftstagung, den 22. Juli 1941, scans 134–35.

Therefore, during the invasion of the Soviet Union he saw himself in a new and significant role. After the invasion, he wrote:

> The victorious march of our glorious Wehrmacht in the east results for us—blessed with honors from the Führer, whose will be that we now become the bridge between the gigantic area of the East, which is opening up before us, and the Reich, the compact seat of our people. This means that we should honor the obligation to devote all our attention only to this complex task in these times of highest heroism and the impressive achievements of the German soldiers.[20]

---

20 Frank, *Okupacja i ruch oporu*, vol. 1, 374.

CHAPTER 6

Jewish Labor in Galicia

During the initial period of the German occupation of *Galizien* [Galicia], authority passed into the hands of the military administration, which was represented by the chief of the civil administration (*Chef der Zivilverwaltung,* CdZ). In Lwów, before the arrival of the Germans, the local Ukrainian Nationalist Organization (OUN) tried to take power into their own hands, but the German authorities were readied against such a possibility. Perhaps, this was the cause that brought about the "Days of Petlura" in late July 1941, nearly a month after the Wehrmacht entered Lwów. This allowed the Ukrainians to celebrate and to organize a pogrom against the Jews, which ultimately reduced social tensions. The "Days of Petlura" occurred shortly before the bitter truth—that there will be no independent Ukraine—was announced. On August 1, 1941, Hitler's decree officially proclaimed the incorporation of the Galicia District (*District Galizien*) into the General Government, which the Germans had created on October 26, 1939.[1] In this way, the General Government acquired additional 51,000 square kilometers and 4.4 million people—mainly Ukrainians, Poles, and Jews. After joining the General Government, the power and legislation structures in the Galicia District were gradually incorporated into the rest of the General Government. The whole district was divided into 16 administrative units: *Stadthauptmannschaft* in Lwów, and another 15 *Kreishauptmannschaften.* Dr. Karl Lasch[2] was nominated as the new district governor. From

---

1 "Verordnung über die Verwaltung von Galizien. Vom 1. August 1941," *VBlGG,* 1941, 443; Pospieszalski, *Hitlerowskie "prawo" okupacyjne,* vol. 2, 71–73.
2 Karl Lasch (1904–1942) was the governor of the Radom District in 1939–1941 and became the governor of the Galicia District in August 1941. He was arrested on January 24, 1942 on charges of corruption, appropriation of goods belonging to the Reich, and trade in foreign currency. He was condemned to death and died in prison in unclear circumstances.

February 1, 1942, *SS-Gruppenführer* Otto von Wächter[3] served as district governor. The head of the governor's office was *Regierungsrat* Dr. Ludwig Losacker. From 1944, commissary manager Dr. Josef Brandl was the head of the district. Friedrich Katzmann[4] was nominated as the SS and police commander. He was later replaced by Theobald Thier, and then Christoph Diehm. The commander Orpo (*Ordnungspolizei*), Paul Worm, was in charge of the military police (*Oberstleutnant der Gendarmerie*); Franz Gansinger was the commander of the Sipo; and Dr. Helmut Tanzmann headed the SD.

Despite annexation of the newly acquired land into the General Government, all indications show that this territory from the very beginning was different from the rest of the General Government. The reason here was not only the ethnic composition of the new district, where the dominant role was played by Ukrainians, but the fact that they considered the Germans their allies, thinking that thanks to them it would be possible to establish an independent Ukrainian state. After August 1, 1941, these hopes faded, but comprehensive cooperation with the Germans still prevailed. This collaboration took place in different fields, but mostly in administration, including local police cooperation with the *Einsatzgruppen* in the murder of Jews and military collaboration. The new district, also from Hans Frank's point of view, had a separate character. For example, in the guidelines of September 15, 1941, Hans Frank recommended the district governor of Galicia, Karl Lasch, to make decisions on all matters regarding the police, because, according to the structure of government, the district governor had full executive authority and had to cooperate with SSPF Katzmann. At the same time, Frank reminded Lasch that the SSPF was not permitted to issue police directives for Galicia.[5]

Jews have been persecuted from the very beginning of the occupation of former Soviet territories. In addition to the previously mentioned pogroms, there were also popular forms of persecution associated with forced labor. First of all, after discovering the murder of prisoners by the NKVD, the work

---

3 Otto Gustav von Wächter (1901–1949) was the governor of the Kraków District in 1939–1942 and the governor of the Galicia District in 1942–1944. In September 1943 he was transferred to northern Italy.

4 Fritz Katzmann (1906–1957) was the SS and police leader in the Radom District in November 1939–July 1941 and held the same post in the Galicia District from August 1941 to April 20, 1943. Then he was nominated to the post of commander of the *SS-Oberabschnitt Weichsel/Danzig-Westpreussen im Wehrkreis XX*. At the end of the war he was responsible for the evacuation of the concentration camp in Stutthof.

5 Frank, *Okupacja i ruch oporu*, vol. 1, 375.

to remove the corpses of those murdered in order to identify and bury them began. Many Jews were engaged in this work. A new massacre of the Jews was linked to this labor because there were frequent incidents of beatings, unpremeditated killings, and abuse of Jewish workers. This was true not only in Lwów, but also in other cities of Eastern Galicia. In places where executions took place, the Jews were engaged in digging mass grave.

Jews were also employed for various humiliating and difficult temporary work. In this case, the 1939 paradigm of Poland was repeated—when during the period of military administration, people were taken from the street for temporary work. Jews were the most common and preferred subject of these arrests.[6] As in central Poland, it was the result of ideological indoctrination of the Germans—of the negative image of the Jews presented in German propaganda. On the other hand, the Polish population was also treated in a humiliating manner. As for the Ukrainians of Eastern Galicia, who were sympathetic to the Nazis, the Polish people, did not have an influential position and often accepted ambivalent attitudes. The Jewish population was again at the bottom of the social hierarchy. As such, the Jews were easy and preferred prey. Moreover, the ideological attitude towards the Jews in the Ukraine was much worse than in Poland, since the Jews were associated with communist ideology and accused of collaboration by the Ukrainians. According to the guidelines issued to the *Einsatzgruppen*, the Jews were destined for liquidation.

ESTABLISHMENT OF THE *DISTRIKT GALIZIEN*

The Germans considered Galicia and especially Lwów their bridgehead to the east. According to Karl Lasch:

> Lwów is the last city with a proper culture far into the East. At the same time, it is the link in the economic interrelations between Southeast Europe and the General Government and the eastern part of the Reich, and especially the great traffic hub of the General Government towards East and Southeast Europe. It cannot be that in this city Jews should be treated differently from Kraków and Warsaw. Therefore, in the next days

---

6 YVA, M.49.E/3773, testimony of Herman Ringer; YVA, M.49.E/4654, testimony of Henryk Szyper; YVA, M.49.E/4950a, testimony of Abraham Schall; YVA, M.49.E/4682, testimony of Izrael Szor; YVA, M.49.E/3551, testimony of Sara Frydman; YVA, M.49.E/1260/100, testimony of Samuel Plutman, YVA; M.49.E/2314, testimony of Aba Reiner.

the Jews in Lwów shall be gathered in Jewish quarters and vanish from the streetscape, as in the other towns in the district of Galicia. This shall take place under consideration of the experiences with the establishment of ghettos and Jewish quarters in other towns of the General Government. The quarter for the approximately 100,000 Jews has been chosen, and the completion of the preliminary work is imminent. Hereafter, this problem will be solved most quickly.[7]

August 1, 1941, and increasing integration of the Galicia District into the rest of the General Government, was followed by unification in legal terms and organizational issues. This also applied to legislation on employment. On August 7, 1941, Governor General Hans Frank issued a decree for the Galicia District regarding the application of his previous regulation of October 26, 1939 and the regulations of December 11 and 12, 1939, issued by the higher SS and police leader in the General Government Friedrich-Wilhelm Krüger. All the male Jewish population of the district between the ages 14 to 60 had to perform forced labor; while boys from 12 were subjected to registration only.[8] In case of the non-Jewish population, initially, regulations were issued, which applied in the General Government in 1939, but on September 6, 1941, Hans Frank signed a new regulation, where one section had been modified to include the duty of work (*Arbeitspflicht*) of the entire non-Jewish population of the district, whereas the regulation of 1939 explicitly mentioned the Polish population.

In terms of organization, forced labor can be divided into four periods.[9] The first was the period of military administration (until August 1, 1941); the second period lasted from the creation of the Galicia District up to the beginning of the deportations to death camps in the spring of 1942; the third period was the time of deportation to death camps from spring 1942 to late 1942—when Jews working in labor detachments (*placówki*) were enclosed in labor camps and small ghettos (*Julag*); and the last period, when all Jews were contained in labor camps. Already at the beginning of the German occupation, guidelines were prepared concerning introduction of forced labor for the Jews.[10]

---

7   YVA-JM.21 (3508214_08004009), *Hans Frank's Diary*, vol. 17, Referat des Gouverneur Dr. Lasch auf Regierungssitzung am Dienstag, den 21. Oktober 1941, scan 807.
8   VBlGG, 1941, 462.
9   Tatiana Berenstein distinguishes three periods, not including the period of military administration, in Berenstein, "Praca przymusowa," 4.
10 "Bericht über die Judenfrage in Lemberg," YVA, JM.15083, PDF frames 2–3.

In terms of forms of forced labor in Galicia we may distinguish between two basic types: labor detachments working in specific places and forced labor camps.[11] However, even here, in addition to these fundamental divisions, other forms of forced labor should be considered. One of these was the collection of raw materials (by people known as rags collectors, or *zbieracze szmat*), in which Jews were involved. The rag collectors were provided with special passes, according to which they were free to move around the district. They could be called individual workers. Organized forced labor, as in other districts of the General Government, can be divided into activities managed by public authorities (government departments of the General Government), the army (Wehrmacht), the war industry, the SS and police, private German enterprises, and non-German companies. This division was blurred by the fact that arms plants were in private hands as well as part of the SS (DAW, OSTI) and the Wehrmacht. In terms of distribution in the different branches of the economy, the division may be as follows: industry, transport, agriculture, water, infrastructure, trade, and services.

ECONOMIC PLANS FOR GALICIA

The Galicia District, as with other districts of the General Government, became the object of interest for the state enterprises, the war industry, the civil administration, and private entrepreneurs. It seems that in this case it was treated as a new area of expansion, where existing industrial plants[12] and other facilities related to the infrastructure could be taken under control, enabling their use for economic expansion.[13] In the case of Galicia, where the model of economic exploitation of newly conquered territory was repeated, it was similar to that of the rest of the General Government. However, in comparison with the General Government in 1939, these processes in Galicia were much faster. First, it was related to the fact that economic aspects of such restructuring were unclear in 1939, when the general Government was created, and the administrative organization of the area proceeded slowly. In 1939 and 1940 a pattern of acquisition

---

11 Berenstein, "Praca przymusowa ludności żydowskiej," 4.
12 Beschaffung von Unterlagen für Planungsarbeiten über die holzbearbeitende Industrie im neuen Ostraum. YVA-JM.12331, scan 126.
13 Bericht des SS-Obersturmführer Gebauer an den SS-und Polizeiführer Brigadeführer Katzmann, Betr. Sägewerke u. Ziegelein in Umkreis von Lemberg, Lemberg, 21. August 1941. YVA-JM.12331, scans 86–87; Bericht und Vorschläge auf Grund der Besichtigungsfahrt des SS-Ustuf. mit SS-Stubaf. Manbach vom 22.–26. September 1941. YVA-JM.12331, scans 90–95; Bericht: Übernahme von geeigneten Objekte, 28. September 1941. YVA-JM.12331, scans 98–100.

and development of industrial facilities had to be worked out, and a legal system along with implementing instructions had to be developed. As far as Galicia was concerned, even if a decision on annexation to the General Government had not yet been taken, the process was much faster, and various German agents, almost immediately after crossing the front line, began to identify business enterprizes which might be suitable for them and planned the takeover of those ventures.[14] This time, DAW was one of the first. The representative of the company, *SS-Obersturmführer* Wolfgang Mohwinkel, arrived in Lwów after its occupation by the Germans to organize new branches of this company.[15] He took over the old mill machine factory and the Steinhaus Company (TBM Building Society) at Janowska Street. Other companies taken over were subject to the *Treuhandstelle* administration being its property.

The role of the district of Galicia, which was annexed by the General Government on August 1, 1941, differed significantly from that of the other districts. The situation in which this district was annexed and its strategic position meant that it remained a separate district in the General Government in terms of its character and the situation of the Jews living there. The fact that Galicia remained under the Soviet rule for two years made the economic situation of the Jews living there different from that of other districts in the General Government and in a way facilitated taking possession of private property by the German authorities. In most cases, the Soviet powers had already nationalized the private property.

The process of nationalization carried out by the Soviet authorities eased the acquisition of numerous factories and other businesses by the occupation forces. In contrast to Poland in 1939, on the territories previously occupied by the Soviet authorities the process of both taking over companies and economic expansion was much faster. First of all, in Poland after the entry of the German troops, there was a period of economic stagnation. Cutting off the General Government from the markets and sources of raw materials, the destruction of transportation and the establishment of a customs border, which separated the area of the General Government from other parts of former Polish territories, struck the economy very hard. Another important factor was the initially unclear

---

14   One of the leading people interested in reconnaissance of different enterprises in Galicia was SSPH in the district Lublin, Globocnik. He was authorized to do this among others as *Beauftragte des RKFDV* in the east. YVA-JM.12331, scan 101.

15   Berenstein, "Praca przymusowa ludności żydowskiej," 5.

concept of exploitation of the Polish territories within the economy of the Reich. Originally proposed was the dismantling and evacuation of industrial equipment from Poland to the Reich in order to give that area a strictly agricultural character and to constitute a reservoir of labor and raw materials for the Reich while providing important strategic functions as a bridgehead. Only the needs of war industry preceding Operation Barbarossa resulted in a change of perception and led to the development of war industry in the territories of the General Government. It should be noted that Poland in 1939 was the first area under direct German occupation, which meant that the German authorities were still inexperienced in the organization of economic life in the occupied territories.

Areas of the Galicia District in 1941 were at the center of various political and military happenings—the general course of events was much more dynamic than in other areas of the General Government. First, the military government of Galicia lasted a relatively short time—only about five weeks. After the advance of the German army and shifting the front lines to the east, Galicia became the immediate hinterland of the Eastern Front. Due to the proximity of the front and the distance from the industrial centres in the Reich, it had to satisfy various needs of the army without waiting for imported goods and resources. In particular, it was necessary to provide all kinds of services for the army, such as repairs of military equipment, military vehicles, and weapons. It was also essential to meet various requirements, such as mending uniforms, providing communication services, and the like. Most towns in the Galicia District were located on transport routes—both rail and road—enabling the supply of war material, fuel, and other goods to the front. Therefore, Lwów became an important railway and road junction, and the transportation lines from the west to Lwów, and further to the east, acquired strategic importance.

Huge frontline requirements concerning military items, food, and services resulted in an immediate expansion of the various elements wishing to exploit the positive economic trend for their own interests. This went according to the rule "first come, first served." Being the first gave priority right to control all domains of production, including the most privileged. An additional factor was the ability to take over existing facilities and adapt them to the necessary production profile. This made possible the use of existing production facilities and equipment with minimum investment from new companies. Therefore, in contrast to Poland in 1939, in Galicia following the occupation, people, wishing to multiply their profits, were interested in starting production based on the existing infrastructure.

THE ORGANIZATION OF FORCED LABOR

On August 22, 1941, Dr. Seifert, head of the Trust Department, had issued instructions to the representatives, managers, and trustees of companies, declaring that it was now possible to keep Jewish employees that were under their control on the condition that

> ... they [the Jews] did not act against the Reich or its citizens and if they were absolutely needed; in exceptional cases that were difficult to settle, it is recommended to communicate with the Trust Department. The Jewish workers left in the enterprises had to—according to the instruction—be reported, on a monthly basis, to the Department of the Trust, including at the same time an exact record containing personal data (name and surname, address, profession and monthly salary).[16]

This order appeared due to practical considerations, because by allowing the former owners to retain the Jews in the workplace as business managers or specialist staff, continued and uninterrupted operation of these enterprises was ensured. Many new managers did not have suitable qualifications or were not able to replace the expert staff in such a short time. However, during the next few months, the replacement of Jewish workers by non-Jewish employees took place. The usefulness or necessity of Jewish workers was checked every month, with appropriate decisions taken.

In September 1941, the authorities of the Galicia District established special branches for employment of Jews (*Judeneinsatz*) in German labor offices (*Arbeitsämter*). At that time, the head of the Labor Department in the district was Dr. Nietzsche. On September 20, 1941, he issued a notice, in which he relied on the decree of Hans Frank from August 7, 1941, and ordered the registration of people aged 14 to 60 who were obliged to perform forced labor. Mayors and the *Judenräte* were responsible for carrying out the registration. The announcement distinguished two forms of employment of the Jews: the first was a call to perform forced labor and the other was a free employment relationship. The registration ordinance required absolute obedience; it called the Jews to come to registration point and to perform forced labor at every summons. A sentence of 10 years in prison could be expected for failing to come forward for registration at the designated time and place; for providing false personal data; for

---

16 Berenstein, "Praca przymusowa ludności żydowskiej," 5.

simulating inability to work; or for failing to appear for work. A similar penalty was expected for members of the *Judenrat* and other people responsible for performing of the registration and organization of work, if they did not perform the task imposed upon them.[17]

The next ordinance, issued by Nietzsche on September 20 (this time as the head of the Labor Office in Lwów), was for implementing the instructions of the first order. According to it, from October 1 until November 15, 1941, registration would take place of all male Jews between the ages of 12 and 60 and women fit for work who had no place of permanent employment. At the same time, the instruction did not specify the age limit of women who were to appear for registration. During the registration, it was necessary to present an appropriate certificate of employment. For not complying with the instruction, a sentence of hard labor for 10 years could be expected.[18]

The Jews were, undoubtedly, a valuable labor force, able to perform many complex jobs in war industry. Other workers, including Ukrainians, could hardly be expected to do the same. We can learn about the high regard of the Jewish labor force from a Wehrmacht report:

> The settling of the Jewish Question in the Ukraine has been made more difficult because in the cities the Jews constituted a major part of the population. [...] The great majority of the Jewish masses remained under the German administration. The entire situation was complicated by the fact that these Jews carried out almost all the work in the skilled trades and even provided part of the labor for small and medium-sized industries; apart from trade, some of which had become superfluous as a result of the direct or indirect effects of the war. [Their] elimination was therefore bound to have profound economic consequences, including even direct effects on the military economy (supplies for troops).[19]

As a consequence of the registration, branch offices for employment of Jews established records (card-index) for all people subjected to forced labor and the registered Jews received their *Meldenkarte*. Since then, these cards were used both as employment certificates and as identity documents. Those branches of employment offices were headed by the Germans and the employees there were

---

17 AŻIH, poster 102.
18 AŻIH, poster 104.
19 From a Wehrmacht report on the extermination of the Jews in the Ukraine. PS-3257; Arad and Gutman, *Documents on the Holocaust*, 417.

mostly Jews. Until the end of June 1942, the branch offices were decisive in all cases involving forced labor of Jews and work in free employment. All authorities, institutions, and private companies interested in engaging Jewish employees had to turn to employment offices. In Lwów, the head of the *Judeneinsatz* was Heinz Weber and his bureau was located on the Zamarstynowska Street.[20] By the end of the year, all Jews in the district obligated to perform forced labor were registered. In Czortków, the registration was conducted in December 1941 and those compelled to perform forced labor were women aged 16 to 45. Similarly, in Stanisławów, women up to age 45 were required to perform forced labor.

At the end of winter 1942, the labor office announced a new registration of Jews obligated to perform forced labor, in order to verify that all people were indeed employed by German authorities and other institutions and companies.[21] Re-registration allowed the creation of an index to exclude people not designated for deportation. This category included all craftsmen and the young and healthy individuals employed by the Germans. All Jews belonging to various groups of professions were also registered, and given documents protecting them from deportation.[22]

In Lwów, on March 13, 1942, on the eve of the first deportation to the camp in Bełżec, an ordinance was issued. Those employed by the authorities, companies and institutions had received a German band with the letter "A" embroidered in the middle of the Star of David, and registration cards, with a photograph and an official stamp. The bands also bore the numbers of the registration cards and a stamp of the labor office. Holders of these special cards and bands were able to obtain permits protecting members of their households from deportation. About fifty thousand people, who constituted about half of all Jews in Lwów, received such new *Meldekarten*. Some of the men who did not receive *Meldekarten* were sent to forced labor camps by the labor office.[23] On April 20, 1942, Nietzsche issued an order stating that as of April 30, all old certificates and registration cards lost validity, and from that time onwards only new registration cards would be honored.[24]

---

20 YVA, M.49.E, rel. 2550, testimony of Joachim Schönfeld.
21 "Offizielle Registerung der jüdischen Händwerker und Fachleute," *Mitteilungen des Judenrates in Lemberg für die Jüdische Gemeinde*, 3 (March 01, 1942): 2 (YVA-JM.15083).
22 "Arbeitsumlage für jüdiechen Heilberufler," *Mitteilungen des Judenrates in Lemberg für die Jüdische Gemeinde*, 3 (March 01, 1942): 2 (YVA-JM.15083).
23 YVA, M.49.E/4691, testimony of Róża Wagner; YVA, M.49.E/4833, testimony of Berl Potruch, AŻIH, 301/44, Leon Weliczkower.
24 AŻIH, poster 12.

The time and manner of the new registration varied in different localities. During the registration in Stanisławów, the physical condition of people was also checked. In this city, a committee composed of Gestapo chief Hans Krüger and his helpers, Brandt and Schott, assessed the physical condition of the individuals and divided them into three categories: A, B, and C. Category A included all craftsmen employed by the Germans, as well as healthy young men. Some of those in category B were sent to labor camps and others were deported to the extermination camp. All Jews who were assigned category C were sent directly to the extermination camp in Bełżec. In Kołomyja, however, the registration was conducted in April 1942 parallel with the selection of Jews for deportation.

JEWISH REACTION TO THE DEPORTATIONS

The actions of the Germans concerning the registration and categorization of employees caused a fierce reaction among the Jews, who understood that in order to survive in their current location they had to seek employment—ideally in companies producing goods for the German army. Facing the deportations to the death camps, the Jews in other districts of the General Government also took initiative, hoping to save their lives. It should be noted that the experience of the Jews in Galicia was different from those in other parts of the General Government. Firstly, the Jews of Galicia passed through the initial period of pogroms and mass executions already in summer 1941, so that now they understood the cruelty of the German occupation and their hostile, predominantly Ukrainian environment. Their initiative to create places of employment came together with the beginning of the *Aktion Reinhardt* in spring 1942, while the Jews in other parts of the General Government initiated development of different forms of employment and creating new places of employment mainly due to hard economic situation, and not to save their lives.

The efforts to obtain supplementary jobs in particular factories, for example, in the German firm Schwartz and Co., came together with the efforts of the Germans to enlarge their activities and exploit the Jewish labor force. However, in the situation of imminent danger of the deportations, the company felt free to require that all applicants bring large sums of money or provide their own equipment, such as sewing machines.[25] In this way, the Jewish employees

---

25   YVA, M.49.E/4648, testimony of Dawid Bertisch; YVA, M.49.E/2171, testimony of Dawid Berber; YVA, M.49.E/1398, testimony of Szaja and Roza Feder.

themselves, in order to obtain the relevant documents protecting them from deportation, financed the activities of the companies employing them. These companies did not have to incur additional expenditure for expensive equipment or tools, and, consequently, further increase their profits at no extra investment. But the actions of the Jews themselves went beyond the individual applications for a job. In Lwów, the Department of Industry and Trade of the *Judenrat* decided to found craftsmanship companies. These companies employed workers of different specialties: shoemakers, tailors, blacksmiths, carpenters, and others. In addition, the Committee of Jewish Mutual Aid Society in Lwów organized workshops, known as urban workshops (Germ. *Städtische Werkstätte*; Pol. *warsztaty miejskie*). These workshops were created in the building of a school at Kazimierzowska Street. In this case also, the person applying for employment provided the machines, tools, and money that facilitated the operation of these workshops. Initially, five thousand jobs were planned there. In the second half of April 1942, 4,300 people were employed in these workshops. The workers received documents and armbands with the letter "A." The workshops secured contracts to sew uniforms and the like from the military authorities. The workshops in Lwów were developed along the lines of similar workshops in Bochnia. For this purpose, a member of the presidium of the Jewish Self-Assistance (ŻSS), Dr. Eliasz Tisch, visited Bochnia on April 12, 1942 and prepared a comprehensive report on this subject. In April 1942, in order to assist in the establishment of the urban workshops, Salo Grajwer visited Lwów.[26] Workshops and enterprises which provided additional jobs were also set up in other cities of the General Government, for instance, in Warsaw and Częstochowa.

In June 1942, when the *Aktion Reinhardt* was already in progress, the ŻSS tried to encourage establishment of collective production workshops in its circular letter:

> A long time ago, collective production workshops in Warsaw, Bochnia, and Tarnów had been organized without our support, and more recently, workshops in Drohobycz, Lwów, and Kraków appeared with our help. Workshops in Warsaw, Bochnia, and Tarnow have gained, in a relatively short period of time, not only the recognition of authorities and companies, but also markets, providing work and bread for thousands of families in Warsaw and

---

26 YVA, M.49.E/4734, testimony of Rudolf Reder; YVA, M.49.E/4630, testimony of Róża Hochberg; S. Szende, *Der Letzte Jude aus Polen* (Zürich: Europa Verlag, 1945), 285.

hundreds of families in Bochnia and Tarnów. These workshops have given employment not only to qualified craftsmen and professional force, but also merchants and white-collar workers, and even lawyers, teachers, and the like, who in a relatively short time learned a craft.[27]

To increase employment, the Jews themselves initiated similar establishments in various cities of the Galicia District: Stanisławów, Drohobycz, Borysław, and others. They were mostly businesses for tailoring, brush making, carpentry, metalwork, basketry, shoemaking, furriers, sheet metal, watchmakers, electrical workshops, sign painting, weaving, and milliners. In some places, service companies, such as laundries and sewing rooms, were set up. For this production, a relatively low investment and low material costs were necessary, but they required much labor. A sewing business could count on military orders and, on the whole, most of the production was intended for the army. In this case, the Jews applying for jobs supplied the sewing machines themselves. A basket maker produced, first of all, baskets for ammunition and artillery shells. A brush production business also required relatively simple and inexpensive materials but involved a large number of workers. An important factor was the low demand for energy, which at that time was a very important factor, because energy was rationed and plants producing marketable goods or items considered unnecessary for the war economy did not receive allocations of energy and fuel. Furthermore, from 1943, these businesses were reviewed by a special committee and closed down by administrative decisions.

Workshops were mostly situated in the ghettos or on the outer edge, but they also existed beyond the walls or fences of ghettos. For example, in Stanisławów and Kołomyja the so-called *Umschlagstellen* were created outside the ghettos.[28] Actions taken by the *Judenräte* and Jewish Self-Assistance were of great importance, because they increased employment of Jews who had no work in German plants, and thereby protected them from deportation. In this case, the Jewish initiative had taken advantage of the existing production capacity that called for relatively low investment. Often it meant simply adapting existing buildings for production purposes. It should be noted that the working conditions of the Jews were very difficult. They worked many hours a day in poorly lit and badly heated rooms. The production program of the

---

27 YVA-JM.1581, ŻSS, Okólnik nr 61. Dotyczy pomocy w dziedzinie pracy, BARDZO PILNE, Kraków, June 11, 1942, scans 702–3.
28 Berenstein, "Praca przymusowa ludności żydowskiej," 12–13.

Jewish community also allowed employment of young people who were unprepared from professional standpoint. They had to learn new skills quickly while performing lighter and simpler jobs. Jewish establishments also had to be competitive: they had to work efficiently and cheaply to secure contracts. That is why they worked many hours a day and were willing to receive very low wages. The newly established plants very often used recycled materials and trash of various kinds. In this case, recovery of raw materials and ingenuity knew no bounds.

TAKEOVER OF JEWISH AFFAIRS BY THE SS AND THE POLICE IN 1942

In mid-1942, all matters pertaining to the employment of Jews were handed over to the higher SS and police commander in the General Government, Friedrich-Wilhelm Krüger. Then the SS and police again began to stamp personal identity documents that had been issued by the labor offices. From that time onwards, only the SS and police determined the assignment of Jewish forced laborers to the German authorities, institutions, and businesses.[29] Therefore, the heads of the major departments in the administrative authorities of the General Government convened on June 22, 1942 to discuss matters regarding the further employment of Jews. Krüger was also present at this meeting. Dr. Max Frauendorfer presented the difficulties associated with acute labor shortages in the General Government and declared that he would not give up Jewish labor. According to him and the Inspector for the Armament in the General Government, General Schindler, Jewish experts and specialists were also indispensable in the armaments industry. Similar views were expressed by Naumann, the head of the Department of Food and Agriculture, who highlighted particular difficulties in recruitment of manpower in the Galicia District, which had caused the collapse of production plants, such as sugar beets. Difficulties in recruiting manpower appeared due to the fact that in Galicia, Ukrainians massively evaded agricultural work because it was hard and poorly remunerated, and therefore, unattractive. However, the problem of labor recruitment in the General Government was far-reaching. First of all, there were not enough professional workers capable of working in the armaments industry. Because there were many professionals among the Jews or because of the threat of deportation, adding to the realization that jobs in the armaments industry could save their lives, Jews undertook the

---

29 Berenstein, "O podłożu," 68–69; Karay, "The Conflict among German Authorities."

work, even in areas where no experience was required. Moreover, they tried to learn the required operations as rapidly as possible, learning from the others and gaining experience directly at the workplace in order not to lose their jobs and, consequently, their lives.

For the non-Jewish population, work in industry, despite the use of various incentives in the form of additional vouchers for food and material necessities, was not very attractive because the official salary tables suggested an amount that did not keep pace with inflation. Those who could find additional earnings in the private sector or trading on the black market clearly preferred this way of life. It should be noted that throughout the occupation, permanent recruitment for forced labor took place in Germany, which caused a large outflow of labor. At the meeting on June 22, 1942, Naumann had asked Krüger to provide Jewish workers for agriculture in Galicia to resolve the employment crisis. If the agricultural work was not done, there would be a risk of incurring large losses and not meeting yield quotas. At that time, the Jews were reported en masse to work, desiring to be protected against actions. Krüger agreed to the allocation of Jewish laborers to work in agriculture, providing they had strict and severe supervision. It was preferable because the police force did not have sufficient manpower to control the Jews.

The extent of the difficulties is evident: 1,800 large farms in Galicia demanded about 30,000 to 40,000 workers. About a month later, Himmler arrived on a visit to Lublin, during which he issued a decree, dated July 19, 1942, ordering to end the deportation of all Jews from the General Government until December 31, 1942. After then, Jews could still inhabit five collective camps in four districts of the General Government. Galicia was not even mentioned in this document, nor were the collective camps in the district.[30] This may have been an oversight, or, more likely, it could have indicated that the SS treated the district differently. Despite the annexation to the General Government in 1941, many facts indicate that Galicia was perceived as a separate entity. First of all, throughout the course of the war and the occupation, the management of Galicia was different. The first period of the occupation was characterized by violent pogroms against the Jewish people and the activities of the *Einsatzgruppen*, which launched the mass destruction of the Jewish population in those areas. Then the process of harmonization of legislation with the General Government went very quickly, albeit with some differences

---

30 Order by Himmler on July 19, 1941 for the completion of the "Final Solution" in the Government-General (NO-5574), in Arad and Gutman, *Documents on the Holocaust*, 275.

due to the ethnic composition of these areas. This led to economic expansion. However, in comparison with other districts, Jewish life in Galicia constantly proceeded in the shadow of death. In summer and autumn months of 1941, actions took place in many locations. For example, in Stanisławów on October 12, 1941, about 12,000 Jews were murdered. In terms of strategic importance, Galicia occupied a significant location because of its railways and roads leading to the east. Thus, the majority of supplies for the army passed through Galicia. Moreover, Galicia also fulfilled the role of the army's rear: production carried out in this district to supply the army could be delivered much faster, better, and cheaper than from the depths of Germany. In order to improve transport capacities, construction of a major road leading to the east was launched. To achieve this goal, a number of Jewish workers were mobilized from forced labor camps along the future road. The Todt Organization (*Organisation Todt*, OT) performed the basic construction work. It is therefore possible that Himmler did not mention Galicia in his order of July 19, 1942, leaving himself and the others freedom of action regarding the Jews in Galicia.

Despite the fact that Galicia was not listed in Himmler's decree, the severe reduction of the Jewish labor force continued to take place there. This process was implemented through a new selection during which the registration cards were either stamped with new stamps, or invalidated. In Lwów in August 1942, certificates of Jews employed in urban workshops were not stamped. In October 1942, about 500 people employed there were liquidated by the Gestapo and 100 other professionals were imprisoned in the Łąckiego Street Jail. Similarly, in Stanisławów, many identity cards of those employed in the German institutions and companies were not stamped. In October 1942, the workshops at the *Umschlagstelle* had been liquidated and the cards already issued were cancelled. Moreover, some employees of the *Judenrat* and the Jewish Self-Assistance did not receive new stamps. The stamps with the inscription *Haushalt* issued earlier by the labor offices were cancelled. Only a few dozen people remained in some locations where several thousand ghetto residents once lived. Those left in the ghettos were the *Kommandos* whose job was to clean up (*Räumungskommando*). Their task was to search the ghetto vicinity after the evacuation of the Jews and to collect items of interest for the Germans. These were primarily hidden treasures, but also valuable and useful furniture, carpets, ceramics, objects of everyday use, and eventually recycled raw materials such as glass, rags, non-ferrous metals, iron, furs, and paper. In addition to the special *Räumungskommando*, so-called rag collectors, were involved. In May 1942, instead of plaques with numbers they received new ID cards and armbands with the letter "A."

During the deportation, their ID cards were stamped again, as they were found indispensable. This was a particularly privileged group, because in the period of the greatest terror, selections, actions, and deportations to the extermination camps, they could move freely within the whole district.

SOCIAL CONDITIONS, REMUNERATION, AND SIZE OF FORCED LABOR IN GALICIA

In the first phase of the occupation, Jews were forced to work in a disorganized and chaotic way. This applied above all to the time of pogroms and the "Days of Petlura" in Lwów, when Jews were brutally murdered on the streets and in houses. Jews were forced to perform different jobs, for example, to remove and bury corpses of murdered prisoners, to clean streets, and so forth. Apart from the period of pogroms, the Jews were apprehended in the streets by the Ukrainian militia, the German police, or the army and herded to different jobs. Their work was often completely useless, and its goal was only humiliation or mistreatment of the Jewish population. In other cases, they were assigned specific jobs such as cleaning up the streets, washing German cars, cleaning offices, transporting, loading or unloading all kinds of materials, and other various services. At that time, there were no standards or regulations on the part of the "employers," and they were free to take advantage of arrested Jews. First of all, this was done under the threat of loss of life or injury, so the Jews could not in any way ignore or refuse to perform work. The only way to avoid such labor was to escape, but that was connected with huge risk. The "employer" did not feel obliged to grant any compensation for their services. The laborers also received no food and often had only basic tools. Moreover, Jews had no possibility of appeal to any authority.

The situation changed after the establishment of the *Judenräte*. The *Judenräte*, seeing the chaos in the field of forced labor, tried to change this situation by providing the required quantity of workers for forced labor, on the one hand, and by handling demands for workers from the authorities, institutions, and German companies, on the other. The *Judenräte* themselves paid the workers' wages, while German firms did not bear any costs. This condition evidently led to financial difficulties for the *Judenräte*. Part of the forced labor expenses was borne by those who paid the appropriate sums for a replacement worker, so that the *Judenrat* only transferred this money to other workers. Each person obliged to perform forced labor had to work one day a week, and later, two days a week. For the poorest, who had no possible earnings except for those from forced labor, that meager salary gave a minimum income to allow their survival. At the end of 1941, the *Judenrat* could not cover expenses of forced labor and introduced special taxes.[31] In addition to payments for work, vouchers for bread were also issued. Initially it was 1 kg of bread per day of work, and then this quantity of bread was systematically reduced. Salaries for work also were low and paid irregularly, and sometimes not at all. After changes in the procurement of forced labor in the summer of 1942 and the adjustments in the financing system of forced labor, German companies and institutions were forced to compensate Jewish employees for the work done. The fixed rate was, in general, about 2 zł for a ten-hour working day. In certain occupations or positions workers earned more, although not significantly. Frequently, the only compensation was free rent. For example, a worker in Kołomyja earned 80 zł; a doctor in Tłuste earned 90 zł; a translator at the print shop in Czortków got 130 zł.[32] The farm workers received food, and often did not receive any monetary remuneration at all. Importantly, food stamps were also issued at the workplace. Prices of bread on the open market were very high, so that a 1 kg loaf of bread costed 3 zł in food coupons, but on the open market it costed 16 zł in the summer and up to 24 zł in the winter. Receiving additional food coupons was sometimes more important than money, because salaries did not keep up with inflation.

GERMAN INSTITUTIONS EMPLOYING JEWISH FORCED LABORERS

In Eastern Galicia, Polish estates were nationalized by the Soviet authorities and collective farms were set up in their place. Some were transformed into Ukrainian cooperatives. The German authorities took over the farms without privatizing them and they were then transformed into agricultural estates under German management called *Liegenschaften*. This form facilitated not only the acquisition of large properties, but also their adaptation for the war economy and food production. The new German administration could freely adjust the profile of agricultural production, moving away from traditional crops to increase the cultivation of selected products, such as sugar beet. The naval blockade of Germany also encouraged the search for substitutes for different inaccessible raw materials that could be found in the fertile areas of Ukraine, for example, a plant called *koksagiz* that was used to produce rubber. To increase

---

31 Berenstein, "Praca przymusowa ludności żydowskiej," 17.
32 Ibid.

the profitability of their vast farms, the German management also used forced labor, including, above all, Jewish forced labor. Towards this objective, a network of labor camps was set up in the German holdings. Jewish labor in these farms was practically free of charge.

In addition to companies engaged in the expansion of construction of new roads, the Eastern Railway (*Ostbahn*) was one of the largest companies employing Jewish workers. Since the beginning of the war between Germany and the USSR, Lwów and other towns in Galicia were on the route of transportation of people, equipment, and supplies to the Eastern Front. In particular, Lwów became an important place of shipment of goods, which required much labor. Work was carried out around the clock. Besides, the Eastern Railway workers had to repair and lay new railway tracks. A large number of workers were needed to repair the rolling stock. They were employed by the railway repair establishments (*Ostbahnhof-Ausbesserungswerk*). Since September 1941, hundreds of well-off Jewish specialists were working at the railway. In addition, many physical laborers were hired for loading and unloading, transporting, and moving different substances, such as coal.[33]

The idea of creating urban workshops arose as a result of the so-called "March Action"—the deportation of "antisocial elements" (*Asoziale Elemente*) in March 1942. In the course of "March Action," a part of Jewish population from Lwów was deported to Bełżec. This action prompted people who had no work cards to find jobs at any price, as only that could protect them from deportation. In this case, the game was no longer about economic survival but about life itself. High public pressure in search of employment meant that the leadership of the Jewish community began to think of how to solve this problem. After the action in March 1942, a Jewish entrepreneur named Grajwer arrived from Bochnia for talks in Lwów. He was a man of experience, since he had founded workshops in Bochnia in which hundreds of Jews worked. In Lwów, the talks on the establishment of urban workshops were attended by a number of people, including *Volksdeutsche* Dormann, Commandant of Lwów, Dr. Heller, his economic adviser, Dr. Rasp, and three Jewish businessmen: Traimski, the lawyer Dr. Rajzler, and David Schechter.[34] The initiative on the establishment of urban workshops was supported by the head of the Department of Jewish Mutual Aid, activist Dr. Landau and the Association of Jewish Artisans in Lwów,

---

33 Ibid., 7.
34 Eliyahu Jones, *Żydzi Lwowa w okresie okupacji 1939–1944* (Lodz: Oficyna Bibliofilów, 1999), 95.

Dr. Maarer. Already in April 1942, the workshops were opened. Grajwer became their general director while the three above-mentioned entrepreneurs became their managers.[35]

The urban workshops were located at 20/22 Kazimierzowska Street and employed about 4,000–5,000 people.[36] Obtaining a job in the workshops was easier for workers who had their own equipment or tools, especially sewing machines. Besides, those interested in working paid money to receive a job. This system meant that the organizers in a short time, without spending their own money, received the necessary equipment and funds for production. Such a situation could have occurred only in exceptional circumstances—at the risk of deportation. Employees received the necessary documents and badges with a letter "W," signifying that they were employed for the Wehrmacht, to be worn on their clothes. The urban workshop primarily produced uniforms and uniform items. Some of the production was also designated for the free market.

In spring of 1942, urban workshops, like those in Lwów, were founded in other cities, such as Borysław, Drohobycz, and Stanisławów. The carpentry workshop established in Borysław produced furniture for German offices. The following workshops: tailoring, linen, producing baskets for ammunition, carpentry, brushes, and toys were established in Drohobycz. In turn, workshops set up in Stanisławów dealt in plumbing, electricity, tailoring, furs, watchmaking, sign painting, and making women's hats. In this last town, workshops were located outside the ghetto in the *Umschlagstelle*.[37] The situation in Kołomyja and Kosów was similar. In Brody, the workshops were called "Craftsman House" and employed 400 people. Later on, the *Judenräte* organized workshops in Jezierzany, Tarnopol, Zbaraż, Złoczów, and other places.[38]

Collecting recyclables remained a special type of employment for Jews. During the war, there was an extensive demand for various raw materials that were lacking for war production. To offset the increasing demand for these resources, the German authorities in occupied territories limited the production of consumer goods for the local population, which resulted in only a slight improvement in those deficiencies. The solution was, on the one hand, the strong growth of a used goods market and, on the other hand, the development

---

35 "Warsztaty dzielnicowe we Lwowie," *Gazeta Żydowska*, April 29, 1942, 1.
36 "Z gmin żydowskich w Generalnym Gubernatorstwie: Warsztaty dzielnicowe we Lwowie," *Gazeta Żydowska*, April 29, 1942, 1; "Wiadomości ze Lwowa: Rzemieślnicy na przedzie," *Gazeta Żydowska*, June 14, 1942, 3.
37 Berenstein, "Praca przymusowa ludności żydowskiej," 12.
38 Ibid., 13.

of illegal production and trade. Additionally, the collection of materials, especially iron, nonferrous metals, paper, rags, and other waste had become an important source of resources. For this purpose, special companies, which handled the collection of desired materials, were formed. The Management Office for Old and Waste Materials (*Bewirtschaftungsstelle für Alt-und Abfallstoffe*) granted special concessions to companies engaged in collecting refuse, garbage, and rubbish. The largest company, founded by Victor Kremin, was called Victor Kremin Old and Waste Materials Collection for the Districts of Lublin and Galicia (*Viktor Kremin Alt- und Abfallstoffe Erfassung für die Distrikt Lublin und Galizien*), and specialized not only in the collection of rags and scrap metal, but also in their sorting, cleaning, and repair. In addition to collecting and processing discarded materials, those companies owned facilities that also dealt in repair and laundering of the uniforms of frontline soldiers. Jewish workers collecting materials had special certificates and were marked with the letter "R" (*Rohstoff*), which allowed them to move around freely. This was a privilege, because at this time most Jews were contained in ghettos and labor camps. There were also two other companies: Lindberger, which collected glass, bottles, and glass packaging, and a business owned by R. Wolf, engaged in collecting waste paper.[39]

LABOR CAMPS IN GALICIA

One of the largest networks of camps was set up along a strategic road DG IV (*Durchgangsstrasse* IV), which ran from Przemyśl, through Lwów, to Kiev.[40] This route was 350 km long. All along the route, camps were established—each managing a separate section of the road. The modernization project involved constructing new roads and repairing railways, old roads, and bridges. In order to implement this plan, the commander of the SS and police (SSPF) in the Galicia District, Fritz Katzmann, created a network of labor camps for Jews. In his report Katzmann wrote about this project:

> The best means for this [evasion of forced labor and black market] was the establishment of Forced Labor Camps by the SS and Police Leader. There was, first of all work on the urgently needed reconstruction of

---

39 Ibid., 9.
40 Andrej Angerick, "Annihilation and Labor: Jews and Thoroughfare IV in Central Ukraine," in *The Shoah in Ukraine: History, Testimony, Memory*, ed. Ray Brandon and Wendy Lower (Bloomington: Indiana UP, 2008), 190–223; Sandkühler, *"Endlösung,"* 137–148.

Dg. 4 [Durchgangstrasse IV], which was extremely important for the entire southern section of the Front and which was in catastrophically bad condition. On October 15, 1941, a start was made on the building of camps along the railroad tracks, and after a few weeks, despite considerable difficulties, 7 camps had been put up, containing 4,000 Jews. More camps soon followed, so that in a very short period of time the completion of 15 such camps could be reported, to the Higher SS and police Leader. About 20,000 Jewish laborers passed through these camps in the course of time. Despite all conceivable difficulties that turned up on this project, about 160 km have now been completed.[41]

At the head of the Board of Labor Camps stood *SS-Obersturmführer* Gustav Bolten and the inspector of the camps was *SS-Untersturmführer* Konrad Hildebrandt. The first four camps were set up in October 1941 in Złoczów County (Kurowice,[42] Lacki Wielkie,[43] Jaktorów,[44] and Płuhów). In December 1941, six camps in the district of Tarnopol (Kamionki,[45] Hluboczek,[46] Stupki, Borki Wielkie,[47] Zborów,[48] and Jezierna[49]) were established, and one camp appeared in the district of Lwów(Winniki[50]). Later on, two other camps (Hermanów, Ostrów[51]) were created in this district. In total, the road construction camps employed about 4,000 people. In May 1942, there were 15 labor camps.[52] To supervise the technical performance of the work, German companies such as Otto Heil of Kissingen and Radebüle, Pohl und Lückel were enlisted. A company from Darmstadt named Auto Carriers for Galicia (*Autotransport für Galizien*) was accountable for transport.[53]

---

41 From the final report by Katzmann, commander of the SS and police in the district of Galcia, on "The Final Solution of the Jewish Problem" in Galicia (L-18) in Arad and Gutman, *Documents on the Holocaust*, 336.
42 YVA-O.3/6822.
43 YVA-O.3/435, testimony of Joel Cygielman; O-3/1818, testimony of Marian Szatkowski; O.3.434, testimony of Dr. Bernard Gerber.
44 YVA-O.3/6822, testimony of Karol Kohan.
45 YVA-O.3/726, testimony of Juda Loewenson.
46 YVA-O.3/3320, collective testimony.
47 YVA-O.3/1813, testimony of Tzadok Mondschein; O.3/3344, testimony of Arieh Czart; O.3/732, testimony of Itzhak Neuman.
48 YVA-O.3/2135, testimony of Natalia Brauner.
49 Ibid.
50 YVA-O.3/3225, testimony of Israel Gleich.
51 YVA-O.3/7524, testimony of Lehrer Mateusz.
52 Berenstein, "Praca przymusowa ludności żydowskiej," 20.
53 Ibid., 22.

These camps were not permanent or built specifically for the purpose of road construction. Rather, they were improvised. Existing large buildings, such as farm buildings, monasteries and public buildings, were used to accommodate the inmates. Some workers were employed directly for the road works while others worked in the extraction of necessary construction material from quarries. Working in the camps, both on the roads and in the quarries, was physically demanding.

DAW was among the first German plants created in Galicia. Immediately after the occupation of Lwów by the German army, *SS-Obersturmführer* Wolfgang Mohwinkel from Lublin arrived in the city to set up a subsidiary company of DAW. Mohwinkel took over the former mill machinery factory and the Steinhaus Company TBM Building Society on Janowska Street. *SS-Obersturmführer* Fritz Gebauer[54] was a branch manager of DAW. He proceeded to organize workshops of different specialties, such as metalwork, carpentry, and auto repair. The haste of the SS men was understandable. Since Mohwinkel was one of the first to come to the area after the German army seized the region, he took advantage of his belonging to the SS and seized the equipment for his future plants. He collected machinery and raw materials in Lwów and carried them into the Janowska Street establishment. In this manner, he took over the administrative authority and authorized seizure of equipment.[55]

Fritz Gebauer immediately launched establishments employing a large number of the pre-war office staff and officials. In order to increase the number of employees, he demanded supplies and additional workers from the *Judenrat*. At the end of August 1941, 150 workers were employed in the plant; by October, up to 500 people worked there. Initially, DAW plants at Janowska Street were called outposts or places of work (*placówka*), where the Jews arrived for work and left afterwards. As early as autumn 1941, roundups took place in the newly created labor camps,[56] apprehending many Jews who willingly volunteered to work in DAW. However, on October 31, 1941, after finishing work the laborers were not allowed to go home, but kept on location. They were placed in uncompleted boarding houses within the factory premises, fenced in with barbed wire, guard towers were set up, and the whole area was secured, thereby turning the DAW plant into a labor camp.

---

54 YVA-O.3/1691, testimony of Artur Wiejski-Weiser.
55 Berenstein, "Praca przymusowa ludności żydowskiej," 5.
56 YVA-O.3/1772, testimony of Jacub Friedman, 2–3.

The Camp on Janowska Street was expanded in February 1942[57] after the expulsion of existing residents. The management set up new workshops in the camp. In the new area adjacent to the old camp, facilities for several thousand prisoners were built. The commander of this camp was *SS-Untersturmführer* Gustav Willhaus.[58] At the end of March 1942, about 400 Jews came from Lwów to this new camp. In April and May, groups of Jews from various towns in the Lwów District arrived at the camp. This was associated with the deportations to the extermination camp at Bełżec, where selections were conducted and able-bodied workers were sent to labor camps. The total number of prisoners amounted to about 2,000. Initially, the prisoners were engaged in building and cleaning the camp. Then, workshops were set up. The inmates of Janowska Street camp were also a reservoir of labor for various German institutions in the city. To work in the city, groups of Jewish workers left their base in the camp every day. The prisoners from Janowska Street worked in railway stations and railway workshops and in factories under the management of military authorities, the police and SS. They also performed clean-up work and construction in the city.

OTHER WORK CAMPS IN THE DISTRICT OF GALICIA

In addition to the labor camps along the strategic transportation routes and the Janowska Street camp, other camps were set up in the district of Galicia. The camps developed especially fast in the spring of 1942, when mass deportations of Jews to extermination camps began. Throughout the period of deportations, selections in the ghettos were carried out, during which young and strong men were sent to labor camps or left in the ghetto to work in offices and help clean out abandoned homes. Many German institutions and plants in this period were transformed into labor camps. Labor camps, in contrast to the ghettos, had a selected workforce and were almost entirely composed of able-bodied workers. Once places of employment were converted into labor camps, the workers there were protected from deportation. Transforming outposts to labor camps was easy, as the outposts already retained permanent detachments of

---

57 Sandkühler, "*Endlösung,*" 185–90; YVA-O.3/2373, testimony of Dr. Efraim Halpern; O.3/3320, collective testimony; O.3/2842, testimony of Szarlotta Nachta (Wach); O.3/2233, testimony of Dorota Seilaender; O.3/1691, testimony of Artur Wiejski-Weiser; O.3/1772, testimony of Jakub Friedman; O.3/3225, testimony of Edward Gleich; O.3/3849, testimony of Shemuel Dreichs; O.3/2373, testimony of Dr. Efraim Halpern.
58 YVA-O.3/1691, testimony of Artur Wiejski-Weiser.

workers, which only had to be put into buildings and guarded. As in other districts of the General Government, in Galicia, the transformation of the ghettos into labor camps took place during the deportation, when Jews were considered nonproductive, they were eliminated. The only difference was the mode of transformation. In some places, small ghettos (Pol. *getto szczątkowe*; Germ. *Restghetto*) were created to house the remaining workers, which de facto became labor camps. In other cases, selected workers were sent to different locations, where they were housed and worked in one or more places. Therefore, the outposts, during the liquidation of the ghettos, were not typically used for resident ghetto laborers, but rather for prisoners from labor camps.

In spring of 1942, the places of work at Czwartaków Street[59] and Grodecka Street in Lwów were converted to labor camps. Similarly, a labor camp was established in Sasów (Złoczów County). The prisoners worked in a quarry in Ruda Kołtowska. However, it was clear that German companies were interested in maintaining Jewish labor force; therefore, they set up labor camps to secure cheap labor and to protect the laborers from deportation. For example, the management of military facilities (*Heeresunterkunftverwaltung*) created a labor camp in Sambor. The District Forestry Office in Złoczów created a camp for their workers as well. The Wehrmacht set up a camp in Sielec Zawonie for 870 prisoners.[60] In Stryj County, labor camps for workers employed at the mills in the villages Delatyn, Mikuliczyn, Nadworna, and Skole were created. A similar process of establishing labor camps in existing facilities was carried out in agriculture; especially in *koksagiz* farms in the Drohobycz County where they hired thousands of girls and young women. Other agricultural labor camps were created in Kazimierówka, Kopanie, Grzęda, and Drohobycz.[61]

The prominent development of German companies working for the Wehrmacht took place in 1942, even though already in 1941 there was a great demand for work on infrastructure development, shipment of goods, and repair of rolling stock. The difference lies in the fact that in 1941 there were reserves of ammunition, equipment, and supplies for the army. However, these materials had been exhausted and German industry could not keep up with the production of items necessary for the army. Moreover, the longer communication lines and the transfer of many supplies for the troops into territory occupied by Germany resulted in an increased demand for services and provisions

---

59 YVA-O.3/1691, testimony of Artur Wiejski-Weiser.
60 Berenstein, "Praca przymusowa ludności żydowskiej," 5.
61 Ibid.

for the army, which in turn led to the development of companies working for the Wehrmacht. In many factories, Jewish workers constituted from 25% to 100% of the workforce. Unsurprisingly, the precise number depended on the specialty, but in some plants, particularly those repairing military uniforms, building carriages (the specialists were called *stelmach* in Polish, or *Stellmacher* in German), or saddles, Jews made up to 100% of the labor force.[62]

Among the plants working for the Wehrmacht were the Military Car Park (*Heereskraftpark*), Army Supply Management (*Heeresunterkunftverwaltung*), Office of Military Construction (*Heeresbauamt*), Training Workshops (*Ausbildungswerkstätte*), Military Forest Office (*Heeresforstamt*), Local Commands (*Ortskommandantur*), Economic Command (*Wirtschaftskommnado*), power plant Booty Storehouses (*Beutesammelstelle*), and Border Protection Corps (*Grenzschutz*). Other facilities included military barracks, camps for prisoners of war, radio stations, et cetera. Among companies working for the Wehrmacht were United Timber Companies (*Vereinigte Holz Betriebe*, VHB) and Schwarz & Co. Among the workshops that dealt with the repair of uniforms were Textilia, Metrowat AG, Holzbau A.G. (Hobag), and others. In Bolechów, furniture factories worked for the army. Karpathen Öl A.G., which dealt with the extraction of oil in Galicia, was particularly important for the German economy.[63]

WAGES AND WORKING CONDITIONS IN THE CAMPS

Living and working conditions of Jewish prisoners in forced labor camps in Galicia were as harsh as in the labor camps in the rest of the General Government. Jewish prisoners were very severely exploited. The institutions responsible for organizing the work were trying to reduce the costs of forced labor as much as possible, and, consequently, attempting to increase their profits. However, this aspect of economic life requires further explanation, because it was not only a result of the policy of the companies that employed prisoners. First of all, we have to consider that the Jews were at the bottom of the social ladder and were practically deprived of all rights. In particular, this could be seen in Galicia from the first days of German occupation, when the wave of pogroms and massacres was carried out by the *Einsatzgruppen* while the Jews were denied of any option of appeal. Despite temporary stabilization, the situation of the Jews remained

---

62 Berenstein, "Praca przymusowa ludności żydowskiej," 22.
63 BA-MA, RW23-14, Rüstungskommando Lemberg, Bericht des Dienststellenleiters zu Ziffer 2c des Kriegstahebuches, Lemberg, den 1 Juli 1943, 10.

very difficult with no great hopes of improvement. Particularly in Galicia in 1941, there was practically no possibility of recourse to any judicial or administrative institution, so that the abuse of Jews continued virtually unpunished.

The situation of Jews in labor camps was difficult not only due to the employment and economic policies of companies that used forced labor, but also because they were exposed to the whole system of corruption within the German administration. With war economy and shortages, all food products became precious commodities, which could be used for consumption, exchanged for other goods, or sold. Jews had already suffered from low standards of food; and food products intended for the Jews did not reach them in their entirety. Some foodstuffs had been appropriated en route by various officials. In addition, the control system, particularly in the labor camps for Jews, did not function properly. As mentioned above, Jews had very limited possibilities to appeal to higher authorities. They could not bring lawsuits against the Germans, which explains why, with the exception of a few well-known cases of anti-corruption investigations by the German authorities against German officers, most of the violations remained unpunished. Jews were the object of ruthless exploitation. Despite the injury inflicted by functionaries that weakened or caused the death of Jewish workers, it was easier to replace those Jews with new workers than to improve their life and work conditions. This repressive system had no mechanism of regulation. It was dominated by a propensity towards unlimited exploitation, thus creating a mechanism which led to the elimination of the labor force, while, at the same time, reservoirs of Jewish labor force seemed endless.

There were, however, differences in the treatment of prisoners between the camps operated by the SS and the camps subject to other administrative authorities. In the camps run by the SS, the situation was much more difficult, because corporal punishment was commonly used and the discipline was very severe. Undoubtedly, the fact that the SS was a repressive organization of police and not an economic organization had an impact on this situation. The treatment of sick Jews in the Jaktorów labor camp in spring of 1942 can illustrate the situation. During epidemics of typhus, instead of providing medical treatment, 80 patients were simply shot to death and thus the epidemic problem was solved.[64]

Prisoners working in the camps did not receive financial compensation. Companies employing Jewish workers from the camps only paid the camp

---

64   Relacja Heryka Charasza, 2299, 6362, in *Dokumenty zbrodni i męczeństwa*, ed. Michał M. Borwicz, Nella Rost, and Josef Wulf (Krakow: CKŻP, 1945), 28

authorities for the Jewish labor and not the workers themselves, which, in effect, turned the Jewish workers into slaves. The work of the prisoners was paid according to daily wage rates, with additional 10% for accommodations in the camp. Daily wages paid by the company for road works were 3.4 zł plus 10%, a total of 3.8 zł for ten hours of work, or 0.38 zł per hour, while Polish workers received 1.2–1.5 zł per hour, and German workers received 3 zł per hour.[65] These tariffs were very advantageous for German companies, since the cost of Jewish labor was about 28% of the Polish worker's labor cost and only 12.6% of the cost of a German worker. Despite the low rates for Jewish workers, their upkeep was profitable for the camp authorities because only a small portion of the sum received was earmarked for feeding the prisoners.

---

65 Berenstein, "Praca przymusowa ludności żydowskiej," 27.

CHAPTER 7

Jewish Labor in the Shadow of the Aktion Reinhardt

After the first two years of the occupation, the economic situation of the Jews in the General Government was very difficult due to economic persecution, high unemployment, and ghettoization. However, after the beginning of Operation Barbarossa the situation began to change quite quickly. The need for more and more war material for the Eastern Front caused rapid development of new enterprises producing for the army. The drainage of Polish forced labor to Germany reduced high unemployment in the General Government. On the other hand, the search for a cheap labor force reached the great ghettos, such as the Warsaw Ghetto in the General Government and Litzmannstadt Ghetto in Warthegau. In both places in 1940, and even at the beginning of 1941, the living conditions of the Jews were catastrophic and the mortality rate was very high. In medium and small towns, the mortality was lower due to better possibilities to obtain food.[1] However, when predominantly German firms began to open workshops in the ghettos, the death rate dropped and living conditions improved. The Jewish inhabitants had hope. This was a change of improvement, and the Jews believed that their work was so important for the German war economy that it would save their lives. Despite this, at the beginning of 1942, the die was cast. During the entire period of *Aktion Reinhardt*, Jews were living between death and hope.

---

1 YVA-JM.814. The mortality rates in Lublin in November 1940 were the following: Poles–68, Jews–61. In November 1939, 120 Poles and 59 Jews died. Lublin, Stadthauptmann, Lagebericht für November 1940, scan 379.

THE GENERAL GOVERNMENT DURING THE WANNSEE CONFERENCE

The Wannsee conference, which took place on January 20, 1942, was attended by Dr. Josef Bühler,[2] representative of the General Government.[3] His statements are of prime importance, since they represented the official position of the General Government and directly referred to the fate of the Jews living there. During the conference, arguments concerning the use of Jews as a labor force were also presented, but these arguments were drowned out by other participants. It is worth quoting part of the protocol:

> As to the question of the effect of the evacuation of the Jews on the economy, Secretary of State Neumann stated that Jews employed in essential war industries could not be evacuated for the present, as long as no replacements were available.[4]

Despite this argument, it should be noted that the Germans were at this time almost at the peak of their power, and despite supply difficulties on the Eastern Front, there were, in fact, no serious labor force shortages yet, and that during the winter of 1941 and 1942 millions of Soviet POWs had died of starvation.

As mentioned, Dr. Josef Bühler was one who took part in the discussion:

> Secretary of State Dr. Bühler put on record that the Government-General would welcome it if the final solution of this problem was begun in the Government-General, as, on the one hand, the question of transport there played no major role and considerations of labor supply would not hinder the course of this *Aktion*. Jews must be removed as fast as possible from the Government-General, because it was there in particular that the Jew as a carrier of epidemics spelled a great danger, and, at the same time,

---

2 JD Josef Bühler (1904–1948) was since November 1939 the chief of the Office of the General Governor (*Chef des Amtes des Generalgouverneurs*) Hans Frank. Since March 1940 he became the secretary of state (*Staatssekretär*), and since June 1940 he was the deputy of the General Governor (*Stellvertreter*). He fled from Kraków on January 18, 1945. Bühler was arrested by Americans on May 30, 1945, extradited to Poland in May 1946, sentenced to death on July 10, 1948, and executed in Kraków on August 21, 1948.
3 AIPN, NTN, 196/239, 193.
4 Protocol of the Wannsee conference, January 20, 1942 (NG-2586-G), in Arad and Gutman, *Documents on the Holocaust*, 260.

he caused constant disorder in the economic structure of the country by his continuous black-market dealings. Furthermore, of the approximately 2.5 million Jews under consideration, the majority were in any case unfit for work.[5]

Bühler's reasoning was the result of an earlier economic policy in the General Government, according to which the nonproductive population should be reduced and only the productive population be allowed to remain. The problem was that in the eyes of the German authorities, members of Jewish families of working people—that is, children under 14 years old, elderly, sick, or anyone unable to work, were also considered to be nonproductive. The remaining arguments concerning the spread of illnesses and the black market were also unfounded, since the spread of disease was the result of living conditions in the ghettos, for which the German authorities were responsible, and black market trade was a result of transforming most manufactures into war production industries, thereby creating shortages of consumer goods and food products in the general market.

Bühler endorsed the "Final Solution," which was consistent with the principles of General Governor Dr. Hans Frank. The minutes of the conference stated:

> Secretary of State Dr. Bühler further states that the solution of the Jewish question in the Government-General was primarily the responsibility of the Chief of the Security Police and the SD and that his work would have the support of the authorities of the Government-General. He had only one request: that the Jewish question in this area is solved as quickly as possible.[6]

To facilitate the action, Jews were persuaded that they were being evacuated to the east in order to transport them to new places of settlement and work. Ultimately, as news of mass destruction spread and the Jewish population reluctantly reported to the transports, the most brutal methods to intimidate, even terrorize, the Jews in order to break any psychological resistance were used. In addition, mass murder, constant shooting, and use of dogs during the evacuation of the ghettos to extermination camps caused additional fear.

---

5 Ibid., 260–61.
6 Ibid., 261.

Deportations from the ghettos took place in stages. Frequently during the first deportation a selection was made, leaving behind a small percentage of able-bodied people. This number was usually from 10% to 30% of the total population of the ghettos. Obviously, it was also dependent on needs and opportunities. For example, before the liquidation of the Jews, the ghetto in Częstochowa had about 42,000 inmates. During the liquidation in September 1942, only about 6,000 people were left, representing approximately 15% of the total population. In some small ghettos, where there were no factories and no particular need for Jewish labor, the special units usually liquidated the entire population. Typically, in small ghettos, a *Räumungskommando* was employed. After completing their work, in general, the team was liquidated or transferred to a labor or concentration camp.[7]

Evacuation of larger ghettos to death camps was via the railway. In localities without a railway station, the Jewish population was usually concentrated in larger towns. Transport took place on foot or with the aid of peasant carts. In remote villages, far away from railroads, mass executions were perpetrated in the nearby forests. Łomazy, in the Lublin District, is an example of the kind of extermination that was implemented by Police Battalion 101. Similar executions took place in Józefów Biłgorajski and other places.

The beginning of the deportations of Jews to extermination camps was also marked by an extensive disinformation campaign. On the one hand, a list of those exempted from evacuation was announced, but on the other hand, the authorities did not keep their word and people who came to the square and presented themselves for document control could not be certain whether they actually would be exempt. An announcement posted in the Warsaw Ghetto contained a long list of people exempt from the evacuation:

> The following are excluded from the resettlement:
> a. All Jewish people employed by German authorities or enterprises, who can show proof of this fact;
> b. All Jewish people who are members or employees of the *Judenrat* (on the day of the publication of this regulation);
> c. All Jewish people who are employed by a German Reich company and can show proof of this fact;
> d. All Jews capable of work who have up to now been brought to their workplaces are to be taken to the barracks in the Jewish quarter;

---

7 Henryk Schönker, *Dotknięcie Anioła* (Warsaw: Ośrodek Karta, 2005), 205–6; AŻIH, 301/4605, testimony of Lejzor Richman, 3.

e. All Jewish people who belong to the staff of the Jewish hospitals. This applies also to the members of the Jewish Disinfection Team;
f. All Jewish people who belong to the Jewish Police (*Jüdischer Ordnungsdienst*);
g. All Jewish people who are first-degree relatives of the person listed under a) through;
f. Such relatives are exclusively wives and children;
h. All Jewish people who are hospitalized in one of the Jewish hospitals on the first day of the resettlement and are not fit to be discharged. Fitness for discharge will be decided by a doctor to be appointed by the Judenrat.[8]

In Lublin, the Germans launched a document exchange. Previous personal documents were canceled and replaced by new ones.

The evacuation of the Jewish population will continue in future with the difference that the valid document permitting a person to remain in Lublin will no longer be the *Arbeitsausweis* with the stamp of the Sipo, but the *J.[uden]-Ausweis*. Those in possession of the *J.-Ausweis* are entitled to remain in Lublin, all others will be evacuated.[9]

The technique of document exchange was used throughout *Aktion Reinhardt* in various forms. This was a relatively simple and effective form of public confusion to prevent forgery of documents.

EXPLOITATION OF JEWISH LABOR DURING AKTION REINHARDT

Liquidation of the ghettos meant the total elimination of the Jewish population, with almost no exceptions. Only the members of the *Raumungskommando* were allowed to live for a few days or weeks and then were also killed. Liquidations took place in a progressive manner, as those who were responsible for carrying out the selection left the healthy and able

---

8   Announcement of the evacuation of the Jews from the Warsaw Ghetto, July 22, 1942, in Arad and Gutman, *Documents on the Holocaust*, 281–82; Eisenbach and Rutkowski, *Eksterminacja Żydów*, 300–302.
9   Protocol of the general meeting of the Lublin *Judenrat* on March 31, 1942, in Arad and Gutman, *Documents on the Holocaust*, 269–72; Blumental, *Documents from Lublin Ghetto*, 314–18.

to work alive. Therefore, the general argument regarding the usefulness of the Jewish workforce was still brought up in various discussions, protocols, and correspondence. Especially in the early days of liquidation actions, even in talks between German officials, it was attempted to keep the elimination totally secret. Therefore, a memorandum of the conversation between the staff of the Lublin District governor's offices, Reuter and Höfle, and the chief of staff of the liquidation action by the SSPF in the Lublin District, Odilo Globocnik, may have caused some consternation. Höfle, apparently, tried to mislead Reuter, which was possible in the first day of the action in the Lublin ghetto. The following is an excerpt of the interview notes:

> It would be right if the Jews from transports coming to Lublin were already divided at the departure station in those able and unable to work. If making this division at the station is not possible, it would eventually be desirable to perform the separation in Lublin.
>
> All Jews unable to work are to be transported to Bełżec, the furthest border station in Zamość County. *SS-Hauptsturmführer* Höfle plans to build a big camp, in which Jews able to work shall be registered according to their occupations and considering the demand.[10]

Further on, Höfle tried to convince the caller that the evacuation of the Jews was irreversible. Nevertheless, Bełżec was located on the edge of the district of Lublin, on the border with Galicia. "In conclusion, he stated that he could take 4–5 daily transports of 1,000 Jews sent to Bełżec station. Those Jews, once they had crossed the border, would never return to the General Government."[11]

SS and police commanders also elaborated on the usefulness of the Jews. On the one hand, they admitted the fact that Jews were useful and needed to work in war production, but on the other hand, they announced that they were willing to follow orders concerning the liquidation of Jews.[12]

---

10 Reuter's note, about a conversation held with Höfle, the future chief of staff of *Operation Reinhard*, in connection with an action of extermination of the Jews, commenced in Lublin, Lublin, March 17, 1942, 281.
11 Eisenbach and Rutkowski, *Eksterminacja Żydów*, 281.
12 From the final report by Katzmann, commander of the SS and police in the district of Galicia, on "The Solution of the Jewish problem" in Galicia (L-18), in Arad and Gutman, *Documents on the Holocaust*, 337.

JEWISH INITIATIVES IN THE FACE OF *AKTION REINHARDT*

Even before the beginning of *Aktion Reinhard*, the Jewish Self-Assistance tried to take initiative of organizing Jewish communities of workers. In one of their circular letters of February 16 [1942], one month before the liquidation of the ghetto in Lublin began, they wrote:

> The branches and institutions of Jewish Self-Assistance, with few exceptions, have so far limited all their activities towards providing so-called "primitive" aid: food, clothing, healing, and to combat or prevent an epidemic. This type of aid inevitably has temporary nature. Every social activity, however, should strive to ensure that after some time help will become unnecessary. Therefore, we warn our centers of the need to address other forms of assistance, more purposeful and constructive. We are thinking in particular about assistance in the field work.[13]

This change in concept of social assistance had not been motivated by the imminent danger of destruction. As the Self-Asistance officials explained:

> Only recently we were able to persuade the central economic authorities to consider the problem of employment of Jewish craftsmen. For larger workshops and craft associations it is possible to receive orders for goods of daily use and some products of small industry. For this we need in the coming days to provide information on production opportunities by Jewish craftsmen in different localities. Primarily, it concerns joiners, coopers, tailors, shoemakers, harness and haberdashery (like toys) makers.[14]

In order to obtain an accurate picture of the production capacity of each locality, the Presidency of the Jewish Self-Assistance asked for a list of bigger workshops or associations of workers in mentioned branches of production or other possibilities of production in every locality: which machines they possessed; the size of orders could they accept; and in what time could they perform those orders. The local committees of Self-Assistance were also asked whether the local communities had before received orders of labor from the

---

13 YVA-JM.1581, ŻSS, Okólnik nr 55, Kraków, dnia 16 lutego 1942, scan 691.
14 Ibid.

German authorities, German institutions, or both German and Polish companies, and how large were these orders. The Presidency of the Jewish Self-Assistance asked for exact and precise data. In that circular letter, the Presidency asked the officials to speak with craftsmen or their associations and make effort to receive orders on the spot. The Presidency also requested the officials to provide the utmost support to artisans and their associations according to their needs and local conditions.[15] The necessary permits to establish labor associations were issued by: Regional Chamber of Crafts (*Gruppe Handwerk in der Abteilung der Distriktkammer Gewerbliche Wirtschaft*) or *Kreishauptmann, Stadthauptmann, Stadtkommissar*, or *Landkommissar*.[16]

After obtaining permission from the authorities, a joint office in every locality shall be formed for the organization of labor community, which will take care of all administrative matters. Next, a community manager shall be chosen, who could be authorized to establish the labor community. The manager was to be responsible for the proper operation of the community and had to sign the appropriate declaration. A text of the membership agreement should be prepared, which also had to be accepted by the supervising authority. The membership agreement recorded the commitment of members to the joint execution of any orders received by the community, joint liabilities for damages, the regulation of working schedule, payment, and the like. Members welcomed into the community were to receive unified identification cards. Next, various professional groups were to be established within the community of labor, run by headmasters, who were to guide the work from technical point of view. The community could divide orders among individual workshops, or execute the orders in joint workshops, where artisans have put their machines. The establishment of a labor community was to be reported to the appropriate territorial Chamber of Crafts. In addition, it had to be registered in the Office of the Governor of the District, Branch of Trade and Industry (*Gewerbliche Wirtschaft*).[17]

The community was to be created regardless of whether the order was obtained or not. According to the experience of the Jewish Self-Assistance, it was much easier to get the order for communities already organized, than for those that were yet to be established. In the localities with closed residential quarters, labor communities were to be established after approval of the

---

15 Ibid.
16 YVA-JM.1581, ŻSS, Instrukcja o organizowaniu wspólnot pracy, Załącznik do okólnika nr 61 z dnia 11 czerwca 1942, scans 700–701.
17 Ibid.

appropriate authority, their branches outside the Jewish quarter in order to take their orders from individual customers. The circular of Jewish Self-Assistance also stated that when applying for the orders, not only the production of new items from normal raw material had to be taken into account. The communities should also apply for material to repair, refresh, and rework damaged clothing to make it fit for use, and eventually for orders, concerning the production of utilitarian objects from waste and substitute materials.[18] According to the circular letter, "People who do not have professional qualifications in the field of handicrafts should be, in consultation with the Labor Office, in part directed to work on the official facilities, and in part allocated to the needs of the existing communities, to perform their assignments after a brief training, which experience has proven possible."[19]

According to the Jewish Self-Assistance, the Division of Labor [of the General Government] supported calls to the local offices of the Jewish Self-Assistance with a drafted plan to use the winter period for the preparatory work related to gardening and farming. Primarily, they had in mind intensive horticultural production, and certain branches of the livestock and agricultural industry. According to the letter of January 5, 1942, "One can use rationally all, even the smallest scraps of land, which makes it easier to accept agricultural youth."[20] In towns, where it was possible, lectures on local conditions for the agricultural and horticultural production were to be arranged, short-term courses organized for landowners, written instructions issued on how to use and exploit the land, and the like. Previously uncultivated areas were prepared for transformation into allotment gardens and large sections of land suitable for cultivation were acquired. Finally, cooperation with all existing institutions of agricultural work—employing candidates for agricultural training or students of agricultural courses at all agricultural facilities—was established.[21]

The Jewish Self-Assistance urged their committees and delegation to organize preparatory work related to gardening and farming. Before starting the work they sent letters to most of their local committees asking to give displaced farmers and youth of both sexes preference when hiring for agricultural work. They also sent a delegate to all villages in the district of Kraków to perform preparatory work and to tour the surrounding mansions, trying to find accomodation for the

---

18 Ibid.
19 Ibid.
20 YVA-JM.1581, ŻSS, Okólnik nr 50, Dotyczy pomocy w dziedzinie pracy dla robotników rolnych. Kraków, dnia 5 stycznia 1942, scans 683–84.
21 Ibid.

Jewish agricultural workers. Thanks to the efforts of the Jewish Self-Assistance, about 2,500 Jews found work in agriculture.[22]

The Jewish Self-Assistance in the face of destruction and total liquidation of smaller ghettos and partial liquidation of larger ghettos wrote:

> We know that in a vast majority of cities and towns inhabited by Jews, Jewish productive forces are not even roughly used. Many people who have lost their livelihood, are forced to use the assistance of our social institutions, confined as it is very common to a bowl of soup a day. Pulling certain parts of dependents to the working process, on the one hand, would relievea large extent our [of the Self-Assistance] institutions, and on the other hand, would provide the opportunity to employ them working in their place of residence. <u>The matters raised by us must be regarded as very urgent.</u> Department Managers of "Work Aid" in the Municipal and District Committees of Assistance and members of the Delegations should strive as soon as possible to engage into the work process the greatest number of Jews—that is their next goal.[23]

In 1942, the Jewish Self-Assistance was also actively engaged in supporting Jewish workers in labor camps. In contrast to other districts, in the district of Kraków during the spring and summer of 1942 many new labor camps for Jews were established. In addition, the camp in Płaszów underwent strong development and received many new inmates. New camps were established frequently without any reasonable infrastructure, in order to perform certain works under the management of civilian firms. This is a fragment of a report concerning new established camp in Prokocim near Kraków:

> In Prokocim, the camp is just being developed. Currently, about 600 Jewish workers, mostly from Biecz, Rymanów, Jasielnica, and Brzozowa live there. In addition, [there are workers from] the small number of closely located villages, such as Myślenice. In this camp, there are no sanitation facilities and we even saw the workers wash themselves in the moat. At the moment there is not even a kitchen, and lunch or dinner is cooked on the open fire. It would be very important if these people could have bath and delousing

---

22 YVA-JM.1581, ŻSS, Okólnik nr 61. Dotyczy pomocy w dziedzinie pracy, BARDZO PILNE, Kraków, June 11, 1942, scans 702–3.
23 Ibid.

in the first place; moreover, they should get a physician assigned by medical insurance company to visit them on-site and eventually arrange a first aid kit. Due to the large distance from their places of residence, these people are not able to receive additional food from their homes. Their journey lasted about a day, so that they came without any inventory and were simply starving. Even having some money they are not able to buy anything themselves because they are not allowed to leave the camp. They work in companies Klug and Vogel. The group from Biecz, who arrived first, had been promised 100 loaves of bread, which for technical reasons they have not yet received. Currently the number of loaves would have to be significantly increased in order to provide for the groups from Rymanów, Jasielnica, and Brzozowa. To organize constant help for these people, it is required to communicate with the companies Klug and Vogel, as well as with the communities they come from. Their home municipalities could bring food to Gorlice, and from there it could be transported to Kraków by road from the Płaszów camp. Clothes and shoes should also be provided, because some people have very tattered clothes and walk barefoot.[24]

Another report of the Jewish Self-Assistance from the labor camp in Koszcz, near Kraków, describes accommodation and nutrition of the workers:

Accommodation. Workers [in the camp Koszcz] live in underground dungeons, disastrous in terms of sanitation. The straw, in which they sleep, is already very old, as it remains after the Russian prisoners. As of yesterday, the 18th of this month [April 1942], 69 people were sent to the second fort to reduce overcrowding. In the fort, there is no straw at the moment, so that the workers are sleeping on the bare ground. Despite this relocating, the workers continue to complain of overcrowding. Due to the deterioration of the water supply tubes, there is lack of water in the dungeons and the toilets are in bad shape. It would be very important for health reasons if the workers could get some mattresses and blankets to cover. For now, it is still chilly in the evenings, the accommodations are very wet, and they do not have coat. They also sleep in their clothes. As workers indicate, the community in Działoszyce has mattresses and blankets, which it would be important to get. Ing. Strauch promised to deliver fresh straw and repair water tubes.

---

24   YVA-JM.1581, ŻSS, Notatka, Kraków, August 6, 1942, scan 295.

Nutrition. During the first days, the workers did not receive any bread. Only on the 18th of this month [April 1942], after the intervention of the head of the works, they were given 200 g of bread and the soup was also more rich and nourishing than in previous days.

During our stay, the delegate of the community of Kazimierz [Wielki] came to visit the camp, and we talked about the food. He stated that he was ready to help the people of his community (9 people). He is only waiting for concrete proposals from our side.

If we can secure assistance with the meals, I hope that the relationship at work will also be improved successfully. Already the 30 or so workers who are employed on Wilga [River] get extra dinners at the local people's kitchen (*kuchnia ludowa*), and the question of accomodation was also favorably resolved, so that there is a good mood among the employees.[25]

The Jewish Self-Assistance was probably also one of few, if not the only body, that could intervene in favor of Jewish workers and bring about real change. The Jewish Self-Assistance had not only direct access to every labor camp, but was also was in constant contact with the German authorities, especially with the Department of Internal Affairs, Group for Population and Welfare (BuF). It must be underlined that interventions of the Jewish Self-Assistance were frequently effective and could bring a real improvement of the workers' conditions.

After the visit to the camp in Koszcz, the representatives of the Jewish Self-Assistance wrote:

> Our current task:
> 1. Firstly, contact with Ing. Strauch in order to find as soon as possible a remedy for the deficiencies in terms of sanitation. It is important to issue passes for some people from among the workers who could then go to the city and carry out errands from all inmates.
> 2. Ensure that food rations for the workers are actually given to them.
> 3. Examination by a physician of all employees on the site, as there is a certain percentage of people completely unable to work, including epileptics. These people were taken off the street and sent [to the labor camp].

---

25   YVA-JM.1581, ŻSS, Notatka z odwiedzin obozu pracy w Koszczu dnia 17 i 18 kwietnia br., Kraków, April 19, 1942, scans 120–21.

4. The most important task is to send a delegate to Działoszyce, who should consult with the local Municipality and the Delegation of the ŻSS in order to determine the best way to help the camp (in previous years the Commune [in Działoszyce] subsidized the same workers, paying them 2 to 3 zł per day).
5. To arrange with Ing. Strauch a weekly bath for the workers (on Sunday). Similarly, to arrange with the local Community that these people can take a bath free of charge.
6. Among the workers there are about 30 people, who are married and have children. The Community of Działoszyce promised that they would be exchanged. This matter is quite urgent.[26]

In other camps, the situation of the Jewish workers was not much better but bearable:

> In the company in Płaszowianka, 59 Jewish workers are employed, coming mostly from Książ Wielki [. . .] and Miechów. Conditions there are bearable, the kitchen has its own board of workers, and the management is reasonable. They have recently been provided 800 kg of potatoes at the maximum price. They only ask for a certain amount of clothing and a certain number of shoes. [. . .] In the company Płaszów Factory of Bricks and Roof Tiles, there are relatively bearable conditions for the workers. Recently people originating from Frysztak and Żmigród were transferred to the company from the camp in Płaszów 12. These people are unable to work and starving.[27]

In order to expand and standardize the care of workers in camps in and around Kraków, Jewish Self-Assistance founded a joint commission after consulting with the commissioner of the Jewish community in Kraków, which managed to establish a direct agreement with the direction of labor camp in Płaszów and discuss the main points of their care—which aimed to improve the position of workers placed in that camp, regardless of the locality they came from. To improve the feeding of the workers, absolute, regular, and disciplined assistance was required from various localities and from the Jewish councils and delegations in these towns, from which groups of workers were recruited.

---

26 Ibid.
27 YVA-JM.1581, ŻSS, Notatka, Kraków, August 6, 1942, scan 295.

It was decided to send a truck from the camp in Płaszów every fourteen days to important towns in the center of the region, such as Działoszyce, Miechów, Bochnia, Jasło, and Gorlice, to receive food, especially bread, and parcels of clothing and underwear. At the request of the management of the camp in Płaszów, partition of bread was to take place centrally—that is, the bread was to be evenly distributed in equal parts to everybody. To do this, each Jewish council had to ensure that for every worker coming from their locality and staying in Kraków, they would be provided with an additional ration of at least 300 g per day or 4.5 kg for fourteen days. Additionally, there were plans to distribute specific quantities of other products, such as marmalade and legumes.[28]

Although the members of the Jewish Self-Assistance tried to avoid unambiguous information concerning liquidation of Jewish ghettos, in a note concerning a discussion with a representative of BuF they noted:

> Activity of the Jewish Self-Assistance (ŻSS). Mr. Stachow was interested in our activity today, all the more that *it is known that the number of neighboring towns in the county of Kraków or other counties of the district of Kraków remained without Jews.* [emphasis mine—W.M.] I have explained that 15–55-years-old men able to perform physical labor have been mostly sent to labor camps. I have portrayed the relations in these camps and added that we are doing everything in our power to come to the rescue of these people. The situation in the camp in Płaszów is so well known to Mr. Stachow that he intervened once to procure better food rations and he knows that the conditions in this regard have changed slightly in favor of [the campers].[29]

It was a very important development because the Presidency of the Jewish Self-Assistance became a central body whose jurisdiction encompassed all of the General Government. It was able to negotiate with the German administration of the General Government. Moreover, it became the central body to initiate and coordinate establishment of new labor communities or craftsmen in the wake of ongoing *Aktion Reinhardt*. The Jewish Self-Assistance, as the central organization of social assistance in the General Government, was probably the only Jewish organization that had

---

28 YVA-JM.1581, ŻSS, Do Rady Żydowskiej Frysztak, Kraków, August 2, 1942, scans 154–55.
29 YVA-JM.1581, ŻSS, Notatka z rozmowy z referentem BuF im Distrikt Krakau p. Stachow. Kraków, September 23, 1942, scan 751.

access to every Jewish ghetto and labor camp, receiving constant and actual reports on the development of events, and had a perspective that permitted them to see a complete and exact picture of what was happening to the Jews in the General Government. As such, the Jewish Self-Assistance tried to avoid the worst: the destruction of Jews in the General Government, providing its assistance to every possible Jewish community, ghetto, labor camp, or other gathering of Jews.

ACTIVITY OF MAX FRAUENDORFER DURING THE *AKTION REINHARDT*

Among the representatives of the civil authorities, one of the most active defenders of the Jews in the high ranks of the General Government was the head of the Labor Department, Dr. Frauendorfer. He was responsible for coordinating the use of the pool of labor in the General Government and providing forced laborers for the Reich. He represented a considerably more rational approach than the police authorities. Frauendorfer held much more balanced views than Frank. While the position of the civil authorities in Jewish affairs in the summer of 1940 was much more powerful, in 1942, when the *Aktion Reinhardt* was already in progress, the police authorities and SS came out victorious from this conflict.

Perhaps, Frauendorfer underestimated his own position, but he tried to preserve the Jews who had employment in their workplaces, as there was a shortage of qualified manpower. On June 22, 1942, the following statement by Dr. Frauendorfer was recorded in the minutes of a meeting:

> According to President Dr. Frauendorfer, resettlement of the Jews, representing a major proportion of the population, would cause far-reaching consequences in all sectors of public life. The country, in terms of labor force, is very exhausted. Approximately 100,000 professionals are employed in the armaments industry, 800,000 workers live in the Reich, and a further 100,000 workers employed in the labor detachments [*Dienststellen*] of the commander of the armed forces in the General Government.[30]

---

30 Statement of Head of the Main Department Labor of the General Government Frauendorfer on a need for further employment of the Jews in the interests of the German economy, Kraków, June 22, 1942, in Eisenbach and Rutkowski, *Eksterminacja Żydów*, 240.

Frauendorfer, undoubtedly, represented the faction that urged care for a skilled labor force, because he realized that it was not possible in such a short time to find or train others who could replace the Jews. Obviously, "far-reaching consequences" in Frauendorfer's speech meant a significant decrease of military production and manufacturing in a difficult time for the economic activity in general, when, in fact, the fate of the war was in balance. We have to bear in mind that at the same time when Frauendorfer warned about a decrease in war production, Albert Speer, nominated by Hitler to the post of Minister of Armaments on February 8, 1942, was reforming the military industry. Clearly, the activities of Himmler and Albert Speer were in conflict; nevertheless, this clash, in the General Government in 1942, could appear as local, without any special significance for the outcome of the war.

The difficulties of mobilizing a labor force became much more acute in 1943 and 1944. Recorded in the protocol of a meeting on June 22, 1942 was the following: "President Dr. Frauendorfer is currently dependent exclusively on the work of the Jews [...]. They are in the absence of Polish professionals, irreplaceable."[31] Despite this, Dr. Frauendorfer was fully aware of the limit of his power and his argumentation, since in his speech he said, "The Jews are not, in fact, to be excluded from the actions conducted by the SS, but during the war we should exploit their work. He [Frauendorfer] is not interested in the withdrawal [entzogen] of Jewish workers from the economy or the industry."[32] As we can assume, Frauendorfer clearly tried to agree with the general political line that the Jews should be "evacuated," but not now—preferably later.

Frauendorfer's speech clearly provoked violent reactions from some SS and police authorities, because only three days later he sent another circular letter to the departments of labor and employment offices in the districts, writing about the need to communicate with the local commanders of the police on matters relating to forced labor of the Jewish population:

> The engagement of the Jews affects the interests of the police. Therefore, ensure immediately that the Jews are allowed to be hired only after consultation with the relevant local police commander. Labor Offices are prohibited, until further notice, to take all the steps needed to offset labor shortages in various districts.[33]

---

31 Ibid.
32 Ibid.
33 Circular of the head of the Main Department Labor of the General Government, Frauendorfer, to the all Labor Departments and Employment Offices in the districts on

It was certainly a setback in comparison to his speech of June 22, 1942. This time he clearly gives up and underlines that the Jews were in the hands of the police, and only the police were authorized to take decisions concerning the exploitation of Jewish forced labor. As this letter goes:

> It is expected that in future the police itself will to some extent use Jewish labor force, especially in the armaments industry. In these circumstances, the role of the intermediary, which Labor Offices currently have, will become redundant. Any eventual police requests for help, addressed to the Labor Offices, shall be fulfilled, of course, as far as possible.[34]

However, he did not urge the labor offices to help the police, but only to comply with their requests to a certain extent.

Harsh criticism from the police can be observed in the report of Friedrich Katzmann, in which he accused the civil administration of being unable to deal with the Jewish problem. Katzmann insisted that only the SS and police were capable of handling Jewish matters.

> As the administration was not in the position to overcome this chaos, and proved weak, the whole issue of Jewish labor was simply taken over by the SS and Police Leaders. The existing Jewish Labor Offices, which were staffed by hundreds of Jews, were dissolved. All work certificates issued by firms and official employers were declared invalid, and the cards given to Jews by the Labor Offices revalidated by the Police.[35]

Katzman, like other SSPF, offered ideological, rather than rational economic considerations, showing a harsh attitude towards the Jews—contrary to the position of the civil administration.

The actions of Dr. Frauendorfer coincided with the activity of Jews who wanted to save their lives by working in factories necessary for the Wehrmacht. But the motives for such conduct were different, because Frauendorfer needed to ensure a sufficient number of qualified laborers, and the most available

---

the need to communicate with local police commanders in matters of Jewish forced labor (Kraków, June 25, 1942), in Eisenbach and Rutkowski, *Eksterminacja Żydów*, 240.
34 Ibid.
35 From the final report by Katzmann, commander of the SS and police in the district of Galicia, on "The Solution of the Jewish problem" in Galicia (L-18), in Arad and Gutman, *Documents on the Holocaust*, 338.

and amenable workers were Jews. The Jews, on their part, had an alternative: either to work or to die. Naturally, a person would try to find a job at all costs. Katzmann referred to that situation in his report:

> Their place of work was often only a means to an end for them: firstly, to escape the sharper measures taken against the Jews; and, secondly, to be able to carry out their black-market dealings without interruption. Only continuous police intervention could prevent these activities.[36]

Katzmann was aware of the corruption prevailing among German officials, who in exchange for various rare goods were willing to arrange work for Jews:

> In addition, Jewish "organizing" on behalf of their "employers" reached catastrophic dimensions [so] that energetic action had to be [performed] in the interest of the reputation of the German people. [...] Draconic measures had to be introduced... after it was noted in increasing numbers of cases that the Jews had succeeded in making themselves indispensable to their employers by providing goods in short supply, etc. [...] It is very sad to have to note that the wildest black-market deals with the Jews were made by Germans who were brought here, and in particular those in the so-called "operating firms" (*Einsatzfirmen*) or the "ill-reputed trustees" (*berüchtigte Treuhänder*), both of which operated Jewish firms, taken from their owners. Cases were known where Jews seeking to obtain some kind of working certificate not only did not ask for pay from their employers but paid [their employers] regularly, themselves.[37]

Katzmann's criticism was directed not only towards the civil administration, but also to the Wehrmacht.

> In the course of this *Aktion* thousands of Jews were again caught in possession of forged certificates or labor certificates obtained fraudulently by means of all kinds of excuses. These Jews were also sent for special treatment (*Sonderbehandlung*). The Wehrmacht authorities in particular aided the Jewish parasites by issuing special certificates without proper control. [...] There were cases where Jews were caught with from 10 to 20 such

---

36 Ibid., 337.
37 Ibid., 337.

certificates. When Jews were arrested in the course of further checks, most of the employers felt obliged to attempt to intervene in favor of the Jews. This was often done in a manner that can only be described as deeply shameful.[38]

He did not refer to the war production, so needed by the Wehrmacht, but rather was willing to accuse the Wehrmacht of corruption and the Jews of forgery and cheating. Needless to say, Katzmann considered himself a soldier, even if until then he had not served even one day at the front line.

COMPLETION OF *AKTION REINHARDT* AND THE CONCENTRATION OF JEWS IN CHOSEN CITIES

The campaign of mass murder of Jews in death camps during the first months ran smoothly. After activating the Bełżec death camp, where Jews from the districts of Lublin and Kraków were murdered, Sobibór death camp opened soon afterwards, and in late July the third death camp in Treblinka started operation. Himmler was pleased with himself. Every day, thousands of Jews were sent to their deaths and the numbers of Jews in the General Government declined dramatically. Some of the ghettos were liquidated completely, and others were converted into so-called small (provincial, reduced) ghettos (*małe getta*) or "remainder" ghettos (Germ. *Restghetto*; Pol. *getto szczątkowe*). The progressive murder of Jews undoubtedly resulted in Himmler's euphoria. To survey his achievements, he visited Katowice, Auschwitz, and then some other cities in the General Government, among them Lublin. On July 19, 1942, he issued an order to complete the Final Solution in the General Government.

Himmler planned to end the "resettlement of the entire Jewish population of the Government-General" by December 31, 1942. According to his order from December 31, 1942, no people of Jewish origin could remain within the General Government outside of the collection camps in Warsaw, Kraków, Częstochowa, Radom, and Lublin. All other work in which Jewish labor is employed had to be finished by that date or, in the event that this was not possible, transferred to one of the collection camps.[39] So at this time, despite

---

38 From the final report by Katzmann, commander of the SS and police in the district of Galicia, on "The Solution of the Jewish problem" in Galicia (L-18), in Arad and Gutman, *Documents on the Holocaust*, 338.

39 Order by Himmler on July 19, 1941 for the completion of the "Final Solution'" in the Government-General (NO-5574), in Arad and Gutman, *Documents on the Holocaust*, 275.

the fact that more and more Jews were sent to labor camps in arms factories in the district of Radom and other places, Himmler did not plan to establish a network of labor camps close to great factories, except for designated areas. Although he envisaged that it might be difficult to accomplish this task, he, apparently, believed that the obstacles could be overcome. Himmler had not forgotten, as usual, to present arguments justifying his conduct, even if it seemed redundant. As he wrote in his order:

> These measures are required with a view to the necessary ethnic division of races and peoples for the New Order in Europe, and also in the interests of the security and cleanliness of the German Reich and its sphere of interest. Every breach of this regulation spells a danger to quiet and order in the entire German sphere of interest, a point of application for the resistance movement and a source of moral and physical pestilence. For all these reasons a total cleansing is necessary and therefore to be carried out. Cases in which the date set cannot be observed will be reported to me in time, so that I can see to corrective action at an early date. All requests by other offices for changes or permits for exceptions to be made must be presented to me personally.[40]

The idea of concentrating the Jews in larger towns, in order to facilitate their management or the actions against them was not something new. It had already been instructed in the telegram from Reinhard Heydrich dated September 21, 1939. Such concentration was also carried out before and during *Aktion Reinhardt*.[41] Moreover, during the discussion at Globocnik's office it was already said that "to the use of Jewish auxiliary forces at the German institutions (*Dienststellen*) are to be put only the Jewish professionals who are indispensable. They should be housed in a special part of their ghetto."[42] Therefore, not only concentration of Jews in determined places but also separation of working forces facilitated further development. However, despite Himmler's order of July 19, 1942, already in the autumn it was clear that full implementation of this idea would not be possible. Therefore, HSSPF issued two orders. The first one was released on October 28, 1942, for the Warsaw and Lublin Districts, setting aside

---

40 Ibid.
41 From a letter of the Deputy Commissioner of the Jewish quarter in Warsaw, Grassler, to the Department *Raumordnung* [Planning] of the Warsaw District on the concentration of Jews in the various counties, Warsawa, March 3, 1942, in Eisenbach and Rutkowski, *Ekstermincja Żydów*, 178–79.
42 YVA-JM.12331, Notiz für Brigadeführer über die Besprechung beim Amtschef am 8. August 1941, 10 Uhr ist festzuhalten, scan 221.

several places where the Jews could stay.⁴³ The second order, dated November 10, 1942, concerned the Radom, Kraków, and Galicia Districts.⁴⁴ These directives were issued in the spirit of Himmler's order of July 19, 1942, since they restricted Jewish places of residence and prohibited living outside the permitted areas. The second paragraph of the October regulation reads as follows:

> From December 1, 1942 it is forbidden for any Jew in the Warsaw and Lublin Districts to stay outside the Jewish quarter, or leave it without police permission. From the date of December 1, 1942 other people [i.e., non-Jews] are allowed to reside in the Jewish quarter, or just come to it only having a police permit. The authorizations are granted in accordance with Jewish residential quarters by *Kreishauptmann*, for the Warsaw Ghetto—by the commissioner of the Jewish residential district.⁴⁵

This order did not concern the Jews working in the armaments industry who lived in closed camps.⁴⁶ The third paragraph of the regulation prohibited the Jews, under penalty of death, from leaving the designated sites and the non-Jewish population from helping the Jews—also under penalty of death.⁴⁷ The result of this residential confinement for Jews was the establishment of closed labor camps. One of them was the camp in Płaszów, where Jewish workers were transferred by order of Scherner—the commander of the SS and police in the Kraków District—dated December 14, 1942.⁴⁸

Limitation of Jewish freedom of residence also affected the Poles, and in some regions the Ukrainians, as it was forbidden to grant Jewish refugees any assistance under penalty of death. As the mayor of Przemyśl announced on July 27, 1942:

> II. Every Ukrainian or Pole who attempts by any conduct to disturb the action of resettlement of Jews will be shot.

---

43 Police regulation on establishing Jewish residential areas in District Warsaw and Lublin, October 28, 1942, in Eisenbach and Rutkowski, *Eksterminacja Żydów*, 313–14.
44 Police regulation of Higher SS and Police Commander Krüger on establishing Jewish residential quarters in some towns in the districts of Radom, Krakow and Galicia, November 10, 1942, in Eisenbach and Rutkowski, *Eksterminacja Żydów*, 316–17.
45 Police regulation on establishing Jewish residential areas in District Warsaw and Lublin, October 28, 1942, in Eisenbach and Rutkowski, *Eksterminacja Żydów*, 313–14.
46 Ibid.
47 Ibid.
48 The commander of the SS and police in the district of Kraków, Scherner to entrepreneurs on the transfer of Jewish workers employed by them to the camp in Płaszów, Kraków, December 14, 1942, in Eisenbach and Rutkowski, *Eksterminacja Żydów*, 253.

III. Every Ukrainian or Pole who will be found in the Jewish quarter looting Jewish homes will be shot.

IV. Every Ukrainian or Pole who tries to hide any Jew or to help him to hide will be shot.[49]

This prohibition also applied to taking possession of Jewish property:

V. The acquisition of Jewish property for money or for free is prohibited. Offences against this ordinance shall be punished as harshly as possible.[50]

Similar regulations were issued by the police in other towns of the General Government, since regulations issued by higher level officials[51] were often repeated by the administration at lower levels. Regulations published by SS and police leaders were frequently repeated by *Stadhaupleute* and *Kreishauptleute*. In the district of Radom, such regulation was issued by SSPF Herbert Böttcher.[52]

THE RESULTS OF DEPORTATIONS ON THE ECONOMY OF THE GENERAL GOVERNMENT

The deportation of Jews from the General Government achieved the desired propaganda effect, of which Frank boasted in his speech on August 15, 1942:

[...] if someone among the visitors of Kraków, Lwów, Warsaw, Radom, and Lublin today would doubt the successful results achieved in this area by the efforts of the German administration, it would not be easy. Formerly,

---

49 Notice of the *Kreishauptmann* of the Przemyśl County, warning Polish and Ukrainian population against assistance to the deported Jews under death penalty, July 27, 1942, in Eisenbach and Ritkowski, *Eksterminacja Żydów*, 298.
50 Ibid.
51 Circular of the SS and police commander in Radom, Böttcher, to the administrative and police authorities ordering to warn the Polish population that hiding Jews and helping them will be punished by death penalty, Radom, September 21, 1942, in Eisenbach and Rutkowski, *Eksterminacja Żydów*, 299.
52 JD Herbert Böttcher (1907–1950) was since August 1939 regiment commander of SS regiment in Memel; then since October 1940 police president (*Polizeipräsident*) in Kassel; and since the beginning of 1942 he held the post of SSPF in Kaunas. At the end of 1942, he was nominated for the post of SSPF in the district of Radom. After the assasination of Franz Kutschera on February 1, 1944, Böttcher was SSPF in the district of Warsaw, and since November 1944 he was the commander of the police in Königsberg.

Jews leisured here. However, this smelly people were only allowed here before 1939! So where are the Jews today? One will see almost no trace of them (applause). Everywhere one only sees working Jews.[53]

From his statement it could be understood that the long-awaited transformation of the Jews into a productive population had finally taken place. All Jews were working, because those who were not able to work were murdered. This was confirmed in Fischer's report: "In the Jewish quarter in Warsaw, about 35,000 Jews remained. These are almost exclusively the workers left behind in munitions factories."[54]

Also, food shortages and the economic situation in the Jewish quarter of Warsaw were due to the new principles:

> [The] SS and police commander who was responsible for the entire Jewish action has obliged firms to pay for Jewish workers—with effect from September 1, 1942—5 zł per day for each remaining Jewish worker. They should transfer 3 zł to the SS and police commander and use the remaining 2 zł to maintain the Jewish worker.[55]

This statement illustrates how the forced workers were transformed into slaves, and the ghettos—into labor camps. From September 1, 1942, Warsaw Jews did not receive any remuneration for their work. The value of their daily work was estimated to be 5 zł, of which the SS received 60%, as holders of slaves; and the remaining 40% was taken by the establishments for themselves, for maintenance costs. Such a system allowed corruption, because with sufficient quantity of workplaces, the establishments could reduce maintenance costs, leaving larger sums for themselves and increasing profitability.

The original success of using Jewish productive capabilities before their liquidation turned out to be unfavorable for the economy afterwards. As Fischer evaluated in his report:

> While in July the value of exports from the Jewish quarter [in Warsaw] exceeded 15 million, in August the total was reduced to 1.9 million, and in

---

53 Keynote speech of Hans Frank on the occasion of the annual meeting of the NSDAP, August 15, 1942, Frank, *Okupacja i ruch oporu*, vol. 1, 510.
54 From the report of the Warsaw District governor for August and September, 1942 to the authorities of the General Government about the situation in the Warsaw Ghetto after the great deportation, Warsaw, October 15, 1942. Dunin-Wąsowicz, *Raporty Ludwiga Fischera*, 305–6.
55 Dunin-Wąsowicz, *Raporty Ludwiga Fischera*, 305–6.

September to 1.1 million, while these are still the old settlement of transactions of goods and services.⁵⁶

Various branches of industry were also in decline:

> Warsaw textile industry suffered heavily after deportation of Jews. This branch of industry was from the end of 1939, with few exceptions, in the hands of the Jews, and most of the crew were also Jewish. Jews did not train Aryans, so that there were almost no skilled Aryan workers. Among 3,500 industrial knitting workers there were formerly at least 3,000 Jews. As a result of resettlement of Jews, a significant decrease in production took place. In August, production dropped from 4.4 million zł to 3.3 million zł, or by about 25%. In fact, however, production dropped by 50%, as companies made a bid for more goods than they had in stock. Returning back to normal production can only occur when a sufficient number of Aryan professionals will be trained.⁵⁷

The consequences for other industries in 1943 will be discussed in subsequent chapters. Undoubtedly, "resettlement" of Jews did not concern only the Jews who were unable to work, but also a large number of laborers. Not always could they provide relevant documents, because sometimes they worked in home-production or illegal manufacture. Even the people running households were useful because it allowed others to work. Therefore, one cannot agree with the notion that only nonproductive Jews were deported. Moreover, motives of deportation were ideological and not economic. Even where economic arguments were presented, the police often did not take them into account.

At the end of 1942, the number of Jews in the General Government dropped significantly compared to the period before *Aktion Reinhardt*. Statistics Officer Korherr of the RFSS reports in his paper "The Final Solution of the Jewish Question in Europe," delivered in Berlin on March 23, 1943,

---

56 Ibid.
57 From the report of the Warsaw District governor for August and September 1942 to the authorities of the General Government about the situation in the Warsaw Ghetto after the great deportation, Warsaw, October 15, 1942, 305–6.

that according to official statistics, 297,514 Jews were still left in the General Government at the end of 1942.[58]

This number is not accurate, because even during this period a number of Jews remained in hiding. However, given the large percentage of able-bodied Jews who were among those nearly 300,000 people, it still was undoubtedly a significant potential labor force, which could be used in the General Government economy, affording a chance to survive for most of those Jews. However, even this limited number of Jews still alive in the General Government, became a bone of contention between the SS and police on the one hand, and the civil administration, the Wehrmacht, and the private sector on the other.

---

58 The paper of Korherr, statistics officer at the RFSS, entitled "Final Solution of the Jewish Question in Europe," Berlin, March 23, 1943, in Eisenbach and Rutkowski, *Eksterminacja Żydów*, 322.

CHAPTER 8

War Industry Requirements in the Face of Annihilation of the Workforce

The beginning of Operation Barbarossa marked a new era of warfare, which was neither limited to the battlefield nor the armed forces. The German-Soviet war directly affected large parts of the population who were subjected to terror, persecution, population transfer, or mass murder. The whole population, under the control of one or another party, was occupied with a total mobilization of all economic resources, including the adoption of war economy and mobilization of labor resources. Apparently, the German army, while occupying new territories, was also reinforcing its economic resources, which included new factories, more food, raw materials, and more labor forces. Those significant elements needed to be used in appropriate ways in order to bolster the war economy. A surplus of resources could, however, lead to misuse or waste. Therefore, we should carefully analyze any declaration of German authorities and verify if the declarative content corresponded to the conduct in practice.

On April 20, 1942, Fritz Sauckel wrote in his labor mobilization program the following:

> The aim of this new, gigantic labor mobilization is to use all the rich and tremendous sources, conquered and secured for us by our fighting Armed Forces under the leadership of Adolf Hitler, for the armament of the Armed Forces and also for the nutrition of the Homeland. The raw materials, as well as the fertility of the conquered territories and their

human labor power, are to be used completely and conscientiously to the profit of Germany and its allies.[1]

Despite these words, we have to examine to what extent the resources of the conquered territories were used "completely and conscientiously." I would argue the opposite: the non-coordinated policy concerning the use of existing human resources led to losing them when they were available. Moreover, even when the shortage of a qualified labor force was clear, the German authorities continued the *opera mortale*, losing millions of workers who were in their hands, while attracting unreasonable funds to mobilize other, much less qualified labor forces. This contradiction was particularly obvious during the *Aktion Reinhardt*, when on the one hand, considerable forces were used to complete the mass murder of the Jews, and on the other hand, significant police and military forces were used in order to forcefully mobilize hundreds of thousands of new workers.

BEGINNING OF LABOR SHORTAGES, 1942–1943

Shortage of manpower began to be progressively acute already in 1942. After the attack on Moscow faltered in December 1941, the Eastern Front stagnated. It became increasingly clear that Germany lost its opportunity to conquer the European part of the Soviet Union. At the same time, the Soviet Union was not strong enough to fully repulse the German forces., being not able to stop the German invasion and to keep it in check. The interval between the attacks on Moscow and the defeat at Stalingrad was a time of frequent local offensives followed by withdrawals. Nevertheless, from an economic point of view, this period marked a depletion of reserves and the beginning of constant growth in the need for war material, which meant the necessity to increase war production. Apparently, the battle was not just on the battlefield: in reality, the fight was no less intense in factories and on the manufacturing belt. The result of war was to be decided not by the quality of soldiers and officers but rather by the production potential. This rather simple fact should have been well understood by the leaders of the Third Reich, and actually it was. But we must

---

1 Sauckel's labor mobilization program sent to Rosenberg on 20 April 1942 (016-PS), in IMT, *Red Series*, vol. 1, 876.

not forget that the regime of Nazi Germany had other priorities as well, which consequentially would lead to the downfall of the Nazi state. In truth, the Nazi regime was able to engage considerable forces in order to realize its plans, which had ideological character and were the raison d'être of Nazism.

The General Government, as an occupied territory, served as a reservoir of manpower for the Reich. This was the first occupied territory, which had a quasi-state organization, but was not annexed to the German Reich and was different in form from the Protectorate of Bohemia and Moravia. The German administration was more ruthless here than in other territories and treated the General Government as a war trophy. Since autumn 1939, there were constant requests from the Reich to provide more and more labor force that was needed in different branches of the economy, mainly in agriculture.

The Polish forced laborers were more preferred in the Reich than the Jews and Soviet POWs. Since the German authorities wanted to get rid of Jews and declare their regions *judenfrei*, which was for them mainly a propagandistic success devoid of any practical value, bringing in Jewish workers would be a contradiction. On the other hand, Soviet POWs were also considered dangerous from an ideological point of view; therefore, during the first months after the beginning of the German-Soviet war, there was a prohibition against bringing Soviet POWs into the Reich's territory. However, this ban was lifted as soon as autumn 1941. According to Göring's statement at a conference at the Air Ministry on November 7, 1941, "The Führer's point of view as to employment of prisoners of war in war industries has changed basically. So far [we keep] a total of 5 million prisoners of war—employed so far are 2 million."[2] Göring was thinking about POWs in general and not former Soviet soldiers who at that time were dying en masse of starvation in temporary POW camps that lacked elementary facilities and even the most primitive barracks.

One year later, in a secret memorandum issued from Hitler's headquarters on October 31, 1942, Wilhelm Keitel directed the execution of Hitler's order to use POWs in the German war economy. "The lack of workers is becoming an increasingly dangerous hindrance for the future the German war and armament industry. The expected relief through discharges from the armed forces is uncertain as to the extent and date; however, its possible extent will by no means correspond to expectations and requirements in view of the great demand.

---

2 Göring's statement at a conference at the Air Ministry on November 7, 1941, where was also discussed the use of POW's in the armament industry (1206-PS), in IMT, *Red Series*, vol. 1, 912–13.

The Führer has now ordered that even the working power of the Russian prisoners of war should be utilized to a large extent by large scale assignment for the requirements of the war industry. The prerequisite for production is adequate nourishment. Also very small wages are to be planned for the most modest supply with a few consumers' goods (*Genussmittel*) for every day's life, eventual rewards for production."[3] The use of POWs in the armament industry violated Geneva conventions that prohibited the exploitation of POWs in warfare and the war industry. However, the above-mentioned directive did not entirely open the possibility of importing Soviet POWs into the Reich. Therefore, the authorities of the Third Reich used to make exchanges of Soviet POWs for Polish workers. In the minutes of the meeting concerning problems of the labor force on September 20, 1941, it was said: "[. . .] as is clear from the letter of the Ministry of Labor, Marshal Göring wishes to provide a further 100,000 Poles in exchange for 100,000 Russian prisoners of war, which are placed in the General Government. The speaker expressed his view that prisoners cannot be considered a full equivalent in exchange for Poles sent to the Reich."[4] Only later, when the shortage of forced laborers became acute, the authorities made the decision to authorize bringing in Soviet POWs and employing them in mining, heavy industry, and the war industry.

Frank and the leadership of the General Government were under constant pressure from the Reich to provide more and more Polish workers. In a Kraków meeting of Frank and the General Plenipotentiary for Labor Deployment Fritz Sauckel on August 18, 1942, the issues of providing additional forced workers from the General Government were raised. During that meeting Hans Frank said:

> I am glad that I can officially report to you, Comrade Sauckel, that until today we have handed over 800,000 workers to the Reich. If we also take into account the number of able-bodied Polish prisoners of war found in the Reich, the total number of manpower greatly exceeds the 1.2 million people from the General Government.[5]

---

3 A secret memorandum issued from Hitler's headquarters on October 31, 1942; Keitel directed the execution of Hitler's order to use POW's in the German war economy (EC-194), in IMT, *Red Series*, vol. 1, 912.
4 Conference of September 20, 1941 on delivery of manpower to Germany, at which were present Frank, Frauendorfer, and Boepple, in Frank, *Okupacja i ruch oporu*, vol. 1, 376–77.
5 Hans Frank's speech on the occasion of the visit of Fritz Sauckel on further supply of forced workers' quotas, Kraków, August 18, 1942, in Frank, *Okupacja i ruch oporu*, vol. 1, 512.

According to Frank's evaluation, about 400,000 Polish POWs coming from the General Government were in the Reich. In fact, the total number of Polish POWs in German hands could have been closer to 450,000, if not only those from the General Government, but also from all of pre-war Polish territories were counted. Since some of the POWs including Jewish soldiers from the Polish army were released, Frank's number is probably more accurate. Frank usually liked to assign himself achievements, even if he had no part in them. However, this number of about 1.2 million Polish laborers was not sufficient. Frank went on to say:

> Recently you reported a demand for manpower counting 140,000 men. I am pleased to declare to you and make it official that under our agreement yesterday I will deliver to the Reich until the end of October 60% of the working force of this new demand, and the remaining 40%—by the end of the year. [...] You may, however, expect in the next year to continue supplying manpower from the General Government because the action will be conducted by the police.[6]

It should be stressed that already in the summer of 1942, a shortage of manpower was felt in the General Government due to the advanced liquidation of ghettos and deportation of hundred thousands of Jews to death camps. Since the Jews could not be brought into the Reich, they were filling in for the deficiency of laborers in the General Government, especially in industry and handcrafts. They performed many important tasks for their communities, towns, etc., which freed Polish workers to perform other jobs. Nevertheless, substitution of Polish workers was only part of the exploitation mechanism of labor force in the General Government. Jews were also employed in many workshops, enterprises, labor camps, and independent labor detachments that were not connected to the management apparatus of the Polish labor force.

We have to mention yet another aspect of the labor force management in the General Government. After the beginning of Operation Barbarossa in the General Government, intensive development of the war industry took place and any labor surplus that had existed during the period of economic stagnation was drained not only by the export of manpower, but also by industrial development. Moreover, due to intensifying aerial bombardment of German territory, many industrial plants were evacuated to safer areas of the General

---

6   Ibid., 513.

Government.[7] Therefore, extermination of Jews within the framework of the *Aktion Reinhardt* created an acute shortage of workers.

Lack of coordination between the extermination of Jews and management of the labor force in all territories occupied by the German Forces created serious difficulties in providing not only a sufficient quantity of workers, but first and foremost, of qualified workers. Frank summed this problem quite clearly:

> For the government of the General Government one particular aspect seems to be important. One of your most difficult tasks was, probably—you are likely to confirm this on the base of your experiences from his last trip—to enable the Reich to settle the central planning concerning labor for the war exigencies once and for all. About the area such as the General Government one may say: "You are a reservoir of labor,"—then you can export work force from here, or, "you are part of the industrial component of the total area of the Reich," then you can build factories here. You cannot do both: export labor and expand the industry of the Reich on the same territory. [...] We have to realize the gigantic investment program of the Reich, including expansion of the rail network. Two-thirds of the general supply for the Eastern Front pass through the General Government.[8]

These objections were quite reasonable. It was the time when *Aktion Reinhardt* was conducted, even though that is not mentioned in the above quotes. That should have been the topic of the conversation during the exchange with Sauckel. However, despite his protests, Frank was actually a conformist. Even though he played the role of a courageous leader, he was rather submissive, especially toward people that were above him in the party hierarchy. Thus, despite expressing his displeasure, he was in fact fulfilling the tasks Sauckel imposed upon him. It would be unlikely for Frank to oppose the mass murder of Jews, even if that were against the interests of the territory under his administration.

In the early months of *Aktion Reinhardt*, Bühler expressed his dissatisfaction with the deportation of the qualified Jewish workforce. At a meeting on May 11, 1942, he said:

> New information is released about the alleged deliberate termination of the Jewish ghettos, when the Jews able to work are stopped and

---

7   BA-MA, RW23-5, Geschichte der Rü In im GG (1. Juli 1940–31. Dezember1941), 115.
8   Frank, *Okupacja i ruch oporu*, vol. 1, 513–14.

transported further to the east. Jews fit for work are to be placed in large concentration camps, which act as production centers. At the first glance, these plans look alluring, but a closer look shows that the damage resulting from the realization of this plan—because it will involve destruction of existing forms of organization—often outweighs the benefits that one could ever promise after such a move. At this time, in any case, such plan, according to the speaker, will not be beneficial. [. . .] Chances that it will free more Polish laborers for the Reich are minimal. As a result of a survey of 27,000 workers of the military industry, only 42 people voluntarily signed up to work in the Reich. But police coercion is used, then many workers do not come to their work at all in fear of shipment to the Reich. The Reich also recommends conducting raids of population on the streets of major cities. It is expected that as a result of this action, we will manage to get 52,000 workers. All these projects are completely meaningless, and actually had such action been taken, it would certainly endanger supply to the front in a significant way.[9]

Despite Bühler's disapproval, the methods he described were widely used after just several months,[10] because, as stated above, the authorities of the General Government were not able to mobilize the laborers for the work in the Reich with incentives or by threats. Special publications describing good working and living conditions in the Reich were issued to convince potential laborers from among the Polish population.[11] These attempts, however, were not favorably embraced.

With increasing difficulties in obtaining the labor force, more and more drastic methods were used to attract forced workers. This happened not only in the General Government, but also in other areas occupied in the east, and above all, in the *Reichskommissariate* Ukraine and Ostland. To round up people to work, in addition to the gendarmerie and the police, the army was engaged. These brutal methods were used not only for Poles, but also for Ukrainians

---

9 Minutes of the 5th meeting of the heads of main departments of the General Government, fragment concerning security and delivery of workers to the Reich, Kraków, May 11, 1942, in Frank, *Okupacja i ruch oporu*, vol. 1, 459–60.
10 Frank, *Okupacja i ruch oporu*, vol. 1, 564–65.
11 Fryderyk Didier, ed., *Europa pracuje w Niemczech: Sauckel mobilizuje rezerwy produkcyjne* (Berlin: Zentralverlag der NSDAP, 1943).

and Belarusians. The Chairman of the Ukrainian Main Committee in Kraków wrote in a letter to Frank in February 1943:

> The wild and ruthless man-hunt as exercised everywhere in towns and country, in streets, squares, stations, even in churches, at night in houses, has badly shaken the feeling of security of the inhabitants. Everybody is exposed to the danger, to be seized anywhere and at any time by members of the police, suddenly and unexpectedly and to be brought into an assembly camp. None of his relatives knows what has happened to him, only months later one or the other gives news of his fate by a postcard.[12]

These complaints could not change the situation, since the problem of labor forces was discussed in the highest echelons of power in the Reich. The new programs of armament led by Speer were based not only on reorganization of industry, but also on developing production, which was only possible on condition that the required number of workers was provided. Therefore, Speer pressed Sauckel, using the authority of his relationship with Hitler, to get what he wanted. Speer's statement in the minutes of conferences with Hitler on August 10, 11, and 12 of 1942 reads as follows:

> Gauleiter Sauckel promises to make Russian labor available for the fulfillment of the iron and coal program and reports that if required, he can supply a further million Russian laborers for the German armament industry up to and including October 1942. So far, he has already supplied 1 million for industry and 700,000 for agriculture. In this connection the Führer states that the problem of providing labor can be solved in all cases and to any extent; he authorizes Gauleiter Sauckel to take all measures required. He would agree to any necessary compulsion (*Zwangsmassnahmen*) in the East as well as in the West if this question could not be solved on a voluntary basis.[13]

However, in 1943 when the shortage of manpower became even more acute, the highest authorities pressured Sauckel and he pushed other regional

---

12 Chairman of the Ukrainian Main Committee to Frank, Cracow, February 1943 (1526-PS), in IMT, *Red Series*, vol. 1, 881.
13 Speer's statement in a record of conferences with Hitler on August 10, 11, and 12, 1942 (R-124), in IMT, *Red Series*, vol. 1, 885.

bodies to obtain more and more workers— it did not matter at what price. In a letter of October 5, 1943, Sauckel wrote:

> The Führer has worked out new and most urgent plans for the armament which require the quick mobilization of two more million foreign labor forces. The Führer therefore has granted me, for the execution of my decree of March 21, 1942, new powers for my new duties, and has especially authorized me to take whatever measures I think are necessary in the Reich, the Protectorate, the General-Government, as well as in the occupied territories, in order to assure at all costs an orderly mobilization of labor for the German armament industry. The additional required labor forces will have to be drafted for the majority from the recently occupied Eastern Territories, especially from the *Reichskommissariat* Ukraine. Therefore, the *Reichskommissariat* Ukraine must furnish: 225,000 labor forces by December 31, 1942 and 225,000 more by May 1, 1943.[14]

The lack of workers was strongly felt not only in industry but also in agriculture— an essential sphere, which provided food for the country. As more and more German men were recruited to the army, numbers of workers needed to replace them at home significantly grew.

> Especially the labor supply for German agriculture and for the most urgent armament production programs ordered by the Führer make the fastest importation of approximately one million women and men from the Eastern Territories within the next four months necessary. Starting March 15 [1943], the daily shipment shall reach 5,000 female and male workers respectively, and at the beginning of April [1943] this number has to be increased to 10,000. This means that most urgent programs shall be implemented, so that the spring tillage and other agricultural tasks are not to suffer, causing detriment of nutrition and bad situation in the armed forces.[15]

The directives from Hitler were passed to Sauckel and then to Rosenberg. Rosenberg instructed his subordinates to use the most severe measures to recruit the forced labor. A secret report of a conference between the Commissioner

---

14 Sauckel to Rosenberg, October 5, 1942 (017-PS), in IMT, *Red Series*, vol. 1, 882.
15 Sauckel to Rosenberg, March 17, 1943 (019-PS), in IMT, *Red Series*, vol. 1, 883.

General of Zhitomir and Rosenberg in Winnica on June 17, 1943 stated the following:

> But as the Chief Plenipotentiary for the mobilization of labor explained to us the gravity of the situation, we had no other device. I consequently have authorized the commissioners of the areas to apply the severest measures in order to achieve the imposed quota. The deterioration of morale in conjunction with this does not necessitate any further proof. It is nevertheless essential to win the war on this front too. The problem of labor mobilization cannot be handled with gloves.[16]

The recruitment in the east in no way was "handled with gloves," but rather with fire and blood. A report from the chief of Main Office III with the High Command in Minsk, dated June 28, 1943, to *Ministerialdirektor* Riecke, a top official in the Rosenberg Ministry, quite vividly described how recruitment of forced laborers looked in the field:

> The recruitment of labor for the Reich, however necessary, had disastrous effects. The recruitment measures in the last months and weeks were absolute manhunts, which have an irreparable political and economic effect. From White Ruthenia, approx. 50,000 people have been obtained for the Reich so far. Another 130,000 are to be obtained. Considering the 2.4 million total population these figures are impossible.[17]

In the course of the mobilization, whole areas were emptied and villages and fields became deserted, which, undoubtedly, caused damage to the German economy. "Due to the sweeping drives (*Grossaktionen*) of the SS and police in November 1942, about 115,000 hectares of farmland is not used, as the population is not there and the villages have been razed."[18] However, this was not a priority, since lack of food in these areas mainly hit the local population—something that did not make any impression on the German authorities.

---

16 Secret report of a conference between the Commissioner General of Zhitomir and Rosenberg, Winniza, June 17, 1943; dated June 30, 1943, and signed by Leyser (265-PS), in IMT, *Red Series*, vol. 1, 890.
17 Report from the chief of Main Office III with the High Command in Minsk, dated June 28, 1943, to Ministerialdirektor Riecke, a top official in the Rosenberg Ministry (3000-PS), in IMT, *Red Series*, vol. 1, 726.
18 Ibid.

The recruitment in some areas looked like hunting for slaves. "Estates of those who refuse to work are to be burned; their relatives are to be arrested as hostages and to be brought to forced labor camps."[19]

Violent methods were also used in the area of the General Government, which unequivocally led to a violent reaction of the population and the Polish underground. Recruitment of the labor force became a rather dangerous job. According to the documents:

> Especially in Poland the situation at the moment is extraordinarily serious. It is well known that vehement battles occurred just because of these actions. The resistance against the administration established by us is very strong. Quite a number of our men have been exposed to increased violence some of them were shot dead, e.g., the Head of the Labor Office of Warsaw who was shot in his office, and yesterday another man again. This is how matters stand presently, and the recruiting itself even if done with the best [efforts] will remain extremely difficult unless police reinforcements are at hand.[20]

The lack of manpower forced the German authorities to search the reserves in every possible area. Already in April 20, 1942, a program was initiated which was outlined as follows in a letter from Pohl to Himmler:

> Today I report about the present situation of the concentration camps and about measures I have taken to carry out your order of March 3, 1942.
> 1. The war has brought about a marked change in the structure of the concentration camps and has changed their duties with regard to the employment of the prisoners. The custody of prisoners for the sole reasons of security, education, or prevention is no longer the main consideration. The mobilization of all prisoners who are able to work for purposes of the war now, and for purposes of construction in the forthcoming peacetime, more and more comes to the foreground.

---

19 Directive of the Commissioner General in Lusk of September 21, 1942, referring to the extreme urgency of the national conscription (290-PS), in IMT, *Red Series*, vol. 1, 889.
20 Statement by Timm (Sauekel's deputy) at the 36th conference of the Central Planning Board (R-124), in IMT, *Red Series*, vol. 1, 881–82.

2. From this knowledge some necessary measures result with the aim to transform the concentration camps into organizations more suitable for the economic tasks, while formerly they were merely politically interested.[21]

This document indicated that two processes were taking place: deterioration of conditions of the prisoners and transformation of the concentration camps into economic enterprises.

Yet another reserve of labor forces had been found by Himmler. He ordered on December 17, 1942 that prisoners who would not otherwise have been bound for concentration camps were to be sent there and used as qualified workers.

> For reasons of war necessity not to be discussed here further, the Reichsführer SS and Chief of the German police on December 14, 1942 has ordered that until the end of January 1943, at least 35,000 prisoners qualified for work are to be sent to the concentration camps. [. . .] *Every single laborer counts!*[22]

The deterioration of conditions was unlimited, as we can see in a document concerning an agreement between the Minister of Justice Thierack and Reichsführer SS Himmler. The judicial system transferred full power over the prisoners into the hands of the SS. The document reads as follows:

> The delivery of anti-social elements from the execution of their sentence to the Reichsführer of SS to be worked to death. [. . .] It is agreed that, in consideration of the intended aims of the Government for the clearing up of the Eastern problems, in future Jews, Poles, Gypsies, Russians, and Ukrainians are no longer to be judged by the ordinary courts, so far as punishable offenses are concerned, but are to be dealt with by the Reichsführer of SS.[23]

---

21 Pohl, *SS Obergruppenführer* and General of the Waffen SS (R-129) to Himmler (dated April 30, 1942), in IMT, *Red Series*, vol. 1, 915.
22 Himmler's order, December 17, 1942 (1063-D-PS), in IMT, *Red Series*, vol. 1, 918.
23 Memorandum of an agreement between Himmler and the Minister of Justice Thierack, September 18, 1942 (654-PS), in IMT, *Red Series*, vol. 1, 916.

In March 1943, yet another document was published: a secret order by the SS concerning the prohibition of releasing prisoners after serving their sentences.

> An agreement was reached stating that, whatever prisoners can be released, they should be put at the disposal of the Commissioner of the Labor Office. When searching (*Überholung*) villages, resp., when it has become necessary to burn down villages, the whole population will be put at the disposal of the Commissioner by force.[24]

Despite mass murder of Jews in the course of the *Aktion Reinhardt*, some Jews sent to Auschwitz were selected and used as forced laborers. In a secret telegram to Himmler evaluating the percentage of Jews able to work out of the transports the following was written:

> In the total of 45,000 the physically handicapped and others (old Jews and children) are included. In making a selection for this purpose, at least 10,000 to 15,000 laborers will be available when the Jews arriving at Auschwitz are assigned.[25]

The percentage, between 22% and 33% of able-bodied workers, was much higher here than during the selection in most ghettos where between 10% and 20% of those able to work were left in special labor detachments.[26]

At the same time, when trains full of Jews rolled into the death camps, Sauckel required a comparable number of workers from the east. In the record of a telephone conversation of the Chief of the OKW Keitel with the Chief of the Economic Staff East of the German Army, dated March 11, 1943, we find the following information:

> The plenipotentiary for the *Arbeitseinsatz*, Gauleiter Sauckel, points out to me in an urgent teletype that the *Arbeitseinsatz* in German agriculture

---

24 Secret SS order (dated March 19, 1943) (3012-PS), in IMT, *Red Series*, vol. 1, 889.
25 RSHA to Himmler (telegram marked "Urgent" and "Secret," dated December 16, 1942) (1472-PS), in IMT, *Red Series*, vol. 1, 989.
26 During the first liquidation action in the Warsaw Ghetto between July 23, 1942 and September 21, 1942, about 300,000 Jews, or about 80% of the ghetto's population, were deported; during the great deportation from the Częstochowa ghetto, between September 22 and October 8, 1942, about 40,000 (83.3%) Jews were deported and approximately 2,000 (4.2%) were killed on the spot. In the small ghetto only less than 6,000 (12.5%) Jews remained; from the ghetto in Lublin between March 16, 1942 and April 11, 1942 about 30,000 Jews (88.2%) were deported.

as well as all the most urgent armament programs, ordered by the Führer, make the most rapid procurement of approx. 1 million women and men from the newly occupied territories an imperative necessity. For this purpose, Gauleiter Sauckel demands the shipment of 5,000 workers daily beginning March 15 [1943], 10,000 workers male and female beginning April 1 [1943] from the newly occupied territories.[27]

Sauckel's *Arbeitseinsatz* was truly impressive. His action brought additional millions of workers to Germany, not counting the other millions that were already employed in the Reich and many more millions who were employed in the war industry, agriculture, and other branches of industry in the occupied territories. In his report Sauckel wrote:

> After one year's activity as Plenipotentiary for the Deployment of Labor, I can report that 3,638,056 new foreign workers were given to the German war economy from April 1, of last year [1942] to March 31, this year [1943]. [...] The 3,638,056 are distributed amongst the following branches of the German war economy: Armament: 1,568,801...[28]

At the same time, the very close number of Jews were executed in the gas chambers of the death camps. However, there were still more Jews to be exterminated and, on the other hand, many more forced laborers were needed for the German economy. In a memorandum of a conference with Hitler which took place on January 4, 1944, concerning allocation of labor, the following request was registered: "The Plenipotentiary for Employment of Labor shall procure at least 4 million new workers from occupied territories."[29]

EMPLOYMENT OF THE JEWS BY THE WEHRMACHT

Jews constituted an important part of the labor force exploited by the Wehrmacht in the General Government. Those workers were essential for various reasons. They were relatively cheap, available, and qualified. Therefore, it was not easy, perhaps even impossible, to substitute them. The beginning of the

---

27 Chief of the OKW Keitel with the chief of the Economic Staff East of the German Army (telephone conversation; dated March 11, 1943) (3012-PS), in IMT, *Red Series*, vol. 1, 930.
28 Sauckel's to Hitler, April 15, 1943 (letter containing a report on one year of Sauckel's activities) (407-VI-PS), in IMT, *Red Series*, vol. 1, 909.
29 Memorandum of conference with Hitler (4 January 1944; concerning allocation of labor) (1292-PS), in IMT, *Red Series*, vol. 1, 927.

Aktion Reinhardt initiated a new era; when two very important factors began to act in two opposite directions. On the one hand, the SS and police started to realize the program of total extermination of the Jews in Europe; on the other hand, the German Army needed qualified workers in order to maintain a high level of war production. Of course, we would be mistaken, if we thought that the Wehrmacht was interested in protecting the Jews. Instead, they were solely concerned about winning the war. We should not forget the fate of millions of Soviet POWs who died of hunger in autumn and winter of 1941 and 1942. They died because this supposedly served the German victory. The dead Soviet POWs could not fight their captors and tons of food, which they otherwise would have consumed, were left for the German army.

However, in 1942, Jews were needed for the war production. Therefore, the Wehrmacht in the General Government became preoccupied with them. The following are a number of quotations confirming the importance of the Jews for the Wehrmacht. "In Kraków, there are 11,000 Jews, who were employed as laborers by the Wehrmacht, Inspection of Armaments and various government departments and companies."[30] Also in Galicia there was an attempt to leave Jewish workers in the military industry:

> The Jewish laborers remained in the *W-Betriebe* for the last quarter of the year, following an agreement of the *Rüstungs-Inspekteur* (armament inspector) of the General Government with the Higher SS and Police Leaders in the General Government. From other strategic enterprises the Jewish laborers were inconsiderately withdrawn and returned only partially on intervention of the *Rüstungskommando*. The company Schwarz & Co., manufacturing clothes for the Wehrmacht exclusively and employing 2.000 Jewish laborers, was taken over by the SS and the Jews were taken to the forced labor camp. The production was merged with the *Deutsche Ausrüstungswerkstätten* and will retain the current volume of output. The former managers were arrested for severe irregularities.[31]

Thousands of Jews were also working for the Wehrmacht in Warsaw:

> Jews are employed in a high percentage. In the ghetto 110 factories are located, which employ 77,000 people, of whom 22,000 work in the arms

---

30 Frank, *Okupacja i ruch oporu*, vol. 1, 487.
31 BA-MA, RW23-14, Rüstungskommando Lemberg, Kriegstagebuch für die Zeit vom 1. April bis 30. Juni 1943, 7–8.

factories. All private production remaining in the ghetto is rearranged into tasks of the importance for the war. Of these 30,000 Jews [not working in the ghetto], a significant number is currently employed outside the ghetto, employment rate will increase, but it would be absolutely necessary to better feed the work force.[32]

Yet another document characterized the development of production for the Wehrmacht in Warsaw in the following manner:

> Contrary to previous views on the matter, so far one has been able to activate the ghetto from an economic point of view that, so far, it was not necessary for state subsidies. In the ghetto work about 25,000 Jews in plants of the importance of war, while 3,000 Jews from the ghetto are employed outside of the ghetto. The second biggest fur company, covering the lion's share of the Wehrmacht demand for these products, has its plants in the ghetto. Monthly turnover between the ghetto and the Aryan quarter now stands at 6 million, to be added to the turnover, which cannot be exactly evaluated and are estimated at 2–3 million. From this turnover the ghetto inhabitants live somehow. The speaker hopes that Warsaw will soon be freed from the ballast of Jews unfit for work.[33]

The last words of this quotation perfectly present the attitude toward the Jews, who were needed only as labor. Similar reference had been made to them in the Radom District: "In Radom and Częstochowa Jewish workers ... in arms factories have to be preserved. Of course, we need to leave the immediate family of such workers, while all others will be displaced."[34] In this case, only the workers employed in arms factories and their families were eligible to remain and thus temporarily avoid deportation to extermination camps. The situation in Galicia was similar: "The Jewish question is no longer a problem. The Jewish labor still used in the armaments factories and in the Karpathen Öl A.G. must, however, remain in any case, because their replacement by local workers at this time seems impossible."[35]

---

32 Meeting of the GG government, Kraków, July 13, 1942, in Frank, *Okupacja i ruch oporu*, vol. 1, 496.
33 Frank, *Okupacja i ruch oporu*, vol. 1, 479.
34 Ibid., 484–85.
35 BA-MA, RW23-14, Rüstungskommando Lemberg, Bericht des Dienststellenleiters zu Ziffer 2c des Kriegstahebuches, Lemberg, den 1. Juli 1943, 10.

BEGINNING OF PERMANENT FACTORY LABOR CAMPS

With the liquidation of the ghettos and the creation of small ghettos, many Jews were looking for a way to save themselves. Many firms were also looking for means to save Jewish workers. As stated by Frauendorfer:

> ... the resettlement of Jews, representing a major proportion of the population, would cause far-reaching consequences [...] The country in terms of labor force is exhausted [...] therefore, at this moment it depends only on the job of Jews; this is the point of view that is also shared by the Inspector of Armaments for the General Government, *Generalleutnant* Schindler.[36]

Frauendorfer stressed that due to a lack of Polish specialists, the Jews were irreplaceable. He did not fail to point out that, "Jews are, in fact, not to be excluded from the actions conducted by the SS, but during the war, we have to use their work."[37] In order to preserve the Jewish workers, it was necessary to protect them by removing them from the jurisdiction of the SS. For this purpose, the Jews had to be put into enclaves where they would be safe. Those enclaves could only be labor camps. Therefore, discussions between the bodies interested in Jewish labor were held on this topic. According to the minutes of one of those meetings,

> [O]n the basis of an agreement with Schindler on the transfer to the arms industry of the Jews, it was completely and clearly explained that he [Frauendorfer] can fully satisfy the wishes of [Schindler]. For this purpose, thousands of Jewish laborers would be put at the disposal of [the armament industry], placed in camps which will be erected near the munitions factories; the SS would take care of them, provide food, and if necessary provide units [of guards]; Reichsführer SS, Reich Minister Speer and the plenipotentiary for employment, Gauleiter Sauckel, attach great importance to the hiring of able-bodied Jews.[38]

---

36 Statement of the head of the Main Department Labor of the General Government, Frauendorfer, on a need for further employment of the Jews in the interests of the German economy (Kraków, June 22, 1942), in Eisenbach and Rutkowski, *Eksterminacja Żydów*, 240.
37 Eisenbach and Rutkowski, *Eksterminacja Żydów*, 240.
38 Ibid.

Frauendorfer's statement announced the creation of permanent labor camps near factories; however, this had, undoubtedly, provoked a strong reaction from the SS. The SS was not interested in the civil administration meddling in matters falling within their competence. Overall, the SS treated the civilian administration dismissively. It was felt that the civil administration was unable to efficiently carry out any decision, and all its actions were chaotic and corrupt. For example, Katzmann wrote in his report on the action in the Galicia District:

> It became increasingly apparent that the civil administration was not in a position to move the Jewish problem to an even reasonably satisfactory solution. Because repeated attempts of the city administration of Lwów, for instance, to move the Jews into a Jewish quarter, failed, this question, too was solved by the SS and Police Leader and his organizations.[39]

In another place, Katzmann wrote:

> As the administration was not in the position to overcome this chaos, and proved weak, the whole issue of Jewish labor was simply taken over by the SS and Police Leader. The existing Jewish Labor Offices, which were staffed by hundreds of Jews, were dissolved. All work certificates issued by firms and official employers were declared invalid, and the cards given to Jews by the Labor Offices revalidated by the Police.[40]

Just three days later, Frauendorfer issued another circular to the departments of labor and employment offices in the districts. He wrote in it about the need to communicate with local police commanders on matters relating to the forced labor of Jews, because "... the employment of Jews affects the interests of the police."[41] Therefore, it was necessary to employ Jews only after consultation with the police. "I order therefore with immediate effect that the Jews

---

39 From the final report by Katzmann, commander of the SS and police in the district of Galicia, on "The Solution of the Jewish problem" in Galicia (L-18), in Arad and Gutman, *Documents on the Holocaust*, 336–37.
40 Ibid., 338.
41 Circular of the Head of the Main Department Labor of the General Government, Frauendorfer, to the all Departments Labor and Employment Offices in the districts on the need to communicate with local police commanders in matters of Jewish forced labor (Kraków, June 25, 1942), in Eisenbach and Rutkowski, *Eksterminacja Żydów*, 240.

are allowed to be hired only after consultation with the police." Frauendorfer banned the labor offices from taking any action to combat labor shortages in various districts. We do not know which precise interests of the police were violated by hiring Jews. There is no doubt that the actions of the labor offices interfered with *Aktion Reinhardt*, since they allowed Jews to find employment.

From the onset of *Aktion Reinhardt*, the Jews formally passed into the hands of the police and SS and became their property, as will be revealed later in our discussion. The labor offices lost their powers, which had been introduced with the agreement of July 4, 1940 between Frank and Krüger. Therefore, Frauendorfer was not sure whether labor of Jews under the SS would be used at all: ". . . it is expected that in the future the police will be dealing with exploitation of the Jewish labor force to some extent, especially in the armaments industry."[42] Frauendorfer ordered that the labor offices no longer be intermediaries in matters of employment of the Jews. However, in cases of requests from the police, the labor offices could, as we remember, provide assistance in these matters.[43]

The conflict between the SS and the Wehrmacht was inevitable, and as the statements above show, the SS had the task of implementing the "Final Solution," while the Wehrmacht was designed to ensure victory at the front. This was essentially contradictory, because the SS did not bear any responsibility for the fate of the war, despite the fact that they created the Waffen-SS troops. The SS was not an organization capable of engaging in economic activity, although some established enterprises, such as DAW and OSTI, were controlled by the SS. However, these companies were founded on the use of virtually free Jewish slave labor, which was very cheap, so that even poorly organized, poorly managed, and unprofitable companies could be lucrative. The SS, only because of the division of powers in Jewish affairs in Germany and in order to maintain the same model of organization in the occupied countries, had been granted full authority over the Jews and the possibility to freely exploit or use them as slaves, whom they could "lend" to other institutions.

During World War II, the Wehrmacht was not merely the German army whose task was to wage war. Through a network of inspectorates in the occupied territories, the Wehrmacht also had to take care of and control the level of production for the war effort, in order to provide enough materials to conduct the war. Despite such an enormous task, the Wehrmacht encountered a

---

42 Ibid.
43 Ibid.

derogatory attitude on the part of the SS, which had the functions of the police and dealt with the criminal activity behind the front line. While the Wehrmacht fought at the front against the enemy, the SS was engaged in murdering defenseless women, children, the sick, and the elderly. In this context we may read Katzmann's statement:

> The Wehrmacht authorities in particular aided the Jewish parasites by issuing special certificates without proper control. ... There were cases where Jews were caught with from 10 to 20 such certificates. When Jews were arrested in the course of further checks, most of the employers felt obliged to attempt to intervene in favor of the Jews. This was often done in a manner that can only be described as deeply shameful.[44]

Katzmann's words were contrary to what he had said earlier about the Jews: "Owing to the peculiarity that almost 90 percent of the artisans in Galicia consisted of Jews, the problem, to be solved could only be carried out gradually, as an immediate removal of the Jews would not have been in the interest of the war economy."[45]

Further in the report, Katzmann wrote about acquisition of control over the Jewish workers by enclosing them in a labor camp that remained under the control of the SS. In this case as well, Katzmann did not hesitate to express his derogatory attitude toward the Wehrmacht:

> The Higher SS and Police Leader gave further instructions to accelerate the total evacuation of the Jews, further considerable work was necessary in order to catch those Jews who were for the time being, to be left in the armaments factories. These remaining Jews were declared labor prisoners of the Higher SS and Police Leader and held either in the factories themselves or in camps erected for this purpose. For Lwów itself, a large camp was erected on the outskirts, which holds 8,000 Jewish labor prisoners at the present time. The agreement made with the Wehrmacht concerning employment and treatment of the labor prisoners was set down in writing.[46]

---

44 From the final report by Katzmann, commander of the SS and police in the district of Galicia, on "The Solution of the Jewish problem" in Galicia (L-18), in Arad and Gutman, *Documents on the Holocaust*, 338.
45 Ibid., 336–37.
46 Ibid., 339.

ORGANIZATIONAL CHANGES IN THE SYSTEM OF SS LABOR CAMPS

The SS only appeared to be a homogeneous organization representing common interests. In actuality, it was split, and different interests of its factions constantly clashed. One of the reasons for these clashes was the use of Jewish labor. Even in the General Government, which was a relatively small area, constant friction existed between forces allied to Himmler, HSSPF, and SSPF, who were the controllers of their area. Especially outstanding was Globocnik, the SSPF in the Lublin District, who for years had been associated with Himmler through ties of friendship. Globocnik constantly fell into trouble and was repeatedly saved by Himmler. He had a great opportunity to repay a debt of gratitude to Himmler, when he was assigned the commander of *Aktion Reinhardt*. It was Himmler's friendship and the task of extermination of millions of Jews in death camps that allowed Globocnik, despite his formal subordination to Krüger and Frank, to avoid the official system successfully and to communicate directly with Himmler. Krüger and Frank, in turn, also dependent on Himmler, had to accept this state of affairs. The same was true of other districts, where the SSPFs often had great power and competed with the governors of the districts. In particular, much power was in the hands of Katzmann, who, like Globocnik, degraded the civilian administration.

Until September 1943, the SSPFs of the districts had Jewish labor camps under their control, but at the beginning of September 1943, an important change concerning subordination of labor camps took place. In Berlin, on September 7, 1943, a conference in the Economic and Administrative Main Office [WVHA] was held in which *SS-Obergruppenführer* Pohl, the *SS-Gruppenführer* Globocnik, *SS-Brigadeführer* Glücks, *SS-Brigadeführer* Lörner, *SS-Obersturmbannführer* Schellin, *SS-Obersturmbannführer* Maurer, *SS-Sturmbannführer* Florstedt, and *SS-Obersturmführer* Dr. Horn were present. It was the last conference of this type attended by Globocnik, who had just completed *Aktion Reinhardt* in the autumn of 1943 and was to be transferred to Yugoslavia, where he would combat the partisans. At the conference on September 7, it was decided by the Main Economic and Administrative Office to take over ten labor camps for Jews, which until then had been under the jurisdiction of SSPF in the Lublin District. These camps were to be subjugated directly to *SS-Sturmbannführer* Florstedt, who was to ensure their safety and efficient management. Important, however, was the second point in Pohl's notes from this conference:

> With the acquisition of [the camps] by the Main Economic and Administrative Office of the SS (Group D), inmates [*Insassen*] of these labor camps have become prisoners in the concentration camp [*Konzentrationslager-Häflinge*]. Allocation of prisoners to workshops that are active or will be established in the future by OSTI in these camps shall be paid and the payment received will be transferred to the Treasury.[47]

From this quotation we may assume that after this conference an SS owned company had to pay for prisoners' labor. This change meant that the OSTI Company suddenly became unprofitable and underwent liquidation.

Although at the beginning of the document only the Lublin District was listed, the order would apply to the entire area of the General Government.

> All the labor camps in the Lublin District, numbering about 10, shall together with other labor camps in the General Government be taken over by the Main Economic and Administrative Department of the SS. SS-*Sturmbannführer* Florstedt will oversee the acquisition of these camps by the Group D at the Main Economic and Administrative Department of the SS.[48]

From now on, all SS labor camps became de facto concentration camps and all the Jews working in them were henceforth prisoners of concentration camps. The document stated: "We should strive to dissolve small camps and those whose production is not significant for the fate of war, or has no decisive meaning for the victory."[49]

One of the most important documents illustrating the attempt to maintain the Jewish workers in the war industry was the memorandum written

---

47 Official note of Oswald Pohl on the takeover of Jewish labor camps in the General Government by the Main Economic and Administrative Office of the SS (WVHA), subordinate until then to commanders of the SS and the police, the Central Office of Economic and Administrative SS (Berlin, September 7, 1943), in Eisenbach and Rutkowski, *Eksterminacja Żydów*, 255–56.
48 Ibid.
49 Ibid.

on September 18, 1942 by General von Gienanth to the General Staff of the Wehrmacht in reaction to the removal of Jews from industrial production.[50] Although this document is called a memorandum, this was in fact a letter of protest. In the beginning, von Gienanth recalls the earlier directive, according to which, "the Polish and Ukrainian workers were to be replaced by Jewish workers, in order to release the former for work in the Reich."[51] However, seeing the growing demand for forced labor in the Reich and the reluctance of Poles to leave to work in the Reich, which made the application of police methods necessary, von Gienanth stated with a bit of irony: "... if the Commissioner General for Labor is prepared to relinquish the 140,000 Poles who were assigned for work in the Reich, and if the police is successful in rounding them up. Previous experience gives cause for doubt in this respect."[52]

In order to employ Jews in war production factories, "... the enterprises concerned will set up camps for the Jews."[53] However, von Giennanth also advised that "... for the full exploitation of Jewish labor for the war effort, purely Jewish enterprises and Jewish sections of enterprises will be established."[54]

General von Gienanth also explained why the work of Jews was so important in war production:

> According to the figures supplied by the Government [General's] Central Labor Office, manpower in industry totals a little over a million, of which 300,000 are Jews. The latest include roughly 100,000 skilled workers. In the enterprises working for the Wehrmacht, the proportion of Jews among the skilled workers varies from 25% to 100%; it is 100% in the textile factories producing winter clothing. In other enterprises—for instance the important motor manufacturing works which produce the "Fuhrmann" and "Pleskau" models—the key men, who do the wheelwork, are mainly Jews. With few exceptions all the upholsterers are Jews. A total of 22,700 workers are employed at the present time on reconditioning uniforms in private firms, and, of these, 22,000 (97%) are Jews. Of these, 16,000 are skilled textile and leather workers. A purely Jewish enterprise with 168 workers

---

50 Memorandum by General von Gienanth to the General Staff of the Wehrmacht in reaction to the removal of the Jews from industrial production (September 18, 1942), YVA, O/4-4-2; Arad and Gutman, *Documents on the Holocaust*, 287–89.
51 Ibid.
52 Ibid.
53 Ibid.
54 Ibid.

produces metal parts for harnesses. The entire production of harnesses in the Government-General, the Ukraine and, in part, in the Reich depends on this enterprise.[55]

As we see from this quotation, the Jews were extremely important in war production, not only because of their number, but also because of their qualifications. It is significant to note that in some industries, especially those with 100% Jewish workers, sudden evacuation of the Jews could result in the total closure of production. In addition, such closure could result in lack of parts and components needed to manufacture other products, which would also affect other areas.

There was also a high percentage of skilled workers among the Jews whose sudden substitution was not possible because there were no reserves of skilled workers and training new workers would take a very long time. Von Gienanth confirmed this in his memorandum:

> Fully skilled labor would first have to be trained. The training of labor drawn mainly from agriculture requires several months to a year, and more in the case of particularly highly qualified workers and craftsmen. Whether the solution to this especially complex problem, on which the continued productivity of the Government General for the war economy depends primarily, can be speeded up by the release of skilled workers from the Reich is beyond my competence to judge. [. . .] Unless work of military importance is to suffer, Jews cannot be released until replacements have been trained, and then only step by step.[56]

Training new workers, however, was very difficult and costly under war conditions. In some cases of highly skilled specialists, it was simply impossible. This was probably why, in the end, compromises in the struggle over the Jewish labor force were made by both sides, and some Jewish workers were left in armament factories.

The German Army, however, struggling with the SS over Jewish workers never used the argument that they wanted to save the Jews, but rather the opposite. Keeping Jewish workers in armament factories was to be only temporary. The Wehrmacht argument was consistent with the policy of elimination of

---

55 Arad and Gutman, *Documents on the Holocaust*, 287–89.
56 Ibid.

the Jews and it seemed that was, in fact, true. We cannot say that there were no individual cases of saving the Jews gratuitously or in exchange of money; nevertheless, this was not representative of the Wehrmacht as a whole. In his memorandum, von Gienanth expressed his view clearly, exclusively employing practical arguments:

> The general policy will be to eliminate the Jews from work as quickly as possible without harming work of military importance. [...] A great variety of Wehrmacht offices have placed military orders of the highest priority, particularly for winter needs, in the Government-General, without the knowledge of the Armaments Department or the Military Commander of the Government-General. The evacuation of the Jews makes it impossible for these orders to be completed in time. It will take some time to register systematically all the enterprises involved. [...] It is requested that the evacuation of Jews employed in industrial enterprises may be postponed until this has been done.[57]

In any case, von Gienanth argued that the evacuation of the Jews, if necessary, should be coordinated with the Wehrmacht. Otherwise: "the evacuation of the Jews without advance notice to most sections of the Wehrmacht has caused great difficulties in the replacement of labor and delay in correct production for military purposes."[58]

In response to von Gienanth's memorandum, Himmler sent a letter on October 9, 1942, where he listed the steps taken in order to preserve the level of production and insisted that the Jewish workers should be closed in concentration camps. However, Himmler warned that employment of Jews was in order to save them and not because it was necessary:

> I have given orders that all so-called armament workers who are actually employed solely in tailoring, furrier, and shoe-making workshops be collected in concentration camps on the spot, i.e., in Warsaw and Lublin, under the direction of *SS-Obergruppenführer* Krüger and *SS-Obergruppenführer* Pohl. The Wehrmacht will send its orders to us, and we guarantee the continuous delivery of the items of clothing required. I have issued instructions, however, that ruthless steps are taken against all those who consider they

---

57 Ibid.
58 Ibid.

should oppose this move in the alleged interest of armaments needs, but who in reality only seek to support the Jews and their own businesses.⁵⁹

Continuing, Himmler argued that the process of removal of Jewish workers would persist, but gradually taper off:

> Jews in real war industries, i.e., armament workshops, vehicle workshops, etc., are to be withdrawn step by step. At the first stage they are to be concentrated in separate halls in the factories. In the second stage in this procedure the work teams in these separate halls will be combined, by means of transformation into closed enterprises wherever this is possible, so that we will then have simply a few closed concentration-camp industries in the Government-General. [...] Our endeavor will then be to replace this Jewish labor force with Poles and to consolidate most of these Jewish concentration camp enterprises into a small number [...] in the eastern part of the Government General, if possible. But there too, in accordance with the wish of the Führer, the Jews are some day to disappear.⁶⁰

The pressure from Himmler towards complete annihilation of Jews found unexpected opposition from Frank. Although he also advocated "sending the Jews to the East," on December 9, 1942, Frank said during a conference:

> Not unimportant labor reserves have been taken from us when we lost our old trustworthy Jews [*altbewährten Judenschaften*]. It is clear that the labor situation is made more difficult when, in the middle of the war effort, the order is given to prepare all Jews for annihilation. The responsibility for this order does not lie with the offices of the *Generalgouvernement*. *The directive for the annihilation of the Jews comes from higher sources* [emphasis mine—W.M.]. We can only deal with the consequences of this situation, and we can tell the agencies of the Reich that the taking away of the Jews has led to tremendous difficulties in the labor field. Just the other day I could prove to *Staatssekretär* Ganzenmüller, who complained that a large construction project in the *Generalgouvernement* had come to a standstill, that it would not have happened if the many thousands of Jews who were employed there

---

59 Himmler's response to the memorandum from General von Gienanth (October 9, 1942) (NO-1611), in Arad and Gutman, *Documents on the Holocaust*, 289–90.
60 Ibid.

had not been taken away. Now the order provides that the armament Jews also are to be taken away. I hope that this order if not already voided, then revoked, because if it is not changed, the situation will be even worse.[61]

The words of Himmler left no doubts: "The Jews were some day to disappear."[62] The only question was when and at what rate. This truly was a question of survival. Nobody knew when the war was to end, but surviving one more day, and then another, was most essential. The race had begun and the question was who would reach their goal faster—the SS with its mechanism of total murder or the Jews with their ability to survive. Those two processes were progressing in parallel. However, only useful and physically able Jews were to survive, since what counted was their work, and their utility to the victory of the Reich—not their lives as such.

---

61 Frank's remarks at the General Government conference (December 9, 1942), in *Hans Frank's Diary* (PS-2233); Hilberg, *The Destruction of the European Jews*, 529.
62 Arad and Gutman, *Documents on the Holocaust*, 289–90.

CHAPTER 9

Harvest Festival (*Erntefest*)—Extermination of the Remaining Jews in the District of Lublin

THE GROWING JEWISH RESISTANCE IN 1943

Since the beginning of 1943, a systematic increase in armed resistance had been noticed with various large gatherings of Jews. The January resistance in the Warsaw Ghetto marked the launch of these events. This occurred a few months after the large-scale deportations from the Warsaw Ghetto in the summer of 1942. Since the Great Action from July to September 1942 and over the coming months, relative calm prevailed. That period was used by the Jews to consolidate various youth movements and political parties in order to create a common organization united in battle. However, a total union did not come about because of too much discord among the Jewish organizations. Eventually, two militant organizations were established: the Jewish Fighting Organization (ŻOB) and the Jewish Military Union (ŻZW). Lack of organized preparation during the large-scale deportations from the Warsaw Ghetto in the summer of 1942 was a painful experience and brought home all the dangers it entailed. They decided to resist deportation at the next attempt. Indeed, such a moment came on January 18, 1943 when another deportation was set in motion. The Jews tried to hide in bunkers and basements, and young people, mainly from the ŻOB, resisted. The Germans managed to deport some thousands of Jews, but it was much fewer than planned. The Jewish fighters had lost many of their people. Finally, the deportation was stopped.

The January experience was used in further preparations for the battle. The underground organizations started to collect funds, often threatening with weapons, resumed intensive construction of shelters, and continued the elimination of Jewish collaborators. They acquired or sequestered weapons and established contacts with the Aryan side. News of resistance in the Warsaw Ghetto quickly began to spread around the country and not only among the Jews. The German authorities collected information about these events and about the mood among the Jews. In addition, knowledge about new places where Jews were being deported also circulated.

Probably not coincidentally, on January 20, 1943, Himmler turned to Ganzenmüller, secretary of state at the Ministry of Communications of the Reich, regarding the need to accelerate the provision of trains for deportation of Jews. Himmler argued as follows:

> The condition for [the establishment] of peace in the General Government, Białystok, and on Russian territory is the deportation of any band of helpers, and suspected of involvement in gangs. It does concern here in the first instance, we think, deportation of Jews [...] because on else case, we expect an increasing number of attacks in those areas.[1]

At the same time, in January 1943, the Jewish Fighting Organization in the Warsaw Ghetto published a call for resistance:

> We have received information from all sides about the destruction of the Jews in the Government-General, in Germany, in the occupied territories. When we listen to this bitter news we wait for our own hour to come every day and every moment. Today we must understand that the Nazi murderers have let us live only because they want to make use of our capacity to work to our last drop of blood and sweat, to our last breath. We are slaves. And when the slaves are no longer profitable, they are killed. Everyone among us must understand that, and everyone among us must remember it always.[2]

---

1 Himmler to the Secretary of State in the Ministry of Communications of the Reich, Ganzenmüller, on the urgent need to supply trains for deportation of Jews, Berlin, January 20, 1943, in Eisenbach and Rutkowski, *Eksterminacja Żydów*, 321.
2 Call to resistance by the Jewish Fighting Organization in the Warsaw Ghetto, January 1943, in Arad and Gutman, *Documents on the Holocaust*, 301–2.

After the great deportation, Jews no longer believed that deportation meant "to work in the East," as it was so often quoted in the German announcements. Therefore, no promise of work in the camps in the district of Lublin, which were announced later, was able to convince the Jews that the Germans' intentions were pure. Armed struggle was suggested as the only alternative. As the Jewish Fighting Organization's pamphlet stated:

> The blood-stained murderers have a particular aim in doing this: to reassure the Jewish population in order that later the next deportation can be carried out without difficulty, with a minimum of force and without losses to the Germans. They want the Jews not to prepare hiding-places and not to resist. Jews, do not repeat these lying tales. Jews in your masses, the hour is near. You must be prepared to resist, not giving yourselves up like sheep to slaughter. Not even a few must go to the train. Let everyone be ready to die like a man![3]

Already on January 22, Ludwik Landau wrote:

> It is said that the deported people are taken to perform fortification works somewhere in the East,[4] but it is also said that some transport go to the prison camp in Trawniki. It does not seem that doing some work was the goal of this action, rather, all the impression is that the point is to destroy the population, its most energetic and most enterprising part in the first place, and in general the urban intelligentsia. Perhaps this fear dictates the deportaion—or maybe just the desire to destroy as much as possible before approaching the end?[5]

In another place Ludwik Landau wrote, "The news about people who have been deported from Warsaw mention constantly the same points of destination: Trawniki, Majdanek, and Bełżec.[6] Escapees from the trains still arrive, but many have died trying to escape."[7]

---

3 Ibid.
4 Such fortification works were done in Bełżec labor camps complex in 1940–1941.
5 Entry of January 22, 1943, in Landau, *Kronika lat wojny i okupacji*, vol. 2, 133.
6 In 1942–1943, a notorious death camp was active in Bełżec. Any news about going to work in Bełżec were misleading. In fact, the transports were destinated to be exterminated in Bełżec death camp.
7 Ibid.

THE EVACUATION OF THE LABOR FORCE FROM THE WARSAW GHETTO TO LABOR CAMPS IN LUBLIN

Formal decisions on the transfer of industrial plants to the Lublin area were soon to be taken. On February 2, 1943, the commander of the SS and police in the district of Warsaw, Ferdinand von Sammern-Frankenegg,[8] wrote to Himmler about relocation of industrial plants and workers from the Warsaw Ghetto to the concentration camp in Lublin:

> Preparations for the translocation of all textile factories employing Jews are in progress and a mobilization plan was completed in cooperation with factory managers. To a concentration camp in Lublin not only Többens and Schultz & Co., but also all other companies will be moved. It is eight plants with a total of approximately 20,000 Jewish laborers. Departure will be made by group departments. *SS-Gruppenführer* Globocnik joined us in the process of taking over these industrial plants.[9]

On February 16, 1943, RFSS Heinrich Himmler issued two important orders. One of them instructed Pohl to create a concentration camp in the Warsaw Ghetto where all Jews living in Warsaw were to be transferred, and dictated the deportation of Jews to the Lublin area.[10] At the same time, Himmler forbade Jews to work in private establishments. All existing private companies in the Warsaw Ghetto were to be transferred to a concentration camp. In the next stage, industrial plants had to be moved to Lublin in such a way that production did not suffer.[11]

The second command was issued to Krüger and concerned the complete destruction of the Warsaw Ghetto after having all its valuables removed.[12]

---

8   JD Ferdinand von Sammern-Frankenegg (1897–1944) since July 1942 was the SSPF in the district of Warsaw, Following the Warsaw Ghetto Uprising he was substituted by Jürgen Stroop. He was transferred in April 1943 to Croatia where he occupied the post of Disrtict Police Leader (*Polizei-Gebietsführer*). He was killed by Jugoslav partisants in Serptember 1944.

9   Letter of the SS and Police Leader in the district of Warsaw, Ferdinand von Sammern-Frankenegg, to Heinrich Himmler on the translocation of industrial companies and workers from the Warsaw Ghetto to the camps in Lublin area, Warsaw, February 20, 1943, in Eisenbach and Rutkowski, *Eksterminacja Żydów*, 250.

10 Himmler's order to the chief of the Main Economic and Administrative Office of the SS, Pohl to set up in Warsaw a concentration camp and deportation of Jews to the Lublin area, Field Headquarter, February 16, 1943 (NO-2494), in Eisenbach and Rutkowski, *Eksterminacja Żydów*, 323.

11 Ibid.

12 Ibid

In this order, Himmler expressed his great contempt for the Jews and their district, while arguing that his actions were for security measures:

> For reasons of security I herewith order that the Warsaw Ghetto be pulled down after the concentration camp has been moved: all parts of houses that can be used, and other materials of all kinds, are first to be made use of. The destruction of the ghetto and the relocation of the concentration camp are necessary, as otherwise we would probably never establish quiet in Warsaw, and the prevalence of crime cannot be stamped out as long as the ghetto remains. An overall plan for the destruction of the ghetto is to be submitted to me. In any case, we must eliminate the living space for 500,000 subhumans (*Untermenschen*) that has existed up to now, but could never be suitable for Germans, and reduce the size of this city of millions, Warsaw, which has always been a center of corruption and revolt.[13]

Together with an attempt to eliminate all Jews from the ghetto in Warsaw, actions intensified in order to eliminate the remnant of the Jewish people hiding in the countryside. On March 13, 1943, von Sammern-Frankenegg issued a circular to mayors in the district, concerning detection and elimination of Jews in hiding:

> I order to take action immediately with all the energy to the detection and transmission of the gendarmerie—in order to liquidate—all Jews who are still in various cities or in villages, especially those who move freely, without armbands, and who therefore could not be included in the course of the deportations of until now conducted actions.[14]

The Polish population was to be used to increase the effectiveness of these activities. Von Sammern-Frankenegg encouraged denunciation of Jews:

> Those who have submitted the appropriate reports for recognition and elimination of these Jews shall receive in each individual case to one-third of the acquired assets of detected Jews. These claims for premiums must

---

13 Ibid.
14 Circular of the SS and police leader in the district of Warsaw Ferdinand von Sammern-Frankenegg to mayors in the district concerning detection and elimination of Jews in hiding, Warsaw, March 13, 1943, in Eisenbach and Rutkowski, *Eksterminacja Żydów*, 326.

be reported to the commander of the gendarmerie, bonuses should be distributed by him after my acceptance. I ask that this action shall organize according to your will, after consultation with the relevant branches of the military police commanders.[15]

The next attempt to deport Jews from the Warsaw Ghetto was met with even greater resistance. After unsuccessful attempts to deport the Jews in January 1943, the Germans prepared for military action under von Sammern-Frankenegg's command to liquidate the ghetto and to deport the remaining Jews. On April 19, 1943, when German forces entered the ghetto, they were met with great opposition. Although scheduled to last a couple of days, the action had to last longer. Failures caused the German side to become enraged, and von Sammern-Frankenegg was immediately replaced by *SS-Gruppenführer* Jürgen Stroop. The new commander applied brutal scorched-earth tactics, which in spite of the fierce resistance of the Jewish fighters, brought results after a few days. The Jews deprived of water, electricity, food, and air (because most of the ghetto was in flames), began to come out and surrender to the Germans. Only well-stocked militant groups, who were ready for anything, survived significantly longer.

The Warsaw Ghetto Uprising had resonance in the highest echelons of Nazi leadership. Even Goebbels recorded in his diary:

> Noteworthy is exceptionally sharp fighting in Warsaw between our Police, and in part even the Wehrmacht, and the Jewish rebels. The Jews have actually succeeded in putting the ghetto in a condition to defend itself. Some very hard battles are taking place there which have gone so far, that the Jewish top leadership publishes daily military reports. Of course this will probably not last long. But it shows what one can expect of the Jews if they have arms. Unfortunately, they also have some good German weapons in part, particularly machine-guns. Heaven only knows how they got hold of them.[16]

The uprising was eventually suppressed, but it served as a warning to the Nazi leadership that the Jews would take up arms in order to defend themselves and to die with honor. This warning was particularly felt by Himmler, who

---

15 Ibid..
16 Extract from Goebbels's diary on the ghetto revolt, May 1, 1943 (Saturday), in Arad and Gutman, *Documents on the Holocaust*, 319.

since then became very careful regarding the Jews. He did not want them to be in the ghettos anymore, but in concentration and labor camps. He wrote, "The condition for [the establishment] of peace in the General Government [...] is [...] deportation of the Jews."[17] Practically since the beginning of 1943, Himmler sought at all costs to liquidate all the Jews in the General Government, regardless of the consequences for the war economy. The new situation created a new relationship, which was essentially different from that during the *Aktion Reinhardt*. Then the Jews believed that the work can save them, this is why they tried hard to get a job and work hard. In 1943, the Jews ceased to believe that their work could save lives and therefore resisted. In turn, resisting resulted in the acceleration of their elimination, due to the fears of the German authorities. It was a relationship that led in one direction only: to the destruction of the last Jews in the General Government. It turned out that desperation, along with good organization, could lead to results that no one could have predicted.

Even before the Warsaw Ghetto Uprising, operational decisions on the transfer of existing factories and the workers from the Warsaw Ghetto were issued. The order was addressed to German firms concerning the transfer of Jewish workers from these establishments to the Lublin region. The directive was issued by Walter Caspar Többens, as the plenipotentiary for the translocation of plants from the Warsaw Ghetto to the Lublin region. Translocation concerned the eight largest plants: W. C. Többens, Schultz & Co. Sp. z. o., Bernard Hallman & Co., Tow. Oskar partnerships Schilling & Co., Hoffman and Curt Roerich Sp. Ltd., Hermann Brauer, Heeresstandortverwaltung, E. Welk, G. Gerlach, Julian Kudasiewicz, and W. v. Schöne.[18] The evacuation of the companies from the Warsaw Ghetto continued during the fighting. Due to the difficult conditions of being in hiding, many reported to the assembly point because of hunger, exhaustion, lack of water, etc. Some plants, which were remote from the main areas of fighting, were evacuated as a whole at the beginning of the uprising. Great risks were associated with the evacuation because no one could really know where the transports were going. When conditions in the ghetto became unbearable, many presented themselves to the transports.

---

17   Letter of Heinrich Himmler to the Secretary of State in the Ministry of Communications of the Reich, Ganzenmüller, on the urgent need to supply trains for deportation of Jews, Berlin, January 20, 1943, in Eisenbach and Rutkowski, *Eksterminacja Żydów*, 321.

18   Order of Többens as a plenipotentiary for translocation industrial plants from the Warsaw Ghetto given to German companies concerning the transfer of Jewish workers of these plants to the Lublin area, Warsaw, April 21, 1943, in Eisenbach and Rutkowski, *Eksterminacja Żydów*, 251–52.

It should be noted that the majority of Jews living in the ghetto did not take part in the battle.

Events in the ghetto led to increased numbers of state police in the General Government. On May 10, Himmler wrote:

> Therefore, the German police force would increase to almost 19,500 people. It should also be noted that I have in the General Government SS units that, although they are replacement units, have in force of 17,000 people. For short-term actions, such as street fighting in the Warsaw Ghetto, these individuals had been and are being used.[19]

Already at that time, despite assurances that the Jews working in factories that produced for the army would be replaced gradually, to avoid any drop in production, Himmler had already decided to liquidate all Jews in the General Government. As he later wrote:

> Evacuation of at least 300,000 Jews remaining in the General Government will not stop, but I will proceed with the utmost haste. Although the evacuation of the Jews at the time of their conduct causes great concern, yet after its end, it will be the primary condition for the establishment of total peace in the territory.[20]

This securement of Himmler was confirmed by the note from Greifeldt on May 12, 1943, who recorded the following words:

> Reichsführer SS has ordered to continue the transplantation continued under the existing possibilities and to accelerate the movement of displaced Poles elsewhere. The primary task of the General Government is to remove 3[00,000]–400,000 Jews still living there.[21]

---

[19] The note of Himmler concerning increase in the number of police force in the General Government and acceleration of the liquidation of the remaining 300,000 Jews in the Geeral Government, Berlin, May 10, 1943, in Eisenbach and Rutkowski, *Eksterminacja Żydów*, 328.

[20] Ibid.

[21] The note of Greifeldt, Himmler's representative for the strengthening of Germanism, on accelerating liquidation of the rest of the Jewish population in the General Government, May 12, 1943, in Eisenbach and Rutkowski, *Eksterminacja Żydów*, 329.

However, it is interesting that a week later, on May 19, 1943, Himmler took the time to write to the head of RSHA, Kaltenbrunner, about organizing a new anti-Jewish propaganda campaign exploiting the alleged trials for ritual murders.[22] It proved Himmler's anti-Jewish obsession. He was looking for new ways to strike at the Jews. His propaganda was also translated to English, and eventually to Russian, and directed to areas not under German control. Presumably, it was also one of the ways to justify his murderous actions.

Himmler's position was opposed by Krüger. The divergence of views became transparent at a high-level meeting, held in Kraków on May 31, 1943. Krüger, the HSSPF elevated to the rank of secretary of state in Frank's domain, took a rather unexpected position:

> The elimination of the Jews did undoubtedly bring about a calming down of the overall situation. For the police, this had been one of the most difficult and unpleasant tasks, but it was in the European interest. [...] Recently he [Krüger] had again received the order to complete the elimination of the Jews in a very short time [*Er habe neulich erst wieder den Befehl erhalten in ganz kurzer Zeit die Entjudung durchzuführen*]. One has been compelled to pull out the Jews from the armaments industry and from enterprises working for the war economy. [...] The Reichsführer wished that the employment of these Jews should stop. He [Krüger] discussed the matter with Lieutenant General Schindler [head of the armaments inspectorate of the OKW, under the command of General von Gienanth] and thought that in the end the Reichsführer's wish could not be fulfilled. The Jewish workers included specialists, precision mechanics, and other qualified artisans, that could not be simply replaced by Poles at the present time.[23]

The difference of positions continued during summer and autumn 1943, until Krüger's removal from the post of the HSSPF in the General Government on November 9, 1943.

---

22 Letter of Himmler to the head of the Reich Security Main Office, Kaltenbrunner on the organization of the new anti-Jewish propaganda campaign by means of the trials of alleged ritual murders, Field Headquarter, May 19, 1943, in Eisenbach and Rutkowski, *Eksterminacja Żydów*, 331. A large text entitled "Warum begehen die Juden Ritualmorde?," used for propaganda purposes, can be found on microflim JM.15083, PDF frames 104–35.
23 Saul Friedländer, *The Years of Extermination: Nazi Germany and the Jews, 1939–1945* (New York: HarperCollins Publishers, 2007), 497.

THE ARMED RESISTANCE IN GHETTOS AND CAMPS

In mid-1943, almost all the Jews were closed in different camps. In the Lublin District, the largest Jewish population centres were at Majdanek, Trawniki, Sobibór, and Poniatowa. After the April uprising in the Warsaw Ghetto and the armed resistance during the evacuation of the Białystok Ghetto, Germans feared that the Jewish resistance movement would emerge in other places of detention for Jews. In addition, there were concerns that the difficulty of suppressing the Jewish resistance could affect the Polish resistance movement. By this time, the Polish resistance was rather passive and beyond armed confrontation, opposing the deportation of the Polish population from the Zamość area. Their activity did not exceed single actions of diversion units. The Jewish struggle in the Warsaw Ghetto and other centers were examples of fighting in a relatively limited area, in which, although not very numerous and poorly armed Jewish forces were involved, but with good preparation they were able to fight relatively large forces of the enemy and resist for a few weeks. These clashes took place in a well-fortified urban area using guerrilla tactics, without significant support but suffering heavy losses among the civilian population. How much more dangerous could guerrilla warfare be in large clusters when enacted in a vast and familiar area? The Germans knew that the difficulty in defeating such an underrated enemy could be deleterious for them. Jews who were concentrated in the remaining centers knew that they had little to lose and at the earliest opportunity of evacuation or attempt at their elimination, they could resist and try to escape.

In the General Government, there were cases of armed resistance, although on a smaller scale. One instance is the armed resistance group of the Jewish Fighting Organization (ŻOB) during the liquidation of a small ghetto in Czestochowa, on June 25, 1943. The event, on a much larger scale, was the rebellion of Jewish prisoners in the Treblinka death camp on August 2, 1943.[24] During this action, prisoners were able to obtain small quantities of arms. They set fire to the barracks that caused confusion in the camp. Although only a few dozen prisoners managed to escape alive from the camp, their resistance meant

---

24 Yitzhak Arad, *Belzec, Sobibor, Treblinka: The Operation Reinhard Death Camps* (Bloomington: Indiana UP, 1987); Yitzhak Arad, "Jewish Prisoner Uprisings in the Treblinka and Sobibor Extermination Camps," in *Nazi Concentration Camps* (Jerusalem: Yad Vashem, 1984), 357–99; Stanisława Lewandowska, "Powstania zbrojne w obozach zagłady w Treblince i Sobiborze," *BGKBZpNP-IPN*, 35 (1993): 115–27.

that the camp ceased to function, and after a short period, was liquidated. In its place, trees were planted and a farm had been set up, which remained fenced in.

Only two weeks later, on August 15 and 16, 1943, the next occurrence of Jewish armed resistance took place. When trying to liquidate the Białystok Ghetto, an armed uprising broke out.[25] Just as in other places, the revolt did not have a chance to change the situation of the Jews. The important thing was fighting and dying with weapons in hand. The leader of the resistance in Białystok was Mordechai Tenenabum-Tamaroff. As in other cases of armed resistance, the equipment of the fighters was very limited: pistols, grenades, and incendiary bottles. Stocks of ammunition soon ran out and the uprising was suppressed.[26]

The Jewish armed resistance and guerrilla attacks were discussed at the highest levels, and the problem was treated very seriously. In the autumn of 1943, there were also many personnel changes in the General Government. On October 10, Himmler sent a telegram to Frank concerning the removal of Krüger from his post, and Wilhelm Koppe[27] was appointed in his place. However, in fact, power was handed over to Koppe only on November 18.[28]

After the conclusion of *Aktion Reinhardt*, Globocnik again fell into disfavor and was dismissed from his commanding post.[29] Along with a significant number of his colleagues at *Aktion Reinhardt* headquarters, Globocnik was transferred to Trieste. In his place SS-*Gruppenführer und Generalleutnant der Polizei* Jakob Sporrenberg[30] was appointed.

---

25 "Odezwa Organizacji Samoobrony Żydowskiej w getcie białostockim z 16 sierpnia 1943 r.," BŻIH 60 (1966): 97–99; Szymon Datner, *Walka i zagłada białostockiego getta* (Lodz: Centralna Żydowska Komisja Historyczna przy CK Żydów Polskich, 1946).
26 Sara Bender, *The Jews of Białystok during World War II and the Holocaust* (Hanover: University Press of New England, 2008), 243–63.
27 Wilhelm Koppe (1896–1975) since October 26, 1949 was higher SS and police leader in Warthegau and Plenipotentiary of the RKFDV Heinrich Himmler. From November 10, 1943 he was higher SS and police leader in the General Government as well as secretary of state (*Staatsekretär*) and deputy (*Stellvertreter*) of the general governor.
28 Frank, *Okupacja i ruch oporu*, vol. 2, 242–46, and 304.
29 Information on the removal of the SSPF in the district Lublin of Odilo Globocnik from his post, Kraków, August 5, 1943, Frank, *Okupacja i ruch oporu*, vol. 2, 191.
30 Jakob Sporrenberg (1902–1952), the participant of the Kapp Putsch, since September 1939 until June 1940 was the HSSPF "Rhein" and then until May 1941 the HSSPF "Nordost." From July to August 1941 he was the SSPF of Belorussia (Weissruthenien) and then transferred to the staff of the Commissar of the Reich for the Reichskommissariat Ukraine. From August 1943 to November 1944 Sporrenberg was SSPF in the district of Lublin. From November 1944 to May 1945 he was SSPF in southern Norway. In May 1945 he was arrested and extradited to Poland. He was sentenced to death in 1950 and hanged in Warsaw in 1952.

Meanwhile, another uprising broke out, this time in the extermination camp at Sobibór, on October 14, 1943.[31] On that day, a group of prisoners under the command of Leon Feldhandler and Soviet POW Alexander (Sasha) Peczerski managed to kill several SS men and guards. Although the original plan to kill all SS men failed, hundreds of prisoners managed to escape. Many prisoners died during the rebellion, or during the escape because of land mines around the camp. Also during the hunt for the escapees, many of those who initially managed to escape were killed. Nevertheless, armed resistance and mass escape of Jewish prisoners from yet another death camp was their great success. For the Germans it was also an important event, about which the SS and police headquarters, including Himmler, were immediately informed.

On October 15, 1943, the day following the uprising in Sobibór, Sporrenberg, accompanied by some 50 SS officers, visited the camp for inspection. Sporrenberg took note of the camp and received a detailed report on the course of events of the previous day and then ordered all the "working Jews," who still remained in the camp, to be shot.[32] After the uprising, it was also decided to liquidate the camp. For the demolition of the camp, Jews from other places in the General Government were brought in. An agricultural farm was established on the camp grounds under the control of the camp staff. Upon completion of the work, these Jews, numbering at least thirty people, were also shot in November 1943.[33]

Four days after the uprising in Sobibór, Hans Frank called a special meeting of the government regarding security. During that meeting, Frank discussed the latest developments and measures that had to be taken. In addition to members of the government, all those responsible for security matters in the General Government were present: *SS-Oberführer* Walter Bierkamp—commander of the SiPo and SD in the General Government, *Generalmajor der Polizei* Hans Dietrich Grünwald—Orpo commander, Gen. Haseldoff—representative of the Wehrmacht, General Sommé from Luftwaffe, and General Schindler, head of the Armaments Inspectorate in the General Government.[34] The following was stated at that meeting, "The Jewish camps in the General Government con-

---

31 A. Peczerski, "Powstanie w Sobiborze," *BŻIH* 1(1952): 3–45; Arad, "Jewish Prisoner Uprisings"; Arad, *Belzec, Sobibor, Treblinka*, 322–33; Jules Schelvis, *Sobibor: A History of a Nazi Death Camp* (London: Bloomsbury Academic, 2007), 145–68.
32 YVA, TR.10/662-II, 301.
33 Ibid.
34 Frank, *Okupacja i ruch oporu*, vol. 2, 242–46.

stitute great danger, as was evidenced by the escape of Jews from one of these camps [Sobibór]."³⁵

During the meeting, Hans Frank ordered Schindler, Bierkampf, and Grünwald to review the Jewish camps in the General Government thoroughly and to evaluate "[. . .] how many Jews being there [in the camps] are used as labor force. Others should be removed from the General Government."³⁶

OPERATION HARVEST FESTIVAL (*AKTION ERNTEFEST*)

The decision to exterminate all Jews in labor camps in the Lublin District was issued by Himmler and referred to Krüger. Krüger, in turn, summoned Sporrenberg and told him to execute Himmler's order. Himmler claimed in his order that all the Jews in the Lublin District should be immediately eliminated, because they had established an underground organization that constituted a threat to security in the district. After returning to Lublin, Sporrenberg received a teletype from Kraków, where he was informed that in order to carry out operations against the Jews, specially assigned SS and police units would come.³⁷ This would suggest that despite the execution of the action by the commander of the SS and police in the Lublin District, the whole operation was planned by Krüger.

At the end of October, preparation for Operation *Erntefest* in the concentration camp at Majdanek began. Three meandering rows of trenches were dug beyond field number 5, south of the crematorium. This work was done by a team of three hundred prisoners. This detachment was divided into three groups that carried out the work around the clock to finish it as soon as possible. In order to allow work at night, the area had been illuminated with special reflectors. In addition, prisoners performing the work were provided with extra food and at night, they were even given unlimited amounts of soup. Various rumours began to circulate through the camp concerning the purpose

---

35 Conference on security affairs, Kraków, October 19, 1943; Frank, *Okupacja i ruch oporu*, vol. 2, 242.
36 Frank's statement shows his lack of insight into the situation and even naivety. In October 1943 the percentage of able-to-work Jews in the labor camps was very high, only in rare cases there were non-working members of the family, mostly children, Frank, *Okupacja i ruch oporu*, vol. 2, 242.
37 Berenstein, "Obozy pracy," 18; Adam Rutkowski, "L'operation 'Erntefest' ou le massacre de 43,000 Juifs les 3–5 novembre 1943 dans les camps de Maidanek, de Poniatowa et de Trawniki," *Le Monde Juif* 72 (October-December 1973): 14.

of these trenches. The official version was that they are anti-aircraft ditches. The ditches were each about 100 meters long, 2 meters deep, and 3 meters wide. All the ditches touched each another at one deep end that led to a sloping descent.[38] After completing the trenches and just before the operation began, SS *Kommandos* from various places of the Lublin District and from other places outside it—Lwów, Kraków, Radom, Warsaw, and Auschwitz—were brought to Majdanek.[39] There, two police cars equipped with big speakers drowned out the shooting during the operation. One of them parked near the trenches and the other at the gate. On the night between November 2 and 3, about 500 police officers from Lublin armed with machine guns arrived at the camp. Before the morning roll-call, they formed a cordon surrounding the prisoners' fields. Moreover, the number of sentries stationed in the guard towers was increased.

ACTION ON NOVEMBER 3, 1943 IN MAJDANEK—"BLOODY WEDNESDAY"

When prisoners went out for roll-call at around 5 a.m., on November 3 it was still dark. At dawn, the prisoners begin to notice the reinforced and heavily armed guards around the prisoners' fields. The roll-call proceeded normally. Only after the roll-call, the command ordering the Jewish prisoners to line up separately was given. At this time, the SS of the Majdanek camp staff entered the field to search the prisoner barracks. The guards were checking whether the number of prisoners corresponded with the camp's prisoner list. After completion, the Jewish prisoners were separated from the rest of the prisoners and sent to the individual field's harvest collection area. Then they were ordered to the field number 5. Similarly, sick Jewish prisoners were separated from others in the infirmary of the camp, loaded onto trucks, and transported to the field number 5. From field number 5, non-Jewish prisoners were transferred to field number 4. After gathering the Jews from fields numbers 1, 3, and 4 to field number 5, which was located near the previously dug trenches, the shooting began. For this purpose, the barbed wire around field number 5 was cut and repositioned nearer the ditches. The German police formed a "guard of honour," through which batches of one hundred prisoners were led to the

---

38 Tadeusz Mencel, *Majdanek 1941–1944* (Lublin: Wydawnictwo Lubelskie, 1991), 258.
39 W. Zyśko, "Eksterminacyjna działalność Truppenpolizei w dystrykcie lubelskim w latach 1943–1944," in *Zeszyty Majdanka* VII (1972): 189–90.

place of execution. The prisoners, before their execution, were put into one of the barracks at field number 5, where they were told to strip naked and so conducted to the place of execution. When the shooting started, the loudspeakers were switched on in order to muffle the gun bursts. On the same day, in the morning, Jewish prisoners from other camps in Lublin and the prison in the castle began to be brought to Majdanek. Specific measures were applied during the transfer of prisoners from the camp at 7 Lipowa Street, many of whom were former Polish POWs.

After leading the group of prisoners from field number 5 to the place of execution, smaller groups of ten men were marched along an earthen ramp that lead to the ditches until, at the opposite end, they were shot. Men and women were shot separately. The action lasted without interruption until 5 p.m. Only the firing squads changed. According to the report by Erich Musfeldt, head of the crematorium at the Majdanek concentration camp, an SD officer, who was in constant contact by means of communication equipment with the command of the SS and police in the district of Lublin, directed the action. It may have been Sporrenberg, but it is also possible that the whole operation was coordinated by Höfle, who was chief of staff of *Aktion Reinhardt*.

Jewish prisoners who gathered in field number 5 understood that the aim of this operation was to eliminate all Jews from Majdanek concentration camp and other places. They reacted very differently. Some, albeit few, people tried to attack the Germans, even though the situation was hopeless. Others fell into despair and attempted suicide in various ways: by cutting their veins, poisoning, or hanging. After the action in field number 5, twenty-three Jews who hid were found alive. They were taken to the crematorium and shot. Jews were also hunted in other fields. Those who were found were shot.

During the action of November 3, 1943, about 300 Jewish women and 300 Jewish men were isolated and left alive. The women were recruited after the action for searching and sorting the clothing of the victims. In mid-April 1944, they were sent to Auschwitz-Birkenau and gassed. The men were at different intervals taken by dozen to Sonderkommando 1005. These Jews were employed to dig up mass graves at execution sites and then to burn the recovered bodies.

According to the testimony of Erich Muhsfeldt, on November 3, 1943, in Majdanek, 17,000 Jews were murdered. According to the Polish-Soviet Commission that gathered the data after the liberation, 18,000 people had been shot, of which 8,100 were inmates of Majdanek. Among the executed prisoners of Majdanek about 1,660 were women. The others annihilated were from other camps of Lublin. In addition to the operation in Majdanek, at the same time similar actions were conducted in the camps in Trawniki, Poniatowa, Annopol-Rachów, Dorohucza, Puławy, and others.[40]

The course of action in Trawniki was described by one of the residents of this city, Władysław Hobot.[41] Just like in Majdanek, so was it in Trawniki. A few days before the action, Jewish prisoners were employed in digging trenches in the garden of a former sugar mill and along the road leading to the Wieprz River. Before the action, the Trawniki camp was surrounded by a ring of police and soldiers. Polish residents living near the camp were displaced and residents that lived farther from the camp were forbidden to leave their homes. Just like in Majdanek, in Trawniki loudspeakers were also used to drown out the gun shot noises. The process began around 7 a.m. and lasted, without a break, until 5 p.m. Naked Jews were driven towards the trenches, and there they were shot, men first, then women and children. After the operation, the trenches were filled with earth. However, several weeks after the action, the place of the mass graves was encircled by a high fence and a special *Kommando* proceeded to extract corpses and burn them.

Esther Rubinstein, who survived the massacre, related the following about the action that took place in the camp in Poniatowa on November 4, 1943.[42] Ten days before the action digging of zigzag trenches began. It was argued that these were anti-aircraft trenches. On November 4, 1943 at 4:30 a.m., the guards began to drive out the prisoners for roll-call. They were joined by the Jewish prisoners in Poniatowa who lived outside the camp, in the so-called settlement (*osiedle*). After collecting all the prisoners, they were driven to their barracks and then taken out in groups of fifty. Then the prisoners were forced to take off their shoes, strip naked and after that, they were driven to the place of execution. In Poniatowa as well, loudspeakers that broadcast noisy music in order to drown out the shots were prepared. During the execution, Esther Rubinstein was wounded. She fell into a trench along with other victims, but was one of the last to drop onto the top layer of dead bodies. After the action, German police checked if anyone was still alive. If they discovered anyone alive, they would shoot those people

---

40 Edward Dziadosz, ed., *Masowe egzekucje Żydów 3 listopada 1943 roku—Majdanek, Poniatowa, Trawniki* (Lublin: UMCS, 1988), 4–5.
41 WładyslawHobot, "3 listopada 1943 roku w Trawnikach", in Dziadosz, *Masowe egzekucje*, 31–32.
42 Relacja Estery Rubinstein, in Dziadosz, *Masowe egzekucje*, 28–31; Nachman Blumental, *Dokumenty i materiały*, vol. 1, *Obozy* (Lodz: Żydowska Centralna Komisja Historyczna, 1946), 261–66.

in the head. Because Rubinstein was splattered with blood, she did not arouse suspicion. Afterwards, the corpses were covered with pine branches. In the darkness, Rubinstein crawled out of the mass grave and scampered into the woods, where she met another naked woman, who had also survived. Both naked, they moved away from the place of execution, but because they were undressed, they provoked fear in the local inhabitants. Only after a chance meeting with Maria Maciąg, a woman from the village of Rogowa, were the two women provided assistance. Maria Maciąg gave them clothes, allowed them to wash, fed them, led them to a doctor, and later helped get them to Warsaw.

As a consequence of Operation *Erntefest*, the Jewish labor force was almost eliminated in the Lublin District. The total number of Jews murdered during Operation *Erntefest* in the Lublin District is estimated at 42,000.[43] This action depleted the three most important clusters of working Jews in Lublin, Poniatowa, and Trawniki. However, in Lublin, there were several different groups of Jews in various places in the city, such as Jewish prisoners from Majdanek, Jewish laborers from the camp at 7 Lipowa Street, and many other smaller installations. In addition to these three major clusters in the district, executions also took place in other smaller towns, such as Annopol-Rachów. Although secondary literature states that this operation was limited to the Lublin District, nevertheless, similar smaller actions during this period also took place in the Galicia District, which probably had a connection to this operation.

Despite Himmler's efforts to liquidate the remaining Jews in the General Government, practically only the Jews in the Lublin District were liquidated. In other districts Jews were still present, even though their number was very small. In the Warsaw District there were virtually no Jews, besides those in hiding. In the Galicia District all labor camps were liquidated during the second half of 1943. In the Lublin District after *Erntefest*, some small groups of Jewish *Kommandos* in Dęblin, Budzyń,[44] and other places remained. However, in two remaining districts—Kraków and Radom—tens of thousands of Jews endured. Most Jews in Kraków were concentrated in Płaszów camp[45] and Emalia

---

43 Dziadosz, *Masowe egzekucje*, 5.
44 WojciechLenarczyk, "Obóz pracy przymusowej w Budzyniu (1942–1944)," in *Erntefest: Zapomniany epizod Zagłady, 3–4 listopada 1943*, ed. Wojciech Lenarczyk and Dariusz Libionka (Lublin: PMM, 2009), 280–82.
45 At the end of 1943 in Płaszów camp there were about 11,500 Jewish prisoners, see Angelina Awtuszewska-Ettrich, "Płaszów-Stammlager," in *Der Ort des Terrors: Geschichte der nationalsozialistischen Konzentrationslager*, ed. Wolfgang Benz und Barbara Distel, vol. 8 (Munich: C.H. Beck, 2008), 274.

factory.[46] Besides, there were also labor detachments at the Kraków airport, a factory in Mielec (Heinkel factory), and some other places. The biggest concentration of Jewish workers was in the Radom District due to the presence of the armament industry and because of General Schindler who headed the Armaments Inspectorate (*Rüstunginspektion*) in the General Government. In the Radom District, many companies were parts of the armament industry; among which the biggest was HASAG, having four factories in Częstochowa (Pelcery, Warta, Raków, and Częstochowianka), one in Skarżysko-Kamienna, and one in Kielce (Granat). Apart from HASAG, in the Radom District companies such as Steyer-Daimler-Puch (Steyer-Daimler-Puch A.G. Waffenfabrik in Radom) and Braunschweig (Stahlwerke Braunschweig GmbH Starachowice) were active. Altogether in the Radom District, at the end of 1943, about 25,000 Jewish prisoners were employed.

The end of 1943 was marked by a very difficult situation at the Eastern Front, where the German troops were entangled in the war without any clear perspective of a breakthrough. The army needed large quantities of supplies, especially arms and munitions. In this emergency situation, the armament industry had to provide a constant supply of large quantities of war material. The only way to continue was to maintain a high level of standardized production as initiated by Speer. Any removal of Jewish workers from the armament industry could provoke a crisis and cut off the vital supply for the army. An emergency meeting on January 4, 1944 in Berlin was called to discuss the question of manpower for the munitions industry. The meeting was attended by Speer, Sauckel, and Himmler. According to Felicia Karay:

> At Speer's insistence, it was decided not to transfer workers out of the munitions plants in the occupied territories so as not to hurt production. This decision also constituted an informal sanction of continued existence of the factory camps. To judge by results, this implication was made clear to Himmler as well. In short, the survival of the factory camps stemmed not from the power of the private concerns operating in the General Government, but from the nature of the plants in which the Jews were employed. The favored status was enjoyed by HASAG,

---

46 In 1943 in Schindlers Deutsche Emalwarenfabrik were employed about 900 Jews, in Edyta Gawron, "Oskar Schindler, Fabryka Naczyń Emaliowanych i jej pracownicy," *Kraków czas okupacji 1939–1945*, ed Monika Bednarek et al. (Krakow: MHMK, 2010), 337; Angelina Awtuszewska-Ettrich, "Emalwarenfabrik," in Benz and Distel, *Der Ort des Terrors*, 289–93.

which in the General Government had a monopoly in the production of ammunition.[47]

HASAG[48] was one of the greatest suppliers of munitions in the General Government; and employed, in early summer 1944, 15,000 Jews in addition to Polish workers. It had Speer's full support and many solid reasons to do that. One of them was the demand for constant supply of munitions, which was used mainly on the Eastern Front. However, the interests of Ministry of Armaments and of HASAG met at another important point: the costs of production. HASAG could lower the cost of production by using Jews who were incarcerated in subhuman conditions and who were reduced to the status of slaves.[49] The Jews received no wages or social benefits; they could be killed at any moment with impunity. The Jews, at the price of suffering those inhuman conditions, achieved a temporary respite from the threat of execution. Speer knew this, but even so, he supported the policy, since due to Jewish labor he could supply munitions at lower prices and in large quantities.[50] It is thus not surprising that in January 1944, an overwhelming majority of the 26,296 Jews employed in the munitions industry in the General Government were working for the companies in the Radom District.[51]

---

47 Karay, "The Conflict among German Authorities," 26.
48 Karay, *Death Comes in Yellow*; Krzysztof Gibaszewski, *Hasag: Historia obozu pracy przymusowej w Skarżysku-Kamiennej* (Skarżysko-Kamienna: Muzeum im. Orła Białego w Skarżysku-Kamiennej), 2011.
49 Róża Bauminger, *Przy pikrynie i trotylu (Obóz pracy przymusowej w Skarżysku-Kamiennej)* (Krakow: CŻKH, 1946), 21–42.
50 Judgement of Albert Speer by the International Military Tribunal, Nürnberg, 1947, in Edward R. Zilbert, *Albert Speer and the Nazi Ministry of Arms: Economic Institutions and Industrial Production in the German War Economy* (Rutherford: Fairleigh Dickinson UP, 1981), 270–74
51 Karay, "The Conflict among German Authorities," 24; Karay, *Death Comes in Yellow*, 52.

Conclusion

From its inception, Jewish forced labor under the General Government was not only the result of economic policy, but rather of ideological considerations that were synchronized with practical opportunity for their implementation. The Nazi ideological platform allows us to understand the development and transformation process of Jewish forced labor in the General Government. The Jews, from the onset, were subjected to the decisions of the HSSPF, that is, police and SS apparatus, and not to the civil administration. Frank's decision of October 26, 1939 gave supreme control to non-economic actors that fully exploited the situation. The Jews in the General Government became, from the beginning, a separate class of people, whose citizenship status remained undefined. The legal system of the General Government alienated them from other ethnic groups and established special laws regarding them exclusively.[1] This legal system erased the Jews from Polish society and pushed them into the hands of the police and SS. The police and SS used instruments of force and persecution in order to compel the Jews to fulfill their orders and wishes. This situation was very grave because in the territory of the General Government, there were about 2,284,000 Jews.[2]

Jews represented an important element of the Polish economy. In some professions Jews, despite their small percentage in the population (about 10%), were overrepresented. Violent removal of the Jews from the General

---

1 As an example may serve one of the first regulations issued by Hans Frank concerning forced labor of Jews, *VBlGG*, 1939, vol. 1, 6–7. For the Poles separate regulationwere issued, *VBlGG*, 1939, vol. 1, 5.

2 Fritz Arlt estimated a number of Jews in the General Government (four districts) as 1.5 milion in 1940, see Fritz Arlt, ed., *Übersicht über die Bevölkerungsverhältnisse im Generalgouvernement*, vol. 3, *Volkspolitischer Informationsdienst der Regierung des Generalgouvernements, Innere Verwaltung, Bevölkerungswesen und Fürsorge* (Krakow: n.p., 1940), 16; At the Wannsee Conference on January 20, 1942 the number of Jews in the Generalgouvernement (five districts) was given as 2,284,000, see Arad and Gutman, *Documents on the Holocaust*, 255.

Government economy, whether by legal methods or through confiscation, robbery, and unlimited exploitation, could not be successful without serious repercussions. Police and SS authorities used administrative methods in order to remove the Jews from society. Through Jewish forced labor, the authorities benefitted from unpaid labor,[3] thus they received services without spending any of the General Government budget.[4] This process, which took place between October 1939 and the summer of 1940, caused the General Government administration to change their system and transfer competences to labor offices, which became solely responsible for the organization of the Jewish labor force.

The civil administration of the General Government was, however, not very stable in its attitude towards the Jews. On the one hand, Frank's circle was well aware of the value of Jewish labor. Even Krüger and Globocnik admitted that the Jews were able workers and performed positive tasks within the General Government's economy, something that had been unknown to them previously.[5] On the other hand, Frank supported eliminationist penchants. Many times in his public speeches, he expressed his wish to get rid of the Jews. For example, when he spoke at The University of Berlin on November 18, 1941, he said:

> ... A problem that occupies us in particular is the Jews. This merry little people (*Völklein*), which wallows in dirt, and filth, has been gathered together by us in ghettos and [special] quarters and will probably not remain in the Government-General for very long.[6]

His ambiguity is understandable. Frank wanted, as many of his officials did, to eliminate nonproductive Jews but, at the same time, to temporarily preserve the productive Jews.

---

3 Only in 1940 the Jews of Warsaw performed 1,934,437 workdays, of which 381,112 workdays were for the benefit of the SS and police and 636,745 workdays for the benefit of the Wehrmacht. Ekspertyza Historycznej Komisji Żydowskiej. AIPN, NTN, 196/59, 187.

4 Minutes of the meeting of the SS and police leader in the district of Lublin, Globocnik with heads of departments at the Lublin District governor's office on the forced labor of the Jewish population, Lublin, April 22, 1940, in Eisenbach and Rutkowski, *Eksterminacja Żydów*, 209.

5 Speech of Friedrich-Wilhelm Krüger from December 8, 1939, in Eisenbach and Rutkowski, *Eksterminacja Żydów*, 204.

6 From a speech by Frank at Berlin University, November 18, 1941, in Arad and Gutman, *Documents on the Holocaust*, 246–47.

Their perceived nonproductiveness, together with eugenic theories, were the main grounds for their execution. In view of that attitude, Frank sent his representative, Bühler, to the Wannsee Conference that fully supported the Final Solution. According to the protocol from the Wannsee Conference:

> ...the Government-General would welcome it if the final solution of this problem was begun in the Government-General, as on the one hand, the question of transport there played no major role and considerations of labor supply would not hinder the course of this Action. Jews must be removed as fast as possible from the Government-General because it was there in particular the Jew as carrier of epidemics spelled a great danger, and, at the same time he caused constant disorder in the economic structure of the country by his continuous black-market dealings. Furthermore, of the approximately 2.5 million Jews under consideration, the majority were in any case unfit for work. Secretary of State Dr. Bühler further states that the solution of the Jewish question in the Government-General was primarily the responsibility of the Chief of the Security Police and the SD and that his work would have the support of the authorities of the Government-General. He had only one request: that the Jewish question in this area is solved as quickly as possible.[7]

However, when *Aktion Reinhardt* began in March 1942, the previous division of competences from July 4, 1940 became obsolete. The civil administration in the General Government lost most of its power concerning the fate of the Jews in favor of the SS. Moreover, Frank had his own Trojan Horse in the person of Globocnik, who was responsible for the realization of *Aktion Reinhardt*.

All existing relations between employers and employees were completely erased with the mass murder of the Jews, the liquidation of the ghettos, and their transformation into so called "small ghettos"—de facto labor camps. Until then, exploitation of workers was without charge or nearly gratis. Forced laborers from provisional camps, who were prisoners only in name, actually held the status lower than slaves that were struggling for their survival. This change of status of the Jewish workers was sanctioned by Himmler. According to the circular of December 1, 1942, all the Jews in the General Government were

---

7 Arad and Gutman, *Documents on the Holocaust*, 260–61.

considered prisoners of HSSPF in the General Government (*Arbeitshäftlinge*).[8] Interestingly, until the end of the General Government, the term used for Jewish forced labor (*Zwangsarbeit*) stuck. This moniker was empty of content, since the Jews were treated as slaves or, as mentioned, even less than slaves. If someone held the status of slave, at least he was permitted to live and even to have a family. In fact, the term *Sklavenarbeit* was rarely used in Nazi jargon.[9] The Jews were working in order to remain alive, if only temporarily. Their final destination was certain death.

In the context of the reflections written above, we may ask the question: what was the rationale behind the elimination of fully available and extremely cheap forced labor in the gravest moments of the Nazi regime? Was the ideological motivation so strong and so important that it overruled rational thinking and behavior needed to preserve the Nazi regime? To what extent were the suicidal tendencies of this regime's ideological factors stronger than rational factors linked to the Wehrmacht, German economists, and industrialists? We may find an answer to these questions as early as the summer and autumn of 1941. According to the Blitzkrieg theory, the Wehrmacht agreed to the *Hungerplan*—mass starvation of millions of Soviet citizens and Soviet POWs in 1941 and 1942.[10] By February 1942, about 2.8 million Soviet POWs died of starvation, lack of elementary hygienic conditions, and a deficiency of accommodations.[11] We do not know how many other Soviet and non-Soviet citizens died at the same time. Concurrently, the Wehrmacht agreed to allow the activities of the *Einsatzgruppen*—the military forces that were farthest from the front—who committed mass murder, mainly of the Jewish population and those suspected to be communists. The *Einsatzkommandos* were even permitted to penetrate POW camps in order to filter out Soviet political commissars. Thus, since the beginning the Nazi regime, it was decided to reach mainly ideological goals, suppressing other considerations in order to attain those aspirations.

---

8   MA, R-H 53-23/87, Substitution of Jewish labor force (*Ersatz der jüdischen Arbeitskrafte*), December 1, 1942.
9   Speer, *Der Sklavenstaat*.
10 Alex J. Kay, "Germany's Staatssekretäre, Mass Starvation and the Meeting of 2 May 1941," in *Journal of Contemporary History*, 41/4 (2006): 685–700; Timothy Snyder, *Bloodlands: Europe between Hitler and Stalin* (London: The Bodley Head, 2010), 162–88; Christian Streit, "The German army and the policies of genocide," in *The Policies of Genocide: Jews and Soviet prisoners of war in Nazi Germany*, ed. Gerhardt Hirschfeld (London: German Historical Institute in London, 1986), 9.
11 G. L. Weinberg, *A World at Arms* (Cambridge: Cambridge UP, 2005), 300.

Those goals may be more easily understood by relating them to some of reflections expressed by Himmler in his famous Poznań Speech of October 3, 1943:

> ... I am referring here to the evacuation of the Jews, the extermination of the Jewish people. [...] This is an unwritten and never-to-be-written page of glory in our history. [...] We had the moral right, we had the duty towards our people, to destroy this people that wanted to destroy us. [...] All in all, however, we can say that we have carried out this most difficult of tasks in a spirit of love for our people. And we have suffered no harm to our inner being, our soul, our character. ....[12]

At the peak of the Barbarossa campaign, decisions regarding the Final Solution had been taken. On January 20, 1942, the Wannsee conference took place, which confirmed the agreement of the highest civil administration institutions to eliminate the Jews. Thus, as early as 1941 and the beginning of 1942, the highest military and civil administration institutions expressed their consent for policies of mass murder of Jews as well as non-Jews, who were simultaneously a valuable labor force.

The attempt to correct the ideologically motivated decisions came later, when the situation of the regime became critical. Even then, ideological factors were a stronger motivation than economic factors, aimed primarily to preserve a high level of production and high profits, and not the Jews. The Jews were only one element, and not the decisive or essential one.

THE TERM "FORCED LABOR"

The term "forced labor" was used since the beginning of the war practically until its end for different kinds of labor performed under coercion. However, its meaning was continuously evolving. Frank, in his decree of October 26, 1939, did not define the term at all. Only in subsequent orders issued by Krüger could it be understood as labor performed for the benefit of the ordering authorities or the society, and this labor was unpaid. However, since the beginning it was not exactly true. This work was paid by the authorities, but it was payed instead by the *Judenräte*, which tried to compensate the Jewish workers. Initially, forced labor meant one day a week of unpaid work performed by the able-bodied Jews.

---

12 From a speech by Himmler before senior SS officers in Poznań, October 4, 1943 (PS-1919), in Arad and Gutman, *Documents on the Holocaust*, 344–45.

Those Jews could be employed on free employment (*Beschäftigung für Belohnung*) during the rest of the week. However, the *Judenräte*, in order to prevent absence in regular places of work and due to a growing number of destitute and unemployed Jews, introduced a system of replacements of those mobilized by others who were unemployed. Thus, certain Jews were not performing forced labor at all, paying instead for this, while the others were working continuously in the framework of forced labor groups or so-called labor battalions. Yet another version of "forced labor," exceeding the original definition, was work in early labor camps, which existed in the General Government from 1940 until 1942, and even until 1943. According to the Agreement of July 4, 1940, the work in the labor camps was unpaid. It was, however, unpaid by the authorities. Moreover, in camps unpaid forced labor was performed not a day per week but continuously, in general, six days a week, while Sundays were dedicated to bath, works in the camp proper, or additional works. Therefore, since the beginning, "forced labor" had different meanings and forms.

Since the beginning of *Aktion Reinhardt* the term "forced labor" acquired new meanings. In the wake of brutal reduction or liquidation of the ghettos and mass deportations to death camps, any employment could save life. At least, the Jews believed that labor would save them from elimination. We will examine this question below in detail. At that time, it was of the utmost importance to find employment, preferably at a firm producing for the army. The best category were firms belonging to armament industry, however, in the spring and summer of 1942, rather few firms from that category were available to Jews due to the prohibition against employing them in armament industry. Nevertheless, during 1942 more and more Jews became employees of the armament industry. The situation of the fronts during 1942 changed from German offensive to stalemate, which resulted in stagnation, as, for example, in the area of Leningrad, or advances and retreats, as it was in the central part of the Eastern Front. In general, the Wehrmacht lost its initiative, and the *Blitzkrieg* had to end. Consequently, the army needed great quantities of supplies in order to maintain the balance of power. The conquest of new territories, new reservoirs of raw material, food, fuel, prisoners of war, and labor forces came to standstill. The economy that sanctioned low armament production, increasing only during the preparation period for a new *Blitzkrieg*, was over. German war production was not ready for this new situation.

After the death of Fritz Todt on February 8, 1942, Hitler's protégé Albert Speer took the post of Minister of Armaments and War Production. Thanks to Hitler's support he became one of key personalities in the Third Reich.

After some time of preparation, he made profound reforms of armaments production and gave it preference over many other tasks within the German economy. Expansion of war production required increase of labor force, which was, generally, in low supply. These changes touched also the General Government, where many new factories producing arms and munitions were established and the existing plants were enlarged. In parallel, however, since the spring of 1942 *Aktion Reinhardt* began, in the wake of which hundred thousands of Jews, including able-bodied men, women, and children were sent to death. These conflicting processes, when shortages of labor force existed, on the one hand, and on the other, thousands of potential workers were exterminated, naturally created tension between the SS and the Wehrmacht. In fact, in late summer and autumn many meetings took place and both sides exchanged much correspondence. In the end, a compromise was reached, which was more or less maintained.

In the wake of total destruction, labor assumed a new meaning and became a synonym for life. Unemployment became a synonym for death. Only relatively small percentage of Jews could escape and find a shelter permitting them to hide until the end of the war. In that situation, Jews searched for any employment and were ready to pay in various ways in order to get work certificates. About this phenomenon Katzmann wrote in his report:

> Owing to the peculiarity that almost 90 percent of the artisans in Galicia consisted of Jews, the solution of our problem could only be carried out gradually, as an immediate removal of the Jews would not have been in the interest of the war economy. Not that one could observe that those Jews who were working made any special contribution by their work. Their place of work was often only a means to an end for them: firstly, to escape the sharper measures taken against the Jews; and, secondly, to be able to carry out their black-market dealings without interruption. Only continuous police intervention could prevent these activities.[13]

In this report from 1943, Katzmann did not spare contemptuous words concerning German firms engaged in war production. At the same time, he tried to give himself more importance, not only elevating his deeds but also boasting of the moral values of his criminal police who used draconian

---

13   From the final report by Katzmann, commander of the SS and police in the district of Galcia, on "The Final Solution of the Jewish Problem" in Galicia (L-18), in Arad and Gutman, *Documents on the Holocaust*, 337.

measures to combat Jewish bribery. However, the most important was his final statement: "There were known cases where Jews seeking to obtain some kind of working certificate not only did not ask for pay from their employers but paid regularly themselves."[14] Thus, we can observe apparently absurd situation when Jews are ready not only to give up the payment for their work but to pay to the employer for their employment.

Raul Hilberg wrote in his book about the will of the Jews to survive at any price:

> The Jews, on their part, sensed what the new arrangement had in store for them. There was no hope for anyone who could not work. Only the best and strongest workers, 'the Maccabees,' as Krüger called them,[15] had a chance to live. All others had to die. There was not even room in the SS-army agreement for dependents. Survival had become synonymous with work. The Jews were grasping labor certificates as a drowning man grasps a straw. How deeply this labor survival psychology had penetrated into the Jewish community is illustrated by a small incident observed by a Pole. In 1943, when an SS officer (*Sturmbannführer* Reinecke) seized a three-year-old Jewish girl in order to deport her to a killing center, she pleaded for her life by showing him her hands and explaining that she could work. In vain.[16]

On the other hand, relatively free Jews in labor camps were gradually enslaved. Many of those Jews who initially escaped *Aktion*, facing lack of possibilities of finding shelter and assistance outside ghettos, returned to small ghettos and infiltrated labor camps in order to survive.[17] Over time, when smaller camps were liquidated, their inmates were transferred to bigger labor camps and concentration camps. Since summer 1942 a new category of camps appears: company camps (*Firmenlager*). Jewish laborers were sent from the ghettos to SS labor camps (*SS Arbeitslager*) and to company camps (*Firmenlager*). It is important to remember that since the beginning of *Aktion Reinhardt*, the SS again took over all the matters concerning the Jews. The *Arbeitsämter* again lost their competences regarding the management of the Jewish labor force. The SS

---

14 Ibid.
15 Krüger's remarks at conference (May 31, 1943) (PS-2233).
16 Hilberg, *The Destruction of the European Jews*, 529.
17 Calel Perechodnik, Spowiedź: *Dzieje rodziny żydowskiej podczas okupacji hitlerowskiej w Polsce* (Warsaw: Ośrodek Karta, 2004).

attempted to establish their own enterprises in the camps (DAW, OSTI), but they did not have much success. However, the SS became the only dispatcher of the Jewish labor force, while many armament industries in the General Government urgently needed Jewish workers. Therefore, the SS supplied workers from ghettos and SS camps to armament companies. All Jews who had left the ghettos were labor prisoners of the SS. This became a very profitable enterprise because the SS and not the state—in this case the government and the treasury of the General Government—became the exclusive dispatcher and proprietor of Jewish labor force. The employers had to pay wages to the SS and police at the agreed rates of 5 zł per each man and 4 zł per each woman minus 1.6 zł for food. The Jews themselves did not receive any wages, becoming de facto "slaves" of the SS. As slaves and not prisoners (*Häftlinge*), they practically did not have any rights. Certainly, they did not have the right to live and their existence depended exclusively on their utility for the SS and the factories. It is important to underline that although armament firms maintained the workers, the only thing important for them was the number of workers. When the workers could be supplied, they had value for the firms; but at any moment, they could be substituted out for others. What counted was their number.[18]

LABOR CAMPS

Labor camps, since the beginning of their establishment in the spring of 1940, were supposed to provide a Jewish labor force for various infrastructure projects that were launched in the General Government: mainly road construction, bridges, railways, queries, regulation of rivers, melioration works, and others. These camps were established by various organizations, including the SS and civil administration on different levels. Local administration also established labor camps at agriculture estates. However, since the very beginning, labor camps became a symbol of persecution due to the appalling conditions in most of the camps. Yet, we should ask why it happened. Was it a general policy of persecution and destruction, or was it a result of other factors? On the basis of this research we may claim that hard conditions in most of the labor camps resulted from lack of proper organization and control by the higher authorities, which permitted many cases of corruption and exploitation of workers. The main goal of those institutions and the firms performing the works for which the camps were created was to complete the works, without proper care about the workers.

---

18   Karay, *Death Comes in Yellow*.

The whole process of mobilization to the labor camps was chaotic and disorganized. Due to bad living and labor condition in the camps, most of the Jews did not want to be sent there. By default, those who found themselves in the camps were poor, physically week, destitute, not adapted to hard work. Naturally, those people in the camps quickly became weaker, sick, and unable to work, as they did not receive any acceptable living conditions, proper tools, clothes, and shoes. Therefore, the performance of those workers was rather poor. Moreover, due to complex organization, when the responsibility for providing food, money, and clothes fell on the *Judenräte*, while private firms were responsible for the works, and the coordinating authority was distant enough, with the rationing or food and other goods, the result was the suffering of workers. However, in the atmosphere of racial policy and propaganda, the Jews had very limited possibilities to complain. It would be difficult to argue that at this early stage of the war, the policy of extermination through labor was already employed. The experience of Jews in those camps could be comparable to concentration camps, which also witnessed periods of better or worse treatment of prisoners.

The number of early camps were reduced during 1942; though, some of them continued to exist. The reason for this reduction was not only poor performance, but also, the limitation of infrastructure works after 1942. At the beginning of the occupation, the German authorities in the General Government had grandiose plans of building or rebuilding the infrastructure, rebuilding the the cities, and constructing new settlements for ethnic Germans. However, after the period of intensive construction as part of the Otto Program, which was supposed to prepare the infrastructure for the invasion against the Soviet Union, and extensive plans of modernizing agriculture, in order to produce more crops with intensive cultivation, those plans became obsolete due to the lack of a labor force and resources, which were directed towards war production.

A new type of camp was created in the summer of 1942, when the armament program, which recognized the urgent need for more workers, was launched by Speer,. The General Government had numerous armament factories, mainly in the District of Radom, Warsaw, and the District of Kraków, and the supply of Polish workers was so insufficient that camps opened near the factories where Jews became inmates. The possibilities of mobilization of Polish workers were reduced because about 500,000 of Polish POWs were already in Germany, many young men and Polish soldiers found themselves in the territory occupied by the Soviets, dozens of thousands of men perished during the war, and a significant number were handicapped. Moreover, from 1939 onward, thousands of Polish men and women were constantly mobilized and sent to work in the Reich. At the same time, in the summer of 1942, thousands of Jews were sent to the death camps. Going to work in factory labor camps was an option to remain alive. However, even in 1942, new camps and labor detachments were created in the district of Kraków. In the district of Warsaw, the Jews from the western parts of the district were transferred in 1940 to the Warsaw Ghetto; and many Jews from Warsaw were dispersed in various labor camps in the district of Lublin and Warsaw. Staying in factory labor camps also had some advantages, despite hard living and working conditions. These camps had fewer selections than regular SS camps.[19] The latter ones were constantly reduced, and the Jews were concentrated in larger camps according to Himmler's decree of July 19, 1942. The transfer of Warsaw Jews, mainly to the labor camps of Poniatowa and Trawniki, began in early 1943. Some became employed at the plants of Schulz and Többens in those camps. The others were employed at the short-lived enterprises of the SS, DAW and OSTI. However, after the rebellion of Jews in Sobibór death camp on October 14, 1943, Himmler decided to murder all the Jews in the district of Lublin. One of the consequences of the murder of about 42,000 Jews was the closing of camps factories of Schulz and Többens in Poniatowa and Trawniki and the liquidation of OSTI. For the time being, Jews in the district of Radom employed at factory camps, among them HASAG, and some other labor camps in the district of Kraków were saved. It is important to mention that from 1942 onward, all the Jews in the General Government became the property of the SS and every institution employing Jewish labor force had to pay the SS for using the Jews and spend a certain sum on their maintenance. The SS, even if they failed in their economic activity, still profited without any effort. The last chapter of the existence of labor camps in the General Government began in 1943. As Raul Hilberg put it:

> The SS camps were originally under the jurisdiction of the SS and Police Leaders, but starting in October 1943 and continuing in 1944, a series of transfers took place in the course of which the camps were taken over by the SS Economic-Administrative Main Office (WVHA), i.e., the agency that controlled the concentration camps. At heretofore undisputed territorial and functional control of the camps by the SS and Police Leaders was now reduced to a purely territorial (disciplinary) jurisdiction. The new master was the WVHA.[20]

---

19 Hilberg, *The Destruction of the European Jews*, 531.
20 Ibid., 532.

JEWS IN THE FACE OF PERSECUTION AND EXTERMINATION

Jews living under the rule of the General Government since the beginning of the occupation were subjected to persecution and looting. Their attitude, however, was never passive, as it frequently appears in the historiography and in the sources. It is frequently repeated that the Jews went to death like sheep to the slaughter. On the basis of this book, I would argue that the Jews were very active from the beginning of the persecutions until the end. They not only reacted in face of the persecution but frequently initiated processes in order to protect themselves and survive. Until the beginning of the *Aktion Reinhardt* in spring 1942, the first and foremost problem was finding means of subsistence. Destruction of economic links, closing of businesses, unemployment, and restrictions of bank accounts (or simply robbery) brought great economic losses to the Jews. Many were transferred or deported. Therefore, only a part of them could use their movable property or even real estate in order to cover their current expenses. For many of them, the one and only solution was work. Avoiding conscription to forced labor, especially in the labor camps, was only a means of protection from exhausting work, which in many cases could hardly provide food for them and their families. Quickly enough, the Jews began to establish workshops and various enterprises under the aegis of the *Judenräte*. However, during the first years of the occupation there was predominant policy of destitution and elimination of the Jews from the economy of the General Government, using them to perform forced labor, frequently without any payment, and pushing them to the margin. In larger ghettos, Jews died of starvation. As a rule, nearly all of them suffered hunger. The situation begun to change only in early 1941 and was improving constantly until the spring of 1942, when *Aktion Reinhardt* begun. The economic considerations were initially not important to the SS. However, during the summer of 1942 the Jews understood that the only possibility of survival was labor. The drive of the Jews to work for the enemy was met by Polish and German entrepreneurs, willing to do business in the General Government, butduring the liquidation of the ghettos in summer 1942, the *Judenräte* were either liquidated or lost their authority. Only few *Judenräte*, which acted as regional umbrella organizations extending their powers on the whole region (like the *Judenrat* in Lublin, Kraków, or Radom), remained. Those *Judenräte* were replaced with the Jewish Self-Assistance (ŻSS in Polish or JUS in German). This was the official self-assistance organization, acting in the framework of the Central Welfare Council (RGO) and having close contacts with the Department of Internal Affairs, Group Population, and

Welfare (BuF). The presidency of the Jewish Self-Assistance sent a number of circular letters asking for data on Jewish workers and prompted the establishment of so-called labor communities in all towns. Despite limited possibilities, the Jewish Self-Assistance made great efforts in order to improve the condition of Jewish workers in the labor camps and frequently proved to be effective, probably thanks to support from the BuF. Those efforts were important on the micro level, but proved to be absolutely ineffective while speaking about the possibilities to save the Jews as a whole from destruction.

JEWS IN THE ARMAMENT INDUSTRY

The Jews were employed in the armament industry at various stages of the war. From this example we may observe the constant struggle between the two most important factors in Nazi Germany: the SS and the Wehrmacht. This struggle over Jewish forced labor depended on changing policy towards the Jews. Various actions were considered: deportations, extermination, prohibition of employment, but also preservation of the Jews due to acute shortages of labor force permitting, and much else. One of the first examples of this struggle is presented in following quotation. It was a telegram dispatched by one of firms employing the Jews to the army on October 14, 1941:

> As a matter of common knowledge, there is now proceeding a new deportation of Jews that affects our Jewish workers who have been arduously trained to become specialists. They have been broken in as electro-welders and zinc-plating experts, and their removal would entail a reduction of production, perhaps by a third. We are therefore telegraphing you in this matter. [...] We would be grateful if, aside from a lot of good advice, a positive contribution would be made for the preservation of our productive capacity, in that you obtain through the OKH a proper directive.
>
> Parenthetically, we should like to observe that these Jewish workers are the most capable and industrious of all, because they are after all the only ones who risk something if their output is not satisfactory, and they are actually achieving such records that one could almost compare the productivity of a Jew with that of two Aryan specialists. For the rest, we can only repeat with emphasis that we do not need, after all, these iron casks for ourselves but that the Wehrmacht needs them, so that it is the business of these agencies to repress such—in our opinion not quite purposeful—ordinances. [...T]he unrest among the Jewish workers is naturally

considerable, since the deportation to Poland without any means of subsistence is more or less equivalent to a quick and certain doom and, under such auspices, their productivity must naturally decline measurably.[21]

Economic considerations did not prevent the deportation of German and Austrian Jews to the east. In the fall of 1942, Hitler himself ordered that the Jews be removed from the armament industry.[22] However, the problem of replacing the Jews in the plants was not solved until the Reich Security Main Office conceived the idea of replacement. Since the Jews could not work in the armament industry, they could be replaced by Polish workers brought to Germany. According to Hilberg:

> The Reich Security Main Office submitted this plan to the official who had overall responsibility for labor recruitment and the labor supply: the plenipotentiary for Labor commitment in the office of the Four-Year Plan, Gauleiter Sauckel. Armed with the RSHA proposal, which seemed reasonable to him, Sauckel ordered the regional labor offices to prepare for a shuttle system of deportations: Jews out, Poles in. Jews performing menial work could be deported as soon as their Polish replacements-arrived. Skilled Jewish workers could be deported as soon as the Polish laborers familiarized themselves with the work.[23]

As a consequence of this order, tens of thousands of Jews were deported to killing centers in 1943.[24] However, the Jews were not the only group, which could not be employed in the armament industry, at least at the beginning of the war. The Soviet POWs were also forbidden to be employed in armament plants. Despite shortages of labor force felt already in 1941, the Soviet POWs

---

21 OKH/Chef HRüst. u. BdE (Replacement Army)/Wa Amt (Weapons Office) to OKW/Wi Rü–Rü V October 22, 1941, enclosing letter by Brunner Verzinkerei/Brüder Boblick (Vienna) to Dr. G. von Hirschfeld (Berlin W62), October 14, 1941, Wi/ID.415, in Hilberg, *The Destruction of the European Jews*, 440.
22 Testimony by Speer, *Trial of the Major War Ciminals*, vol. 16 (Nuremberg: n.p., 1948), 519. According to Speer, many Jews were then employed in the electrical industry (AEG and Siemens). Speer and Labor Plenipotentiary Sauckel attended the conference during which Hitler gave the order.
23 Sauckel to regional labor offices, November 26, 1942, L-61. The RSHA plan is summarized in the Sauckel's directive. Hilberg, *The Destruction of the European Jews*, 442.
24 See letter by Sauckel to the regional labor offices, inquiring how they were getting along without their Jews, March 26, 1943, L-15. Hilberg, *The Destruction of the European Jews*, 442

died en masse in the winter of 1941 and 1942. The labor replacement theory conceived by RSHA had, though, one weak point. According to Hilberg:

> the Reich had an absolute labor shortage. If all available foreign laborers, prisoners of war, and concentration camp inmates had been added to the Jewish labor force, the labor gap could still not have been filled. It is true that the labor supply increased with German conquests in the West and East, but it is also true that with the great industrial expansion of the 1940s the demand for labor increased faster than the supply. If Jews were "replaced" in one plant, the only result was that another plant, which needed laborers to expand production, went short. It is therefore not surprising that industrial firms clamored for increasing allocations of skilled workers and heavy laborers. The clamor began in 1940 and grew more insistent in 1941 and 1942.[25]

Until 1942, Jews had been employed mainly in ghetto workshops and construction projects in labor camps, but, beginning from 1942, due to shortages of labor force, Jews had to be employed in war industry, including aircraft plants, munitions works, and the steel industry. This replacement program was just getting under way when the SS and police liquidated the ghettos and deported the Jews to the death camps. The army found itself in the impossible position of trying to replace the Poles departing to Germany with the disappearing Jews. Ironically enough, some of the Poles were replacing Jewish workers deported from Germany to the east. This was quite a chaotic situation, as the Wehrmacht tried to maintain the armament production on the highest level and fight on the fronts, while the SS was pursuing its ideological goals, and at the same time sabotaging the war effort of the Wehrmacht.

The labor situation in the General Government was very serious, because of the constant pressure from the part of Sauckel to provide more and more workers to Germany. At the same time, the armament industry and the economy of the General Government had also to realize its own goals, among them maintaining high level of war production, exporting food to Germany, providing accomodations to German troops based in Poland, and maintaining the German administration and police apparatus. Therefore, the biggest struggle over a remnant of thousands of skilled Jewish workers took place. Among the participants in this struggle were the civil administration,

---

25 Hilberg, *The Destruction of the European Jews*, 443.

the *Ostbahn*, private firms under contract to the military commander or the Armament Inspectorate, and the SS itself— all of them were making use of Jewish labor in various business ventures. Among the offices attempting to preserve irreplaceable Jewish workers, who were regularly sent into the killing centers, were the military commander, General von Gienanth, and the armament inspector, General Schindler.

Already in July 1942, Schindler came to an understanding with Krüger, according to which Jewish workers in armament enterprises were to be held in plant barracks and the SS labor camps in order to continue production. On July 19, 1942 Himmler accepted the agreement; the same day, though, he ordered the resettlement of the entire Jewish population in the General Government to be carried out and completed by December 31, 1942. According to his order, no people of Jewish origin could remain within the territory of the General Government except for the collection camps in Warsaw, Kraków, Częstochowa, Radom, and Lublin. "All other work in which Jewish labor is employed must be finished by that date or, in the event that this is not possible, it must be transferred to one of the collection camps."[26] These measures, according to Himmler, "were necessary for the new order in Europe as well as for the 'security and cleanliness' of the German Reich and its spheres of interest. Every violation of this regulation would endanger peace and order and would create in Europe 'the germ of a resistance movement and a moral and physical center of pestilence.'"[27]

According to Raul Hilberg:

> The military offices soon found out that Himmler's concessions were even more restrictive than they appeared to be in the agreed stipulations. The army had not protected its own installations. An army supply depot, loading cattle and flour for the front, lost half of its Jewish labor force overnight even while empty freight cars were waiting on the sidings.[28]

---

26 Order by Himmler on July 19, 1941 for the completion of the "Final Solution" in the Government-General (NO-5574), in Arad and Gutman, *Documents on the Holocaust*, 275.
27 Himmler to Krüger, July 19, 1942, NO-5574.
28 Militarbefehlshaber im GG/oQu via oFK Krakau to vo/Mic, August 5, 1942, Polen 7502219a. See also incident at Przemysl on July 26, 1942, during which army personnel were actually shooting at police taking away their Jewish workers. Report by KdS Kraków / Grenzpolizeikommissariat Przemyśl (signed Benthin) July 27, 1942, Israel Police, 1113; Grenzpolizeikommissariat to OKW Kommission, August 23, 1942, Israel Police, 1114; Himmler to Bormann, October 3, 1942, Israel Police, 1155. The episode infuriated Himmler.

Also he writes:

> Soon another, more serious omission was felt. The generals discovered that their understanding with Krüger covered only a part of the armament industry, the so-called *Rüstungsbetriebe*, or armament plants under contract with the Armament Inspectorate. Apparently, the agreement did not cover armament enterprises that were filling orders placed directly by agencies in the Reich or by the myriads of small repair shops and finishing plants that were under contract with the military commander (*Wehrkreisbefehlshaber im Generalgouvernement*).[29]

The struggle with the Wehrmacht over Jewish labor force had also its impact on Himmler and the SS when he decided to develop his own business on the field of armament production. Since the SS had no knowledge and experience in the real armament industry, they developed enterprises that principally manufactured uniforms. In the case of armament production, the SS was in charge of labor supply. This was arranged by establishment of labor camps. As said above, the payment was made to the SS and not to the workers. In order to make the final arrangement on October 14 and 15, 1942, Oberst Forster, the *Oberquartiermeister* of the military commander in the General Government, met with Krüger to explain several contentious issues. The new agreement also covered the firms operating under contract with the army (i. e., the Armament Inspectorate or the *Wehrkreisbefehlshaber*), and not only the armament industry plants.

The most important thing, however, was the arrangement to undertake the reduction of the Jewish labor force only after mutual consultation, and no disturbance of production was to be expected. In addition, for the first time, the SS was to be paid for camp labor at a daily rate.[30] It has to be underlined that Krüger was much more ready to make concessions and reach an agreement than Himmler. The October 1942 agreement was a last-minute arrangement to save the Jewish labor force for military needs, but this agreement did not concern civilian firms, the *Ostbahn*, or civil administration enterprises. Jews were withdrawn from projects and plants outside the scope of the written agreement with the Armament Inspectorate.

---

29 Hilberg, *The Destruction of the European Jews*, 526.
30 Ibid., 528.

The effects of the deportations were consequently felt everywhere except in the narrowly defined armament industry. Even there the Jews were to remain only temporarily. On December 9, 1942, Frank said during a conference:

> We can tell the agencies of the Reich that the taking away of the Jews has led to tremendous difficulties in the labor field [...] a large construction project in the *Generalgouvernement* had come to a standstill; that would not have happened if the many thousands of Jews who were employed there had not been taken away. Now the order provides that the armament Jews also are to be taken away. I hope that this order if not already voided, will be revoked, because then the situation will be even worse.[31]

Himmler's order of July 19, 1942 for the deportation of nonproductive Jews in the General Government by the end of 1942 could not be executed. In December 1942, there were still about 300,000 Jews in the General Government itself. From the small ghettos of the General Government, the SS and police selected the strongest and the best-trained workers to preserve them as forced labor reservoir that lasted for about two years. Many firms not included in the agreement between the Armament Inspectorate and the SS also attempted, however, to preserve their Jewish labor force. According to Katzmann's report of July 1943: "When Jews were arrested in the course of further checks, most of the employers felt obliged to attempt to intervene in favor of the Jews. This was often done in a manner that can only be described as deeply shameful."[32] As Himmler write in the letter of October 9, 1942:

> Jews in real war industries, i.e., armament workshops, etc. are to be withdrawn step by step. As a first stage they are to be concentrated in separate halls in the factories. In a second stage in this procedure the work teams in these separate halls will be combined so that we will then have simply a few closed concentration camp industries in the General Government. Our endeavor will be to replace this Jewish labor force with Poles and to

---

31 Frank's remarks at the General Government conference (December 9, 1942), in *Hans Frank's Diary* (PS-2233).
32 From the final report by Katzmann, commander of the SS and police in the district of Galcia, on "The Final Solution of the Jewish Problem" in Galicia (L-18), in Arad and Gutman, *Documents on the Holocaust*, 338.

consolidate most of these Jewish concentration camp enterprises-in the Eastern part of the General Government, if possible. But there, too, in accordance with the Führer wish, the Jews are some day to disappear.[33]

By saying that the Jews would be consolidated in concentration camp enterprises-in the Eastern part of the General Government, Himmler meant his ambitious plans to establish the SS-owned enterprises exploiting Jewish labor force, among the Deutsche Wirtschaftsbetriebe (DWB), DAW, and Ostindustrie GmbH (OSTI). The latter company had been set up by Globocnik according to Pohl's and Himmler's directives. Those newly established SS workshops would be financed by the assets of the victims murdered in the *Aktion Reinhardt*.

In the meantime, within the framework of the *Aktion Reinhardt*, thousands of Jews who were able to work were sent to death. In order to illustrate this murderous mentality of the SSPF, brutally liquidating thousands of Jews willing to work and to save themselves, we bring a quotation from Katzmann's report July 1943, where he presents himself as a kind of "savior." He wrote:

> As the [civil] administration was not in the 'position' to overcome this chaos, and proved weak, the whole issue of Jewish labor was simply taken over by the SSPF [Katzmann]. The existing Jewish Labor Offices, which were staffed by hundreds of Jews, were dissolved. All work certificates issued by firms and official employers were declared invalid, and the cards given to Jew by the Labor Offices revalidated by the Police.[34]

Obviously, his goal was to murder all the Jews in his district, without any reflection or consideration. He presented himself as a man abiding the law and pursuing forgery. He still regarded the Jews, even when they were willing to work, according to his ideological clichés, as fraudulent parasites, nothing more. He permitted himself also to criticize the Wehrmacht, which struggled for the survival of the state, while he continued to perform his murderous tasks on the rear. He continued:

> In the course of this *Aktion* thousands of Jews were again caught in possession of forged certificates or labor certificate: obtained fraudulently

---

33 Friedländer, *The Years of Extermination*, 495–96.
34 From the final report by Katzmann, commander of the SS and police in the district of Galcia, on "The Final Solution of the Jewish Problem" in Galicia (L-18), in Arad and Gutman, *Documents on the Holocaust*, 338.

by means of all kinds of excuses. These Jews were also sent for special treatment (*Sonderbehandlung*). The Wehrmacht authorities in particular aided the Jewish parasites by issuing special certificates without proper control.[35]

With the establishment of the SS enterprises like OSTI, Himmler's ideological conviction in total extermination of forced labor became somewhat shaky. According to Hilberg:

> The SS industries in the General Government were organized in a typical fashion, and their short life is an ironic postscript to the history of Polish Jewry under the Nazis, for in these enterprises Himmler himself attempted at the last moment to slow down the deportations—to hold up the works, as it were—and to make some profits. Originally, SS enterprises had been set up in the concentration camps with a view to exploiting the cheap inmate labor supply. Now that the end phase of the Polish deportations had arrived, one of the SS firms, *Deutsche Ausrüstungswerke* (DAW), emerged from the concentration camps and stretched out its arms for a share of the surviving labor force.[36]

Although on October 3, 1943 Himmler still glorified the extermination conducted by the SS, it seems that already then, he was himself not convinced about the truth of his own words.[37] About ten days later, on October 14, 1943, a mutiny at Sobibór took place, during which several SS men and some Hiwi guards were killed, the death camp burned down, and about 300 men escaped from the camp. Himmler's reaction was imminent. To prevent further rebellions he ordered the execution of all the Jews in the district of Lublin. Ironically enough, he murdered the Jews who were employed in his enterprises as well as in factories inside the camps of Poniatowa and Trawniki, which brought about liquidation of those enterprises. For the time being, the Jews employed at the armament industry and various camps in the district of Kraków were saved.

Like Himmler, Goebbels also dreamed about a *judenfrei* Germany. He wrote in his diary: "When Berlin is free of Jews, I shall have completed

---

35 Ibid.
36 Hilberg, *The Destruction of the European Jews*, 532–33.
37 From a speech by Himmler before senior SS officers in Poznań, October 3, 1943 (PS-1919), in Arad and Gutman, *Documents on the Holocaust*, 344–45.

one of my greatest political achievements."[38] However, according to Saul Friedländer:

> German policies regarding the fate of the remaining Jews became increasingly inconsistent. On the one hand, Hitler himself and part of the SS apparatus directly involved in the implementation of the "Final Solution" did not waver to the very end in the policy of extermination, although it was delayed at times by last-minute need for slave labor. In fact, in early 1944 already, Hitler had been ready to compromise regarding the presence of Jewish slave laborers on German soil. Speer confirmed, in a memorandum dated April 1944, that the Nazi leader authorized the use of 100,000 Hungarian Jews in urgent building projects for munitions factories to be located in the Protectorate. In late 1944, Himmler's hesitant search for a way out becomes apparent. It seems that at some stage the Reichsführer countermanded the steps taken by his underlings (and approved by his master) to pursue the "Final Solution," but was unable to sustain this alternative, afraid as he was of Hitler's reaction. Nonetheless, from early 1945 on, in order to find an opening to the west, Himmler was ready to give up some small groups of Jews to prove his goodwill.[39]

Already since 1943, every possible effort was made in order to hide the mass murder of civil population by the Nazi regime, since the corpses constituted proof. To hide that proof was the main task of Kommando 1005, created especially for the purpose of opening burial pits and burning corpses of mass murder victims. Therefore, Himmler gave the order for the complete evacuation of all the camps in the east which, according to several testimonies, included ominous warning to the camp commanders: "The Führer holds you personally responsible for [...] making sure that not a single prisoner from the concentration camps falls alive into the hands of the enemy."[40] As Friedländer writes,

> ... in a basic directive that had already been issued in July 1944, [Richard] Glücks had stated clearly that in an 'emergency situation' (evacuation) the camp commanders were to follow the directives of the regional HSSPFs.

---

38 Entry of April 19, 1943, in Louis Lochner, trans. and ed., *The Goebbels Diaries 1942–1943* (Garden City: Doubleday, 1948), 335.
39 Friedländer, *The Years of Extermination*, 646.
40 Ibid., 648.

In other words, nobody seemed to know who was in charge of the evacuations. But in the rapidly increasing chaos, the marches westward started.[41]

During the marches approximately 250,000 of these Jewish prisoners perished from exhaustion, freezing, shooting, or being burned alive.[42]

EXTERMINATION THROUGH LABOR (*VERNICHTUNG DURCH ARBEIT*)

Among the historians researching problems of forced labor and exploitation of laborers during the Nazi period, some present the thesis of "extermination through labor" (*Vernichtung durch Arbeit*), which, according to their arguments, was one of the methods of extermination of Jews and other unwanted groups of people. As we know today, the conditions reigning in labor camps in the General Government, as well as in other areas, led to the quick destruction of laborers who got sick, injured, starved, and then died. I argue that this was not the initial purpose of those labor camps and, in fact, bad conditions were only a consequence of lack of proper organization, control, shortages of food, and clothes. However, as already discussed above, many SS labor camps became places of physical destruction of workers, as it was in the case of Bełżec complex. In those camps the conditions were much worse than in civil administration camps due to the profile of the personnel. Most of the SS men were trained and indoctrinated in the spirit of persecution of Jews. Many among the staff went through education in concentration camps. Moreover, the staff of those camps was subordinated to the SSPF in the district and received his full support. The exploitation of Jewish workers in the camps of Bełżec complex caused conflicts between the SS and the civil authorities who had to take care of laborers unable to work.

Still, we cannot deny that there were plans to exterminate Jews and other groups through hard labor and weather hardships. In part, it remained the long-term plan. The *Generalplan Ost* provided that in the future, millions of people would be transferred to the east and forced to work there in labor camps:

> According to Heydrich's reference to the decimation of the Jews by way of forced labor, particularly in road building in the East, has for years been regarded as code language designating mass murder. It is likely, however, that

---

41 Ibid.
42 Ibid.

at this stage (and of course only in regard to Jews capable of working) the RSHA chief meant what he said: "Able-bodied Jews would first be exploited as slave labor given the escalating manpower needs of the German war economy." "Road building" was probably an example of slave labor in general; it may also have been a reference to the building of Durchgangstrasse IV, in which, as we saw, Jewish slave laborers were already used en masse and where they also perished en masse. Moreover, either at the end of 1941 or in early January 1942, Hitler ordered the use of Jewish slave labor for the building of roads in the northern part of the occupied Soviet Union.[43]

In another occasion on February 2, 1942 Heydrich said:

> ... when we further open up the area of the Arctic Sea (*Eismeer*), where we will take over the concentration camps of the Russians, which according to our present knowledge hold some 15–20 million deported inmates and which could become the ideal homeland for the 11 million European Jews.

According to Saul Friedländer: "In any case, as Heydrich made amply clear at Wannsee, none of the working Jews would eventually survive."[44]

What Heydrich presented as a plan, the Wehrmacht already put into practice beginning in the summer of 1941. According to the Wermacht's *Hungerplan*, many Soviet citizens were to die in order to free up the food resources for the German army. According to Wolfgang Benz: "In the camps of the General everyday died from 3.000 to 4.000 [Soviet] prisoners [of war]."[45] An unknown number of Soviet citizens died of starvation. Thus, the fantasy of Heydrich was not so distant from reality. This was not the case, however, of the labor camps in the General Government. Even the camps such as the HASAG camp in Skarżysko Kamienna, where many prisoners were employed for production of explosives (and eventually died of exhaustion, exposure to chemical substances, or lack of proper nourishment), death was not the purpose. The prisoners died because the management was interested in profit and output, and death was rather a by-product. According to Friedländer:

> The German concentration and extermination camp system was geared to send its Jewish victims either to immediate extermination or to slave labor

---

43 Ibid., 342.
44 Ibid., 343.
45 Benz, "Zwangsarbeit im nationalsozialistischen Staat," 6.

that would end in extermination after a short time. Yet some of the smaller labor camps attached to enterprises working for the armaments industry, whether under control of the SS or not, sometimes kept their Jewish slaves alive for longer stretches of time, either due to essential production imperatives or (and) for the personal benefit of local commander.[46]

Over time, however, when shortages of the labor force became more and more acute, mobilization of workers in general also became more aggressive. The gauleiter of Thuringia, who was appointed plenipotentiary for employment of labor in March 1942, understood his duties as follows: "I have received my order from Adolf Hitler, and I will bring the millions of *Ostarbeiter* to Germany regardless of their feelings, whether they want it or not."[47] Prisoners in the SS camps died, however, not only because of the condition but because of their treatment by the staff. SS-*Oberscharführer* Josef Schwammberger, who from October 1941 was a staff member of the SSPF in the Kraków District, SS-*Oberführer* Julian Scherner, once said to the prisoners: "I am your God. When I say you live, then you live, and when I say you're dead, then you die. (*Ich bin euer Gott. Wen ich sage Du lebst, dann lebst Du, und wenn ich sage Du bist tot, dann stirbst Du.*)"[48] Deterioration of conditions in the last stages of war took place independently of the plans to exterminate the labor force. For example, "OT rapidly proved itself equal to the SS in its mistreatment of the slave laborers, and by the fall of 1944, hundreds had been killed or were too weak to continue working."[49]

During the last stages of war, thousands of prisoners died in many construction projects: in the construction of Durchgangstrasse IV,[50] in Mittelbau-Dora, Gross Rosen, Neuengamme,[51] and other camps. However, even then, performance was the goal—finishing projects of underground armament factories and other enterprises on time. It was a race against time, and the result was either a complete

---

46 Friedländer, *The Years of Extermination*, 582.
47 Benz, "Zwangsarbeit im nationalsozialistischen Staat," 7.
48 Mario Wenzel, "Ausbeutung und Vernichtung: Zwangsarbeitslager für Juden im Distrikt Krakau 1942–1944," *Dachauer Hefte* 23 (2007): 199.
49 Friedländer, *The Years of Extermination*, 646–47.
50 Manfred Grieger, "Extermination and Work under the Nazi System of Forced Labor," in *Forced Labor: The Germans, the Forced Laborers and the War*, ed. Volkhard Knigge et al. (Weimar: Stiftung Gedenkstätten Buchenwald u. Mittelbau-Dora, 2010), 209–12; Andrej Angerick, "Annihilation and Labor: Jews and Thoroughfare IV in Central Ukraine," in *The Shoah in Ukraine: History, Testimony, Memory*, ed. Ray Brandon and Wendy Lower (Bloomington: Indiana UP, 2008), 190–223.
51 Hermann Kaienburg, *"Vernichtung durch Arbeit": Der Fall Neuengamme* (Bonn: JHW Dietz, 1990).

defeat or, as it was often believed, victory. In a situation of struggle for survival, Nazi Germany was ready to sacrifice not only thousands of prisoners, but also thousands of its own citizens.

The central question of this book is whether labor could save life. Another question, which is closely linked to it, is this: if Jews were really so important for the war industry, why did the Nazis liquidate a great part of them in the General Government as well as in other territories? The General Government as an administrative unit, even if had some characteristics of an independent state (government, judicial system, custom border, and currency), was strongly dependent on the policy of the German Reich. In the wake of destruction, liquidation of the ghettos, and deportations of the productive Jews to the labor camps, to produce goods necessary for the German war industry seemed to be the only way leading to survival. Most Jews still living in 1942 could rightly think so. They already had a long experience of persecution, destitution, and Nazi propaganda that treated them as parasites. They correctly understood that only work could save life. After all, it was in line with the Nazi propaganda. If non-productive Jews were useless, then productive Jews could live. The Jews, as it was already proved, could contribute greatly to the Nazi war effort. Many of them were specialists in different fields of production; they had experience, capacity to learn fast, and were cheap and disposible. Apparently, they were perfect workers. Nevertheless, the SS, the organization carrying out such an absurd program of annihilation of the Jews—not only from a moral and human point of view, but also from an economic, strategic and logistical viewpoint—was finally able to almost fully realize that annihilation plan. The answer to those questions was already given above. However, it is important to sum it up.

According to Wolfgang Benz:

> The contestation between economic efficacy, important for the war efforts, and National Socialist racial politics constituted the pivotal problems connected to the employment of foreign workers in the Second World War. The recruiters categorically demanded maximal work performance, but their demands were not rationalized by any renouncement of racial principles. The improvement of living conditions of the *Ostarbeiter* in spring 1942, as ordered by Hitler, remained a single episode.[52]

The question of Jewish forced labor remained a subject of dispute almost until the war's end. On the one hand, there was consent of the leadership of the

---

52 Benz, "Zwangsarbeit im nationalsozialistischen Staat," 9.

Nazi state to exterminate, as it was Hitler's will until the end. On the other hand, there were "temporary" concessions to retain Jews in the armament industry and concentration camps. This temporariness eventually saved lives of many Jews, who survived until liberation. Those dilemmas could be also observed in the case of Hitler himself, who at the same time wanted to have Germany *judenrein* and also wished to preserve his county's force by means of the Wehrmacht, and for that purpose, needed supplies of war production. Thus, in 1944 approximately "100,000 Hungarian Jews were ordered by Hitler as slaves into the German Reich, which shortly before had been triumphantly reported *judenfrei*."[53] As time progressed, this divergence between wishes and reality became more and more visible. Moreover, Himmler, one of the leaders of the Nazi state and the main perpetrator of Nazi crimes, became shaky in his convictions at the end of the war. However, on the other side was Speer, who was intensively pursuing his goals of armament production, and for the sake of that production he was able to protect Jewish labor force in armament plants. We should in no way be mistaken and think that he protected Jews for moral reasons. In the case of the Mittelbau-Dora complex, for instance, thousands of Jews perished during the construction of underground factories. Speer had plans that were implemented without any other considerations. It seems plausible that he was not interested in protecting Jews and he surely did not want to ask Hitler to change his mind. Thus, among the military as well as within the industrial complex there was lack of willingness to raise ideological questions. Nobody wanted to admit openly their interest in protecting the Jews.

In the General Government, the situation was no less complex. However, on the ground the lines of divisions passed between many different authorities and no less frequently within the same institutions. The decisions to exterminate the Jews in the General Government came from above and was carried out by the staff of Globocnik and the other SSPFs. Most of them were willing executioners and they acted quite independently of the civil administration. In this case, Krüger's role is rather interesting. Although he could not compete with Himmler, he at least tried to have his own opinion and policy concerning the question of forced labor of the Jews. He was able to agree with the Armament Inspection on the preservation of Jewish labor force. It seems also that the independence of Globocnik, who received orders directly from Himmler, undermined his competences. On the other hand, he was in conflict with Frank, and that resulted in his removal from the post of the HSSPF in the General Government. Frank, who tried to imitate Hitler as the supreme leader of the

---

53 Ibid., 15.

General Government, was rather powerless and inconsistent. He expressed many times his wish to remove all the Jews from the General Government, but at least during the first years of his rule, he was constantly receiving hundreds of Jewish transports for the old Reich and from Warthegau. On the other hand, in December 1942 he expressed his regret that the Jews were removed and that he could not realize many important projects. Globocnik and Katzmann in their activity did not have any economic considerations and were willing executors of the "Final Solution."

The civil administration of the General Government, especially on the level of Main Offices and different divisions, sections, and agencies, was much more humane than the apparatus of the SS. The BuF subdivision in particular had close contacts with the Jewish Self-Assistance and were frequently efficient in helping the Jews. On the other hand, the private firms were quite powerless, and their wish to protect Jewish forced labor failed completely.

On the basis of my research, I argue that the thesis of extermination through labor is not fitting to the realities of the General Government, although there were cases of high death rate in labor camps. Forced labor was rather used in concentration camps and at the end of the war, first of all, to achieve certain economic goals and not in order to exterminate the prisoners. I would also like to recall that millions of Soviet POWs died in POW camps without doing any work, but rather because of the weather conditions, lack of housing and food. It is quite striking that the SS did not adapt this model of mass extermination. Contrarily, researchers like Götz Aly, Susanne Heim, and others argue that Jewish labor had no value to the Germans, and that the Jewish population in Poland was seen in terms of overpopulation, as a structural obstacle to modernization, so that there was a consensus from below to murder the Jews as an act of economic rationality.[54] This is not plausible, since the decisions concerning the "Final Solutions" came from above, and there is no direct link between high-level decision makers and low-level functionaries. There is nothing important that the high-ranking leaders did not know that the people on the ground knew. Frank and his entourage wanted to realize their grandiose plans and transform the General Government into a kind of exemplary state (*Musterstaat*). Naturally, they supported the idea of removing the Jews, but they preferred that this job was done by somebody else. Even so, the question of modernization

---

54 Aly, *Sozialpolitik und Judenvernichtung*; Aly and Heim, "The Economics of the Final Solution"; Aly and Heim, *Bevölkerungsstruktur und Massenmord*; Aly, *Endlösung: Völkerverschiebung und der Mord*; Aly and Heim, *Vordenker der Vernichtung*; Aly, "Final Solution."

and remodelling of the population using hard labor and bad living conditions was often raised, as seen in sending of thousands of Polish forced laborers into the Reich for the development of the war industry.

Wolf Gruner[55] and Christopher Browning,[56] among others, state that the Nazi policies toward Jewish labor varied according to time, place, and circumstances. Their approach is the most reasonable. While many Germans wanted to use Jewish labor productively, the others focused primarily on destruction. The Jews also found themselves facing those two options and tried to manoeuvre between them. For the Jews, labor was the key strategy for survival. Labor could save life, but only in some cases, and it was not a question of choice, but rather a question of fate. Those who were in the labor camps belonging to armament industry (and were lucky enough), survived, despite subsequent deportations and death marches. The others did not.

The state of affairs in the General Government mirrored the situation in Nazi Germany and the occupied territories. The General Government became one of the main battlefields of conflicted interests that intersected civil administration, the Wehrmacht, private enterprises, and institutions, such as the SS and police. Those institutions were predominantly interested in safeguarding their competencies and interests, and not in protecting the Jews. As long as the Jews were functional and profitable, they were preserved. Most Jews believed, as any rational people would, that labor could be an important factor in saving their lives. The fact that this belief did not manifest itself was determined by political actors, who self-destructively implemented Nazi convictions, even as they resulted in disastrous military and moral consequences.

---

55 Gruner, *Die Organisation von Zwangsarbeit*; Gruner, *Jewish forced labor under the Nazis*.
56 Browning, "Jewish Workers in Poland."

Abbreviations

AAN	Archiwum Akt Nowych
AG	Aktiengesellschaft
AIPN	Archiwum Instytutu Pamięci Narodowej
APL	Archiwum Państwowe w Lublinie (State Archives in Lublin)
AZS	Akademicki Związek Sportowy
AŻIH	Archiwum Żydowskiego Instytutu Historycznego
BA-MA	Bundesarchiv-Militärarchiv
BGKBZHP	Biuletyn Głównej Komisja Badania Zbrodni Hitlerowskich w Polsce
BGKBZpNP-IPN	Biuletyn Głównej Komisji Badania Zbrodni Przeciwko Narodowi Polskiemu Instytutu Pamięci Narodowej
BuF	Bevölkerung und Fürsorge
BŻIH	Biuletyn Żydowskiego Instytutu Historycznego
CdZ	Chef der Zivilverwaltung
CŻKH	Centralna Żydowska Komisja Historyczna
DAF	Deutsche Arbeitsfront
DAW	Deutsche Ausrüstungswerke
DWB	Deutsche Wirtschaftsbetriebe
EG	Einsatzgruppe
EK	Einsatzkommando
EVZ	Stiftung Erinnerung, Verantwortung und Zukunft (Foundation "Remembrance, Responsability and Future")
FPO	Fareinigte Partizaner Organizatsye
GBA	Generalbevollmächtigter
GG	Generalgouvernement (General Government)
GmbH	Gesellschaft mit beschränkter Haftung

GULAG	Glavnoye upravleniye lagerey i koloniy
HASAG	Hugo Schneider Aktiengesellschaft
HKP	Heereskraftpark
HSSPF	Höhere SS- und Polizeiführer
HTO	Haupttreuhandstelle Ost
IMT	International Military Tribunal, Nuremberg
IPN	Instytut Pamięci Narodowej
KZ	Konzentrationslager
MHMK	Muzeum Historyczne Miasta Krakowa
NKVD	Narodny Kommissariat Vnutriennych Diel
NSDAP	Nationalsozialistische Deutsche Arbeiterpartei
OFK	Oberfeldkommandantur
OKH	Oberkommando des Heeres
OKW	Oberkommando der Wehrmacht
ORT	Association of Propagation of Professional Work among the Jews
OSTI	Ostindustrie
OT	Organsation Todt
OUN	Organization of Ukrainian Nationalists
POW	Prisoners of War
RAD	Reichsarbeitsdienst
RKFDV	Reichskommissar für die Festigung deutschen Volkstums
RGBl	Reichsgesetzblatt
RSHA	Reichssicherheitshauptamt
RŻL	Rada Żydowska w Lublinie (The Jewish Council in Lublin)
SB	Służba Budowlana
SD	Sicherheistdienst
SS	Die Schutzstaffel der NSDAP
SSPF	SS- und Polizeiführer
TN	Technischa Nothilfe
UMCS	Uniwersytet Marii Curie-Skłodowskiej
USSR	Union of Soviet Socialist Republics
VBlGG	Verordnungsblatt des Generalgouvernements
VHB	Vereinigte Holz Betriebe
Wi Rü	Wirtschaft Rüstung
WVHA	Wirtschafts- und Verwaltungshauptamt
YVA	Yad Vashem Archives

ZOM	Zakład Oczyszczania Miasta
ŻIH	Żydowski Instytut Historyczny
ŻOB	Żydowska Organzacja Bojowa
ŻSS	Żydowska Samopomoc Społeczna
ŻZW	Żydowski Związek Wojskowy

Archival Sources

YAD VASHEM ARCHIVES (YVA)

Collections:

O.3	Yad Vashem testimonies
O.33	Diaries, memoirs, testimonies
O.6	Collection on Poland
M.49.E	Copy of testimonies from the Archives of the Jewish Historical Institute in Warsaw (collection 301)
M.49.P	Copy of diaries and memoirs from the Archives of the Jewish Historical Institute in Warsaw (collection 302)
M.54	Archives in Poland
TR.10	Investigation files from the Zentrale Stelle der Landesjustizverwaltungen in Ludwigsburg
TR.17	Investigation files from the Main Commssions for Investigation of Nazi Crimes in Poland (GKBZHP)

ARCHIVES OF THE INSTITUTE OF NATIONAL REMEMBRANCE IN POLAND—MAIN COMMISSION FOR THE INVESTIGATION OF CRIMES AGAINST THE POLISH NATION (AIPN)

Collections:

196	Najwyższy Trybunał Narodowy (NTN)—Trial of Ludwig Fischer
196	Najwyższy Trybunał Narodowy (NTN)—Trial of Josef Bühler
196	Najwyższy Trybunał Narodowy (NTN)—Trial of Arthur Greiser
891	Records of the SS and Polizeiführer in Distrikt Lublin
185	Records of the Kommandeur der Sicherheitspolizei und Sicherheitsdienst in Lublin.
184	Kommandeur der Sipo und des SD für den Distrikt Radom.

100	Records of the Amt des Distrikts Radom.
880	Records of the Generalgouvernment—Kraków.
113	Records of the Institut für Deutsche Ostarbeit, Kraków

ARCHIVES OF THE JEWISH HISTORICAL INSTITUTE (AŻIH)

Collections:

29	Podziemne Archiwum Getta Warszawskiego (Ringelblum Archives)
32	Zbiór dokumentów z obozów hitlerowskich 1939–1945
33	American Jewish Joint Distribution Committee (AJDS) 1940–1941
34	Żydowska Samopomoc Społeczna (Jüdische Soziale Selbsthilfe) 1940–1942
36	Rada Starszych w Częstochowie
54	Obwieszczenia i zarządzenia władz okupacyjnych
301	Testimonies
302	Diaries and Memoirs

THE STATE ARCHIVES IN LUBLIN (APL)

Collections:

891	The Jewish Council in Lublin (Rada Żydowska w Lublinie)
498	Urząd Okręgu Lubelskiego (Amt des Distrikts Lublin)
499	Starostwo Miejskie w Lublinie
510	Dowódca SS i Policju Okręgu Lubelskiego

ARCHIVES OF NEWS RECORDS (AAN)

Collections:

1335	Niemieckie władze okupacyjne, Zbiór akt

MILITARY ARCHIVES IN FREIBURG IM BREISGAU (BA-MA)

Collections:

RH53-23-27

RH53-23-56
RW5-150
RW5-699
RW23-2
RW23-5
RW23-7
RW23-8
RW23-14

INSTYTUT ZACHODNI W POZNANIU (IZ)

Collections:

Stadhaupt- und Kreishaupleute Lageberichte (copy YVA-JM, 814)

ARCHIVES OF THE CAPITAL CITY WARSAW (AMSTW)

Collections:

483	Przewodniczący Rady Żydowskiej w Warszawie
125	Der Kommissar für den jüdischen Wohnbezirk in Warschau (copy JM.1882–1894; 3646; 10016)

Maps

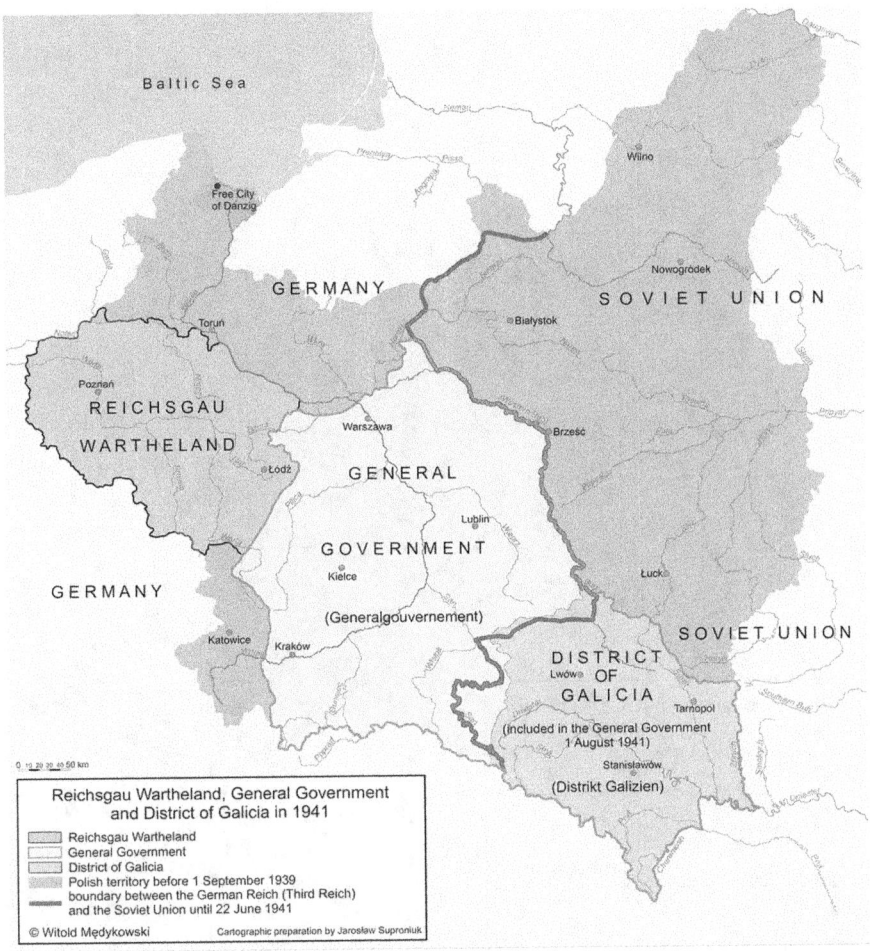

Maps | 329

THE DISTRICT OF LUBLIN - LABOR CAMPS NEAR BEŁŻEC

CAMPS OF THE WATER INSPECTION IN THE DISTRICT OF LUBLIN

Maps | 331

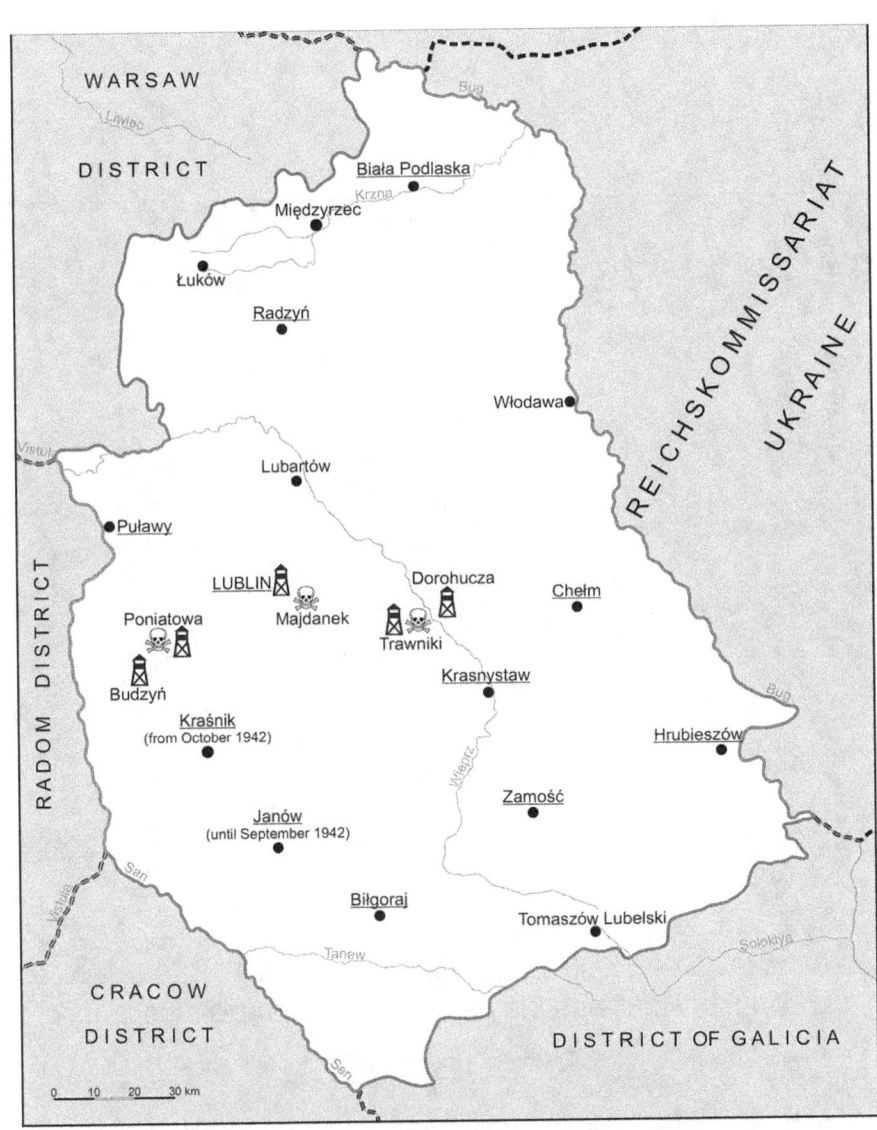

AKTION ERNTEFEST - MURDER OF JEWS
IN THE DISTRICT OF LUBLIN ON NOVEMBER 3-4, 1943

━━━━ boundary of the District of Lublin from 1.08.1941 to July 1944

Zamość capitals of counties 🛖 camps
━ ━ ━ other boundaries   ☠ exterminations sites

Cartographic preparation by Jarosław Suproniuk

© Witold Mędykowski

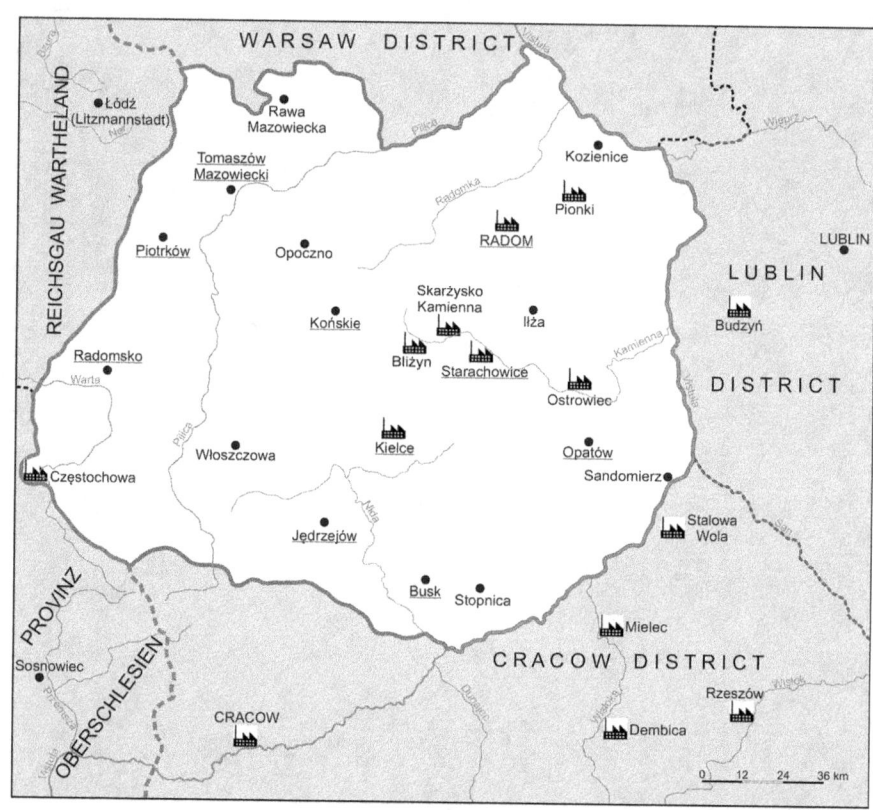

ARMAMENT FACTORIES IN THE DISTRICT OF RADOM (1942-1944)

― boundary of the District of Radom from October 1939 to January 1945
--- boundary of the German Reich
🏭 armament factories
Opatów capitals of counties

© Witold Mędykowski
Cartographic preparation by Jarosław Suproniuk

Tables

Table 1. Number of workdays performed by Jewish men and women in Lublin from October 24, 1939 to August 31, 1940.[1]

Month	Year	Men	Women	Total
October 24, 1939–August 31, 1940	1939	4564	139	4703
December	1939	7771	877	8648
January	1940	8884	1999	10883
February	1940	6365	2427	8792
March	1940	9696	2795	12491
April	1940	12380	3578	15958
May	1940	15051	3773	18824
June	1940	19134	5748	24882
July	1940	22134	7854	29988
August	1940	5435	1778	7213
Total		**111414**	**30968**	**142382**

1 APL, RŻL-40, 2.

Table 2. Maximal and minimal number of workers performing forced labor in Lublin from October 24, 1939 to August 31, 1940.[2]

Month	Year	Maximum		Minimum		Average number of workers		
		Men	Women	Men	Women	Men	Women	Total
		Daily		Daily		Daily		
October 24–August 31, 1940	1939	240	20	30	2	120	4	124
December	1939	535	43	17	12	251	28	279
January	1940	463	158	98	29	287	64	351
February	1940	337	127	118	56	219	84	303
March	1940	435	147	95	49	313	90	403
April	1940	474	153	352	93	413	119	532
May	1940	668	146	134	64	485	122	607
June	1940	850	258	417	90	638	191	829
July	1940	983	331	407	132	714	253	967
August	1940	533	149	14	2	175	57	232
October 24, 1939–August 31, 1940		983	331	14	2	361	101	462

[2] APL, RŻL-40, 2.

Table 3. Wages paid by Judenrat in Lublin to forced laborers in 1940.[3]

Category of worker	Daily wages in zł	
	until March 1940	since April 1940
Unmarried man	2.5	3.5
Married man	3	4
Married man, supporting more than 4 children	3.5	4.5
Unmarried woman	2.5	2.5
Married woman	3	3

Table 4. Employment of workers in the industry of Radom District in December 1939 in comparison to August 1939.[4]

Industry	August 1939		December 1939		Index
	no. of plants	no. of workers	no. of plants	no. of workers	August = 100
Metallurgy	3	20,233	3	2,385	11.8
Cast Iron foundry	9	3,291	7	953	18.9
Metal industry	15	4,276	8	937	21.9
Chemical industry	6	656	3	250	38.1
Textile	16	19,343	16	8,005	41.4
Ceramic and mineral industry	30	5,319	11	590	11.4
Wood industry	14	1,585	8	450	28.4
Leather	6	457	6	206	45.1
Food processing	19	977	17	675	69.1
Paper industry	1	220	1	30	13.6
Other	8	935	5	267	28.6
Total	127	57,290	86	14,748	25.7

3   APL, RŻL-40, 3.
4   Meducki, *Przemysł i klasa robotnicza*, 99.

Table 5. Quantity of Polish workers from General Government sent to work in Reich before June 1943.[5]

District	Number of forced workers
Kraków	304,000
Lublin	112,000
Radom	207,000
Warsaw	168,000
Galicia	304,000
Total	**1,095,000**

Table 6. Numbers of Jewish men registered for forced labor in Lublin in 1939/1940 according to year of birth.[6]

Year of birth	Number of registered Jewish men
1928	66
1927	384
1926	421
1925	**505**
1924	457
1923	463
1922	403
1921	288
1920	346
1919	305
1918	210
1917	232
1916	180
1915	209
1914	248
1913	309
1912	258
1911	295
1910	309

5   Madajczyk, *Polityka III Rzeszy w okupowanej Polsce*, vol. 1, 254.
6   APL, RŻL-7, 55–56.

Year of birth	Number of registered Jewish men
1909	305
1908	279
1907	288
1906	261
1905	307
1904	305
1903	329
1902	278
1901	286
1900	271
1899	259
1898	245
1897	274
1896	215
1895	227
1894	275
1893	238
1892	231
1891	209
1890	221
1889	222
1888	178
1887	167
1886	206
1885	175
1884	160
1883	167
1882	168
1881	121
1880	104
Total	**12859**

Table 7. Professional division of registered men and women in Lublin in 1939/1940.[7]

Professional category	Jewish men	Jewish women
Merchants and traders	2388	427
Medium and small-scale industrialists	84	
Householders	293	90
Agriculturers	28	
Unskilled workers	3339	1132
White-collar workers and trade workers	884	160
Craftsmen	4739	667
Freelancers	177	38
Total	**11932**	**2514**

Table 8. Categories of craftsmen (partial data) registered in Lublin in 1939/1940.[8]

Category of craft	Number
Tailors	1726
Shoemakers	595
Carpenters	327
Bakers	268
Hairdressers	196
Painters	163
Butchers	159
Locksmiths	136
Furriers	126
Total	**3696**

---

7   APL, RŻL-7, 59.
8   APL, RŻL-7, 59.

Table 9. Number of workers presenting themselves to perform forced labor in Lublin from January to August 1940.[9]

Day of month	January	February	March	April	May	June	July	August
1		894	635	838	752	992	1121	603
2		422	527	876	737	478	915	561
3		651	451	853	752	1157	1062	568
4		184	833	791	961	1090	1039	395
5		693	717	748	513	1244	997	572
6		692	511	693	1096	1097	1055	672
7		820	759	508	1184	1051	495	372
8		869	702	536	1276	412	957	425
9		881	520	724	1086	526	1047	501
10		575	375	778	944	1084	1104	468
11		173	1287	737	1088	1018	1068	356
12		897	674	691	370	1051	970	413
13		712	825	690	302	814	956	397
14		795	763	598	974	919	533	
15		752	1295	714	1022	859	819	

9 APL, RŻL-7, 55.

Day of month	January	February	March	April	May	June	July	August
16		778	1295	814	948	446	608	
17		846	630	805	897	1037	568	
18		287	1480	808	945	970	567	23
19		844	1118	761	416	1170	567	62
20		731	1111	833	1162	1114	490	90
21		794	933	516	836	1100	270	51
22		841	856	670	871	1085	456	71
23		833	628	669	817	538	525	45
24		860		596	750	1141	507	43
25		451		773	727	1052	495	31
26		840	762	798	438	1140	489	61
27		807	686	750	793	1102	427	79
28		1662	675	478	785	991	293	62
29	1075	679	553	747	1011	988	513	76
30	920		698	730	933	457	487	63
31	907		450		867		523	40
Total workdays	2902	21263	22641	21523	26253	28123	21923	7100	151728

Table 10. Budget of General Government.[10]

Department	Expenditure of ordinary budget of the GG in million zł				
	1940	**1941**	**1942**	**1943**	**1944**
General Governor, Government of the GG and District offices	120.7	157.4	164.7	161.2	135.4
Treasury	36.0	43.5	65.9	65.4	72.1
Internal administration	85.2	253.8	324.6	526.4	541.8
Police	70.6	293.0	369.1	380.4	397.3
Propaganda	9.8	25.9	31.9	34.3	36.8
Judicial system	34.4	43.8	71.3	69.2	65.8
Science and education	94.9	141.7	218.9	214.3	227.5
Alimentation and agriculture	81.0	118.9	231.8	391.9	429.2
Forestry	71.5	91.7	156.1	126.7	135.5
Economy	8.7	20.9	26.6	44.1	53.9
Labor	56.7	70.9	96.0	111.2	122.2
Construction	44.7	50.4	156.0	250.0	276.1
Transportation	0.0	0.5	0.0	0.0	0.0
Provision	0.0	91.0	125.7	142.1	127.3
General tax administration	324.8	364.2	662.1	1138.3	1075.0
Total	**1039.0**	**1767.6**	**2700.7**	**1138.3**	**3695.9**

10 AAN, zespół rząd GG, syg 719; Skalniak, *Polityka pieniężna i budżetowa*, 36–37.

Table 11. Civil construction in General Government (except for projects with exclusively military purposes), in million zł.[11]

Type of construction	1940	1941	1942	1943	1944	1945	Together
Railways (Ostbahn) [payment of Emissionbank]	62.5	192.4	430.6	360	520	0	1565.5
Road Construction [payment of Emissionbank]	45.2	26	70	86	147	0	374.2
Regulation of rivers and waterways [payment of Emissionbank]	14.6	0	22.4	75.2	17.5	8	137.7
Construction [payment of Emissionbank]	0	0.6	3.2	0	0	0	3.8
Water management [paid from special budget of the GG]	37.2	82	90.3	0	0	0	209.5
Regulation of Wisła river [paid from special budget of the GG]	11.2	18	29.5	0	0	0	58.7
Dams construction [paid from special budget of the GG]	10.6	22	32	0	0	0	64.6
Construction of houses for German functionaries [paid from special budget of the GG]	10	14	35	75	40	0	174
Enlargement of refineries [paid from special budget of the GG]	0	0	0	0	38	0	38
Total	191.3	355	713	596.2	762.5	8	2626

11 AAN, zespół rząd GG, syg 719; Skalniak, *Polityka pieniężna i budżetowa*, 70.

Table 12. Payments by *Emissionbank in Polen* (General Government), in million zł.[12]

Total	1940	1941	1942	1943	1944	1945	Together
	169,760	338,457	589,767	631,576	845,214	8,014	2,582,788
Railway	62,541	192,427	430,620	360,000	520,000		1,565,588
SS and police	38,576	62,739	58,123	87,444	155,594		402,476
Road construction	45,190	26,000	70,000	86,000	147,000		374,190
Regulation of rivers and water construction	14,639	0	22,435	75,182	17,500	8,000	137,756
Military Chemical Plant in Krosno	3,600	42,780	0	0	0		46,380
Resettlement action	2,364	10,011	1,651	8,000	4,000		26,026
Strengthening of Germanhood	0	0	0	12,800	0		12,800
Departments of the GG Government	2,850	1,860	3,750	2,150	1,120	14	11,744
Construction	0	640	3,188	0	0		3,828
Committee of Refugees of the German-Soviet war	0	2,000	0	0	0		2,000

12 AAN, zespół rząd GG, syg 720; Skalniak, *Polityka pieniężna i budżetowa*, 25.

Table 13. Income of Jewish community in Lublin from September 1, 1939 to August 31, 1940.[13]

Income in zł of the Jewish Community in Lublin from September 1, 1939 to August 31, 1940	
One-time services I	342535.4
One-time services II	349684.59
Community tax	124520.5
Fees for forced labor of men / fees for replacement	497276.34
Fees for forced labor of women / fees for replacement	153320.43
Fees for the postal department	23880.85
Fees for the population registration department	6398.2
Fees for the emigration department	1842.54
Fees for the legal department	718.6
Fees for funerals	75382
Fees for monuments (*matzevot*)	3507
Fees for weddings	2091.5
Fees for birth certificates	3757.1
Secretarial fees	4817
Donations	20232.54
Miscellaneous	7815.7
Total	**1617780.29**

Table 14. Expenses of Jewish Community in Lublin from September 1, 1939 to August 31, 1940 in zł.[14]

Expenses in zł of the Jewish Community in Lublin from September 1, 1939 to August 31, 1940				
Expenses on command of authorities	Direct payments	260000		
	Delivery	47232.33		
	Payment for workers	591872.7		
	Maintenance of workshops	343202.7	1242307.79
Social assistance				108318.26
Purchase of land for cemetery				10713.5
Salaries				143165.27
Administrative expenses				21426.57
Miscellaneous				93507.48
Total				**1619438.87**

13 APL, RŻL-8, 5.
14 APL, RŻL-8, 6.

Table 15. Expenses of *Judenrat* in Lublin for forced laborers between October 24, 1939 and August 31, 1940, in zł.[15]

Month	Year	Permanent workers and daily workers	POWs	Workers in Chelm	Replacing workers	Total
October 24–August 31, 1940	1939	17913				17913
December	1939	28519.6				28519.6
January	1940	33178				33178
February	1940	20097			10391	30488
March	1940	23903.75	2234		23015.5	49153.25
April	1940	26036.75	50	2514	36417.5	65018.25
May	1940	28785.5		291	41969.5	71045
June	1940	46373			51255.5	97628.5
July	1940	61667.75			49628	111295.75
August	1940	32214.5			11877	44091.5
Together		**318688.85**	**2284**	**2805**	**224554**	**548330.85**

---

15 APL, RŻL-40, 3.

Table 16. Quantity of workdays performed by labor battalions and labor detachments in Warsaw from October 1939 to July 1942.

Month	Year	Workdays			Total
		Labor detachments at German institutions	Labor detachments working for the *Judenrat*	Labor detachments working for ZOM	
October	1939				4,191
November	1939				29,963
December	1939				49,108
Total, 1939	**1939**				**83,262**
January	1940	37,600	620	12,950	51,170
February	1940	69,500	3,390	50,960	123,850
March	1940	150,500	13,610	56,170	220,280
April	1940	187,600	11,360	14,510	213,470
May	1940	224,600	8,430	13,920	246,950
June	1940	218,400	910	6,710	226,020
July	1940	216,000	1,470	5,620	223,090
August	1940	266,500	4,850	16,000	287,350
September	1940	164,500	6,380	6,910	177,790
October	1940	134,200	4,890	2,070	141,160
November	1940	142,100	9,290	810	152,200
December	1940	123,000	14,990	670	138,660
Total, 1940	**1940**	**1,934,500**	**80,190**	**187,300**	**2,201,990**

Month	Year	Workdays			Total
		Labor detachments at German institutions	Labor detachments working for the *Judenrat*	Labor detachments working for ZOM	
January	1941	94,630	5,800	8,550	108,980
February	1941	72,500	6,300	2,100	80,900
March	1941	20,500	19,500		40,000
April	1941	36,780	2,900		39,680
May	1941	59,400	2,300		61,700
June	1941	52,420	780		53,200
July	1941	42,250	200		42,450
August	1941	41,900	100		42,000
September	1941	49,520	100		49,620
October	1941	27,500	3,920		31,420
November	1941	16,700	7,400		24,100
December	1941	13,750	6,500		20,250
Total, 1941	**1941**	**527,850**	**55,800**	**10,650**	**594,300**
January	1942				19,740
February	1942				17,590
March	1942				18,530
April	1942				40,000
May	1942				70,000
June	1942				84,100

Month	Year	Workdays			Total
		Labor detachments at German institutions	Labor detachments working for the *Judenrat*	Labor detachments working for ZOM	
July	1942				160,000
Total, 1942	1942				409,960
Total	1939–1942				3,289,512

Table 17. Number of notifications sent by Labor Department of *Judenrat* in Lublin in 1940.[16]

Month	Year	Number of notifications	Number of undelivered notifications due to change of address	Number of cancelled notifications due to poverty or deregistration	Number of people who appeared to work	Number of people who did not appear to work	Number of people who paid for replacement
February	1940	12215	721	1588	320	2858	6773
March	1940	11280	625	470	165	3734	6326
April	1940	11675	845	960	65	3718	6087
May	1940	10817	793	874	77	2703	6370
June	1940	9315	489	655	27	1171	5711
July	1940	9185	744	478	40	1664	6253
August	1940	9346	1214	998	33	2509	4592
Total		**73833**	**5431**	**6023**	**727**	**18357**	**42112**
Percent		**100%**	**7.35%**	**8.15%**	**0.98%**	**24.90%**	**57%**

16 APL, RZL-8, 45.

Table 18. Quantity of workdays performed by Jewish workers in the framework of labor detachments in German institutions in Warsaw in 1940.[17]

Month	Total workdays	Labor detachments (Dienststellen)					
		Wehrmacht	SS and Police	Railways and Post	Administration	Raw materials collection	Industry
January	37,600	5,900	12,000	12,800	6,900		
February	69,500	35,700	9,600	20,200	3,300		700
March	150,500	65,100	17,200	35,600	13,000	17,600	2,000
April	187,600	62,500	26,400	52,700	17,400	26,400	2,200
May	224,600	58,400	38,600	61,200	30,800	30,300	5,300
June	218,400	44,500	45,000	46,100	36,000	41,900	4,900
July	216,000	46,900	48,400	49,500	45,000	20,700	5,500
August	266,500	68,500	64,100	72,300	53,700	4,500	3,400
September	164,500	65,900	30,200	44,500	18,400	3,000	2,500
October	134,200	65,100	23,200	32,600	9,800	1,500	2,000
November	142,100	66,900	32,000	25,600	15,300	750	1,550
December	123,000	51,300	34,600	18,600	17,800	300	400
Total	1,934,500	636,700	381,300	471,700	267,400	146,950	30,450

17 Zestawienie ilości robotników dostarczonych poszczególnym instytucjom w 1940 r., AŻIH, Ring I/28; Berenstein, "Praca przymusowa Żydów w Warszawie," 54.

Table 19. Quantity of paid and non-paid workdays performed by forced labor detachments for German institutions in Warsaw in 1940–1941.[18]

Month	Year	Total—workdays	%	Non-paid	%	Paid By the Judenrat	%	By the German employers	%
January	1940	37,600	100			37,600	100		
February	1940	69,500	100	32,900	47.5	36,600	52.5		
March	1940	150,500	100	109,700	72	40,800	28		
April	1940	187,600	100	136,400	73	51,200	27		
May	1940	224,600	100	169,800	76	54,800	24		
June	1940	218,400	100	156,100	71.5	54,800	25.1	7,500	3.4
July	1940	216,000	100	157,300	72.8	55,900	25.9	2,800	1.3
August	1940	266,500	100	228,400	85.7	32,200	12	5,900	2.3
September	1940	164,500	100	127,600	77.6	3,900	2.3	33,000	20.1
October	1940	134,200	100	66,000	50	5,300	4	62,100	46
November	1940	142,100	100	70,800	49.3	5,100	3.5	66,200	47.2
December	1940	123,000	100	62,600	50.4	4,500	3.7	55,000	45.9
Total	**1940**	**1,934,500**	**100**	**1,318,400**	**68**	**382,700**	**20**	**233,400**	**12**

18 Berenstein, "Praca przymusowa Żydów w Warszawie," 66, 84.

Tables | 351

						Paid			
Month	Year	Total—workdays	%	Non-paid	%	By the Judenrat	%	By the German employers	%
January	1941	94,630	100	54,000	57	3,000	3	37,900	39.3
February	1941	72,500	100	41,000	57	3,000	4	28,370	39
March	1941	20,500	100	7,000	34	3,000	15	10,580	51
April	1941	36,780	100	820	2	2,190	6	33,770	92
May	1941	59,400	100			3,450	6	55,950	94
June	1941	52,420	100			2,910	6	40,510	94
July	1941	42,250	100			3,840	9	38,610	91
August	1941	41,900	100			3,400	8	38,500	92
September	1941	49,520	100			3,630	7	45,890	93
October	1941	27,500	100			3,350	12	24,150	88
November	1941	16,700	100			3,300	20	13,400	80
December	1941	13,750	100			3,120	23	10,630	77
Total	1941	527,850	100	102,820	20	38,190	7	387,150	73
Total	1940/1941	2,462,350		1,421,220	57.7	420,890	17.1	620,550	25.2

Table 20. Employment growth in the workshops conducted by employment agencies in Warsaw in 1941.[19]

Month	Number of workers	Turnover in zł
May	220	64,074.00
June	1,377	
July	2,134	484,697.39
August	2,424	1,830,000.00
September	3,055	

Table 21. Number of worker's cards issued in Warsaw between November 1941 and June 1942.[20]

Month	Year	Number of issued worker's cards
November/December	1941	20,000
January	1942	7,187
February	1942	10,438
March	1942	13,309
April	1942	8,959
May	1942	13,027
June	1942	2,475
Total	**1941–1942**	**75,395**

---

19 Dunin-Wąsowicz, *Raporty Ludwiga Fischera*, 123.
20 Berenstein, "Praca przymusowa Żydów w Warszawie," 77.

Table 22. Official and free market (black market) prices in 1942, in zł.[21]

Product	Unit	Oficial price	Official price			Multiplication of official price		
			GG	Warsaw	Krakow	GG	Warsaw	Krakow
Rye bread	zł/kg	0.45	17.81	10.23	11.00	39.6	22.7	24.4
Wheat flour	zł/kg	0.70	23.98	27.30	17.41	34.2	39.0	25.0
Sugar	zł/kg	1.60	54.44	64.68	52.70	34.0	40.4	32.9
Beef	zł/kg	3.00	33.10	42.80	22.20	11.0	14.3	7.4
Eggs	zł/kg	0.12	2.87	3.28	1.96	23.9	27.3	16.3

Table 23. Free market (black market) prices in Warsaw.[22]

Product	Unit	Month and year					
		July 1939	July 1940	April 1941	February 1942	July 1943	June 1944
Beef	kg	1.56	8.92	10.31	20.00	82.89	94.23
Pork	kg	1.60	11.74	13.62	30.08	130.94	132.31
Bacon	kg	1.61	16.09	20.56	51.11	199.17	177.54
Butter	Kg	2.73	20.83	27.89	60.78	196.66	213.32
Milk	liter	0.27	1.52	1.86	4.84	12.63	15.49
White cheese	Kg	0.83	6.32	7.30	18.23	59.88	77.03

21 Skalniak, *Stopa życiowa społeczeństwa polskiego*, 39.
22 Tomasz Szarota, *Okupowanej Warszawy dzień powszedni: Studium historyczne* (Warsaw: Czytelnik, 1978), 262.

Product	Unit	Month and year					
		July 1939	July 1940	April 1941	February 1942	July 1943	June 1944
Eggs	item	0.08	0.52	0.80	2.51	4.33	5.09
Sugar	Kg	1.00	7.10	9.70	33.46	37.37	95.66
Wholemeal rye bread	Kg	0.30	1.51	4.27	6.88	12.00	5.04
Wheat flour	Kg	0.51	4.16	8.37	16.97	39.35	33.60
Barley grits	Kg	0.38	3.58	6.28	14.02	21.26	18.41
Peas	Kg	0.35	5.57	7.66	17.38	24.10	25.56
Potatoes	Kg	0.14	0.92	1.49	2.80	4.91	4.19
Onion	Kg	0.11	1.00	4.29	7.12	33.87	25.01
Fresh cabbage	Kg	0.22	0.88	1.29	1.59	5.70	11.53
Vodka (alc. 40%)	Liter			60.00	60.00	170.00	

Table 24. Abandoned property in Przemyśl County in 1940.[23]

Quantity of real estates	Type of property	Value in zł	Currency
165	Former Jewish land worth approx.	6,250,000.00	zł
62	Former Aryan land worth approx.	1,700,000.00	zł
10	Abandoned former Church properties. The collection order can, however, only be maintained for 3 plots worth approx.	500,000.00	zł
16	Former Jewish plants worth approx.	820,000.00	zł
22	Former Jewish mortgages worth approx.	32,948.27	zł
2	Mortgages	1,150.00	Dollar
2	Mortgages	7,089.00	Austrian Kronen
	Pieces of furniture and movable objects worth approx.	10,000.00	zł
Total		9,312,948.27	zł

23 Lagebericht, Der Stadthauptmann Deutsch-Przemyśl, 13.7.1940–31.8.1940. YVA-JM-814, scan 38.

Table 25. Official hourly wages of male and female workers in General Government, 1941, in zł.[24]

Salary group	Skilled workers		Semi-skilled workers				Unskilled workers			
	Non-Jews	Jews	Non-Jews, men	Jews, men	Non-Jews, women	Jews, women	Non-Jews men	Jews, men	Non-Jews, women	Jews, women
older than 21 full years	1	0.8	0.76	0.61	0.61	0.49	0.65	0.52	0.52	0.42
older than 20 full years	0.9	0.72	0.68	0.54	0.55	0.44	0.59	0.47	0.47	0.38
older than 19 full years	0.8	0.64	0.61	0.49	0.49	0.39	0.52	0.42	0.42	0.34
older than 17 full years	0.7	0.56	0.53	0.42	0.43	0.34	0.46	0.37	0.36	0.26
older than 16 full years			0.46	0.37	0.37	0.3	0.39	0.31	0.31	0.25
younger than 16 years			0.38	0.3	0.31	0.25	0.33	0.26	0.26	0.21

24 APL, RŻL-6, Stundenlöhne der Arbeiter und Arbeiterinnen—Lohnordnung, 1941, 80.

Table 26. Food standards for the population in General Government introduced from November 1, 1940.[25]

Kind of product	Unit	Regular	Employed in plants A	Card A	Employed in plant B	Card B	Children until the age of 10	Jews
Bread	Kg	4.2	8.4	4.2	5.6	1.4	2.89	2.8
Flour	Kg	0.4	0.8	0.4	0.8	0.4	0.4	0
Grain coffee	Kg	0.16	0.48	0.32	0.24	0.08	0.16	0.16
Meat	Kg	up to 0.5	up to 1.3	0.8	up to 0.5	0	up to 0.5	0
Sugar	Kg	up to 0.4	up to 0.64	0.24	up to 0.5	0.1	0.4	0.2
Marmalade	Kg	up to 0.4	up to 0.5	0.1	up to 0.5	0.1	0.4	0
Eggs	Item	up to 4	up to 12	8	up to 8	up to 4	4	0
Butter, fat	Kg		0.12	0.13	0.12	0.12	0	0
Groats, pasta, oatmeal	Kg		0.8	0.8	0.4	0.4	0.4	0

25 Meducki, *Przemysł i klasa robotnicza*, 141.

Table 27. Energy value of food rations in the General Government, calories.[26]

Term	1940		1941	
	Poles	Jews	Poles	Jews
January-March	609	503	611	237
April-June	704	449	553	219
July-September	698	331	531	198
October-December	938	369	981	360
Average annual	**737**	**413**	**669**	**253**

Table 28. Expenses of *Judenrat* in Lublin for labor camps in the area of Bełżec between June and September 1, 1940, in zł.[27]

Expenses in zł for labor camps between June and September 1, 1940	
Nutrition	910.99
Medical assistance	813.3
Lodging	574.5
Post and telegraph	54.26
Transportation of laborers	3821.6
Maintenance of the services	1461.5
Travel expenses of administration	1249.7
Office materials	22.05
Long-distance calls	41.6
Camp equipment	429.1
Money paid to the German authorities for the maintenance of laborers	27800
Together	**37178.6**

---

26 Szarota, *Okupowanej Warszawy*, 240.
27 APL, RŻL-17, 11.

Table 29. Demand for Jewish labor force in General Government (August 6, 1940).[28]

Institution	Project	Quantity of workers		
		I stage	II stage	Together
Border fortifications		15,000	15,000	30,000
Water Inspection	Projects in the District Lublin	3,000		3,000
Water Inspection	Hydroelectric dam in Rożnów	1,800		1,800
Water Inspection	small construction projects	2,000		2,000
Ostbahn	n.d.			
Road construction		3,000		12,000
Department of Woods	n.d.			
Together				**48,800**

28 YVA-JM.2700, Protokoll über die Judeneinsatzbesprechung vom. 6 August 1940 [...] bei der Abteilung Arbeit im Amt des Generalgouverneurs, scan 8.

Table 30. Quantity of Jewish workers from Lublin sent to work in agriculture from mid-June to mid-August 1940.[29]

Estate	Number of men	Number of women	Together
Jastków	55	15	70
Dys Dominium	6		6
Dys Dwór	7		7
Piotrków	15		15
Radawiec Duży	29	13	42
Motycz	18	11	29
Jakubowice Murowane	25		25
Wola Sławińska	15	2	17
Rury	15		15
Matczyn	40		40
Pólko	38		38
Kawenczyn	20	2	22
Łuszczów	17		17
Krzesimów	23		23
Osmolice	30		30
Sobianowice Wieś	11	4	15
Wola Sławińska	23		23
Elizówka	14	5	19
Nasutów	15	5	20
Baśka	3		3
Dziuchów	5		5
Pliszczyn	2		2
Zakrzów	4	2	6
Konopnica	6		6
Łemszczyzna	3		3
Snopków	24		24
Jabłonna	5		5
Świdnik	2		2
Estates in Hrubieszów County	300		300
Together	**770**	**59**	**829**

29 APL, RŻL-47, 54–55. Report on the activity of the Central Camps Council in Bełżec for the period June 13 until December 5, 1940.

Table 31. Number of Polish forced workers from General Government in Third Reich in the years 1939–1943.[30]

Year	Number of workers from the GG in the Third Reich		
	in agriculture	in industry	Together
1939	32,540	7,135	39,675
1940	259,096	42,866	301,962
1941	157,496	65,932	223,428
1942	265,461	133,498	398,959
1943	115,919	59,799	175,718
First half of 1944			52,445
Together	830,512	309,230	1,192,187

Table 32. Number of Jews placed in small ghettos in General Government on December 31, 1942.[31]

District	Number of Jews
Kraków	37,000
Radom	29,000
Lublin	20,000
Warsaw	50,000
Lwów	161,514
Total in the General Government	297,514

Table 33. Employment in DAW in 1940–1944.[32]

Year	Employment in DAW in general—annual average	Employment in DAW Lublin	Employment in DAW Lublin—percentage of all DAW employees
1940	1220	221[1]	18.1
1941	3650	2000	54.8
1942	7402	2756	37.2
1943	15498	5486	35.4
1944	15799	649[2]	4.1

---

30 Skalniak, *Stopa życiowa społeczeństwa polskiego*, 25.
31 Eisenbach and Rutkowski, *Eksterminacja Żydów*, 322.
32 Mencel, *Majdanek 1941–1944*, 381.

Table 34. Plan and artillery ammunition production in Stahlwerke Braunschweig GmbH in Starachowice in 1943.[33]

Month	Artillery ammunition caliber					
	37 mm	40 mm	75 mm	105 mm	150 mm	152 mm
Monthly plan	20,000	40,000	200,000	20,000	15,000	25,000
January, February	no data	38,000	116,500	17,500	16,000	no data
March	no data	40,000	130,000	21,500	20,000	1,500
April	no data	21,287	102,000	15,250	12,000	4,497
May	no data	28,820	85,100	4,650	8,100	14,100
June	500	28,793	75,392	9,037	8,194	10,062
July	21,277	40,000	100,788	17,863	8,430	16,262
August	26,427	26,000	115,638	18,565	8,430	16,262
September	25,436	23,583	144,403	20,005	9,258	16,014
October	21,396	no data	122,703	20,202	9,133	13,850
November	22,752	no data	63,999	14,377	6,259	11,448
December	no data	no data	no data	no data	no data	no data
Together	117,788	246,483	1,056,523	158,949	105,804	103,995

Table 35. Production of artillery ammunition in HASAG Munitionsfabrik in Skarżysko Kamienna.[34]

Period	Artillery ammunition caliber						
	20 mm	40 mm	75 mm	88 mm	105 mm	Howitzer 105 mm	150 mm
Monthly average 1941	500,000	50,000	50,000				12,000
November 1942				37,600	23,200		9,400
December 1942				39,500	26,500		11,500
First half of January 1943		26,000	9,000	6,610	14,405		18,952

33 Meducki, *Przemysł i klasa robotnicza*, 79.
34 Ibid., 66–73.

Period	Artillery ammunition caliber						
	20 mm	40 mm	75 mm	88 mm	105 mm	Howitzer 105 mm	150 mm
August 1943						30,000	
Monthly average 1943			39,636	46,000	28,272		12,454
December 1943		320,000				88,500	
February 1944	417,000		62,800		40,000		7,200
March 1944	417,000		80,700		42,000		12,700

Table 36. Rifle and pistol ammunition production in HASAG Munitionsfabrik in Skarżysko Kamienna.[35]

Period	Rifle ammunition	Pistol ammunition
July 1941	3,417,000	3,993,600
November 1–15, 1941	5,747,000	6,267,000
Monthly average in 1941	2,000,000	2,500,000
November 15–December 31, 1943	21,604,000	18,472,780
Total, year 1943	149,767,000	86,500,000
Monthly average in 1943	12,480,583	7,208,333
February 1944	10,450,200	3,748,600
March 1944	12,985,400	3,898,890

Table 37. Labor forces in the armament industry in the General Government 1943–1944.[36]

Month	Year	Jews	Jews %	non-Jews	non-Jews %	Together	Together %
January	1943	15,091	12.50	105,632	87.50	120,723	100
April	1943	15,538	12.13	112,499	87.87	128,037	100
July	1943	21,643	14.90	123,588	85.10	145,231	100
October	1943	22,444	14.64	130,808	85.36	153,252	100
January	1944	26,296	15.80	140,057	84.40	166,353	100
April	1944	28,537	13.73	179,244	86.27	207,781	100
May	1944	27,439	13.70	172,781	86.30	200,220	100

---

35 Ibid.
36 Karay, *Death Comes in Yellow*, 52.

Photographs

Demolition works at a destroyed tenement house. Warsaw, 1939. (*Zeitungs-Verlag Krakau-Warschau.*) Archival signature: 2-199. National Digital Archives (NAC), Warsaw.

Construction of a bridge over the Narew River by German troops, September 28, 1939. Author: Becke. (*Zeitungs-Verlag Krakau-Warschau.*) Archival signature: 2-61. National Digital Archives (NAC), Warsaw.

Jews at forced labor digging a pit in order to bury a dead horse. Rzeszów. Submitter: Mosinger. Archival signature: 1024_34. Yad Vashem Archives.

Jewish forced laborers digging a pit, under the supervision of an armed guard, Kraków, printed in the periodical *Illustrierter Beobachter*, November 1939. Archival signature: 1573_37. Yad Vashem Archives.

Jewish women in New Sandez, July 1942. Stadtarchiv München, FS-WKII-KB, photographer: Wilhelm Nortz. Image taken during a trip for journalists through the Generalgouvernement.

Hans Frank—Governor of the General Government. (*Zeitungs-Verlag Krakau-Warschau.*) Archival signature: 2-2732. National Digital Archives (NAC), Warsaw.

Governor Hans Frank (second from right) in the company of General Walther von Brauchtisch (first from left) and General Johannes Blaskowitz (on the right side of Hans Frank, with a mustache) on the cloisters of Wawel. In the background, you can see Governor Otto Wachter and German officers. Kraków. (*Zeitungs-Verlag Krakau-Warschau.*) Archival signature: 2-2902. National Digital Archives (NAC), Warsaw.

Josef Bühler (on the left) receives from Hans Frank the appointment as deputy governor of the General Governorship. In the background you can see Hermann Senkowsky (in the dark) and Friedrich Wilhelm Krüger (first from the left). Kraków, July 1941. Photographic bet: Otto Rosner. (*Zeitungs-Verlag Krakau-Warschau.*) Archival signature: 2-2848. National Digital Archives (NAC), Warsaw.

SS-Obergruppenführer Friedrich Wilhelm Krüger, December 1939. (*Zeitungs-Verlag Krakau-Warschau.*) Archival signature: 2-4469. National Digital Archives (NAC), Warsaw.

Heinrich Himmler (on the right) in conversation with the SS and police commander of the Lublin district Otto Globocnik. Author: Bruno Wiśniewski. (*Zeitungs-Verlag Krakau-Warschau.*) Archival signature: 2-4665. National Digital Archives (NAC), Warsaw.

Families meeting near the fence of the Biała Podlaska Camp, June 1940. Archival signature: 7711_4. Yad Vashem Archives.

First group of workers from Międzyrzec coming back from work, 1940. Archival signature: 7711_13. Yad Vashem Archives.

Prisoners in the labor camp. Bełżec, 1940. Archival signature: 5318_170. Yad Vashem Archives.

Photographs | 371

A work battalion. Krychów, 1942, (submitter Z. Kratzak). Archival signature: 72BO2. Yad Vashem Archives.

A group of workers from Międzyrzec working to divert the Krzna River, 1940. Archival signature: 7711_21. Yad Vashem Archives.

Construction of drainage channels in the Krzna valley in the vicinity of Biała Podlaska. (*Zeitungs-Verlag Krakau-Warschau.*) Archival signature: 2-6918b. National Digital Archives (NAC), Warsaw.

Forced labor in a labor camp. Kraków-Prokocim, probably 1942. The photograph was given to Yosef Getner after the war by the German Kapo in charge of the work battalion. Submitter Yosef Getner. Archival signature: 3260. Yad Vashem Archives.

Photographs | 373

First group of workers from Międzyrzec in the camp in Biała Podlaska, 1940. Archival signature: 7711_23. Yad Vashem Archives.

Construction of a hydroelectric dam on the Dunajec River in Rożnów, 1941. (*Zeitungs-Verlag Krakau-Warschau.*) Archival signature: 2-7763, National Digital Archives (NAC), Warsaw.

Forced laborers washing in the Vistula River after work. Archival signature: 3116_102. Yad Vashem Archives.

Food distribution in a labor camp in Płaszów. Archival signature: 139fo5. Yad Vashem Archives.

Construction of the wall around the ghetto. Kraków, 1941. Archival signature: 4797_109. Yad Vashem Archives.

Jewish forced laborers in a roll call prior to receiving food, Warsaw, 1941. Propaganda company (*Propaganda-Kompanie*) photographer. Archival signature: 6AO1. Yad Vashem Archives.

A Jewish woman operating a spinning-wheel in a workshop situated at 65 Niska Street in the Warsaw ghetto, probably 1941. Foto Forbert. Archival signature: 3119_216. Yad Vashem Archives.

A sewing room in a workshop situated at 28 Nalewki Street, Warsaw, probably 1941. Foto Forbert. Archival signature: 3119_35. Yad Vashem Archives.

Stroop instructing Ukrainian auxiliary police during Warsaw Ghetto Uprising, Warsaw, April-May, 1943. Author: Franz Konrad. Archival signature: 2807_31. Yad Vashem Archives.

People constructing a barbed wire fence at a labor camp, Poniatowa. Archival signature: 76FO6. Yad Vashem Archives.

Walter Caspar Többens textile factory at a labor camp in Poniatowa, 1943. Archival signature: 76F02. Yad Vashem Archives.

Women at forced labor, Płaszów, 1943. Archival signature: 139fo8. Yad Vashem Archives.

The Reich Minister Albert Speer (left) and field marshal Erhard Milch (right) are examining new weapons, September 1943. Author: Kobierowski (*Zeitungs-Verlag Krakau-Warschau.*) Archival signature: 2-12936. National Digital Archives (NAC), Warsaw.

Workers at an ammunition factory, September 1940. Author: Dieck. (Zeitungs-Verlag Krakau-Warschau.) Archival signature: 2-6352. National Digital Archives (NAC), Warsaw.

German policemen supervising deportees. Międzyrzec Podlaski, May 26, 1943. Archival signature: 77EO2. Yad Vashem Archives.

Bibliography

PRINTED SOURCES

Ajzensztajn, Betti, ed. *Ruch podziemny w gettach i obozach (Materiały i Dokumenty)*. Warsaw: CŻKH, 1946.

Albert, Walter. *Die Ernährungswirtschaft des Generalgouvernements*. Krakow: Agrarverlag, 1942.

Arad, Yitzhak, Yisrael Gutman et al., eds. *Documents on the Holocaust: Selected Sources on the Destruction of the Jews of Germany and Austria, Poland and the Soviet Union*. Jerusalem: Yad Vashem, 1987.

Arad, Yitzhak, Shmuel Krakowski, and Shmuel Spector, eds. *The Einsatzgruppen reports: Selections from the Dispatches of the Nazi Death Squads' Campaign Against the Jews, July 1941–January 1943*. New York: Holocaust Library, 1989.

Amtliches Gemeinde- und Dorfverzeichnis für das Generalgouvernement auf Grund der summarischen Bevölkerungsbestandsaufnahme am 1. März 1943. Krakow: Statistisches Amt des Generalgouvernements, Burgverlag, 1943.

Appenszlak, Jacob, ed. *The Black Book of Polish Jewry*. New York: The American Federation for Polish Jews, 1943.

Archiwum Państwowe w Lublinie i jego oddziały: Przewodnik po zasobie archiwalnym, vol. 1. Lublin: Wyd. UMCS, 1997.

Arlt, Fritz. *Die ukrainische Volksgruppe im Generalgouvernement*. Krakow: Regierung des Generalgouvernements, 1940.

———. *Polen-, Ukrainer-, Juden-politik im Generalgouvernement für die besetzten polnischen Gebiete 1939/40 und im Oberschlesien 1941/43 und im Freitheitskampf der unterdrückten Ostvölker: Errinerungen eines Insiders*. Lindhorst: Täge, 1995.

Auf Vorposten: Drei Jahre Aufbau im Arbeitsbereich Generalgouvernement der NSDAP. Krakow: Hauptarbeitsgebiet Presse im Arbeitsbereich Generalgouvernement der NSDAP, Typ. Zeitungsverlag, 1943.

Bauen und Kämpfen: Gedichte und Bilder vom Einsatz der Frontarbeiter. Munich: Georg D.W. Callway, 1942.

Becker, Bruno, ed. *Das Devisenrecht des Generalgouvernements: Die Devisenrechtlichen Verordnungen, Anordnungen, Erlasse und Bekanntmachungen des Generalgouvernements*. Krakow: Burgverlag Krakau, 1941.

Behrend, Else Rahel (Rosenfeld), ed., *Lebenszeichen aus Piaski: Briefe Deportierter aus dem Distrikt Lublin 1940–1943*. Munich: Biederstein Vlg, 1968.

Bericht über die Aufgaben und Ergebnisse auf dem Gebiet des Arbeitseinsatzes vom 1. Januar bis 30. Juni 1943. Berlin: Generalbevollmachtigter für den Arbeitseinsatz, Elsnerdruck, 1943.

Best, Werner. *Die Verwaltung in Polen vor und nach der Zusammenbruch der Polnischen Republik.* Berlin: Verlag Decker, 1940.

Bestimmungen über die Getreidewirtschaft im Wirtschaftsjahr 1943/1944. Krakow: Hauptverband der Getreide- und Futtermittelwirtschaft, Typ. "Styl," 1944.

Biernacki, Stanisław, Czesław Madajczyk, and Blanka Meissner, eds. *Generalny plan wschodni, Zbiór dokumentów.* Warsaw: Główna Komisja Badania Zbrodni Hitlerowskich w Polsce, 1990.

Biernat, Andrzej, and Anna Laszuk, eds., *Archiwa państwowe w Polsce: Przewodnik po zasobach.* Warsaw: Wydawnictwo DiG, 1998.

Blumental, Nachman, ed. *Documents from the Lublin Ghetto: Judenrat without Direction.* Jerusalem: Yad Vashem, 1967.

Blumental, Nachman, and Józef Kermisz, eds. *Dokumenty i Materiały do Dziejów Okupacji Niemieckiej w Polsce,* vol. 3. Lodz: Centralna Żydowska Komisja Historyczna, 1946.

Borwicz, Michał M., Nella Rost, and Josef Wulf. *Dokumenty zbrodni i męczeństwa.* Krakow: CKŻP, 1945.

Bühler, Joseph. *Das Generalgouvernement: Seine Verwaltung und seine Wirtschaft. Sammlung von Vortragen der ersten wissenschaftlichen Vortragsreihe der Verwaltungs-Akademie des Generalgouvernements.* Krakow: Burgverlag, 1943.

Ciepielewicz, Mieczysław, and Eugeniusz Kozłowski, eds. *Obrona Warszawy 1939 we wspomnieniach.* Warsaw: MON, 1984.

———. *Wojna obronna Polski 1939.* Warsaw: MON, 1968.

———. *Wrzesień 1939 w relacjach i wspomnieniach.* Warsaw: MON, 1989.

Cyprian, Tadeusz, and Jerzy Sawicki, eds. *Siedem procesów Najwyższego Trybunału Narodowego.* Poznań: Instytut Zachodni, 1962.

Das Generalgouvernements. Ein Jahr Aufbauarbeit im Distrikt Krakau. Krakow: Zeitungsverlag Krakau, 1942.

Das Recht der Kommunalfinanzen im Generalgouvernement. Krakow: Amt für Gesetzgebung, Generalgouvernement, Typ. Stadtdruckerei, 1943.

Datner, Szymon, Janusz Gumkowski, and Kazimierz Leszczyński. "Einsatzgruppen (Wyrok i uzasadnienie)." *BGKBZHP* XIV (1963): III–199.

Didier, Friedrich, ed. *Europa pracuje w Niemczech: Sauckel mobilizuje rezerwy produkcyjne.* Berlin: Zentralverlag der NSDAP, 1943.

———. *Handbuch für die Dienststellen des Generalbevollmachtigen für den Arbeitseinsatz und die interessierten Reichsstellen, im Auftrage der GBA.* Berlin: Generalbevollmachtigte für den Arbeitseinsatz, 1944.

Domarus, Max, ed. *Hitler—Reden und Proklamationen 1932–1945.* Neustadt: Schmidt, 1962–1963.

Du Prel, Max Freiherr, ed. *Das Deutsche Generalgouvernement Polen: Ein Überblick über Gebiet, Gestaltung und Geschichte.* Krakow: Buchverlag Ost, 1940.

———. *Das Generalgouvernement, Im Auftrage und mit einem Vorwort [von] Dr. Frank.* Wurzburg: Konrad Triltsch Verlag, 1942.

Dunin-Wąsowicz, Krzysztof. *Raporty Ludwiga Fischera gubernatora dystryktu warszawskiego 1939-1944*. Warszawa: Książka i Wiedza, 1987.
Eisenbach, Artur, Adam Rutkowski, and Tatiana Berenstein, eds. *Eksterminacja Żydów na ziemiach polskich w okresie okupacji hitlerowskiej: Zbiór dokumentów*. Warsaw: Żydowski Instytut Historyczny, 1957.
Eisenbach, Artur, Adam Rutkowski, Tatiana Berenstein, and Bernard Mark, eds. *Faschismus—Getto—Massenmord: Dokumentation über Ausrottung und Widerstand der Juden in Polen während des zweiten Weltkrieges*. Berlin: Rütten & Loenig, 1960.
Fischer, Karl, ed. *Die Wehrmacht: Der Freiheitskampf des grossdeutschen Volkes, Hrsg. vom Oberkommando der Wehrmacht*. Berlin: Die Wehrmacht, 1940.
Fischer, Ludwig, and Friedrich Gollert. *Zwei Jahre Aufbauarbeit im Distrikt Earschau*. Krakow: Dt. Osten, 1941.
Forstreuter, Adalbert. *Deutsches Ringen um den Osten, Kampf und Anteil der Stämme und Gaue des Reiches*. Berlin: C.A. Weller, 1940.
Frank, Hans. *Auszüge aus dem Tagebuch von Hans Frank, Generalgouvernor für die besetzten polnischen Gebiete*. Tel Aviv: n.p. 1960.
———. *Hans Frank's Diary*. Warsaw: Państwowe Wydawnictwo Naukowe, 1961.
———. *Okupacja i ruch oporu w dzienniku Hansa Franka 1939-1945*, vol. 1-2. Warsaw: Książka i Wiedza, 1970.
Friedrich, Klaus-Peter, Susanne Heim et al., eds. *Die Verfolgung und Ermordung der europäischen Juden durch das nationalsozialistische Deutschland 1933-1945*. Munich: Oldenbourg, 2008-12.
Geisler, Walter. *Deutscher!: Der osten ruft dich! Die Wirtschaftlichen Entwicklungsmöglichkeiten in den eingegliederten Ostgebieten des Deutschen Reiches*, vol. 1. Berlin: Volk und Reich Verlag, 1941.
Gliksman, William M. *Daily Records Sheet of the Jewish Police (Distrikt I) in the Częstochowa Ghetto 1941-1942*. Jerusalem: Yad Vashem, 1967.
Grohmann, Viktor. *Der Arbeitseinsatz nach den Arbeitseinsatz-politischen Massnahmen des Beauftragten für den Vierjahresplan: Die Mittel und Formen der Staatlichen Einflussnahmen auf das deutsche Arbeitsleben Beidem Arbeitseinsatz*. Dresden: Buchdruck M. Dittert, 1939.
Hofer, Walther, ed. *Der Nationalsozialismus: Dokumente 1933-1945*. Frankfurt a.M.: Fischer Bücherei KG, 1957.
Janczewska, Marta, ed. *Obozy pracy przymusowej. Archiwum Ringelbluma. Konspiracyjne archiwum getta Warszawy*, vol. 24. Warsaw: Żydowski Instytut Historyczny, 2015.
Jóźwik, Marek. "Akta Żydowskiej Samopomocy Społecznej (1940-1942) w Archiwum Żydowskiego Instytutu Historycznego w Warszawie (ze szczególnym uwzględnieniem miasta Radomia)." In *Biuletyn Kwartalny Radomskiego Towarzystwa Naukowego XXXIII: Żydzi w dystrykcie radomskim w okresie II wojny światowej*, no. 1 (1998): 43–49.
Kasperek, Józef. *Kronika wydarzeń w Lublinie w okresie okupacji hitlerowskiej*. Lublin: Wydawnictwo Lubelskie, 1989.

Katzmann, Friedrich, and Andrzej Żbikowski, eds. *Rozwiązanie kwestii żydowskiej w Dystrykcie Galicja*. Warsaw: Instytut Pamięci Narodowej, 2001.

Kermish, Joseph, ed. *To Live with Honor and Die with Honor: Selected Documents from the Warsaw Ghetto Underground Archives "O.S." (Oneg Shabbath)*. Jerusalem: Yad Vashem, 1986.

Kuppers, Hans, and Rudolf Bannier. *Arbeitsrecht der Polen im deutschen Reich: Private Wirtschaft und offentlicher Dienst*. Berlin: O. Elsner, 1942.

Melies, Heinz, ed. *Das Arbeitsrecht des Generalgouvernements: Die Regelungen der Arbeitsbedingungen, insbesondere der Lohngestaltung im Generalgouvernement*. Krakow: Burgverlag, 1943.

Mozołowski, Rafał, ed. *Inwentarz archiwalny b. Statistisches Amt 1939–1944. Statystyka w dokumencie archiwalnym 2*. Warsaw: GUS, 1968.

———. *Inwentarz archiwalny spisu ludności Generalnego Gubernatorstwa 1943. Statystyka w dokumencie archiwalnym 5*. Warsaw: GUS, 1970.

Madajczyk, Czesław, ed. *Zamojszczyzna—Sonderlaboratorium SS: Zbiór dokumentów polskich i niemieckich z okresu okupacji hitlerowskiej*. Warsaw: Ludowa Spółdzielnia Wydawnicza, 1977.

Noakes, Jeremy, and Geoffrey Pridham. *Nazism 1919–1945: A Documentary Reader*, vol. 3: *Foreign Policy, War and Racial Extermination*. Exeter: University of Exeter, 1997.

Piotrowski, Stanisław. *Dziennik Hansa Franka*. Warszawa: Wydawnictwo Prawnicze, 1956.

———. *Misja Odyla Globocnika: Sprawozdania o wynikach finansowych zagłady Żydów w Polsce*. Warszawa: Państwowy Instytut Wydawniczy, 1949.

Pospieszalski, Karol Marian. *Hitlerowskie "prawo" okupacyjne w Polsce: Wybór dokumentów*, vol. 1: *Ziemie "wcielone."* Doccumenta Occupationis V. Poznań: Instytut Zachodni, 1952.

———. *Hitlerowskie "prawo" okupacyjne w Polsce*, vol. 2: *Generalna Gubernia: Wybór dokumentów i próba syntezy*. Doccumenta Occupationis VI. Poznań: Instytut Zachodni, 1958.

Proces ludobójcy Amona Leopolda Goetha przed Najwyższym Trybunałem Narodowym. Warsaw: Centralna Żydowska Komisja Historyczna, 1947.

Rauschning, Hermann. *Hitler Speaks: A Series of Political Conversations with Adolf Hitler on His Real Aims*, London: Butterworth, 1940.

Rejestr miejsc i faktów zbrodni popełnionych przez okupanta hitlerowskiego na ziemiach polskich w latach 1939–1945. Warsaw: GKBZHP-IPN, 1985.

Ruppert, Josef, ed. *Richtlinien für die Krankenernährung im Generalgouvernement*. Krakow: Burgverlag, 1942.

Schindler, Dietrich, and Jiří Toman, eds. *The Laws of Armed Conflicts: A Collection of Conventions, Resolutions and Other Documents*. Geneva: Henri Dunant Institute, 1988.

Schulte-Wissermann, Fritz. *Das Devisenrecht des Generalgouvernements*. Krakow: Verlag des Instituts für deutsche Ostarbeit, n.d.

Seraphim, Hans-Jürgen, and Carl Heymann, eds. *Ostraum-Berichte: Schriftenreihe für Wirtschaftskunde und Wirtschaftspolitik Osteuropas*. Berlin: n.p., 1942.

Seraphim, Peter-Heinz, and Gerald Fischer. *Polen und seine Wirtschaft*. Königsberg: Institut für osteuropaische Wirtschaft, 1937.

Seraphim, Peter-Heinz. *Das Judentum im osteuropäischen Raum*. Essen: Essener Verlagsanstalt, 1938.

———. *Die Wirtschaftsstruktur des Generalgouvernements*. Krakow: Burgverlag, 1941.
Skibińska, Alina, and Robert Szuchta, eds. *Wybór źródeł do nauczania o Zagładzie Żydów na okupowanych ziemiach polskich*. Warsaw: Stowarzyszenie Centrum Badań nad Zagładą Żydów, 2010.
Stothfang, Walter. *Arbeitseinsatz im Kriege*. Berlin: Junker und Dunnhaupt, 1940.
Święcicki, Witold, and Feliks Zadrowski, eds. *Zbiór rozporządzeń władz niemieckich obowiązujących na terenie Generalnego Gubernatorstwa ze szczególnym uwzględnieniem Okręgu Szefostwa Warszawskiego*. Warsaw: Typ. "Presshaus," 1940.
Syrup, Friedrich. *Arbeitseinsatz im Krieg und Frieden*. Essen: Essener Verlagsanstalt, 1942.
Umińska, Apolonia, ed. *Inwentarz zbioru "Pamiętniki Żydów" 1939–1945*. Warsaw: Archiwum Żydowskiego Instytutu Historycznego, 1994.
Walbaum, Jost, ed. *Kampf den Seuchen!: Deutscher Ärzte-Einsatz im Osten; Die Aufbauarbeit im Gesundheitswesen des Generalgouvernements*. Krakow: Deutscher Osten, 1941.
Weh, Albert. *Das Recht des Generalgouvernements: Nach Sachgebieten geordnet mit Erläuterungen und einem ausführlichen Sachverzeihnis*. Krakow: Burgverlag, 1941.
———. *Ein Jahr Generalgouvernement*. Berlin: C. Heymann, 1940.
———. *Übersicht über das Recht des Generalgouvernements*. Krakow: Burgverlag, 1943.
Witte, Peter, et al., eds. *Himmlers Dienstkalender*. Hamburg: Christians, 1999.
Wörmann, Emil. *Die Europäische Ernährungswirtschaft in Zahlen*, vol. 2. Berlin, 1944.
Zelinkovsky, Issachar, ed. *Ghetto Bochnia: On the Trail of the Family I Never Knew*. Ontario: n.p., 1995.

ENCYCLOPEDIAS AND LEXICONS

Angolia, John R., and David Littlejohn, eds. *Labor Organizations of the Reich*. Mountain View, CA: R. J. Bender Pub., 1999.
Benz, Wolfgang, et al., eds. *Enzyklopädie des Nationalsozialismus*. Stuttgart: Klett-Cotta, 1997.
Borzymińska, Zofia, and Rafał Żebrowski, eds. *Polski słownik judaistyczny: Dzieje, kultura, religia, ludzie*. Warszawa: Proszynski i S-ka, 2003.
Charny, Israel W., ed. *Encyclopedia of Genocide*, vols. 1–2. Santa Barbara: ABC-Clio, 1999.
Encyclopaedia Judaica. Jerusalem: Keter Publishing House, 1971.
Encyclopedia of Nationalism, vols. 1–2. San Diego: Academic Press, 2001.
Gutman, Yisrael, ed. *Encyclopedia of the Holocaust*, vols. 1–4. New York: Macmillan, 1990.
MacLean, French L., *The Field Men: The Officers Who Led the Einsatzkommandos—The Nazi Mobile Killing Units*. Atglen, PA: Schiffer Military History, 1999.
Pilichowski, Czesław, ed. *Obozy hitlerowskie na ziemiach polskich 1939–1945: Informator encyklopedyczny*. Warsaw: Państwowe Wydawnictwo Naukowe, 1979.
Rossi, Jacques, William A. Burhans, and Robert Conquest, eds. *The Gulag Handbook: An Encyclopedia Dictionary of Soviet Penitentiary Institutions and Term Related to the Forced Labor Camps*. New York: Paragon House, 1989.
Roszkowski, Wojciech, and Jan Kofman, eds. *Słownik biograficzny Europy Środkowo-Wschodniej*. Warszawa: ISP PAN-RYTM, 2004.

Rozett, Robert, and Shmuel Spector, eds. *Encyclopedia of the Holocaust*. Jerusalem: Yad Vashem-Facts on File Inc., 2000.

Snyder, Louis Leo. *Encyclopedia of the Third Reich*. New York: Paragon House, 1976.

Spector, Shmuel, ed. *The Encyclopedia of Jewish Life before and during the Holocaust*, vols. 1–3. New York: New York University Press, 2001.

Tomaszewski, Jerzy, and Andrzej Żbikowski, eds. *Żydzi w Polsce: Dzieje i kultura—Leksykon*. Warsaw: Wydawnictwo Cyklady, Warszawa, 2001.

Weinmann, Martin, Ane Kaiser, and Ursula Krause-Schmidt, eds. *Die Nationalsozialistische Lagersystem (CCP)*. Frankfurt a.M.: Zweitausendeins, 1998.

Wistrich, Robert S. *Who's Who in Nazi Germany*. London: Routledge, 2002.

Zentner, Christian, and Friedemann Bedürftig, eds. *The Encyclopedia of the Third Reich*. New York: Da Capo, 1997.

PERIODICALS

Amtsblatt des Chefs des Distrikts Warschau im Generalgouvernement
Biuletyn Informacyjny
Gazeta Żydowska
Verordnungsblatt des Generalgouverneurs für die besetzten polnischen Gebiete
Verordnungsblatt für das Generalgouvernement

DIARIES AND MEMOIRS

Adamczyk, Ryszard. *Izbicy dni powszednie: Wojna i okupacja—pamiętnik pisany po latach*. Lublin: Norbertinum, 2007.

Adler, Stanisław. *In the Warsaw Ghetto 1940–1943: An Account of a Witness*. Jerusalem: Yad Vashem, 1982.

Bauminger, Róża. *Przy pikrynie i trotylu*. Krakow: CŻKH, 1946.

Berg, Mary. *Warsaw Ghetto: A Diary by Mary Berg*. New York: L. B. Fischer, 1945.

Biberstein, Aleksander. *Zagłada Żydów w Krakowie*. Krakow: Wydawnictwo Literackie, 1985.

Birenbaum, Halina. *Nadzieja umiera ostatnia*. Warsaw: Czytelnik, 1967.

Blatt, Thomas (Toivi). *Sobibor, the Forgotten Revolt*. Issaquah: HEP, 1998.

Borwicz, Michał. *Uniwersytet zbirów*. Krakow: CKŻP, 1946.

Brener, Liber. *Widersztand un umkum in tszenstohower geto*. Warsaw: ŻIH, 1950

Bryskier, Henryk. *Żydzi pod swastyką, czyli getto w Warszawie w XX wieku*. Warsaw: Aspra, 2006.

Chodźko, Mieczysław. *Ucieczka z Treblinki*. Montreal: Polish-Jewish Heritage Foundation of Canada, 2004.

Decker, Willed. *Mit dem Spaten durch Polen: Der Reichsarbeitsdienst im Polnischen Feldzug*. Leipzig: v. Hase & Koehler, 1939.

Diamant, Ita. *Moja cząstka życia*. Warszawa: Twój Styl, 2001.

Donat, Alexander. *The Holocaust Kingdom: A Memoir*. London: Secker & Warburg, 1965.

Frank, Hans. *Das Diensttagebuch des deutschen Generalgouverneurs in Polen 1939–1945*, Hrsg. von Werner Praeg und Wolfgang Jacobmeyer, Deutsche Verlags-Anstalt, Stuttgart, 1975.

Fuks, Marian, ed. *Adama Czerniakowa dziennik getta warszawskiego 6 IX 1939–23 VII 1942*. Warsaw: Państwowe Wydawnictwo Naukowe, 1983.

Glazar, Richard. *Trap with a Green Fence: Survival in Treblinka*. Evanston, IL: Northwestern University Press, 1995.

Gruber, Sam (Mietek). *I Chose Life*. New York: Shengold, 1978.

Hirszfeld, Ludwik. *Historia jednego życia*. Warszawa: Czytelnik, 1946.

Kaplan, Chaim. *The Warsaw Diary of Chaim A. Kaplan*. New York: Collier, 1973.

———. *Scroll of Agony: The Warsaw Diary of Chaim Kaplan*. Bloomington: Indiana University Press, 1999.

Klukowski, Zygmunt. *Dziennik z lat okupacji Zamojszczyzny, 1939–1944*. Lublin: LSW, 1958.

———. *Diary from the Years of Occupation 1939–1944*. Urbana: University of Illinois Press, 1993.

Kulski, Julian, *Zarząd miejski Warszawy 1939–1944*, Państwowe Wydawnictwo Naukowe, Warszawa, 1964.

Landau, Ludwik. *Kronika lat wojny i okupacji, vol. 1, wrzesień 1939–listopad 1940*, Warsaw: Państwowe Wydawnictwo Naukowe, 1962.

———. *Kronika lat wojny i okupacji, vol. 2, grudzień 1942–czerwiec 1943*, Warsaw: Państwowe Wydawnictwo Naukowe, 1962.

———. *Kronika lat wojny i okupacji, vol. 3, lipiec 1943–luty 1944*, Warsaw: Państwowe Wydawnictwo Naukowe, 1963.

Lewin, Abraham. *A Cup of Tears: A Diary of the Warsaw Ghetto*. Oxford: Blackwell, 1989.

Lewin, Kurt I. *Przeżyłem: Saga Świętego Jura spisana w rou 1946 przez syna rabina Lwowa*. Warsaw: Fundacja Zeszytów Literackich, 2006.

Lochner, Louis, ed. and trans. *The Goebbels Diaries 1942–1943*. Garden City, NY: Doubleday, 1948.

Milch, Baruch. *Testament*. Warsaw: Karta, 2001.

Peczorski, Aleksander. "Powstanie w Sobiborze." *BŻIH* 1 (1952): 3–45.

——— (as Pechersky, Alexander). "Revolt in Sobibor." In *They Fought Back; The Story of Jewish Resistance in Nazi Europe*, ed. Yuri Suhl, 7–44. New York: Schocken, 1975.

Perechodnik, Calel. *Spowiedź: Dzieje rodziny żydowskiej podczas okupacji hitlerowskiej w Polsce*. Warsaw: Ośrodek Karta, 2004.

Peter, Janusz. *Tomaszowskie za okupacji*. Tomaszów: Nakł. Tomaszowskiego Towarzystwa Regionalnego, 1991.

Reder, Rudolf. *Bełżec*. Krakow: Wojewódzka Żydowska Komisja Historyczna, 1946.

Ringelblum, Emmanuel. *Notes from the Warsaw Ghetto*. New York: Schocken, 1974.

———. *Kronika getta warszawskiego: wrzesień 1939–styczeń 1943*, ed. Artur Eisenbach. Warszawa: Czytelnik, 1988.

Ronikier, Adam. *Pamiętniki 1939–1945*. Krakow: Wyd. Literackie, 2001.
Rosenfeld, Else, and Gertrud Luckner, eds. *Lebenszeichen aus Piaski: Briefe Deportierter aus dem Distrikt Lublin 1940–1943*. Munich: Biederstein, 1968.
Szereszewska, Helena. *Krzyż i mezuza*. Warsaw: Czytelnik, 1993.
Wdowinski, David. *And We Are Not Saved*. London: W.H. Allen, Philosophical Library, 1963.
Weingarten, Niusia. *Lo vivido*. Montevideo: Editorial Universitaria de Buenos Aires, 1996
Wiernik, Yankel. *A Year in Treblinka*. New York: American Representation of the General Jewish Workers' Union of Poland, 1944.
Willenberg, Shmuel. *Bunt w Treblince*. Warszawa: Res Publica, 1991.
———. *Rebelion en Treblinka*. Jerusalem: La Semana Publicaciones, 1988.
Wolkowicz, Shlomo. *Das Grab bei Zloczow: Geschichte meines Überlebens, Galizien 1939–1945*. Berlin: Wichern Verlag, 1996.
Żbikowski, Andrzej, ed. *Archiwum Ringelbluma: Konspiracyjne Archiwum Getta Warszawy*, vol. 3: *Relacje z Kresów*. Warsaw: ŻIH, 2000.
Zuckerman, Yitzhak ("Antek"). *A Surplus of Memory: Chronicle of the Warsaw Ghetto Uprising*. Berkeley: University of California Press, 1993.
——— (as Cukierman, Antek). *Nadmiar Pamięci (Siedem owych lat): Wspomnienia 1939–1946*. Warszawa: Państwowe Wydawnictwo Naukowe, 2000.
Zylberberg, Michael. *A Warsaw Diary 1939–1945*. London: Vallentine-Mitchell, 1969.
Zylberberg, Perec. *This I Remember*. Montreal: Concordia University Chair in Jewish Studies, 2000.

SECONDARY LITERATURE

Alberti, Michael. *Die Verfolgung und Vernichtung der Juden im Reichsgau Wartheland 1939–1945*, Wiesbaden: Harrassowitz, 2006.
Allen, Michael Thad. *The Business of Genocide: The SS, Slave Labor and the Concentration Camps*. Chapel Hill, NC: University of North Carolina Press, 2002.
Aly, Götz, and Susanne Heim. *Architects of Annihilation: Auschwitz and the Logic of Destruction*. London: Weidenfeld and Nicolson, 2002.
———. "The Economics of the Final Solution: A Case Study from the General Government," *Simon Wiesenthal Center Annual* 5 (1988): 3–48.
Aly, Götz. *"Final Solution": Nazi Population Policy and the Murder of European Jews*. London: Arnold, 1999.
Aly, Götz, et al., *Sozialpolitik und Judenvernichtung: Gibt es eine Ökonomie der Entlösung?* Berlin: Rotbuch Verlag, 1983.
Angrick, Andrej. "Annihilation and Labor: Jews and Thoroughfare IV in Central Ukraine." In *The Shoah in Ukraine: History, Testimony, Memorialization*, ed. Ray Brandon and Wendy Lower, 190–223. Bloomington: Indiana University Press, 2008.
Arad, Yitzhak. *Belzec, Sobibor, Treblinka: The Operation Reinhardt Death Camps*. Bloomington: Indiana University Press, 1999.

———. *History of the Holocaust: Soviet Union and Annexed Territories* [Hebrew], vol. 1–2. Jerusalem: Yad Vashem, 2004.

———. "Jewish Family Camps in the Forests—An Original Means of Rescue." In: *The Nazi Holocaust*, vol. 7: *Jewish Resistance to the Holocaust*, ed. Michael R. Marrus, 219–39. London: Meckler, 1989.

———. "Jewish Prisoner Uprisings in the Treblinka and Sobibor Extermination Camps." In *Nazi Concentration Camps*, 357–99. Jerusalem: Yad Vashem, 1984.

Arbeitsmarkt und Sondererlass: Menschenverwertung, Rassenpolitik und Arbeitsamt. Berlin: Rotbuch Vlg., 1990.

Barkai, Avraham. *Nazi Economics: Ideology, Theory and Policy*. New Haven, CT: Yale University Press, 1990.

Bender, Sara. *"Be-Eretz Oyev," The Jews of Kielce and the Vicinity during World War II: 1939–1945*. Jerusalem: Yad Vashem, 2012.

Bender, Sara. "Jewish Slaves in Forced Labor Camps in Kielce, September 1942–August 1944." *Polin* 23 (2011): 437–63.

Bennett, Giles. "Die Arbeitsbedinungen der Warschauer Juden 1941–1942. Max Bischof und die Transferstelle Warschau." In *Arbeit in den nationalsozialistischen Ghettos*, ed. Jürgen Hensel und Stephan Lehnstaedt, 91–110. Osnabrück: Fibre, 2013.

Benz, Wolfgang. "Zwangsarbeit im nationalsozialistischen Staat: Dimensionen—Strukturen—Perspektiven." *Dachauer Hefte* 16 (2000): 3–17.

———. "Ghetto: Topographie—Strukturen—Funktion." In *Lebenswelt Ghetto: Alltag und Soziales Umfeld während der nazionalsozialistischen Verfolgung*, ed. Imke Hansen, Katrin Steffen, and Joachim Tauber, 24–36. Wiesbaden: Harrassowitz Vlg., 2013.

Berenstein, Tatiana, and Adam Rutkowski. "Prześladowania ludności żydowskiej w okresie hitlerowskiej administracji wojskowej na okupowanych ziemiach polskich (1 IX 1939 r.–25 X 1939 r.)," parts 1–3. *BŻIH* 38 (1961): 3–38.

Brustin-Berenstein, Tatiana. "Hitlerowskie dyskryminacje gospodarcze wobec Żydów w Warszawie przed utworzeniem getta." *BŻIH* 2 (1952): 156–90.

———. "O hitlerowskich metodach eksploatacji gospodarczej getta warszawskiego." *BŻIH* 4 (1953): 3–52.

———. "O niektórych zagadnieniach gospodarczych w tzw. Generalnej Guberni w świetle 'Dziennika Franka.'" *BŻIH* 9–10 (1954): 236–87.

——— (as Berenstein, Tatiana). "Eksterminacja ludności żydowskiej w dystrykcie Galicja (1941–1943)." *BŻIH* 61 (1967): 3–58.

——— (as Berenstein, Tatiana). "Obozy pracy przymusowej dla Żydów w dystrykcie lubelskim." *BŻIH* 24 (1957): 3–20.

——— (as Berenstein, Tatiana). "Praca przymusowa Żydów w Warszawie w czasie okupacji hitlerowskiej." *BŻIH* 45–46 (1963): 42–93.

——— (as Berenstein, Tatiana). "Praca przymusowa ludności żydowskiej w tzw. Dystrykcie Galicja (1941–1944)." *BŻIH* 69 (1969): 3–45.

———— (as Berenstein, Tatiana). "Prześladowania ludności żydowskiej w okresie hitlerowskiej administracji wojskowej na okupowanych ziemiach polskich (1 IX 1939 r.–25 X 1939 r.)," parts 4–5. *BŻIH* 39 (1961): 63–87.

Blatman, Daniel. *For Our Freedom and Yours: The Jewish Labour Bund in Poland 1939–1949*. London: Vallentine Mitchell, 2003.

Böhler, Jochen, ed. *"Größte Härte… ". Verbrechen der Wehrmacht in Polen Septembe–Oktober 1939*. Osnabrück: Fibre, 2005.

Böhler, Jochen. *Auftakt zum Vernichtungskrieg: Die Wehrmacht in Polen 1939*. Frankfurt a.M.: Fischer, 2006.

————. "Totentanz. Niemieckie śledztwa w sprawie akcji 'Erntefest.'" *Erntefest 3–4 listopada 1943—zapomniany epizod Zagłady*, ed. Wojciech Lenarczyk, Dariusz Libionka, 327–46. Lublin: Państowe Muzeum na Majdanku, 2009.

————. *Zbrodnie Wehrmachtu w Polsce: Wrzesień 1939: Wojna totalna*. Krakow: Znak, 2009.

Breitman, Richard. *The Architect of Genocide: Himmler and the Final Solution*. London: Bodley Head, 1991.

Brener, Liber. "O pracy przymusowej ludności żydowskiej w Częstochowie w okresie okupacji hitlerowskiej." *BŻIH* 22 (1952): 45–60.

Broszat, Martin. "Nationalsozialistische Konzetrationslager 1933–1945." In *Anatomie des SS-Staates*, ed. Martin Broszat. Freiburg: Walter-Verlag, 1965.

Browning, Christopher Robert. *Fateful Months: Essays on the Emergence of the Final Solution*. New York: Holmes and Meier Publishers, 1985.

————. "'Alleviation" and "Compliance": The Survival Strategies of the Jewish Leadership in the Wierzbnik Ghetto and Starachowice Factory Slave Labor Camps." In *Gray Zones: Ambiguity and Compromise in the Holocaust and Its Aftermath*, ed. Jonathan Petropoulos and John K. Roth, 26–36. New York: Berghahn Books. 2005.

————. "Jewish Workers and Survivor Memories: The Case of the Starachowice Labor Camp." In Christopher R. Browning, *Nazi Policy, Jewish Workers, German Killers*, 89–115. Cambridge: Cambridge University Press, 2000.

————. "Jewish Workers in Poland: Self-Maintenance, Exploitation, Destruction." In Christopher R. Browning, *Nazi Policy, Jewish Workers, German Killers*, 58–88. Cambridge: Cambridge University Press, 2000.

————. "Nazi Germany's Initial Attempt to Exploit Jewish Labor in the General Government: The Early Jewish Work Camps 1940–41." In *Die Normalität des Verbrechens: Bilanz und Perspektiven der Forschung zu den nationalsozialistischen Gewaltverbrechen*, ed. Helge Grabitz, Klaus Bästlein, and Johannes Tuchel, 171–85. Berlin: Edition Hentrich, 1994.

————. *Ordinary Men: Reserve Police Battalion 101 and the Final Solution in Poland*. New York: Harper Perennial, 1998.

————. *Remembering Survival: Inside a Nazi Slave Labor Camp*. New York: W. W. Norton, 2010.

————. *The Path to Genocide: Essays on Launching the Final Solution*. Cambridge, MA: Cambrdige University Press, 1998.

――――― (with contributions by Jurgen Matthaus). *The Origins of the Final Solution: The Evolution of Nazi Jewish Policy, September 1939–March 1942.* Lincoln, NE: University of Nebraska Press, 2004.

Bullock, Alan. *Hitler and Stalin: Parallel Lives.* London: HarperCollins, 1991.

Czyńska, Zofia, and Bogumił Kupść. "Obozy zagłady, obozy koncentracyjne i obozy pracy na ziemiech polskich w latach 1939–1945." *BGKBZNwP* I (1946): 11–62.

Conquest, Robert, Paul R. Gregory, and Valery V. Lazarev. *The Economics of Forced Labor: The Soviet Gulag.* Stanford: Hoover Institution Press, 2003.

Datner, Szymon. *55 dni Wehrmachtu w Polsce: Zbrodnie dokonywane na polskiej ludności cywilnej w okresie 1.IX–25.X.1939 r.* Warsaw: MON, 1967.

―――――. "Obozy jenieckie na Lubelszczyźnie w latach okupacji niemieckiej." *Zeszyty Majdanka* 3 (1969): 235–37.

―――――. "Sonderkommando 1005 i jego działalność ze szczególnym uwzględnieniem okręgu białostockiego." *BŻIH* 2 (1976): 63–78.

―――――. "Wywóz ludności polskiej na roboty niewolnicze do Niemiec." *BGKBZHP* XVI (1967): 17–64.

―――――. "Zbrodnie Wehrmachtu na jeńcach wojennych w zakresie pracy." *BGKBZHP* XVII (1967): 7–100.

Dąbrowa-Kostka, Stanisław. *W okupowanym Krakowie: 6 IX 1939–18 I 1945.* Warsaw: MON, 1972.

Dean, Martin. "Regional Pattern of Ghettoisation in the Annexed and Occupied Territories of the Third Reich." In *Lebenswelt Ghetto: Alltag und Soziales Umfeld während der nationalsozialistischen Verfolgung*, ed. Imke Hansen, Katrin Steffen, and Joachim Tauber, 37–51. Wiesbaden: Harrassowitz Vlg., 2013.

Dębnicki, Kazimierz. *Akcja Hasag.* Warsaw: Ruch, 1969.

Dempsey, Patrick. *Einsatzgruppen and the Destruction of European Jewry.* Eastbourne: P.A. Draigh Publishing, 2003.

Dobroszycki, Lucjan. *Reptile Journalism: The Official Polish-Language Press under the Nazis, 1939–1945.* New Haven, CT: Yale University Press, 1994.

Domańska, Regina. "Obozy w getcie warszawskim." *BGKBZPMP-IPN* XXXIV (1992): 124–35.

Dunin-Wasowicz, Krzysztof. "Forced Labor and Sabotage in the Nazi Concentration Camps." *The Nazi Concentration Camps*, ed. Yisrael Gutman, and Avital Saf, 133–42. Jerusalem: Yad Vashem, 1984.

Dziadosz, Edward, and Marszałek Józef. "Więzienia i obozy w dystrykcie lubelskim w latach 1939–1944." *Zeszyty Majdanka* 3 (1969): 54–125.

Dziadosz, Edward, ed. *Masowe egzekucje Żydów 3 listopada 1943 roku: Majdanek, Poniatowa, Trawniki, Lublin.* Lublin: Państwowe Muzeum na Majdanku, 1988

Echtenkamp, Jörg. *Die deutsche Kriegsgesellschaft: 1939 bis 1945: Politisierung, Vernichtung, Überleben*, vol. 1. Suttgart: DVA, 2004.

Eisenbach, Artur, *Hitlerowska polityka eksterminacji Żydów jako jeden z przejawów imperializmu niemieckiego.* Warsaw: ŻIH, 1953.

Eisenblatter, Gerhard. *Grundlinien der Politik des Reichs gegenüber dem Generalgouvernement, 1939–1944.* PhD Thesis. Frankfurt a.M.: n.p., 1979.

Engelking, Barbara, and Jacek Leociak, *Getto warszawskie: Przewodnik po nieistniejącym mieście*. Warsaw: Wydawnictwo IFiS PAN, 2001.

Engelking, Barbara. "Życie codzienne Żydów w miasteczkach dystryktu warszawskiego." In *Prowincja noc: Życie i zagłada Żydów w dystrykcie warszawskim*, ed. Barbara Engelking et al., 119–221. Warsaw: Wydawnictwo IFiS PAN, 2007.

Fear, Jeffrey. "The Business of Genocide: The SS, Slave Labor and the Concentration Camps." *Business History Review*, June 30, 2004.

Finder, Gabriel N. "Jewish Prisoner Labour in Warsaw after the Ghetto Uprising, 1943–1944." *Polin* 17 (2004): 325–51.

Florian, Dierl, and Janjetović Zoran, Linne Karsten. *Pflicht, Zwang und Gewalt: Arbeitsverwaltungen und Arbeitskräftspolitik im deutsch besetzten Polen und Serbien 1939–1944*. Essen: Klartext, 2013.

Förster, Jürgen. "The German Army and the Ideological War against the Soviet Union." In *The Policies of Genocide: Jews and Soviet Prisoners of War in Nazi Germany*, ed. Gerhard Hirschfeld, 15–29. London: The German Historical Institute, 1986.

Friedländer, Saul. *The Years of Extermination: Nazi Germany and the Jews, 1939–1945*. New York: HarperCollins, 2007.

Friedman, Filip. *Zagłada Żydów lwowskich.*, Lodz: Wydawnictwo Centralnej Żydowskiej Komisji Historycznej, 1945.

Friedrich, Klaus-Peter. *Die deutsche polnischsprachige Presse im Generalgouvernement (1939–1945): NS-Propaganda für die polnische Bevölkerung*. Wiesbaden: Westdeutscher Vlg., 2001.

Friedrich, Klaus-Peter. *Publizistische Kollaboration im sog. Generalgouvernement: Personengeschichtliche Aspekte der deutschen Okkupationsherrschaft in Polen (1939–1945)*. Marburg: Herder-Institut, 1999.

Führerhauptquartier Wolfschanze 1940–1945: Zeitgeschichte in Farbe. Kiel: Arndt, 2001.

Gawacki, Henryk. "Liban: Obóz karny służby budowlanej." *BGKBZHwP* VI (1951): 131–67.

Geiss, Imanuel, ed. *Deutsche Politik in Polen 1939–1945: Aus dem Diensttagebuch von Hans Frank*. Opladen: Leske & Budrich, 1980.

Georg, Enno. *Die Wirtschaftlichen Unternehmungen der SS*. Stuttgart: Deutsche Verlags-Anstalt, 1963.

Gerlach, Christian. *Krieg, Ernährung, Völkermord: Forschungen zur deutschen Vernichtungspolitik im Zweiten Weltkrieg*. Hamburg: Hamburger Edition, 1998.

Gibaszewski, Krzysztof. *HASAG: Historia obozu pracy w Skarżysku Kamiennej*. Skarżysko Kamienna: Muzeum im. Orła Białego, 2011.

Gicewicz, Ryszard. "Obóz pracy w Poniatowej (1941–1943)." *Zeszyty Majdanka* 10 (1980): 88–104.

———. "Obóz pracy w Poniatowej (1941–1943)." In *Ernftefest 3–4 listopada 1943 – zapomniany epizod Zagłady*, ed. Wojciech Lenarczyk and Dariusz Libionka, 211–28. Lublin: Państowe Muzeum na Majdanku, 2009.

Gil, Idit. "The Exploitation of Jewish Labor in the Radom District during the First Months of the War." *Yad Vashem Studies* 45 (2017): 69–95.

Glińska, Alina. *Zamojszczyzna w okresie okupacji hitlerowskiej.* Warsaw: Pax, 1968.

Goschler, Constantin. "The Struggle for Recognition and Compensation of Forced Laborers." In *Forced Labor: The Germans, the Forced Laborers and the War*, ed. Volkhard Knigge et al., 230–41. Weimar: Buchenwald and Mittelbau-Dora Memorials Foundation, 2010.

Grabitz, Helge. *Letzte Spuren: Ghetto Warschau, SS-Arbeitslager Trawniki, Aktion Erntefest: Fotos und Dokumente über Opfer des Endlösungwahns im Spiegel der historischen Ereignisse.* Berlin: Edition Hentrich, 1988.

Grelka, Frank. "Rural Hubs of Early Destruction. The Waterworks' Camps in the Lublin District, 1940–1942." *Yad Vashem Studies* 45 (2017): 39–67.

Grieger, Manfred. "Extermination and Work under the Nazi System of Forced Labor." In *Forced Labor: The Germans, the Forced Laborers and the War*, ed. Volkhard Knigge et al., 208–19. Weimar: Buchenwald and Mittelbau-Dora Memorials Foundation, 2010.

Gross, Jan Tomasz. *Polish Society under German Occupation: The Generalgouvernement, 1939–1944.* Princeton, NJ: Princeton University Press, 1979.

Grudzińska, Marta, and Violetta Rezler-Wasielewska. "Lublin, Lipowa 7: Obóz dla Żydów—polskich jeńców wojennych (1940–1943)." *Kwartalnik Historii Żydów* 4 (2008): 490–514.

Gruner, Wolf. "Der Beginn der Zwangsarbeit für arbeitslose Juden in Deutschland 1938–39." *Zeitschrift für Geschichtswissenschaft* 37 (1989): 135–51.

———. *Der geschlossene Arbeitseinsatz deutscher Juden: Zur Zwangsarbeit als Element der Verfolgung 1938–1943.* Berlin: Metropol Vlg., 1997.

———. *Die Organisation von Zwangsarbeit für Juden in Deutschland und im Generalgouvernement 1939–1943, eine vergleichende Eestandsaufnahme.* Berlin: Stiftung Topographie des Terrors, 1995.

———. *Jewish Forced Labor under the Nazis: Economic Needs and Racial Aims, 1938–1944.* Cambridge: Cambridge University Press, 2006.

———. *Juden bauen die "Strassen des Führers": Zwangsarbeit und Zwangsarbeitslager für nichtdeutsche Juden im Altreich 1940 bis 1943/44.* Berlin: Metropol, 1996.

———. "Terra Incognita?: The Camps for Jewish Labor Conscription (1938–1943) and the German Population." *Yad Vashem Studies* 24 (1994): 3–42.

Gumkowski, Janusz. *Zbrodniarze hitlerowscy przed Najwyższym Trybunałem Narodowym.* Warsaw: Wyd. Prawnicze, 1961.

Gutman, Yisrael. "The Concept of Labor in Judenrat Policy." In *Patterns of Jewish Leadership in Nazi Europe, 1933–1945*, ed. Yisrael Gutman, 151–80. Jerusalem: Yad Vashem, 1979

———. *Żydzi warszawscy 1939–1943: Getto—Podziemie—Walka.* Warsaw: Rytm, 1993.

Gutman, Yisrael, and Cynthia J. Haft, eds. *Patterns of Jewish Leadership in Nazi: Proceedings of the Third Yad Vashem Internatonal Historical Conference, April 1977.* Jerusalem: Yad Vashem, 1979.

Gutman, Yisrael, and Avital Saf, eds. *The Nazi Concentration Camps: Structure and Aims, The Image of the Prisoner, the Jews in the Camps.* Yad Vashem, Jerusalem, 1984.

Gutterman, Bella, ed. *Days of Horror; Jewish Testiomonies from German Occupied Lemberg 1941–1943.* Tel Aviv: Tel Aviv University, 1991.

Hamburger, Ludwig. *How Nazi Germany Has Mobilized and Controlled Labor.* Washington: Brookings Institution, 1940.

Heim Susanne, and Götz Aly, eds. *Bevölkerungsstruktur und Massenmord: Neue Dokumente zur deutschen Politik der Jahre 1938–1945.* Berlin: Rotbuch Verlag, 1991.

Held, Thomas. "Vom Pogrom zum Massenmord: Die Vernichtung der jüdischen Bevölkerung Lembergs im Zweiten Weltkrieg." In *Lemberg, Lwów, Lviv*, ed. Peter Fäßler, Thomas Held, and Dirk Sawitzki, 113–16. Cologne: n.p., 1993.

Hempel, Adam. *Pogrobowcy klęski: Rzecz o policji 'granatowej' w Generalnym Gubernatorstwie, 1939–1945.* Warsaw: PWN, 1990.

Hepp, Michael. "Deutsche Bank, Dresdner Bank—Erlöse aus Raub, Enteignung und Zwangsarbeit 1933–1945." *Zeitschrift für Sozialgeschichte* 15, no. 1 (2000): 64–116.

Herbert, Ulrich. *Hitler Foreign Workers: The Forced Foreign Labor in Germany under the Third Reich.* Cambrigde: Cambrige University Press, 1997.

———. "Zwangsarbeiter im 'Dritten Reich' und das Problem der Entschädigung: Ein Überblick." In: *Die politische Ökonomie des Holocaust*, ed. Dieter Stiefel, 203–38. Munich: R. Oldenbourg Verlag, 2001.

———. "Zwangsarbeit im 20. Jahrhundert." In *Zwangsarbeit in Hitlers Europa: Besatzung-Arbeit-Folgen*, ed. Dieter Pohl und Tanja Sebta, 23–36. Berlin: Metropol, 2013.

Heusler, Andreas. "Forced Labor in the Nazi War Economy: The Genesis of a Research Genre." In *Forced Labor: The Germans, the Forced Laborers and the War*, ed. Volkhard Knigge et al., 194–201. Weimar: Buchenwald and Mittelbau-Dora Memorials Foundation, 2010.

Hilberg, Raul, *The Destruction of the European Jews.* Chicago: Harper & Row, 1961.

Hoffenberg, Sam. *Le camp de Poniatowa: La liquidation des derniers Juifs de Varsovie.* Paris: Bibliophane, 1988.

Homze, Edward L. *Foreign Labor in Nazi Germany.* Princeton, NJ: Princeton University Press, 1967.

Honigsman, Iakov. *Katastrofa evreistva Zapadnoi Ukrainy: Evrei Vostochnoi Galitsii, Zapadnoi Volyni, Bukoviny i Zakarpatia v 1933–1945 godakh.* Lviv: n.p., 1998.

———. *Katastrofa l'vovskogo evreistva.* Lviv: n.p., 1993.

Hryciuk, Grzegorz. *Przemiany narodowościowe i ludnościowe w Galicji Wschodniej i na Wołyniu w latach 1931–1948.* Torun: Wydawnictwo Adam Marszałek, 2005.

Janczewska, Marta. "Obozy pracy przymusowej dla Żydów na terenie dystryktu warszawskiego." In *Prowincja noc: Życie i zagłada Żydów w dystrykcie warszawskim*, ed. Barbara Engelking et al., 271–320. Warsaw: Wydawnictwo IFiS PAN, 2007.

Jansen, Christian. "Zwangsarbeit für das Volkswagenwerk: Häftlingsalltag auf dem Laagberg bei Wolfsburg." In *Ausbeutung, Vernichtung, Öffentlichkeit*, ed. Norbert Frei and Sybille Steinbacher, 75–107. Munich: Saur, 2000.

Jaskot, Paul B. *The Architecture of Oppression: The SS, Forced Labor and the Nazi Monumental Building Economy.* New York: Routledge, 2000.

———. "Concentration Camps and Cultural Policy: Rethinking the Development of the Camp System, 1936–41." *Lessons and Legacies* VI (2004): 5–20.

Jastrzębowski, Wacław. *Gospodarka niemiecka w Polsce 1939–1944*. Warsaw: Czytelnik, 1946.

Jones, Eliahu. *Żydzi Lwowa w okresie okupacji 1939–1945*. Lodz: Oficyna Bibliofilów, 1999.

Kaczanowski, Longin. *Hitlerowskie fabryki śmierci na Kielecczyźnie*. Warsaw: Książka i Wiedza, 1984.

Kahane, David. *Lvov Ghetto Diary*. Amherst: University of Massachusetts Press, 1990.

Kaienburg, Hermann. "Zwangsarbeit von Juden in Arbeits- und Konzentrationslagern." In *"Arisierung" im Nationalsozialismus*, ed. Irmtrud Wojak, Peter Hayes, 219–40. Frankfurt a.M.: Campus Verlag, 2000.

Kaienburg, Hermann. *Die Wirtschaft der SS*. Metropol: Berlin, 2003.

Karay, Felicja. "The Conflict among German Authorities over Jewish Slave Labor Camps in the General Government." *Yalkut Moreshet* (1999): 1–28.

———. *Death Comes in Yellow: Skarżysko-Kamienna Slave Labor Camp*. Amsterdam: Harwood Academic Publishers, 1996.

———. "Heaven or Hell? The Two Faces of the HASAG-Kielce Camp." *Yad Vashem Studies* 32 (2004): 269–321.

———. "Spór między władzami niemieckimi o żydowskie obozy pracy w Generalnej Guberni." *Zeszyty Majdanka* 18 (1997): 27–44.

———. "Women in the Forced-Labor Camps." In *Women in the Holocaust*, ed. Dalia Ofer and Lenore J. Weitzman, 285–309. New Haven, CT: Yale University Press, 1998.

———. "Żydowskie obozy pracy w czasie 'akcji Reinhardt.'" In *Akcja Reinhardt. Zagłada Żydów w Generalnym Gubernatorstwie*, ed. Dariusz Libionka, 248–60. Warszawa: IPN, 2004.

Kasperek, Józef. "Metody werbunku do przymusowych robót w III Rzeszy na terenie dystryktu lubelskiego w latach 1939–1944." *Zeszyty Majdanka* 8 (1975): 52–99.

———. "Początki organizacji i działalności urzędów pracy na Lubelszczyźnie (październik 1939–styczeń 1940)." *Zeszyty Majdanka* 6 (1972): 130–50.

———. "Zarys organizacyjny Arbeitsamtów w dystrykcie lubelskim w latach 1939–1944." *Zeszyty Majdanka* 7 (1973): 94–117.

Kiełboń, Janina. "Deportacje Żydów do dystryktu lubelskiego (1939–1943)." *Zeszyty Majdanka* 14 (1992): 61–92.

———. "Deportacje Żydów do dystrykty lubelskiego (1939–1943)." In *Akcja Reinhardt. Zagłada Żydów w Generalnym Gubernatorstwie*, ed. Dariusz Libionka, 161–81. Warszawa: IPN, 2004.

———. *Migracje ludności w dystrykcie lubelskim w latach 1939–1945*. Lublin: Państwowe Muzeum na Majdanku, 1995.

———. "Przemieszczenia Żydow między dystryktami radomskim i lubelskim (1940–1944)" in: Żydzi w dystrykcie radomskim w okresie II wojny światowej." *Biuletyn Kwartalny Radomskiego Towarzystwa Naukowego* XXXIII, no. 1 (1998): 35–42.

Klein, Peter, ed. *Die Einsatzgruppen in der besetzten Sowjetunion 1941/1942. Die Tätigkeits- und Lageberichte des Chefs der Sicherheitspolizei und des SD*. Berlin: Edition Hentrich, 1997.

Kłosinski, Tadeusz. *Polityka przemyslowa okupanta w Generalnym Gubernatorstwie*. Poznań: Instytut Zachodni, 1947.

Konieczny, Alfred, ed. *Praca przymusowa Polakow pod panowaniem hitlerowskim, 1939–1945*. Poznań: Instytut Zachodni, 1976.

Kopówka, Edward. "Obozy pracy przymusowej w Szczeglacinie i Bartkowie Nowym k. Siedlec." *Kwartalnik Historii Żydów* 204 (2002): 515–19.

Kostrowicka, Irena, Zbigniew Landau, and Jerzy Tomaszewski. *Historia gospodarcza Polski XIX i XX wieku*. Warsaw: Książka i Wiedza, 1985.

Kotek, Joel, and Pierre Rigoulot, eds. *Das Jahrhundert der Lager: Gefangenschaft, Zwangsarbeit, Vernichtung*. Berlin: Propyläen, 2001.

Kranz, Tomasz. "Egzekucja Żydów na Majdanku 3 listopada 1943 r w świetle wyroku w procesie w Düsseldorfie." *Zeszyty Majdanka* 19 (1998), 139–50.

———. "Egzekucja Żydów na Majdanku 3 listopada 1943 r." In *Erntefest 3–4 listopada 1943—zapomniany epizod Zagłady*, ed. Wojciech Lenarczyk and Dariusz Libionka, 25–35. Lublin: Państowe Muzeum na Majdanku, 2009.

Krausnick, Helmut. *Hitlers Einsatzgruppen: Die Truppe des Weltanschauungskriege 1938–1942*. Frankfurt a.M.: Fischer Taschenbuch Verlag, 1985.

Krausnick, Helmut et al. *Anatomy of the SS State*. London: Collins, 1968.

Kroll, Bogdan. *Rada Główna Opiekuńcza 1939–1945*. Warsaw: Książka i Wiedza, 1985.

Król, Eugeniusz Cezary. *Polska i Polacy w propagandzie narodowego socjalizmu w Niemczech 1919–1945*. Warsaw: ISP PAN.

Kuwałek, Robert. "Das Durchgangsghetto in Izbica." *Theresienstädter Studien und Dokumente* 10 (2003): 321–51.

———. "Die Durchgangsghettos im Distrikt Lublin (u.a. Izbica, Piaski, Rejowiec und Trawniki)." In *Aktion Reinhardt: Der Völkermord an den Juden im Generalgouvernement, 1941–1944*, ed. Bogdan Musiał, 197–232. Osnabrück: Fibre, 2004.

———. "'Erntefest' w świetle polskich materiałów śledczych (1944–1968)." In *Erntefest 3–4 listopada 1943—zapomniany epizod Zagłady*, ed. Wojciech Lenarczyk and Dariusz Libionka, 287–325. Lublin: Państowe Muzeum na Majdanku, 2009.

———. "Getta tranzytowe w dystrykcie lubelskim." In *Akcja Reinhardt. Zagłada Żydów w Generalnym Gubernatorstwie*, ed. Dariusz Libionka, 138–60. Warszawa: IPN, 2004.

———. "Obóz zagłady w Sobiborze w historiografii polskiej i obcej." *Zeszyty Majdanka* 21 (2001): 115–160.

Kwiet, Konrad. "Forced Labour of German Jews in Nazi Germany." *Leo Baeck Institute Year Book* 36 (1991): 389–410.

Lehnstaedt, Stephan. "Coercion and Incentive. Jewish Ghetto Labor in East Upper Silesia." *Holocaust and Genocide Studies* 24 (2010): 400–30.

———. "Die deutsche Arbeitsverwaltung im Generalgouvernement und die Juden." *Vierteljahrshefte für Zeitgeschichte* 60 (2012): 409–40.

———. "Generalgouvernment: Ideologie und Ökonomie der Judenpolitik," In *Arbeit in den nationalsozialistischen Ghettos*, ed. Jürgen Hensel und Stephan Lehnstaedt, 159–80. Osnabrück: Fibre, 2013.

———. *Geschichte und Gesetzesauslegung: Zu Kontinuität und Wandel des bundesdeutschen Wiedergutmachungsdiskurses am Beispiel der Ghettorenten*. Osnabrück: Fibre, 2011.

———. "Ghetto Labour Pensions. Holocaust Survivors and Their Struggle for Compensation in the 21st Century." *Kwartalnik Historii Żydów* 283 (2011): 191–210.

———. "Jewish Labor in the Smaller Ghettos in the Warthegau Region." *Yad Vashem Studies* 38 (2010): 47–84.

———. "Jüdische Arbeit in Generalgouvernement, Warthegau und Ostoberschlesien." In *Lebenswelt Ghetto: Alltag und Soziales Umfeld während der nationalsozialistischen Verfolgung*, ed. Imke Hansen, Katrin Steffen, and Joachim Tauber, 210–25. Wiesbaden: Harrassowitz Vlg., 2013.

———. "Zwischen Profitgier, Überleben und Rente: Überlegungen zur einer Geschichte der Arbeit in nationalsozialistischen Ghettos." In *Arbeit in den nationalsozialistischen Ghettos*, ed. Jürgen Hensel and Stephan Lehnstaedt, 11–29. Osnabrück: Fibre, 2013.

Lenarczyk, Wojciech. "Obóz pracy przymusowej dla Żydów przy ul. Lipowej w Lublinie (1939–1943)." In *Erntefest 3–4 listopada 1943—zapomniany epizod Zagłady*, ed. Wojciech Lenarczyk and Dariusz Libionka, 37–71. Lublin: Państowe Muzeum na Majdanku, 2009.

———. "Obóz pracy przymusowej w Budzyniu (1942–1944)." In *Erntefest 3–4 listopada 1943—zapomniany epizod Zagłady*, ed. Wojciech Lenarczyk and Dariusz Libionka, 261–86. Lublin: Państowe Muzeum na Majdanku, 2009.

Lenarczyk, Wojciech, and Dariusz Libionka, eds. *Erntefest 3–4 listopada 1943—zapomniany epizod Zagłady*. Lublin: Państowe Muzeum na Majdanku, 2009.

Lewandowska, Stanisława. "Powstania zbrojne w obozach zagłady w Treblince i Sobiborze." *BGKBZPNP-IPN* 35 (1993): 115–27.

Libionka, Dariusz, ed. *Akcja Reinhardt: Zagłada Żydów w Generalnym Gubernatorstwie*. Warsaw: Książka i Wiedza, 2005

———. "Polska konspiracja wobec Żydów w dystrykcie warszawskim." In *Prowincja noc: Życie i zagłada Żydów w dystrykcie warszawskim*, ed. Barbara Engelking et al., 443–504. Warsaw: Wydawnictwo IFiS PAN, 2007

Linne, Karsten. "Struktur und Praxis der deutschen Arbeitsverwaltung im besetzten Polen und Serbien." In *Zwangsarbeit in Hitlers Europa: Besatzung-Arbeit-Folgen*, ed. Dieter Pohl and Tanja Sebta, 39–61. Berlin: Metropol, Berlin, 2013.

Linne, Karsten, and Florian Dierl. *Arbeitskräfte als Kriegsbeute. Der Fall Ost- und Südosteuropa 1939–1945*. Berlin: Metropol, 2011.

Lipgens, Walter, ed. *Europa-Föderationspläne der Widerstandsbewegungen 1940–1945: Eine Dokumentation*. Munich: R. Oldenbourg, 1968.

Longerich, Peter, and Dieter Pohl, eds. *Die Ermordung der europaeischen Juden: Eine umfassende Dokumentation des Holocaust 1941–1945*. Munich: Piper Verlag, 1990.

Loose, Ingo. "Credit Banks and the Holocaust in the 'Generalgouvernement,' 1939–1945." *Yad Vashem Studies* 34 (2006): 177–218.

———. "Die Bedeutung der Ghettoarbeit für die nationalsozialistische Kriegswirtschaft." In *Arbeit in den nationalsozialistischen Ghettos*, ed. Jürgen Hensel and Stephan Lehnstaedt, 71–90. Osnabrück: Fibre, 2013.

Lower, Wendy. "Facilitating Genocide: Nazi Ghettoization Practices in Occupied Ukraine, 1941–1942." In *Life in the Ghettos during the Holocaust*, ed. Eric J. Sterling, 120–44. Syracuse, NY: Syracuse University Press, 2005.

Łuczak, Czesław. *Polityka ludnościowa i ekonomiczna hitlerowskich Niemiec w okupowanej Polsce*. Poznań: Wydawnictwo Poznańskie, 1979.

——— (as editor). *Położenie polskich robotników przymusowych w Rzeszy 1939–1945*. Poznań: Instytut Zachodni, 1975.

———. *Przyczynki do gospodarki niemieckiej w latach 1939–1945*. Poznań: Instytut Zachodni, 1949.

Łukaszewicz, Zygmunt. "Obóz pracy w Treblince." *BGKBZNwP* III (1947): 107–22.

Macior-Majka, Beata. *Generalny Plan Wschodni: Aspekt ideologiczny, polityczny i ekonomiczny*, Krakow: Avalon, 2007.

Madajczyk, Czesław. *Die deutsche Besatzungspolitik in Polen (1939–45)*. Wiesbaden: F. Steiner, 1967.

———. *Faszyzm i okupacje 1938–1945: Wykonywanie okupacji przez państwa Osi w Europie*, vol. 1: *Ukształtowanie się zarządów okupacyjnych*, Poznań: Wydawnictwo Poznańskie, 1983.

———. *Faszyzm i okupacje 1938–1945: Wykonywanie okupacji przez państwa Osi w Europie*, vol. 2: *Mechanizmy realizowania okupacji*. Poznań: Wydawnictwo Poznańskie, 1984.

———. *Generalna Gubernia w planach hitlerowskich: Studia*. Warsaw: Państwowe Wydawnictwo Naukowe, 1961.

———. *Generalplan Ost*. Poznań: Instytut Zachodni, 1962.

———. "Lubelszczyzna w polityce okupanta." *Zeszyty Majdanka* 2 (1967): 5–18.

———. *Polityka III Rzeszy w okupowanej Polsce*. Warsaw: Państwowe Wydawnictwo Naukowe, 1970.

———. *Nazistowska realizacja doktryny panowania rasowej w Zamościu i na Zamojszczyźnie*. Wroclaw: Ossolineum, 1983.

Madajczyk, Czeslaw, Stanislaw Biernacki et al., eds. *Vom Generalplan Ost zum Generalsiedlungsplan*. Munich: K.G. Saur, 1994.

Majer, Diemut. "'Narodowo obcy' w Trzeciej Rzeszy: przyczynek do narodowo-socjalistycznego ustawodawstwa i praktyki prawniczej w administracji i wymiarze sprawiedliwości ze szczególnym uwzględnieniem ziem wcielonych do Rzeszy i Generalnego Gubenatorstwa." *GKBZHwP-IPN* (1989).

———. *"Non-Germans" under the Third Reich: the Nazi Judicial and Administrative System in Germany and Occupied Eastern Europe, with Special Regard to Occupied Poland, 1939–1945*. Baltimore, MD: John Hopkins University Press, 2003.

Mallmann, Klaus-Michael, and Bogdan Musiał, eds. *Genesis des Genozids: Polen 1939–1941*. Darmstadt: Wissenschaftliche Buchgesellschaft, 2004.

Malmgreen, Gail. *Labor and the Holocaust: The Jewish Labor Committee and Anti-Nazi Struggle*. Silver Spring, MD: George Meany Memorial Archives, 1991.

Mańkowski, Zygmunt. "Obozy zagłady na terenie dystryktu lubelskiego, ich system i funkcje." *Zeszyty Majdanka*. 17 (1996): 39–49.

———. "Odilo Globocnik und die Endlösung der Judenfrage." *Studia Historiae Oeconomicae* 21 (1994): 147–55.

———. "Strategiczne znaczenie Lubelszczyzny i polityka represyjna okupanta." *Zeszyty Majdanka* 4 (1969): 9–17.

Marszałek, Józef. "The Camp of Zarzecze near Nisko in the System of Jewish Labour Camps." In *Akce Nisko*, 139–47. Ostrava: Rondo, 1995.

———. "Labor Camps in the General Government, 1939–1945." *Pro Memoria* 11 (2001): 37–42.

———. *Obozy pracy w Generalnym Gubernatorstwie w latach 1939–1945*. Lublin: Państwowe Muzeum na Majdanku, 1998.

———. "RozPoznańie obozów śmierci w Bełżcu, Sobiborze i Treblince przez wywiad Armii Krajowej i Delegatury Rządu Rzeczypospolitej Polskiej na Kraj." *BGKBZHP*, XXXV (1993), s. 36–52.

———. "System obozów śmierci w Generalnym Gubernatorstwie i jego funkcje (1942–1943)." *Zeszyty Majdanka* 17 (1996): 17–35.

Meducki, Stanisław. "Ekonomiczne aspekty eksterminacjii Żydów w dystrykcie radomskim." *Biuletyn Kwartalny Radomskiego Towarzystwa Naukowego* XXXIII, no. 1: *Żydzi w dystrykcie radomskim w okresie II wojny światowej* (1998): 19–34.

———. *Przemysł i klasa robotnicza w dystrykcie radomskim w okresie okupacji hitlerowskiej*, Krakow: Państwowe Wydawnictwo Naukowe, 1981.

Mędykowski, Witold. "Der jüdische Kampf um Lebensunterhalt in den Ghettos des Generalgouvernements." In *Lebenswelt Ghetto: Alltag und Soziales Umfeld während der nationalsozialistischen Verfolgung*, ed. Imke Hansen, Katrin Steffen, and Joachim Tauber, 226–41. Wiesbaden: Harrassowitz Vlg., 2013.

———. "Obóz pracy dla Żydów w Trawnikach." In *Erntefest 3–4 listopada 1943— zapomniany epizod Zagłady*, ed. Wojciech Lenarczyk and Dariusz Libionka, 183–210. Lublin: Państowe Muzeum na Majdanku, 2009.

———. "Pogromy 1941 roku na terytorium byłej okupacji sowieckiej (Bukowina, wschodnie województwa RP, państwa bałtyckie) w relacjach żydowskich." In *Świat niepożegnany: Żydzi na dawnych ziemiach wschodnich Rzeczypospolitej w XVIII–XX wieku*, ed. Krzysztof Jasiewicz, 761–813. Warsaw: ISP PAN–RYTM, 2004.

———. "Pomiędzy euforią a klęską: Polityka zatrudnienia jeńców wojennych w przemyśle zbrojeniowym III Rzeszy." *Łambinowicki Rocznik Muzealny* 31 (2008): 7–28.

——— *W cieniu gigantów: Pogromy 1941 r. w byłej sowieckiej strefie okupacyjnej. Kontekst historyczny, społeczny i kulturowy*. Warsaw: ISP PAN, 2012.

———. "Wie überdauerte ein Ghetto? Mikroökonomische Aspekte." In *Arbeit in den nationalsozialistischen Ghettos*, ed. Jürgen Hensel and Stephan Lehnstaedt. Osnabrück: Fibre, 2013.

Meissner, Blanka. *Ewakuacja niemieckich wladz administracyjnych i niemieckiej ludnosci z okupacyjnych ziem polskich w latach 1944–1945.* Warsaw: IPN, 1987.

Mencel, Tadeusz, ed. *Majdanek 1941–1944.* Lublin: Wydawnictwo Lubelskie, 1991.

Milch, Baruch. *Can Heaven be Void?*, ed. Shosh Milch-Avigail. Jerusalem: Yad Vashem, 2003.

Milward, Alan. *Die deutsche Kriegswirtschaft 1939–1945.* Stuttgart: Deutsche Verlagsanstalt, 1966.

Misiuna, Władysław. "Wspomnienia o dziewczętach z obozu pracy dla Żydów w Radomiu." *BŻIH* 1 (1989): 91–99.

Młynarczyk, Jacek Andrzej. *Judenmord in Zentralpolen: Der Distrikt Radom im Generalgouvernement 1939–1945.* Darmstadt: Forschungstelle Ludwigsburg der Universität Stuttgart, 2007.

Motyka, Grzegorz, and Rafał Wnuk. "Żydzi w Galicji Wschodniej i na Wołyniu." In *Europa nie prowincjonalna: Przemiany na ziemiach wschodnich dawnej Rzeczypospolitej (Białoruś, Litwa, Łotwa, Ukraina, wschodnie pogranicze III Rzeczypospolitej Polskiej) w latach 1772–1999*, ed. Krzysztof Jasiewicz. Warsaw: Instytut Studiów Politycznych PAN, 1999.

Musiał, Bogdan, ed. *Aktion Reinhardt: Der Völkermord an den Juden im Generalgouvernement, 1941–1944.* Osnabrück: Fibre, 2004.

———. *Deutsche Zivilverwaltung und Judenverfolgung im Generalgouvernement: Eine Fallstudie zum Distrikt Lublin, 1939–1944.* Wiesbaden: Harrassowitz Verlag, 1999.

———. "Die Verfolgung und Vernichtung der Juden im Generalgouvernement: Die Zivilverwaltung und die Shoah." In *Täter der Shoah: Fanatische Nationalsozialisten oder ganz normale Deutsche?*, ed. Gerhard Paul, 187–203. Göttingen: Wallstein Verlag, 2002.

———. *Konterrevolutionäre Elemente sind zu erschiessen: Die Brutalisierung des deutsch-sowjetischen Krieges im Sommer 1941.* Berlin: Propylaeen, 2000.

———. "The Origins of 'Operation Reinhardt': The Decision-Making Process for the Mass Murder of the Jews on the Generalgouvernement." *Yad Vashem Studies* 18 (2000): 113–53.

Neander, Joachim. "The SS and the Economics of Genocide." *Yad Vashem Studies* 32 (2004): 449–67.

Oberlaender, Theodor. *Die Überwindung der Deutschen Not.* Darmstadt: C. W. Leske, 1954.

Orenstein, Benjamin. *Churban Czenstochow.* N.p.: Central Farwaltung fun der Czenstochower Landsmanschaft in der Amerikaner Zone in Dajczland, 1948.

Ostrowski, Karol. *Hitlerowska polityka podatkowa w Generalnym Gubernatorstwie.* Kraków: Państwowe Wydawnictwo Naukowe, 1977.

Overy, Richard James. *War and Economy in the Third Reich.* Oxford: Clarendon Press, 1994.

Petersen, Hans-Christian. *Bevölkerungsökonomie—Ostforschung—Politik: Eine biographische Studie zu Peter-Heinz Seraphim (1902–1979).* Osnabrück: Fibre, 2007.

Petzina, Dieter. *Autarkiepolitik im Dritten Reich: Der nationallsozialistische Vierjahresplan.* Stuttgart: Deutsche Verlags-Anstalt, 1968.

Piątkowski, Sebastian. "Judenraty w dystrykcie radomskim (ze szczególnym uwzględnieniem miasta Radomia)." In *Biuletyn Kwartalny Radomskiego Towarzystwa Naukowego* XXXIII, no. 1: *Żydzi w dystrykcie Radomskim w okresie II wojny światowej* (1998): 51–70.

Piątkowski, Sebastian. "Obóz pracy w Bliżynie (1942–1944)." *Zeszyty Majdanka* 21 (2001): 97–112.

———. "Żydowscy robotnicy przymusowi w radomskiej fabryce obuwia 'Bata' (1941–1943)." *Kwartalnik Historii Żydów* 227 (2008): 322–33.

Pietrzykowski, Jan. *Łowy na ludzi: Arbeitsamt w Częstochowie.* Katowice: Wydawnictwo Śląsk, 1968.

Pohl, Dieter. "Die 'Aktion Reinhard' im Licht der Historiographie." In *Aktion Reinhardt: Der Völkermord an den Juden im Generalgouvernement, 1941–1944*, ed. Bogdan Musiał, 15–47. Osnabrück: Fibre, 2004.

———. "Die Ermordung der Juden im Generalgouvernement." In *Nationalsozialistische Vernichtungspolitik*, ed. Herbert Ulrich, 98–121. Frankfurt a.M.: Fischer Taschenbuch Verlag, 1998.

———."Die Grossen Zwangsarbeitslager der SS- und Polizeiführer für Juden im Generalgouvernement 1942–1945." In *Die nationalsozialistischen Konzentrationslager: Entwicklung und Struktur*, ed. Christopher Dieckmann, 415–38. Göttingen: Wallstein Vlg, 1998.

———. *Die Herrschaft der Wehrmacht: Deutsche militaerbesatzung und einheimische Bevoelkerung in der Sowjetunion, 1941–1944.* Munich: R. Oldenbourg Verlag, 2008.

———. "Die Stellung des Distrikts Lublin in der 'Endlösung der Judenfrage.'" In *Aktion Reinhardt: Der Völkermord an den Juden im Generalgouvernement, 1941–1944*, ed. Bogdan Musiał, 87–107. Osnabrück: Fibre, 2004.

——— (with Andrej Angrick). *Einsatzgruppen C and D in the invasion of the Soviet Union.* London: Holocaust Educational Trust, 2000.

———. "Forced Labor in Occupied Eastern Europe—A Research Overview." In *Forced Labor: The Germans, the Forced Laborers and the War*, ed. Volkhard Knigge et al., 202–7. Weimar: Buchenwald and Mittelbau-Dora Memorials Foundation, 2010.

———. *Holocaust: Die Ursachen, das Geschehen, die Folgen.* Freiburg: Herder, 2000.

———. *Nationalsozialistische Judenverfolgung in Ostgalizien 1941–1944: Organisation und Durchfürung eines staatlichen Massenverbrechens.* Munich: R. Oldenbourg Verlag, 1997.

———. "Rola dystryktu lubelskiego w 'ostatecznym rozwiązaniu kwestii żydowskiej.'" *Zeszyty Majdanka* 18 (1997): 7–24.

———. "Ukrainische Hilfskräfte beim Mord an den Juden." In *Täter der Shoah: Fanatische Nationalsozialisten oder ganz normale Deutsche?*, ed. Gerhard Paul. Göttingen: Wallstein Verlag, 2002.

———. *Von der "Judenpolitik" zum Judenmord: Der Distrikt Lublin des Generalgouvernements 1939–1944.* Frankfurt a.M.: Lang, 1993.

Pohl, Dieter, and Tanja Sebta, eds. *Zwangsarbeit in Hitlers Europa: Besatzung—Arbeit—Folgen.* Berlin: Metropol, 2013.

Pohl, Dieter, and Tanja Sebta. "Nationalsozialistische Zwangsarbeit außerhalb des Deutsches Reiches und ihre Folgen." In *Zwangsarbeit in Hitlers Europa: Besatzung—Arbeit—Folgen*, ed. Dieter Pohl and Tanja Sebta, 13–22. Berlin: Metropol, 2013.

Polskie Siły Zbrojne w drugiej wojnie światowej, vol. 1: *Kampania wrześniowa 1939*, part 2: *Przebieg działań od 1 do 8 września*. London: Instytut Historyczny im. Gen. Sikorskiego, 1959.

Polskie Siły Zbrojne w drugiej wojnie światowej, vol. 1: *Kampania wrześniowa 1939*, part 3: *Przebieg działań od 9 do 14 września*. London: Instytut Historyczny im. Gen. Sikorskiego, 1959.

Połomski, Franciszek. *Aspekty rasowe w postepowaniu z robotnikami przymusowymi i jeńcami wojennymi III Rzeszy (1939–1945)*. Wroclaw: Ossolineum, 1976.

Popiński, Krzysztof, Aleksander Kokurin et. al., eds. *Drogi śmierci: Ewakuacja więzień sowieckich z Kresów Wschodnich II Rzeczypospolitej w czerwcu i lipcu 1941*. Warsaw: Karta, 1995.

Poprzeczny, Joseph. *Globocnik—Hitler's Man in the East*. London: McFarland & Company, 2004.

Price, John. *Organised Labour in the War*. New York: A. Lane, 1940.

Proces ludobójcy Amona Leopolda Goetha przed Najwyższym Trybunałem Narodowym. Krakow: Centralna Żydowska Komisja Historyczna, 1947.

Przybysz, Kazimierz. *Chlopi polscy wobec okupacji hitlerowskiej, 1939–1945: Zachowania i postawy polityczne na terenach Generalnego Gubernatorstwa*. Warsaw: Ludowa Spoółdzielnia Wydawnicza, 1983.

Radzik, Tadeusz. *Lubelska dzielnica zamknięta*. Lublin: Wydawnictwo UMCS, 1999.

———. "Praca przymusowa ludności żydowskiej na przykładzie obozu pracy w Bełżcu w 1940 r." In *Żydzi i judaizm we współczesnych badaniach polskich: Materiały z konferencji, Kraków, 21–23 XI 1995*, ed. Krzysztof Pilarczyk, 307–319. Krakow: Księgarnia Akademicka Wydawnictwo Naukowe, 1997.

Rajca, Czesław. "Lubelska filia Niemieckich Zakładów Zbrojeniowych." *Zeszyty Majdanka* 4 (1969): 237–300.

———. "Podobozy Majdanka." *Zeszyty Majdanka* 9 (1977): 83–103.

Rieger, Berndt. *Creator of Nazi Death Camps: The Life of Odilo Globocnik*. London: Valentine-Mitschell, 2007.

Ringelblum, Emanuel. *Stosunki polsko-żydowskie w czasie drugiej wojny światowej: Uwagi i spostrzeżenia*, ed. Artur Eisenbach. Warsaw: Czytelnik, 1988.

Rossino, Alexander B. *Hitler Strikes Poland: Blitzkrieg, Ideology and Atrocity*. Lawrence: University Press of Kansas, 2003.

———. "Nazi Anti-Jewish Policy during the Polish Campaign: The Case of the Einsatzgruppe Woyrsch." *German Studies Review* 24 (2001): 35–54.

Roth, Karl Heinz. "Bevölkerungspolitik und Zwangsarbeit im 'Generalplan Ost.'" *Dokumentationsstelle zur NS-Sozialpolitik: Mitteilungen* 1 (1985): 70–93.

Rutkowski, Adam. "Hitlerowskie obozy pracy dla Żydów w dystrykcie radomskim." *BŻIH* 17–18 (1956): 106–26.

———. *L'opération "Erntefest" ou le massacre de 43.000 Juifs les 3–5 novembre 1943 dans les camps de Maidanek, de Poniatowa et de Trawniki*. *Le Monde Juif* 72 (October–December 1973): 13ff.

———. "Ruch oporu w Sobiborze." *BŻIH* 65–66 (1968): 3–49.

Sandkühler, Thomas. "Das Zwangsarbeitslager Lemberg-Janowska 1941–1944." In *Die nationalsozialistischen Konzentrationslager; Entwicklung und Struktur*, vol. 2, ed. Ulrich Herbert, Karin Orth, and Christoph Dieckmann, 606–35. Göttingen: Wallstein-Verlag, 1998.

———. *"Endlösung" in Galizien: Der Judenmord in Ostpolen und die Rettungsinitiativen von Bertold Beitz, 1941–1944*. Bonn: Dietz, 1996.

———. "Rozpoczęcie 'ostatecznego rozwiązania kwestii żydowskiej' w Generalnym Gubernatorstwie na przykładzie dystryktu galicyjskiego w latach 1941–1942." *Zeszyty Majdanka* 19 (1998): 7–33.

———. "Zwangsarbeit und Judenmord im Distrikt Galizien des Generalgouvernements: Die Rettungsinitiativen von Berthold Beitz." In *Konzentrationslager und deutsche Wirtschaft 1939–1945*, ed. Hermann Kaienburg, 239–62. Opladen: Springer, 1996.

Sarid, Levi Aryeh. *Ruin and Deliverance: The Pionier Movements in Poland throughout the Holocaust*, vol. 1: *The Road of Torment and Rebellion*. Tel Aviv: Moreshet, 1994.

Schelvis, Jules. *Sobibor: A History of a Nazi Death Camp*. New York: Berg, 2007.

Schenk, Dieter. *Hans Frank: Biografia generalnego gubernatora*. Krakow: Znak, 2009.

Schmalhausen, Bernd. *A Man of Courage in an Inhuman Time: Berthold Beitz in the Third Reich*. Jerusalem: Yad Vashem, 2006.

Schminck-Gustavus, Christoph U., ed. *Hungern für Hitler: Erinnerungen polnischer Zwangsarbeiter im Deutschen Reich, 1940–1945*. Hamburg: Reinbek, 1984.

Schulte, Jan Erik. "Zwangsarbeit für die SS—Juden in der Ostindustrie GmbH." In *Ausbeutung, Vernichtung, Öffentlichkeit*, ed. Norbert Frei and Sybille Steinbacher, 75–107. Munich: Saur, 2000.

———. *Zwangsarbeit und Vernichtung: Das Wirtschaftsimperium der SS: Oswald Pohl und das SS-Wirtschafts-Verwaltungshauptamt 1933–1945*. Padeborn: Ferdinand Schöningh, 2001.

Seeber, Eva. *Robotnicy przymusowi w faszystowskiej gospadarce wojennej Deportacja i wyzysk obywateli polskich z tzw. Generalnego Gubernatorstwa (1939–1945)*. Warsaw: Książka i Wiedza, 1972.

———. *Zwangsarbeiter in der faschistischen Kriegswirtschaft: die deportation und Ausbeutung polnischer Burger unter besonderer Berucksichtigung der Lage der Arbeiter aus dem sogenannten Generalgouvernement (1939–1945)*. Berlin: VEB Deutscher Verlag der Wissenschaften, 1964.

Seraphim, Hans Juergen. *Theorie der allgemeinen Volkswirtschaftspolitik*. Gottingen: Vandenhoeck & Ruprecht, 1955.

Seraphim, Peter Heinz. *Bevölkerungs- und wirtschaftspolitische Probleme einer europaeischen Gesamtlösung der Judenfrage*. Munich: Hoheneichen, 1943.

———. *Das Judentum im osteuropäischen Raum*. Essen: Essener Verlagsanstalt, 1938.

———. *Das Judentum: Seine Rolle und Bedeutung in Vergangenheit und Gegenwart*. Munich: Deutscher Volks-Verlag, 1944.

———. *Das Ostjüdische Ghetto*. Königsberg: Institut für Osteuropäische Wirtschaft am Staatswissenschaftlichen Institut der Universität Königsberg, 1938.

———. *Die Wanderungsbewegung des jüdischen Volkes*. Heidelberg: K. Vowinckel, 1940.

Seyda, Marjan. *Poland and Germany and the Post-War Reconstruction of Europe*. London: Barnard and Westwood, 1942.

Silberklang, David. *Gates of Tears: The Holocaust in the Lublin Disctrict*. Jerusalem: Yad Vashem, 2013.

———. *The Holocaust in the Lublin District*. PhD thesis. Jerusalem: n.p., 2003.
Silling, Victor. *Die Hintergruende des Falles Oberlaender*. Gross Denkte: Grenzland-Vlg., 1960.
Singer, Hedwig. *Organisation Todt*. Osnabrück: Biblio, 1998.
Skalniak, Franciszek. *Polityka pieniężna i budżetowa tzw. Generalnego Gubernatorstwa narzedziem finansowania potrzeb III Rzeszy*. Warsaw: Ministerstwo Sprawiedliwości. Główna Komisja Badania Zbrodni Hitlerowskich w Polsce, 1976.
———. *Stopa życiowa społeczeństwa polskiego w okresie okupacji na terenie Generalnego Gubernatorstwa*, Warsaw: Ministerstwo Sprawiedliwości. Główna Komisja Badania Zbrodni Hitlerowskich w Polsce, 1979.
Smelser Ronald. *Robert Ley Hitler's Labor Front Leader*. Oxford: Berg, 1988.
Speer, Albert. *Erinnerungen*. Frankfurt a.M.: Propyläen, 1969.
Spoerer, Mark. *Praca przymusowa pod znakiem swastyki. Cudzoziemscy robotnicy, jeńcy wojenni i więźniowie w Niemczech i okupowanej Europie w latach 1939–1945*. Gdansk: Muzeum II Wojny Światowej, 2015.
Statistisches Gemeindeverzeichnis des bisherigen polnischen Staates: Mit Berücksichtigung der am 28. September 1939 festgelegten Grenze der deutschen und sowjetrussischen Reichsinteressen. Berlin: Selbstverlag der Publikationsstelle, 1939.
Stein, Harry. "Juden im Konzentrationslager Buchenwald 1938–1942." In *Pogromnacht und Holocaust, Frankfurt, Weimar, Buchenwald, die schwierige Erinnerung an die Stationen der Vernichtung*, ed. Thomas Hofmann, Hanno Loewy, Harry Stein, 81–171. Weimar: Böhlau, 1994.
Steinert, Dieter. *Deportation und Zwangsarbeit: Polnische und sowjetische Kinder im nazionalsozialistischen Deutschland und im besetzten Osteuropa 1939–1945*. Essen: Klartext, 2013.
Streit, Christian. "The German Army and the Policies of Genocide." In *The Policies of Genocide: Jews and Soviet Prisoners of War in Nazi Germany*, ed. Gerhard Hirschfeld, 1–14. London: The German Historical Institute, 1986.
Stroop, Jürgen. "Raport o likwidacji getta warszawskiego w 1943 r." Janusz Gumkowski and Kazimierz Leszczyński, ed. *BGKBZHP* XI (1960).
Szarota, Tomasz. *U progu Zagłady: Zajścia antyżydowskie i pogromy w okupowanej Europie—Warszawa, Paryż, Amsterdam, Antwerpia, Kowno*. Warsaw: Wydawnictwo Sic!, 2000.
Szczepańczyk, Czesław. "Centralny Urząd Rolniczy—Landwirtschaftliche Zentralstelle." *Zeszyty Majdanka* 7 (1973): 121–58.
Szulc, Wacław, ed. "Wysiedlanie ludności polskiej z tzw. Kraju Warty i na Zamojszczyźnie oraz popełnione przy tym zbrodnie." *BGKBZHP* XXI (1970): 7–322.
Szurgacz, Herbert. *Przymusowe zatrudnianie Polaków przez hitlerowskiego okupanta w latach 1939–1945: Studium prawno-polityczne*. Wroclaw: Ossolineum, 1971.
Tomaszewski, Jerzy, and Zbigniew Landau. *Historia gospodarcza Polski*, Warszawa, 1986.
———. *Żydzi w Polsce do 1950 roku*. Warsaw: Państwowe Wydawnictwo Naukowe, 1993.
Tooze, Adam. *Wages of Destruction: The Making and Breaking of Nazi Economy*. London: Allen Lane, 2006.

Tregenza, Michael. "Bełżec—okres eksperymentalny, listopad 1941–kwiecień 1942." *Zeszyty Majdanka*, 21 (2001): 165–206.

———. "Christian Wirth a pierwsza faza 'Akcji Reinhard.'" *Zeszyty Majdanka* 14 (1992): 7–35.

Trunk, Isaiah. *Judenrat: The Jewish Councils in Eastern Europe under Nazi Occupation*, New York, 1972.

Umbreit, Hans. *Deutsche Militärverwaltungen 1938–39: Die militärische Besetzung der Tschechoslowakei und Polens*. Stuttgart: Deutsche Verlags-Anstalt, 1977.

Urynowicz, Marcin. *Adam Czerniaków: Prezes getta warszawskiego*. Warsaw: IPN, 2009.

Wagner, Jens-Christian. "Forced Labor in the National Sozialist Era—An Overwiev." In *Forced Labor: The Germans, the Forced Laborers and the War*, ed. Volkhard Knigge et al., 180–93. Weimar: Buchenwald and Mittelbau-Dora Memorials Foundation, 2010.

Walczak, Marian. *Walka ekonomiczna narodu polskiego 1939–1945*. Warsaw: MON, 1983.

Weiss, Aharon. "Jewish-Ukrainian Relations in Western Ukraine during the Holocaust." In *Ukrainian-Jewish Relations in Historical Perspective*, ed. Peter J. Potichnyj and Howard Aster. Edmonton: Canadian Institute of Ukrainian Studies University of Alberta, 1988.

Wenzel, Mario. "Ausbeutung und Vernichtung: Zwangsarbeitslager für Juden im Distrikt Krakau 1942–1944." *Dachauer Hefte* 23 (2007): 189–207.

———. *Arbeitszwang und Judenmord. Die Arbeitslager für Juden im Distrikt Krakau des Generalgouvernements 1939–1944*. Berlin: Metropol: 2017.

———. "Die Arbeitslager für Juden im Distrikt Krakau des Generalgouvernements 1940–1941." In *Zwangsarbeit in Hitlers Europa: Besatzung—Arbeit—Folgen*, ed. Dieter Pohl and Tanja Sebta, 173–94. Berlin: Metropol, 2013.

———. "Die Umwandlung von Ghettos in Zwangsarbeitslager für Juden: Das Beispiel des Distrikts Krakau im Generalgouvernement 1942–1944." In *Arbeit in den nationalsozialistischen Ghettos*, ed. Jürgen Hensel and Stephan Lehnstaedt, 361–73. Osnabrück: Fibre, 2013.

Wilhelm, Hans-Heinrich. *Die Einsatzgruppe A der Sicherheitspolizei und des SD 1941/42*. Frankfurt a.M.: P. Lang, 1996.

———. *Rassenpolitik und Kriegsführung: Sicherheitspolizei und Wehrmacht in Polen und in der Sowjetunion 1939–1942*. Passau: Wissenschaftsverlag Richard Rothe, 1991.

Wróblewski, Bronisław. "Obóz w Budzyniu." *Zeszyty Majdanka* 5 (1971): 179–89.

Wróblewski, Mścisław. *Służba Budowlana (Baudienst) w Generalnym Gubernatorstwie 1940–1945*. Warsaw: PWN, 1984.

Wrzosek, Mieczysław. "Raporty Hütera i O. Fitznera o sytuacji w Zagłębiu Śląsko-Dąbrowskim (w okresie 3 września–20 października 1939 r.)." *BGKBZHP* 18 (1968): 165–245.

Yahil, Leni. *The Holocaust: The Fate of European Jewry*. New York Oxford University Press, 1991.

Zbrodnicza ewakuacja więzień i aresztów NKWD na Kresach Wschodnich II Rzeczypospolitej w czerwcu–lipcu 1941 roku. Warszawa: IPN, 1997.

Zimmerer, Katarzyna. *Zamordowany świat: Losy Żydów w Krakowie, 1939–1945*. Krakow: Wydawnictwo Literackie, 2004.

Ziółkowska, Anna. "Obozy pracy przymusowej dla Żydów w Poznańskiem w czasie okupacji Hitlerowskiej." *Żydzi i judaizm we współczesnych badaniach polskich* II (2000): 313–23.

———. *Obozy pracy przymusowej dla Żydów w Wielkopolsce*. Poznań: Wydawnictwo Poznańskie, 2005.

Żbikowski, Andrzej. "Local Anti-Jewish Pogroms in the Occupied Territories of Eastern Poland, June–July 1941," In *The Holocaust in the Soviet Union. Studies and Sources on the Jews in Nazi-Occupied Territories of the USSR, 1941–1945*, ed. Lucjan Dobroszycki and Jeffrey S. Gurock, 173–79. London: M.E. Sharpe, 1993.

———. "Lokalne pogromy Żydów w czerwcu i lipcu 1941 roku na wschodnich rubieżach II Rzeczypospolitej." *BŻIH* 2–3 (1992): 3–18.

Index

A
Adam, Peter, 9n32
Adamczyk, Ryszard, 116n142
Afghanistan, 182
Aircraft factories/plants, 64, 306
Aktion Reinhardt, viii–ix, xi, xiv, xxix, 63, 203–204, 221, 225–227, 234–245, 247, 251, 258, 260, 264, 266, 279, 283, 287, 294, 297–299, 303, 310
Albert, Andrzej, 5n20
Allen, Michael T., xxx, **139n18**
Alvensleben von, Ludolf, 138
Aly, Götz, xxvi, xxviin82, 10n35, 135n2, 318
Angerick, Andrej, 213n40, 315n50
Annopol-Rachów, 287, 289
Arad, Yitzhak, xin6, 5n19, 12n41, 26n33, 36n70, 39n83, 75n1, 76n2–4, 127n171, 128n176, 143n30, 185n7–8, 187n13, 188n14, 189n15–16, 201n19, 207n30, 214n41, 222n4, 225n8–9, 226n12, 237n35, 239n38–39, 263n39–40, 268n50–54, 269n55–56, 271n59–60, 272n62, 274n2, 278n16, 282n24, 283n31, 292n2, 293n6, 294n7, 296n12, 298n13, 307n26, 309n32, 310n34, 311n37
Arlt, Fritz, 40n88, 292n2
Armament industry (enterprises, plants), ix–x, 22, 183–184, 206, 235–237, 241, 248–249, 253–254, 259–265, 269–272, 281, 289–290, 297–309, 311, 315, 317, 319
Aryanization, 29, 78, 90, 110, 112, 114–115
Auerswald, Heinz, 128, 176
Auschwitz, xxiii, 239, 258, 285, 287
Auto Carriers for Galicia (*Autotransport für Galizien*), 214
Awtiszewska-Ettrich, Angelina, 289n46

B
Backe, Herbert, 183–184
Bartetzko, Franz, 65, 138
Bednarek, Monika, 289n46
Będzin, 92

Bekker, Henryk, 148
Belgium, 66
Bełżec, 64–65, 71, 138, 142, 144–154, 160–163, 170–171, 178–180, 202–203, 211, 216, 226, 239, 275, 313
Bender, Sara, xxx–xxxi, 283n26
Bennett, Giles, xxxiin116
Benz, Wolfgang, ix, xxx, xxxiin117, 289n45–46, 314, 315n47, 316
Berber, Dawid, 203n25
Bertisch, Dawid, 203n25
Biberstein, Aleksander, 102n93, 113n128, 166, 169
Berenstein, Tatiana, xx–xxi, 13n41, 26n29, 36n73, 70n170, 71n181, 196n9, 197n11, 198n15, 200n16, 205n28, 206n29, 210n31, 212n37–38, 214n52–53, 215n55, 217n60, 218n62, 220n65, 285n37, 344n16, 347n18, 348n19, 350n21
Biała Podlaska, 158
Białowicz, Lena, 90n47
Białystok, 274, 281–283
Bień, Marian, 8n31
Bierkamp, Walter, 284
Biecz, 230–231
Biuletyn BGKBZHP (Bulletin of the Main Commission for Investigation of Nazi Crimes in Poland), xxi
Biuletyn ŻIH (BŻIH) (Bulletin of the Jewish institute), xxi
Black market, 82, 99–100, 110, 125, 207, 213, 223, 238, 294, 298
Blitzkrieg, 143, 295, 297
Blumental, Nachman, xxvin73, 225n9, 288n42
Bochnia, 72n184–185, 90, 111–112, 114, 138n15, 204–205, 211, 234
Boepple, Ernst, 249n4
Böhler, Jochen, 8n29–30, 10n33–34, 13n42, 16n56,
Bolechów, 218
Bolshevism, 181–182, 185
Bolten, Gustav, 214

Borysław, 205, 212
Borwicz, Michal M., 64n160, 219n64
Böttcher, Herbert, 242
Brandl, Josef, 194
Brandon, Ray, xxxn98, 213n40, 315n50
Brandt, Oskar, 203
Brauchitsch von, Walther, 12, 18, 58
Brauner, Natalia, 214n48
Braunschweig, 289, 360
Breitman, Richard, xxviin85
Brenner, Liber, xxin29, 17n58, 34n66
Brones, Mieczysław, 20n10, 22n16–17, 24n26
Broszat, Martin, xxvi, 136n8
Browning, Christopher, xxviii, xxx, 128n175, 138n17, 319
Brustin-Berenstein, see Berenstein
Bryskier, Henryk, 107, 108n107, 114, 157n87, 177n153–154, 178n157
Brzozowa, 230–231
Buchbender, O., 11n36
Buchheim, Hans, xxvi
Budzyń, xxv, 289
BuF (Department of Internal Affairs: Group for Population and Welfare), 65, 159, 232, 234, 303–304, 318
Bug (river), 60, 66, 142–145
Bühler, Josef, 157, 180, 222
Bührmann, Arnold Julius, 22

C

Chamberlain, Neville, 3
China, 182
Ciepielewicz, Mieczysław, 6n24
Cieszanów, 152
Crafts/men/ship, 14, 47, 50, 60, 80, 108, 110, 113–115, 118–121, 129–130, 155, 188–189, 202–205, 212, 227–229, 234, 250, 269, 336
    Basketry, 205, 212
    Blacksmithing, 110, 204
    Brush making, 121, 124, 131–132, 205, 212
    Carpentry/joiners, 112, 120, 124, 130, 132, 137, 164, 204–205, 212, 215, 227, 336
    Electrical workshops, 205, 305n22
    Food processing/baking, 92, 116, 333, 336
    Furriers, 113, 205, 212, 270, 236
    Leather processing/saddler, 92, 110, 115–116, 121, 268, 333
    Metalwork, 92, 115, 124, 205, 215, 269
    Shoemaking/repair (cobblers), 110, 113, 137, 204–205, 188, 227, 270, 336
    Tailor(ing), 110–111, 113, 123, 137, 204–205, 212, 227, 270, 336
    Watchmaking/repair, 15, 115, 137, 205
    Weaving, 120, 205
Cygielman, Joel, 214n43
Czart, Arieh, 214n47
Czerniaków, Adam, xxvi, 36, 79–80, 86, 97–99, 111, 176
Częstochowa, 16, 26, 34, 44, 90, 101, 109, 111, 115, 120, 178, 204, 224, 239, 258n26, 261, 282, 289, 307
Czortków, 202, 210
Czyńska, Zofia, xixn19, 139n18–19

D

Dąbrowice, 177
Daladier, Edouard, 3
Datner, Szymon, xxi, 4n15, 282n25
DAW (Deutsche Ausrüstungswerke), 66n162, 179, 198, 215, 264, 300, 302, 310–311, 359
"Days of Petlura," 193, 209
Dean, Martin, xxxiin117
Dęblin, 60, 289
Dempsey, Patrick, xin6, 187n13
Deighton, Len, 143n34
Deutsche Ausrüstungswerke (DAW), see DAW
Deutsche Wirtschaftsbetriebe (DWB), 310
Diamant, Henoch, 17n59
Diamant, Ita, 116n143
Didier, Fryderyk, 252n11
Dieckmann, Christopher, xxviin86
Diehm, Christoph, 194
Distel, Barbara, xxx, 289n45–46
Dniestr, 191
Dobroszycki, L., 6n24
Dolp, Hermann, 64
Domarus, Max, 6n23
Donat, Alexander, 115
Dormann, 211
Dorohucza, xxv, 287
Dreichs, Shemuel, 216n57
Drohobycz, 204–205, 212, 217
Drohobycz County camps,
    Grzęda, 217
    Kazimierowka, 217
    Kopanie, 217
Drozdowski, M. M., 6n24
Dunin-Wasowicz, Krzysztof, xxiii, 47n110, 85n27, 89n43, 91n53–55, 92n60, 93n65,

Index

98n79, 100n88–89, 107n106, 127n172, 128n174, 243n54–55, 350n20
Du Prel, Max Freiherr, 44n103, 45n104–105, 47n112, 59n145, 60n148
Durchgangstrasse IV, 214, 314–315
Dziadosz, Edward, 139n19, 287n40–41, 288n42–43
Działoszyce, 141n24, 168, 231, 233–234
Dzików, 152–153, 165

E

Eastern Front, 199, 211, 221–222, 247, 251, 290, 297
Eastern Railway (*Ostbahn*), 58, 71, 144n36, 211, 307–308, 340, 357
Echtenkamp, Jörg, xxxn98
Eichmann, Adolf, xxv
Einsatzgruppen (operational groups), xi, 7–8, 19, 26–30, 36, 43–44, 185, 187–189, 194–195, 207, 218, 295
Eisenbach, Artur, xxn24, 13n41, 26n29–33, 28n36–37, 29n41–42, 50n121, 62n153, 65n161, 67n163–164, 70n174, 73n186, 76n2–4, 77n5–6, 84n22, 100n87, 105n100, 111n116, 135n3–4, 143n32, 144n36, 145n38, 160n101, 161n104–105, 163n110–111, 165n114, 166n117, 170n129, 172n135, 175n145, 176n147–148, 177n152, 225n8, 226n11, 235n30, 237n33–34, 240n41, 241n43–48, 242n49–51, 245n58, 262n36–38, 263n41, 267n47–49, 274n1, 276n9–12, 277n13–15, 278n17, 279n18, 280n19–22, 293n4–5, 359n32
Elsässer, 22
Engelking, Barbara, xxiv, 102n94, 106n103, 107n105, 108n108–110, 116n138–139, 117n145–146, 119n150, 125n165, 126n170
Enno, George, xxvi
Erntefest (Harvest Festival), *see* Operation Erntefest

F

Fear, Jeffrey, xxx
Feder, Roza, 203n25
Feder, Szaja, 203n25
Fefer, Ester, 34n68
Feifermacher, Jozef, 32n49, 32n54
Feldhandler, Leon, 283
"Final Solution," xxviii, 223, 239, 244, 264, 294, 296, 312, 318
Finder, Gabriel N., xxx
Fischer, Ludwig, 70, 85, 89, 91, 93, 97–98, 100, 142n27, 145n41, 177, 243
Fitzner, Otto, 23
Flemming, Marian, 13n44–45, 15n51
Flick, Friedrich, xxv
Florian, Dierl, xxiin112
Florstedt, Hermann, 266–267
Forster, Albert, 20, 308
Foundation "Remembrance, Responsibility and Future" (*Stiftung Erinnerung, Verantwortung und Zukunft*, EVZ), xxxi
Four-Year Plan, 28–29, 184, 305
Frajman, Jerychem, 13n43, 14n46
France, 66
Frank, Hans, x, xxv, 20–24, 37, 41, 43, 47–49, 57, 63, 65, 68, 70n176, 72, 76, 81, 94–95, 128, 146, 151, 153–154, 162, 190–192, 194, 196, 200, 223, 235, 242–243, 249–253, 264, 266, 271–272, 281, 283–284, 292–296, 309, 317–318
Frank, Jacob, 138n17
Frauendorfer, Max, 41, 45, 47, 69–70, 94–95, 144n36, 149–150, 206, 235–239, 249n4, 262–264
Frei, Norbert, xxixn97
Friedländer, Saul, xxvin80, 281n23, 310n33, 312, 314–315
Friedman, Jakub, 215n56, 216n57
Friedman, Tuvia, 138n17, 215n56
Frydman, Sara, 195n6
Fuks, Marian, 79n11–12, 86n29–32, 97n76, 98n80, 99n85, 111n117–118, 176n149–150

G

Galicia, Galicia District, xi, xx, xxix, 27, 97, 181–219, 226, 237n35, 239, 241, 260–265, 289, 298, 310n34, 327, 334
Ganzenmüller, Albert, 271, 274, 278n17
Gansinger, Franz, 194
Garfinkiel, Mieczyslaw, 90n47, 104n99, 105n101, 109n113–114, 112n125, 116n140, 122n158
Gawron, Edyta, 289n46
Gazeta Żydowska, 77, 97
Gdańsk, 1, 10
Gebauer, Fritz, 215
General Government (*Generalgouvernement*)
   Department of
      Construction, 144n36
      Forestry, 144n36

Food Supplies and Agriculture, 144n36
Economy, 144n36
Labor Office (department of Employment Jews), 144n36
"Labor Department" (Abteilung Arbeit/ Hauptamt Arbeit), 44–45
Arbeitsämter, 44
Arbeitseinsatz, 45
Sozialversicherung, 45
Treuhänder, 45
Wohnung-und Siedlungswesen, 45
Regional Planning Department (*Abteilung Raumordnung*), 60
Gerber, Bernard, 214n43
Geneva conventions, xiv, 249
Gerlach, Christian, xxvii
German War Economy Organization, 183
Gestapo, 7, 15, 44, 75, 86, 109n114, 122, 203, 208
Getter, M., 6n24
G. Gerlach (plant), 279
Ghetto, viii, xii–xvii, xxxii, 18, 64, 72–74, 79, 87, 90, 96, 99–133, 146, 156, 170n132, 190–191, 196, 205, 208, 212–213, 216–217, 221–230, 234–235, 239–224, 250–251, 258–262, 273–282, 293–294, 297–300, 302–303, 306, 309, 316, 359
Białystok, 281–282
Bochnia, 111–112
Częstochowa, 109, 111, 115, 282
Kołomyja, 205
Krakow, 112–113
Litzmannstadt, *see* Warthegau
Lublin, xxiii, xxvi, 226–227
Stanisławów, 205
Warsaw, xxiv, 102, 109, 114–117, 121–122, 124–125, 127–133, 156, 158, 178n156, 190–191, 221, 224, 243–244, 258n26, 260–261, 273–282, 302
Warthegau, 221
Zamosc, 105, 111–112, 114, 122
Gibaszewski, Krzysztof, xxiv, 290n48
Gicewicz, Ryszard, xxiii, xxvn66
Gienanth von, Curt Ludwig, 268–271, 281, 307
Gleich, Edward, 216n57
Gleich, Israel, 214n50
Globocnik, Odilo, xxx, 62–73, 79, 90, 137–138, 141n25, 144–148, 151–152, 161–162, 172, 198n14, 226, 240, 266, 276, 283, 293–294, 310, 317–318

Glücks, Richard, 266, 312
Goldhust, Blanka, 32n53, 34n65
Goschler, Constantin, xxxiin118
Göring, Hermann, xxv, 2, 24, 28, 57, 182, 184, 248–249
Gorlice, 72n185, 103, 231, 234
Gottong, Heinrich, 65
Grabitz, Helge, 123n159
Grajwer, Salo, 204, 211–212
Greifelt, Ulrich, 280
Greiser, Arthur, 20, 191, 328
Grieger, Manfred, xxxin111, 315n50
Grinabaum, Diana, 15n52–53
Grochów, 92
Gross Rosen (labor camp), 315
Grudzińska, Marta, 137n12, 138n17
Gruner, Wolf, xxix, 139n18, 319
Grünwald, Hans Dietrich, 284
Grünwald, Israel, 103
Grynwald, Rywka, 31n45
Gumkowski, Janusz, 23n20
Gunst, Walter, 138
Gutman, Yisrael, 5n19, 12n41, 26n33, 36n70, 39n83, 75n1, 76n2–4, 127n171, 128n176, 143n30, 185n7–8, 187n13, 188n14, 189n15–16, 201n19, 207n30, 214n41, 222n4, 225n8–9, 226n12, 237n35, 239n38–39, 263n39–40, 268n50–54, 269n55–56, 271n59–60, 272n62, 274n2, 278n16, 283n31, 292n2, 293n6, 294n7, 296n12, 298n13, 307n26, 309n32, 310n34, 311n37
Gypsies, 139, 145, 257

H

Hague Convention, The, xiv
Halpern, Efraim, 216n57
Hanneken von, Hermann, 183
Hansen, Imke, viiin1, xxxii
Hartglas, Apolinary, 35, 36n70
HASAG (Hugo Schneider Aktiengesellschaft), xxviii–xxix, 289–290, 302, 314, 360–361
Haseloff, Kurt, 284
He-Chalutz, 92
Heim, Susanne, xxvi, xxvii, xxxi, 10n35, 135n2, 318
Heinkel factory, 289
Heitz, Walter, 20
Heller, 211
Hensel, Jürgen, xxxii
Herbert, Ulrich, xxvii, xxxi
Hermanów (camp), 214

Heusler, Andreas, xxxin111
Heydrich, Reinhard, 7–8, 12, 26–30, 36, 43, 75–76, 135n3, 143, 145n38, 185, 187, 240, 313–314
Hilberg, Raul, xxv, 272n61, 299, 302, 305–308, 311
Himmler, Heinrich, 7, 25, 63, 143, 174, 185, 207–208, 236, 239–241, 256–258, 266, 270–272, 274, 276, 278–285, 289–290, 294, 296, 302, 307–312, 317
    Poznań Speech (of October 3, 1943), 296, 311
Hirschfeld, Gerhardt, 295n10
Hirszman, Chaim, 32n51, 32n55
Hitler, Adolf, 1–6, 9–10, 16, 20, 22–25, 41, 58, 181–182, 190–191, 193, 236, 246, 248–249, 253–254, 259, 297, 305, 312, 314–317
Hitler Youth, 9–10
Hobot, Władysław, 287
Hochberg, Róża, 204n26
Hofbauer, Karl, 65, 150
Höfle, Herman, 226, 287
Holzbau A.G. (Hobag), 218
Homze, Edward, xxvi
Horn, Max, 266
Hrubieszów, 171, 358
HSSPF (Higher SS and Police Commander), 42, 50, 52, 54, 56–57, 62–63, 65, 68, 139, 144, 154–155, 240, 266, 281, 292, 295, 312, 317
Huberband, H., 157n91
Hungarian
    Jews, 312, 317
    troops, 185
Hungerplan, 295, 314
Hutter, 23

I

Ilgner, Max, 22
Inspectorate of War Economy, *see* War Economy Inspection
International Convention on Forced Labor (1930), 30
Izbica, 14

J

Jachimowicz, Jakow, 171n134
Jaktorów labor camp, 214, 219
Janczewska, Marta, xxiv
Janiszowcie, 72n184
Japan, 182
Jasielnica, 230–231
Jasło, 45–46, 83, 93–94, 234
Jastrzębowski, Wacław, xx
Jaworzno, 14
Jędrzejów, 26, 38, 81–82
Jewish Councils of Elders, 28, 148, 161–162
Jewish Fighting Organization (ŻOB), 273–275, 282
Jewish labor camps,
    administrative labor camp (*Verwaltungarbeitslager*), 139
    camp for certain tasks (*Einsatzlager*), 139
    collective camp (*Sammellager*), 139
    Forced labor camp (*Zwangsarbeitslager*), xii, xiv, xviii, xxiii–xxiv, 69, 84–86, 90, 93, 103, 122, 133, 139–140, 147, 154, 167–173, 197, 202, 208, 213, 218, 256–260
    Jewish camp or camp for Jews (*Judenlager, Julag*), xvii–xviii, 69, 71, 139–140, 147, 168, 174, 180, 196, 284
    Permanent factory labor camps, 262–265, 302
    SS labor camps, 141, 266–272, 299, 307, 313
Jewish Military Union (ŻZW), 273
Jewish Mutual Aid, 204, 211
Jewish pogroms, 187, 194, 203, 207, 209, 218
Jewish police, 108, 177, 225
Jewish Self-Assistance (ŻSS), 68n165, 70n173, 112n123, 166–168, 204–205, 208, 227–235, 303–304, 318
Jezierzany, 212
Jones (Yones), Eliyahu, 211n34
Judeneinsatzstelle (Jewish Forced Labor Office), 69
Judenrat, xxvi, 14, 36–37, 51–55, 69–70, 75–94, 108–117, 123–125, 136, 138, 146, 153, 155, 158, 164, 168, 176–178, 200–205, 208–212, 215, 224–225, 296–297, 301, 303, 333, 343–346, 348–349, 356

K

Kaczanowski, Longin, xxii
Kaienburg, Hermann, xxixn93, xxx, 315n51
Kaiser, Ane, xxixn96, 139n18
Kaltenbrunner, Ernst, 280
Kaplan, Chaim A., 32n50, 33–34, 78, 80, 83, 88n42
Karay, Felicja, xxviii, 23n21, 73n187, 162n108, 206n29, 290–291, 300n18, 361n37

Karpathen Öl A.G., 218, 261
Kasperek, Józef, xxin33
Katowice, 239
Katzmann, Friedrich, 194, 213–214, 226, 237–239, 263, 265–266, 298, 309–310, 318
Kay, Alex J., 295n10
Kazimierz (Wielki), 93, 232
Keitel, Wilhelm, 2, 25, 248–249, 258–259
Kermish, Joseph, 102n95, 108n111, 146n46, 155n83, 157n91, 158n93–94, 168n128, 170n130, 173n139, 174n140, 175n144, 178n160
Kisielewicz, S., 137n11
Kiełboń, Janina, 152n70
Kielce, xxii, xxxi, 22, 44, 59, 90, 105n100, 289
Klausner, L., 75n1
Kleeberg, Franciszek, 7
Klein, Paulina, 14n47
Klein, Peter, xin6, 187n13
Kłosiński, Tadeusz, xx
Knigge, Volkhard, xvn14–15, xxxin111, xxxiin118, 315n50
Kohan, Karol, 214n44
Koksagiz, 210, 217
Kołomyja, 203, 205, 210, 212
Konieczny, Alfred, xxii
Königsberg, 158, 242n52
Końskie, 16, 44, 46, 176–177
Kopciowski, Adam, 111n122, 114n130
Kopówka, Edward, xxiv
Koppe, Wilhelm, 283
Korherr, Richard, 244–245
Körner, Hellmut, 61–62, 183
Korniło, Jozef, 31n45, 35n69
Kosow, 212
Kostrze, 141n24, 169
Koszcz (camp), 231–232
Kotek, Joel, xxxn98
Kozłowski, Eugeniusz, 6n24
Kraków, 20, 22, 26, 28, 34, 39, 59, 61, 85, 92–93, 102, 112–113, 147, 149–151, 164, 166–172, 195, 204, 229–239, 241–242, 249, 252, 260, 281, 285, 289, 301–303, 307, 311, 315, 334, 351, 359
    Krakusa Street, 113
    Targowa Street, 113
    Węgierska Street, 113
Krakowski, Shmuel, xin6, 64n158, 137n11, 187n13
Kraśnik, 14
Krausnick, Helmut, xin6, 26n24, 136n8, 187n13

Krause-Schmidt, Ursula, xxixn96, 139n18
Kreikamp, Hans-Dieter, xxxi
Kremin, Victor, 97, 213
Kripo (*Kriminalpolizei*), 7
Kristallnacht, 144
Krohn, Johannes, 48–49
Król, Eugeniusz Cezary, 10n35
Krupp, Alfred, xxv
Krüger, Friedrich-Wilhelm, x, 42, 50–51, 62–63, 65, 68, 79, 95, 135n3–4, 136, 143n32, 144–146, 151, 153, 155, 161–162, 196, 203, 206–207, 241n44, 264, 266, 270, 276, 281, 283, 285, 293, 296, 299, 307–308, 317
Kupść, Bogumił, xixn19, 139n18–19
Kurland, Bernard, 178
Kwiet, Konrad, xxviin85

L
Labor battalions, xix, 36, 53, 80–83, 85–86, 88, 297, 344
Labor detachments, 81, 196–197, *see also* Labor battalions
Landau, Ludwik Maurycy, 12n40, 16, 32–33, 85, 95, 275
Landau, Lejb (Dr.), 211
Łańcut, 15
Lasch, Karl, 193–195
Lebensraum, 1, 3, 10
Lehnstaedt, Stephan, xivn16, xxxii
Lehrer, Mateusz, 214n51
Lenarczyk, Wojciech, xxiv–xxv, 138n16, 154n81, 289n44
Leningrad (today St. Petersburg), 297
Leociak, Jacek, xxiv, 102n94, 106n103, 107n105, 108n108–110, 116n138–139, 117n145–146, 119n150, 125n165, 126n170
Leszczyński, Kazimierz, 23n20, 27n35
Libionka, Dariusz, xxiv–xxv, xxviiin91, 289n44
Linne, Karsten, xxxiin112, xxxii
Lipowa street 7 (camp), xxv, 64–65, 67, 90, 137–138, 153, 286, 289
Lipsk, 152–154
List von, Wilhelm, 20
Litzmannstadt Ghetto (Warthgenau), 221
Łódź, 20, 114, 120–121
Loewenson, Juda, 214n45
Loewenstein, Artur, 64n159
Loose, Ingo, xxx, xxxiin116
Lörner, Georg, 266
Losacker, Ludwig, 94, 194

Lower, Wendy, xxxn98, 213n40, 315n50
Lublin, xxiii, xxv–xxvi, 14, 22, 30–31, 36–37, 52, 59–67, 70, 79–81, 86–90, 95, 112, 121, 137–138, 144n36, 145–172, 177n156, 207, 213, 215, 221n1, 224–227, 239, 242, 258n26, 270, 285–288, 302–303, 307, 331–337, 342–343, 346, 356–359
   Lipowa Street , *see* Lipowa street 7 (camp)
Lublin District, xx, xxvii, xxxi, 63–67, 71, 91–92, 96–97, 107, 117, 129, 140n23, 149–172, 180, 224–226, 240–241, 266–267, 274–281, 285, 288–289, 302, 311
   Józefów Biłgorajski, 224
   Łomazy, 224
Lubliniec, 44
Łukaszewicz, Zdzisław, xxn20, 139n18, 141n26, 154n79
Łuczak, Czesław, xx, xxii
Łuków, 151
Lwów, 64, 138, 186, 193, 195–196, 198–199, 201–204, 208–209, 211–217, 242, 263, 265, 285, 359
   Czwartaków Street, 217
   Grodecka Street, 217
   Janowska, Street, 64, 138, 198, 215–215
   Kazimierzowska Street, 204, 212
   Łąckiego Street Jail, 208
   Zamarstynowska Street, 202

M
Maarer (Dr.), 212
Maciąg, Maria, 288
   Macior-Majka, Beata, xxiv
MacLean, French L., xin6, 187n13
Madajczyk, Czesław, xxi–xxii, 5n20, 143n31, 334n5
Majdanek, xxi, xxiii–xxv, 275, 281, 285–291
Majewski, Ryszard, 7n26
Mandelbaum, Franciszek, 14n48, 31n45
Mańkowski, Zygmunt, 63n157, 139n19
Marszałek, Józef, xxiii, 71n181, 139–140, 154n80
Matthaus, Jurgen, xxviiin89
Mayzel, Maurycy, 78
Meducki, Stanisław, xxii, 125n164, 333n4, 355n26, 360n34
Mędykowski, Witold, viiin1, xxiv, xxvn67, xxxiin116–117, 187n11
Meldekarten, 202
Mencel, Tadeusz, 285n38, 359n33

Metrowat AG, 218
Miechów, 168, 233–234
Międzyrzec, 90, 96
Mielec, 289
Mińsk Mazowiecki, 47, 71
Mintz, B., 75n1
Misiuna, Władysław, xxiii
Mittelbau-Dora (concentration camp), 315, 317
Młynarczyk, Jacek Andrzej, xxxi
Mohwinkel, Wolfgang, 65, 138, 198, 215
Mondschein, Tzadok, 214n47
Moscow, 247
Muhsfeldt, Erich, 286–287
Müller, Horst, xxxi
Munition factories/works/industry, 243, 262, 290–291, 298, 306, 312
Musial, Bogdan, xxix
Mussolini, Benito, 1

N
Nachta, Szarlotta, 216n57
Nadel, Chaim, 33n57
Nagel, Wilhelm, 22
Narol, 169, 174
Neander, Joachim, xxxn103
Netherlands, 66
Neuengamme (concentration camp), 315
Neuman, Itzhak, 214n47
Neumann, Erich, 183, 222
Nieprześno, 72n184
Nietzsche, Dr., 200–202
NKVD, 194–195
Nobel, Hejnoch, 15n50
Norway, 184
Nowa Osada, 104–105

O
Oberländer, Theodor, 187n12
Ofer, Dalia, xxviiin91
Okęcie, 97
Olender, Abraham, 14n49
Olkusz, 31
Opatów, 101, 157–158
Operation Barbarossa, xi, 64, 91, 129–130, 181–185, 189–190, 199, 221, 246, 250
Operation *Erntefest*, xxiv–xxv, 273–291
Organisation Todt (OT), xv, xxix, 134, 208
Ostindustrie GmbH (OSTI), 66, 197, 264, 267, 300, 302, 310
Ostjuden (Eastern Jews), 9
Ostrów (camp), 214
Ostrowiec, 101, 152n70, 156

Ostrowski, Karol, xxii
Oszczów (camp), 160n101, 166, 171–172, 178
"Otto Program", 70–71, 180, 189–190, 301

P

Parasol, Efraim, 31n46
Paul, Gerhard, xxviiin86
Peczerski, Alexander (Sasha), 283
Penal labor camps (*Strafarbeitslager*), xix, 140
Perechodnik, Calel, 299n17
Petersen, Hans-Christian, xxxn103
Petzina, Dieter, xvi
Piaski, 145
Piątkowski, Sebastian, xxiv
Pietrzykowski, Jan, xxii
Pilarczyk, Krzysztof, xxiiin56, 145n43, 148n51–52, 153n75
Pilichowski, Czesław, xxiin49, 139n18–19
Pinkus, Dawid, 31n47
Piotrków, 44, 358
Plage-Laśkiewicz (aircraft factory), 64
Plaszow (camp), 103, 169, 172n137, 230, 233–234, 241, 289
Płazów (camp), 152–154, 174
Plutman, Samuel, 195n6
Podgórze District, 112
Pohl, Dieter, xin6, xxvii, xxviiin86, xxxi, 139n18,
Pohl, Oswald, xxv, 256, 266–267, 270, 276, 310
Pohl and Lückel (company), 214
Polish
    Intelligentsia/leadership, 7, 21, 25
    Territories, viii, xn4, xxii, 23, 25, 37, 88, 186, 190, 198–199, 250
    Workers, xv, xix, 45–48, 69, 100, 155, 175–176, 220, 249–250, 290, 301, 305, 334
Polesie, 6–7
Pomorze, 7
Poniatowa, xxiv–xxv, 281, 285n37, 287–288, 302, 311
Poprzeczny, Joseph, xxxn104, 63n157, 138n17
Porwit, Marian, 6n24
Pospieszalski, Karol Marian, 18n4, 19n5–6, 25n28, 37n77–78, 39n83, 40n87, 41n91–93, 42n97–98, 43n99–100, 44n101, 50n122, 51n124, 52n127, 53n128–129, 54n130, 55n133, 68n166, 136n5–7, 153n78, 193n1
Potruch, Berl, 202n23
POW(s), xv, xviii, xxi, xxiv, 158, 248–250, 343
    Camps, xviii, 63–64, 137–138, 248, 295, 318
    Jewish, 137, 141n25, 158–159
    Polish, 137, 250, 286, 301
    Soviet, 188, 222, 248–249, 260, 295, 305, 318
Poznań, xx, 7, 20, 296
Price, John, xxvn69
Production, xii, xvi, 22–23, 29–30, 53, 55–58, 61, 73, 90, 91, 97, 107, 110–111, 123–126, 133, 181–183, 190, 199, 204–206, 208, 212, 223, 226–229, 236, 244, 247, 252–254, 260, 268–270, 280, 290, 296–298, 301, 304, 306–308, 314, 317, 360–361
    Agricultural, 1, 57, 99, 210, 229
    In ghettos, 110–112, 114–122, 127–133, 261
Prokocim (camp), 230
Przemyśl, 8, 213, 241, 307n28
Przyrów, 176
Puławy, 46, 60, 69, 93, 96, 140n22, 287

R

Radom, xxviii, xxxi, 38, 59, 61, 72, 144n36, 150, 152, 239–242, 261, 285, 289, 290–291, 301–303, 307, 333–334, 359
Radomsko, 44, 176
Radzik, Tadeusz, xxiii, 70n175, 142n28, 145n39, 147n49, 148n51, 151n66, 152n70, 153n77
Raeder, Erich, 2
Rajca, Czesław, xxin33
Rajzler, Isidor, 211
Rasp (Dr), 211
Räumungskommando, 97, 197, 208, 224–225
Raw materials, viii, xvi, 1, 3, 20–24, 30, 38, 53, 56–59, 71, 80, 99, 106–109, 113, 115–122, 126, 130–132, 135, 182–184, 190, 198–199, 206, 208, 210, 212, 215, 229, 246, 297, 347
    Collectors of, 95–98, 197
Reder, Rudolf, 204n26
Reich Labor Service (*Reichsarbeitsdienst*, RAD), xix, 134

Reich Security Main Office (*RSHA*), 44, 305
Riedel, Horst, 65, 138
Reiner, Aba, 195n6
Restghetto (small, remainder ghetto), xii, 217, 239
Reuter, Ernst, 226
Rezler-Wasielewska, Violetta, 137n12, 138n17
Rhodes, Richard, xin6
Rieger, Berndt, xxxn104, 63n157, 138n17
Riecke, Hans-Joachim, 255
Riftlep, Rohan, 3n13–14
Rigoulot, Pierre, xxxn98
Ringelblum, Emanuel, 84n22–24, 86n28, 87, 88n40, 90n52, 93n64, 95–97, 98n82, 99, 100n87, 114, 115n133, 121n154–156, 133, 156n85, 167, 177n155, 178n158, 179–180
Ringer, Herman, 195n6
Rogowa, 288
Rohstoffstelle [raw material office], 97
Romane, Patrick, 6n23
Romanian troops, 185
Rosen, N., 146n46, 156n84, 157n87, 158n93
Rosenberg, Alfred, xxv, 247n1, 254–255
Rosenberg, Stefania, 19n9, 34n64
Rosenblum, Rywka, 32n48
Rosenzweig, Dr., 168
Rosenzweig, Maria, 32n52
Rosh Hashana, 34, 87
Rossino, Alexander B., 8n29, 11n36–37, 26n34
Rost, Nella, 219n64
Roszkowski, Wojciech, *see* Albert, Andrzej
Rożnów, 62, 150, 357
Rubinstein, Esther, 288
Ruda Kołtowska, 217
Rüdiger, General, 29n40
Rundstedt von, Gerd, 20
Rutkowski, A., xxi, 13n41, 26n30, 28n36, 29n41, 50n121, 62n153, 65n161, 67n163, 70n174, 72n183, 73n186, 76n2, 77n5–6, 84n22, 100n87, 105n100, 111n116, 135n3–4, 143n32, 144n36, 145n38, 160n101, 161n104–105, 163n110–111, 165n114, 166n117, 170n129, 172n135, 175n145, 176n147–148, 177n152, 225n8, 226n11, 235n30, 237n33–34, 240n41, 241n43–48, 242n49–51, 245n58, 262n36–38, 263n41, 267n47–49,
274n1, 276n9–12, 277n13–15, 278n17, 279n18, 280n19–22, 293n4–5, 359n32
Rymanów, 230
Rzeszów, 19, 22, 59

S
Sammern-Frankenegg von, Ferdinand, 276–278
San (river), 66, 142–145, 191
Sandkühler, Thomas, xxix, 64n160, 114n131, 213n40, 216n57
Sauckel, Fritz, xxv, 42n96, 246, 249, 251–254, 258–259, 262, 290, 305–306
Schall, Abraham, 195n6
Schechter, David, 211
Schellin, Erich, 266
Schenk, Dieter, 20n11
Schepers, Hansjulius, 60–61
Scherner, Julian, 241, 315
Schindler, Dietrich, 13n44–45, 15n51
Schindler, Maximillian, 206, 262, 281, 284, 289, 307
Schindler, Oskar, 289n46
Schön, Waldemar, 127
Schönfeld, Joahim, 202n20
Schönker, Henryk, 90n51, 224n7
Schott, Heinrich, 203
Schwammberger, Josef, 315
Schwarz and Co., 203, 217–218, 260
Schulte, Jan Erik, xxix
Schultz & Co., (company), 100, 123, 276, 279
Sebta, Tanja, xxxi
Seeber, Eva, xxvi
Seifert, Helmut, Dr., 200
Seilaender, Dorota, 216n57
Selbstschutz (self-defense units), 66–67, 138, 154, 160
Seyss-Inquart, Arthur, 20, 23, 145n38
Shukhevich, Roman, 187n12
Siedlce, 47
Siedlicze (correctly Siedliszcze), 88n39, 163–164
Sielec Zawonie (camp), 217
Siemianowice, 31
Silberklang, David, xxxi, 138n17, 142n28
Singer, Hedwig, xxix
Skalniak, Franciszek, xxii, 339n10, 340n11, 341n12, 351n22, 359n31
Skarżysko Kamienna, xxviii, 23, 289, 314
Skierniewice, 47, 152, 177
Skorwider, Danuta, 47n110

Śląsk, 7
Słomczyński, A., 6n24
Slovak troops, 185
Śmigły-Rydz, Edward, 6
Snyder, Timothy, 295n10
Sobibór, 239, 281–284, 302, 311
Sochaczew, 47
Sommé, Walter, 284
Soviet POWs, *see* POWs, Soviet
Soviet troops, 6, 27, 104, 185–186
Soviet Union, xi, 3, 27, 66, 71, 130, 137, 142–143, 149, 181–183, n185, 187–189, 192, 247, 301, 314
Spała, 20
Speer, Albert, xiiin10, xxv, 236, 253, 262, 290–291, 295n9, 297, 301, 305n22, 312, 317
Spector, Shmuel, xin6
Sporrenberg, Jakob, 283–285, 287
Stalag II B Hammerstein, 158
Stanisławów, 186, 202–205, 208, 212
Stąporków (Końskie County), 176
Starvation, 117, 127–128, 178, 181, 222, 248, 295, 303, 314
Steinert, Dieter, xxxin112
Steffen, Katrin, viiin1, xxxii
Sterz, R., 11n36
Steyer-Daimler-Puch A.G. Waffenfabrik, 289
Stalingrad, 247, 290
Stahlwerke Braunschweig GmbH, *see* Braunschweig
Starachowice (camp), xxviiin88, 38, 289
Streckenbach, Bruno, 161–162
Streit, Christian, 295n10
Stroop, Jürgen, 276n8, 278
Stryj County, 217
    Delatyn, 217
    Mikuliczyn, 217
    Nadworna, 217
    Skole, 217
Strzemieszyce, 13–14
Stutthof, xxiii, 194n4
Święcicki, Witold, 18n1–3, 39n84, 41n95, 48n113–114, 49n116–119, 51n123, 116n144, 136n7
Szatkowski, Marian, 214n43
Szczepańczyk, Czesław, xxin35
Szende, S., 204n26
Szor, Izrael, 195n6
Szurgacz, Herbert, xxii
Szyper, Henryk, 195n6

T

Tanzmann, Helmut, 194
Tarnopol, 186, 212, 214
    Borki Wielkie, 214
    Hluboczek, 214
    Jezierna, 214
    Kamionki, 214
    Stupki, 214
    Zborów, 214
Tarnów, 31n45, 35, 90, 92–93, 204–205
Tarnowiec, 44
Tauber, Joachim, viiin1, xxxii
Technische Nothilfe (TN) (German technical services), 134
Tenenabum-Tamaroff, Mordechai, 283
Thier, Theobald, 194
Thierack, Otto, 257
Thomas, Georg, 23, 183–184
Thomas, Max, 187
Timm, Max, 256n20
Tisch, Eliasz, 204
Tłuste, 210
Többens, Walter Caspar, 279, 302
Többens, W. C. (company), 123, 276, 279, 302
Todt, Fritz, 297
Todt Organization, see *Organisation Todt*
Toman, Jiří, 13n44–45, 15n51
Tomaszów Mazowiecki, 120, 174
Trawniki, xxiv–xxv, 65, 275, 281, 287–288, 302, 311
Treblinka, 142n27, 239, 282
Trials of War Criminals before the Nuerenberg Military Tribunals, 187n13
Trimborn, Jürgen, 9n32
Trunk, Yeshayhu, xxvi
Türk, Richard, 65

U

Ukraine, 6, 186–189, 193–195, 201–203, 210, 252–254, 269
Ukrainian
    Authorities, 186
    Battalions/formations, 160, 187
    Cooperatives, 210
    Militia, 188, 209
    State, 194
Ukrainian Nationalist Movement/ Organization (OUN), 186n10, 193
Ukrainians, xix, 2, 5, 39–40, 139, 154, 173n138, 180, 186, 193, 195, 201, 206, 241–242, 252–253, 257, 268

Umiastowski, Roman, 6
Umschlagstelle, 205, 208, 212
Ungerer, A., 139n18
United Timber Companies (*Vereinigte Holz Betriebe*, VHB), 218
Unternehmen Tannenberg (Operation Tannenberg), 7–8
Urban workshops (Städtische Werkstätte), 89, 112, 204, 208, 211–212
USSR, 6, 27, 96, 143, 149, 181–187, 190, 211, *see also* Soviet Union

V

Victor Kremin Old and Waste Materials Collection, 213, *see also* Kremin, Victor
Vollard-Bockelberg von, Alfred, 20
Volksdeutsche (ethnic Germans), 40, 154, 211

W

Wagner, Eduard, 185
Wagner, Jens-Christian, xiv–xv, xxxin111
Wächter, Otto, 39, 72n185, 194
Wagner, Roza, 202n23
Wannsee Conference (January 20, 1942), 222–225, 292n2, 294, 296, 314
War Economy Inspection (*Wehrwirtschaftsstelle*), 22, 184
Warlimont, Walter, 25
Warsaw, xx, xxiii–xxiv, 6–7, 12, 18, 22, 32–36, 39, 47, 52, 59, 61, 70, 75, 79, 81, 84–85, 89–92, 97–98, 111–114, 120–121, 145n41, 150, 152–153, 163–164, 165n116, 169, 171–172, 179–180, 195, 204, 239–244, 256, 260–261, 270, 276, 283, 288–302, 307, 334, 344, 347–348, 350–351, 359
  Twarda Street, 115
  Gęsia Street (Gęsiówka), 120–121
  Niska Street, 121
Warsaw Ghetto, 75–79, 102–105, 109, 116–117, 123–133, 156, 158, 178n156, 190, 221, 224–225, 241, 244, 258n26, 273–281, 302
Warsaw Ghetto Uprising, 278, 281–282
Warschauer Zeitung, 95
Warthegau, viii, xv, xxiv, xxxii, 27, 70n173, 91n56, 135n3, 143–145, 191, 221, 318
Water Inspection Office (*Wasserwirtschaftsamt*), 71, 88n39, 164n112, 357
Weber, Hartmut, xxxi

Weber, Heinz, 202
Weliczkower, Leon, 202n23
Weinberg, Gerhard L., 5n20, 295n11
Weinmann, Martin, xxixn96, 139n18
Weitzman, Leonore, J., xxviiin91
Wenzel, Mario, xxx, xxxiin114, xxxiin116, 315n48
Wehrmacht, x, xvii, 2, 10, 15, 18, 21–24, 30, 43, 57–58, 61, 63, 70, 78, 89, 100, 129, 142, 147, 158–159, 185–189, 192–193, 197, 201, 212, 217–218, 237–239, 245, 259–261, 264–265, 268–270, 278, 293n3, 295, 297–298, 304–311, 314, 317, 319, 347
Wiejski-Weiser, Artur, 215n54, 216n57–58, 217n59
Wieliczka, 90
Wieluń, 44
Wieprz (river), 71, 287
Wild roundups, 56, 90
Wilhelm, H. H., 187n13
Willhaus, Gustav, 216
Winkler, Jerzy, 114n132, 115n135, 116n137, 118n149, 119n151–152, 124–125, 129n178, 130, 132
Winnica, 169, 255
Winniki (Lwow district), 214
Wi Rü [*Wirtschaft Rüstung*—Armament Production Management], 182–183, 188n14
Wisła River, 60, 72, 84, 191
Włodawa, 87, 164n112
Wolf, R., 213
Woodward, E. L., 3n13–14
World War I, 7, 10
Worm, Paul, 194
Woyrsch von, Udo, 8
Wróblewski, Bronisław, xxin32
Wróblewski, Mścisław, xixn18, xxin33
Wrzosek, Mieczysław, 23n20
Wulf, Josef, 219n64

Y

Yom Kippur, 87

Z

Żabno, 93
Zadrowski, Feliks, 18n1–3, 39n84, 41n95, 48n113–114, 49n116–119, 51n123, 116n144, 136n7
Zakład Oczyszczania Miasta, ZOM (cleaning enterprise), 88, 344–346

Zamość, 59, 90, 104–105, 111–112, 114, 122, 138, 147, 226, 282
Zavrel, B. John, 9n32
Zbaraż, 212
Zentralstelle II/P (Polen), 7
Zeszyty Majdanka, xxi
Zhitomir, 255
Zimmerer, Katarzyna, 113n127
Ziółkowska, Anna, xxiv
Zipser, Zygmunt, 112

Złoczów (county), 212, 214, 217
   Jaktorów, 214, 219
   Kurowice, 214
   Lacki Wielkie, 214
   Płuhów, 214
   Sasów, 217
Zwangsarbeit (forced labor), vii, xiii, xvii–xviii, 47, 69, 295
Zyśko, W., 285n39

www.ingramcontent.com/pod-product-compliance
Lightning Source LLC
Chambersburg PA
CBHW071355300426
44114CB00016B/2073